DEMOGRAPHY
The Science of Population

SECOND EDITION

Jay Weinstein
Emeritus, Eastern Michigan University

Vijayan K. Pillai
University of Texas at Arlington

ROWMAN & LITTLEFIELD
Lanham • Boulder • New York • London

Executive Editor: Nancy Roberts
Associate Editor: Molly White
Senior Marketing Manager: Karin Cholak
Marketing Manager: Deborah Hudson
Interior Designer: Andrea Reider
Cover Designer: Chloe Batch
Cover Art: Bolkins / Thinkstock

Published by Rowman & Littlefield
A wholly owned subsidiary of The Rowman & Littlefield Publishing Group, Inc.
4501 Forbes Boulevard, Suite 200, Lanham, Maryland 20706
www.rowman.com

Unit A, Whitacre Mews, 26-34 Stannary Street, London SE11 4AB

British Library Cataloguing in Publication Information Available

Library of Congress Cataloging-in-Publication Data

Weinstein, Jay A., 1942–
    Demography : the science of population / Jay Weinstein and Vijayan K. Pillai. — Second edition.
        pages cm
    Includes bibliographical references and index.
    ISBN 978-1-4422-3519-9 (cloth : alk. paper) — ISBN 978-1-4422-3520-5 (pbk. : alk. paper) — ISBN 978-1-4422-3521-2 (electronic)
    1. Demography. 2. Population. I. Pillai, Vijayan K. II. Title.
    HB871.W445 2015
    304.6—dc23   2015020166

Printed in the United States of America

BRIEF CONTENTS

CONTENTS

PART I: AN OVERVIEW OF POPULATION SCIENCE

PART II: POPULATION DYNAMICS: VITAL EVENTS AND GROWTH

PART III: POPULATION MODELS

CHAPTER 9   The Life Table: An Introduction   213

LIST OF FIGURES

LIST OF TABLES

LIST OF BOXES

PREFACE

One aspect of being a well-informed person in today's rapidly changing world is knowing about populations and the field that specializes in their study, demography. Newspapers, magazines, television, and the Internet are filled with discussions about demographic issues. These include such headline-making events as the rapid population growth now occurring in Asia, Africa, and Latin America, the aging of the U.S. population, and the flows of immigrants—official and undocumented—into the industrialized countries. Most of us are also aware that the methods and the data of demography are used extensively in business, in government, and in professions such as actuarial science, city planning, and public health. For these reasons, it is unlikely that you need to be convinced that population science is an important—and useful—field of study.

NEW TO THE SECOND EDITION

This second edition is divided into four main parts; each part begins with a short introduction, and all chapters include end-of-chapter summaries. All tables, related narrative, and graphics have been updated to include data from the 2000 and 2010 census counts, more recent estimates for the United States—especially the American Community Survey, and comparable new data from international sources (e.g., World Bank, Population Research Bureau *World Data Sheet*). Several new figures have been added throughout the text.

Part I: An Overview of Population Science introduces the field of demography and provides a summary of its subject matter. The chapters in this part have been reorganized to reflect changes in the discipline. Chapter 1 now includes a new "the study of populations" section, a shorter Chapter 2 covers population size, and its former discussion of structure has been moved to Chapter 3. This de-emphasizes the history of population science to some extent and increases emphasis on population size as the key demographic variable. Chapter 4 presents some of the main principles and analytical techniques associated with the third "static" characteristic of populations: geographic distribution.

Part II: Population Dynamics: Vital Events and Growth reflects the wealth of data and analytical techniques now available from The U.S. Centers for Disease Control and Prevention (CDC) and its "Wonder" utility. The first three chapters focus on the vital events of birth, death, and migration. The final chapter in this part brings this material together in a discussion of population growth: its measurement, its history, and current related policy concerns.

Part III: Population Models, introduces the principles of life table analysis, population estimation, and projection. This material has been simplified and updated. Chapter 9 ("The Life Table: An Introduction") has been revised to accord with the new federal alignment for vital statistics between the CDC and National Institute for Health Statistics. Life tables from non-U.S. sources are increased in number and in detailed functions.

Part IV: Demography in Application, provides overviews of population policy, the environment, and demographic resources, along with a brief postscript on population in the larger scheme of things. What appeared as two appendices in the first edition, one on the history of population policy and one on tourism as a type of international migration, have been combined to create a new Chapter 14.

The end-of-chapter material has been shortened and now contains a summary, key terms, and notes.

WHY STUDY DEMOGRAPHY?

You are about to embark on a course that will deepen your understanding and your appreciation of demographic principles, techniques, and facts. It might be worthwhile to consider *why* we seem to pay so much attention to these matters; for they certainly are not what most people would think of as high-priority issues. Nor is it immediately apparent how growth rates in Africa, for instance, can actually affect us personally. This is true enough. Although obviously worth knowing about, the characteristics and dynamics of populations do seem somewhat remote and abstract in relation to our daily concerns.

Despite this appearance, it is our belief and the belief of most demographers that, in ways that are often silent and invisible, population affects nearly every aspect of our social lives: economic conditions, the quality of our environment, political affairs, and even our ethics and morality. Moreover, economic conditions, environmental quality, and so on, react in turn to demographic pressures in helping to determine the size, the structure, the geographic distribution, and other features of our populations. Thus, population functions as a link in a vital causal chain, a basic and essential part of a larger system that shapes our public and private worlds.

It is these connections that make populations newsworthy and that underlie demography's wide application. The public is interested in rapid population growth not because we have a special fascination with percentages and rates, but because every increase in the number of persons on this planet places a strain on scarce resources. People discuss current immigration policy not because they are especially curious about how the Immigration and Naturalization Service (INS) operates. Rather, it is because they know that the size of the groups that enter the country and the places from which they emigrate will affect the labor force, the schools, and our language and culture.

As social scientists, demographers study *collective* experiences: how people relate to one another, the ways in which individuals affect the larger groups to which they belong, and how others influence the individual. In this respect, it has much in common with anthropology, sociology, and similar fields. It is true that demography has close ties both with biology and mathematics, as we discuss in the first chapter. But these are not its nearest intellectual relatives. The study of the vital processes—reproduction, death, and aging—and the skills associated with quantifying our observations are very important aspects of population science. But, at root, demography is one of the humanities.

In the human populations we study, the processes of growth and structural change and the dynamics of geography do not operate mechanically or merely organically. Nor do they function independently. Instead, they are always part of a broader set of forces that include, norms, values, stratification, organizations, and—most significant of all—human purpose. Populations are very much part of our collective lives, an essential and formative part. And they always and everywhere intermingle with our cultures and our societies. This makes population science one of the most interesting and, at the same time, one of the most challenging fields in the academic world. If you can say after reading this book that you agree, that you have been introduced to a fascinating and a worthwhile subject, the authors will feel that they have accomplished the goals they established when they set out to write it.

ABOUT THE BOOK

Demography: The Science of Population, Second Edition is designed to be used in a wide range of courses, including sociology, geography, economics, and related professional disciplines. Over the past several decades, two alternative approaches to teaching the subject have been developed. The first, *population studies* (also called "social demography"), emphasizes substantive matters. It focuses on the history of naturally occurring human populations, current demographic characteristics of nations and regions, and population policies and problems such as family planning and migration law. The second, *demography* as such (also known as "formal demography"), is primarily methodological. It emphasizes principles and techniques for measuring the size and other characteristics of populations, analyzing the components of population structure and change, and producing projections and forecasts.

Although all existing textbooks touch on both of these approaches, a distinction has generally prevailed such that the former is considered to be most appropriate for beginning undergraduates whereas the latter is offered at advanced undergraduate and graduate levels. This book reflects, but also seeks to go beyond, this tradition. Our decision concerning what to emphasize was made in view of the prevailing need of instructors to introduce key demographic facts and concepts and to reserve much of the technical side of demography for more advanced courses.

At the same time, we have attempted to be responsive to the increasing demand for practical, career-oriented undergraduate curricula and the growth of service courses for nonmajors—especially at regional comprehensive universities like Eastern Michigan University and The University of Texas at Arlington where the authors teach. The material in the following chapters is aimed at the sophomore level and above, and its main emphasis is on the facts and contemporary issues in population studies. In fact, the entire last section of the book is devoted exclusively to these concerns. However, this material is integrated with a preliminary look at technique and at the analytical tools commonly employed in academic demography and applied in numerous professional fields.

Thus, the chapters on population structure, geographic distribution, mortality, and the like begin with substantive concerns, but they also include discussions of data sources and measurement techniques. In addition, two chapters—9 and 10—feature technical aspects not ordinarily covered in such detail in undergraduate texts: the life table and population estimation/projection, respectively.

Our principal instructional objective in pursuing this approach is to strengthen the students' skills as *consumers* of demographic information. In particular, we seek to improve the abilities of readers in interpreting research reports with demographic content and in understanding what ratios and rates can (and cannot) tell us about population structure and dynamics.

We also stress the importance of assessing the strengths and limitations of population projections and the qualitative meaning of quantitative data. Secondarily, the book introduces the elements of population *analysis*; pointing students to a base of resources that will help them formulate and pursue their own research projects on population relevant to their chosen future careers. These objectives are reflected in the general selection of topics, numerous illustrative examples, a chapter specifically devoted to the uses of demographic resources in school and professional contexts (Chapter 13), and an extensive list of references.

INSTRUCTOR AND STUDENT RESOURCES

This book is accompanied by a teaching and learning package designed to enhance the experience of both instructors and students.

Instructor's Manual and Test Bank. For each chapter in the text, this author-written resource provides chapter summaries, key terms with definitions, Doing Demography exercises, web sites to bookmark, and suggested further readings. The test bank section includes multiple choice and true/false questions. The Instructor's Manual and Test Bank are available to adopters for download on the text's catalog page at www.rowman.com/isbn/9781442235205.

Testing Software. The Test Bank is also available in Respondus 4.0©. Respondus 4.0© is a powerful tool for creating and managing exams that can be printed to paper or published directly to the most popular learning management systems. Exams can be created offline or moved from one LMS to another. **Respondus LE** is available for free and can be used to automate the process of creating print tests. **Respondus 3.5**, available for purchase or via a school site license, prepares tests to be uploaded to an LMS. Go to http://www.respondus.com/products/testbank/search.php to submit your request.

Additional study tools. Respondus StudyMate© is available to help students master the basics of course material through learning activities, self-assessments, and games. A dozen activities—such as flash cards, crosswords, and quizzes—engage students with course content in an individualized way. Students can access StudyMate activities using computers, smartphones, and tablets. StudyMate also integrates seamlessly with the most popular learning management systems.

Lecture Slides. A set of PowerPoint® slides provides lecture outlines as well as the tables and figures from the text. The slides are available to adopters for download on the text's catalog page at www.rowman.com/isbn/9781442235205.

Enhanced eText. The Enhanced eText allows students to access this textbook anytime and anywhere they want. The eText for *Demography: The Science of Population, Second Edition*, includes everything that is in the print edition but also features direct links to a student Companion Website, where you will find flash cards, self-quizzes, and additional activities designed to enhance the concepts in each chapter. The Enhanced eText can be purchased at www.rowman .com/isbn/9781442235205 or at any other eBook retailer.

Companion Website. Accompanying the text is an open-access Companion Website designed to engage students with the material and reinforce what they've learned in the classroom. For each chapter, flash cards, self-quizzes, and additional activities help students master the content and apply that knowledge to real-life situations. Students can access the Companion Website from their computer or mobile device; it can be found at textbooks.rowman.com/weinstein2e.

ACKNOWLEDGMENTS

The authors would like to acknowledge with thanks, the late Alan McClare, with whom the idea of a second edition was first discussed, Sarah Stanton, who put the idea into action, and Nancy Roberts and Molly White for seeing it through. I (JW) dedicate this edition to my wife, Lauren. I (VKP) dedicate this edition to my parents, C. K. U. Pillai and J. Chandramathi and my wife, Ann C. Kelley.

It is our hope that this selection of topics and the manner in which they are organized will provide a comprehensive and comprehensible introduction to the major tools and resources of our discipline. Of course, there may be subjects or techniques we have not covered here that other demographers might view as important. And there are surely some items that we have included that others would view as superfluous. This is only to be expected in a book of this size and scope. However, we do believe that, with our reference list, the many of Internet sites cited, and the other resources beyond these pages to which we have directed you, it will be possible to make up for some of the deficiencies you may find in our presentation. Of course, we assume final responsibility for all errors in the material. And we would like to hear from you by e-mail with any comments or questions.

JW: jay.weinstein@comcast.net and VKP: drpillai@yahoo.com

ABOUT THE AUTHORS

Jay Weinstein is a native of Chicago and received his B.A. and Ph.D. degrees from the University of Illinois at Urbana–Champaign. His M.A. is from Washington University–St. Louis, and he pursued additional graduate studies at McGill University (Montreal) and Madras (now Chennai) University in India. He served on the faculties of the University of Iowa, The Georgia Institute of Technology, and Eastern Michigan University, where he now holds the rank of Professor of Sociology, Emeritus. He is the author of numerous articles and books, including *Social Change 3e* and *Applying Social Statistics*. During the course of his nearly fifty-year career, he has been active with the American Sociological Association, as Chair of the Section on Sociological Practice and cofounder of the Section on Altruism, Morality, and Social Solidarity. He also served as President of the Michigan Sociological Association, The North Central Sociological Association, and The Society for Applied Sociology. He edited the journal, *Studies in Comparative International Development* for ten years and is the founding editor of the *Journal of Applied Social Science*. He is the recipient of many awards of recognition for his teaching, research, and service to the profession, including two Fulbright Professorships in India.

Vijayan K. Pillai received the M.S.W. from the University of Indore; Post Graduate Diploma in Planning from the School of Planning, Ahmedabad, India, and the Ph.D. from the University of Iowa. He started his teaching career at the University of Zambia, Lusaka Campus. Before joining the University of Texas at Arlington, where he is currently a professor of Social Work, he taught at the University of North Texas. He has published extensively in demography journals and has coauthored several books including *Women's Reproductive Rights in Developing Countries* and *Reproductive Health in Yemen*. He is actively involved with the International Consortium for Social Development where he has assumed leadership positions. He is currently the editor of *Social Development Issues* and has received several awards for research as well as mentoring at the University of North Texas and the University of Texas at Arlington.

AN OVERVIEW
OF POPULATION
SCIENCE

The world's population has now surpassed the 7-billion mark, its largest size ever. Of these 7 billion people, two-thirds live in the less-developed countries of Africa, Asia, and Latin America. Led by the true population giants of China with 1.4 billion people and India with over 1.3 billion, the poorer nations are growing at an average rate of 2 percent per year. At that rate, their population sizes will have doubled by the year 2045. In contrast, many countries in Europe are experiencing no population growth at all, and many—led by Russia—are actually losing people at rates of up to 0.5 percent annually. The United States' population stands between these two extremes. With approximately 308.7 million people enumerated by Census 2010, its growth rate is approximately 0.7 percent per year.

Although there are obvious and substantial demographic gaps between these sets of nations, there are also many important connections. The most significant, of course, is that we all occupy the same, finite planet. And, because changes in population size are bound to affect our environment and resource base, one nation's growth rate will impact on the standard of living and quality of life of all other nations.

Migration is another factor that links the fates of countries now experiencing rapid population increase with those that are barely growing at all. As a rule, the less-developed nations are rural, with only a small proportion of their populations living in one or a few very large cities. In contrast, the industrialized countries are nearly completely urbanized, with more than 80 percent of their populations living in numerous cities of various sizes. Yet, the metropolises of Asia, Africa, and Latin America are dramatically overcrowded and they continue to expand by the day, as seemingly endless streams of migrants from the impoverished countryside continue to arrive in search of the "good life." As a result of this rapid urban growth, frequent shortages of food, housing, and basic amenities regularly emerge. In turn, political violence often breaks out, all of which places demands on the industrialized countries for emergency assistance, long-term development aid, and diplomatic or military intervention.

The rapid urban growth in the poorer nations creates a strong incentive for people to emigrate to Europe and especially the United States and Canada, in search of jobs and security. Although the number of those who do find haven is just a fraction of those who want to come to Europe and America, each year hundreds of thousands do manage to make the trek. On arrival at their destinations, the new immigrants increase the size of and change in other ways their host populations. Many European populations would be experiencing even more rapid decrease were it not for the inflows of migrant workers from Africa and Western Asia. And immigrants, especially from Latin America and Eastern Asia, account for as much as 40 percent of the total annual increase in the United States' population.

The four chapters that make up our overview of population science are designed to provide a foundation for exploring these remarkable and critical demographic trends of our times. Because these topics and issues will be considered and reconsidered at several points in later chapters, Part I will also serve as a framework for the discussion that follows in the remainder of the book.

The purpose of Chapter 1, "The Nature of Populations," is to help us begin using and feeling comfortable with the uniquely demographic way of looking at the world. With this perspective our attention is directed not to individual human beings but to groups of them as they are aggregated—either naturally or for statistical purposes. Although demographers do not deny the importance of individuals, they are primarily concerned with the size, the structure, the territorial features, and the dynamics of the *collective* wholes that individuals form and in which they participate. These include especially certain kinds of aggregates, such as nations and cities, we call "populations." These have characteristics that set them apart from mere collections and give them the power to affect and be affected by key aspects of our social lives and our natural environments.

Thus, much of the first chapter is devoted to considering the ways in which aggregates and populations have a real, concrete existence above and beyond the individuals that make them up. To help in making this point, and in understanding the implications of a collective ("trans-individual") level of reality, we introduce several well-known demographic principles, including ecological correlation and ecological fallacy, structural effects, demographic determinism, and the use of populations as units of observation. The chapter continues with a section on the study of population, outlining the principal ways in which population research is conducted. Included here is a history of the discipline that focuses on the early founders and originators, such as Thomas Robert Malthus.

Chapter 2 begins with a focus on the tools of contemporary demography, including its main sources of data: census information and vital statistics. Next we consider the basic demographic variable, population size. Here we compare the sizes of various types of populations and aggregates: nations, continents, counties, and cities. The chapter concludes with a survey of the procedures associated with the measurement of population size and related characteristics.

Chapter 3, on demographic structure, discusses the elements that make up a population and the many ways in which populations can be disaggregated into their component parts. Here we introduce the two types of structures, biological and sociocultural. In this context, several key variables are introduced, including age, gender (sex), and a range of sociocultural structures and stratification systems: family, ethnicity, occupation, wealth, and income. Throughout the chapter, we discuss key principles in demographic analysis, issues in data collection, the major measures and indexes for analyzing structure, and relevant structural characteristics of the United States and of nations throughout the world.

Chapter 4, "Geographic Distribution: Population and Territory," considers how populations are dispersed over space, sometimes in highly concentrated areas and sometimes very sparsely. Among the main topics covered are density and its measurement and consequences, territorial units—both administrative and technical—and the current urban distribution in the United States. Much of the latter portion of the chapter presents the major highlights of a millennia-long trek that has eventuated in "the urbanization of the human population." As noted, today, the industrialized nations of the world are approaching a point at which virtually all of their inhabitants live in cities, and in which little urban growth is occurring. In the less-developed regions, however, urbanization rates are generally low but explosive urban growth is placing a tremendous strain on already-scarce resources.

THE NATURE OF POPULATIONS

Demography, the science of population, is a field of study that lies at the intersection of the social and the biological sciences. It is a distinct discipline with a long, rich, and interesting history; a well-articulated body of theory; and a set of specialized techniques for data collection and analysis. Although often classed as a branch of sociology, demography actually incorporates insights and methods drawn from numerous fields, ranging from biology to mathematics. It is employed extensively in basic scientific research and, at the same time, it is one of the most frequently applied of all the social sciences.

THE FOCUS ON AGGREGATES

The name of the field comes from the Greek word, *demos*, meaning "the people (collectively)." Accordingly, as this first chapter will make clear, its chief concern is with the characteristics of **aggregates** of living individuals. Generally speaking, an aggregate is a collection of two or more objects or units: sheets of paper, stones, items of clothing, and so forth. However, we stress that in the case of demography the objects or units that make up the aggregates of interest are alive. They are born, they age, they move from place to place, they reproduce, they become ill, and they die.

Our main goal in this chapter is to become better acquainted with the field and with the concepts, materials, and methods commonly employed in demographic research today. The discussion begins with some basic observations on demographic aggregates. Next, we move to a review of the history of population studies. In this context, we note that humans have been interested in the size, structure, geographic distribution, and dynamics of their populations for a very long time. This look backward is then followed by a discussion of contemporary sources of demographic information, in which we identify recent innovations in survey approaches and in **vital registration** systems—including national censuses, CD-ROM files, the controversy surrounding using sample information for the decennial census count, and Census-related Internet sites.

Populations and Other Aggregates

In the demographic sense, there are many different kinds of aggregates, depending in part on the extent to which the individuals it contains interact with one another, share the same geographic territory, and maintain prolonged contact over the course of one or more generations. At one extreme, some aggregates are mere classifications, created by the researcher for analytical purposes, such as the aggregate of all female persons aged 15 to 45 living in the state of Georgia. Other aggregates are truly interacting groups, such as the specific household that now resides at 105 E. Main St., in Mytown, U. S. A. Whereas many of the principles and techniques of demography can be, and routinely are, applied to all types of aggregates, demographers do give major consideration to the special type of aggregate known as a **population.**

Naturally Occurring Populations: Human and Nonhuman

Because nearly all species of living organisms, including human beings, form naturally occurring populations, demography has a unique position in academe: sometimes administered as part of a social science department such as sociology or geography, sometimes administered as a natural science, such as ecology, and sometimes given its own department. In fact, at some major universities, courses and training in population studies are offered in more than one department at the same time. The fact that populations are not unique to humans should also help remind social researchers that the people they study are part of nature and that their field is, after all, a branch—albeit a very special branch—of biology (Forsman 2011; Carey 1993).[1]

A naturally occurring population, human or not, has certain defining features that set it off from other kinds of aggregates. Primary among these features are:

1. Populations are relatively *endogamous*; their individual members tend strongly to mate and to reproduce with one another. The "relatively" qualification distinguishes a population from a species. The latter is absolutely endogamous and its members are, under ordinary circumstances, incapable of reproducing with members

Figure 1.1 Home Page for the University of California-Davis Center for Population Biology

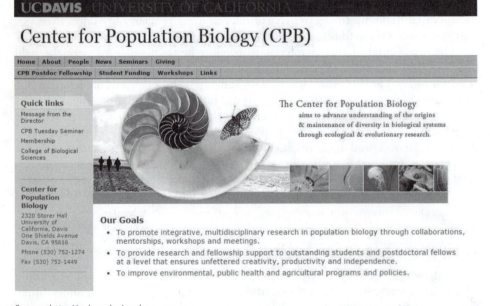

Source: http://cpb.ucdavis.edu.

of another species. Every species, including *Homo sapiens*, is thus composed of several (possibly hundreds of) populations. Each member of a given human population is most likely to mate and reproduce with another member. However, anyone can, and some people do, mate and reproduce outside of their own population (Coleman 1993). The trait of relative **endogamy** also helps distinguish between populations and other aggregates of demographic interest that do not have this trait, such as all people of a certain age or sex who live in Asia.

The following excerpt from an article published in 2006 both defines the term "endogamy" and connects with the biological/genetic features of naturally occurring populations.

> The development of demographic studies in anthropology is directly linked to the success of population genetics. The anthropodemographic or anthropogenetic approach is thus underpinned by questions of genetics. While demographers focus on population dynamics and renewal in quantitative terms, population geneticists refer not to individuals but to the sets of genes carried by individuals in a population. Their aim is to detect the factors and processes which influence the genetic evolution of a group, i.e. which modify gene frequencies from one generation to the next. Among them are the factors which affect modes of reproduction. (Cazes 2006: Abstract)

2. Populations share a bounded geographic territory. Other aggregates, such as the set of all persons born into the human species in the past year, are not defined by their locale as such. Naturally occurring populations, on the other hand, tend to establish an intimate, reciprocal relationship with their territories, which is of special concern to evolutionary biologists and ecologists. Nutritional habits, reproductive characteristics, annual physiological changes, and other aspects of their members' existence are shaped in accord with the opportunities and limitations imposed by the population's territorial environment.

In most species, including ours, the population-territory relationship tends to be an exclusive one, wherein it is unusual for two or more populations (of the same species) to share the same territory for a prolonged period of time. More often, because endogamy is only relative (members of different populations of the same species can and do reproduce under certain circumstances), two populations that occupy the same territory would likely merge, thus experiencing *demographic assimilation* in becoming a new, larger, and more heterogeneous unit. We consider the territorial aspect of human populations in some detail in Chapter 4, where we discuss geographic distribution, classification, density, and related topics.

The two traits of endogamy and territoriality provide each population with a distinctive, shared gene pool uniquely developed under the specific conditions of its home range. Thus, in any given territory, members of populations of a particular species have common physical and behavioral traits that are distinct from those of the members of populations of the same species that occupy other territories. Taken together, these features give naturally occurring populations a real, concrete, collective existence. They certainly are aggregates—and not merely single individuals. But, in contrast to other important collective entities such as societies and cultures, they can be readily observed and their characteristics directly measured.

3. Human populations are especially complex because, in addition to having a common gene pool and territory, their members also share a sociocultural heritage:

tools, language, or other knowledge that is transmitted from parents to offspring and from peer to peer through imitation and/or learning. Comparative research indicates that the *degree* of complexity and many qualitative features, as well, differ considerably from population to population.[2]

The field of demography is affected in several ways by the fact that human populations do have such distinct sociocultural heritages. Most generally this characteristic divides the field into two branches. One branch is **formal demography**, which focuses on population size, composition, geographic distribution, and the interplay of **vital events** as such. These concerns apply to all species, human and nonhuman. The other is **social demography**, essentially the study of human aggregates. This branch explores the relationships among a population's size, structure, and geographic distribution, its vital events, and social and cultural factors such as the norms and values shared and the intergroup conflict and cooperation experienced by members. Although this book is clearly a text in *social* science whose focus is on sociocultural factors such as policy issues, environmental impacts, and population ethics, the earlier chapters do introduce some basic formal principles.

The relatively elaborate organization of human populations is reflected in the kinds of population *structures* studied in social demography, which are more inclusive than those in formal demography. Whereas the latter deals with biological structures only, that is, age and sex, the former must also consider such variables as social class, ethnicity, and language. In addition, social demographers, unlike their formal counterparts, seek to *relate* demographic features and processes to sociocultural phenomena. For instance, they might explain a change in a population's birth rate as the result of a change in its members' norms defining what constitutes the "proper" number of offspring—referred to as a "stopping rule" (something obviously not of direct interest to the formal demographer).

Social demographers must also be ever alert to the possibility that the characteristics and changes that they observe in a given population may well be the result of conscious acts undertaken by members of the population, acts designed to affect its demographic character and fate. For example, migration rates in human populations often vary from time to time because the (human) members of those populations pass and enforce laws that encourage or limit the flow of migrants. Death rates may decline because health officials purposely distribute life-saving medication, and so on.

Finally, and perhaps of greatest significance, the presence of a sociocultural heritage means that members of a population inherit the traits that make them similar and that distinguish them from members of other populations. This occurs in two separate, but related, ways. One of these is biogenetic inheritance, which is a feature of every population, regardless of species. The other is cultural inheritance through enculturation and acculturation (that is, learning), which is characteristic only of populations of humans and other species rightly deemed to have cultures. In such populations, members may look alike and share other physical traits (such as being susceptible or immune to the same diseases); *and* they may behave and think in similar ways, and speak the same language. But they do so for very different reasons. In the first case, it is because of a common gene pool; in the second, it is the result of common learning experiences.

We make this explicit point about the two sources of inheritance in human populations to illustrate what may already be quite obvious to you: That is, the study of human populations is an especially difficult and challenging branch of demography. For centuries, scientists and the general public alike have been especially puzzled by this particular aspect of population dynamics; seeking to determine how much of a person's heritage is biogenetic and how much is sociocultural. Indeed, this brings us close to the notoriously perplexing "nature versus nurture" controversy.

It is not possible to give fair consideration in a book like this to the many problems and issues associated with the fact that human populations do have a dual inheritance, each part of which is subject to different principles. We can note that some serious errors have been made in the past (distant and recent) by those who gave *too much* emphasis to one or the other factor. The characteristics and dynamics of a human population—its size, birth rate, and the like—are clearly shaped in part by biogenetic processes, wherein Darwin's principles of evolution, adaptation, and competition apply. But it is equally true that these characteristics and dynamics are affected by human interpretation, human will, and human error; and that individuals can, in **Lamarckian** fashion,[3] acquire new traits in their lifetimes, such as a new language. They can also transmit those traits to their offspring, for instance, by teaching them the new language from birth. To one degree or another, both "nature" and "nurture" play a role in shaping human (and possibly other culture-bearing) populations, a role whose proportions are not yet entirely understood. Among other things, this makes all of the "laws" and "exact predictions" concerning our kinds of populations subject to considerable skepticism.

The Principles of Demographic Analysis

The characteristics of populations and other aggregates with which demography is most directly concerned can be classed into four categories:

- Size: the number of individuals included in an aggregate or a population;
- Structure: the various ways in which subaggregates and subpopulations are formed;
- Geographic Distribution: how an aggregate or population is dispersed over physical space; and
- Changes in Size, Structure, and/or Geographic Distribution: the dynamic aspects of these characteristics, as they vary with the passage of time.

As we will see, each of these categories can be further divided according to types, subtypes, and other special features.

Like other sciences, demography is interested in both description and explanation. That is, it consists of tools and concepts designed to aid in carefully observing the size and the other characteristics of aggregates, and in conveying such observations to other scientists, consumers of scientific information, and the public. This is the field's *descriptive* phase, which, as we will emphasize throughout this text (but especially in Part IV, "Demography in Application"), is applied in a wide range of contemporary professions and businesses, from public administration to wildlife management, from marketing to city planning.

In addition, much basic research in demography has been dedicated to understanding population dynamics, to explaining why some aggregates grow faster than others, why population structures vary from time to time and place to place, and so forth. This is the field's *explanatory* phase. Throughout the many decades since the field was founded (more about the history of demography later in this chapter), the results of these explorations have contributed significantly to the body of scientific theory in biology, sociology, anthropology, and other disciplines.

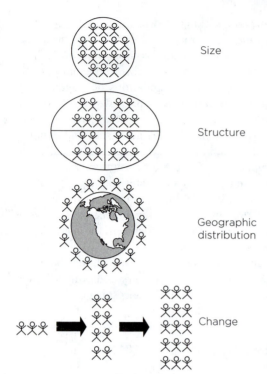

Size

Structure

Geographic
distribution

Change

**Figure 1.2   Four Applications of
Demographic Analysis**

The task of explanation begins with an examination of the *vital events* of demography: birth, death, and migration. These are the variables in the "basic balancing equation" of demography (Shryock and Siegel 1976:4):

Formula 1.1 The Basic Balancing Equation of Demography

$$P_t = P_0 + (B-D) + (I-O)$$

where P_0 is the size of a population at an earlier or initial date, Pt is the size at a later date, B is the number of births that occur between the two dates, D is the number of deaths, I is the number of in-migrants, and O is the number of out-migrants. These four factors, birth, death, in-migration, and out-migration, entirely determine the magnitude and rate of population growth. In Part III, we return to this equation and discuss how it is used in the process of demographic explanation, with a chapter devoted to each type of event. At that point we will also examine the conditions that determine how each varies (or remains constant) in specific populations.[4]

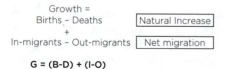

**Figure 1.3   The Four Components of
Population Growth**

AGGREGATES AND INDIVIDUALS

We have already emphasized that demography focuses on the aggregate and not the individual level of human (and other forms of) life. So, for example, in this book we are concerned with understanding such things as the size or the age structure or the growth rate of a population, but not the heights or "growth rates" or ages of specific children who belong to such a population. Although somewhat obvious, this is an important distinction, which we discuss and illustrate in this section.

A population or other aggregate surely is made up of individuals. But at the same time, as demographers and other social scientists like to stress, "the whole is greater than the sum of its parts." In practical terms, this means that although there always is a connection between individuals and the aggregates to which they belong, the connection can be tricky; we can make mistakes if we simply add up observations of individuals to draw conclusions about population characteristics and dynamics. In this context, we introduce two concepts well known to population scientists. The first is **ecological fallacy**. As the name would suggest, it refers to a common type of error, in this case an error made in translating between aggregate and individual levels of observation. The other is **structural effect**, a concept first introduced by Emilé Durkheim (1858–1917), which demonstrates the potential impact that aggregate characteristics can have on individuals.

Ecological Fallacy

An ecological fallacy is an unwarranted (and possibly false) statement about individual characteristics based on information that relates to characteristics of an aggregate. The study of voting behavior is especially prone to such problems (see Scott 1998; Johnson, Shively, and Stein 2002). Research in this area has established that electoral districts (precincts, wards, counties, and states) that have large concentrations of members of certain ethnic groups tend consistently to vote for candidates of one party and to defeat other candidates. This observation has often led to the conclusion that ethnic group members overwhelmingly support their favorite party. Although this may be true, it does not necessarily follow. For it is possible that members of the ethnic group are not especially inclined to vote for a particular candidate, but that all of the *other* residents of the district support the party. Knowledge about how members of a specific group vote depends on data that refer to those individuals, not to the electoral district as a whole.

The problem of ecological fallacy affects most academic disciplines and public policy areas. Moreover, it is a problem with a long pedigree. Information about official areal units (counties, census districts, and cities) is especially prone to ecological fallacy because these units tend to be arbitrary, and to coincide poorly with natural *social* areas. The latter are formed according to principles of proximity, which makes it quite likely that group boundaries will spill over official district and municipal lines—especially those of artificially drawn census tracts. Similarly, residents of a particular district may have little in common except their addresses (see Chapters 4 and 7 for more on this issue).

Structural Effects: An Introduction

One of the most interesting discoveries of "hidden" relationships among individual and aggregate characteristics is credited to the great demographer and sociologist

This member of the aggregate is wealthy; therefore he votes Republican.

A high percentage of wealthy members of the aggregate vote Republican.

Figure 1.4   The Ecological Fallacy is the attempt to conclude information concerning an Individual from related characteristics observed at an aggregated level.
Source: Designed using an image from VectorSilhouettes/Thinkstock.

of the 1900 era, Emilé Durkheim. The discovery is known today as the principle of *structural effects* (see Blau 1960; Kendall and Lazersfeld 1955; and Matras 1973:162–67).

Durkheim's Study of Suicide

Throughout his illustrious career as founder of academic sociology in France, Durkheim was engaged in a project to establish that a true aggregate level of reality exists and that this level is worthy of scientific study unto itself. In this respect, he was part of a movement, also championed by his contemporaries Herbert Spencer in England, Max Weber in Germany, and Vilfredo Pareto in Italy, to free social science from its prescientific origins in moral philosophy and at the same time to distinguish it from psychology. Durkheim and the others argued that the characteristics and dynamics of population, culture, and society studied in social science are legitimate scientific objects. But, they stressed, these objects cannot be reduced simply to physical, biological, or psychological phenomena (you may recall that Durkheim referred to these as "social facts," to distinguish them from physical, biological, or psychological facts). Rather than accept this **reductionist** position, he sought to show that aggregate phenomena do have an independent **emergent** existence.

Durkheim's best-known search for structural effects focused on comparisons between the suicide rates of individuals with given characteristics, for instance Protestants, unmarried persons, and so on, who reside in aggregates that have those characteristics (e.g., with a majority of the population Protestant, a high proportion unmarried, etc.). These were then compared to the rates of those who reside in aggregates that lack the characteristic (e.g., where the majority is Roman Catholic, a high proportion married, etc.). A structural effect exists if individual suicide rates are higher for all groups (for instance, Protestant and Catholic) in a largely Protestant state or province and lower in a largely non-Protestant one. In symbols, where DRS_{pp} is the death rate by suicide among Protestants in largely Protestant states, DRS_{pc} is the suicide rate for Protestants in predominately Roman Catholic aggregates, and so on, a structural effect exist when:

$$DRS_{pp} > DRS \text{ and}$$
$$DRS_{pc} > DRS \text{ and}$$
$$DRS_{pp} > DRS \text{ and}$$
$$DRS_{cp} > DRS.$$

Durkheim did find that, in addition to having higher individual suicide rates than Catholics, Protestants have higher suicide rates in predominately Protestant aggregates than they do in Catholic ones. He observed that Catholics in predominately Protestant countries and provinces have higher rates than Catholics in predominately Catholic countries and provinces; and so on. From these kinds of findings, he concluded that structural effects do exist.[5] In this specific case, it would appear that the less anomic, Roman Catholic character of the state dampens the effect of anomie even on Protestants, with the result that they are less prone to take their own lives than are their counterparts living in largely Protestant states. Similar results held for the other characteristics, such as marital status, indicating that one's social environment has a general, independent influence on one's individual predispositions: In brief, some kinds of populations are more conducive to suicide than others.

Figure 1.5   Emilé Durkheim introduced the concept of structural effects into social demography
Source: Pictorial Press Ltd/Alamy.

Demographic Determinism and "Laws" of Population

We have defined demography as the study of naturally occurring populations and other living aggregates. We have also noted that populations are relatively endogamous, territorial, and are structured along biological (e.g., age) dimensions and, in the case of human populations, sociocultural (e.g., social class, ethnicity) dimensions as well. We have seen that populations can be divided into subpopulations according to one or more of several criteria, including gender, region, age, and social class. In the course of this discussion, we also pointed out that populations are part of nature, with a visible concrete existence in space and time; and, as emphasized in the last section, with their own effects that transcend the behavior of their individual members.

In this section, we follow out the implications of a point made earlier to the effect that, because of their concreteness, populations (and subpopulations) are especially appropriate macro-level (larger) units of observation and analysis in social science. Here we stress that one needs to be careful not to take this point too far. For to say that populations are appropriate units of observation does not mean that population dynamics *determine* our collective lives. This latter view is known as **demographic determinism** and was first introduced in modern academic circles by Thomas Robert Malthus (1766–1834). It is a fairly common error that we now know should be avoided.

Malthus's is perhaps the most prominent name in the history of the field of demography (James 1979; Winch 1987; Turner 1986). He is well remembered for his belief that the alternating periods of population growth and decline he observed in demographic records of *his* past (the period up to about 1800) would continue forever. This boom-and-bust kind of population change, which is now referred to as **Malthusian** growth, is illustrated in Figure 1.7. As you may know, Malthus based this forecast on what he considered to be immutable laws of population. These are principles whereby populations naturally and automatically worked: (1) that the needs for food and for sexual expression are permanent parts of the human condition, and (2) that food supplies always increase more slowly than populations grow. In fact, his word for these principles was *postulata*, a logical term even stronger than "law" because it implies logically necessary truths. These *postulata* are quoted in full in Chapter 14, as we return to Malthus and his influence on past and current population policy.

Figure 1.6   Thomas Robert Malthus
Source: Photos.com/Thinkstock.

Over the years, these views have become the foundation of the doctrine of demographic determinism; that is, that human existence is ultimately determined by population dynamics. This doctrine has had an enormous impact on both scientific and popular thinking. In particular, it has given considerable credence to the view held by some pessimistic commentators that human population dynamics always run a certain, disastrous course no matter what we do about it, the "classic Malthusian" position. As we shall note in Chapter 11, the doctrine also underlies the more common understanding that populations may well be on a general runaway course, but that certain measures, like fertility control, can be taken to mitigate or avoid the worst consequences—the "**neo-Malthusian**" position.

What many people, including some scientists, fail to notice, however, is that Malthus's argument is false. There may well be inevitable, necessary, and unavoidable outcomes in populations of other species, but human beings long ago took the matters of food production and the expression of the sexual passions in hand. By exerting conscious control over formerly natural processes, through agriculture and with mortality- and fertility-control beliefs and technologies, humans have so altered things that no one can really say what the "logically necessary" connections may be. We do know that in the years following Malthus's dire prediction to the effect that food would increase only arithmetically (the line in Figure 1.7) and population would increase geometrically (the curve in Figure 1.7), the *reverse* actually occurred!

Figure 1.7   Malthusian Growth

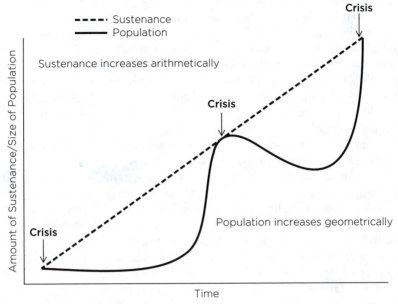

Food production, of every grain crop and of most meat products, shot up geometrically. Meanwhile, population growth became arithmetic, then it dampened further until, today, growth rates in Malthus's England and other parts of Europe are at *zero or below*.

Malthus's forecasts specifically were mistaken, as are all such views that assume that demographic factors determine everything else, because they ignore the important role that society and culture play in human populations. Malthus's name and work will be well remembered; in large part because he directed the attention of all future social scientists to populations as key units of observation and analysis in human affairs (he became England's first professor of a social science—"Political Economy"—in 1805). But his record as a prophet is less impressive, in part because he took his own insights about the power of population too far. Human affairs surely do take place within and between populations, but in these affairs demographic factors are always constrained by sociocultural ones, and *vice versa*.

THE HISTORY OF DEMOGRAPHY: AN OVERVIEW

The creation of a Chair in Political Economy and Modern History at London's East India College in 1805 marks the formal beginning of the academic study of population. The fact that Malthus, an Anglican Minister trained at Cambridge University, was the first occupant of that chair has shaped the field in many ways that are apparent to this day. In a discussion of Malthus's continuing importance, Geoffrey McNicoll (1998:309) asks rhetorically: "So, should Malthus therefore be retired . . . with gratitude or disdain, but in either case with acknowledgement that the issue [of overpopulation] is all but dead—a piece of intellectual history rather than a continuing controversy? As with most important thinkers, the answer is 'no.'"

Despite his prestigious appointment and unquestionable influence, Malthus was not England's first population scientist. According to several sources, including a recent editorial in *Population and Development Review*, his fellow countryman, Sir James Steuart (1713–1780), anticipated many of his ideas on the race between sustenance and birth rates (Archives 1998; also see Sullivan 1997). And it is likely that Malthus's views would have been quite different had they not been formed in debate with William Godwin (1756–1836), as we discuss in Chapter 11. Reaching back even earlier, many historians credit John Graunt (1620–1674) with the honor of being the founder, based on his extensive (privately sponsored) studies of death statistics in Metropolitan London, some of which were published as the first treatise in demography, *Observations on the Bills of Mortality*. Other contemporary scholars prefer to recognize a contemporary of Graunt, William Petty (1623–1687) as the first true demographer, based on his book, *Political Arithmetic* (Strauss 1954). In fact, a controversy has brewed for more than a century about whether it was Petty and not Graunt who actually wrote the *Observations* (Hull 1896).

Another very important figure in early-modern population research was Edmund Halley (1656–1742; see Figure 1.8). Halley is, of course, best remembered for his careful study of charts indicating the positions of comets, one of which now bears his name (Cook 1998). But he was also fascinated with charting the changes in the size of human populations, especially as their rates of death varied from one to another, and from age group to age group (or what is termed a *cohort*) within a given population (Halley 1693 [1942]). A major invention resulting from Halley's demographic research, the life table, is today an essential tool in demography, actuarial science, and in the life and health insurance industries in which actuarial science is extensively applied. We will have occasion to mention Halley again in our discussion of his life table in Chapter 9.

The contributions of Steuart, Malthus, Graunt, and Halley certainly represent landmarks in the creation of modern population science. But they were by no means the first people ever to take an interest in the study of population. As you probably know, information about the size and characteristics of populations has been gathered for as long as we have written records; in fact, demographic information is included among the very first items ever recorded by the ancient civilizations of Egypt, Sumer, Babylon, and Israel.

Based on what we now know of these ancient societies, the oldest of which were established in the Near East more than 5,000 years ago, it is apparent that their populations had grown to great size, geographic reach, and structural complexity. As a result, it was necessary for the rulers to make a conscious effort to take a count of their subjects accurately and on a regular basis. In the very earliest times, the need to count led, in many cases, to the invention of methods of keeping track of these accounts: that is, systems of numerals and writing itself. Without such information, captured in some more-or-less permanently preserved form, the two cornerstones of the ancient empires (and of most societies to this day), military power and taxation, would be impossible to manage. These needs thus led to the first widespread *census* operations. In fact, the word *census* comes from a Sanskrit word meaning to assess or tax.

The Egyptian Empire and many other ancient civilizations kept censuses counts. The importance of the census in the traditions of the Western world, as well, is evident in the Hebrew Bible, in which God is said to have *commanded* his people through His Prophet Moses to count their numbers:

On the first day of the second month, in the second year following the exodus from Egypt, the Lord spoke to Moses in the wilderness of Sinai, in the Tent of Meeting, saying: "Take a census of the whole Israelite community by the clans of its ancestral houses, listing the names, every male, head by head. You and Aaron shall record them by their groups, from the age of twenty years up, all those in Israel who are able to bear arms. Associated with you shall be a man from each tribe, each one the head of his ancestral house. (Numbers 1, 1–4)[6]

And, of course, Christians are well aware of the importance of these early censuses because, according to the New Testament, Christ was born in Bethlehem during a taxation count:

Figure 1.8 Edmund Halley, a pioneering demographer as well as an astronomer
Source: Georgios Kollidas/Thinkstock.

And it came to pass in those days, that there went out a decree from Caesar Augustus that all the world should be taxed. (And this taxing was first made when Cyrenius was governor of Syria.) And all went to be taxed, every one into his own city. And Joseph also went up from Galilee, out of the city of Nazareth, into Judaea, unto the city of David, which is called Bethlehem; (because he was of the house and lineage of David) to be taxed with Mary his espoused wife, being great with child. (King James Version: Luke 2, 1–5)

Even today, census operations in the United States and throughout the world are treated as a serious matter. They are universally conducted by national governments under stringent legislative authority and, for virtually all of the world's countries that belong to the United Nations (U.N.), in accord with strict U.N. standards of reliability and comparability. In most countries, a resident is required to respond to the census survey by law.

As the story of Christ's birth indicates, the Roman Emperor's subjects reported *to* the census-taker, often at the place of one's birth. This ordinarily meant that a man would return to his father's home, if he had ever left it, with his wife (or wives) and children, and physically present himself to an officer of the King or Emperor. There he would convey his name and probably other information such as his age, the number of his children, their sexes, and information about his wife and other relatives. Under the conditions of life for the vast majority of the people of these ancient empires (over 95 percent of whom were illiterate, rural, and lived at or near subsistence levels), the results of the census surveys must have been highly inaccurate. Nevertheless, they were good enough to allow the authorities to estimate their pools of military manpower and to have some idea about the size of the tax base they could draw upon to support their regimes.

During the centuries between the fall of Rome and the time of Graunt, Petty, and Halley, religious organizations in Europe and the Near East assumed the major responsibility for keeping track of population characteristics and dynamics. Churches, mosques, and synagogues became the recorders and repositories of demographic data through their ceremonial registers marking key life events, what the anthropologist Arnold Van Gennep (1977) first labeled *rites de passage* ("rites of passage"): births, baptisms, ritual circumcisions, religious confirmations, illnesses, and deaths.

Most of this information was maintained at the local level, especially at parishes in the case of Christian churches (Cambridge Group 1974); it was rarely centralized or collated by official bodies. The faiths with the more centralized organizations, such as the Roman Catholic Church, did have access to information about larger regional and (what we would today consider) "national" aggregate populations; but, in other cases, the information that survives exists in many small, village-level "packets" (Drake 1982). The historical demographer E. A. Wrigley was one of the first contemporary students of population to work extensively with these records (Wrigley 1986; 1997). Wrigley's innovations in piecing together the many packets of information to form a coherent picture about populations that existed four or more centuries ago are considered to be among the major achievements in the field of social demography.

The end of the Middle Ages is marked by the rise of the modern nation-state, among many other significant social innovations. One of these innovations is closely tied to the creation of the nation, that is, modern censuses. The first official total population count was probably conducted in 1665 in the area that is today Quebec (Petersen 1975:21). In 1749, the new constitutional monarchy of Sweden produced the first in a series of continuous government-sponsored reports on the population of a country. In fact, Sweden's was a compilation of locally collected (city, town, and village) information on population size and other characteristics, along with local registration data. But because it was the product of a centralized operation, and because it was tied to representative government, some historians designate it as the first modern census.

All things considered, the U.S. Census of 1790, conducted by authority of an Act of the First Congress, is the more appropriate choice as the model of its type. It was the first population count actually undertaken, from design to data analysis and interpretation, by a national government for its entire populace; and its explicit purpose was to apportion the electorate in a representative manner.[7] Thus, since that time, the connection between demo*graphy* and demo*cracy*—*government by* the people collectively—has been more than just linguistic. As the founders of the United States and leaders of the other democratic nations that were to follow their lead were aware, a strong representative government requires free access to accurate and timely information about population characteristics and dynamics.

At about the time of the first U.S. Census, the elementary concepts of population studies had found their way into various courses in history, natural science, and mathematics in colleges and universities in the United States, England, and France (Sullivan 1997). From the time of Malthus's appointment to this day, demography has been taught as a branch of social science. It is offered in various departments, especially sociology and geography, at universities throughout the world; and population scientists are employed at all levels of government, in private industries, and in academic settings.

CONTEMPORARY SOURCES OF DEMOGRAPHIC INFORMATION

As this brief review of the history of demography suggests, developments in methods of data collection have closely paralleled the growth of the field as an academic discipline. Halley's case is illustrative in that it emphasizes how important the careful collection and observation of data are in scientific research, whether the objects are comets or human populations. This section expands on the role of data collection in population science by highlighting the main sources of information employed in the field today. These include traditional sources, censuses and other types of surveys, and vital registration.

Census and Registration Data

We noted that religious organizations served as the collectors and keepers of demographic information for many centuries in Europe and other parts of the world. But this is not to say that the practice does not continue, nor that these records are no longer of interest to demographers. To the contrary, churches, mosques, synagogues, and—in this increasingly secular world—many nonreligious social organizations routinely collect and keep track of much useful information about their members and clients. Much of this information is unique, especially because it tends to cover small, local populations that might be overlooked (or undersampled) in surveys.

Although they are valuable sources of data, local religious and service organizations such as churches, synagogues, and welfare agencies no longer collect most population information. Rather, since the late eighteenth century this has been a task assigned to government agencies at national and local levels. The United Nations Fund for Population Activities (UNFPA) and several constituent U.N. agencies also collect some data on an international level and, more often, they compile nationally collected information into international data sets.

The main generators of demographic information today are the national census counts, one of which is now regularly held in at least one hundred nations. In most countries, the national census operation, located in the capital city, keeps track of two types of data and distributes both in a similar manner. These are: (1) survey data, based on mailed questionnaires or in-person interviews held between the census-taker and the members of the national population; and (2) registration information, based on entries of vital events in official registers (births, deaths, and other items). In this instance, however, the United States is the exception.

Although the U.S. Census was the first of its kind, it has always been viewed as a purely survey research operation, with the principal aim of taking a periodic (every 10th year) count or **complete enumeration** of the population. Until the early 1900s, this was its only activity; for the organization ceased functioning between surveys. As indicated in a Bulletin from the U.S. Census, reproduced in Box 1.1, today, the U.S. Census Bureau, a branch of the Department of Commerce, collects, analyzes, and distributes vast amounts of information on a daily basis, much of which can be found online at the Census Bureau web site (http://www.census.gov). This includes the results of a monthly survey of a *panel* of 50,000 households throughout the nation.

Box 1.1   History and Function of the U.S. Census

The first census began more than a year after the inauguration of President Washington and shortly before the second session of the first Congress ended. Congress assigned responsibility for the 1790 Census to the marshals of the U.S. judicial districts. The pay allowed for the 1790 "enumerators" was very small, and did not exceed $1 for 50 people properly recorded on the rolls.

The First Federal Congress established a special committee to prepare the questions to be included in the first census. The suggestions were likely debated in the House, and according to a report in a Boston newspaper, Virginia Representative James Madison recommended at least five of the initial six questions.

The six inquiries in 1790 called for questions on gender, race, relationship to the head of household, name of the head of household, and the number of slaves, if any. Marshals in some states went beyond these questions and collected data on occupation and the number of dwellings in a city or town.

The 2010 questionnaire is one of the shortest in history, and comes very close to the length and scope of inquiries asked in 1790. Everyone in the household answers seven questions: name, gender, race, ethnicity, and whether they sometimes live somewhere else. The head of household answers how many people live in the residence, whether it is a house, apartment, or mobile home, and provides a telephone number for Census workers to follow up if any information is incomplete or missing.

Questions Beyond a Simple Count are Constitutional

It is constitutional to include questions in the decennial census beyond those concerning a simple count of the number of people. On numerous occasions, the courts have said the Constitution gives Congress the authority to collect statistics in the census.

Source: U.S. Census Bureau, "Census in the Constitution" http://www.census.gov/2010census/about/constitutional.php.

Indeed, as the Census Bureau puts it, "[t]oday the Census Bureau's demographic and economic programs are an invaluable planning tool for citizens, businesses, and government officials."[8]

Despite this enormous increase in the scale of the operation, as in the past, all of the data collected directly under U.S. Census auspices comes from in-person interviews and mailed questionnaires. On the other hand, the function of keeping records of vital information in the United States was reserved for, and remains, in local jurisdiction, a practice based in part on the principle of state's rights. In fact, for many years after the founding of the Republic, local church parish records were employed as a source of official registration data. Today, births, deaths, marriages, and divorces are registered by governments at the municipal, county, and state levels. These records are then transmitted under a cooperative agreement to the Center for Disease Control and Prevention (CDC) in Atlanta. The CDC publishes its findings in several documents, the most important of which are the annual *Vital Statistics of the United States* and the *Monthly Vital Statistics*. Its URL (Uniform Resource Locator or address) is http://www.cdc.gov/nchwww. Box 1.2 discusses the types of registration systems maintained by the states and local governments, along with other information about the work of the CDC.

Data on international migration to the United States is collected and distributed by the Immigration and Naturalization Service (INS). This information is obtained from visas and other forms, and it is circulated in the annual *Statistical Yearbook of the Immigration and Naturalization Service*. Several different categories of immigrants have been created, and a substantial body of legislation and regulations has been developed to administer the immigration process, as we discuss in Chapter 7. In any case, nonnationals admitted to the country for legal permanent residence are considered to be part of the United States population; and they are counted during decennial enumerations and included in Census Bureau estimates.

As you may know, information about internal migration in the United States, county to county or state to state, is not officially recorded, again by virtue of law and conventions that prohibit such monitoring of citizens. In contrast, thorough internal migration records are kept in Canada and many other countries throughout the world.[9] Of course, migration registration information on state-to-state and other internal population movements in the United States is available, but because of the restrictions noted, it is based on unofficial sources (for example, utility records and driver's license applications). The other official sources of migration information produce only estimates of population movements based on (a) comparisons between successive census counts—to which we return in Chapter 7 in connection with the *components* method of estimation, or (b) surveys. In the latter instance, as part of its decennial enumerations and the CPS, mentioned above, the U.S. Census Bureau regularly samples households to provide information about recent moves, as discussed further when we return to the subject of migration data.

The fact that there is a difference between survey and registration data obviously has practical consequences, at least in the United States. These include issues of limited access to registration data, problems of comparability between Federal **sample survey** and state registration findings, and concerns over the levels of reliability of the two methods of data collection. That is, surveys and registration are both subject to undercount, but for different reasons. In addition, the existence of two types of data parallels an important theoretical distinction in population studies and other social sciences, indicated by the paired concept: *synchronous*, at the same time, for survey data; and *diachronic*, through time, for registration data.

Samples and Complete Enumerations

Before leaving this subject for the time being, let us consider one further aspect of contemporary data collection: sample surveys. In all fields of social research and in population studies especially, sampling techniques have helped to increase our knowledge base in a highly cost-effective, yet still controversial, way.[10] Since the 1970s, or even earlier, this controversy has affected the operation and public image of the U.S. Census Bureau.

Most academic and private researchers routinely collect demographic information from relatively small samples as part of marketing, attitude, and public opinion surveys. In fact, in summarizing what it is about the respondents (or "subjects") that survey researchers *survey*, most texts in research methods identify four categories, captured by the mnemonic: D-KAP: "Demographics, Knowledge, Attitudes, and Practices." The first, of greatest interest to us, includes age, gender, place of birth, occupational status, ethnicity, health characteristics, and the like. Although these questions are posed in terms of individual characteristics, from a demographic perspective, they represent major criteria in the study of population **structure.**

Box 1.2 Centers for Disease Control and Prevention, Source of Vital Statistics for the United States

National Vital Statistics System

- About NVSS
- What's New
- Birth Data
- Mortality Data
- Fetal Death Data
- Linked Birth and Infant Death Data
- Marriages and Divorces
- National Maternal and Infant Health Survey
- National Mortality Followback Survey
- Instruction Manuals
- Publications and Information Products
- Listserv

The National Vital Statistics System (NVSS) provides the Nation's official vital statistics data based on the collection and registration of birth and death events at the state and local levels. These data are provided through contracts between NCHS and vital registration systems operated in the various jurisdictions legally responsible for the registration of vital events, producing critical information on such topics as teenage births and birth rates, prenatal care and birth weight, risk factors for adverse pregnancy outcomes, infant mortality rates, leading causes of death, and life expectancy.

Sources: Centers for Disease Control and Prevention, National Vital Statistics System (NVSS), http://www.cdc.gov/nchs/nvss.htm; "Celebrating 50 Years," National Center for Health Statistics, http://www.cdc.gov/nchs/about/50th_anniversary.htm.

In these and related ways, most contemporary survey research includes a "mini-census" that is of considerable value. We have already mentioned the work of large research institutes, but many lesser-known organizations are involved in similar activities. In fact, most new careers in population research are oriented more to smaller surveys, such as those conducted by commercial market-research firms, than to working with the Census Bureau. Of course, information collected in this manner cannot *replace* official Census data. But, because it tends to be local and to cover unique subpopulations, it can be a significant supplement to official population data.

As was the case for the previous 70 years, the U.S. Census count for the year 2010 included two different types of data collection procedures: (a) a sample survey,[11] and (b) a complete enumeration. The sample survey, as the name indicates, drew its findings from questionnaires and interview schedules (which are called *survey instruments*) completed by less than the entire population—with varying sample sizes. The enumeration was based upon a direct count, presumably of every member of every household residing in the country. Just one in every six households (17 percent) answered some sample survey items, whereas in some areas the *sampling fraction* was one-half.

The Census 2010 survey produced far more information than the enumeration, in terms of the number of variables and the sheer volume of facts and figures that can be extracted from the questionnaires. Its findings were used extensively and definitively in legislation, in court decisions, and in government, academic, and private research until the results of the 2010 enumeration became available. But, until 2010, according to the members of the 105th Congress and the U.S. Supreme Court, the sample survey approach was *not* good enough to satisfy the mandate of the First Congress to count every member of the population for the sake of apportioning members of the House of Representatives.

Proposed legislation (in the form of several bills and amendments) that would allow the total population size to be *estimated* from sample survey data was deliberated for several years. In June 1998, House Speaker Newt Gingrich authorized a lawsuit challenging sampling, which was heard in two jurisdictions, including the Federal District Court in Roanoke, Virginia (Sample 1998; National Desk 1998). President Clinton responded by appointing as new Director of the Census Bureau Kenneth Prewit, former head of the Social Science Research Council and a strong supporter of sampling (El Nasser et al. 1998). Focusing on the fact that the results of sample surveys always have a known margin of error, an antisampling interest group, Citizens for an Honest Count Coalition, made an emotional appeal. Their spokesperson argued that "Census 2000 initiatives are continuing to push their unconstitutional and illegal plan to use statistical sampling to adjust the 2000 Census. . . . This fundamental flaw, the margin of error rate, would violate our time-honored principle of one man one vote. This principle should not be sacrificed to the partisan agenda of a select few" (Cleary 1998).

In an attempt to provide academic perspective on the debate, Norman Bradburn of the University of Chicago made these observations.

> The proposed use of sampling as part of Census 2000 has led to a fierce political battle. Conventional wisdom has it that the Democratic Party will be favored by sampling because it will result in a higher count of minorities and urban dwellers who are more apt to vote Democratic. Opponents of sampling cite, with alarm, for instance, estimates by unnamed "experts" that such a result may cause as many as 22 House seats to shift from Republican to Democratic, threatening Republican control of the House. Such estimates, like opposition to census sampling in general, are based on a faulty understanding of the use of sampling. . . . [P]artisan political advantage has much more to do with the ability to gerrymander legislative districts than it does with whether the Census Bureau uses sampling and statistical methods to produce better counts of the population. An accurate census serves the best interests of all of the population and both political parties. (Bradburn 1998)

Despite such arguments, the two lower courts ruled against the proposed change, declaring it "unlawful" (AP 1999:3). And, via a "fast-track" procedure, the case was automatically appealed to the United States Supreme Court. On January 25, 1999, The Court ruled that:

> The Federal census law bars use of statistical methods intended to make the national population count more nearly accurate. . . . When the census law was

amended in 1976, "At no point did a single member of Congress suggest that the amendments would so fundamentally change the manner in which the (Census) Bureau could calculate that population for the purposes of apportionment," Justice Sandra Day O'Connor wrote for the court. (AP 1999:3)

The court was, in fact, split 5 to 4 on the decision—along ideological lines, with the majority consisting of conservative Justices O'Connor, Chief Justice William H. Rehnquist, and Justices Antonin Scalia, Anthony M. Kennedy, and Clarence Thomas. The dissenting votes came from moderate-to-liberal Justices John Paul Stevens, David H. Souter, Ruth Bader Ginsburg, and Stephen G. Breyer. In his dissenting opinion, Breyer wrote, "The Census Act . . . unambiguously authorizes the Secretary of Commerce to use sampling procedures when taking the decennial census." Nevertheless, the majority prevailed and the complete enumeration strategy was undertaken as definitive.

By 2010, however, a complete reversal occurred, in the absence of lawsuits and lengthy court proceedings and appeals. The 2010 survey design included a postenumeration sampling, which was conducted in the absence of political conflict. Ironically, "The U.S. Census Bureau released today results from its postenumeration survey, providing a measure of the accuracy of the 2010 Census. The results found that the 2010 Census had a net overcount of 0.01 percent, meaning about 36,000 people were overcounted in the census. This sample-based result, however, was not statistically different from zero" (U.S. Census Bureau 2012). In this case, the actual count and the adjusted account were essentially identical.

Of course, inaccuracy is a concern to census officials throughout the world, not only in the United States. Problems of undercounting, and overcounting as well, have been documented in several countries in Asia, Africa, Europe, and Latin America. This includes some fairly recent cases of blatant political manipulation of census findings by government officials. In fact, the U.S. Census remains a model for other nations. The most recent count was certainly the most expensive, and one of the most highly organized and highly computerized social research projects in history. It is also among the world's most accurate population studies.

SUMMARY

Each of the sections of this chapter has explored an aspect of population studies. The first section introduced several aspects of the distinctively demographic way of thinking, which we have called the "focus on aggregates." We began with a definition of some of the basic terms in the field of demography, including the name of the field itself, *aggregate*, *population*, and *endogamy*, and we examined the character of naturally occurring, especially human, populations at some length. Following this, we looked at some of the ways in which the distinction between aggregate- and individual-level characteristics is apparent, including ecological fallacy and the technique of analysis of structural effects. This led to a brief concluding discussion of demographic determinism and an introduction to the classic theory of Thomas Robert Malthus. At several points, mention was made of the vital demographic events, such as birth and death and the three basic dimensions of a population: size, structure, and geographic distribution. We now return to these with an examination of the ways in which naturally occurring populations are and have been studied.

KEY TERMS

aggregate
complete enumeration
demographic determinism
ecological fallacy
emergent
endogamy
formal demography
Lamarckian
Malthusian
National Vital Statistics System (NVSS)

neo-Malthusian
population
reductionist
sample survey
social demography
structural effect
structure
vital events
vital registration

NOTES

1. Included among several general studies of population biology are Hastings (1997) and McKinney (1998). The collection by Cappuccino and Price (1995) is of special interest because of its emphasis on the manner in which *insect* populations grow (including insect pests).

2. At this point, it should be apparent that we do not believe that human beings are unique in having cultures, or at least tools, symbols, "languages," and other rudiments of culture. Thus, strictly speaking, demographers interested in certain nonhuman populations—primates and cetaceans, for example—might be as concerned with sociocultural heritage as those who specialize in *Homo sapiens.*

3. You may recall that Lamarck proposed the "law of use and disuse," which allows for the possibility of an organism acquiring (or losing) a physical trait during its life and then passing the change on to the next generation. This view is generally understood to have been thoroughly refuted by Darwin's theory of evolution in the case of biogenetic inheritance. However, it *does* apply to sociocultural traits. The acquisition or loss of norms, values, languages, tools, and the like and the consequent passing of such changes to offspring is a legitimate and major source of sociocultural change.

4. Demographers study these events using *rates* of occurrence: for example, the **crude birth rate** is the rate at which births occur during a year (or other interval of time) per each one thousand members of a population.

5. Durkheim generalized these findings in coining the term "social fact"—as opposed to an *individual* fact.

6. Online English translation of the Tanakh (Jewish Bible) with Rashi's commentary (Brooklyn, NY: The Judaica Press). The section continues with a count, tribe by tribe and household by household, until in verse 46 we learn that "all who were enrolled came to 603,550." Assuming one adult woman and three children for every man counted, this would bring the total to about 3 million.

7. Data from the first Census count of 1790 are available for several states in a series of Census Bureau *Staff Paperbacks.* See, for example, United States Bureau of the Census (1992).

8. For this and other information about the Bureau's history and operations, visit the Census Bureau site. Also, see McCave and Koeth (1998).

9. In the Netherlands, population registers have been maintained since 1800s. Events such as births, deaths, change in residence, and name are recorded in each person's registration card (Rees et al. 1998).

10. A substantial body of literature on survey sampling exists in printed and electronically accessible forms. However, most researchers continue to rely on the definitive text on the

subject by Leslie Kish (1995). The U.S. Census Bureau maintains a site on survey sampling at https://www.census.gov/prod/2006pubs/tp-66.pdf.

11. In enumeration years, the Census Bureau conducts a set of related surveys, some of which had been ongoing for some time prior to the count.

CHAPTER TWO

DEMOGRAPHIC VARIABLES

Size, Structure, and Vital Events

In this and the following two chapters, we turn to the basic tools and techniques used to summarize and communicate the demographic information that has been collected via a **census** count or other sources (e.g., estimates).[1] This chapter in particular is devoted to an exploration of the most fundamental features of a population: size, structural measures, and rates of vital events.

POPULATION SIZE

The size of a population is defined as the number of individual elements contained in the aggregate. It is measured by a count of these elements. We symbolize population *size* with an upper case P, and include a subscript for a date, such as P_{2010}, P_t, or P_0, indicating the total number of persons in the aggregate alive in the year 2010, at a general date t, or at an initial date, 0. The population clocks at the U.S. Census Bureau, which keep a running estimate of population sizes at https://www.census .gov/popclock/, reported that for the United States, as of t = July 12, 2014, P_t = 328,429,106. And for the world, P_t = 7,178,505,260.

When we think about the size of a population we ordinarily focus on the number of individual organisms it contains. In the case of human populations, of course, this means individual *persons*. It is therefore clear that when we say that the official size of Georgia's population as of 2013 was 10.0 million, we mean that 10 million people—women, men, boys, and girls—resided in the state at that date. On the other hand, the U.S. and other national censuses (and most unofficial population studies as well) are designed to interview and/or send survey questionnaires to *households*, not to individuals. Thus, the 2013 estimate for Georgia, based on the number actually contacted at the most recent census was actually about 3 million households, which contained an average of 2.70 persons (see Table 2.1). Moreover, the Census Bureau has for some time recognized the family unit as distinct from an individual and a household. A family corresponds to all related members of a household. Using this criterion, the estimated size of Georgia's Census population was 2.04 million families.[2]

Table 2.1.   Persons and Households in Georgia and Texas, 2000 to 2012-2013

Place	Persons 2000	Persons 2012-2013	Percent Increase	Households 2000	Households 2012-2013	Percent Increase	PPH 2000	PPH 2012-2013	Percent Increase
U.S.	281.4	316.1	12.3	105.5	115.2	.09	2.59	2.61	.07
Georgia	8.3	10.0	20.4	3.0	3.5	16.7	2.65	2.70	.02
Texas	20.9	26.4	26.3	7.4	8.8	18.9	2.74	2.80	.02

Source: U.S. Bureau of the Census 2010 enumeration and 2012–2013 estimates, www.census.gov.

These differences between individuals, households, and families are evident in comparisons between states in the United States. Although there have been considerable gains in the number of individuals, especially in "sunbelt" states such as Georgia and Texas, the number of households is increasing even more rapidly.

Table 2.2 reflects these changes to some extent.

Table 2.2.   Population Sizes of the States

Rank by Populations			Rank by Populations		
Rank	State	Population	Rank	State	Population
	All United States	308,745,538	27	Oregon	3,831,074
1	California	37,253,956	28	Oklahoma	3,751,351
2	Texas	25,145,561	29	Connecticut	3,574,097
3	New York	19,378,102	30	Iowa	3,046,355
4	Florida	18,801,310	31	Mississippi	2,967,297
5	Illinois	12,830,632	32	Arkansas	2,915,918
6	Pennsylvania	12,702,379	33	Kansas	2,853,118
7	Ohio	11,536,504	34	Utah	2,763,885
8	Michigan	9,883,640	35	Nevada	2,700,551
9	Georgia	9,687,653	36	New Mexico	2,059,179
10	North Carolina	9,535,483	37	West Virginia	1,852,994
11	New Jersey	8,791,894	38	Nebraska	1,826,341
12	Virginia	8,001,024	39	Idaho	1,567,582
13	Washington	6,724,540	40	Hawaii	1,360,301
14	Massachusetts	6,547,629	41	Maine	1,328,361
15	Indiana	6,483,802	42	New Hampshire	1,316,470
16	Arizona	6,392,017	43	Rhode Island	1,052,567
17	Tennessee	6,346,105	44	Montana	989,415
18	Missouri	5,988,927	45	Delaware	897,934
19	Maryland	5,773,552	46	South Dakota	814,180
20	Wisconsin	5,686,986	47	Alaska	710,231
21	Minnesota	5,303,925	48	North Dakota	672,591
22	Colorado	5,029,196	49	Vermont	625,741
23	Alabama	4,779,736	50	Washington, D. C.	601,723
24	South Carolina	4,625,364	51	Wyoming	563,626

Source: Resident Population Data, U.S. Census 2010.

Table 2.3. Population Sizes (in Millions) of 60 Nations

Country	Population Size	Country	Population Size
Albania	2.8	Liberia	5.2
Antigua	0.1	Lithuania	3.2
Australia	22.0	Macedonia	2.1
Bahamas	0.4	Malaysia	29.0
Barbados	0.3	Mauritania	3.6
Belize	0.3	Moldova	4.1
Bolivia	10.8	Mozambique	23.7
Brazil	194.3	Nepal	30.9
Burkina Faso	17.5	New Caledonia	0.3
Cameroon	20.9	Niger	16.3
Central African Rep	4.6	Oman	3.1
China	1350.4	Panama	3.6
Cuba	11.2	Peru	30.1
Denmark	5.6	Portugal	10.6
Dominican Republic	10.1	Reunion	0.9
El Salvador	6.3	Rwanda	10.8
Estonia	1.3	Saudi Arabia	28.7
Fiji	0.8	Sierra Leone	6.1
French Guyana	0.2	Slovenia	2.1
Gambia	1.8	South Africa	51.1
Ghana	25.5	Sudan	33.5
Guadalupe	0.4	Sweden	9.5
Guinea	11.5	Taiwan	23.3
Iceland	0.3	Thailand	69.9
Iran	78.9	Tunisia	10.88
Israel	7.9	Uganda	5.6
Japan	127.6	United Kingdom	63.2
Kenya	43.0	Uzbekistan	68.0
Kuwait	2.9	Vietnam	29.8
Latvia	2.0	Yemen	25.6

Source: The World Factbook: Country Comparisons by Population. Online at https://www.cia.gov/library/publications/the-world-factbook/rankorder/2119rank.html.

Variations in Population Size

Regardless of the element selected, it is obvious that some human populations are very large, others are relatively small, and others span the entire range from the least to the most numerous. At the national-aggregate level, for example, we find the island nation of Antigua with an estimated population size of less than 100,000 at one extreme and, at the other, the People's Republic of China, with an estimated total of approximately 1.4 billion persons (see Table 2.4). The state-levels of the U.S. populations (shown in Table 2.2) exhibit a similar range, from 563,626 in Wyoming to 37,253,956 in California (2010 Census).

As shown in Figure 2.1, size also varies at the county level within each state. Each bar on the chart represents the size (in number of persons) of one of the 13 counties of Massachusetts—whose 2010 total population size was 6.55 million. Even in this relatively small state the range is quite large. The average county population size of the state is 457,690. Nantucket County is the smallest, with only 10,000 persons. In

Table 2.4. Population Sizes (in Millions) of 60 Nations and Other Demographic Indicators

Country	Population Size	Infant Mortality	Percent Urban	Per-Capita Income	Average Life Expectancy
Albania	2.8	18.0	54.0	8520.0	75.0
Antigua	0.1	12.0	30.0	20400.0	77.0
Australia	22.0	3.9	68.0	36910.0	82.0
Bahamas	0.4	12.0	84.0	30620.0	75.0
Barbados	0.3	12.0	45.0	25900.0	74.0
Belize	0.3	17.0	71.0	6200.0	76.0
Bolivia	10.8	42.0	66.0	4640.0	67.0
Brazil	194.3	7.9	84.0	11000.0	74.0
Burkina Faso	17.5	65.0	24.0	1250.0	55.0
Cameroon	20.9	62.0	49.0	2270.0	51.0
Central African Rep	4.6	101.0	38.0	790.0	48.0
China	1350.4	17.0	51.0	7640.0	75.0
Cuba	11.2	4.5	75.0	10200.0	78.0
Denmark	5.6	3.5	72.0	41100.0	79.0
Dominican Republic	10.1	27.0	66.0	9930.0	73.0
El Salvador	6.3	20.0	63.0	6550.0	72.0
Estonia	1.3	3.3	69.0	19810.0	75.0
Fiji	0.8	45.0	51.0	4510.0	69.0
French Guyana	0.2	10.4	81.0	8390.0	79.0
Gambia	1.8	70.0	59.0	1300.0	58.0
Ghana	25.5	47.0	44.0	1620.0	64.0
Guadeloupe	0.4	7.6	98.0	21780.0	80.0
Guinea	11.5	89.0	28.0	1020.0	54.0
Iceland	0.3	0.9	94.0	28270.0	82.0
Iran	78.9	43.0	69.0	11490.0	70.0
Israel	7.9	3.4	92.0	27660.0	82.0
Japan	127.6	4.3	86.0	34610.0	83.0
Kenya	43.0	47.0	32.0	1640.0	62.0
Kuwait	2.9	8.0	98.0	56374.0	75.0
Latvia	2.0	5.7	68.0	16320.0	74.0
Liberia	5.2	83.0	47.0	340.0	56.0
Lithuania	3.2	4.3	16.7	17840.0	73.0
Macedonia	2.1	8.0	66.0	11070.0	72.0
Malaysia	29.0	7.0	63.0	14220.0	74.0
Mauritania	3.6	74.0	42.0	2410.0	58.0
Moldova	4.1	11.0	42.0	3360.0	69.0
Mozambique	23.7	86.0	31.0	930.0	52.0
Nepal	30.9	46.0	17.0	1210.0	68.0
New Caledonia	0.3	47.0	58.0	37700.0	77.0
Niger	16.3	81.0	20.0	720.0	58.0
Oman	3.1	16.0	73.0	25190.0	74.0
Panama	3.6	17.0	65.0	12770.0	76.0
Peru	30.1	16.0	74.0	8930.0	74.0
Portugal	10.6	2.5	38.0	24590.0	79.0
Reunion	0.9	8.0	94.0	4800.0	78.0
Rwanda	10.8	50.0	17.0	1150.0	54.0
Saudi Arabia	28.7	17.0	81.0	22750.0	74.0
Sierra Leone	6.1	109.0	40.0	830.0	47.0
Slovenia	2.1	3.0	50.0	26530.0	80.0

Table 2.4.   Continued

Country	Population Size	Infant Mortality	Percent Urban	Per-Capita Income	Average Life Expectancy
South Africa	51.1	38.0	62.0	10360.0	54.0
Sudan	33.5	67.0	41.0	2030.0	60.0
Sweden	9.5	2.1	84.0	37030.0	82.0
Taiwan	23.3	4.2	78.0	39059.0	79.0
Thailand	69.9	12.0	34.0	8190.0	74.0
Tunisia	10.88	20.0	66.0	9060.0	75.0
Uganda	35.6	54.0	15.0	1250.0	53.0
United Kingdom	63.2	4.3	80.0	35840.0	80.0
Uzbekistan	68.0	51.0	51.0	3110.0	68.0
Vietnam	29.8	36.0	31.0	3070.0	73.0
Yemen	25.6	48.0	29.0	2500.0	65.0

Sources: Table 2.3 The World Factbook: Country Comparisons by Population. Online at https://www.cia.gov/library/publications/the-world-factbook/rankorder/2119rank.html and Population Reference Bureau World Fact Sheet, 2013.

contrast, Middlesex (which includes Boston) is more than 150 times larger, with 1.5 million persons.

Population Size and Other Variables

Ever since the first censuses were taken as *head counts* intended principally to estimate a nation's "manpower," it has been assumed that the size of a population is in some respects a measure of its strength. In considering the possible relationship between demographic and cultural factors it is important to stress that a population's size is related to, but is not the same as (a) its density or (b) its rate of growth. We return to the topic of population density in the following chapter. There we note that, because density combines population size with size of territory, it may indeed have a substantial role to play—as cause and as effect—in a nation's well-being. Similarly, population growth (discussed in Part III) is today closely related to the wealth, levels of education, and other welfare variables. In particular, today's nations with slowly growing (or contracting) populations tend to be better off (often far better off) than those with rapid rates of population growth. Although this has not always been the case, it is currently one of the most widely discussed demographic facts.

Tables 2.4 and 2.5 focus on the population sizes of today's nations. They also include some key variables that were once believed to be associated with size. The first of these tables lists a sample of 60 countries drawn from Table 2.3 and the Population Reference Bureau's 2013 Data Sheet. In addition to the population sizes of these nations, the table contains data on four other variables: the infant mortality rate (IMR), percentage urban (URB), per-capita income (PCINC), and life expectancy at birth (AVELIFEEX). Table 2.5 contains the sample means for these variables.

The average population size for the sample is 35.3 million, ranging from 100,000 in Antigua and Barbuda to nearly 1.4 billion in the People's Republic of China. Infant mortality rates average 30.5 per 1,000 births, ranging between 0.9 in Iceland and 109.0 in Sierra Leone. The percentage urbanization rate for the entire sample is approximately 57. This ranges between 15 percent in Uganda and 98 percent in Guadalupe and Kuwait.

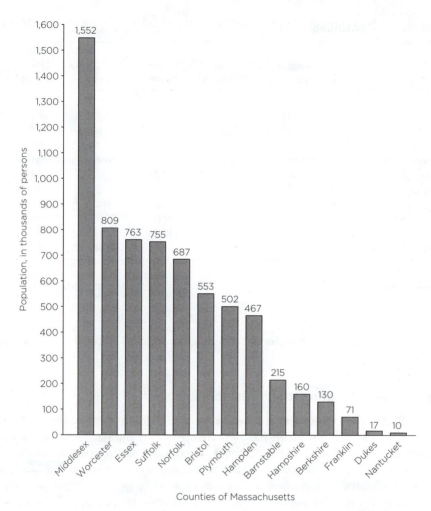

Figure 2.1. Population Sizes of the Fourteen Counties of Massachusetts (in Thousands of Persons), 2012-2013 Estimates

Source: Data from http://quickfacts.census.gov/qfd/states/25/25027.html (revised March 27, 2014).

The average per-capita income for the sample is $13,793. These vary substantially, with Niger at one extreme with $720 and Kuwait, exceeding Niger by a factor of 78 to 1, with $56,374. Finally, for the entire sample, the average life expectancy is just under 70 years, with a low of 47 years in Sierra Leone to a high of 83 in Japan (note the close connection between IMRs and average life expectancies).

From these comparisons, it is clear some of the largest nations in the world are very wealthy, highly urban, and have low IMRs (e.g., Japan), some are in the middle in these respects (e.g., China), and some are quite poor, rural, and have high IMRs (e.g., Thailand). On the other hand, some of the smallest nations (e.g., Kuwait) are very well off, while others (e.g., Albania) are very poor. Indeed, the more closely we examine data such as those shown in Tables 2.5, the more evident it becomes that the size of a contemporary national aggregate is something of an historical accident that has little to do with the "strength" of its members.

Table 2.5.   Population Size (in Millions) and Related Variables, 60 Nations

Variable	Minimum	Maximum	Mean	Standard Deviation
Population Size	.10	1350.4	35.3	1744.7
Infant Mortality	.90	109.0	30.5	29.2
Urbanization	15	98.0	56.9	22.9
Income $US	340	55,374	13,793	13.538
Average Life Expectancy	67	83.00	69.9	9.9

Source: Based on data from Table 2.4.

In brief, a nation's population size is essentially unrelated to the quality of life of its citizens. However, while noting that size, per se, appears to be a rather insignificant aspect of a nation's well-being, we also need to be clear about what we are *not* saying. That is, we are not saying that this lack of relationship necessarily holds for all aggregates. It is possible that size is a factor at other levels of aggregation: for instance, at the state, or county, or city level within nations. Perhaps nations are too artificial (because they are constructed for political as well as demographic purposes) to exhibit any advantages—or disadvantages—associated with size; but such a pattern may show up in smaller populations. Moreover, we have not yet examined the relationship between levels of population density or rates of population growth and socioeconomic well-being. So, although we will just have a little more to say about the "size equals strength" thesis, we will return to the impacts of density and growth.

Recently, demographers have shown interest in another issue related to population size, that is, the question of which nation has the largest population. As of 2012, both China and India were "billionaires," with population sizes of 1.35 billion and 1.26 billion, respectively. Taken together, these two make up nearly 40 percent of the world's population. It is likely that at some point in the year 2015, India surpassed China because of India's higher birth rates. A few comparisons can provide a clearer idea of how enormous these populations are. The third largest national population, after India and China, is that of the United States with 314 million persons in 2012. Thus, China and India have population sizes that are between four and five times that of the United States.

As Table 2.6 indicates, of the 28 states and seven Union Territories that make up India, the three largest states—Uttar Pradesh, Maharashtra, and Bihar—all have population sizes exceeding 100 million. In fact, the two largest states have a combined population size nearly equal to that of the entire United States. With a land area of approximately 1.3 million square miles, India is more than 11 times more densely populated than the United States (whose area is 3.7 million square miles). Table 2.7 lists the population sizes of China's 33 provinces. As of 2007, Guangdong had the largest population size, approximately 94.5 million, followed by two provinces, Shandong and Henan, with population sizes approaching 94 million. China's geographical area is approximately 3.3 million—close to that of the United States. But because of its larger population, its density exceeds that of the United States by a factor of 4.3. With these facts in mind, it is clear that much of the current and future population dynamics of the world depends upon demographic events in India and China (which, incidentally, share a long and not always peaceful border).

Table 2.6. Population Sizes of India's States and Union Territories

Rank	State or Union Territory	Population (2011 Census)
01	Uttar Pradesh	199,581,477
02	Maharashtra	112,372,972
03	Bihar	103,804,637
04	West Bengal	91,347,736
05	Andhra Pradesh	84,665,533
06	Madhya Pradesh	72,597,565
07	Tamil Nadu	72,138,958
08	Rajasthan	68,621,012
09	Karnataka	61,130,704
10	Gujarat	60,383,628
11	Odisha	41,947,358
12	Kerala	33,387,677
13	Jharkhand	32,966,238
14	Assam	31,169,272
15	Punjab	27,704,236
16	Haryana	25,353,081
17	Chhattisgarh	25,540,196
18	Jammu and Kashmir	12,548,926
19	Uttarakhand	10,116,752
20	Himachal Pradesh	6,856,509
21	Tripura	3,671,032
22	Meghalaya	2,964,007
23	Manipur	2,721,756
24	Nagaland	1,980,602
25	Goa	1,457,723
26	Arunachal Pradesh	1,382,611
27	Mizoram	1,091,014
28	Sikkim	607,688
UT1	Delhi	16,753,235
UT2	Puducherry	1,244,464
UT3	Chandigarh	1,054,686
UT4	Andaman and Nicobar Islands	379,944
UT5	Dadra and Nagar Haveli	342,853
UT6	Daman and Diu	242,911
UT7	Lakshadweep	64,429
Total	India	1,210,193,422

Source: http://www.indiaonlinepages.com/population/state-wise-population-of-india.html.

MEASURING STRUCTURAL CHARACTERISTICS

Like population size, information about structural characteristics comes from survey data, both census and unofficial surveys. The structural variables can be classed into two types: **biological** (age and gender) and **sociocultural** (social class, race or ethnicity, level of education, etc.). In both cases, they are measured with ratios, proportions, percentages, and averages. Beginning with *biological* characteristics, the simplest variable is the **sex ratio** (SR), a measure of the **sex structure** of an aggregate. Its formula is:

$$SR = (m/f) \times 100$$

Table 2.7. China's Province Populations, 2007

Name	Population	Name	Population
Anhui	61,200,000	Jiangxi	43,700,000
Beijing	16,300,000	Jilin	27,300,000
Chongqing	28,200,000	Liaoning	43,000,000
Fujian	35,800,000	Macau	500,000
Gansu	26,200,000	Neimongol	24,100,000
Guangdong	94,500,000	Ningxia	6,100,000
Guangxi	47,700,000	Qinghai	5,500,000
Guizhou	37,600,000	Shaanxi	37,500,000
Hainan	8,500,000	Shandong	93,700,000
Hebei	69,400,000	Shanghai	18,600,000
Heilongjiang	38,200,000	Shanxi	33,900,000
Henan	93,600,000	Sichuan	81,300,000
Hong Kong	6,900,000	Tianjin	11,200,000
Hubei	57,000,000	Tibet	2,800,000
Hunan	63,600,000	Xinjiang	21,000,000
Jiangsu	76,300,000	Yunnan	45,100,000
Jiangxi	43,700,000	Zhejiang	50,600,000

Source: Data from *The State of China* Atlas. Publisher: SACU (Society for Chinese American Understanding).

where m is the number of males in a population and f is the number of females. The ratio is expressed as the number of males "for every 100 females." For example, in the United States, the SRs for (1) 2000 and (2) 2010 were:

1. $(138,053,563/143,368,343) \times 100 = 96.29$ males for every 100 females;
2. $(151,781,326/156,964,212) \times 100 = 96.67$ males for every 100 females.

Here, as in many other populations, we find a "surplus" of women, reflecting an aging population (for reasons to be discussed in Chapter 3).

Several measures are used to indicate a population's age structure, including median age, which summarizes much information in a single number. This is the age that divides a population or other aggregate in two halves, one older and the other younger. For example, in 2010, the median age of the populations of Georgia and Texas, respectively, were 35.3 and 33.6 years (the median age of the United States was 37.2), indicating that by this criterion Georgia's population was older (see Table 2.8). In 2000, the medians were 33.4 and 32.3 years, respectively (the median for the United States was 35.3). This makes it clear that the populations of both states are getting older, and that Texas's is aging slightly more rapidly. By comparison with the median ages of the entire U.S. population at these two dates, both Georgia and Texas are somewhat younger.

Another set of age-related measures divides a population into subaggregates containing all individuals born at the same time (the same year, the same five-year period, or the same decade). These are known as **cohorts.** To continue our illustrations with state-level data, Table 2.9 shows the age and sex structure of the states of Georgia and Texas based on the 2010 Census. We see that for Georgia there are 686,785 persons under 5 years of age (350,673 males and 695,161 persons aged 5–9). For Texas, the size of the under-5 cohort was 1,948,234 and the number of those aged 5–9 was 1,268,136.

Table 2.8. Median Age of the Entire United States, Each State, and the District of Columbia, 2010

Rank	Median Age	State / Population	Rank	Median Age	State / Population
U.S.	37.2		27.	37.90	South Carolina / 4,625,364
1.	29.20	Utah / 2,763,885	27.	37.90	Alabama / 4,779,736
2.	33.60	Texas / 25,145,561	27.	37.90	Missouri / 5,988,927
3.	33.80	District of Columbia / 601,723	30.	38.00	Maryland / 5,773,552
3.	33.80	Alaska / 710,231	30.	38.00	Tennessee / 6,346,105
5.	34.60	Idaho / 1,567,582	30.	38.00	New York / 19,378,102
6.	35.20	California / 37,253,956	33.	38.10	Kentucky / 4,339,367
7.	35.30	Georgia / 9,687,653	33.	38.10	Iowa / 3,046,355
8.	35.80	Louisiana / 4,533,372	35.	38.40	Oregon / 3,831,074
9.	35.90	Arizona / 6,392,017	36.	38.50	Wisconsin / 5,686,986
10.	36.00	Kansas / 2,853,118	37.	38.60	Hawaii / 1,360,301
10.	36.00	Mississippi / 2,967,297	38.	38.80	Ohio / 11,536,504
12.	36.10	Colorado / 5,029,196	38.	38.80	Delaware / 897,934
13.	36.20	Nebraska / 1,826,341	40.	38.90	Michigan / 9,883,640
13.	36.20	Oklahoma / 3,751,351	41.	39.00	New Jersey / 8,791,894
15.	36.30	Nevada / 2,700,551	42.	39.10	Massachusetts / 6,547,629
16.	36.60	Illinois / 12,830,632	43.	39.40	Rhode Island / 1,052,567
17.	36.70	New Mexico / 2,059,179	44.	39.80	Montana / 989,415
18.	36.80	Wyoming / 563,626	45.	40.00	Connecticut / 3,574,097
19.	36.90	South Dakota / 814,180	46.	40.10	Pennsylvania / 12,702,379
20.	37.00	Indiana / 6,483,802	47.	40.70	Florida / 18,801,310
20.	37.00	North Dakota / 672,591	48.	41.10	New Hampshire / 1,316,470
22.	37.30	Washington / 6,724,540	49.	41.30	West Virginia / 1,852,994
23.	37.40	Arkansas / 2,915,918	50.	41.50	Vermont / 625,741
23.	37.40	Minnesota / 5,303,925	51.	42.70	Maine / 1,328,361
23.	37.40	North Carolina / 9,535,483			

Source: Census of Age and Sex, http://www.census.gov/prod/cen2010/briefs/c2010br-03.pdf.

According to the Census Fact Finder, SRs for these younger cohorts indicate a surplus of males, despite the fact that in both states the SRs for all ages combined favor females. In Georgia, the SR for the entire population was $4,729,171/4,958,482 \times 100 = 95$, indicating a surplus of females. The ratios for the two youngest cohorts are $(66,614/63,578) \times 100 = 104.8$ and $(276,585/264,624) \times 100 = 104.5$. For Texas, these ratios are 104.5 and 104.8. This apparent discrepancy illustrates a general but not universal demographic principle: males outnumber females at birth by a ratio of about 105 to 100, but as people age, the death rate for males exceeds that for females; and the oldest cohorts have a surplus of females. For example, in Georgia and Texas in 2010 the SRs for 75–79-year-olds were: Georgia $(77,156/105,579) \times 100 = 73.07$ and Texas: $(208,530/268,715) \times 100 = 77.60$. A closely related measure of age structure is the percentage of a population at a given age. This is calculated by dividing the cohort size by the population size, P, and then multiplying by 100.

Following similar procedures, the various *sociocultural* structures are measured in terms of the numbers and percentages of specifically identified individuals contained in a larger whole, in this case identified by features other than age or gender.

Table 2.9. Age Structure, Texas and Georgia, 2013

Age	TEXAS		GEORGIA	
	Persons	**%**	**Persons**	**%**
Total population	25,145,561	100.0	9,687,653	100.0
Under 5 years	1,928,473	7.7	686,785	7.1
5 to 9 years	1,928,234	7.7	695,161	7.2
10 to 14 years	1,881,883	7.5	689,684	7.1
15 to 19 years	1,883,124	7.5	709,999	7.3
20 to 24 years	1,817,079	7.2	680,080	7.0
25 to 29 years	1,853,039	7.4	673,935	7.0
30 to 34 years	1,760,434	7.0	661,625	6.8
35 to 39 years	1,763,587	7.0	698,059	7.2
40 to 44 years	1,694,795	6.7	699,481	7.2
45 to 49 years	1,760,467	7.0	722,661	7.5
50 to 54 years	1,674,869	6.7	668,591	6.9
55 to 59 years	1,422,924	5.7	573,551	5.9
60 to 64 years	1,174,767	4.7	496,006	5.1
65 to 69 years	853,100	3.4	356,007	3.7
70 to 74 years	619,156	2.5	250,422	2.6
75 to 79 years	477,245	1.9	182,735	1.9
80 to 84 years	347,206	1.4	129,048	1.3
85 years and over	305,179	1.2	113,823	1.2
Median Age	33.6		35.3	

Source: U.S. Bureau of the Census, 2013 American Community Survey 1-Year Estimates, http://factfinder.census. gov/faces/tableservices/jsf/pages/productviewxhtml?pid=ACS_13_1YR_S0101&prodType=table.

According to estimates published by the Population Reference Bureau (PRB) for the year 2012, approximately 3.6 billion people in the world now live in cities. This can be expressed as a proportion or a percentage. With a total world population size (P_{2012}) of about 7.1 billion, the proportion of urban dwellers (U_{2012}) is 3.6/7.1 = 0.51 as a proportion or 51 percent, or just over one half of the world's population lives in cities (a landmark that we discuss further in Chapter 4).

Another example is the percentage of a (working) population unemployed—the "unemployment rate," symbolized as UR (see Table 2.10) where U is the number of persons unemployed and seeking jobs and TLF is the size of the total labor force,[3] then

$$UR = U/TLF \times 100$$

where U is the number of persons seeking jobs. TLF is the size of the total labor force. In December 2015, the U.S. Department of Labor estimated the size of the U.S. labor force at 157.2 million and job seekers at 8.8 million. This gave a rate/ percentage of: 8.8/157.4 × 100 = 55.7 percent. This is a high but declining level of unemployment, following a serious recession in 2007. As the table indicates, the rate reached 10.0 in October 2009.

Another important and, as we will discuss in the next chapter, highly contro-versial structural factor is racial and ethnic composition. This is measured by the

Table 2.10. Unemployment Rates, 2005-2015

Year	Jan	Feb	Mar	Apr	May	Jun	Jul	Aug	Sep	Oct	Nov	Dec
2005	5.3	5.4	5.2	5.2	5.1	5.0	5.0	4.9	5.0	5.0	5.0	4.9
2006	4.7	4.8	4.7	4.7	4.6	4.6	4.7	4.7	4.5	4.4	4.5	4.4
2007	4.6	4.5	4.4	4.5	4.4	4.6	4.7	4.6	4.7	4.7	4.7	5.0
2008	5.0	4.9	5.1	5.0	5.4	5.6	5.8	6.1	6.1	6.5	6.8	7.3
2009	7.8	8.3	8.7	9.0	9.4	9.5	9.5	9.6	9.8	10.0	9.9	9.9
2010	9.8	9.8	9.9	9.9	9.6	9.4	9.4	9.5	9.5	9.4	9.8	9.3
2011	9.2	9.0	9.0	9.1	9.0	9.1	9.0	9.0	9.0	8.8	8.6	8.5
2012	8.3	8.3	8.2	8.2	8.2	8.2	8.2	8.0	7.8	7.8	7.7	7.9
2013	8.0	7.7	7.5	7.6	7.5	7.5	7.3	7.2	7.2	7.2	7.0	6.7
2014	6.6	6.7	6.6	6.2	6.3	6.1	6.2	6.1	5.9	5.7	5.8	5.6
2015	5.7											

Calculation of rate for January 2015:
Unemployed = 8.98 million; Labor force = 157.18 million
Unemployment rate = 8.98/ 157.18 = .057 x100 = 5.7 percent

Source: Labor Force Statistics from the Current Population Survey Series ID: KNS14000000.

percent of individuals in a larger population or other aggregate who identify themselves as members of specific racial and ethnic groups. For example, according to the 2000 U.S. Census, there were 4,119,301 people, 1.5 percent of the total population, who identified themselves as being of Native American (Indian, Eskimo, and Aleut) origin. In 2010, the number increased to 5,220,579, or 1.7 percent of the total population. By way of comparison, for the 2000 Census a total of 36,419,434 persons identified as black (African American), which was 12.9 percent of the total population. For the 2010 Census, the number had increased to 41.72 million or 13.2 percent of the total population. Until 2010, the U.S. Census distinguished between race—such as Native American and African American—and ethnicity. Prior to 2010 the two recognized ethnic groups were: Hispanic and non-Hispanic. Beginning in 2010, each of these groups is then classified according to race.[4]

In later chapters, we will encounter additional rates, proportions, and percentages. Census findings and other types of population information are often presented directly in one or more of these forms, although in most instances researchers must derive them indirectly from raw data. Certainly, demography is not the only field that uses rates and the like, but population scientists are perhaps uniquely dependent on—and even well known for their use of—such measures, especially rates. The main reason for this is that rates are so extensively employed when working with vital statistics, a topic to which we now turn.

RATES OF VITAL EVENTS

Vital events—births, deaths, and migration—are all measured by rates that reflect the relative number of persons added to or subtracted from a population *over* a period of time (see Figure 2.2). The period is usually one year, in which case they are *annual* rates. Although other periods are used, ranging from several years to one second, as shown in Table 2.11 we will usually assume that the rates discussed in this and later

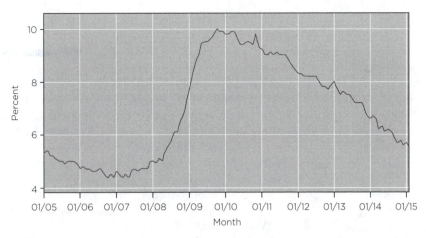

Figure 2.2. Resident Population Growth of the United States, 2005-2015

Source: Resident Population Data, U.S. Census 2010

chapters are annual. Each vital event has several different rates associated with it, depending on the larger aggregate to which the events are viewed as relative. The simplest, or **crude**, **rates** compare events to the entire population, whereas **specific rates** refer only to persons of an appropriate subpopulation. For instance, gender-specific rates separate events between males and females and age-specific rates refer only to particular cohorts.

Death (*mortality*) is the least complex of the vital events to measure, as we discuss in Chapter 6. The best-known measure is the annual crude rate,

$$CDR_t = D_t/P_t \times 1,000$$

where CDR_t is the crude death rate of a given population during year t, D_t is the number of deaths that occurred during the year, and P_t is the total population size at midyear.

To illustrate, PRB reported that approximately 1.28 million deaths occurred in Japan during the year 2012. With a total midyear population size of 128 million, this yields a crude death rate of: $CDR_{2012} = D_{2012}/P_{2012} \times 1,000 = 128/1.28 \times 1,000 = 10.0$

Table 2.11. Vital Events for Different Time Intervals

Time Interval	Births	Deaths	Natural Increase
Year	140,541,944	56,238,200	84,303,942
Month	11,711,830	4,688,5001	7,025,329
Week	2,788,531	1,115,833	1,672,697
Day	385,046	154,077	238,952
Hour	16,045	6420	9,624
Minute	267	107	160
Second	4.5	1.7	2.7

Number of births, deaths, and natural increase in the world per different units of time (2012 data).

Source: The yearly rates are from Population Research Bureau *World Population Data Sheet, 2013.*

deaths per 1,000 persons. For the sake of comparison, the southern African nation of Zimbabwe, with a total population size of 12.6 million, reported 1.89 million deaths in 2012. This gives a CDR_{2012} of 1.89/12.6 × 1,000 = 150, which is 15 times that of Japan.

Because crude rates (of death and other vital events) "average out" the number of events that occur in different subpopulations, specific rates are more precise in conveying a sense of actual conditions. In midyear 2010, the total population size of the United States, according to Bureau of the Census, was 308.74 million. CDC vital statistics indicate that during the year, 2.46 million deaths occurred, and a CDR of 8.0 per 1,000. The Census reported a total of 156.96 million females and 151.78 million males in the population. For that year, 1.32 million and 1.40 million deaths occurred for females and males, respectively; the gender-specific rates provide more detail. For females, the sex-specific death rate was 8.41 and for males it was 9.22 (CDC, *National Vital Statistics Report*, Vol. 61, No. 4: Table 1).[5]

Another type of death rate is of considerable importance in demographic analysis and application. This is the *age-specific* death rate ($ASDR_x$). For this and related measures (e.g., age-specific fertility rates), the subscript that to this point identified the calendar year is now replaced by a lowercase "x." This identifies the year or range of years of age of the subpopulation of interest (a cohort).

$$ASDR_x = (D_x/P_x) * 1,000$$

where D_x is the number of deaths occurring to persons aged x and P_x is the total number of persons at that age (we use the * to indicate multiplication here to avoid confusion with the "x" that symbolizes age). The rates can be calculated for any age, but the one that refers to the 0–1 cohort, D_0/B × 1,000, where B is the number of births during a year, is especially important.[6] This is the infant mortality rate, IMR, and it is one of the most sensitive indicators of general social and economic conditions available. For example, in Adams County, Colorado, 4,855 births occurred in 1996. Of these, 24 did not survive to the end of the year. Thus, the County IMR was:

$$(D_0/B) \times 1,000 = 24/4,855 \times 1,000 = 4.9 \text{ infant deaths per 1,000 births}$$

Other age-specific death rates are calculated similarly. For instance, in 1995, the state of Arkansas reported a total of 26,695 deaths and a midyear population size of 2,480,119. This yields a CDR of 10.76 per 1,000. In that same year, for the 0–4 cohort, the size and number of deaths were P_{0-4} = 175,256 and D_{0-4} = 388. For the 15–24 cohort, these figures were P_{10-15} = 363,936 and D_{10-15} = 444. Thus, the age-specific death rates were: 388/175,256 × 1,000 = 2.21; and 444/363,936 × 1,000 = 1.22, respectively.

One final type of specific rate is illustrated in Table 2.12; that is, place-specific rates. Here, too, we focus on **crude birth rates** (**CBR**s), defined as the number of births during a year (B_t) divided by the mid-year population size (P_t) multiplied by 1,000: B_t/P_t × 1,000. In 2012, the northeast region of the United States had a total population size of 54.1 million and had nearly 637,000 births, for a CBR of 11.8 per 1,000.

Because the Northeast is so large, consisting of two major subregions and nine states, this rate cannot possibly capture all of the variations in population sizes and

Table 2.12. Region- and State-Specific Crude Birth Rates, 2012

Region/State	Total Population	Number of Births	Crude Birth Rate
Northeast	54,093,025	636,762	11.8
New England	13,250,812	142,144	10.6
Connecticut	3,557,358	37,708	10.6
Maine	132,347	1,297	9.8
Massachusetts	6,564,414	72,865	11.1
New Hampshire	1,313,673	12,874	9.8
Rhode Island	1,054,434	11,177	10.6
Vermont	628,586	6,223	9.9
Middle Atlantic	40,842,213	494,618	12.1
New Jersey	8,764,098	106,922	12.2
New York	19,394,841	244,375	12.6
Pennsylvania	12,683,274	143,321	11.3

Source: *National Vital Statistics Reports*, Volume 61, Number 1, August 28, 2012; see Tables 11 and 12, pages 42 and 43.

numbers of births in the region as a whole. For example, the New England subregion has a lower CBR than the Middle Atlantic, by nearly one and one half births per thousand. And at the state level, the differences are even greater: with CBRs ranging from 9.8 in New Hampshire and Maine to 12.6 in New York. It should be clear from this illustration, and from the other examples in this section, that crude rates are adequate to begin an analysis but rates that are specific to place, age, gender, and so on are necessary if we seek a deeper understanding of vital events.

SUMMARY

In highlighting the study of the size and other characteristics of populations, this chapter has addressed the question: How are populations studied? The last section, in particular, focused on techniques for measuring size, structure, and vital events—with illustrations from counties and states in the United States and from several other nations. The next two parts of this book expand and elaborate on contemporary population characteristics and trends, using the measures discussed here and adding some new ones. In this light, the next chapter continues our exploration of a topic we have just introduced and one that logically follows our comments on population size: the many ways in which populations are structured along biological and sociocultural dimensions.

KEY TERMS

biological (structure)
census
cohorts
crude birth rate (CBR)
crude rates

sex ratio
sex structure
sociocultural (structure)
specific rates

NOTES

1. Data in this section come from several sources, including *The Statistical Abstract of the United States 1997*, Tables 34 and 92; the U.S. Census Bureau (state level) and NCHS web sites; PRB (1997) and PRB (1998); and the Colorado State web site: https://dola.colorado.gov/demog_webapps/dashboard.jsf?county=1.

2. The comparable U.S. figures for the 1990 Census were 248,765,140 persons, approximately 91,946,000 households (thus, 2.63 persons per household—"p.p.h.") and 64,517,947 families. Sources: U.S. Bureau of the Census, Internet release date, May 28, 1998; Population Estimates Program, Population Division, U.S. Bureau of the Census, release dates December 30, 1996 and July 7, 1997.

3. In the United States, this is currently defined as all persons age 16 and above who are employed or seeking employment.

4. "Overview of Race and Hispanic Origin 2010," http://www.census.gov/prod/cen2010/briefs/c2010br-02.pdf.

5. CDC *National Vital Statistics Report* 61 (4): Table 1.

6. For infant mortality rates, we use the number of births during the reference year (B) as the denominator, not K0—the number of persons aged 0 to 1 at midyear of the reference year. These are not the same, because the latter includes persons born between July 1 and December 31 of the previous year, and it does not include infants born during the reference year who did not survive to midyear. See Chapters 6 and 9 for more on this technicality.

CHAPTER THREE

HOW
POPULATIONS
ARE STRUCTURED

Populations and other demographic aggregates can be divided in several different ways to produce *subpopulations* or *subaggregates*: males and females, married and single persons, and so on. Taken together, each set of these subparts constitutes a structure. This chapter examines some of the principal ways in which naturally occurring populations are structured. The first of two main sections discusses biological structures; those that are based on purely physical characteristics. The characteristics considered here, sex and age, are of special interest because they have a significant and direct influence on the rates at which births and other vital events occur. The second main section focuses on sociocultural factors, including marital status and social class. The several types of sociocultural structures featured in this section are divided into two categories: those that underlie social differences and those that produce social inequalities. In the course of this discussion we present brief case studies and current data from the United States and other nations, emphasizing the diversity that exists within and between today's populations.

BIOLOGICAL STRUCTURE: AGE AND SEX

We introduced some of the most basic structures in Chapter 2, including one of the simplest, sex. You will recall that a population's sex *structure* is made up of two subaggregates taken together: one consisting of all of the males and the other consisting of all females. In this same way, we spoke of the *age structure* as the combination of the several special subaggregates called *cohorts*, each of which consists of persons born at the same time (e.g., during the same calendar year). In this section, we take a closer look at these important demographic variables.

Sex Structure: Some Comparisons

As noted in Chapter 2, the sex ratio, SR, is equal to the number of males in a population (M) divided by the number of females (F) times 100:

$$SR = (M/F) \times 100.$$

This ratio is especially sensitive to the age of a population, with the general rule being the younger the population, the higher the ratio.

To illustrate, according to the estimates shown in Table 3.1, the total 2010 population sizes of the United States, Afghanistan, and Russia were 309,326,225; 29,120,727; and 142,526,896 respectively. The sex ratios for these three countries were:

United States: $(152,088,297/157,237,928) \times 100 = 96.72$
Afghanistan: $(14,786,133/14,334,594) \times 100 = 103.14$
Russia: $(66,002,772/76,524,124) \times 100 = 86.25$

Russia's low ratio reflects an older population and the residue of male casualties at the front during World War II. Afghanistan's high sex ratio indicates a young population and/or lower survival rates for women, probably because of poorer standards of nutrition and health care compared to males. The U.S. rate, which lies between the other two, is typical of industrialized nations, although compared to most Western European nations the U.S. population is younger and its sex ratio is somewhat higher.

A comparison between the sex ratios at different ages provides further detail, and it dramatizes the differences between the populations. For example, the ratios for the 0 to 4 age groups were:

United States: $(10,313,172/9,876,246.0) \times 100 = 104.42$
Afghanistan: $(2,384,471.0/2,311,337.0) \times 100 = 103.16$
Russia: $(4,177,236.0/3,950,530.0) \times 100 = 105.73$

For persons aged 35–39, the ratios were:

United States: $(9,993,268.0/10,084,236) \times 100 = 99.09$
Afghanistan: $(769,479.0/739,626.0) \times 100 = 104.03$
Russia: $(5,054,189.0/5,110,271.0) \times 100 = 98.90$

And for those aged 75–79, they were:

United States: $(3,186,542.0/4,132,580.0) \times 100 = 77.10$
Afghanistan: $(51,325.0/60,912.0) \times 100 = 84.26$
Russia: $(1,091,825.0/2,641,306.0) \times 100 = 41.33$

Afghanistan's age-specific sex ratios tell a rather astounding story. Although its population is the youngest of the three, and among the youngest of any country, this fact does not explain the overall surplus of males. For its sex ratio *increases* with age, so that at ages 75–79, there are nearly 84.3 men per 100 women (compared to 77.1 in the United States). In Russia, the situation is nearly the opposite. Although the ratios at the youngest and middle age groups are within the normal range, the ratio for those aged 75–79 falls to an exceptionally low 41.3 men for every 100 women. This is less than one-half of the ratio for this age group in the United States. However, with just over 77 males for every 100 females in this older age group, it is clear that despite a higher incidence of stress-related diseases, smoking, and the like, women still do live longer than men in the United States.

Table 3.1. Gender and Age Structures of Afghanistan, Russia, and the United States, 2010 (Numbers of Persons in Millions)

Age(x)	Afghanistan Total	Male	Female	Russia Total	Male	Female	United States Total	Male	Female
0–4	4.69	2.38	2.31	8.13	4.18	3.95	20.19	10.31	9.88
5–9	4.06	2.06	2.00	6.98	3.59	3.40	20.33	10.38	9.95
10–14	4.12	2.10	2.03	6.36	3.26	3.10	20.68	10.58	10.10
15–19	3.40	1.73	1.67	8.00	4.10	3.90	21.98	11.28	10.70
20–24	2.68	1.37	1.31	12.04	6.11	5.93	21.70	11.07	10.63
25–29	2.02	1.04	0.99	11.96	6.01	5.95	21.14	10.66	10.48
30–34	1.75	0.90	0.85	10.89	5.41	5.48	20.07	10.05	10.02
35–39	1.50	0.77	0.74	10.16	5.05	5.11	20.08	9.99	10.08
40–44	1.23	0.63	0.60	9.35	4.61	4.74	20.90	10.40	10.50
45–49	1.01	0.51	0.49	11.32	5.40	5.92	22.64	11.18	11.46
50–54	0.80	0.41	0.40	11.56	5.31	6.25	22.35	10.96	11.39
55–59	0.62	0.31	0.32	9.98	4.36	5.62	19.79	9.59	10.21
60–64	0.47	0.23	0.24	7.00	2.86	4.14	16.99	8.16	8.83
65–69	0.32	0.16	0.17	4.60	1.72	2.88	12.52	5.90	6.63
70–74	0.20	0.10	0.11	6.20	2.08	4.12	9.34	4.27	5.06
75–79	0.11	0.05	0.06	3.73	1.09	2.64	7.32	3.19	4.13
80+	0.06	0.03	0.03	2.83	.65	2.17	11.30	4.12	7.18
Total	29.12	14.79	14.33	142.5	66.00	76.52	309.3	152.1	157.2

Source: Census Bureau's International Data Base (IDB), located at www.census.gov/population/international/data/idb. http://www.census.gov/population/international/data/idb/region.php?N=%20Results%2&T=10&A=separate&RT=0&Y=2010&R=-1&C=US.

Age Structure and Population Pyramids

Demographers graphically represent the age structure of a population with a special kind of bar graph or histogram, the familiar **population pyramid**.[1] As Figures 3.1, 3.2, and 3.3 indicate, population pyramids usually combine age and sex structures, with males on the left side and females on the right. This allows us to view simultaneously the relative numbers of men and women and the relative sizes of cohorts.

Each of the three populations illustrated here has a distinctive "signature" reflected in its pyramid. Afghanistan's displays the classic isosceles triangle shape. Note the wide base, representing a high birth rate and thus a large cohort of infants, and the sharp point at the top, indicating high death rates and a small cohort of the aged. You can also see the unusual phenomenon of the sex ratio increasing with age. This situation is expected to continue for several decades, with continued high birth rates and relatively small older cohorts under conditions of rapid general growth.

Russia's pyramid is highly asymmetric, reflecting abrupt periodic changes in both death and birth rates—including war and a postwar recovery. One of its most obvious features is the relative surplus of women, especially in the older cohorts. Also, at the very bottom, we see the cohort sizes decreasing as age decreases, showing a falling birth rate. This is a middle-aged to older population, as indicated by the "bulges" at ages 45 to 59 and again, for women, at ages 55 to 74. Russia's is also a population experiencing negative growth, as death rates now exceed birth rates. This trend is expected to continue into the future, as the population gets progressively older.

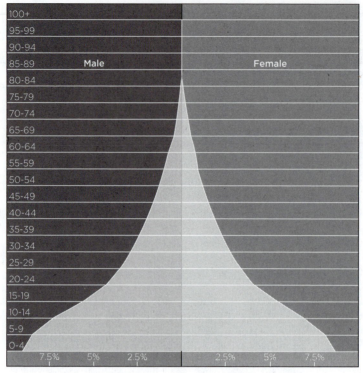

Figure 3.1. Population Pyramid for Afghanistan, 2010

Source: Based on the pyramid visual by Martin De Wulf at http://population pyramid.net/afghanistan/ and data from United Nations, Department of Economic and Social Affairs, Population Division. World Population Prospects: The 2012 Revision.

In the United States, the number of those 25 to 29 years old is as large as or larger than that of the younger cohorts. But perhaps the most prominent aspect of the U.S. population pyramid is the large bulge between ages 45 and 65. This is the "baby boom" generation, the group born during the post–World War II era. Birth rates were clearly very high during those years. They were high in comparison to the older cohorts, consisting of the parents of the "boomers," and in comparison to those younger. This young group, especially the 25–30 cohort, includes the children of the boomers, whose relatively large size has been identified as a ripple effect: Large numbers of persons born after World War II had many children in absolute terms during the 1970s and 1980s, despite relatively low birth rates. The projections for the United States foresee continued growth and continued aging, as the boomers age to the point at which the 85+ cohort (especially women) is expected be the largest of all at midcentury.

Proportional and Average Ages

In addition to population pyramids, there are several other ways to measure the age structure of a population. One of these was introduced in Chapter 2 and is, in fact, a

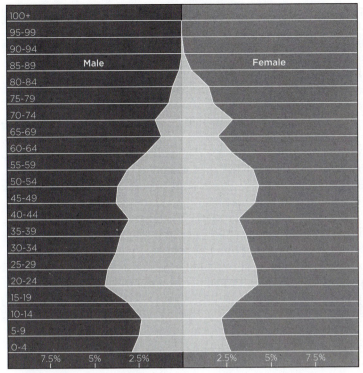

Figure 3.2. Population Pyramid for Russia, 2010

Source: Based on the pyramid visual by Martin De Wulf at http://populationpyramid.net/russian-federation/ and data from United Nations, Department of Economic and Social Affairs, Population Division. World Population Prospects: The 2012 Revision.

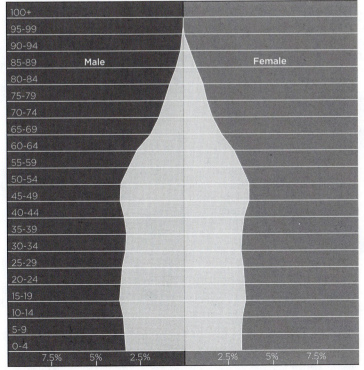

Figure 3.3. Population Pyramid for the United States, 2010

Source: Based on the pyramid visual by Martin De Wulf at http://population pyramid.net/united-states-of-america/ and data from United Nations, Department of Economic and Social Affairs, Population Division. World Population Prospects: The 2012 Revision

set of measures that represent the proportions or percentages of individuals at various ages. These can be read directly from the pyramid.

Using the information from Table 3.1, this set of measures shows that 0.024 of Afghanistan's population is age 65 and above (or, multiplying by 100, 2.43 percent), whereas the respective figures for Russia and the United States are 0.122 and 0.131. The proportions of the three populations that are ages 0–4 are Afghanistan, 0.1613; Russia, 0.0570; and the United States, 0.0653. These measures underscore the conclusion we drew from the population pyramids: that Afghanistan's population is quite young and Russia's is quite old.

Two other closely related measures of age are the median and mean age, both of which are referred to as averages. The median, introduced in Chapter 2 and illustrated below in Table 3.2, is the age that divides a population's age structure into two equal parts. Thus, if a population's median age were 35 years, we would know that there are as many individuals below 35 as there are above 35. We use the estimated U.S. population in 2010, shown below, to illustrate. Beginning with the list of cohorts and cohort sizes, we first cumulate, from the bottom, to find the number of persons at a given age (x) or older. Looking at the cumulative age distribution, we see that nearly 160 million were ages 35 and above and 140 million were ages 40 and above. Therefore, the middle person is in the 35–39 cohort.

With this established, we need to estimate the age between 35 and 39 the middle person is likely to be, which turns out to be 38.51 years. This same method indicates that the median age in Afghanistan was approximately 17.78 years—less than one-half that of the United States, and Russia's was a little lower than that of the United States, at 37.29.

The mean age is calculated in three steps as shown in Table 3.3: (1) First, multiply the midpoint of each age interval by the number of persons at the age. (2) Next, add together all of the products found in the first step. (3) Finally, divide the sum

Table 3.2. Age Structure Table for Creating Median Age

Age (x)	P_x	Cumulative P_x
0–4	20.19	306.09
5–9	20.33	285.90
10–14	20.68	265.57
15–19	21.98	244.89
20–24	21.7	222.91
25–29	21.14	201.21
30–34	20.07	180.06
35–39	20.08	159.99
40–44	20.9	139.92
45–49	22.64	119.01
50–54	22.35	96.38
55–59	19.79	74.02
60–64	16.99	54.23
65–69	7.32	37.24
70–74	11.30	29.92
75–79	7.32	18.62
80+	11.30	11.30
Total	306.09	

Source: Based on data from Table 3.1 from the Census Bureau's International Data Base (IDB).

found in the second step by the total population size. We illustrate with Russia's population in the preceding table.

The second column contains the midpoints of the age intervals and the fourth contains the cohort sizes, with the sum of the cohort sizes—the total population size—in the last row of the fourth column. The last column contains the products of these two numbers, and the last row of the last column shows the sum of these products. The quotient of these last two entries gives us the mean age in Russia: 5,484.4/141.1 = 38.87 years. This method yields the mean ages for Afghanistan and the United States as 22.09 and 38.03, respectively. Russia's population proves to be the oldest of the three, slightly older than the United States. Afghanistan's population, by this measure, is almost 16 years younger than that of the United States.

A set of measures that combines proportions at various ages and has important welfare implications is the **dependency ratio**. There are various versions of this measure but they are all similar in attempting to grasp the number of nonemployed persons—the very old and the very young—who must be supported by one member of the labor force. For example, according to World Bank 2010 figures, 0.67 of the U.S. population is working age (by this definition). In comparison, a slightly smaller proportion of the world's population is in this category, 0.65, whereas 0.68 of Switzerland's and 0.55 of Kenya's populations are working age. The respective proportions for the persons aged 15 and below are: 0.20 in the United States, 0.26 for the world, 0.15 in Switzerland, and 0.43 in Kenya.

These yield the following child dependency ratios: 0.30 for the United States, 0.41 for the world, 0.5 for Switzerland, and 1.28 for Kenya. As can be easily seen, this measure is not only sensitive to age structure, it reveals quite a bit about the relative well-being of the populations. Wealthier, more industrialized countries have proportionately fewer children and the working-age segment of these populations support less than one-third as many young dependents as those of poorer, rural nations.

Table 3.3. Age Structure Table for Creating Mean Age

Age(x)	M	P_x	M_xP_x
0–4	2.5	8.13	20.32
5–9	7.5	6.98	52.37
10–14	12.5	6.36	79.45
15–19	17.5	8.00	139.94
20–24	22.5	12.04	270.96
25–29	27.5	11.96	329.01
30–34	32.5	10.89	353.92
35–39	37.5	10.16	381.17
40–44	42.5	9.35	397.4
45–49	47.5	11.32	537.79
50–54	52.5	11.56	606.77
55–59	57.5	9.98	573.76
60–64	62.5	7.00	437.79
65–69	67.5	4.60	310.78
70–74	72.5	6.20	449.4
75–79	77.5	3.73	289.32
80+	90.0	2.83	254.3
Total		141.1	5,484.44

Source: Based on data from Table 3.1 from the Census Bureau's International Data Base (IDB).

1. Child dependency ratio = Children/Working age
2. Elderly dependency ratio = Elderly/Working age
3. Elderly and children dependency ratio = (Children + Elderly)/Working age
   - "Children" refers to the proportion of the population aged 15 and below.
   - "Working age" refers to the proportion of the population aged 16 to 64.
   - "Elderly" refers to the proportion of the population aged 65 and above.

A related measure includes in the numerator not only the very young but also the very old, on the grounds that the elderly must also depend on members of the work force for their needs. The formula for this dependency ratio adds together persons 15 and below and those 65 and above, and divides this total by the working-age population. With the proportion of elderly in the United States at 0.13, the world at 0.07, Switzerland at 0.17, and Kenya at .03, the respective ratios are 0.49, 0.51, 0.47, and 1.19. We see that in the United States and Switzerland, the addition of the large older segment of the population increases the dependency ratio considerably; but in Kenya, with relatively few persons over age 65, there is a small increase in an already high ratio.[2]

SOCIOCULTURAL STRUCTURE: SUBPOPULATIONS AND STRATA

The biological structures of gender and age apply to virtually all populations, certainly to all species that experience sexual reproduction. In addition to these, however, there is a set of structures that are more or less distinctly human. These are distinguished by social and cultural definitions. For a variety of scientific and practical reasons, it is important to know the numbers that constitute such subaggregates. Membership in them is closely associated with one's standard of living. And, through a process of indirect causation, the sociocultural subaggregates to which one belongs—especially ethnicity and economic status—affect demographic characteristics such as birth and death rates. The very first U.S. Census of 1790 asked what was then an all-important question: who in the population was free and who was a slave. By 1840, questions were being asked about who in the household was employed in each of six classes of industry and about one's occupation, who was literate, who was a pensioner, and so on (see United States Bureau of the Census 1992; also Shryock and Siegel 1976:16).

The Constituents of Population: Marriage and Family, Ethnicity and Race

Demographers and other social scientists employ several criteria in analyzing populations along social structural lines. These criteria can be roughly divided between those that produce social *differentiation*—qualitative differences—between groups and those associated with social **stratification**, that is, inequality between groups. This section presents two of the major forms of differentiation: (1) marriage and family structure and (2) ethnicity and race. The following section focuses on the two principal forms of stratification: (1) occupation and (2) income and wealth. To illustrate the fact that group differentiation can for various reasons lead to inequality, the first section ends with a comparative discussion of ethnic stratification.

In 2010, the total population size of the United States was approximately 309.33 million; of these, 229.1 million (74.06 percent) were aged 18 and over. Taking this later group as our subpopulation, Table 3.4 shows that 129.5 million of them were married and the reminder were either never married or they were widowed or divorced. Expressing these categories as proportions, we see that the proportion married = 0.56, the proportion never married = 0.27; the proportion widowed = 0.06; and the proportion divorced = 0.10. The length of these bars in Figure 3.4 represents these proportions. All of the subaggregates of this marital structure taken together make up the base population (and of course, the base population plus those under 18 constitute the entire population): $0.56 + 0.27 + 0.06 + 0.10 = 1.0$, or all persons 18 and above.

Among the many other aspects of the changing U.S. family structure worth exploring, perhaps none has received as much attention in the press and in public forums as the growth in the number of single-parent and unmarried-parent households (e.g., Gibb et al. 2014; Cherlin 2010; London 1998; Moffitt, Reville, and Winkler 1998). As the proportion of married persons has declined, the proportion of all households that consist of married couples with children has also declined, from about 0.42 in 1980 to .22 in 2010. Conversely, increases have occurred in the proportion of unmarried couples without children, unmarried couples with children, and single-parent households (both male and female headed) with and without children.

As the percentage of married persons has declined, the percentage of all households that consist of married couples with children has also declined, from about 37 in 1990 to 20 in 2010. The percentages of married couples without children are larger than percentages of married persons with children. Table 3.5 shows some of the details of these trends, with data from 1990, 2000, and 2010. According to these figures, male-only households with children grew from 1.1 million in 1990 to 2.8 million in 2010. This is a relatively small group, but it increased at a rate of over 3.0 percent per year during the period. Finally, although considerable interest has been shown in the growth of female-only households with children, this category increased slowly, from slightly fewer than 6.6 million in 1990 to a little more than 8.4 million—a growth rate of only 0.8 percent per year.

These illustrations have focused almost exclusively on marriage and family in the United States. This is because our purpose was to introduce the concepts and techniques of structural demography, not to explore comparative issues. We will have an opportunity to return to marriage and family outside of the United States (and in the past as well) when we discuss fertility and family size in Chapter 5 and comparative

Table 3.4. Marital Status of the U.S. Population Aged 18 and Over, 1990-2010 (Number of Persons in Millions)

Marital Status/Year	1990	2000	2005	2010
Never married	40.4	48.2	53.9	61.5
Married	112.6	120.1	127.4	129.5
Widowed	13.8	13.7	13.8	14.3
Divorced	15.1	19.8	22.1	23.7
Total	181.8	201.8	217.2	229.1

Source: Table 56: Marital Status of the Population by Sex, Race, and Hispanic Origin, 1990 to 2010. U.S. Census Bureau, Statistical Abstract of the United States: 2012, http://www.census.gov/compendia/statab/2012/tables/12s0056.pdf.

and historical aspects of population growth in Chapter 8. Meanwhile, some of these comparisons can be summarized in a few words by saying that family characteristics in the United States are fairly typical of those in other wealthy, industrialized countries (Bailey and Dynarski 2011; Choi and Jackson 2011; Clarke, Cooksey, and Verropoulo 1998). In the less-developed nations, on the other hand, the situation is quite different. There, nearly all adults are married, marriages occur at younger ages, and are more likely to be arranged. Also, families are larger—with more children and with grandparents and other relatives in the household (see Schoeni 1998), and divorce is far less common. Nevertheless, as these countries strive to achieve the levels of industrialization and standards of living found in the United States, Japan, and Western Europe, their family structures will almost surely shift in those directions as well.

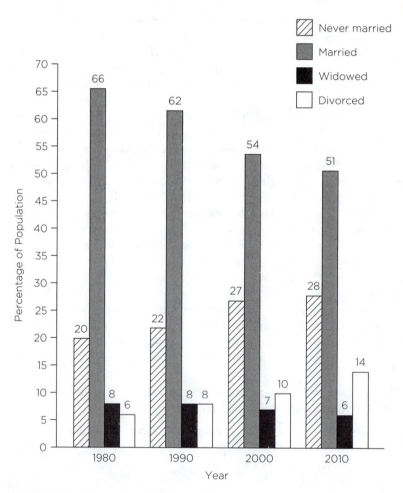

Figure 3.4. Percentage of U.S. Population by Marital Status 1980-2010

Sources: Statistical Abstract of the United States, 1997: Table 58; U.S. Bureau of the Census, Marital Status 2000: Census 2000 Brief; Pew Research Center analysis of Decennial Census (1960–2000) and American Community Survey Data (2008–2010).

Table 3.5.   Changes in Family Types, 2000–2010 (Numbers in Millions)

Family Type	1990 Number	1990 Percent	2000 Number	2000 Percent	2010 Number	2010 Percent
Couples with children (Married)	24.54	37.1	24.83	23.5	23.59	20.2
Couples without children (Married)	25.79	39.0	29.66	28.1	32.92	28.2
Males only (with children)	1.15	1.7	2.19	2.1	2.79	2.4
Females only (with children)	6.56	10.0	7.56	7.2	8.36	7.2

Source: Statistical Abstract of the United States (Households and Families: 2010 Census Briefs); http://www.census.gov/prod/cen2010/briefs/c2010br-14.pdf.

Ethnicity

Two of the most important social structural variables are (1) race/ethnicity and (2) socioeconomic class. In the United States and in virtually every other country, these characteristics not only separate members of the general population into aggregates and subpopulations, but they also include a dimension of ranking, or inequality. For this reason, the structures formed according to such criteria are referred to as *stratification* systems, and the aggregates are known as **strata**. This metaphor, borrowed from geology, suggests a structure that is hierarchical (it has a top, a middle, and a bottom). It is made up of layers that are different from one another but the elements of each (individuals, households, or families) are alike in important ways. This section focuses on race/ethnicity and the next on class. In both instances, we use some of the techniques of structural analysis already presented, and we will introduce a few additional ones. In both sections we also examine some of the implications of the stratification aspect.

Issues in the Classification of Race

Prior to and during Census 2000, race and ethnicity once more proved to be the most difficult to measure and the most politically controversial of all the social structural variables. Beginning with the first Census of 1790, black slaves and "Indians" were included as special categories. This lasted until 1850, when for the next eight enumerations (through 1920) an attempt was made to count among the newly liberated African Americans "mulattos," that is, people with both white and black ancestry (Shryock and Siegel 1976:146). Even after this practice was abandoned, African Americans (under the label "Negroes," and then "Blacks") have constituted by far the largest official ethnic minority group in the United States (Preston et al. 1998). The 1990 enumeration reported approximately 30 million members of this group, out of a total of 255 million persons, or nearly 12 percent of the population. Estimates indicate that the percentage grew to nearly 13 percent by the late 1990s. Following years of considerable resistance to labeling people as "mulattos" and the like, the practice was in effect reintroduced in 2000, as respondents were allowed to report mixed ("multiracial") heritage. Moreover, since 1990, respondents have been given the option of indicating "other" under the race category.

Considerable confusion now exists in academic and in government circles throughout the world on the question of what constitutes a race and how it differs from an ethnic group, if at all (see Petersen 1997). To complicate matters further, the U.S. Census Bureau and similar agencies in other countries recognize a separate form of classification, "nativity," indicating where a person was born (the two categories included in the United States are "native" and "foreign born"). A directive issued in 1977 by the **U.S. Office of Management and Budget** (**OMB**), Statistical Policy Directive No. 15, guides the Census Bureau's approach to racial classification. This document "provides standards on ethnic and racial categories for statistical reporting to be used by all Federal agencies. According to the directive, the basic racial categories are American Indian, Alaskan Native, Asian or Pacific Islander, Black, and White" (U.S. Census Bureau 2004:4). This classification considers people of Hispanic "origin" (later revised to "background") to be members of an ethnic group who could be of any race.

Experts and ordinary citizens as well have expressed concern about the practice of categorizing people by race. For example, as Sharon M. Lee (1998:4) has pointed out, "Most immigrants from Asian countries identify themselves by their national or ethnic origin—Chinese, Korean, or Indian—not as 'Asian.' Asian is a label used by the majority United States population and officially recognized by the Office of Management and Budget." In response to such concerns, on August 28, 1995, the OMB issued a 40-page notice on "Standards for the Classification of Federal Data on Race and Ethnicity" (OMB 1995). In this document, the authors acknowledge that "[d]uring the past several years, the standards have come under increasing criticism from those who believe that the minimum categories set forth in Directive No. 15 do not reflect the increasing diversity of our Nation's population. Some have also proposed changing the names of certain categories [including Hispanics, many of whom prefer the labels "Latino and Latina]."[3] The notice then identifies several specific issues and discusses how they have been addressed. Part of the OMB approach was to hold public hearings in various parts of the country and to review the findings from the hearings and from other sources, including academic research findings. With this information in hand, and additional research, some changes were made—including the new category of multiracial heritage. However, the 1977 standards remained essentially intact.

The critical demographer, Hayward Derrick Horton (1998a; 1998b) has observed that such apparently technical exercises as redefining racial categories have their roots in a cultural history of racism. Despite the neutral tone of the OMB directive, the categories themselves and the data collection and reporting practices associated with them are effective in shaping attitudes, practices, and even legislation in ways that are deemed offensive (Burton et al. 2010; Horton 1998a). It is as if those who create and revise the categories are oblivious to the serious social problems associated with racism in this country. According to Horton, "The inclusion of racism as a variable of explanation would only enhance the area of racial and ethnic demography. Rather than ignoring racism, it should be operationalized and measured so as to document the changes thereof relative to the racial differentials that characterize the studies in this area" (Horton 1998a:17). For some, these practices recall the so-called Nuremberg laws of 1938 in Nazi Germany. There, authoritative government agencies developed a scheme of official racial classifications, including a category of "mixed race" (*mischlinge*), and then proceeded to use the laws to justify discrimination, imprisonment, and ultimately genocide (see Burleigh and Wipperman 1992; Jung and Kwon 2013).

Of course, times have changed considerably; and such abuses are virtually impossible under a democratic political system. In contrast to the Nazi regime, in the United States today: "The concept of race the Bureau of the Census uses reflects self-identification by respondents; that is, the individual's conception of his/her racial identity. The concept is not intended to reflect any biological or anthropological definition" (U.S. Department of Commerce, Bureau of Statistics 1997:5). Nevertheless, the very idea of promulgating official directives that define racial categories strikes many as mischievous and prone to abuse. Certainly, no scientific basis exists for continuing the practice. The prominent anthropologist Ashley Montague "led a lifelong campaign to rid science of the term 'race.' Most race theorists would [agree]. Although the person on the street may still believe that races are biologically real, science has proven otherwise" (Andreasen 1998:200; see also Bonilla-Silva 2013).

The classification system that is stipulated in OMB Statistical Directive No. 15 identifies what are in fact subpopulations within the general U.S. population. Each group can trace its roots to a geographic region whence its ancestors originated: Europe, Asia, North America, and so on. In these ancestral homelands, each of the groups constituted a set of partly but not entirely endogamous populations: English and French, Howsa and Ibo, Japanese and Korean, Chippewa and Huron, and so on. Each population shared a distinctive culture and a distinctive gene pool, although within the population sets there was considerable overlap. For this reason, some physical and cultural similarities as well as differences existed. When these groups came together (some via migration and others by absorption) to become the constituent parts of the U.S. population, they continued to be relatively endogamous and to share somewhat distinct subcultures. Thus "minority groups," or, when European Americans are included, "ethnic groups" are probably the most appropriate terms. But neither today nor for some time has any of them been "pure" in either the biological or the sociocultural sense. We may continue to classify these groups as "races," but we will therefore also continue to ignore the fact that the boundaries between them are highly permeable, and are becoming more so.

The blending of ethnic groups under conditions such as those in the contemporary United States can come about in either or both of two ways. One is **cultural assimilation**, whereby a group increasing uses the language and adopts the customs of another. This process has, of course, been a hallmark of our "melting pot" heritage for generations. The other way in which so-called racial barriers are crossed is through intermarriage. Although this has always been practiced to some extent, by the end of the twentieth century it had become increasingly common.

In 2010, nearly 2.1 million marriages were consummated in the United States, of which nearly 15 percent were interracial. The percentage of interracial marriages in 2010 was almost double the 1980 percentage (Wang, Parker, and Taylor 2012). There has been a steady increase in the percentage of interracial marriages over the last three decades. The steady increase in interracial marriages can be attributed to the flow of immigrants as well as an increase in the propensity of native populations to marry out. Seventy percent of the interracial marriages in 2010 involved either a European American male or female. As impressive as this might appear, Euro-Americans are far less likely to marry out than other racial groups. Only 2.1 and 2.3 percent of married European American women and men respectively are interracially married. Among all the couples in interracial marriages, 43 percent were Euro-American married to Hispanic; 14.4 percent were European Americans married to Asians, and 11.9 percent were European American married to African American. The likelihood of interracial marriage varies along gender. Among the 24 percent of all African Americans married in 2010, males were most likely to marry out, compared with just 9 percent of African American females. Asian American females were most likely to marry European American men. One percent of all married European American men have Asian spouses (Wang and Taylor, 2012). Almost twice the percentage of Asian females compared to Asian men married out.

Ethnic Structure and Change in the United States

According to the OMB classification, more than 250 million European Americans account for about 79.6 percent of the total population, and 40.7 million African Americans make up less than 13 percent. "The US Census Bureau considers Hispanic to mean persons of Spanish/Hispanic/Latino origin including those of Mexican, Cuban, Puerto Rican, Dominican Republic, Spanish, and Central or South American origin living in the US who may be of any race or ethnic group. This category constitutes about 15.2 percent of the total estimated US population."[4]

As Table 3.6 indicates, over 63.7 percent of the members identify themselves as white, although nearly 37.7 million indicate that they are black.

Another smaller but highly diverse group is the Asian and Pacific Islander category. With just under 4.8 percent of the nation's population, these people trace their origins from areas as different as China, the Philippines, Japan, India, and Korea. Finally, there are the Native Americans, including Indians, Eskimos (Inuit), and Aleuts, contributing to less than 1 percent of the total population. Some of the most disadvantaged persons in the nation are in this group, despite the fact that they were here first.

One of the most widely discussed aspects of ethnic stratification in the United States is the rapid growth of the non-European-background peoples (see Table 3.7). In 1980, 80 percent of the U.S. population was European American, 12 percent was African American, 6 percent was Hispanic, and 2 percent was Asian. By 2010, the European American share had dropped to just over 67 percent and the Hispanic and Asian groups had increased their shares to 15.3 and 4.4 percent, respectively.

Table 3.7 shows the changes in size and the percentage of the total population of the several groups between 2000 and 2010. For purposes of comparison, the Hispanic subpopulation is separated from the statutory races, listing each racial group minus the Hispanic component. Although each of the groups is growing amidst general increases in the size of the U.S. population, the rates of growth are

Table 3.6. U.S. Population Race/Ethnic Composition, 2010

	European American	African American	Native American	Asian and Pacific Islander	Hispanic	Others
Number	196,817,552	37,685,848	2,247,098	14,465,124	50,577.494	6,570,746
Percent	63.7	12.2	0.7	4.7	16.3	2.1

Numbers in '000

Source: K. Humes, N. A. Jones, and R. R. Ramirez. 2011. *Overview of Race and Hispanic Origin, 2010*. U.S. Department of Commerce, Economics and Statistics Administration, U.S. Census Bureau.

quite different. Of even greater significance, the relative proportions are shifting in a consistent manner. The percentage shares of African American and American Indians remained fairly constant during this period, while the proportion of European Americans declined steadily.

In contrast, the percentage share of the Hispanic American component (of all races) increased from 12.0 to 15.3, surpassing that of African Americans (some of whom are classified as Hispanic). During the period, the number of Hispanic Americans increased by 15 million, with an absolute growth rate of 3.6 percent per year. But the fastest-growing group of all is the Asians. Its percentage share increased from 3.5 to 4.4, as 4.4 million people in this group were added to the population through natural increase and migration. This represents a 3.7 percent annual rate of absolute population growth. By way of comparison, the rate of absolute growth for European Americans was 0.56 percent, just one-seventh as rapid; and for African Americans the growth rate was 1.2 percent, considerably less than one-half that of the Asian group. If these trends continue, as they are likely to do, Hispanic Americans will soon surpass African Americans as the nation's second-largest ethnic group, and the Asian category will eventually equal and then surpass both of these in the long run.

As noted earlier, most members of this category do not use the label "Asian" because it obscures significant national and ethnic differences. Figure 3.5 illustrates the considerable diversity among Asian Americans with a representation of their countries of origin and the percentage shares of each country in 2010. The largest group is from China, amounting to over 16 percent of Asian immigrants in 2010. In Chapter 7 on migration, we examine how the Chinese Americans came to this country (and we discuss the obstacles against which they had to struggle in order to migrate). The second-largest group is from the Philippines, representing over 15 percent of Asians. Korea and Vietnam have also contributed substantial proportions to this growing Census category.

The regional population concentrations of Asian Americans within the country is uneven. The western states, and California in particular, clearly have the largest proportion with 54 percent of all Asian Americans in the West. Geography is certainly a factor, because access to the United States from China and the Philippines

Table 3.7. Change in the U.S. Ethnic Composition, 2000-2010 (Numbers in Millions)

Group	2000 Number	2000 % of Population	2010 Number	2010 % of Population	Change 2000 to 2010 Number	%
African American	34.66	11.8	38.93	11.8	4.27	12.3
Asian	10.24	3.5	14.67	4.4	4.43	43.3
European American	211.46	71.9	223.55	67.6	12.09	5.7
Hispanic	35.30	12.0	50.47	15.3	15.17	43.0
American Indian/Alaska Native	2.47	0.9	2.93	0.9	0.46	18.4

Source: Population by Hispanic or Latino Origin and by Race for the United States: 2000 and 2010. Overview of Race and Hispanic Origin: 2010 Census Briefs; http://www.census.gov/prod/cen2010/briefs/c2010br-02.pdf.

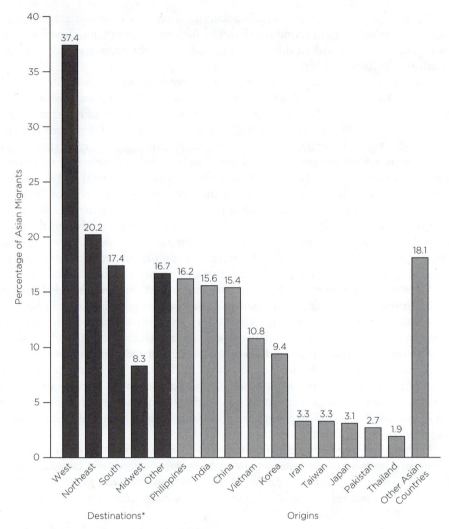

Figure 3.5. Origin and Destinations of Asian Americans (by Percentage)
Sources: Data from Migration Policy Institute at http://www.migrationpolicy.org/data/state-profiles/state/demographics/US and Jeanne Batalova, "Asian Immigrants in the United States," May 24, 2011 at http://www.migrationpolicy.org/article/asian-immigrants-united-states. Note: The percentage of immigrants in the destination only is 83.3 percent of the total immigrants. That is 83.3 percent of the total Asian immigrants are accounted for by their distribution across the four regions. The remaining 16.7 percent are unidentified.

is most direct via the West Coast. But economic opportunities, especially the availability of jobs during various eras in U.S. migration history, are equally important, as we shall see in Chapter 7.

A Comparative Perspective

Although the United States has rightfully earned its reputation as a nation of immigrants, it is only one among many ethnically diverse nations in the contemporary world. As William Petersen (1997) has observed, India is at least as heterogeneous, if not more so.[5] Moreover, India has struggled, as has the United States, in trying to develop a system of ethnic and racial classification that is at once accurate, just, and acceptable to all interested parties. Canada, too, is a nation of immigrants. In fact, its immigration policies have generally been more liberal than those of the United States, with the result that it is ethnically (if not racially) more diverse. Although the number of ethnic groups in most of the Latin American countries is not large, Native people make up a higher proportion of these populations than in the United States and Canada. And there is a substantial African-background component in many of the Caribbean and South American populations, especially Cuba and Brazil. At the other extreme are Japan and some of the countries of northern Europe, which have very small minority subpopulations.

Comparisons among set of countries like Canada, Zambia, and Israel are of interest because they are all former colonies of England; and they are among the most ethnically diverse nations in the world. Yet, they came to be that way via quite different routes. Let us briefly consider their respective ethnic structures.

1. Canada. Like the United States, Canada is a nation created on land that was originally the territory of numerous small-scale societies, whom Canadians now refer to as "First Nations." Most of them were agricultural or based on hunting and fishing. Subsequent to a series of wars of conquest by British and French settlers, these original inhabitants came to be categorized as a single minority group. During the mid-eighteenth century, war over territory broke out between the British and the French in which the French were defeated (in 1753). This led to their marginalization, despite the fact that people of French descent were and continue to be the vast majority in Quebec and a substantial minority in Nova Scotia. As a result of this conflict, the land now known as Canada remained a British dependency until 1867, when the "Dominion" of Canada was created.

During the entire period up to and including the 1861–1865 era of Civil War in the United States, Canada never had slavery. In fact, it was the terminus of the Underground Railroad used by fugitive slaves from the United States. The small African Canadian population (945,665 persons or 2.8 percent of the total population [NHS 2011]) partly consists of descendants of fugitive slaves. But most of this group emigrated from Caribbean nations. From the Civil War era to the present, Canada has been a net receiver of immigrants from the British Isles, France, other parts of Europe and, more recently, from the Caribbean, Asia, and Africa (see Hiller 1991; see Krahn, Hughes, and Lowe 2010).

Canada's 2011 Census enumeration reported a total of nearly 33 million persons. The basic questionnaire included 15 categories and three write-in spaces for the item on ethnicity. According to Statistics Canada, this method yielded 126 different types of responses, including one labeled "American!" Some of these are nationalities (Chinese, Hungarian, and Turkish). Some are regional or ethnic groups from abroad (Basque, Arab, Kurd, Punjabi, and Tamil). Some are domestic ethnic groups (Acadian, Inuit, and Quebecois). Some are what the U.S. Census would classify as races (African black, black, and Polynesian). And still others refer to general parts of the world (North American, Scandinavian, and West Asian). Many observers reacted to this variety quite positively, considering it to be an accurate reflection of the Canadian "mosaic" (Porter 1971). Other people found it to be impossibly complex and poorly organized. But, in either case, the outcome does indicate what happens when the matter of racial and ethnic identification is left entirely in the hands of the respondent rather than being influenced by predesigned, mutually exclusive categories.

Table 3.8 lists the 10 most frequently reported Canadian groups in 2006, along with an updated listing from the 1996 Census based on a 20 percent sample. Notice that the ethnicity item was somewhat simplified for the latter survey, although respondents were permitted to give more than one answer, and the number of groups remained large. The table also indicates that amidst the great diversity of ethnic, national, and racial backgrounds, groups with origins in England and France still essentially dominate the Canadian population.

2. Israel. Israel's ethnic structure is unique in several ways (see Figure 3.6). Most obvious is that it is the only country in the world in which the majority of the population is Jewish (you will recall that Jews make up between 2 and 3 percent of the U.S. population, and in Canada the official count is less than 1 percent). Despite this apparent homogeneity, the Jews of Israel have emigrated from all over the world. From Europe, of course, but people have also come to claim their citizenship from Africa, Latin America, India and other parts of Asia, and from North America as well (Okun 1997; Okun and Kagya 2012). Like India, The State of Israel was created following a civil insurrection against the British, who controlled the territory. Thus, the act of drawing postindependence maps had much to do with determining the ethnic mix of the country; for not all of Israel's residents entered the country from abroad.

One of the less well-known features of the Israeli population is that it consists of a significant segment of non-Jews who were living in the territory under British mandate. In fact, there is even a very small group of Palestinian Jews who were indigenous people since long before Israel became a state—perhaps dating back to biblical times. Because native groups were incorporated into the State when it was created, and because the exact boundaries have been affected by a series of regional

Table 3.8. Canada's Ethnic Structure, 2006

Group–2006	Single Response	Percent	1996 Census Survey
Portuguese	262,230	1.43	
Polish	269,375	1.47	
Ukrainian	300,590	1.64	1,026,475
Dutch (Netherlands)	303,400	1.65	
Filipino	321,390	1.75	
Irish	491,030	2.68	3,787,610
North American Indian	512,150	2.79	
Scottish	568,515	3.10	4,260,840
German	670,640	3.66	2,757,140
Italian	741,045	4.04	1,207,475
East Indian	780,175	4.25	
Chinese	1,135,365	6.19	921,585
French	1,230,535	6.71	5,597,845
English	1,367,125	7.46	6,832,095
Canadian	5,748,725	31.38	8,806,275
Others	1,470,229	20.8	
Total	18,319,580	100.0	28,528,125

Source: Ethnic origins, 2006 counts, for Canada, provinces, and territories—20% sample data. Source: Statistics Canada: http://www12.statcan.ca/census-recensement/2006/dp-pd/hlt/97-562/pages/page.cfm?Lang=E&Geo=PR&Code=01&Data=Count&Table=2&StartRec=1&Sort=3&Display=All&CSDFilter=5000.

wars—and are still in dispute today, the image of Israel as a "purely Jewish" nation is greatly exaggerated.

As shown in Figure 3.6, this relatively small nation of about 8.0 million people is an amalgam of more than 20 different nationalities and four religions. The Arabic segment of the population consists of Muslims, Christians, and Druze people, and constitutes about 18 percent of the total. Just over 14 percent of Israelis are Muslim, which makes it the third-largest ethnic group after Israeli-born Jews and Jews who migrated from Europe. Although the largest segment of the Jewish population is from Russia and other parts of Europe, large groups from Morocco, Iraq, Yemen, and Algeria have diversified the population. And these non-European Jews have for many years had the highest rates of immigration and natural increase.

3. Zambia.[6] Until October 1964, the southern African nation of Zambia was the British Colony of Northern Rhodesia. At that time, its total population size was about 4 million. Nearly all of these were native people who shared a Bantu cultural background. One percent of the population was European, which made Zambia one of the most extreme instances of "minority rule." As was the practice in British Africa, two additional classifications were employed to designate ethnicity: Asian—mostly people from Gujarat and other parts of India—and colored/mixed. These two

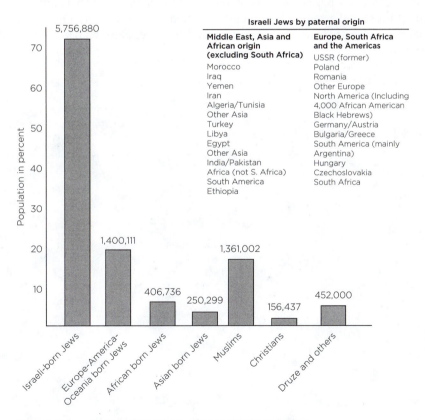

Figure 3.6.   Ethnic Structure of Israel's Population

Sources: *CIA World Factbook* (data in the public domain). Statistical Abstract of Israel, 2009, CBS. "Table 2.24—Jews, by country of origin and age" (PDF). Retrieved March 22, 2010. World Bank, Washington. D.C. "Data" online: http://data.worldbank.org/indicator/SP.POP. TOTL. Accessed August 31, 2015. Graph by author.

groups did and still do constitute about 0.25 and 0.10 percent of the population, respectively. An apartheid system maintained the tiny group of Europeans at the top of the stratification system, the Africans (blacks) at the bottom, and the Asians and coloreds between them.

In the years immediately following independence, the number of Europeans in Zambia declined steadily, from 43,400 in 1969, to 29,000 in 1974, to 18,000 in 1980. By the 2010s, however, the size of this group had increased to nearly 105,000. Between 1969 and 1980, the size of the general population increased from 4.1 million, to 4.7 million, to 5.7 million. In July 2010, Zambia's population size stood at 13,092,680. Of these, 93.4 percent were Bantu and 105,000 were European.

The European colonists introduced the practice of categorizing all of the local people as black or African, and the category persists in the current census definitions in Zambia and many other African nations. Even the Bantu classification is overly broad, as there are about 80 Bantu-speaking ethnic groups in the country. The largest of these are the Bemba, Nyanja, and Tonga; although the Kanoda, Lozi, Lunda, and Luvale peoples also make up substantial segments of the population. In addition to the four racial categories and 80 ethnic groups, the Zambian Census also reports religion. According to this classification, in 2010, 75.3 percent were Protestant and 20.2 percent were Catholic. Among the Christians, approximately one-half attend syncretic churches that combine Christianity with traditional beliefs and practices. Finally, substantial regional groupings exist that do not entirely correspond with ethnicity or religion. Thus, there are cultural differences between people who live in

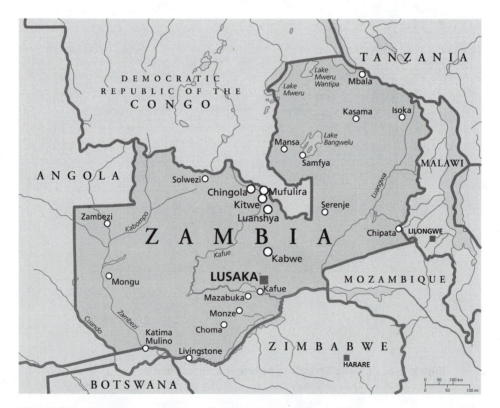

Figure 3.7. Zambia, population estimated at 13.1 million in 2010.
Source: PeterHermesFurian/Thinkstock.

and around the capital Lusaka and those in one of the other nine provinces: Luapula, Copperbelt, Western, and so on.

Zambia's diversity stems from decisions made by the British concerning what would constitute a specific colony, and thus which local groups would be included in and which excluded from the territory that later became a nation. Its ethnic structure was also shaped by the colonial practices associated with apartheid, including the importation of people from other parts of the empire such as India. The linguistic and ethnic diversity that had existed in the region before colonization also played a role. As in Canada and Israel, the Government has recognized several different ways to define ethnicity/race. Unlike them, immigration has not been a significant factor in Zambia (except for the small Asian group). In any case, Zambia's experience, like those of India and Israel, helps to provide perspective on the challenges the United States faces in attempting to account for its version of ethnic diversity.

Ethnic Stratification

Throughout the world, one's ethnic group membership makes a considerable difference in the things that count. In the United States, members of the five statutory categories differ from one another not only in terms of ancestral origins but also with respect to values, beliefs, and other subcultural characteristics—or what the pioneering sociologist Max Weber first referred to as **life styles.** Moreover, these groups are significantly *unequal* in standards of living, or **life chances.** As of 2000, for example, the median annual family income of European Americans was about $54,620. In that same year, the median income for African American families was just under $34,000. That is, the latter group was earning about 62.2 percent of the former. In 1990, African American incomes were only 58.0 percent as large.

Nevertheless, the gap between these two groups is not the largest ethnicity-specific income differential in the nation. In 2000, the median family income for Hispanic Americans, $37,795, was 69.0 percent of that for European Americans ($54,620). And the difference has been even greater between European and Native Americans. According to the 2000 Census, the median income for the latter group was only $35,662. This means that Native Americans, including Indians, Eskimos, and Aleuts, were earning less than the European American median. Part of the difference may reflect the fact the European Americans are the oldest of the groups (as measured by median age) and are likely to be closer to realizing their maximum income potential. In contrast, Native Americans are the youngest and are likely to have a lower proportion of its members in the labor force. But this hardly accounts for the magnitude of the income gap.

In fact, all things considered, these comparisons would certainly suggest that European-background people are the wealthiest Americans. But, as you may know, that is not the case. Rather, the group labeled Asian and Pacific Islander had the highest earnings of all in 2000. This is despite the fact that it consists of very wealthy, highly educated nationalities (e.g., Japanese) along with some of the poorest immigrant Americans (e.g., Vietnamese). In 2000, the median for this group was $67,022. Thus, they earned an average of $1.23 for every $1.00 earned by European Americans and $1.9 for every $1.00 earned by Native Americans.

In terms of education, 29.3 percent completed college in 2000, whereas 17.7 percent of African Americans were in this category. The comparable figures for Hispanics and Native Americans are 13.0 and 14.4, respectively. However, as you might expect by now, the group with the highest percentage of members who have completed college is the Asian American. Nearly 50 percent of this group has completed four or more years of college, which is also the highest among the five including European Americans (see Table 3.9). The next highest is that of European Americans (29.3), followed by African Americans, Native, and Hispanic Americans, in that order. In addition, Asian Americans have the highest proportion employed, the lowest infant mortality rate, and the lowest proportion of female-headed households. On all three measures, African Americans are most disadvantaged.

It seems clear that a consistent pattern of ethnic stratification exits in the contemporary United States. The small group of Asian Americans is relatively well off. The small group of Native Americans has the highest rates of poverty. And between them in the stratification system are the European, African Americans, and Hispanic Americans, in that order on most indicators.

Class and Income Differentials

This final section of the chapter continues our examination of socioeconomic inequality. Our attention now turns from what sociologists call ascribed characteristics to those that are achieved. The former are statuses with which we are born or (like age and some disabilities) that befall us through no will of our own. The latter result from concerted effort: getting an education, pursuing a career, and the like. As we have just seen, ascribed characteristics such as race and ethnicity can have considerable influence on what a person is able to achieve in life (e.g., education) and how one does so. Obviously, the two categories are closely, and interestingly, related. Nevertheless, the achieved characteristics on which we are focusing here, occupation and income, are generally treated separately for purposes of analysis.

Table 3.9. Comparative Characteristics of U.S. Minority Groups

	Percent Distribution of Median Household Income	Percentage Below the Poverty Level	Infant Mortality Rate*	Percentage of 12th-Grade Students at Basic (Lowest) Achievement Level	Percentage 20 and Above Unemployed
All groups	49,445	14.3	6.14	27	5.4
Asian	63,408	12.1	4.27	26	3.7
Black	32,068	25.8	11.46	40	6.7
Native	35,062	27.0	8.28	33	11.3
Hispanic	37,758	26.6	5.25	46	9.8
White	54,620	12.1	5.18	21	4.7

*Per 1,000 population

Sources: BLS Labor Force Statistics from the Current Population Survey, http://www.bls.gov/web/empsit/cpsee
_e16.htm; National Council for Educational Statistics, Assessment of Educational Progress, https://nces.ed.gov/
pubs2010/2010015/tables.asp; National Vital Statistics Reports 62, no. 8 (December 18, 2013), reported by: Marian
F. MacDorman, PhD, http://www.cdc.gov/nchs/data/nvsr/nvsr62/nvsr62_08.pdf; U.S. Census Bureau, (a) Income,
Poverty and Health Insurance Coverage in the United States: 2009, Current Population Reports, P60-238, and
Detailed Tables—Table FINC-07, September 2010: http://www.census.gov/hhes/www/cpstables/032010/faminc/
new07_000.htm; (b) Poverty Rates for Selected Detailed Race and Hispanic Groups by State and Place: 2007–
2011 American Community Survey Briefs https://www.census.gov/prod/2013pubs/acsbr11-17.pdf.

This first part of this discussion, on occupation, introduces classification systems as shown in Table 3.10, composition of the workforce, and other workforce-related characteristics of populations. In the context of the discussion of income, in the following section, we introduce a measure of structure with which you may already be familiar. It is the **Gini index** of inequality, and it has been used extensively by demographers, sociologists, economists, and geographers.

Occupation

Most social scientists agree that occupation is the main determinant of a person's socioeconomic class membership. Where people work, how they work, what they work at, and how much they earn from their work have as much if not more effect on their life styles and life chances than any other set of factors. Questions concerning occupation have been included in the U.S. Census enumerations and its Current Population Surveys for many years, since 1790 in the case of enumerations. And most other countries have similar items on their census questionnaires. The U.S. Department of Labor, through its **Bureau of Labor Statistics** (**BLS**), regularly collects and analyzes information on employment, including some of the data included here. State agencies throughout the country are also valuable sources of information on employment and occupation, and most now have useful Internet sites.

Based on the industrial classification and other information shown in Tables 3.10 and 3.11, we see that the service sector (Financial activities and Other services) is the largest and fastest-growing segment of the workforce. With just less than 16 million employees in 2000, accounting for 20 percent of the workforce, the number increased to slightly over 16 million and its proportional share to just less than 22 percent in 2010. During 1990–2010, this sector grew at an average rate of 8 percent per year. The service industry includes a wide range of occupations, from business services, education, health, to automobile repair, to motion pictures. It also includes computer and data-processing services, whose workforce size *quadrupled* between 1980 and 2010 from 300,000 to 1.4 million. As if further proof were needed that the United States (and the world) has entered the information age, the average hourly earnings in the computer industry increased by 267 percent during the period, from $7.16 to $19.11. In contrast, the number of workers in agriculture declined from 3.7 million in 1983 to just over 2 million in 2010 and its share of the labor force fell from 3.7 to 1.5 percent. Similarly, the number of workers and the proportional shares in mining, durable goods manufacturing, nondurable goods manufacturing, and wholesale trade all declined during the 1990s and 2010.

With these major shifts as a backdrop, by the mid-1990s, retail trade had taken over as the second-largest employer, with more than 21.5 million persons working in the sector. For many years Government, at federal, state, and local levels together, had employed the second-largest share of the workforce, until retail trade overtook it around 1990 with the Government sector experiencing considerable shrinkage by 2010. In 2010, Government employed a little over 9 percent of all workers. The index of dissimilarity between the 1990 structure and the 2010 structure is .29, indicating a substantial rearrangement of the workforce in a relatively short time span.

These changes are characterized by rapid growth in services, moderate growth in financial activities, small declines in durable and nondurable goods, and a dramatic decline in Government labor force during the last decade. This situation has been the subject of public discussion and academic research for some time, at least since the sociologist Daniel Bell (1976) coined the term "postindustrial society."

Table 3.10. Occupational Structure by (Nonfarm) Industry, United States, 2000-2010 (Numbers in Thousands)

	2000		2005		2010	
Mining	475.0	0.01	624.0	0.01	731.0	0.01
Construction	9931.0	0.13	11197.0	0.14	9077.0	0.12
Durable goods	12519.0	0.16	10333.0	0.13	8789.0	0.12
Nondurable goods	7125.0	0.09	5919.0	0.07	5293.0	0.07
Wholesale trade	4216.0	0.05	4579.0	0.06	3805.0	0.05
Retail trade	15763.0	0.2	16825.0	0.21	15934.0	0.22
Transportation and utilities	7380.0	0.09	7360.0	0.09	7134.0	0.1
Financial activities	9374.0	0.12	10203.0	0.13	9350.0	0.13
Other services	6450.0	0.08	7020.0	0.09	6769.0	0.09
Government workers	6113.0	0.08	6530.0	0.08	6983.0	0.09
total	79346.0	1.0	80590.0	1.0	73865.0	1.0

Sources: Bureau of Labor Statistics, http://www.bls.gov/opub/mlr/2012/01/art4full.pdf (table 1) page 66 of Monthly Labor Review.

Table 3.11. Average Hourly Earnings by Private Industry Group

Industry	2000 Earnings	2010 Earnings	Proportional Increase
Total private	14.02	19.07	0.360
Mining and logging	16.55	23.83	0.439
Construction	17.48	23.22	0.328
Manufacturing	14.32	18.61	0.299
Trade, transportation, and utilities	13.31	16.83	0.264
Wholesale trade	16.28	21.53	0.322
Retail trade	10.86	13.24	0.219
Transportation and warehousing	15.05	19.17	0.273
Utilities	22.75	30.04	0.320
Information	19.07	25.86	0.356
Financial activities	14.98	21.49	0.434
Professional and business services	15.52	22.78	0.467
Professional and technical services	20.61	29.93	0.452
Management of companies and enterprises	15.28	23.79	0.556
Administrative and waste services	11.69	15.82	0.353
Education and health services	13.95	20.12	0.442
Health care and social assistance	13.98	20.43	0.461
Leisure and hospitality	8.32	11.31	0.359
Arts, entertainment, and recreation	10.68	15.28	0.430
Accommodations and food services	7.92	10.68	0.348
Other services	12.73	17.08	0.341

Source: https://www.census.gov/compendia/statab/cats/labor_force_employment_earnings.html.

Demographers have sought to understand this trend with numbers, proportions, percentages, and the like—as we are doing here. In any case, there is no question that the nature of work is changing rapidly during the late twentieth and early twenty-first centuries.

Of all the other dimensions of occupational structure that might be explored, the one of greatest interest is undoubtedly relative compensation, that is, which jobs make the most money. The BLS reports salaries, wages, and benefits currently earned in all industries and occupations. Table 3.11 contains some of this information, reported by industrial category. Unlike occupational classification, this system combines the characteristics of all employees in a specific industry, from managers to laborers and from the lowest to the highest paid. With this in view, the information, utilities, professional, and construction sectors have the highest per-hour earnings, with nearly $19.00 on the average in 2000 and an average of $25.00 in 2010. The lowest-paid jobs are those in the leisure and hospitality sector. In 2010, the average pay per hour in the leisure and hospitality sector was $11.30, or $2,010 per month.

The managerial professions held their position in the distribution of hourly earnings presented in Table 3.11. The lowest-paid occupations in 2000 were in retail trade; arts, entertainment, and recreation; leisure and hospitality; and the accommodation and food services industries. These occupations did not register any improvement in their rankings in the occupational distribution in 2010. There was only a 35-percent increase in the average hourly pay between 2000 and 2010. As the increase is below inflation rates during the decade, workers in the lowest-paid sectors experienced a decline in their standard of living. By contrast, managers not only experienced a significant increase in their hourly earnings, but also maintained their relative positions in the occupational distribution. In general, those who were paid well in 2000 improved their wages over time and those who were poorly paid lost their ability to keep up with inflation, contributing to the growing wage inequalities between the well paid and the poorly paid.

Wealth and Income

The last two of the stratification criteria to be considered here are perhaps the most important, wealth and income. These are closely related concepts, but they are not identical. Income refers to money (or in-kind goods and services such as housing) that is regularly received; for example, the hourly earnings just discussed in connection with occupational structure. Wealth is the sum total of all of the valuables possessed by a person or group, which includes savings from income along with other holdings and investments: land, shares of stock, precious metals and gems, and so on. When a financial institution seeks to establish a person's "net worth," it is focusing on wealth—not income. Of the two, wealth is clearly the more significant in determining life style and life chances, although it tends to be highly correlated with income (income is the "flow" and wealth the "stock").

This section begins with a look at the distribution of wealth. Our units here are national aggregates, the sample of 50 nations of the world shown in Table 3.12. The measure of wealth used is gross domestic product (GDP). GDP is defined as the monetary value of all the finished goods and services produced on an annual basis. It includes all of private and public consumption, government outlays, investments and exports minus imports that occur. In some ways it is a very crude measure that has serious drawbacks frequently discussed in scholarly literature. Nevertheless, it is reported and used extensively.

The World Bank dataset from which the sample was drawn was published in 2012, and the GDP figures are for 50 of the 66 nations for the year 2012. The mean per-capita GDP is $15,253, with a standard deviation of $20,499. With a ratio of the standard deviation to the mean of 1.3:1, there is clearly a wide range of values among the 50 nations. In fact, the lowest-reported per-capita GDP is $399, for Niger, and the highest is $103,858, for Luxemburg. This range of $103,463 is substantial, to say the least. To get an even clearer sense of how unequally the wealth of the world is distributed, Table 3.12 shows the 50 nations divided into 10 categories according to GDP, from the poorest five to the wealthiest five, along with the average for each category. Each group of five represents 0.10 or 10 percent of the sample. Just below each list of names, in boldface, is the cumulative proportion, which indicates that the

Table 3.12. 50 Nations Ranked According to GDP $US, 2010

Fifty countries were selected randomly from a list of 194 countries for which GDP data were available.

Country	Key	Country	Key
Eritrea	Group = 1	Azerbaijan	Group = 6
Vanuatu	Ave GDP = 979.0	Croatia	Ave GDP = 15,012
St. Vincent and the Grenadines	Pct. Ave GDP = 0.002	Estonia	Pct. Ave GDP = 0.0121
São Tomé and Principe	Cumulative Pct.= 0.002	Uruguay	Cumulative Pct. = 0.0163
Tuvalu		Slovenia	
Haiti	Group = 2	Kazakhstan	Group = 7
Tajikistan	Ave GDP = 6,421	Kuwait	Ave GDP = 18,266
Niger	Pct. Ave GDP = 0.0014	Hungary	Pct. Ave GDP = 0.0307
Guinea	Cumulative Pct. = 0.0016	Puerto Rico	Cumulative Pct = 0.0470
Barbados		Ecuador	
Mozambique	Group = 3	United Arab Emirates	Group = 8
Congo, Rep.	Ave GDP = 12,079	Denmark	Ave. GDP = 28,869.4
Chad	Pct. Aver GDP = 0.0026	Egypt, Arab Rep.	Pct Ave GDP = 0.0626
Madagascar	Cumulative Pct. = 0.0042	Philippines	Cumulative Pct = 0.1097
Macedonia, FYR		Ireland	
El Salvador	Group = 4	Saudi Arabia	Group = 9
Nepal	Ave GDG = 18,236	Iran, Islamic Rep.	Ave GDP = 22,380.0
Brunei Darussalam	Pct. Ave. GDP = 0.0040	Poland	Pct Ave GDP = 0.1155
Georgia	Cumulative Pct. = 0.0083	Argentina	Cumulative Pct = 0.2252
Papua New Guinea		Austria	
Lithuania	Group = 5	China	Group = 10
Ethiopia	Ave GDG = 35,455	Germany	Ave GDP = 19,316.4
Turkmenistan	Pct Ave. GDP = 0.0078	France	Pct Ave GDP = 0.7626
Jordan	Cumulative Pct = 0.0161	Brazil	Cumulative Pct = 1.00
Bolivia		Turkey	

Source: http://data.worldbank.org/data-catalog/GDP-ranking-table (World Bank Data 2012).

first group constitutes 0.10, the first and second make up .20, the first, second, and third, .30, and so on.

To the right of each list of countries are four figures. The one at the top is the group number. The second is the average of the GDP for the group in millions of dollars. For example, the first group, with Eritrea, Vanuatu, and so forth has an average of $979, and the last, which includes Germany and France, has an average of $34,612. The third number on the list is the proportion of the total GDPs each group has: that is, .0002 for the first group, .0014 for the second, .0026 for the third, and so on. This number was derived by adding together all of the GDPs for the 50 countries and dividing by sum for the five in each group. The lowest number on the list, in boldface, is the cumulative percentage of GDP. According to these, the first group has .002, the first and second has .0016. The first, second, and third have .0042, and so on.

Using the last two numbers, we can determine the proportion or percentage of countries with a given share of the wealth. For example, the poorest 10 percent have 0.02 percent of the wealth, the poorest 20 percent have 0.16 percent of the wealth, and the poorest 50 percent have 1.61 percent of the wealth. This means that the richest 50 percent of the nations have 98.4 percent of the wealth. To focus in detail on the wealthiest nations, we simply cumulate in the other direction. This shows that the richest 10 percent have 76.2 percent of the wealth, the richest 20 percent have 87.81 percent of the wealth, and so on. It is a vivid picture of how deeply stratified is the "world of nations."

A distribution such as this can be summarized in one powerful and widely employed measure known as the Gini index, or the Gini "concentration ratio," after the statistician and demographer Corrado Gini (1884–1965). This measure has been used in many fields since the early twentieth century when it was invented. Here we apply it to the distribution of wealth, which is its most common application. But it can help in understanding geographic distributions of populations by size of place and virtually anything else to which the concepts of equality and inequality can apply (see Milanovic 2011; Crowell 1995; Shryock and Siegel 1976:98–100).

The ratio is a number between 0 and 1.0 that measures inequality. The closer to 1.0, the greater is the inequality; the closer to zero, the greater the equality. A ratio of 0.5 or above indicates significant inequality, whereas a score below 0.25 reflects a fairly equal distribution. Another way to understand what the Gini index measures is to look at the distance between the line and the curve in the diagram below, known as the Lorenz curve, after M. O. Lorenz (1905; see Figure 3.8). The straight line is called the "line of equality." It depicts a situation in which 1.0 percent of the countries have 1.0 percent of the wealth, 2.0 percent have 2.0 percent, all the way to 99 percent of the countries with 99 percent of the wealth and, of course, 100 percent have 100 percent. The closer the curve is to the line, the lower the Gini index.

For the sample of 50 nations the Gini index was calculated and found to equal .7032. By the criteria just stated, this is a very high score, which means that the distribution of wealth in this sample is extremely unequal, as we have already seen.

The Gini index and other measures of inequality can be applied to income as well as to wealth, and they can be used with any type of population and its elements. This includes measurements of the distribution of individual and household incomes within a national population, such as that of the United States. We have already examined differences among the incomes of the four statutory races and the one ethnic group in the United States, and we have also considered the hourly earnings of different sectors of industry. To extend these observations here we use current data to examine the U.S. income distribution by region of the country, family type, age,

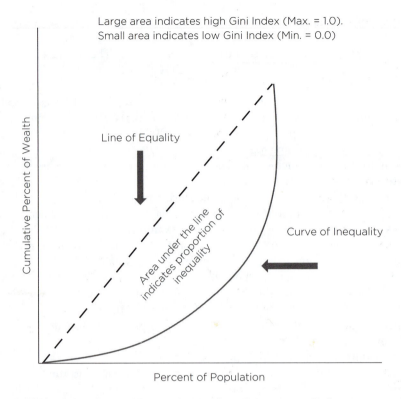

Large area indicates high Gini Index (Max. = 1.0).
Small area indicates low Gini Index (Min. = 0.0)

Figure 3.8. Lorenz Curve Illustrating Measurement of Gini Index

and ethnicity (once again). We conclude with a look at the level of inequality for the entire population.

In its *Current Population Reports*, the U.S. Census Bureau regularly publishes data on income. The information comes from the monthly Current Population Surveys. Over the years, it has been discovered that "income" is not an easy term to define. People receive money on a regular basis from many different sources, which apply to some groups but not to others—the elderly, welfare recipients, or people with capital investments. Thus, it is difficult to compare individuals and households on an equivalent basis in determining earnings. In an effort to resolve these issues, over the years the Bureau has created alternative definitions of "income"; and it publishes separate sets of figures for each definition. By the late 1990s, 15 different definitions had been developed, one of which is designated as official:

Definition 1. Money income excluding capital gains. This can be contrasted with the definition that had the lowest median in 1996 and in 1997 ($29,647 and $30,250).

Definition 8. Money income, less government cash transfers, plus health insurance supplement to wage or salary income, less social security payroll taxes, plus federal income taxes (including the earned income credit), less state income taxes. The definition that had the highest median in those two years ($37,194 and $37,623) was specifically designed to count as income all government benefits received by people on public welfare.

Definition 15. All sources in Definition 8 plus non-means-tested government cash transfers, plus the value of Medicare, plus the value of regular-price school lunches, plus means-tested government transfers, plus the value of Medicaid, plus the value of other means-tested government noncash transfers, plus imputed return on equity in your home (U.S. Bureau of the Census 1998:xvi).

Between 2011 and 2012, the median annual income for households (Definition 1) decreased from $51,100 to $51,017. As Table 3.13 indicates, the Northeast had the highest median of all regions in 2011 and 2012. The South has been the poorest region for decades, and it maintained this position between 2011 and 2012 with a 1997 median that was $3,000 below that of the nation as a whole. Comparing family types, we see that married couples were far better off than households headed by one person. In fact, there is $17,000 gap between married couples' incomes and those of female-headed households. Also shown in Table 3.13 are the medians for three age categories of householders: 15–24, 34–44, and 75 and above. As might be expected, the median for the middle group, in its most productive years, is by far the highest. In 2012, the median was 1.9 times greater than that of the poorest group, the most elderly.

The various definitions do make a difference in the medians. As in past years, Definition 8 yielded the lowest incomes, as a result of subtracting government transfers, social security taxes, and state taxes. All of the ethnic groups are affected by this shift in definition, but the relative ranking does not change. The most affected are European Americans, whose income by Definition 8 is only 81 percent of the official figure. Least affected are Hispanic Americans, whose Definition 8 income is 89 percent of its Definition 1 income. Married couples with children are affected more than female-headed families, with the latter's Definition 8 income more than 93 percent of the official figure.

Definition 15, which adds all government payments in cash or in kind, raises the income of every group and family type except Asian Americans and married couples—both of whom receive relatively little from public sources. The ethnic groups most affected are African and Hispanic Americans, whose Definition 15 incomes are about 107 percent of their official incomes. But the greatest increase of all is among female-headed households. This group's Definition 15 median is 118 percent that of the official figure. That is, when all of the transfers are added, this group seems better off that it first appeared; although even the Definition 15 median is still only 62 percent of the national average.

In considering the general population, the Bureau determined that the 20 percent of Americans earning the least reported 3.6 percent of the incomes (officially defined) and that the 20 percent with the highest incomes earned 49.3 percent (U.S. Bureau of the Census 1998: Table E). Although the degree of inequality of this distribution is not as high as that between nations of the world (the respective figures are 0.8 and 77.7 percent), it is certainly not low. Using Definition 1, the Gini index = .448, which indicates a substantial concentration of incomes at the top. The highest concentration occurs with the use of Definition 4, which adds capital gains. By this standard, the Gini index = .513. According Definition 8, Gi = .487; and with Definition 15, which includes all government benefits, Gi = .397, the lowest of all. To the

Table 3.13. Median Incomes by Group, United States, 2011–2012

Size and Income/ Category	2011		2012	
	Percent of Total Households	Median Income	Percent of Total Households	Median Income
All Households	100	51,100.0	100	51,017.0
Region				
Northeast	17.98	54,989.0	18.06	54,627.0
Midwest	22.18	49,740.0	22.12	50,479.0
South	37.66	47,879.0	37.51	48,033.0
West	22.16	53,470.0	22.29	55,157.0
Family Type				
Married Couples	48.68	75,678.0	48.34	75,694.0
Female, no husband	12.94	34,340.0	12.63	34,002.0
Male, no wife	4.86	50,602.0	5.08	48,634.0
Age of the Householder				
15–24	5.10	31,096.0	5.15	30,604.0
35–44	17.54	63,209.0	17.42	63,629.0
75+	22.17	33,810.0	22.80	33,848.0

Median Incomes by Group, U.S. 2011–2012. Source: Data from Table 1 Income and Earnings Summary Measures by Selected Characteristics: 2011 and 2012 from Carmen DeNavas-Walt, Bernadette D. Proctor, Jessica C. Smith, "Income, Poverty, and Health Insurance Coverage in the United States: 2012," U.S. Census Bureau, September 2013. http://www.census.gov/prod/2013pubs/p60-245.pdf.

extent that government transfers are intended to equalize income distribution, they appear to be working, at least to some extent—according to these results.

SUMMARY

We began the chapter with some definitions and basic concepts that are used in the measurement and analysis of populations and other aggregates. We continued by analyzing populations into their various parts, including subpopulations, cohorts, ethnic groups, occupational categories, and social hierarchies. We ask: How many men are there compared to women? How many elderly persons are there compared to the very young? And how many people are rich and how many are poor? In answering such questions about the structure of populations, we use percentages, proportions, indexes, and ratios that are all based on the relative sizes of aggregates and subpopulations.

We continue and conclude this introduction to the basic features of population (as distinct from the vital events) with a look at geographic distribution. Many of the ideas and techniques present here will be used again in Chapter 4. Size, of course, will figure prominently, as will structural characteristics such as family type and age structure. Now however, these principles are applied to one of the most interesting and persistent aspects of humans in aggregate contexts, the territorial imperative.

KEY TERMS

Bureau of Labor Statistics (BLS)
cultural assimilation
dependency ratio
Gini index
life chances
life styles

U.S. Office of Management and Budget
   (OMB)
population pyramid
strata
stratification

NOTES

1. Of course, these are not pyramids, which are three-dimensional forms. They are the two-dimensional *faces* of pyramids: that is, triangles. As we discuss in the text, even the classic triangular shape is not universal but rather reflects one (traditional) type of population.

2. In this section, we did not consider longevity or average life expectancy because they are *not* direct indicators of age structure. *Longevity* refers to the oldest age reached in a population, and it is generally around 90 to 100. For example, in 1997, Jeanne Louise Calment died in France at a documented age of 122. It is an idiosyncratic measure having little to do with average age. For more on longevity, see http://www.llma.org/files/documents/LLMA_Longevity _Index_Technical_Document_19.3.12_v1_final.pdf. Average life expectancy, as we shall discuss later, is a set of figures or a *vector* that indicates the number of years a typical person at a given age is expected to live. It is based on a special population model, the life table, and it does not measure age but rather mortality conditions.

3. http://www.whitehouse.gov/sites/default/files/omb/fedreg/race-ethnicity.html.

4. http://www.immigration-usa.com/world_fact_book_2012/united_states/united_states _people.html.

5. India and the United States are diverse for quite different reasons, which have affected their respective experiences with democratic pluralism. With the exception of the Native peoples, the United States became diverse by way of migration, even if it was forced migration as in the case of the ancestors of African Americans. India, like many developing countries, became diverse through the process of creating a single, large new nation out of many different smaller sovereignties and tribal areas.

6. Data for this section are from http://data.un.org/CountryProfile.aspx?crName=zambia.

C H A P T E R
FOUR

GEOGRAPHIC DISTRIBUTION
Population and Territory

This chapter examines the ways in which populations are distributed in space. We begin with a catalog of the political and administrative divisions used in demographic analysis, from continents and nations to census tracts and blocks (Figure 4.1a–b). This is followed by an introduction to the most basic variables in population geography, size of place and population **density**. The exploration of density and its effects takes us in two related but separate directions. First is a discussion of various measures of the spatial distribution of populations, including the Gini index introduced in Chapter 3. Second is a summary of the long-range trends of urban growth at international and national levels, including the United States. The chapter concludes with a brief overview of the technology in the study of the spatial distribution of populations, **geographic information systems** (**GIS**).

Like size and structure, geographic distribution is a concept that refers to populations and other aggregates at a particular time. When we move on to Part II and the dynamic components of demographic analysis, we will examine the ways in which the vital events of birth, death, and especially in-migration and out-migration contribute to changes in geographic factors.

HOW TERRITORY IS DIVIDED: ADMINISTRATIVE AND STATISTICAL AREAS

In Chapter 1, we identified three features that distinguish a naturally occurring human population (or a part thereof) from other kinds of aggregates: relative endogamy, a shared set of biological and sociocultural structures, and shared territory. The last of these is important in several ways, some of which we have touched on already in relation to populations as units of observation and in our discussion of ethnicity. In fact, the universal practice of human beings aggregating in distinct territories with culturally defined boundaries that designate "inside/ours" and "outside/not ours" has shaped our beliefs, practices, and institutions profoundly. Based on an influential and much-discussed study published several years ago, the sociobiologist Robert Ardrey (1966 [1997]) argued that master concepts such as property, nationality, and

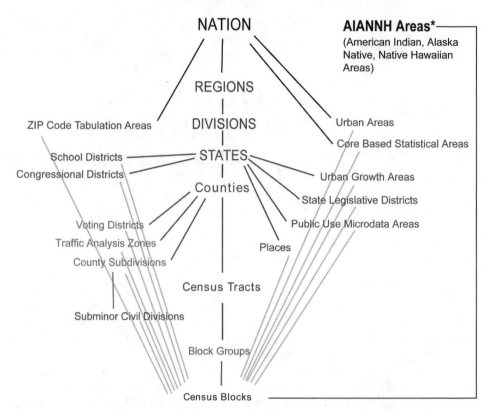

Figure 4.1a.   Standard Hierarchy of Census Geographic Entities
Source: U.S. Census Bureau, http://www2.census.gov/geo/pdfs/reference/geodiagram.pdf.

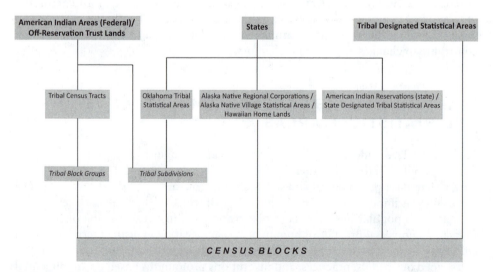

Figure 4.1b.   Hierarchy of American Indian, Alaska Native, and Native Hawaiian Areas
Source: U.S. Census Bureau, http://www2.census.gov/geo/pdfs/reference/geodiagram.pdf.

stratification stem from this aspect of human life, one that it is shared with other territorial animals that have analogous "institutions." To emphasize the power of this impact, Ardrey coined a term that has become part of common usage, the **Territorial Imperative** (Young 2014).[1]

Populations (and many kinds of subpopulations) express the territorial imperative by having their members live and work close to one another, by defining *migration* as entering or exiting a stipulated region, and in other ways. Most populations conceive of their territories informally, by virtue of tradition and natural growth or expansion. However, *official* units are also established by law, administrative directive, and other formal means. This is of some importance because the latter do not consistently correspond to the former, with the result that official boundaries are often approximations of natural domains. With very few exceptions, demographic information that refers to naturally bounded areas is not available. Instead, the data we use to determine the size of places, their densities, their concentrations of ethnic and other kinds of groups, their population centers, and the like are almost always based on legal and/or administrative definitions. Therefore, they are always approximate to greater or lesser degrees.

In many cases, the problem is not serious: the geographic boundaries of the United States, for example, closely define the U.S. population (although even here some overlap exists at the northern and southern borders; see Hiller 1991). In the new nations of the developing world, however, significant discrepancies exist between official international borders and the territories recognized—some for centuries—by local people (Herzfeld 2014; Teune 1990). And everywhere, boundaries between one neighborhood and the next and between city and suburb are somewhat arbitrary.

These observations should be understood as a caution against taking some of the concepts and measures that are to follow too literally. Often, we mean them to apply to continuous, natural areas, but the information employed refers to officially designated, discrete units such as nations, states, and counties. In this regard, two types of geographic units are recognized as distinct units (referred to in Figure 4.1 that begins this chapter): (1) administrative and political areas and (2) statistical areas. Areas of the first type have legal standing, hold charters, and are administered by public officials. All individuals and households in such an area are held accountable for obeying its laws and ordinances and, in turn, are entitled to services rendered by the unit. Included in this category are nation states, national subdivisions such as states or provinces, counties or other units of states or subdivisions, villages, towns, cities, subunits such as wards, and crosscutting units at the interurban, intercounty, or interstate levels (see Youngs 1991). Population data at many of these levels—nation, state/province, and city, at a minimum—are available in most countries.

The second category, statistical areas, includes geographic units that are created by census bureaus and like organizations for the sole purpose of collecting data. In some instances, they coincide with other preexisting units, such as in England where small areas are also electoral districts. More often, however, they are established anew for the convenience of the enumerator, as is the case with the smallest areas in the United States. Generally, the boundaries of statistical areas are more artificial than those of administrative and political units and are especially prone to ecological fallacy (Fasel, Green, and Sarrasin 2013; see Chapter 1; also, Oppenshaw 1984). In the United States and most other countries that employ such areas, data collection occurs at a combination of the two types of levels: for instance, counties *and* census districts. Since 2000, the entire United States has been divided into the common small-area geographies of block group, census tract, and ZIP Code Tabulation Area (ZCTA). A ZCTA approximates the delivery area for a five-digit or a three-digit (Census 2000 only) ZIP code. The Census Bureau allocates each block that contains addresses to a single ZCTA. The ZCTAs do not clearly define the area within which mail deliveries associated with that ZIP code occur. Since the 2010 Census, ZCTAs do not have nationwide coverage.

The following are the geographic areas selected by the U.S. Census Bureau in the United States and their official definitions (statistical areas in italics).

1. *Census block*. These are the smallest units. A city block bounded by streets may be made up of several census blocks each with a population size of approximately 200 persons. In the rural areas, a census block may contain several square miles of area and may have boundaries other than streets and roughly correspond to a city block.

2. *Block group or cluster*. This is a "reasonably compact and contiguous cluster of census blocks." Their boundaries "should follow visible and identifiable features such as roads, rivers." The population size of a block cluster ranges between 600 and 3,000 persons. A block group is geographically smaller than a census tract defined below, but larger than a census block. A block group is the smallest geographic unit for which the Census Bureau tabulates sample data. Statistics about socioeconomic characteristics such as income and education are available at the block groups level.

3. *Census tracts*. These are "small, relatively permanent geographic subdivisions of a county or equivalent entity." They consist of from one to nine block groups, and their population size ranges between 1,200 and 8,000. Like block groups, tract boundaries follow roads and other visible features. A community may be constituted by several census tracts and there may be several hundreds of census tracts in a large city.

4. Cities and towns. These come next in geographic scale, and are political/administrative units, not statistical areas. A city, now called a Census Designated Place (CDPs). These are areas delineated to provide data for settlements that are identifiable by name but are not legally incorporated under the laws of the state in which they are located. Prior to Census 2000, a minimum population size of 2,500 was required. The boundaries usually are defined in cooperation with local or tribal officials and generally updated prior to each decennial census. Towns are either unincorporated (e.g., villages and townships) or their populations usually fall below 2,500.

5. *Urban agglomerations*: metropolitan areas (MAs), **metropolitan statistical areas (MSAs)**, **consolidated metropolitan statistical areas (CMSAs)**, and primary statistical metropolitan areas (PMSAs). These are defined below.

6a. Minor civil divisions (MCDs). The primary legal subdivision of counties, usually towns or townships, used in 28 states.

6b. *Census county divisions* (CCDs, used in 21 states). These are artificial subdivisions of counties used in states without townships or similar administrative units.

7. Counties. These are administrative units that constitute the primary subdivisions of every state (although their counterparts are called boroughs in Alaska and parishes in Louisiana).

8. States (and territories). Data from all lower levels are collated in separate state statistics.

9. *Regions.* There are four regions, each divided into two or thee subregions: Northeast, Midwest, South, and West. At Census 2000, the South had the largest population and the Northeast the smallest.
10. The nation. See Figure 4.2.

As the number and size of U.S. cities have grown, especially during the period of baby boom and rapid suburbanization following World War II, the practice of defining the urban component of the population as those who resided within official city limits has become obsolete. In response, the Census Bureau developed a new statistical unit, the Standard Metropolitan Area (SMA). It includes all persons who live within or near a city and who could reasonably be treated as participants in the same economic market. In practice, this means a city and its suburban ring.

With each Census enumeration of the last half of the twentieth century, the definition of this unit, along with its name, had to be revised to keep up with population trends. By the time of the 1980 Census, the old SMAs (later changed to SMSAs, then to MSAs) had so grown in size and geographic expanse that many had converged on one another to create massive conurbations and megalopolises. Anticipating the need to redefine the urban statistical area, the U.S. Office of Management and Budget

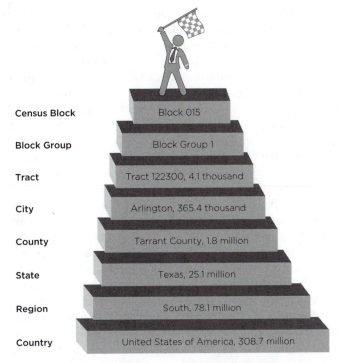

Census Block	Block 015
Block Group	Block Group 1
Tract	Tract 122300, 4.1 thousand
City	Arlington, 365.4 thousand
County	Tarrant County, 1.8 million
State	Texas, 25.1 million
Region	South, 78.1 million
Country	United States of America, 308.7 million

Figure 4.2. Levels of Geographic Aggregation and Population Sizes by Census Area Types

The person at the top of the pyramid lives in a specific block of Arlington, Texas, with a total population size of 125 persons. At the same time, he lives in seven other levels of aggregation—as the 2010 Census viewed him.

Source: U.S. Bureau of the Census, 1990 and "The Official Statistics." Participant Statistical Areas Program, U.S. Bureau of the Census, Washington, D.C. (accessed December 5, 2013).

(OMB) issued directives updating the criteria and names that would be used to collect and report population data. Since 2000, the entire United States has been divided into the common small-area geographies of block group, census tract, and ZCTA.

The OMB has demarcated a number of core-based statistical areas (CBSAs) consisting of counties or equivalent units containing an urbanized area or an urban core with a population of at least 10,000 that also demonstrates a high degree of socioeconomic integration. The concept of "core-based statistical area" includes several types of statistical areas such as MSAs, micropolitan statistical, combined statistical areas (CSAs), and metropolitan divisions. When the urbanized area has a population more than 50,000, it is called a metropolitan statistical area, and those with population between 10,000 and 50,000 are called micropolitan statistical areas. The 2010 Census identified 381 metropolitan statistical areas and 536 micropolitan statistical areas in the United States. CSAs consist of CBSAs with strong employment-related interconnections. The largest of all the 2010 Census CSAs is New York-Newark, NY-NJ-CT-PA with an estimated population of 23,484,225. As of 2013, about one out of every 15 Americans resided in this region.

Metropolitan divisions consist of either counties or similar units within an MSA containing a single core with a population of 2.5 million or more. According to 2007 U.S. Census Bureau estimates, the Dallas-Fort Worth-Arlington MSA contained two metropolitan divisions, Dallas-Plano-Irving and Fort Worth Arlington, with a total population of 6.4 million. Nearly 94 percent of the U.S. population lived in either MSAs or micropolitan statistical areas at the 2010 Census count, which makes it one the most thoroughly urbanized nations in the world. The 2010 Census identified 929 CBSAs, 169 CSAs, 388 metropolitan statistical areas, and 541 micropolitan statistical areas.

In 2013, the metro areas contained 269.9 million people, adding about 2.3 million from 2012. The largest gain in population of about 138,000 was registered by Houston between 2012 and 2013. Of the 10 fastest-growing metropolitan statistical areas in 2013, six were within or near the Great Plains, including Odessa, Texas; Midland, Texas; Fargo, North Dakota-Minnesota; Bismarck, North Dakota; Casper, Wyoming; and Austin-Round Rock, Texas. New York continued to be the most populous with 19.9 million in 2013, followed by Los Angeles and Chicago. In terms of counties, Harris County, Texas (Houston) had the largest numeric population increase between mid-2012 and mid-2013, adding almost 83,000 people. Following Harris were Maricopa County, Arizona (Phoenix), Los Angeles County, California; King County, Washington (Seattle), and San Diego County, California.

Table 4.1 lists 10 CSAs rank ordered by population size. One of the first impressions one gets is how huge these urban areas are, in population and physical sizes. Another evident fact is how these urban areas reflect and shape the region of the country they dominate, with slow growth in the Northeast and Midwest and rapid growth in the South. Finally, despite all of the work that has gone into creating and refining classification systems, America's largest CSAs of the twenty-first century are the same, familiar big cities of the past: New York, Los Angeles, Chicago, and so on.

POPULATION DENSITY: CONCEPTS AND CONSEQUENCES

The distribution of the MSAs on the map in Figure 4.3 vividly illustrates one of the key features of cities, the density of their populations. This impression is even

Table 4.1. Combined Statistical Areas, 2010 to 2013, Rank Ordered by Population Size

Rank	(2010 to 2013) Constituent Core Based Combined Statistical Area	2013 Estimate	Change
1	New York-Newark, NY-NJ-CT-PA Combined Statistical Area	23,076,664	+1.77%
2	Los Angeles-Long Beach, CA Combined Statistical Area	17,877,006	+2.66%
3	Chicago-Naperville, IL-IN-WI Combined Statistical Area	9,840,929	+0.73%
4	Washington-Bal-Arlington, DC-MD-VA-WV-PA Combined Statistical Area	9,051,961	+4.32%
5	San Jose-San Francisco-Oakland, CA Combined Statistical Area	8,153,696	+3.88%
6	Boston-Worcester-Providence, MA-RI-NH-CT Combined Statistical Area	7,893,376	+1.87%
8	Philadelphia-Reading-Camden, PA-NJ-DE-MD Combined Statistical Area	7,067,807	+1.12%
7	Dallas-Fort Worth, TX-OK Combined Statistical Area	6,817,483	+5.70%
9	Miami-Fort Lauderdale-Port St. Lucie, FL Combined Statistical Area	6,166,766	+4.55%
10	Houston-The Woodlands, TX Combined Statistical Area	6,114,562	+6.44%

Source: "Annual Estimates of the Resident Population: April 1, 2010 to July 1, 2013—United States—Combined Statistical Area; and for Puerto Rico," U.S. Census Bureau, Population Division.

stronger when we look out the window of an airplane flying at a high altitude at night. As the lights on the ground alternatively disperse and cluster together, we can clearly see when we are near a city, and approximately how large the population of the city is. These patterns indicate why the concept of density is the starting point for the exploration of the relationship between people and space. This section examines several aspects of density, including its measurement, its relationship to socioeconomic structure and behavior, and its role in the process of urban growth. This last topic will bring us back to another look at how the United States became 80 percent urbanized since the first census, when only 5 percent of the population of the new nation lived in cities.

Measuring Density

According to *Webster's Third International Dictionary* (1961), density is "the distribution of a quantity per unit, usually of space (area, volume, etc.)." In this general sense, any set of items or objects can display one degree of density or another, depending on how closely compacted they are. These include galaxies in outer space, particles in the nucleus of an atom, and strands of yarn in a carpet. And, in each instance, the number of objects per unit has practical consequences. When we consider density in demographic contexts, these same general principles hold. In this case, however, the quantities of interest that are distributed in space are individual persons, groups of individuals, or artifacts created by people.

The simplest and most familiar kind of demographic density is the number of persons per areal unit, square miles, square kilometers, and acres. Other commonly used measures are households per unit, families, and types of structures (schools, hospitals,

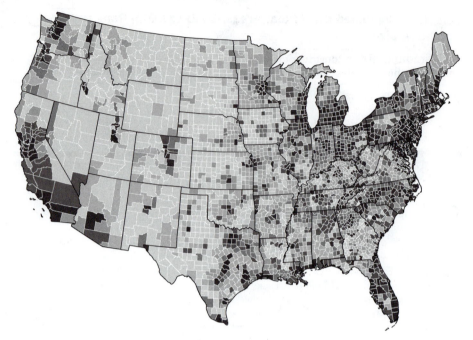

Figure 4.3.   U.S. Population Density Map
Source: mapofusa.net.

office buildings, stores, and so on). For specialized purposes, it is often relevant to know the concentration of certain types of individuals or groups, such as families in poverty, ethnic group members, or physicians. The method of calculation is always the same, and it is one that everybody has performed at least once in his or her life. Where Q is the quantity (of persons, etc.), A is the areal unit, and D is density,

$$D = Q/A$$

Table 4.2 shows the population size in number of persons, the land area, and the population density of the United States at 11 census dates between 1790 and 2010. The densities were calculated according the above formula. So, for example, the 2010 figure was derived by dividing the 2010 population by the 2010 area:

$$D = Q/A. \quad D = 308.74/3.53 = 87.4 \text{ persons per sq. mi.}$$

The growth of the U.S. population has been steady and positive since the first census, when the enumerated total was just under 4 million persons. Similarly, population density has increased regularly during the period, with two exceptions. Between 1800 and 1810, and again between 1960 and 1970, density declined slightly: from 6.1 to 4.3 persons per square mile in the first case and from 60.1 to 57.4 in the second. Both times, the declines were the result of acquiring additional territories whose population densities were lower than that of the nation as a whole; the latter instance is the period when Alaska and Hawaii became states.

From what has been said thus far about density, it is evidently related to level of urbanization. Cities are denser than nations, industrial cities within a CMSA are more densely populated than nearby "bedroom suburbs," and so on. Certainly, high

Table 4.2. Land Area and Population Density, United States, 1790-2010

Year	Population Size (in Millions)	Area (in Millions of Square Miles)	Density (in Persons Square Mile)
1790	3.93	0.87	4.5
1810	7.24	1.68	4.3
1830	12.87	1.75	7.4
1850	23.19	2.94	7.9
1870	39.82	2.97	13.4
1890	62.95	2.97	21.2
1910	91.97	2.97	31.0
1930	122.78	2.98	41.2
1950	150.70	2.97	50.7
1970	203.30	3.54	57.4
1990	248.71	3.54	70.3
2000	281.42	3.54	79.6
2010	308.74	3.53	87.4

Source: Population and Housing Counts, U.S. Bureau of the Census, 2010.

density appears to be condition for determining whether a place is or is not urban. But, we might ask, does density make a difference in other respects? If two geographic areas, for instance counties, or states, or nations, happen to have different levels of density—one high and the other low—what else can be expected? Would one be more likely to be wealthier than the other, or to be more urbanized, or to differ in similarly important ways? Demographers and other social scientists have pondered such questions for many years, and a considerable amount of research has been conducted in seeking the answers. Of course, this is at once a very general and a very complex kind of inquiry. For the answer hinges, in part, on how we define *density* and other terms, and on what methods we employ to establish whether and what kinds of relationships exist.

One approach that can shed some light on the consequences of density is to compare nations, some densely and some sparsely populated, and to compare them with respect to other variables. For this purpose, we can draw upon a sample of countries. Table 4.3 shows 50 nations categorized into 10 groups, according to the number of persons per square mile. These density figures, like the others we have used in this section, are averages. They assume that all of the people in each country have been spread out evenly over the country's territory, so that each square mile contains the number shown. Obviously, this is a fiction; we know that in every nation, many people crowd around big cities and very few live in deserts or mountainous regions. This fact certainly affects the validity of comparisons such as these.

Nepal, for example, has a total population size of 25 million, an area of 52,800 square miles, and a density of 184 persons per square kilometer. The island nation of Antigua and Barbuda, with a population of about 88,000 and an area of only 170 square miles, has a density of 201 persons per square kilometer. Based on this information, we would say that the two countries are about equally as dense, and that Antigua and Barbuda is somewhat denser. Whereas this is true on the average, it is also a fact that a large portion of Nepal is uninhabitable because it is so mountainous, even though the Himalayan region is included in the country's total land area. Although the amount of land occupied by the people of Antigua and Barbuda is

Table 4.3. 50 Countries in Order of Density (Persons Per Square Kilometer) and Proportion of Per-Capita GNI

Australia	3.0	Niger	14.0	Mozambique	31.0	Estonia	29.0
Iceland	3.0	Belize	16.0	United States	33.0	Latvia	31.0
Mauritania	4.0	Sweden	22.0	Zimbabwe	38.0	South Africa	44.0
Central African Republic	8.0	Brazil	24.0	Guinea	47.0	Cameroon	48.0
Bolivia	9.0	Peru	24.0	Yemen	49.0	Panama	52.0
0.10	.1097	0.20	.2160	0.30	.2528	0.40	.3231

Lithuania	45.0	Tunisia	67.0	Slovenia	102.0	Albania	104.0
Fiji	47.0	Macedonia	80.0	Ghana	113.0	Denmark	131.0
Burkina Faso	65.0	Sierra Leone	88.0	Portugal	113.0	China	143.0
Uzbekistan	69.0	Malaysia	91.0	Thailand	129.0	Antigua and Barbuda	201.0
Kenya	74.0	Costa Rica	93.0	Uganda	161.0	Dominican Republic	213.0
0.50	.3878	0.60	.4793	0.70	.5518	0.80	.6705

Nepal	184.0	St. Vincent and the Grenadines	273.0
United Kingdom	266.0	El Salvador	303.0
Vietnam	273.0	Marshall Islands	304.0
Comoros	335.0	Israel	371.0
Haiti	387.0	Rwanda	421.0
0.90	.8200	1.00	1.0000

Note: GNI indicates proportion of per-capita gross national income for each group of countries. Countries are ranked in ascending order by density. The countries are in groups of five. Following each country's name is its density. Just below the last country name in each group are two numbers. The one at the left is the group's cumulative percentage out of fifty countries (10 percent for the first group, 20 percent for the second and so on.) The number on the right is each group's cumulative proportion of the total of the gross national incomes of the fifty countries.

Sources: "GNI per capita, PPP (current international $)," World Bank, International Comparison Program database, http://data.worldbank.org/indicator/NY.GNP.PCAP.PP.CD; "Density (people per sq. km.)," Population Reference Bureau 2014, World Population Data Sheet, www.prb.org/DataFinder/Topic/Rankings.aspx?ind=30.

small, it is also nearly entirely habitable. With this factor considered, the concentration of Nepal's population in the parts of the country where people do live is clearly much greater than that of the Antigua.

With this caution in mind, the densities in the sample range from three persons per square kilometer in Australia to 421 in Rwanda. Calculations were performed to determine the strength of the relationship between the density of these countries and five other variables: crude death rate, infant mortality rate, average life expectancy at birth, percent urban, and per-capita GNP. In each case, the relationship proved to be weak or nonexistent. By these criteria, population density appears to have little or no impact on the wealth—or health—of nations.

Two of the relationships are of special interest. First is the lack of a connection between the density of a country and its level of urbanization. Some very dense countries are highly urbanized, as in the case of Israel. Others, such as Rwanda, have very small percentages of their populations living in cities. Some countries with low densities, for example, Australia and Iceland, are highly urbanized, whereas others whose populations are equally sparsely distributed—such as Central African Republic and Niger—have low urbanization rates. This lack of a connection reflects the situation just noted. Population densities as ordinarily reported do not account for the amount of land that is actually habitable and/or inhabited. If one could imaginatively eliminate Australia's vast Outback, it would be a densely population continent—because most of the settled areas are metropolitan centers.

The second point of interest is the lack of a relationship between population density and wealth. From one theoretical standpoint, density should have advantages in the concentration of resources and the workforce for their most efficient utilization. This perspective is related to the concept of **central place theory**, which we discuss below. From another standpoint, high densities could mean overcrowding, and thus bring on psychological problems and economic shortages. This idea is related to the theory of behavior sink, which we will also examine in a later section. But in any case, the fact that no apparent advantages or disadvantages follow from variations in density (at the national level) is something of a surprise.

By way of verifying this weak relationship, Table 4.3, above, provides the cumulative frequencies for the proportion of (1) countries, shown in the last row of the first column of each set and (2) wealth, as measured by GNI per capita, shown in the last row of the second column. The lack of an association is clear. We see that the least-dense 10 percent of the countries have 11 percent of the wealth but that the densest 10 percent have about 18 percent of the wealth. The densest one-half of the countries have 61 percent of the wealth and the least-dense one-half have 39 percent. The Gini index turns out to be a very low .314, indicating that density is neither an advantage nor a disadvantage. Some wealthy countries have very sparse population distributions, such as Australia and Sweden, and others are densely populated. Some poor countries have low densities, for example, Bolivia and Belize, and others are very densely populated, such as Vietnam and Haiti.

Density and Behavior

If the impact of density at the national level is inconsequential in relation to other sociodemographic factors, it does not necessarily follow that density at lower levels of aggregation has no effects. For example, we might wonder, is there a difference between the behavior of people whose cities, neighborhoods, or homes differ in the number of persons/households per square mile, or per acre, or per square yard? This kind of question has been the subject of speculation and research for many years. In fact, during the period between the early 1960s and the early 1980s, an entire field of study developed around the topic of the behavioral effects of population density and crowding.

The main event that sparked this upsurge in the amount of research on density's effects was the 1962 publication of an article by the psychologist John Calhoun in *Scientific American* (Calhoun 1962). The article, entitled "Population Density and Social Pathology," introduced the concept of *behavioral sink* to the public and to many scientists as well. In it, Calhoun reported on a series of experiments that he had conducted with rats, designed to determine what happens if the animals are subjected to conditions of extreme crowding.

In these experiments, the researcher began by placing a small number of rats in a spacious enclosed cage. They were provided with food, water, an adequate supply of air, and clean surroundings. Their behavior was monitored on a regular basis. Then, at predetermined intervals, more rats were added to the cage, and the food and water supply was increased to account for their needs. This procedure continued until the rats were packed in so tightly that they had difficulty in navigating around the floor of the cage. With the addition of more animals, unusual behavior began to occur. The rats became aggressive (see Calhoun 1962), they began to simulate copulation with members of the same sex, mothers stopped nursing and nurturing their offspring, they no longer had normal sexual intercourse, and they stopped reproducing. Eventually, the animals started dying off, they began to practice cannibalism, and the members of the colony were either dead or in a state of total chaos. In contrast, nothing of the kind occurred in a control group, which received identical treatment to that of the experimental group, except that its density was maintained at a constant, low level.

Calhoun referred to this phenomenon as **behavioral sink**. He concluded that pathological behavior is a consequence of high densities, that the frequency and severity of such behavior increases in direct proportion to increased density, and that at some threshold behavioral sink sets in as a prelude to population collapse. Following his early experiments, he replicated the procedure with rats and he and other researchers confirmed the results with mice, birds, fish, deer, and other animals.[2]

Following the publication of Calhoun's findings, social scientists in several countries undertook research designed to establish the extent to which the density-pathology connection exists in *human* populations (e.g., Wohlwill and VanVliet 2013; Dunstan 1976; Rosenberg 1982). Because some of our more significant social problems are related to aggression, sexual behavior, or inadequate nurturing, it seemed reasonable that high densities could explain these phenomena. Of course, no exact replications of the behavioral sink studies were performed, because of practical, ethical, and legal issues. (This is a common occurrence in studies that seek to test laboratory results and/or studies of animals in the real world.) Instead, most of the research focused on examining the effects of crowding in actual urban neighborhoods.

In this work, two principal types of density were used as the independent variable, or cause. These are (1) areal density, as measured by the persons per square mile in various sections of a city or cities; and (2) in-dwelling density, as measured by persons per house, per room, or per square foot of floor space. Among the most frequently studied dependent variables were crimes of various types, mental and physical disorders, and dysfunctional family relations. Results varied from study to study and a general pattern emerged in which densities, of both types, and the behavioral problems of interest were found to be correlated, not extremely so but often at statistically significant levels. So, it appeared, even if Calhoun's results could not be shown to apply strictly to human populations, some interesting parallels did exist.

However, upon careful examination of these results, it turned out that all or nearly all of the relationships were spurious. Harvey Choldin (1978) of the University of Illinois conducted one of the most thorough restudies of the research on the effects of urban density. He found that many of the conclusions drawn were ecological fallacies, in which aggregate effects were mistakenly translated into individual behavior. In some of the studies, the research design was faulty, and there were other problems as well. But the most important point made by Choldin is that the effects attributed to high density could consistently be explained by poverty, lack of education, inadequate socialization, and similar socioeconomic conditions that happen to prevail in some high-density neighborhoods. When statistical controls are introduced to include neighborhoods that are equally densely populated as those with high rates of crime and other social problems, but that are relatively affluent, the relationship disappears. And, by the same token, not all "problem" urban neighborhoods are densely populated.

One of the major conditions in Calhoun's experiments has no counterpart in human populations, and this may partly explain the lack of comparability. Between each increment in the number of rats, the animals lived at the same, single level of density, night and day. The situation is never as static among people (Fernández and Langhout 2014; Gillis 1973). Neighborhoods have different densities at different times of day (for instance, at noon and at midnight). Inhabitants of neighborhoods come and go, experiencing one level of density at work, another during recreational activities, another at home. Moreover, not only do we distinguish between areal and in-dwelling densities, but each of these categories can be broken down further. The area near one's house or apartment may be sparsely populated. But the street as a whole might have a high density, and the surrounding block may be moderately dense, and the surrounding one-quarter mile may be very dense again. Similarly, one's apartment building may be packed with people, but one's own apartment may have plenty of space—except that one sleeps in a room with two siblings. Under such conditions, which of the density conditions is supposed to influence our behavior? Things are simply too complex in naturally occurring human populations to demonstrate behavioral sink.

In view of the lack of a relationship between population density and other likely factors (1) at the level of nations and (2) in neighborhoods and cities, should we conclude that density has no effects? Before we do that, let us consider one last perspective. At a symposium on the effects of population density organized by Choldin,[3] the participants observed that the relationship between density and crime, although statistically insignificant with controls, was not entirely spurious. Research in New York City had demonstrated that in densely populated neighborhoods in which socioeconomic conditions were bad (low incomes, lack of education, etc.) crime rates were higher than in similar neighborhood with lower densities. In contrast, among the wealthy neighborhoods with low crime rates, those with high densities had *lower* crime rates than neighborhoods that were less dense.

The tentative conclusion drawn was that in this case and perhaps in other instances, density does not *cause* certain behaviors, but it *intensifies* whatever tendencies are present. If conditions are bad, high density makes them worse. If things are good, high density makes them better. By way of analogy, think of a party. If people are having a great time, then "the more, the merrier." If it's a boring party, then more guests will probably increase the misery—at least for the host.

The idea of density as an intensifier was first elaborated by the late-nineteenth and early-twentieth-century sociologist Georg Simmel (1858–1918). In his masterwork, *The Philosophy of Money* (1990), Simmel sought to explore the impact of the city and urban life on human thought and behavior. As indicated in his title, he traced the invention of money to the conditions and challenges people faced at the dawn of urban society. In fact, the process of adapting to urban life brought many inventions, of which a monetary economy was both cause and effect. Perhaps most fundamental for Simmel is the innovation of a particular way of thinking that does not—cannot—exist without cities and money (Simmel 1969). The twin hallmarks of the urban mind-set are the tendency toward abstraction and the habit of rationalization (analyzing and calculating). Money symbolizes these because, compared to bartered goods and precious metals, it is not "real" and it can be subdivided into parts.

In explaining how the mental life of the metropolis developed, Simmel gives density a key role. In comparison to other kinds of settlements, the daily round of experiences in cities is intense. An individual comes in contact with many more people, of many different types. Strangers (another one of Simmel's favorite topics) pass by, and in an instant they are gone. Sounds, sights, and seemingly endless varieties of "little worlds" assault the individual every day and from all directions.

In response to this onslaught of sense experiences and human interactions, urban dwellers begin to seek refuge within themselves. They learn how to perceive selectively, seeing only what is necessary and ignoring what is not. They withdraw their emotions from their everyday affairs to protect themselves from the otherwise impossible range of demands. They become "cold," inattentive, and disinterested in the concrete world around them. In exchange, they learn how to deal in abstractions, how to intellectualize. "Intellectuality is thus seen to preserve subjective life against the overwhelming power of Metropolitan life, and intellectuality branches out in many directions and is integrated with numerous discrete phenomena" (Simmel 1969:49). And, associated with these changes, urban dwellers replace the tendency to react emotionally with rationality. "[I]n rational relations man is reckoned with like a number, like an element which itself is indifferent. Only objective measurable achievement is of interest" (Simmel 1969:49).

So, it seems that population density does have effects, and profound ones, too. But they are not to be found at the macroscopic level of nations, nor are they especially pathological. Rather, the effects of density at levels typical of cities operate in shaping a certain social psychology, which we call "urbaneness," or "cool." From this, as Simmel noted, many things follow, including the invention of money. With such connections in mind, then, let us take a closer look at cities and urban life.

THE URBANIZATION OF THE HUMAN POPULATION

Following Simmel's observations, it appears that the characteristics and dynamics of a population are strongly influenced by the locations and sizes of its urban centers. Consider, for example, India, with world's second-largest population. Like most developing countries, India is predominately rural, with about 32 percent of its population living in cities (this comes to 406 million persons, larger than the size of the total U.S. population). Yet, it has 18 cities of over 1 million population, three of which are among the world's largest: Mumbai, with a metropolitan area population of 18.1 million; Calcutta, with 14.1 million; and the Delhi region, with more than 16.3 million.[4]

India's rate of general population growth reached a peak during the late 1980s, with an estimated 2.8 percent per year (Census of India 1991; also Weinstein 1991/92). At that time, its rate of urban growth was nearly 4.4 percent. During the 1990s, general growth slowed to less than 2.0 percent (Lutz 2013; PRB 1998), but the urban sector continued to expand. Most of the increase in the urban population came from migration from the countryside, where the growth rate continued to be well above 2 percent—more than twice that of the total U.S. population. In addition to having large and rapidly growing cities, India's economic and political life are—as in virtually every other country—dominated by the urban sector.

At the turn of the twenty-first century, approximately 45 percent of the world's population was urbanized. In the industrialized countries of Europe, in Japan, in Australia, and in North America, the urbanization rates were approximately 80 percent. Iceland reported 95 percent urban, Denmark and Australia 87 percent, and Japan 91 percent. However, in most of Asia, Africa, and much of Latin America, the average is about 35 percent, with rates as low as 17 percent in Nepal and in Rwanda. As in India, many poorer, rural counties have large cities, an indication of the phenomenon known as *primacy.*[5] The largest urban agglomeration is in the world's wealthiest nation, Japan: Tokyo-Yokohama, with nearly 35 million persons. The eleventh-largest urban area is the New York CMSA, with more than 21 million. But between these two are Mexico City (22 million); Manila, Philippines (22.4 million); and Karachi, Pakistan (23 million)—all relatively poor nations.

The relationship between urbanization and socioeconomic development is reflected in our sample of 50 nations. For the 50 countries for which urbanization rates were available, the mean is 55.1 percent. These range between Rwanda's 17 percent and 95 percent for Iceland. In examining the correlation between percent urban and other factors, it was found that where urbanization rates are low death rates are high, infant mortality rates are high, per-capita gross national product is low, and average life expectancy is low. Clearly, the more urbanized nations are better off in some very important ways.

A Historical Overview of Urban Growth

The story of how the world became so urbanized, and how it did so in such an uneven fashion, is a fascinating one. In part this is because it is the story of the development of human civilization, which itself means "city culture." It is difficult to establish an exact date at which human beings first appeared on the earth. Most anthropologists agree that it was well before the species *Homo sapiens* evolved some 38,000 years ago. In any case, for hundreds of thousands of years people lived in a variety of settlement types, including temporary encampments of peripatetic ("nomadic") groups and several kinds of relatively permanent homesteads. These were generally based on extended kin relations, and the economies—whether hunting, gathering, herding, or horticultural—barely provided for a subsistence standard of living. Thus, for at least 95 percent of human existence, no settlement existed that was structurally more complex than a large village.

Then, beginning about 10,000 years ago, the first cities were established in the Middle East (see Figure 4.4). These served, in part, as trading centers, and included a market place for the regular exchange of goods from the hinterland. The oasis city of Jericho, which is the present-day West Bank town also known as Ariha, is the oldest city for which we have firm archaeological evidence. It was settled in 7500 BCE. By 7000 BCE, a population exceeding 2,000 persons lived within its walls, and the citizens had created a political administration. During the subsequent several centuries of Neolithic Revolution, other urban settlements were founded throughout the region, most of them walled and all about the size of Jericho. By 4000 BCE, some of the most famous ancient cities had been established; these included Babylon, Thebes, and Sumer. To the east, in the Indus Valley region of present-day India and Pakistan, the inhabitants built the monumental twin settlements of Mohenjo-Daro and Harappa, seats of the legendary Sanskrit/Aryan civilization.

Conditions for the Development of Cities

Although such places were relatively large and densely populated, these were not their defining characteristics. For some villages were (and still are) larger and at least as crowded. Rather, what distinguished them from other settlement types was that:

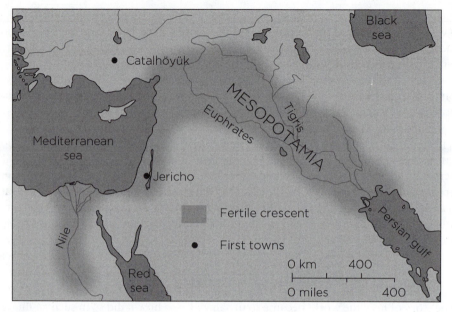

Figure 4.4. The Cradles of Civilization, Sites of the First Cities, 8,000-10,000 Years BCE
Sources: Dorling Kindersley/Thinkstock.

(1) a substantial portion of their populations worked at occupations that did not involve food or raw material production.[6]

In addition, although the household remained the basic unit of social organization, as it had been prior to the shift to cities,

(2) new groups developed that were based on political and occupational specialization and which went beyond pure kinship relations.

According to the classical sociologist, Max Weber (1900 [1958c]), these factors, combined with

(3) a separate political system,
(4) the prevalence of fortress-like walls (the German word *Berg* means both "fortress" and "city"), and
(5) a marketplace

constitute the essential conditions of cities everywhere and in all eras. These conditions also provide a clue as to why cities first developed when and where they did. Approximately 10,000 years ago, in the valleys of the Jordan and other rivers in the Middle East, some groups discovered new tools and principles that could be used in food production: the plow, irrigation, and technologies of animal husbandry. As these innovations were applied, and as knowledge of them diffused from population to population, a qualitative leap occurred in the ability of people to sustain themselves and to reduce death rates enough to initiate a period of relative growth. Now called the *first* **Agricultural Revolution**, it produced enough surplus with sufficient regularity to free some people from direct production, permitting them to pursue trade, manufacturing, and other activities on a more-or-less full-time basis. It also created the conditions for a new division of labor to develop that involved separation of work from family activities. This combination of a reliable surplus and a new level of social complexity made it possible and, in some respects, made it necessary for the affected populations to establish the first cities.[7] Thus, agricultural revolution preceded urban revolution. This sequence was to be repeated many times throughout the world.

Between the Neolithic period and the beginning of the Common Era, the number of cities increased, as did their influence on the surrounding regions. Many other social, cultural, and economic changes that accompanied the spread of urban settlements contributed to this influence, including the development of the institution of the state. Not only did the ancient cities have an autonomous form of administration, they were states unto themselves, **city-states** (*polis* in Greek). Vestiges of this system exist today in Singapore, Monaco, and Luxembourg. Through this political institution, the cities were able to tax, draft for military service, and conduct census counts of the population in the hinterlands. One of the more interesting demographic features of these early city-states is that approximately 5 percent of the population under their control actually lived within the city walls. The other 95 percent remained in the countryside, farming or pursuing other primary occupations. This 18:1 rural-urban ratio indicates how meager the surplus was upon which the cities depended.

Western scholarship has tended to focus on the rise of cities in the Middle East and India. However, it is clear that the sequence of agricultural revolution, increases in population size and level of social complexity, generation of economic surplus, and thus the establishment of urban settlements occurred as independent innovations in many places. In addition to Thebes and other ancient Egyptian cities, Africa had urban settlements since well before 1 AD (Fage 2013; Shinne 1965). These included the cities of the Kush Empire established about 800 BCE, and the Ghana and Mali peoples some years later. By 221 BCE, all of present-day China, under the Ch'in Dynasty, was unified with Peking (Beijing) as its capital (Mu 1982). During this same period, the populations of Indochina created several city-states. And, in the New World, groups from whom the Mayas, Incas, and other great civilizations were descended built great stone cities throughout central and South America (Aveni 2013; Coe 1985; Mason 1968).

Like the early urban settlements in the Middle East, these cities were established in river valleys and in the wake of agricultural revolutions. They, too, developed political structures along the lines of city-states. And they were settled by a tiny fraction of their regional populations—3 to 5 percent—whom they nevertheless dominated in political, cultural, and economic realms. The principle whereby these small populations could control the affairs of much larger groups is known to geographers as *central place theory*, and it has been shown to apply to a wide range of phenomena.

Central Place Theory

Although the idea that central location has advantages is more or less intuitive, its first formal and precise expression came in the 1930s in the work of Walter Christaller (1893–1969). The basic premise of the theory is that the center of an area, such as a city or state, is the most efficient point from which to gain access to

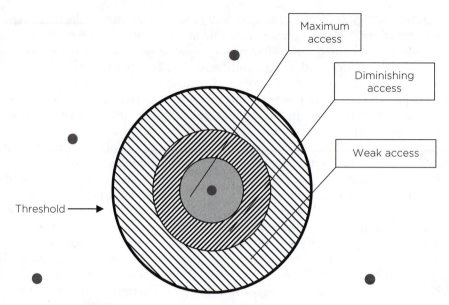

Figure 4.5. Central Place Theory
The center is the optimum location for access to peripheral areas. Access decreases with distance to a threshold, at which point other centers exert greater influence.

the populations in that area (see Figure 4.5; Christaller 1972). In economic terms, this means that a business located at the center of its market is more likely to profit from its activities than a business located elsewhere, all else equal. When the first cities developed, they took advantage of this principle and capitalized on it. They were capable of making contact with large numbers of people and whatever the people produced, from all directions. Thus, urban dwellers could coordinate the activities of many more nonresidents, and do so more efficiently than was possible when settlements were smaller and more dispersed.

The form of control from the center identified in central place theory gave rise to a new type of geographic stratification, the core-periphery system. With this system, socioeconomic inequality is achieved through large-scale access. In fact, no other type of spatial arrangement allows for so few to coordinate the activities of so many. In addition, it is a system of territorial dominance and subordination; the core rules the periphery. As cities grew in numbers and size, the advantages of centrality created ever more powerful core-periphery relations throughout the world, and the scope of control of urban settlements grew to enormous proportions. At its peak, Rome, with perhaps 800,000 inhabitants, ruled an area of millions of square miles and the millions of people who occupied this territory. And, by the eighteenth century AD, a few cities in Europe—principally London—were capable of creating a core-periphery system that was truly worldwide in scope (see Wallerstein 1974, 2013).

Central place theory has been referred to as one of the "geographic ideas that changed the world" (Ogborn, Blunt, and Gruffudd 2014; Hanson 1997); and it has been widely celebrated among geographers and others (e.g., Berry and Harris 1970; Preston 1985). Much research has been guided by the theory, and perhaps even more theoretical work has been dedicated to exploring its implications (Berry 1965). It has also been subject to critical scrutiny on several grounds. For example, it appears not to distinguish carefully between a territory's geographic center and its population center (or centers), the latter of which is the valid central point in terms of the theory's basic principle. Also, Christaller himself and the theory as a potential tool for territorial domination have been questioned for their ties to the Nazi regime in Germany (Roessler 1989).

Setting aside the merits and limitations of the theory and its author, it is increasingly clear that the notion of central advantage was once very important—even the driving force of urban development—but that it is rapidly becoming obsolete. In most metropolitan areas of the United States, the suburbs dominate the core. Not only has the majority of urban residents migrated from the center, so have the businesses, factories, and cultural facilities. With innovations in electronic communication, home offices, and the like, there is less and less of an advantage to being at the center.

This is certainly not to deny the ingenuity of central place theory, nor of the important research it has inspired. But in the twenty-first century, being some*where* matters relatively little. Many of us use the Internet in our work, especially sites such as the Worldcat online library service (*https://www.worldcat.org/advancedsearch*). But how many of us know if it is centrally located or, for that matter, what its location is? Some populations, such as that of the United States, Japan, and Western Europe, have become so urbanized that they have transcended many of the hard-and-fast rules of city life, including central place theory.

Urbanization before the Industrial Revolution

In combination, the two factors of central advantage and a small agricultural surplus kept the number and sizes of cities relatively small—by contemporary standards—from prehistoric times through the Middle Ages (Ioannides and Skouras 2013). According to the comprehensive compilation of information on the rise and fall of cities by Tertius Chandler and Gerald Fox (1974), almost all of the cities in the ancient world were small. However, some approaching population sizes of 100,000 may have existed as early as 1360 BCE. Babylon's population was almost surely larger than 50,000 and ancient Thebes had about 225,000 persons (see Petersen 1975:chap. 11; also Davis 1974). During the Golden Era of 500 BCE, fewer than 100,000 people lived within the walls of the great city-state of Athens (not including the port of Piraeus). By 1 AD, Rome had reached a size variously estimated between 350,000 and 1 million. In any case, it was the largest city in the world at the time and, as events turned out, it was to be the largest city in Europe for many centuries.

With the fall of the Roman Empire in 455 AD, the population of the city of Rome dwindled to less than 100,000. From that point until the 1300s, social life in Europe was centered in the countryside, as the land-based feudal system developed. The center of urban civilization thus shifted to the east and to the two great successor regimes to Rome, Imperial China and the Turco-Muslim Empire. By 361 AD, Constantinople had a population size of 350,000, and Peking was probably as large. As the capitals and urban areas of these empires expanded in size and influence, growth proceeded slowly in London, Paris, and Europe's other walled towns and cities. At the time of the Norman Conquest in 1066, London had only 18,000 inhabitants. And, as late as 1300, Paris's population size was less than 60,000. The exceptions to this pattern were to be found in the Iberian region, where cities like Cadiz, Lisbon, and Barcelona had grown large and economically important. Yet, although they were geographically located in Europe, these were actually Muslim cities and part of the Moorish Empire until 1411.

Toward the end of the fourteenth century, feudalism began to weaken and a pre-capitalist economic system emerged at the peripheries of the Turco-Muslim world. This sparked a renaissance, not only in cultural terms but also in relation to urban growth in Europe. In northern Italy, several towns evolved into cultural and banking centers. They were chartered as city-states and soon came to exert considerable influence on the region—and on the world. These included Padua, Bologna, Venice (whose population size in 1363 was 78,000), and Florence (pop. 55,000). London had grown by this time, but it was still smaller than the Italian cities, with a population size of about 35,000.

Constantinople and Peking remained the world's largest cities through the fifteenth and sixteenth centuries, and Italy, Spain, and Portugal continued to be the major urban centers of Europe. The economic position of the Iberian region was greatly enhanced by its expanding colonial empire in the newly discovered areas in the New World, Africa, and Asia. This, in itself, represented a revolutionary development, because the potential maximum size of a city's hinterlands had thus expanded exponentially with the acquisition of overseas territories. England was not yet a major player in the colonial system, but by about 1550 London's population had reached 100,000. At about this time Rome—with no empire at all—still had only 55,000 inhabitants, or about one-tenth of its maximum prior to its fall. Even as late as 1650, and including Iberia, less than 2 percent of Europe's population lived in places with population sizes greater than 20,000.

The Industrial City Emerges

At that point, as the seventeenth century was drawing to a close, the center of colonial power shifted northward to Holland, where the port city of Amsterdam became a dominant force in world affairs, and to England. There, technological innovations in fertilization and irrigation converged with ever-increasing wealth from the new overseas Empire and with political changes that, in effect, destroyed the feudal system. The result was a *second* agricultural revolution. In this case, between unprecedented levels of domestic productivity and seemingly endless supplies of raw materials from abroad, economic surpluses were generated that were enormous by previous standards. This made it possible, and necessary, for masses of people to leave the countryside and move to the cities.

Events cumulated, as change in one realm initiated change in others, which then rebounded to affect the first. The principles of physics that Newton had elaborated in the seventeenth century were put into effect in the eighteenth. In about 1740, the steam engine was invented, and it quickly took hold of the imagination of manufacturers, farmers, and merchants. This further increased agricultural productivity and, at the same time, created a demand for urban laborers. These workers streamed into the cities where they helped to raise levels of industrial productivity, while wealth continued to flow in from America, India, and Africa. Thus, in the wake of an agricultural revolution, England experienced an industrial revolution and an urban revolution. By 1750, London had reached a population size of 750,000, at an average annual rate of increase of more than 10 percent per year. Only Peking was larger. And by 1800, when Peking's population size reached 1 million, London's did as well, making them the first million-plus cities in the world. By that date, 10 percent of England was urbanized, also a then-unprecedented figure (the new nation of the United States had an urbanization rate of 6.1 percent).

It was during this period, at the turn of the nineteenth century, that the discrepancy was established between the levels of urbanization in the industrialized countries and those in what are today the less-developed nations. As the industrial revolution spread throughout the United Kingdom to continental Europe and to North America, it was everywhere accompanied by rapid urban growth. Towns became cities and cities became metropolises throughout these regions. By the end of the nineteenth century, there were 16 million-plus cities, 12 of which were in Europe and one in North America (New York). And 50 percent of England's population was living in cities.

However, the industrial revolution was not exported to India, nor did it diffuse to Latin America or to Africa. For these were the areas whose human and natural resources were fueling the great changes in Europe. Consequently, urban growth there was uneven and generally slow. Great port cities such as Bombay were established, but they were not designed to contribute to domestic growth. Rather, they were exporting "nodes" that faced outward to London and the other colonial capitals (Wallerstein 1974). The interior of these colonized areas, where the vast majority of the populations lived, was largely ignored. This pattern has persisted to this day when, with very few exceptions, we find the most highly urbanized countries at the core of the colonial system and low levels of urbanization at the peripheries.

By virtue of this same pattern, however, urban growth rates are the highest where levels of urbanization are lowest. As we mentioned in the case of India, the press of general population growth, along with industrialization and economic changes, has created huge and increasing streams of rural to urban migration, especially to the primary cities like Mumbai, Lagos, Nairobi, and Mexico City. With only 30 to 35 percent of the populations of these countries urbanized at the turn of the twenty-first century, the explosion of cities is likely to continue for many decades (Kundu 2013; Jones and Visaria 1997). Meanwhile, the highly urbanized countries, including England and the United States, have reached a point of saturation. There is very little scope for more urban growth, as most of the population already lives in cities. In these places, the process of urbanization traces an "S" curve of logistic growth.

During the course of several thousands of years of urban growth, humanity has experienced a reversal. Once, more than 95 percent of the population of a territory was required to sustain fewer than 5 percent who lived in cities. Today, less than 5 percent of the population is engaged in agriculture, as the urban sector in many countries approaches the 90-percent mark. The proportion of the labor force employed in agriculture in the United States has fallen steadily. As of 2008, less than 2 percent of the population was employed in the agricultural sector. Yet, these few farmers not only supply the nation's urban population, they feed many other nations as well.

Urban Growth in the United States[8]

Now one of the most highly urbanized countries, the United States began as a nation of farmers. The issuing of the Declaration of Independence coincided with the very beginnings of the Industrial Revolution. Although it would be impossible to prove such speculation, had not the Americans freed themselves from British colonialism, the nation might have gone the way of India. That is, it would have continued to supply the "Motherland" and to have delayed its trek to the cities until the mid-twentieth century. However, this did not occur, and the new nation had the double advantage of being sovereign and having the resources to initiate its own process of industrialization. The nation was relatively small at the beginning, with a total population size at the first census of 3,929,214, of which 201,655 were living in cities. For this reason, and because it had such a vast frontier to be settled, its experience with urban growth began later and, at first, proceeded somewhat more slowly than that of England, France, and some other European countries.

Between the first and second censuses, the total U.S. population grew to 5.3 million, at a rate of 3.0 percent per year. However, the urban sector increased to 203,000, at a rate of 4.7 percent. The period of the most rapid urban growth was between 1840 and 1860. During the earlier year, the number living in cities was just under 1.9 million, constituting 10.8 percent of the population. By 1860, just prior to the Civil War, more than 6.2 million persons were living in cities, making up nearly 20 percent of the total population. The average annual rate of urban growth during this period was 6.1 percent.

The nation reached 50 percent urban at the 1920 Census, when 54.3 million of 106 million (51.2 percent) were living in cities. The period exhibiting one of the slowest urban growth rates is the most recent, because of the saturation effect. Between 1970 and 1980, the growth rate averaged 1.1 percent per year, and between 1980 and 1990 it was also 1.1. At the latter enumeration, 75.2 percent of the population was urban. The slowest period of all, however, came during the Great Depression. Between 1930 and 1940, the rate of urban growth was only 0.8 percent per year.

Along with the increase in the urban component of the population has come steady growth in the number of cities (defined as places with a population size greater than 2,500). At the first census there were 24 such places; by 1840 there were more than 100 (131); by 1890 more than 1,000 (1,351); and by 1960 there were over 5,000 (5,023). As of the 1990 Census, the United States had 8,500 urban places, of which more than 20 have populations greater than 1.5 million and an additional 252 have at least 57,000 persons. Only in 1920 did the population living in cities surpassed rural population. By 2010, the number of urban places with population greater than 1.5 million increased to 32.

At the end of the twentieth century, the regional distribution of the urban population in the United States was fairly even. The subregional percentages ranged between 56.2 for the East South Central (Kentucky, Tennessee, Alabama, and Mississippi) and 88.6 for the Pacific (California, Oregon, Washington, and Hawaii). Among the main regions, the South had the largest number of urban dwellers, with 58.7 million out of the nation's total of 187.0 million, and an urbanization rate of 68.6 percent. The West, with 45.5 million persons living in cities, had the highest urbanization rate: 86.3 percent. California, which has three CMSAs entirely within its borders and is the most urbanized state in the nation, accounts for most of this regional pattern in the West. But part of the high rate comes from states—like Nevada—that have a small population but virtually no rural sector. Although the Northeast is the locale of two enormous CMSAs (New York and Boston), it has the fewest urban dwellers in absolute terms: 40 million, or 78.9 percent of the region's total. The Midwest has a relatively low urbanization rate of 71.7 percent, although it includes one of the country's most urbanized states (Illinois).

Of the 10 most densely populated areas in the United States, nine are in the West. At the state level, California, whose urbanization rate was 92.6 percent and which had 26.8 million persons living in cities, led the nation in both categories. Vermont, with a total population size of 563,000 and 181,000 urban dwellers, had the lowest rate: 32.2 percent. Even with this kind of variation, the United States is clearly a nation of cities, as only three states had urbanization rates below 40 percent and 23 had rates above 70 percent. The regional pattern of urbanization was maintained through the 2010 Census year as well. California and New Jersey had the highest urbanization rates in 2010. The lowest rates in 2010 were in Maine, Vermont, and West Virginia with both Kansas and Michigan in the middle range of urbanization rates. The Northeastern region had 39.4 million, the Midwest 43.6 million, the South 78.1 million, and the West 58.8 million urban dwellers. The urbanization rates for the four regions were 71 percent, 66 percent, 68 percent, and 82 percent, respectively.

GEOGRAPHIC INFORMATION SYSTEMS

It would be difficult to name an innovation in social science research technology that has had greater impact since the early 1990s than geographic information systems (GIS). In fact, its scope extends far beyond the social sciences, to city planning, physical geography and geology, environmental studies, engineering, and business (Lakhan 1996). In the last instance, the prevailing view is that "every industry needs GIS," as noted by Edward Lollis, a partner in GeoVisual Business Services in the Washington, D.C. area (Stahl 1995:33).

Thousands of books and articles have been published on the subject, an international symposium on GIS advances has been held annually since 1992 (ACM 1998), software is widely available (e.g., ESRI 1998), and the Internet abounds with GIS-oriented sites. "Of all the technology-related online sources . . . the most abundant are of one type—GIS" (Jeer 1997:22; also Harder 1998). Although many of these sources are useful and informative, perhaps the premier source is the U.S. Census Bureau's TIGER (Topologically Integrated Geographic Encoding and Referencing) database web site.

The concept of GIS is the result of the convergence of knowledge and technology from many fields. In some respects, it is a form of cartography, because its focus is on the production of visual maps that convey information to the viewer. It also is the product of innovations in computer hardware and software technology. Several aspects of GIS are strongly computer-dependent, especially the speed and graphics that allow the maps that are produced to be displayed on a monitor, printed, and stored in compressed-format files. With the appropriate remote sensing software, the user can employ live satellite maps (LSU 1990).

Perhaps the most important computer-related breakthrough is the digitizing workstation, the most widely used of which is Arc/Info©. This system allows a programmer to stand or sit at a monitor with a hard-copy map of an area affixed to a nearby drawing table. The programmer then uses a specialized pointer-shaped mouse to make contact with the map and to have the contact point input to a file and appear on the monitor. This "Automatic Digitizing System (ADS)" has turned a tedious and time-consuming task into a simple and effective form of geographic data management (BLM 1993).

One of the leading GIS organizations, the Environmental Systems Research Institute (ESRI) in Redlands, California, has innovated in combining these various approaches and disseminating information to professionals and the public. In 1995, an ESRI researcher, Michael Michelsen Jr., observed that "GIS has existed in a crude form for 25 years, but came of age 12 to 15 years age with improvements in computers. . . . Much of the early GIS work was performed by governments, utilities, geologists, and environmental groups, which used these systems for purposes of tracking land parcels, rock formations, old-growth forests, and water management" (Stahl 1995:32).

Obviously, GIS is not exclusively concerned with the mapping of demographic information, although this is one of its principal applications (Cockings et al. 2013; Martin and Higgs 1997).[9] One of the major advances in mapping technology that GIS has made possible is the ability of the researcher to display several kinds of information simultaneously: demographic, geological, civil engineering data, and more. This is accomplished with the technique of "layering." Once the position of the subareas of a city, state, or other geographic unit are determined, data are input in linked files: say one for population size, one for income level, one for land elevation, and one for access to sewage lines. When reading out the file on screen, in hard copy, or to a storage location, the user requests both the location set and one of the data subfiles. Once this has been examined, another subfile can be called up and presented, either overlaid on the first or as a replacement. The data from one set can be mathematically correlated with location, or those from two or more sets can be correlated with one another.

Thus, we can know—and *see*—things such as where the larger population concentrations are, the location of wealthy and poor households, and which areas have the best and the worst access to sewer lines. And we can know if wealthy people have better access than poor people, if the large population concentrations are found in hilly regions on in flat places, and so on. Once the appropriate data have been input, all of this can happen instantaneously and in vivid colors. Also, because the data are stored in independent but linked files, they can be updated regularly. By saving files between updates, one can call up and display the same variables at different points in time. This provides an efficient and effective way to perceive changes, such as how the population concentrations of an area are shifting, and if these shifts are correlated with changes in access to utilities.

The field of geographic information systems has captured the imagination of experts and laypersons alike. So much has been said, written, and posted about it that one would have to be very inattentive not to have some knowledge of it. It is relevant for demography and for many other disciplines; and it is taught in several departments at most universities. Perhaps most important, it is a field with a future that is looking for people to develop and apply hardware and software. At least four web sites are devoted exclusively to providing job-search information in GIS. One site that has a comprehensive listing, including specialization and geographic location, is Indeed: One Search All Jobs.

SUMMARY

Cities and urbanization now typify the territorial nature of human populations, whether that territory is a census block, one of the other administrative and statistical units introduced—including the CMSA, or the entire planet. As noted, in the larger scheme of things, this is a relatively recent development; for cities were invented many thousands—perhaps hundreds of thousands—of years after people began to inhabit the earth. Today, there is little doubt that the trend of rapid urban growth, especially in the less-developed parts of the world, will continue and accelerate for many years to come.

With this introduction to geographic distribution, we have covered three of the four major categories that make up the field of demography. The fourth, *changes* in size, structure, and geographic distribution, is the focus of the next several chapters. There we consider how and why populations, subpopulations, cities, states, and other aggregates grow or diminish. Appropriately, we begin with birth in Chapter 5.

KEY TERMS

Agricultural Revolution
behavioral sink
central place theory
city-state
consolidated metropolitan statistical
    area (CMSA)

density
geographic information systems (GIS)
metropolitan statistical area (MSA)
Territorial Imperative

NOTES

1. For a critique of Ardrey's book by an extremely competent opponent of biological explanation in the social sciences (including explanations that use "race," as noted in Chapter 3), see Montague (1970).

2. Not every animal study confirmed Calhoun's findings. For example, Lobb and McCain (1978) showed that rats will adapt to high densities with time, and will exhibit competitive but not aggressive behavior under such circumstances.

3. "The Correlates of Population Density." Population Association of America, 69th Annual Meeting." Boston. April 1–3. H. M. Choldin Chair, J. Weinstein, Discussant.

4. These estimates for 1997–1998 come from various sources, including several web sites, Almanacs, and yearbooks. They are not official figures.

5. This concept, introduced by the influential geographer, Mark Jefferson (1863–1949), refers to the tendency for virtually the entire urban population of a country to reside in the one, capital capitacity—called the "primate" city (Jefferson 1909).

6. At the same time, many urban dwellers between the period of the ancient civilizations until, and even after, the medieval era continued to work at agriculture and related pursuits (see Petersen 1975:401–10). "(O)ccupational specialization characteristic of town life was often incomplete, related to a continuing osmosis between rural and urban worlds" (Petersen 1975:402).

7. We emphasize that some populations were affected because the extent of the Agricultural Revolution's spread was not great by today's standards. Most populations in the region and most members of the populations that did make the agricultural breakthrough remained rural for millennia.

8. Data for this section are from U.S. Bureau of the Census, "United States Urban and Rural." United States Summary, *Population and Housing Unit Counts*; and *Statistical Abstract of the United States, 1997*: Table 44.

9. As Martin and Higgs point out, GIS has caused census officials—in their native U.K. and in the United States as well—to rethink their approach to small-area (tract, block, etc.) definition and use. Because GIS is point-specific, tract boundaries are to some extent irrelevant. This is a problem yet to be worked out. The U.S. Census Bureau's TIGER service has proceeded under the assumption that tracts and blocks are adequate for present purposes.

PART TWO

POPULATION DYNAMICS
Vital Events and Growth

The four chapters in this part are arranged according to the fundamental equation of demography: births (Chapter 5) – deaths (Chapter 6) ± net migration (Chapter 7) = growth (Chapter 8). These are the components that determine population dynamics, the changes in size, structure, and geographic distribution that all naturally occurring populations experience from moment to moment.

The first two of these chapters, Chapter 5, "Birth and Fertility: Measures, Theories, and Trends," and Chapter 6, "Mortality: Causes and Consequences" constitute natural increase and are organized in a parallel fashion. Each begins with some basic definitions and then moves on to a presentation of the major methods and measurements demographers employ in studying these vital events. Each then concludes with a discussion of the social and historical factors associated with the respective events, in the United States and internationally.

Chapter 7, "Migration: Geographic and Social Psychological Components," also begins with a discussion of measurement, with special emphasis on the difficulties in tracking and accurately accounting for population movements. Much of the chapter is devoted to substantive matters in the field of migration studies: episodes of internal migration in the United States, patterns and changes in immigration flows, and issues in international migration, with special emphasis on the refugee problem. Also included is a review of several major theories in the field. Finally, in the context of international migration, the reader is referred to Chapter 14, where the related but separate subject of tourism is discussed.

Chapter 8 draws on the material in the earlier chapters in focusing on population growth. It begins with discussions and illustrations of the major growth models, both the "difference" and the "components" types. It then focuses on the concepts and historical data associated with demographic transition, dramatic changes in growth patterns. With this section emphasizing long-range, past trends in the populations of today's industrialized nations, the discussion then turns to current growth in developing nations and to future growth prospects at the global level. The chapter (and Part II) ends with data and commentary on the aging of the world's population, a major consequence of current growth patterns, and an historical overview of population growth in the United States.

BIRTH AND FERTILITY

Measures, Theories, and Trends

The size and other characteristics of naturally occurring populations are always changing. Ordinarily, such change is gradual and barely discernible from day to day; much like the hands of a clock that we know to be moving but at too slow a pace to be easily observed. Occasionally, populations are transformed dramatically and quickly as the result of natural disasters, technological breakthroughs, and the like. In such instances we describe the process vividly with terms like "explosion," "boom," or "collapse." But regardless of the rate of change, from gradual to explosive and all points in between, the root cause ultimately can be traced to the interactions among the four vital events: **birth**, death, in-migration, and out-migration. We are now about to begin an examination of these events in some depth with the first and in some ways the most challenging, birth.

One source of these challenges is that demographers employ many terms to describe what is essentially the same phenomenon: birth, **fertility**, **reproduction**, and **natality**. This is because it can be viewed from several different points of view. A birth is the event from the perspective of the newborn; an individual comes into the world at a certain time and day, and it happens *once* in a lifetime. *Fertility* describes the status of a parent, almost universally the mother.[1] When a birth occurs, the fertility level of the parent increases by one (or more in the case of multiple births). This is referred to as a change in *parity*, the number of children born to the parent. A woman who has never given birth is at 0 parity, having one child raises her parity to 1, and so on. From the mother's standpoint, births can happen *several* times during the course of her reproductive life. One consequence of this difference between birth and fertility is that rates measuring the frequency of the event employ different base populations. Birth rates, of which the best known is the CBR (crude birth rate), are measured in relation to the general or total population. Fertility rates are measured in relation to an aggregate of fertile women.

Reproduction refers to the capacity for a population or subpopulation to sustain its size from generation to generation. Thus, its measurement not only accounts for births but also for the probability that some newborns will die before they reach adulthood and bears children. Our final term, *natality*, refers to the effect that birth and fertility have on a population as a whole. It is conceived as a risk factor or probability that an individual (again, ordinarily a fertile woman) will change birth parity within a year or other unit of time. These probabilities vary substantially according to the age of the mother and other factors.

With these various concepts and in view, the remainder of this chapter examines the aspects of fertility of greatest interest to population scientists. We begin with an introduction to several of the most common measures and indicators in the field, such as rates of birth and fertility. Next is a discussion of theories of fertility, general summaries and models that attempt to explain why birth rates vary from time to time and from one population to another. These theories and measures are then used to describe general past and current trends in world fertility levels. The chapter ends with a brief overview of the historical variations in fertility in the United States from the 1940s to the turn of the twenty-first century.

MEASURING FERTILITY

A woman's level of fertility refers to the number of live births she has actually experienced at a specific point in her life. This should not be confused with a related phenomenon, **fecundity**, which is the physical capacity of a woman to give birth. In principle, this number is something in the range of 15 (Petersen 1975:199; Abel and Kruger 2012) not counting multiple births, although it is rarely, if ever, achieved.[2] The opposite of fecundity, sterility, is the inability to conceive. This condition affects approximately 10 percent of the U.S. population, varying according to age and other factors. It is obvious that fecundity and the prevalence of sterility contribute to a population's overall fertility level. But today, especially in the industrialized nations, their influence is negligible in comparison to the effects of contraception. That is, the birth rates observed in the United States, Canada, Europe, and Japan—among other places—are principally the result of social and economic conditions, not organic ones.

The three major sources of data for the analysis of fertility are vital statistics, censuses, and sample surveys. As we saw in Chapter 2, vital statistics are collected on a continuing basis and are available from local sources and national governments, especially the Center for Disease Control and Prevention (CDC) in the United States. Census enumerations provide several useful types of information for fertility analysis, such as the age distribution of a population and the number of children ever born to women of various ages. Demographic surveys, including the Current Population Surveys (CPS) conducted by the U.S. Census Bureau, are a preferred source of fertility data. These studies provide detailed information on the number of births in the most recent year, the number of children ever born, and the respondents' ages at marriage.[3]

As in the case of life tables (see Chapter 9), birth and fertility can be measured in two alternative ways, by *period* or by *cohort*. **Period measures**, based on a synchronous model, account for births that occur to women in one or more age groups during a specific calendar year (or other period). **Cohort measures**, based on a diachronic model, track the fertility performance of a specific group of women of similar ages—an age cohort—through the duration of their reproductive years. When we ask how many children were born in a population during a year (or month, etc.), we are seeking a period measure. When we ask how many children a woman delivered during her lifetime, we are framing the question in terms of cohort measures.

COMMON PERIOD MEASURES

Crude Birth Rate (CBR)

The well-known annual crude birth rate, CBR, is a period measure that employs both vital registration and census or survey data. It is defined as the total number of births to mothers of all ages that occur during a year (B, a vital statistic) per 1,000 persons in the general population (P, based on enumeration). The formula, as first presented in Chapter 2 is:

$$CBR = B/P \times 1,000$$

According the U.S. Census Bureau estimates, the total midyear 2011 population size of the country was 311,591,917. During that year, there were an estimated 3,953,590 live births. This yields a CBR of (3,953,590/311,591,917) × 1,000 = 12.68 births per 1,000 persons. In comparison, India's total estimated midyear population size was over 1 billion, at 1,210,193,422. With 25,377,756 live births, its CBR was 20.97 per 1,000. This, of course, is a substantial difference that helps to explain why India's population is growing at about twice the rate as that of the United States

Table 5.1 lists the CBRs for our sample of 66 nations introduced in Chapter 3 along with information on three other variables. One of these, the **total fertility rate** (**TFR**), is another period measure of fertility to be discussed in the following section. The remaining variables shown are per-capita GDP and "birth control," the

Table 5.1. Birth Rates and Their Correlates for 66 Nations, 2011

Country	CBR	TFR	GDP ($)	Birth Control
Albania	12.65	1.748	4556.14	-
Antigua and Barbuda	16.76	2.115	12785.16	-
Australia	13.29	1.87	62080.98	71
Bahamas, The	15.47	1.898	21490.36	-
Barbados	12.80	1.842	15503.33	-
Belize	24.09	2.756	4707.85	31
Bolivia	26.20	3.308	2319.6	34
Brazil	15.33	1.822	12576.2	77
Burkina Faso	41.97	5.781	649.93	15
Cameroon	38.18	4.939	1204.7	14
Central African Republic	34.76	4.538	494.93	9
China	11.93	1.657	5447.31	84
Comoros	36.47	4.85	871.69	19
Costa Rica	15.50	1.827	8704.11	72
Cuba	9.74	1.459	6051.22	73
Denmark	10.60	1.75	59911.9	-
Dominican Republic	21.54	2.551	5462.7	70
El Salvador	20.34	2.236	3698.55	66

Table 5.1. Continued.

Country	CBR	TFR	GDP ($)	Birth Control
Estonia	11.00	1.52	16982.3	56
Fiji	21.19	2.641	4324.69	-
French Polynesia	16.77	2.092		-
Gambia, The	43.18	5.789	517.75	13
Ghana	31.79	3.985	1594.03	17
Guadalupe				-
Guinea	37.76	5.088	454.0	4
Haiti	26.37	3.28	749.22	24
Iceland	14.10	2.02	44019.39	-
Iran, Islamic Rep.	19.11	1.912	7006.05	59
Israel	21.4	3.0	33250.51	-
Japan	8.30	1.39	46203.7	44
Kenya	36.10	4.538	816.44	39
Kuwait	21.10	2.652	51396.85	34
Latvia	9.10	1.34	13827.36	56
Liberia	36.56	4.945	376.93	10
Lithuania	11.30	1.76	14158.01	33
Macedonia, FYR	10.85	1.443	4940.95	10
Malaysia	17.62	1.986	10058.04	-
Malta	10.30	1.38	21985.34	46
Mauritius	11.50	1.45	8749.58	39
Moldova	12.31	1.469	1970.84	43
Mozambique	40.03	5.338	510.46	11
Nepal	22.27	2.496	694.14	43
New Caledonia	16.70	2.172		-
Niger	49.92	7.581	388.33	5
Oman	21.65	2.899	23132.94	25
Panama	20.06	2.521	8895.18	-
Peru	20.26	2.479	5759.4	51
Portugal	9.20	1.35	22532.51	83
Reunion				64
Rwanda	36.37	4.728	574.89	45
St. Vincent	16.84	2.046	6191.07	-
Saudi Arabia	20.32	2.763	24116.17	-
Sierra Leone	37.69	4.861	499.92	6
Slovenia	10.70	1.56	24478.35	63
South Africa	21.31	2.438	7830.51	60
Sudan	34.37	4.563	1617.45	-
Sweden	11.80	1.900	56724.36	65
Taiwan				-
Thailand	10.74	1.427	5192.12	77
Tunisia	18.60	2.130	4305.04	52
Uganda	44.15	6.060	440.8	26
Uzbekistan	21.40	2.499	38927.07	84
United Kingdom	12.90	1.98	1544.83	49
Vietnam	16.15	1.794	1543.03	60
Yemen, Rep.	31.87	4.348	1253.31	19
Zimbabwe	31.90	3.643	820.15	57

Note: "Birth Control" identifies the percentage of eligible females who regularly use birth control.

Source: Population Reference Bureau, World Population Data Sheet 2011.

percentage of women in the country who report using any form of contraception. You can see that in this sample, countries with high birth rates also have low per-capita GNPs, high rates of infant mortality (IMR), low rates of urbanization, low average life expectancies, and low percentages of women using contraception.

Thus, the difference between the CBRs of India and the United States reflects a pattern that will be discussed later in this chapter and at several other points throughout the remainder of the book. That is, today's populations with high birth rates are in the less-developed countries of South and West Asia, parts of Latin America, and especially Southern Africa. Low fertility, in contrast, is a characteristic of the industrialized nations, especially in Central and Western Europe. For example, note the CBRs of Niger, Uganda, Burkina Faso, and Mozambique, which are all in the range of 40 per 1,000. Compare these to the rates of Latvia, Japan, Denmark, Slovenia, and Portugal, which—in the range of 10 per 1,000—average about one-fourth of those in the former group.

Age-Specific Fertility Rates (ASFR)

Age-specific fertility rates (ASFR) are defined as the number of births per year by women of a specified age, such as 15 to 19, 35 to 39, and so forth. Thus, for any population during a specific year, we have not one ASFR but rather a set of rates, depending on the number of age cohorts we use. The general formula that applies to any cohort of women between ages x and x + n is:

$$\text{ASFR}_{x \text{ to } x+n} = (B_{x \text{ to } x+n}/W_{x \text{ to } x+n}) \times 1{,}000$$

where Bx to x+n is the number of births to women between ages x and x+n, Wx to x+n is the number of women between ages x and x+ n alive at midyear, and n ordinarily equals 5 years. So, in practice, with x = 15, 20, 25, and so on, ASFRs are calculated for women ages 15–19, 20–24, . . . 40–44, and sometimes 45–49. For example, in our comparison between the United States and India (2011 estimates), we find that in the 20–24 cohort, the U.S. population at midyear included 10,843,755 women and in India the number was 53,839,529. During that year, in the United States, 925,200 births occurred to women between ages 20 and 24; and in India there were 9,983,517 such births. The respective ASFRs are:

United States: ASFR_{20-24} = (925,200/10,843,755) × 1,000 = 85.0 births per 1,000 women

India: ASFR_{20-24} = (9,983,517/53,839,529) × 1,000 = 185.43 births per 1,000 women

A graph obtained by plotting ASFRs against age groups reveals the pattern of fertility in a population. In general, the curve rises from 0 at the 10–15 years age group and peaks at one of the two groups between 20 and 30 years—depending upon the average age of marriage. Thereafter, it declines until it reaches 0 at some point between 45 and 50 years. Figure 5.1 shows the average ASFRs for three continents during 2013, based on United Nations population estimates. Here we can vividly see the rise-peak-decline character of fertility by age, regardless of the actual fertility level. It is also quite obvious that Africa is in the midst of a birth explosion, with its ASFRs the highest in the world at every age. Note, too, how births in

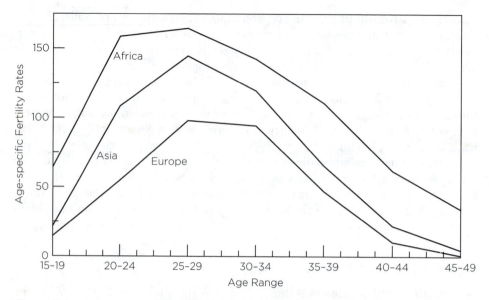

Figure 5.1. Age-Specific Fertility Rates for Africa, Asia, and Europe

Note: Only countries with complete data in each of the three continents for all age cohorts were selected for calculating ASFRs

Source: *Demographic Year Book, 2013.* Table 10. New York: United Nations.

Europe drop to 0 at age 45 to 49 but in Asia they are still in the 4 per 1,000 range and in Africa they are above 30 per 1,000. Another interesting feature of this figure is that women in Africa begin giving birth before age 15, and that during the 15–19 interval, the fertility rate is higher than most ASFR in Europe, including its peak at around 165 per 1,000 in the 24–29 cohort.

Total Fertility Rate

The total fertility rate (TFR) is calculated from ASFRs. In fact, it is a weighted sum obtained by adding together the ASFRs for each cohort. If, as is usually the case, the size of each age interval is five years, then the sum is multiplied by 5 (again, assuming that all births in the interval are evenly distributed among the specific ages). The number that is produced indicates the average number of children born to each 1,000 women at all childbearing ages. In finding the mean age of childbearing, we saw that the sum of the ASFRs for the United States was 414 and for India it was 523.2. Multiplying each of these by 5, we derive the TFR for each country.

United States: TFR = 416.7 × 5 = 2,083.5 per 1,000
or, dividing by 1,000, 2.08 children per woman

India: TFR = 2,616, per 1,000; or 2.6 children per woman

Table 5.2 contains the total fertility rates for the United States and each of the states for the year 2011. For the nation as a whole, the rate was 2.08 (recall that

**Table 5.2. U.S. Birth and Fertility Rates by State, 2011
(Ranked in Order of GFR)**

State/Territory	GFR	CBR	TFR	State	GFR	CBR	TFR
Guam	95.9	20.6	2575.5	California	63.4	13.3	1900.0
American Samoa	95.3	22.8	3095.0	Delaware	62.9	12.4	1904.5
Utah	83.6	18.2	2377.5	Colorado	62.7	12.7	1854.5
Alaska	78.5	15.9	2277.0	Tennessee	62.3	12.4	1566.0
South Dakota	77.1	14.4	2253.0	Ohio	62.1	11.9	1881.5
N. Marianas	74.0	19.8	2169.0	Wisconsin	62.0	11.9	1573.0
North Dakota	72.4	13.9	2060.0	Virginia	61.9	12.7	1553.0
Idaho	72.3	14.1	2145.5	Alabama	61.8	12.4	1836.5
Virgin Islands	72.2	4.1	2344.0	South Carolina	61.8	12.3	1539.5
Nebraska	72.0	14.0	2112.0	Illinois	61.5	12.5	1838.5
Hawaii	71.9	13.8	2114.0	North Carolina	61.5	12.5	1860.0
Kansas	71.2	13.8	2091.0	Maryland	61.3	12.5	1854.0
Oklahoma	70.4	13.8	2039.5	New Jersey	61.3	12.0	1884.0
Texas	69.8	14.7	2074.5	West Virginia	60.7	11.2	1542.5
Wyoming	69.1	13.0	1576.0	Michigan	59.9	11.5	1543.5
New Mexico	68.2	13.1	2001.5	New York	59.8	12.4	1786.0
Arkansas	67.8	13.2	1995.5	Florida	59.6	11.2	1799.0
Arizona	67.3	13.2	1999.5	Oregon	59.4	11.7	1756.5
Montana	66.7	12.1	1961.5	Pennsylvania	58.8	11.2	1600.0
Louisiana	66.4	13.5	1910.0	D.C.	56.0	15.0	1636.5
Iowa	66.1	12.5	1572.5	Connecticut	54.3	10.4	1708.0
Mississippi	66.0	13.4	1940.0	Massachusetts	54.3	11.1	1666.0
Minnesota	65.5	12.8	1547.0	Puerto Rico	53.6	11.1	1596.5
Indiana	65.0	12.8	1551.5	Maine	53.1	9.6	1665.0
Missouri	64.8	12.7	1915.0	New Hampshire	51.9	9.7	1671.5
Kentucky	64.7	12.7	1939.0	Vermont	51.8	9.7	1627.0
Nevada	64.2	13.0	1911.5	Rhode Island	51.5	10.4	1602.5
Georgia	63.8	13.5	1527.0				
Washington	63.7	12.7	1886.0				

Source: *National Vital Statistics Reports* 62 (1): Table 12, June 28, 2013.

the 45–49 cohort was omitted). Utah's TFR was the highest at 2.37, reflecting the fact that it also had the highest CBR (and the highest general fertility rate (GFR)— see below). Rhode Island and Vermont reported the lowest rates of 1.60 and 1.63, respectively. This is also consistent with their low birth rates.

In our earlier discussion of crude birth rates, we noted that Table 5.1, above, also listed the TFRs for the sample of 66 nations. For this set of data, the range of total fertility values is enormous. At one extreme we have Niger, Burkina Faso, and Uganda, all in the range of six children per women and above. At the other extreme are Latvia, Portugal, and Cuba, all well below 1.5 children per woman. Of all the measures discussed thus far, this provides the most dramatic sense of the differences in the fertility levels of today's world: a ratio of nearly 6 to 1 between the most- and the least-fertile populations. Because the TFR and the CBR are very closely related, we should expect that they would each be similarly related to other variables, such as

GDP. As Table 5.1 indicates, this is indeed true. Where the TFR is high, it is usually negatively correlated with both GNP and infant mortality rates. When TFR is high, it is negatively correlated with urbanization rates, with average life expectancy, and with low use of birth control. Thus, we see the close connection between high fertility and underdevelopment.

This point is underscored in Table 5.3, in which six countries are compared according to their ASFRs, their TFRs, and their general fertility rates. Two of the countries, the United States and India, have already been compared in illustrating other fertility measures. The other three represent types of populations that differ somewhat from these two. Italy is included because its fertility level is below that of the United States. In fact, the country was at or just below **zero population growth** (**ZPG**) at the turn of the twenty-first century. Lithuania is included because its fertility level is also low, nearly as low as Italy. The fifth country shown is Rwanda. Its fertility level is very high; in fact, it is nearly twice that of India and three and a half times that of Italy.

Overall, Latvia has the lowest TFR and GFR, and Rwanda's are the highest. In these and other respects, the United States stands somewhere in the middle between the low-fertility countries of Europe and the high-fertility developing nations. In greater detail, the ASFRs for the youngest (15–19) cohort do not follow any particular pattern. This is because ages at marriage differ among the countries and because the United States has relativity high pregnancy rates among teenaged and unmarried women. However, the rates for the 20–24 and 25–29 cohorts are more telling, as both India and Rwanda are nearly in the 200-births-per-1,000 range. Most significant, however, is the pattern of continued high fertility in the older cohorts. For example, in Rwanda, the ASFR for the 40–44 cohort is nearly 100 per 1,000. Such a high rate is not achieved at even the most fertile ages in the three industrialized nations included in the table.

Table 5.3. Age-Specific Fertility Rate, Total Fertility Rate, and Gross Reproduction Rate for Low- and High-Fertility Populations, 2011

Age	India	Lithuania	Italy	Rwanda	United States	Latvia
15-19	39.7	19.5	7.1	5.1	31.3	22.7
20-24	185.4	72.5	34.4	187.1	85.3	83.5
25-29	160.2	81.5	73.1	247.1	107.2	83.4
30-34	81.7	51.9	93.7	221.7	96.5	51.3
35-39	36.1	21.1	57.7	181.3	47.2	21.6
40-44	14.7	5.3	12.5	90.3	10.3	5.4
45-49	5.4	0.1	0.7	17.1	0.7	0.3
TFR	2.62	1.25	1.39	4.9	1.89	1.32
GRR	1.23	0.61	0.68	2.41	1.00	0.64

Sources: The following URL gives GRR for more than 100 countries for 2011: http://www.geoba.se/population.php?pc=world&type=9&year=2011&st=rank&asde=&page=3.

Data in Table 5.3 is from the U.S. Census Bureau International Data Base; however, the GRR for the United States was taken from the URL for GRR given above.

Other Period Measures

General Fertility Rate (GFR)

Another widely used measure of fertility that, like the TFR, is adjusted for age is the **general fertility rate**, or **GFR**. It is defined as the number of births that occur in a population during a year per 1,000 women of childbearing ages alive at midyear. The childbearing ages are assumed to be 15 to 44 or 49. Of course, women are capable of giving birth prior to age 15 and above age 49. But such events are considered to be rare enough to be disregarded. In fact, the NCHS does report births to women age 10 to 14, whereas the 45–49 cohort is often omitted because its fertility levels are generally very low. The formula (with 44 as the upper limit) is:

$$GFR = \frac{B}{W_{15-44}} * 1000$$

W_{15-44} is the total number of women of childbearing age 15–44 at midyear; and B is the number of births per year.[4]

To illustrate, we again use the 2011 population estimates for the United States and India. In the countries, 3,953,590 and 25,377,756 births, respectively, occurred resulting in CBRs 12.08 and 20.97 respectively. To find the GFRs, we will need to know the number of women of childbearing age for each country—in this case those aged 15–49 because the total births included those to mothers in the 44–49 cohort. For the United States, this number was 73,874,470. Dividing the size of this group by the total population size of nearly 308 million, we see that 23.92 percent of the U.S. population consisted of women between ages 15 and 49. India's total in this category was 311,681,858, or about 25.7 percent of its billion-plus population. With this in view, we should expect the difference between the GFRs for the two countries to be about the same as the difference between their CBRs. Using the above formula, we find that for the United States,

GFR = 3,953,590/7,384,470 = 53.58 per 1,000

For India, the rate is:

GFR = 25,377,756/311,681,858 = 81.42 per 1,000

As expected, India's GFR was considerably higher, in fact 1.52 times that of the United States.

Gross Reproduction Rate (GRR)

The **gross reproduction rate** (**GRR**) measure is very similar to the TFR. The difference is that in calculating the GRR, only *female* births are considered. As the name indicates, here we are concerned with reproduction—the ability of a population to sustain its size over the generations. Thus, we assume that if every woman had at least one daughter who had at least one daughter, and so on, reproduction would be achieved. The reason that we refer to the measure as "gross" is that it does not account for the fact that not every female child will survive to bear children; that is, mortality is not taken into consideration. The rate can be calculated directly by summing the age-specific female birth rates and dividing by 1,000 to obtain a ratio. It can also be estimated fairly closely by multiplying the TFR by the proportion of females born. The sex ratio at birth is conventionally assumed to be 105 males per 100 females, although this differs somewhat from population to population. Based on this, the proportion of males at birth is .5122 and that of females is .4878.

Net Reproduction Rate (NRR)

The **net reproduction rate** (**NRR**) is derived from the GRR. It is based on calculations that reduce the size of the GRR in accord with known mortality experiences of women in their reproductive ages. It is interpreted as the average number of daughters a woman will have if (1) she has children during her reproductive years according to current ASFRs and (2) her daughters survive to an age at which they can bear at least one daughter. If the value of NRR is 1, it implies exact replacement of the mother by one daughter. An NRR greater than one implies that a mother is replaced by more than one daughter. And an NRR less than 1 implies negative growth in the long run. If we assume that in India, a woman can be expected to have borne one daughter by age 44 and that 97.5 percent of daughters can be expected to reach childbearing age, the NRR can be estimated. Using the 2011 GRR of 1.23, NRR = 1.23 × 0.975 = 1.199. This indicates that the Indian population is above the level at which it is replacing itself.

Child-Woman Ratio (CWR)

The last of our period measures is also one of the most frequently employed: **child–woman ratio** (**CWR**). All of the information necessary to obtain it is available from national censuses or surveys; that is, vital statistics are not used. The formula is:

$$CWR = P_{0-5} / W_{15-49} \times 1,000$$

where P_{0-5} is the number of children under age 5 at midyear and W_{15-49} is the number of women age 15–49 at midyear. The ratio accounts for the general fertility experience of all women of childbearing age in relation to the number of living children. It is neither a birth rate nor a fertility rate, because it does not track births through the course of a year (or other interval). However, it is an accurate reflection of the overall force of natality, and it is highly correlated with the other measures we have considered.

Returning to the comparison between the United States and India, the number of women between ages 15 and 49 in each country (as of 2011) was 73,874,470 and 311,681,858, respectively. The U.S. Census Bureau also estimated that that the total number of children alive at midyear who had not yet reached their fifth birthday was 19,041,110 in the United States and 118,195,193 in India, according to 2011 Census of India. These figures yield the following child–woman ratios:

United States: CWR = (20,201,362/73,874,470) × 1,000 = 273.45

India: CWR = (112,806,778/311,681,858) × 1,000 = 361.92

Once more, the difference in fertility levels of the two populations is reflected in the ratio between their respective values on a quantitative indicator—approximately

Table 5.4.   Comparing Different Measures of Fertility: India and the United States, 2013 Base Year

Measure	United States	India	Ratio
CWR	278.77	374.18	1.34
TFR	1.90	2.55	1.34
GRR	0.98	1.20	1.22
CBR	13.0	22.0	1.69

Sources: PRB World Population Data Base for CBR (crude birth rate) and TFR (total fertility rate); U.S. Census Bureau, International Programs, International Data Base (IDB) for GRR (gross reproduction rate) and CWR (child-woman ratio).

1.3 to 1. Listed below along with the CWRs are some of the other period measures used in this section (see Table 5.4). The close correspondence between the measures, as seen in the ratios of the values for India to those of the United States, shows that they are all tapping in to the force of natality, but from slightly different perspectives.

Cohort Measures

Cohort measures account for the fertility experience over time (diachronically) of a birth or a marital cohort; that is, an aggregate of women born during the same year or five-year interval or who were married on approximately the same date. These rates are used because period measures are often inappropriate for long-term, longitudinal analyses. When, for example, we say that the total fertility rate of Utah is 2.38, we are basing the measure on the number of births that occurred and the number of women who had achieved various ages during a single year (2011 in the example cited). But this does not mean that a group of 1,000 women married in that state in 2011 will have 2,6377 children during their reproductive lives. Nor, of course, does the rate apply to women *born* in Utah in 2011. In general, the use of period rates such as these to project future population characteristics is not justified unless we can assume that nothing will happen to alter the force of mortality during the projection interval: no changes in marriage patterns, no changes in contraceptive use, and so on. Obviously, such an assumption is unrealistic in today's dynamic populations.

The fact that there are several forces at play which either decrease or increase the risk of childbirth among the population in the denominator lead to controlling for the most influential sources of risk. In the case of childbirth, customs and traditions in most societies tend to restrict premarital childbirth. For this reason, new fertility measures may be obtained by restricting the denominator to only those who are married. ASFRs that control for marital status are called age-specific marital fertility rates. They are obtained by dividing the number of births per year to married women belonging to a specified age range. Such marital-status-specific rates may be obtained for all the measures we have discussed so far. This refinement for marital status obviously reduces the size of the denominator to only those married among all the women. Consequently, the values of ASFRs are smaller than age-specific marital fertility rates.

Within marriage, women are faced with the decision of timing the birth of their first child. In the United States, the mean age of mother at first birth increased to 25.4 years from 25.2 in 2009. The mean age rose for nearly all racial groups.[5] In most developed countries, the interval between marriage and motherhood has increased for a variety of reasons such as labor-force participation and education (see Lesthaeghe 2010). With the postponement of childbirth, the number of children born to women in a specified age range reduces, resulting in the reduction of period fertility measures. In the long run, as postponement of motherhood becomes a norm across generations of daughters, TFRs are likely to reduce in tandem.

In principle, the CBR and the other rates we discussed above can be derived for relevant cohorts. If an actual birth cohort were followed from birth until the last member died, its CBR could be calculated as follows:

$$CBR = (B/P) \times 1,000$$

Here, B is the total number of births that occurred to all women in the cohort and P is the total number of person years lived by the cohort. This latter total, like survival rates, is derived from the life table. It is calculated by summing the number of persons in the cohort alive at midyear during each year. For example, if 1,000 members were born and 990 survived to midyear of year 0, 988 survived to the middle of year 1, and 985 survived to the middle of year 2, we would count 990 + 988 + 985 = 2,963 person years. The process continues until the last person dies, with one person-year credited to the individual's last midyear alive.

In practice, the derivation of this type of CBR and the other cohort rates requires access to the fertility history of the cohort, which is usually published for one-, five-, or 10-year periods. These records must be collated to derive the necessary, grand total number of births. The person year data are derived from periodic census enumerations or surveys. As these are collated, one can track the declining size of the cohort. You can see that it is more realistic to consider deriving such rates retrospectively; for example, for a cohort born in 1900 or married in 1950, rather than prospectively—for a cohort born or married in, say, 2000. Unfortunately, the further back one delves into population history, the less reliable is information at small levels of aggregation such as birth or marital cohorts.

THEORIES OF FERTILITY

By this point you should have a pretty clear idea about what fertility is and how it is related to birth, reproduction, and natality. And you are now fairly well acquainted with the various techniques used to measure these phenomena. In this section, we place such concerns in the background as we consider *why* the force of natality varies between populations, among different groups within a population, and historically—from the past to the present. Several years ago, the sociologist and demographer Geoffrey Hawthorn developed a framework for "explaining human fertility" that included economic, cultural, and technological factors (Hawthorn 1968, 1970; Yeatman, Sennott, and Culpepper 2013). In this context, he cautioned that the manner and pace at which people bear children cannot be easily understood from one standpoint alone, and that a *multivariate* explanation is necessary. As we present here several different theories of fertility and reproduction, it will be useful to keep this observation in mind. No one theory can be judged "right" and the others "wrong," because they are not mutually exclusive. Instead, they should be thought of as cumulative, with each providing a distinctive piece to a complex puzzle.

The Theory of Multiphasic Demographic Response

High fertility was the normal condition for most of the 38,000 years that human beings *(Homo sapiens)* have inhabited the earth. Until relatively recent times—no earlier than the late eighteenth century, total fertility levels everywhere were at or above the very highest observed today in places such as Niger, Rwanda, and Burkina Faso; that is, TFRs averaging at least 7.0 children per woman. Even then, NRRs hovered around and frequently fell below the 1.0 replacement level because of very high death rates, especially infant deaths. Then, some time after 1650 in parts of Western Europe, innovations in sanitation and nutrition that were modest by today's standards began to have an impact in the form of reductions in infant mortality. Ultimately this led to population explosion that peaked during the mid- to late nineteenth century. As events proceeded, these changes were to become part of a three-stage historical cycle now known as the European demographic transition. An extended discussion of the demographic transition is featured in Chapter 8, at which point we will fill in some additional details and update related events to the present. Here, however, we want only to set the stage for one of population science's most influential explanations of fertility. This is the theory of multiphasic response, developed in a landmark study by the leading U.S. demographer, Kingsley Davis (1963).

With declining mortality rates and consequent rapid population growth, high fertility becomes a problem. In fact, in Europe during its early stages of demographic transition, it was an historically unprecedented problem. The large family had traditionally been viewed as a necessary resource for the sake of reproduction but also as a labor force on the family farm, a source of caretaking for ill and elderly relatives, and for numerous other services. With most infants now surviving to adulthood and most adults surviving to an advanced age, large families had become unnecessary and, in some cases, an obstacle. Davis viewed this situation as a *stimulus*, a negative one perhaps, but a source of motivation nonetheless. Thus, he characterized the changes that ensued as a *response*. And, universally, that response was a decline in fertility levels and a reduction in family size.

The response did not come immediately. In Europe there was a lag of between five and 10 generations—about 150 years. And, although the initial reduction in the number of children resulted in families that were about as large as they had been under conditions of high infant mortality, the fertility declines continued (to this day) to the point at which we are approaching the norm of one child per couple. But, the main response—fertility decline following mortality decline—was clear and well documented (in Europe and eventually in North America, Japan, Australia, and New Zealand as well).

Davis notes that the response to "too high" levels of fertility can be approached not in only one way but that several strategies are available. In England and other parts of Europe in the mid-nineteenth century, the ideals of family planning and well-known but previously frowned-upon methods of contraception (douching, *coitus interruptus*, and condoms) became acceptable. In post–World War II Japan, fertility decline was achieved with a number of equally important birth-control methods, induced abortion, postponement of marriage, and contraception. This multimethod approach was the key in many Western and Eastern European countries as well. Davis also observed that in some places, at least for a limited period, the response was not fertility decline by any means but rather sustained population growth under conditions of positive economic growth. That is, with too many mouths to feed, some societies grew more food rather than eliminating mouths. Thus the term "multiphasic" is used, indicating a variety of demographic, social, cultural, technological, and economic approaches to managing the negative consequences of large family size.

According to this theory, the people most likely to lead the way in responding to such negative consequences are also in a position to seek social and economic mobility—that is, members of the middle classes. It is the fear of **relative deprivation** rather than the likelihood of famine or starvation that motivates such couples to limit family size. Other groups may ultimately follow the lead of their upwardly mobile fellow citizens, for their own reasons or merely for the sake of conformity. But the innovations must begin with a core group, and in Europe and other parts of the world where fertility levels have fallen, this core consisted of largely urban middle- and upper-middle-class families.[6] In this light, Davis identifies six principal demographic responses that are compatible with the avoidance of *relative deprivation*. They are:

1. An increase in the proportion of those who are permanently celibate.
2. A substantial increase in the age at marriage.
3. The use of contraception within marriage.
4. An increase in abortion and sterilization rates.
5. International migration.
6. Rural to urban migration.

It is important not only to isolate the most common responses to sustained population growth but also to understand the timing of such responses. For example, in the short run, the migration responses (points 5 and 6) appear to be more widespread than fertility control, in part because migration to high-wage areas enables large families to maintain their income. In addition, young adults are more likely to migrate than are older adults. This relieves the economic demands on the family and considerably improves the standard of living of older adults through remittances. Migration is also easier to accomplish than changes in fertility and it does not immediately challenge the existing traditional family structure. Ultimately, however, more potent measures are required, as migration proves to be a temporary solution—or, for some families, an impossibility. At that point, one or more of the remaining alternatives is pursued.

The Theory of Intermediate Variables

Most theories of fertility indicate that an increase in a woman's birth parity, from no children to one, one to two, and so on, is determined by social and economic factors. However, according to the perspective developed by Kingsley Davis and Judith Blake (1956), the influence of these factors is not direct. Rather, three biological processes that occur in sequence mediate it: intercourse, conception, and gestation. In support of this view, Davis and Blake provided a list of variables that are affected by cultural norms and socioeconomic conditions, on one hand, and which affect the probabilities of intercourse, conception, and gestation, on the other. As shown in Table 5.5, there are 11 variables in all. Of these, six are associated with the stage of intercourse, three are related to the stage of conception, and the remaining two affect gestation.

These are referred to as *variables* because they differ from society to society and tend to change over time. Moreover, several of them are subject to conscious intervention. For example, early marriage is characteristic of rural, traditional culture,

Table 5.5.   The Intermediate Variables

Stage	Variables
Intercourse	1. Age of entry into union
	2. Permanent celibacy (Proportion of women never entering into marriage)
	3. The amount of time spent outside of union (Divorce, separation, death of a spouse)
	4. Voluntary abstinence within marriage
	5. Involuntary abstinence within marriage (Impotence, illness)
	6. Coital frequency within marriage
Conception	7. Fecundity or infecundity from involuntary causes (Sterility caused by STD, breast-feeding)
	8. Use or nonuse of contraception
	9. Fecundity or infecundity from involuntary causes (Sterility)
Gestation	10. Fetal mortality through involuntary causes (Involuntary abortion)
	11. Fetal mortality through voluntary causes (Induced abortion)

Source: Adapted from Kingsley Davis and Judith Blake, "Social Structure and Fertility: An Analytic Framework," *Economic Development and Cultural Change* 4:211–35, 1956.

but as levels of urbanization increase so does age at marriage. The use or nonuse of contraception is strongly correlated with economic conditions and the status of women; but it is also a matter of conscious choice. Thus, the intervening variables are prime targets for family-planning programs and other types of population policy initiatives.

Family planning has played a role in determining family size in today's industrialized countries since the mid-nineteenth century. In most of the developing nations of Asia, Africa, and Latin America, knowledge and the technologies of planned parenthood have been available for at least several decades. Thus, it would be unrealistic to attempt to explain fertility in today's world without taking account of these innovations. Clearly, socioeconomic development was in the past essential for lowering the demand for children. However, it is now evident that fertility decline can occur without significant social change—in the presence of strong family-planning programs, as in the case of Thailand (whose CBR was 18 per 1,000 and TFR 1.9 per woman in the late 1990s). For these reasons, we return to the theory of intermediate variables in Chapter 11, where we take a closer look at these and several other policy issues.

Economic, Structural, and Cultural Theories

G. S. Becker: Quality of Children

In traditional societies, large families were universally desired. Thus, as family income increased, the number of children was also likely to increase. However, in modern industrial societies, reproduction has come to involve a considerable expenditure of time and other resources. Most parents now must decide either to discontinue participating in the labor force or at least to limit the amount of time spent working in the absence of childcare. The amount of potential income lost in the process, the "opportunity cost," can be considerable.[7] And, as the opportunity cost increases, family size is likely to decrease. The family-studies specialist G. S. Becker proposed an explanation of fertility that emphasizes such rational economic choices. From this perspective, family size is determined by (1) a couple's income and (2) the costs (including opportunity costs) they incur in having children (Becker 1981). Here, the cost factor is also related to the relatively modern idea of the *quality*, as opposed to quantity, of offspring.[8] In seeking to maximize quality, prospective parents calculate the amount of market goods and services and the time investments required to bear and to rear an additional child. Ordinarily, all family members are involved in this process, as improving child quality is assumed to be a cooperative venture.

R. Easterlin: Relative Income

Another widely used economic approach is Richard Easterlin's theory of relative income (Easterlin 1978a, b; Easterlin and Crimmins 1985; Kodzi, Johnson, and Casterline 2012; Becker, Cinnirella, and Woessmann 2013). Easterlin argues that the effect of income on family size depends on how couples view their current income with respect to their demand for child quality. The parents' desire to provide for their children is influenced by their own standard of living during their childhood, as they aspire to give their children at least as much as they had when they were young. Easterlin assumes that tastes are formed during adolescence. "For material aspirations, I use the income situation in the young adult's families of orientation, specifically, their parent's families when they were growing up, on the theory that the period of adolescent development is critical in the formation of the material aspirations of young adults" (Easterlin 1978a:315). If the current income of prospective parents is deemed inadequate by these standards, then family size will be small. If the family's resources are considered to be more than sufficient, families will be large.

Coale: The Role of Values and Custom

Researchers have known for many years that cultural factors influence birth rates (Coale and Hoover 1958; Williams 2014). However, renewed interest in the role that culture plays in fertility decline has emerged from the findings of the Princeton European Fertility Project, spearheaded by Ansely Coale. This work opposes economic explanations in suggesting that small-family-size norms might simply have diffused among social groups that had other cultural traits in common. In this light, the number of children women bear in their lifetimes (assuming access to contraception) is a matter of style and custom rather than economic choice. Thus, instead of cost-benefit analyses, cultural theories stress shared ideas, values, beliefs, customs, and material artifacts as the main determinants of fertility.

The recent fertility declines in several states of India have been attributed to cultural factors. The leading hypothesis proposes that where the autonomy of women is greatest, fertility levels will be the lowest. In India, a North–South divide has been observed with respect to the sex ratios, as well as mortality and fertility rates (Alexander 1998; Dyson and Moore 1983; Nalwadda et al. 2010; Pillai and Salehin 2012). In the North, women suffer from social, economic, and political neglect; and they have much less autonomy in decision making at the household level than women in the South. As a result, South Indian women live longer, enjoy higher levels of reproductive health, and have fewer children than their counterparts in the North. Both William Alexander and Barbara Miller (1981) argue that the North Indian cultures, and (for Alexander) the subculture of the leading Rajput community in particular, are antifemale.

Social Structural Theories

Social structural theories focus on the role of modernization and industrialization in process of fertility decline.[9] Most of these explanations stress the close association between fertility and mortality. Mortality declines, which virtually always precede fertility declines, are the product of improved access to social services, medical care, public knowledge about the causes of maternal and child health, and nutrition. When infant mortality is common, high fertility levels enable families to achieve their desired family sizes. Thus, structural changes in the economy that result from lower death rates ultimately lower the demand for large families, given the availability of birth-control technology. Under the socioeconomic conditions of an industrial society, large families become a burden, especially for parents who seek upward social mobility. If, at the same time, the status and employment prospects for women increase, the value of children is diminished even further, pronatalist values erode, and fertility decline sets in.

J. Caldwell: Wealth Flow Theory

John Caldwell (1982) developed the wealth-flow theory of fertility in the course of his extensive demographic fieldwork in West Africa. His conclusions are based on assumptions about family organization and economic structure that combine the structural and cultural approaches. The theory focuses on the role of nondemographic causes, such as the acquisition of a Western education and the assimilation of Western values in the presence of opportunities for socioeconomic mobility, in producing a demographic effect. Such conditions trigger a reversal in wealth flows—from child → parent to parent → child—paving the way for fertility decline.

Diffusion Theories

The spread, or diffusion, from one population to another of new ideas and behaviors associated with family planning has been credited with lowering fertility levels. Diffusion theory suggests that information is exchanged through both public and informal channels. A successful transfer occurs when the adoption of innovative ideas by some individuals increases the likelihood of adoption of these ideas by others. In general, the first group of innovators is likely to be a community elite. The pace of diffusion depends upon costs and benefits of modeling new behaviors with respect to fertility. The emergence of new beliefs and practices that affect fertility levels, such as preference for small family size, become cultural norms under the influence and leadership of the initial innovators. Although extensive research has established the effectiveness of innovation diffusion in a wide range of contexts (especially agriculture; see Weinstein 2010: chap. 8), there is little direct evidence for its effects in relation to family planning. Several studies are currently underway to test the validity of the diffusion hypotheses with respect to fertility reduction.

WORLD FERTILITY: LEVELS AND TRENDS

This section presents a comparative overview of fertility trends between the middle of the twentieth century to the present. The discussion is divided into three main parts: First is a summary of recent fertility trends throughout the world. This is followed by a profile of the less-developed countries, by continent. The section concludes with an overview of fertility trend and differentials in the United States.[10]

During the 1950s, fertility levels in the industrialized countries remained steady at about 2.8 children per woman. But by the early 1960s, a decline had begun that continues to the present, as TFRs fell from 2.8 in 1960–1965 to 1.9 in 1985–1990 to 1.7 (or below) at the end of the twentieth century. Of the 113 less-developed countries considered by the CFSC, 95 also experienced fertility decline between 1968 and 1975. During this period, China's TFR fell from 4.2 to 3.2, a decline of 24 percent. In contrast, declines in India and Pakistan were much smaller, from 5.67 to 5.24 in the former and from 6.84 to 6.57 in the latter. One of the most dramatic fertility reductions occurred in Indonesia, where the TFR fell from 6.46 in 1968 to 4.57 in 1975, a decline of nearly 30 percent. Brazil as well as most of the countries of Africa experienced some of the smallest changes during this early period. In fact, it is estimated that Nigeria's TFR was increasing slightly through the mid-1970s.

With such exceptions noted, the last few decades of the twentieth century nevertheless saw steady—and in some cases substantial—reductions in fertility throughout the world, in both the less- and the more-developed nations. As of the mid-to-late 2000S, TFRs still varied significantly among regions, as shown in Table 5.6: with the highest rates in Africa and the lowest in Europe. However, in all of the world's populations, fertility is now at its lowest levels in history (and probably in prehistory as well).

Fertility Decline in Asia

Between 1980 and 2011, the general worldwide pattern of fertility reduction continued and, in the less-developed regions, it accelerated. In Asia, the continent that contains the two demographic giants, China and India, TFRs fell an average of 0.7 children per woman, from 3.7 to 3.0. Within the continent, however, there was considerable variation in both rates and levels of fertility. Fertility rates in East Asia (including Japan) are similar to those in Europe (see Table 5.7). In this part of the continent, TFRs fell from 2.4 to 1.5 between 1980–2011. By the latter date, all of the East Asian countries, with the exception of Mongolia, had fallen below replacement levels. In Southeast Asia (including Thailand), TFRs were reduced by 22 percent over

Table 5.6.   Total Fertility Rate (per Woman) for the World and Its Regions, 1980-1985 and 2005-2010

Region	1980–1985	2005–2010
World	3.6	2.5
More-developed regions	1.8	1.7
Less-developed regions	4.2	2.7
Least-developed regions	6.4	4.5
Africa	6.3	4.9
Asia	3.7	2.2
Europe	1.9	1.5
Latin America/Caribbean	3.8	2.3
North America	1.8	2.0
Oceania	2.6	2.5

Source: *World Population Prospects*: The 2012 Revision File, U.N. Department of Economic and Social Affairs. Total fertility by major area, region and country, 1950–2100 (children per woman) estimates, 1950–2010, June 2013.

Table 5.7. Total Fertility Rate (per Woman) and Age-Specific Fertility Rates for the World and Its Regions, 2011

Fertility Rates for Region Summary

ASFR	15-19	20-24	25-29	30-34	35-39	40-44	45-49	TFR
Africa	95.8	201.54	221.32	188.78	129.31	64.55	18.4	4.6
Eastern Africa	105.7	230.46	240.73	204.95	151.83	81.88	24.75	5.2
Middle Africa	105.81	218.19	240.97	220.82	149.75	78.05	21.44	5.2
Northern Africa	44.66	138.86	171.03	139.31	79.06	34.08	8.88	3.1
Southern Africa	42.15	105.39	124.3	105.52	63.08	25.53	6.47	2.4
Western Africa	118.18	222.58	252.4	215.65	150.44	76.33	22.53	5.3
Asia	31.05	130.32	136.89	86.33	39.23	14.79	5.63	2.2
Eastern Asia	5.42	92.88	105.68	62.78	24.95	9.77	5.86	1.5
South-Central Asia	44.66	165.52	158.91	93.17	43.61	17.41	5.77	2.7
South-Eastern Asia	35.13	109.95	137.34	101.64	51.84	20.24	3.9	2.3
Western Asia	36	125.16	156.65	123.12	67.97	27.82	7.33	2.7
Europe	16.69	64.48	95.35	85.47	40.9	8.94	0.74	1.6
Eastern Europe	24.03	79.79	93.12	63.56	26.11	5.87	0.65	1.5
Northern Europe	19.6	65.64	104.12	111.52	57.31	11.17	0.65	1.9
Southern Europe	11.78	47.59	81.62	89.28	49.94	10.39	0.86	1.4
Western Europe	8.32	49.68	105.8	110.41	52.3	11.08	0.81	1.7
Latin America/Caribbean	51.54	109.64	120.47	90.45	44.59	14.95	2.47	2.2
Caribbean	46.03	105.95	124.24	100.73	47.11	16.14	2.22	2.2
Central America	60.8	129.19	127.53	95.55	50.48	17.01	2.79	2.4
South America	47.93	101.47	117.18	87.6	41.98	14.02	2.38	2.1
Northern America	(NA)	(NA)	(NA)	(NA)	(NA)	(NA)	(NA)	(NA)
Oceania	28.42	86.39	122.2	125.07	65.58	18.66	3.43	2.2

Source: U.S. Census Bureau International Data Base.

the decade, primarily as the result of economic development. The rate for this region as of 1995 was 3.3, and by 2011 it had fallen below 2.4.

South Central and Western Asia continue to have the highest fertility levels as well as some of the weakest family-planning programs on the continent. In the former, the TFR in 1990–1995 was 4.1, although it declined by 2011 to 2.7. Western Asia's rate in 1995 was 4.4, and the area experienced a similar decline to approximately 2.7. The Gaza portion of the Palestinian Authority has high fertility, with an average of approximately 4.7 children per woman as of the year 2011. Other countries with high levels of fertility in this region include Yemen with 2011, TFR = 4.6. In contrast, nearby countries, such as Armenia, Azerbaijan, Cyprus, and Georgia are in the below replacement category, except Israel and Turkey. Clearly, effective family-planning programs backed by strong government support (and possibly coercion) have played a major role in Asia, despite limited socioeconomic development. Examples of this approach include Vietnam and Myanmar. At least five countries in East and Southeast Asia have below-replacement fertility levels. These include Japan, the Republic of Korea, Singapore, Taiwan, and Thailand (the Chinese territory of Hong Kong is also in this category). Several others countries are close to replacement: Myanmar, Democratic Republic of Korea, Sri Lanka, and Turkey. As we discuss at some length in Chapter 11, the transition from high to low fertility in the Peoples Republic of China is largely the outcome of the "One Child Policy" pursued by the government since the early 1970s.

Delayed Transition in Africa

With a TFR in the range of 5.7 during the late 1990s, Africa continues its birth explosion that began during the last years of the colonial era. The major exceptions are the largely Muslim countries north of the Sahara, which were the earliest to register signs of diminishing family size. Egypt, Morocco, and Tunisia had already reported declines by the 1970s, and in Algeria the total fertility rate dropped from 6.8 in the early 1980s to 2.8 in 2011. In contrast, in the sub-Saharan regions, fertility levels remained very high through the 1980s, and in most countries they were still at 6.0 or above during the late 1990s. Three countries that appear to be at the forefront of fertility transition in the region are Botswana, Kenya, and Zimbabwe (Cleland, Onuoha, and Timaeus 1993; Foote, Hill, and Martin 1993; Habimana Kabano, Broekhuis, and Hooimeijer 2013; Cho and Tien 2014). These are also among the pioneers in government-supported family-planning programs. For example, Kenya's TFR fell from 8.0 in 1977 to 4.2 in 2011 (Njogu and Castro Martin 1991; Magadi and Agwanda 2010). More recently, fertility declines have been reported in countries such as Ghana, Senegal, and Zambia (with 2011 TFRs of 4.2, 4.8, and 5.9, respectively).

Latin America: Low Fertility, High Variability

The Latin America/Caribbean region has few very high-fertility populations, and most countries experienced only modest fertility reductions during the 1980s and 1990s. Overall, total fertility rates fell from 3.8 in 1980–1985 to 3.1 in 1990–1995 and to less than 3.0 by century's end. For several years, the Caribbean island nations have had the lowest fertility levels within the region, with an average of 2.7 children per woman during the late 1990s. Seven of these countries are now at or below replacement. Nevertheless, the variations within the region are great. At one extreme are Barbados and Cuba, with TFRs well below replacement, at about 1.5 during the late 1990s. At the other extreme is Haiti, whose TFR was 4.8, more than triple that of some of its closest neighbors.

Moreover, despite the general trend, between 1990 and 1998 Central America experienced some of the most rapid fertility declines in the world, at an annual rate of approximately 2.3 percent per year. The greatest share of this decrease occurred in Costa Rica, Panama, and Mexico, the wealthiest countries in the poorest subregion in Latin America. TFRs for these three were at 3.0 or below at the turn of the century, whereas total fertility rates in the least-developed nations—Honduras and Guatemala remained above 5.0.

In South America, TFRs fell from 3.7 in 1980–1985 to 3.0 in 1990–1995 and to 2.1 by 2011. Most of the countries in this subregion have achieved moderate-to-low levels of fertility. These include Argentina, Uruguay, and Chile, where TFRs as of 1997–1998 were 2.8, 2.3, and 2.4, respectively. Brazil, the most populous nation in Latin America, had a 1997 TFR of 2.5.

Toward Negative Growth in the Industrialized Nations

As noted in earlier sections, most of the industrialized nations were at or below the replacement level at the end of the twentieth century, as birth rates continued to fall (see Table 5.8 for 2012 data). The overall TFR in Europe declined from 1.9 in

Table 5.8. Countries with TFRs (per Woman) below Replacement Levels, 2012

Country	TFR	Country	TFR
Macau	1.1	Puerto Rico	1.6
Portugal	1.2	Belarus	1.6
Andorra	1.2	Canada	1.6
Hong Kong	1.3	Russian Federation	1.6
Singapore	1.3	Denmark	1.7
Korea, South	1.3	Netherlands	1.7
Bosnia and Herzegovina	1.3	China	1.7
Spain	1.3	Trinidad and Tobago	1.8
Italy	1.4	Finland	1.8
Japan	1.4	Belgium	1.8
Germany	1.4	Barbados	1.8
Thailand	1.4	Georgia	1.8
Mauritius	1.4	Albania	1.8
Lebanon	1.5	Virgin Islands (U.S.)	1.8
Macedonia	1.4	Chile	1.8
Moldova	1.5	Vietnam	1.8
Switzerland	1.5	Norway	1.9
Cuba	1.5	Saint Lucia	1.9
Liechtenstein	1.5	Iran	1.9
Bulgaria	1.5	Norway	1.9
Slovenia	1.6	Saint Lucia	1.9

Source: The Word Bank Data. fertility rate total (births per woman, 2012 data), http://data.worldbank.org/indicator/SP.DYN.TFRT.IN.

1980–1985 to 1.6 in 1990–1995 and to 1.4 or below by the late 1990s. Southern Europe experienced the most substantial reduction on the continent (an average of more than 2.2 percent per year between 1985 and 1995) and, as of 2011, its TFR was 1.4. In 1997–1998, Spain and Italy reported the world's lowest rates of 1.2 children per woman. Most Eastern European nations also are well below the replacement levels, including The Czech Republic and Bulgaria, with TFRs of 1.2 as of the late 1990s. Their TFRs improved to 1.4 in 2011. The United States has one of the highest levels of fertility among all of the more-developed countries. However, following an increase in its TFR from 1.8 to 2.1 between 1980 and 1995, the rate declined to 2.0 by the end of the century. And, as we saw in our discussion of the net reproduction rate, by 1999 the U.S. population had fallen below replacement in terms of that crucial indicator.

FERTILITY IN THE UNITED STATES

Between the colonial era and the 1940s, average family size in the United States declined almost continuously. Estimates of the years prior to the Revolutionary War indicate a TFR of about eight children per married woman, several of whom were likely to die at a very young age (Rindfuss and Sweet 1977). At that time, the

CBR was above 50 live births per 1,000 persons (U.S. Department of Commerce 1975). Through the nineteenth and early twentieth centuries, the TFR fell below 4.0. The trend continued through the Depression years of the 1930s, as U.S. birth rates dropped to their lowest levels since records had been kept. Following a slight recovery, as of 1940 the TFR was still less than 2.9 per 1,000.

Postwar Trends and the Baby Boom

Following World War II, the United States experienced very rapid economic growth, a **baby boom**, in sharp contrast to the prewar period. The demand for workers was high and the supplies low, as few young people were on the labor market because of the low birth rates of the 1920s and 1930s. The distinct bias against married women working outside the home, which had been temporarily suspended during the war, once more took effect. This applied especially to women with young children. Incomes were rising rapidly and continued to do so into the 1950s. All of these conditions favored employable males who found relatively well-paid positions, married early, had children, and still achieved the lifestyles to which they aspired. The result, now known as the "baby boom," brought total fertility rates back to the 3.0 level and above, reaching 3.27 by 1947. By 1953, the rate had climbed to just under 3.5 children per 1,000 women and it peaked in 1957 at 3.8. The boom lasted for about 12 years, between 1946 and 1964, with the highest CBR recorded around 1955. By 1965, the CBR declined to about 18 per 1,000 and the TFR fell below 3.0, where it has remained ever since.

At the end of the twentieth century, total fertility in the United States was at or near the replacement rate of 2.0. However, the trajectory of the decline between

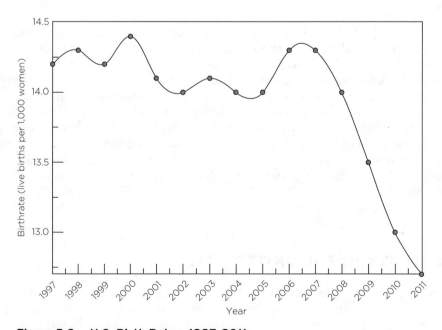

Figure 5.2. U.S. Birth Rates, 1997–2011
Source: *National Vital Statistics Reports*, 62, no. 1 (June 28, 2013): Table 12.

the mid-1960s and the present was not steady. Rather, fertility levels dropped consistently until the mid-1970s, at which point they began to increase once more, although relatively slowly. The 1976 TFR of 1738 live births per 1,000 women and the CBR of 14.0 are the lowest ever recorded in the nation, and they represent reductions of almost 50 percent from the 1957 rates. Another way to envision this pattern is to consider the total numbers of live births. In 1945, 2.7 million babies were born in the United States. By 1957, this number had increased to 4.3 million, but by 1973 it had declined to 3.1 million (Rindfuss and Sweet 1977).

To summarize, U.S. fertility levels during the postwar period were dominated by two important trends. (1) The first is the boom of the late 1940s that lasted through the 1950s. Not only were these levels the highest in our history, but most of the world's industrialized countries also experienced rising marriage and fertility rates during this period. Nevertheless, the increases were more sustained in the United States and Canada than in Europe (Kiser, Grabill, and Campbell 1968). (2) Second is the drop in birth and fertility rates that began in the late 1950s and has continued, in the rather uneven manner noted, to the present.

The pattern of minor oscillations at relatively low levels is especially apparent in the CBRs and GFRs. Between 1980 and 1983, both sets of rates declined, from 15.9 to 15.6 and from 68.4 to 65.7, respectively. Then, between 1984 and 1990, fertility levels increased, with the CBR going from 15.6 to 16.7 and the GFR from 65.5 to 70.9 (an increase of about 1.4 percent per year). This was followed by another period of decline between 1990 and 1996, as the CBR dropped from 16.7 to 14.7—at a rate of 2.0 percent per year, and the GFR went from 70.9 to 65.3. Between 1997 and 2008, the CBRs remained below 14.4 followed by precipitous declines to 12.7 in 2011; and Figure 5.2 shows the birth rates for the same period.

Table 5.9. Births, Birthrates, and Fertility Rates, United States, 1997-2011

Year/Variable	Live Births	CBR	GFR	TFR
1997	3880894	14.2	63.6	1971.0
1998	3941553	14.3	64.3	1999.0
1999	3959417	14.2	64.4	2007.5
2000	4058814	14.4	65.9	2056.0
2001	4025933	14.1	65.1	2030.5
2002	4021726	14.0	65.0	2020.5
2003	4089950	14.1	66.1	2047.5
2004	4112052	14.0	66.4	2051.5
2005	4138349	14.0	66.7	2057.0
2006	4265555	14.3	68.6	2108.0
2007	4316233	14.3	69.3	2120.0
2008	4247694	14.0	68.1	2072.0
2009	4130665	13.5	66.2	2002.0
2010	3999386	13.0	64.1	1931.0
2011	3953590	12.7	63.2	1894.5

Source: *National Vital Statistics Reports* 62, no. 1 (June 28, 2013): 18 and 22.

Contemporary Fertility Differentials

For as long as data have been available, variations in fertility levels by ethnic group, socioeconomic status, and urban-rural residence have existed in the United States (and in most other nations as well). For most of recent U.S. history, European Americans have had fewer children than members of minority groups—as shown in Table 5.10. Detailed data on the comparative fertility of five groups are shown in Table 5.11. Hispanic Americans (of all "races") report the highest levels, with a CBR of 17.6 and a TFR of 2.24. At the other extremes are Native Americans and European Americans (including a portion with Hispanic backgrounds), whose CBRs and TFRs 10.7 and 1.37 and 10.8 and 1.77, respectively. The other groups, listed by fertility level from low to high, are Asian American and African American.

In addition to these differences, fertility rates in urban areas tend to be lower than in rural areas and lower among married women in the labor force than women not in the labor force. Recent studies also show that fertility differentials by religion have widened. These variations arise from two sources: (1) differences in the number of children couples want and (2) differences in their willingness and/or ability to control fertility. With this in view, presented below are a few other selected aspects of current fertility in the United States.

- In both 1990 and 1994, 42 percent of American women 15 to 44 years old were childless (married and never-married women included).
- About 42 percent of the American women who gave birth between July 1993 and June 1994 reported that birth as their first. This was up slightly from 39 per cent for the year ending in June 1990. Of the 6.5 million Hispanic American women 15 to 44 years old in 1994, 4 million reported that they were of Mexican ancestry. The general fertility rate for Mexican American women in 1994 was

Table 5.10. Total Fertility in the United States by Ethnicity, 2000-2008

Year	European Americans	Minority Groups	Difference
2000	2,051	2,129	0.078
2005	2,056	2,071	0.015
2008	2,067	2,132	0.061

Source: U.S. Census Bureau, Statistical Abstract of the United States: 2012, http://www.census.gov/prod/2011pubs/12statab/vitstat.pdf.

Table 5.11. Births, Birthrates, and Fertility Rates by Ethnicity of Mother, United States, 2011

Group	Live Births	CBR	GFR	TFR
Asian American	253,915	14.5	59.9	1706.5
European American	2,146,566	10.8	58.7	1773.5
Hispanic	918,129	17.6	76.2	2240.0
African American	582,345	14.7	65.4	1919.5
Native Americans	46,419	10.7	47.7	1373.5
All groups	3,947,374	12.7	63.2	1894.5

Source: *National Vital Statistics Reports* 62, no. 1 (June 28, 2013): 4 and 41.

111 births per 1,000, a rate about twice as high as for the non-Hispanic population (61 per 1,000). Women of Mexican ancestry averaged 1.6 children ever born, about 0.4 children higher than non-Hispanic women.

- General fertility rates of women of Mexican ancestry born in the United States (85 per 1,000) were significantly lower than the rates of women born in Mexico (143 per 1,000).[11]
- In 1994, the proportion of U.S. children born out of wedlock was 0.26.
- Sixty-six percent of all African American women who gave birth in 1994 were unmarried (that is, women never married, widowed, or divorced at the survey date). This was more than triple the rate of European American women (19 percent) and more than twice that of Hispanic women (28 percent).
- About 38 percent of women 15 to 44 years old in 1994 had never been married. Of these 22.7 million never-married women, 22 percent had given birth to at least one child by the time of the survey.
- About 7 percent of never-married teenagers have borne at least one child. Among women in their 30s, about 4 out of every 10 had borne at least one child out of wedlock.

Vital statistics data indicate that over 30 percent of the births in the United States are to unmarried women and that the practice is becoming more common among all groups. As Table 5.12 indicates, in 2008, 72.3 percent of births to African American women were of this type, as were 57.0 percent of the births to Native Americans. The group with the lowest rate is Asian Americans, with 16.9 percent. The national average in 2008 was 40.6 percent.

Table 5.12. Birth Characteristics by Ethnic Group, United States, 2000, 2005, and 2008

Birth Characteristic	All Groups	African American	Asian American	European American	Hispanic American	Native American
Total Births 2000	4,058	604	201	2,363	816	42
2005	4,138	584	231	2,280	966	45
2008	4,248	623	253	2,268	1,041	50
To Teenage Mothers (pct.)						
2000	11.8	19.7	4.5	10.6	16.2	18.7
2005	10.2	16.9	3.3	9.3	14.1	17.7
2008	10.4	17.0	3.3	9.5	14.1	18.0
To Unmarried Mothers (pct.)				22.1	42.7	58.4
2000	33.2	68.7	14.8	25.3	48.0	63.5
2005	36.9	69.9	16.2	28.7	52.6	65.8
2008	40.6	72.3	16.9	7.2	43.1	57.0
With Low Birth Weights (pct.)						
2000	7.6	13.1	7.3	6.6	6.4	6.8
2005	8.2	14.0	8.0	7.3	6.9	7.4
2008	8.2	13.7	8.2	7.2	7.0	7.4

Notes: All percentages are of total births for each group; Hispanic includes members of all other groups.

Source: U.S. Census Bureau, Statistical Abstract of the United States: 2012, Table 86, https://www.census.gov/compendia/statab/2012/tables/12s0086.pdf.

SUMMARY

From a purely biological perspective, the activities associated with reproduction—intercourse, conception, and gestation—are among the most natural processes in the world. Yet, as we have seen, in contemporary human populations a range of social, cultural, psychological, and economic factors now influence these activities. In the not-too-distant past, nature more or less did take its course with regard to fertility. But under such conditions, the threat of death to infants was also ever present. Moreover, in the absence of modern institutions and technologies, a large family was universally understood to be an economic asset of the highest possible value. Today, from sub-Saharan Africa to Southern Europe, conditions have made high birth rates and large families increasingly burdensome. Thus, in every human population on earth, fertility levels are at an all-time low and are continuing to decline.

This, at least, is the broad picture. At a more detailed level, however, vast differences exist in the rates of birth, fertility, and reproduction, both between and within contemporary populations. In some less-developed areas of the world, TFRs are in the range of seven children per woman, whereas these ratios are approaching only a single child in many parts of Europe. In some places, women marry late in life, or not at all, thus ensuring that they will bear relatively few children. Elsewhere, girls begin to reproduce while still in their teens and continue to do so into their forties. In our own nation, some groups rarely have children out of wedlock, marry late, and stop giving birth at parity one or two. Other groups of Americans experience higher rates of birth to unmarried women than to married women and frequently bear children as teenagers. As of early 2010s, the CBR of the highest fertility U.S. ethnic group exceeded that of the lowest by a ratio of more than 1.63 to 1.

As demographers look ahead to the middle and latter years of the twenty-first century, both the macro- and the micro-level trends in fertility will be carefully monitored. As we shall see in Chapters 8 and 10, the art and the science of population projection include the cautious practice of producing not one but a series of (usually three) scenarios of the future based on alternative assumptions. Among such assumptions, the most important ones focus on the very issues underscored in this chapter. These are, (1) the extent to which universal fertility decline will continue, for how long, and a what rate; and (2) the extent to which the differences between the fertility of the rich and the poor, the urban and the rural, and the black and the white will be narrowed. In the view of most observers, what is now only a concept of a single human population with a common level of fertility is almost certain to become a reality. The only serious question is, "When?"

We now move on to Chapter 6 and the other vital event that contributes to natural increase, mortality. There we will find that many of the basic concepts introduced in our discussion of fertility are reintroduced in a new context: the difference between crude and age-specific rates, sources of vital statistics, the long-range trend of declining levels, and the variations between and within different regions of the world. Also, as we have noted several times, the principles and techniques of fertility analysis are applied at several other points in later chapters. For these reasons, you might consider this introduction to the force of natality to be just that, an introduction that will be expanded upon as we continue our exploration of the science of population.

KEY TERMS

age-specific fertility rate (ASFR)
baby boom
birth
child-woman ratio (CWR)
cohort measures
fecundity
fertility
general fertility rate (GFR)

gross reproduction rate (GRR)
natality
net reproduction rate (NRR)
period measures
relative deprivation
reproduction
total fertility rate (TFR)
zero population growth (ZPG)

NOTES

1. Male or "paternal" fertility rates typically differ somewhat from female, "maternal" rates. They are obviously less reliable because the father of a child is not necessarily present at the birth. Nevertheless they are of interest and are occasionally used. See Shryock and Siegel (1976:293–94).

2. Because it depends on periodic ovulation, the capacity to bear children varies according to the health and other physiological factors of a woman. Male fecundity, on the other hand, is virtually unlimited. Several individual records exceeding 30 children per woman have been claimed, all of which involve multiple births. One of the most frequently cited cases, a staple of *The Guinness Book of World Records*, is that of a Russian woman who lived in the eighteenth century and produced more than 65 offspring. No naturally occurring population has ever come close to this level, although several very high-fertility groups have been documented. These include the Hutterites of the United States and Canadian Plains and the Cocos Keeling Islanders of south central Asia. Both of these groups average between 10 and 12 children per woman (see Eaton and Mayer 1954; Smith 1960; Weinstein 1978:82–83; Westoff and Westoff 1971; Franklin 2013; Volk and Atkinson 2013; Butler et al. 2013).

3. One of the earliest systematic studies of in this field was a survey conducted in 1941 as the Indianapolis Fertility Survey. Although the sample used was limited to urban European Americans, it established a valuable record of reproductive practices during the 1930s. The first large-scale post–World War II survey was conducted in 1955 as "The Growth of American Family Study." Designed to provide estimates of several relevant variables for the entire United States, it was followed-up by a similar study in 1960. Another major postwar survey was the Princeton Study of 1957 and 1960, to be discussed in a later section. It was designed to test hypotheses related to social and psychological factors affecting fertility. This was followed by the 1965 National Fertility Survey on family planning, which, like the 1955 Growth of American Families Study, collected data from a nationwide sample of the population of reproductive age. The National Survey of Family growth has been conducted by the CDC sine 1973. It is an excellent data source for researchers interested in studying Hispanics, African Americans, and teenagers. During the 1980s and 1990s, the most important research on U.S. fertility levels and differentials was conducted as part of the Current Population Surveys (CPS) program.

4. This aggregate does contain unmarried, divorced, and widowed women who have a low risk of fertility.

5. *National Vital Statistics Reports* 61, no. 1 (August 28, 2012), see page 2.

6. We stress *middle* class because of what Hawthorn (1968; 1970) refers to as the "J" curve phenomenon. That is, during some periods (if not permanently), the middle classes have the lowest fertility levels, lower than those of the working class and even lower than those

of the upper class. For both of these groups, traditional values and economic considerations favor large families, although for different reasons. Because the fertility levels of the upper class are higher than those of the middle class but not as high as those of the working class, we have the "J" shape (as opposed to a " / " or a "U").

7. Empirical studies have consistently reported a negative net relationship between women's level education and family size. Because level of education is highly (positively) correlated with earning power, opportunity costs will increase and family size will decrease as level of education increases.

8. Quality, in this sense, is associated with the child's good health, high level of education, and economic well-being. Contemporary families would thus prefer to have one or two children who are healthy and so forth, than several who are lacking in these characteristics.

9. Frank Notestein (1945) provided one of the earliest formulations, as a corollary to demographic transition theory. Harvey Leibenstein (1974) developed a revised model that incorporated a microeconomic framework.

10. The main sources of these data are national census bureaus. As discussed in Chapter 2, the organized collection of enumeration data and vital statistics extends back two centuries or more in the United States and the other industrialized countries. But census-taking in most of the developing world, especially in sub-Saharan Africa, was initiated far more recently: between the 1950s and 1970s in the wake of the independence movements that ended colonialism. During the earliest period for which reliable information is available, 1960 to 1975, the Community and Family Study Center (CFSC) at the University of Chicago undertook a large-scale project of tracking TFRs. Here, we use the results of this research, as reported by the Population Reference Bureau (PRB 1978). For the periods between 1980 and 1985 and between 1990 and 1995, fertility rates are drawn from United Nations publications. The most recent data are from PRB (1997; 1998).

11. The fact that residence in the United States lowers the fertility level of Mexican-background women suggests that a structural effect is at work. See Chapter 2.

CHAPTER SIX

MORTALITY
Causes and Consequences

Whereas birth is the very first human experience, death is the last. It is not ordinarily desired, but we are all aware that it is inevitable. Thus, attitudes toward death are ambivalent. The lack of preparation for death among people and their families is widespread. This can bring about an array of problems, depending upon such things as the age at which death occurs, its cause, and for how long it had been anticipated. In the United States, about 80 percent of the deaths every year occur in hospitals, hospices, or nursing homes. And among these, 70 percent occur after a decision is taken to forgo life-sustaining treatment. The practice of terminating life unnaturally through means such as suicide, assisted suicide, and voluntary or involuntary euthanasia is widely contested, even in the few countries where these procedures are legal. The grieving and bereavement processes that take place over the loss of a loved one are virtually universal, but the form they take is strongly influenced by cultural factors. It is possible to learn to accommodate the occurrence of death more effectively; and perhaps this is something that would benefit individuals and society at large. But ultimately there is nothing that can be done to avoid it.

For these reasons, a detailed discussion of death may not be the most pleasant subject to which one devotes a chapter in a textbook. However, it is of central importance to the material to be covered from this point on. In Chapter 2, we saw that the origins of demography in the seventeenth century coincided with the earliest attempts to account scientifically for the impact of death on the size and structure of populations. Similarly, many of the important innovations in the history of demographic research are associated with the study of death and mortality, including the invention of the life table, the use of parish records, and the quantification and computerization of population data. It is also in the study of death that our field overlaps most thoroughly with the disciplines of actuarial science and public health. Thus, it would not be redundant to say that mortality is an especially vital characteristic.

Mortality refers to the process of the depletion of a population through death. Death comes as the result of diseases, accidents, homicide, and, in about one of every 70 cases (in the United States), it is self-inflicted. And death comes at all ages, although some age groups are at greater risk than others. The term *general mortality* is used when referring to the occurrence of death regardless of cause or age, and cause-specific and **age-specific mortality** are used when such details are of interest.

The related concept of **morbidity** refers to an abnormal or pathological state. Its immediate root is in the Latin word *morbus*, meaning "diseased." In demographic applications, the term is nearly always used in combination with mortality, because of the linkage between certain kinds of pathologies and death. In this respect, its meaning is more akin to "*deadly* illness," and it is closer to the Greek root *marainien*, which means "to waste away." The connection between the two terms is reflected in the leading U.S. publication on the subject, *Morbidity and Mortality Weekly Report*, published by the CDC.[1] Like fertility and mortality, morbidity is measured in terms of rates, proportions, and ratios, as we shall see in a moment.

Our survey of mortality begins with the topic of measurement. This discussion focuses on the rates and ratios that allow us to quantify the occurrence and risks of illness and death. Next we take up the causes of mortality, both social and environmental. Here we get a direct introduction to the public-health perspective on demographic studies. The chapter concludes with two sections on the facts of mortality, past, present, and in various parts of the world. The first of these sections focuses specifically on mortality in the United States. The second, and last of the chapter, looks at international trends. At the conclusion of this discussion we will have a chance to reflect for a moment on the place of mortality in the larger demographic scheme of things. There we will consider the mutual impact of mortality and fertility. It is this impact, known a **natural increase**, which combines with migration—the subject of Chapter 7, to determine the amount and rate of population growth.

MEASURING MORBIDITY AND MORTALITY

Dorland's Illustrated Medical Dictionary (25th edition) defines death as the irreversible cessation of (a) total cerebral function, (b) spontaneous function of the respiratory system, and (c) spontaneous function of the circulatory system. As we all know, medical science has made it possible to sustain a person artificially even when one or more of these functions has stopped. Thus, for demographic purposes, we operationally define a death as the event as verified in writing (in a document known as a "certificate of death") by a licensed physician or other competent authority. This means that a person being sustained by life-support systems is demographically alive until and unless a doctor certifies otherwise, and that someone whose whereabouts are unknown following an accident is considered to be alive until a formal declaration is made that the accident was fatal. Once a death is certified, it is recorded in a national, state, or local register of vital statistics and thus it becomes demographic data.[2]

Extending and preserving life has been one of the oldest concerns of humankind. In order to prevent death, it is essential to learn about all causes of death that are either diseases or events leading to death as recorded in death certificates. They provide valuable data that may be analyzed for discerning demographic correlates. Given the universal interest in the causes of death, the World Health Organization has developed a system of statistical classification of diseases along with a coding system known as the International Classification of Diseases (ICD).[3] The current version, ICD-10, came into being in 1994, with the next revision envisioned for 2017. The latest version of ICD-10-CM is now being used in the United States.[4]

ICD-10 classification groups similar diseases under a unique block. For example, diseases of the digestive system are assigned the block identifier k00-k93. Each of the identifiers such as k00 is constituted by subblocks, k00.1 to K00.9 and each subblock consists of a number of similar diseases. Assignment of accurate ICD codes will depend upon the presence of medical personnel at the time of death as well as cause of death.

Measures of morbidity describe the occurrence of illness in a population. Such measures are important because an understanding of the conditions that lead to death is essential in describing and explaining mortality patterns. The two approaches to measuring how frequently a disease occurs are the **prevalence** and the **incidence** methods. Prevalence measures indicate the proportion of individuals in a population who have a specific disease at a particular point in time or during a specified interval. Incidence refers to the number cases of a disease *newly diagnosed* during a specified period of time, usually one year.

Morbidity Rates

The most straightforward demographic measure of illness is the simple proportion of those affected, symbolized by "pr," where pr = number of individuals with particular disease/total population size.

For example, in 2004, the number of persons with one of the two of the leading causes of death in the United States, heart diseases and hypertension (high blood pressure), was 26.84 million and 56.58 million, respectively (*Statistical Abstract of the United States, 2012*: Table 197). These numbers refer to all persons who were diagnosed with either or both of these diseases during the year of interest or before it, perhaps many years before. To find the prevalence proportions, the totals are divided by the midyear population size, which in 2009 was 307.44 million. Thus,

$pr_{\text{heart conditions}}$ = 26.84/307.44 = .087 or 8.7 percent; and

$pr_{\text{hypertension}}$ = 56.58/307.44 = .184 or 18.4 percent

With rates approaching 9 and 19 percent, respectively, you can see why these two conditions are of such serious concern in the medical community.

The incidence rate, symbolized by "I," is the number of new cases of a disease that occur per 100,000 persons in the population.[5] The duration is measured from the time the disease is positively diagnosed to the point at which the person either dies or is cured. One of the most closely followed sets of incidence rates is for cancer. The CDC lists 10 specific categories of the disease according to the site of onset: colon, rectum, pancreas, lung and bronchus, and so on. Table 6.1 lists the incidence rates for the two most common sites for men and women between 2006 and 2011. Lung and prostate cancer are by far the most common types among men, and breast and colon cancer lead among women. To illustrate the incidence rate, let us consider breast cancer among African American women during 2010. That year, 24,513 new cases of the disease were diagnosed among this group. With a Census 2010 total of 20,155,262 African American women in the U.S. population,

I = 24,513/20,155,262 = 0.00121,62 or 121.6 per 100,000

As Table 6.1 indicates, the breast cancer incidence rate for this group remained steady at the 125-per-100,000 level between 2006 and 2011. The rate for European American women was consistently higher during this period, but it did exhibit a general decline.

Table 6.1.   Incidence Rates for Cancer, United States, 2006-2011

Group/Site	2006	2007	2008	2009	2010	2111
EA Males (all)	562.60	571.40	551.11	541.14	528.22	513.05
Lung	73.07	72.70	70.67	69.55	67.24	64.40
Prostate	167.84	169.23	152.40	149.29	141.03	133.39
AA Males (all)	641.14	663.54	658.40	632.26	606.67	577.75
Lung	100.60	100.07	102.69	96.63	85.06	85.29
Prostate	252.30	264.20	249.62	240.86	226.23	214.83
EA Females (all)	433.64	434.55	436.74	439.26	429.33	426.99
Breast	130.32	132.33	131.23	134.00	130.24	132.58
Colon	30.57	30.19	29.73	28.09	25.41	24.86
AA Females (all)	414.21	413.34	415.71	419.23	402.69	406.52
Breast	124.56	124.47	127.55	128.40	121.62	126.69
Colon	41.48	39.35	36.14	36.72	32.67	31.28

Note: "All" refers to all sites; *EA* is European American and *AA* is African American.

Source: National Institutes of Health, National Cancer Institute: *SEER Cancer Statistics Review* 1975–2011 Incidence Tables 2006–2011. Surveillance Epidemiology and End Results Program, National Institutes of Health, *www.cancer .gov.*

Crude Death Rates

As is true of birth and morbidity, the most important sources of data on death and mortality are vital registration systems. Various types of registration systems are used in the industrialized countries, but all are considered to be reliable. In the United States, states and local governmental units are assigned the primary responsibility for registering and recording deaths. Then, through a cooperative agreement, this information is conveyed to the Federal Government and to the National Center for Health Statistics (NCHS), where it is made available to researchers and the general public. The NCHS and the counterpart organizations (usually the national census bureaus) in Europe, Japan, Canada, Australia, and New Zealand also provide data on important correlates of mortality such as age, gender, cause, marital status, and occupation. In contrast, in most less-developed countries, the vital registration systems are incomplete. Deaths go unreported and the causes of death are often not clearly entered. These limitations constrain our ability to measure mortality accurately on a worldwide basis; and they should serve to caution us to treat such data from such areas as approximate.

We speak of the *force of mortality* when referring to the probability that member of a population will die at some specific moment (compare this with the force of *natality* introduced in Chapter 5). This force, or likelihood, varies with time and from person to person depending on variables such as gender, age, and socioeconomic status (SES). The most common measure is the *annual crude death rate* (CDR). It is defined as the number of deaths that occur in a population during the course of one year for every 1,000 persons alive at midyear. The formula is:

$$CDR = (D/P) \times 1,000$$

where D is the number of deaths and P is the total population size (see Table 6.2). To illustrate, in the year 2009 Canada's midyear population size was approximately

33.7 million, and about 210,700 deaths were reported for the period. Thus, we find its CDR:

$$CDR = (239,461/33,726,915) \times 1,000 = .007 \times 1,000 = 7 \text{ (per thousand)}.$$

For the sake of comparison, for the same year, the total population size of the United States was 306.7 million, and about 2,576,881 deaths were recorded. This yields a CDR of 2576/306,771 × 1000 = 8.4 (per thousand) By this criterion, then, we can say that the *overall* probability of dying was lower in Canada than in the United States (at least for the year 2009). But does it mean that Canada's mortality level (the rate at which its population is being depleted by death) is lower than that of the United States? Unfortunately, the answer is "maybe yes and maybe no."

Because the CDR is not a "pure" measure, it alone cannot determine the actual force of mortality or other important aspects of the incidence of death. So we would be misled if we were to compare the CDRs in Table 6.2 to determine (for instance) the quality of medical care in the countries shown—that is, on the assumption that high CDRs go with poor medical care and low CDRs are associated with good care. If this were true, then we would conclude that Sweden and Gambia were about equal in health care access, or that Albania surpassed Japan in this respect. Obviously, the CDR is measuring something else.

Like all demographic indicators, the CDR incorporates certain assumptions in the absence of facts. Some of these are relatively trivial, and some have significant consequences. One fairly inconsequential (and commonly made) assumption is that the size of the midyear population is the same as the yearly average size: the number one would get by summing the sizes of the population on each and every day of the year and then dividing by 365. Of course, we do not know that this is the case, but it seems to be a reasonable guess. It is a much more serious matter to assume, as the CDR does, that each member of a population has the same chance as every other member to die during the course of the year. That is, by taking total deaths divided

Table 6.2. Crude Death Rates for Selected Countries, 2009

Country	Deaths	Population Size	CDR
Albania	20,376.0	3.0	6.0
Australia	139,384.0	22.0	6.0
Bolivia	73,631.0	10.0	7.0
China	9,425,321.0	1331.0	7.0
Cuba	83,266.0	11.0	7.0
Gambia, The	16,746.0	2.0	10.0
Israel	38,925.0	7.0	5.0
Japan	116,0777.0	128.0	9.0
Portugal	104,198.0	11.0	10.0
Rwanda	87,828.0	11.0	8.0
Saudi Arabia	89,125.0	27.0	3.0
South Africa	703,157.0	49.0	14.0
Sweden	90,196.0	9.0	10.0
Yemen, Rep.	168,923.0	22.0	8.0

Population size in millions, crude death rate per 1,000 persons.

Source: World Bank, Crude death rates, http://data.worldbank.org/indicator/SP.DYN.CDRT.IN.

by total population, the rate "averages out" the risk of dying. But we know that this is not true: some cohorts are at greater risk than others are, the risks for men differ from those of women, and so on.

The practical consequence is that a population may have a high CDR in comparison to another (say the United States and Canada) for any of several reasons. It might be because the risk of dying in the first population is truly greater *or* it might be because the first population has proportionately more members in high-risk categories—say, many very elderly people.

Because of this "averaging out" characteristic, we refer to the rate as *crude*. Here, "crude" means unrefined or unspecific. To avoid this crudity, several adjustments are made that provide us with a set of other, more specialized measures of mortality. The first of these is a simple procedure that accounts for the instability of the CDR. The value of this rate depends on the level of mortality, the age structure, the sex, structure, and several cause-specific factors (incidence of morbidity, etc.). Each of these elements varies somewhat each year, and in combination they cause the CDR to fluctuate. To account for this, we can calculate a stable or **central crude death rate** for a specific year, y, by taking the average of the CDR for Y and for the preceding and the following year, y − 1 and y + 1, respectively (Shryock and Siegel 1976:225). The formula for this rate is:

$$[(D_{y-1}/P_{y-1} + D_y/P_y + D_{y+1}/P_{y+1})/3] \times 1,000 = (CD_{y-1} + CDR_y + CDR_{y+1})/3$$

Although the CDR for the United States has, in fact, been very stable for many years at less than 9 per 1,000 (between 7.94 and 8.54), during 2005 there was sufficient fluctuation to justify calculating this kind of rate. In 2008, the total (midyear) population size was 304,798,000 and 2,471,984 deaths were reported, which yields a CDR of 8.11 per 1,000. For the preceding year, 2007, the CDR was 8.02, and for the following year, 2009, the rate was 7.43. Adding these three rates together and dividing by 3, we get 8.02: not very different from the observed rates, but more likely to be accurate.

An alternative measure of the central CDR is to add the deaths for the three years (the target year, the one preceding, and the one following) and multiply by one-third. This gives the average number of deaths. Then, divide by the population size of the target year, on the assumption that it is the average population—and multiply by 1,000. With a total of 2,471,984 deaths in 2008 and 2,437,163 in 2010, we calculate the CDR for the United States as follows:

1. Average number of deaths = (1/3) × (2,471,984 + 2,423,712 + 2,437,163) × 1000

1/3 × (7,332,859) = 2, 444, 286

2. CDR = (2,444,286/304,798,000) × 1,000 = 8.01

which is probably the best estimate (and the lowest).

Specific Death Rates

Demographers adjust for the manner in which the CDR treats all members of the population alike with respect to the risk of dying with the use of *specific* rates. As the name suggests, these rates refer to the deaths that occur among a specific subpopulation or subaggregate whose members are known to have a common level of exposure to disease and other causes of death. For any subpopulation, "S," the specific (annual) death rate for that group, DR_s is:

$$DR_s = D_s/P_s \times 1,000$$

where D_s is the number of deaths that occur to members of that subpopulation, and P_s is the size of the group at midyear. Note that the group of interest, not the general population, is represented in both the numerator and denominator of this fraction.

Tables 6.3 and 6.4 contain information about four major subpopulations in the United States: African Americans, both male and female, and European Americans, male and female. During the year for which the data in Table 6.3 were collected (2009), the CDR for the nation was 8.12 per 1,000. But that figure conceals the fact that the gender-specific rate for men was well above the average and that for women well below it. The CDR also doesn't indicate that European American males had the highest death rates and African American females the lowest. The African American male death rate experienced significant declines between 1995 and 2010. Table 6.4 shows that in general, death rates for all groups declined during the last quarter of the twentieth century, although European American women saw a fairly steady increase during the period.

Table 6.3. Group-Specific Death Rates, United States, 2009

Group	Persons	Deaths	Death Rate
Males	151,777	1,232	8.12
European American	121,408	1,051	8.66
African American	20,044	145	7.25
Females	157,027	1,236	7.87
European American	124,021, 027	1,036	8.58
African American	21,963	141	6.42

Source: Sherry L. Murphy, Jiaquan Xu, and Kenneth D. Kochanek, Division of Vital Statistics. "Deaths: Final Data for 2010," *National Vital Statistics Reports* 61, no. 4 (May 8, 2013).

Table 6.4. Group-Specific Death Rates (per 1,000 Persons), 1995–2010

Group	1995	2000	2005	2010
Males	9.01	8.53	8.32	8.12
European Americans	9.21	8.73	8.73	8.66
African Americans	9.60	7.96	7.96	7.25
Females	8.37	8.25	8.25	7.87
European Americans	8.43	8.81	8.81	8.57
African Americans	7.43	6.99	6.99	6.42

Source: Sherry L. Murphy, Jiaquan Xu, and Kenneth D. Kochanek, Division of Vital Statistics. "Deaths: Final Data for 2010," *National Vital Statistics Reports* 61, no. 4 (May 8, 2013): Table 1, p. 18.

Age-Specific Rates

Age-specific death rates (**ASDR**s) measure the incidence of death among members of the same cohorts. They are the most widely used specific rates, and the ones most sensitive to the force of mortality. The ASDRs allow us to speak of deaths among persons who are 40 years old, or those age 20, and so on. Data that refer to single years in this manner, single-year cohorts, are collected as "unabridged" data—as we discuss in Chapter 9. However, it is more common to use larger intervals of five or 10 years, such as 24 to 29, or 20 to 29. An exception is made in the case of the very youngest cohorts, ages 5 and below, because death rates at these ages are high and because the variation between single years, say between ages 1 and 2, is significant. In addition, the oldest cohort is usually treated as an open-ended interval: 65 and above or 85+. Table 6.5 compares ASDRs for the United States, Canada, and Mexico.

The formula for the ASDR is:

$$ASDR_x = (D_x/P_x) \times 1,000$$

where x is a specific age or age interval. As you can see, this is quite similar to the formula for CDR, except that we specify the age to which we are referring. We will illustrate with data from the state of California. Suppose, for example, we are interested in the death rate for persons between ages 25 and 29, for a specific year—2010. Then the rate we wish to find is symbolized as $ASDR_{25-29}$. To calculate it, we first need to know the number of persons in the state alive at midyear in that cohort, which was estimated to be 2,668,604. This is expressed as $P_{25-29} = 2,668,604$, indicating the size of the cohort. Next, we need to know the number of deaths at that age that occurred in the state during the year. This total is 1,836, symbolized as $D_{25-29} = 1,836$. Therefore,

$$ASDR_{25-29} = (D_{25-29}/P_{25-29}) \times 1,000 =$$
$$(1,836/2,668,604) \times 1,000 = 0.68 \text{ (per 1,000)}$$

Table 6.5. Age-Specific Deaths and Death Rates for Mexico, the United States, and Canada

Age	Mexico (2010)			United States (2009)			Canada (2008)		
	Persons	Deaths	ASDR	Persons	Deaths	ASDR	Persons	Deaths	ASDR
1–4	8.06	5.64	0.7	14.83	4.45	0.3	1.33	0.27	0.2
5–9	9.56	2.87	0.3	25.23	2.52	0.1	2.01	0.2	0.1
10–14	11.97	3.59	0.3	15.64	3.13	0.2	2.46	0.25	0.1
15–24	21.08	23.01	1.09	44.04	30.42	0.69	4.34	2.16	0.5
25–34	17.31	30.21	1.74	40.51	42.5	1.05	4.43	2.66	0.6
35–44	15.38	38.1	2.48	41.60	74.67	1.79	4.9	5.46	1.11
45–54	11.05	54.46	4.93	44.95	187.57	4.17	5.3	14.44	2.72
55–64	7.01	77.21	11.01	34.64	303.31	8.76	3.94	25.94	6.58
65–74	4.19	102.16	24.36	20.76	401.03	19.31	2.41	39.48	16.37
75–84	2.04	120.63	59.04	13.15	627.73	47.72	1.57	69.21	44.06
85–94	0.62	82.52	133.29	5.64	733.18	129.97	0.54	64.45	118.92

Source: United Nations Department of Economic and Social Affairs, *Demographic Yearbook 2013*, Table 19.

Table 6.6. Age-Specific Death Rates for the State of California, 2010

Age Cohort	Persons	Deaths	ASDR
below 1	568,771	2419	4.25
1–4	2,201,909	436	0.20
5–9	2,745,233	239	0.09
10–14	2,691,330	307	0.11
15–19	3,054,118	1,127	0.37
20–24	2,915,575	1,869	0.64
25–29	2,668,256	1,836	0.69
30–34	2,487,744	2,040	0.82
35–39	2,658,460	2,600	0.98
40–44	2,830,879	4,102	1.45
45–49	2,904,236	6,893	2.37
50–54	2,724,228	10,152	3.73
55–59	2,330,002	13,433	5.77
60–64	1,948,855	15,994	8.21
65–69	1,375,945	16,689	12.13
70–74	1,012,104	19,236	19.01
75–79	784,016	24,562	31.33
80–84	611,691	32,789	53.6
85–89	401,966	37,900	94.29
90–100	226,306	38,492	170.09
Total	39137,325	233,143	5.96

ASR per 1,000 persons except for below 1 category.

Source: State of California, Department of Public Health, Death Records, Table 5-4, "Deaths and five-year age-specific death rates by sex, California, 2010."

Table 6.6, which contains the entire set of ASDRs for California, 2010, indicates that the state's CDR for that year was 5.9 per 1,000. Although this is well below the CDR for the nation during 2009 (that is, 8.1), it certainly is much higher—more than 12 times higher—than the age-specific rate for persons between ages 25 and 29. The reason for this discrepancy can be seen in the table. The CDR is based on the deaths to persons in every cohort, not only the 25–29 year olds but also the very elderly groups, with ASDRs as high as 170, and the infants who have a rate of 4.2. When deaths are distributed by age, as in Figure 6.1, the highly variable nature of the force of mortality becomes very clear. The ASDRs represent the probability that a person who has reached exact age x will die before reaching exact age x+1; and these rates are used for constructing life tables.[6]

The risk of dying among persons age 5 and below is very high. In virtually every population, the only death rates that are higher are those of the very oldest cohorts. Moreover, because the very young are the most vulnerable to infectious disease, malnutrition, and other illnesses that can prove fatal, the rate at which deaths occur among them is an especially sensitive indicator of socioeconomic conditions. To account for these conditions, several special rates have been devised, including:

1. **Neonatal mortality rate** (**NMR**), which focuses on the first 28 days of life.
2. **Infant mortality rate** (**IMR**), covering the first year of life.
3. **Child mortality rate** (**CMR**), which measures death among persons one to five years old.

Figure 6.1. Age-Specific Mortality Rates for the United States, 2012

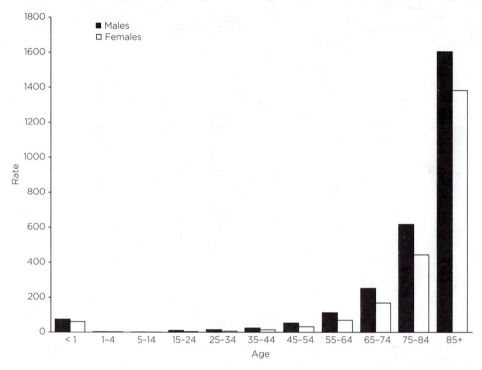

Source: Centers for Disease Control and Prevention, National Center for Health Statistics. Compressed Mortality File 1999–2012 on CDC WONDER Online Database, released October 2014. Data are from the Compressed Mortality File 1999–2012 Series 20 No. 2R, 2014, as compiled from data provided by the 57 vital statistics jurisdictions through the Vital Statistics Cooperative Program.

Unlike most other age-specific death rates, the annual neonatal mortality rate is calculated by dividing the number of deaths to persons age 1 to 28 days that occur during a year by the number of live births, not by the size of the cohort. The formula for this rate (NMR) is

$$NMR = (D_{1-28} \text{ days/B}) \times 1,000,$$

where B is the number of births. The source from which the age-specific data on California were derived also provided information on neonatal mortality. According to the Department, in 2008, 2,015 infants died before reaching their 29th day of life and a total of 544,594 children were born. Thus, the NMR = (2,015/544,594) × 1,000 = 3.7. Table 6.7 lists neonatal mortality rates for the U.S. population between 1995 and 2009. These rates are given for the general population and for European Americans and minority groups (combined). The fact that these rates have steadily declined among the general population, from 4.91 to 4.18 deaths per 1,000 live births, is evidence of steadily improving health conditions. The fact that rates among the ethnic minority groups have been consistently twice as high as rates among the majority is a clear indication of the level of social and economic inequality that persists in the United States (as discussed in Chapter 3).

Table 6.7. Neonatal Mortality Rates, United States, 1995-2009

Year	Total	European American	All Minorities
1995	4.91	4.08	8.13
1998	4.80	3.98	7.91
1999	4.73	3.88	7.94
2000	4.63	3.82	7.60
2001	4.54	3.78	7.37
2002	4.66	3.89	7.55
2003	4.62	3.87	7.40
2004	4.52	3.78	7.19
2005	4.54	3.79	7.18
2006	4.45	3.72	7.00
2007	4.42	3.70	8.86
2008	4.29	3.62	6.54
2009	4.18	3.48	6.48

Source: *National Vital Statistics Reports* 60, no. 3 (December 29, 2011): Table 20.

The practice of using births instead of cohort size in the denominator is based on the fact that the 1- to 28-day cohort at midyear is only one small part of the population base in which neonatal deaths occur. Every month there is a different set of babies who are in their first month of life; yet neonatal mortality refers to deaths throughout the year. Because births are counted from January 1 to December 31—and not just on July 1 as in the case of cohort size, they provide the correct subpopulation to which neonatal mortality is referred.

This same convention applies to measures of infant mortality, for a similar but slightly different reason. In this case, the numerator, D_{0-1}, or the number of infant deaths, is not confined to the number of infants born during the year for which infant mortality rate (IMR) is computed. In any year, a number of infants born during the preceding calendar year may die. Therefore, using cohort size to measure infant mortality does not produce an accurate indication of the actual probabilities of dying. This is especially true if the number of births changes significantly from one calendar year to another. The widely used IMR is thus defined as:

$$(D_{0-1}/B) \times 1,000$$

the number of deaths that occur annually to members of a population during their first year of life, divided by the number of live births during the year (times 1,000). As we saw in the case of California, there were 2,419 infant deaths during 2010 and 568,771 births. Thus, the IMR was:

$$(2,419/568,771) \times 1,000 = 4.2$$

You have probably noticed that neonatal deaths are a component of infant deaths. That is, in the latter case, the first 28 days of life are considered to be part of the first year. Consequently, the neonatal mortality rate for a population is always lower than its IMR. The other component of infant mortality, deaths that occur between the 29th and the 365th day of life, is referred to as "postneonatal mortality." The associated rate is, of course, calculated by subtracting the neonatal mortality rate from the IMR. Thus, for Colorado, 1996, the postneonatal mortality rate is equal to (6.6 − 4.4), or 2.2 deaths per 1,000 live births.

Table 6.8 gives the percentage distribution of infant deaths in the United States for selected years between 1980 and 2005. Here, neonatal mortality is divided between the categories "early" (less than 7 days) and "late" (7 to 27 days), and these are compared with postneonatal mortality. As you can see, the period of highest risk is by far the first week of life. Although only one-third the length of the late neonatal period, and less than one-tenth the length of the postneonatal period, more than one-half of all infant deaths occur before the age of 7 days. This proportion remained steady during the years shown, whereas there was a decline in the percentage of postneonatal deaths.

Analyzing Infant Mortality

Table 6.9 and Figure 6.2 feature comparative IMRs. The table, which is modeled after Table 6.7, contains trends in the IMR for the U.S. population, for European Americans, and for all minority groups combined, between 1993 and 2010. IMR declined steadily during the period, from 8.4 to 6.1 per 1,000 births for the population as a whole. Nevertheless, the rates for minorities remained consistently almost twice as high as the rates of European Americans.

The data on which Figure 6.2 is based came from the sample of 66 nations introduced in Chapters 3 and 4. The mean IMR for the entire sample is 23.35 per 1,000 live births, and there is a substantial amount of variation between countries. The values range between 3.8 for Japan and 50 per 1,000 for Gambia. As these values and Figure 6.2 indicate, a very close, inverse relationship exists between level of socioeconomic development and infant mortality: the higher the per-capita gross national product (GNP), the lower the IMR. The CIA World Fact Book indicated that the average IMR for the world was 49.4 per 1,000. For the more-developed countries, the rate was 9; and for the less-developed countries it was more than *seven* times higher, at 64 per 1,000. Africa, the continent with the lowest per-capita GNP and the highest IMR had a rate of 89 per 1,000—10 times the average of the more-developed nations. The highest IMRs in the world today are in the range of 100 to 150 deaths per 1,000 live births.

Table 6.8. Infant Deaths by Age of Infant, United States, 1980-2005 (in Percentages)

Year	Early Neonatal	Late Neonatal	Postneonatal
1980	56.35	11.11	32.54
1990	52.17	10.87	36.96
1995	52.63	11.84	35.53
2000	53.62	13.04	33.33
2001	52.94	13.24	33.82
2002	52.86	14.29	32.86
2003	53.62	13.04	31.88
2004	52.94	13.24	33.82
2005	52.17	13.04	33.33

Source: U.S. Census Bureau, Statistical Abstract of the United States: 2012, Table 112; U.S. National Center for Health Statistics, *Health, United States, 2008*. See also http://cdc.gov/nchs/hus.htm.

Table 6.9. Infant Mortality Rates, United States, 1993-2010 (Rates per 1,000 Births)

Year	Total, All Groups	European American	African American
2010	6.15	5.20	9.28
2007	6.75	5.64	10.55
2006	6.69	5.56	10.60
2005	6.87	5.73	10.92
2004	6.79	5.66	10.92
2003	6.85	5.72	11.09
2002	6.97	5.79	11.41
2001	6.85	5.65	11.33
2000	6.91	5.68	11.44
1999	7.06	5.77	11.94
1998	7.20	5.95	11.92
1997	7.23	6.03	11.76
1996	7.32	6.07	12.18
1993	8.37	6.82	14.07

Source: Sherry L. Murphy, Jiaquan Xu, and Kenneth D. Kochanek, Division of Vital Statistics. "Deaths: Final Data for 2010," *National Vital Statistics Reports* 61, no. 4 (May 8, 2013): Table 20, p. 91.

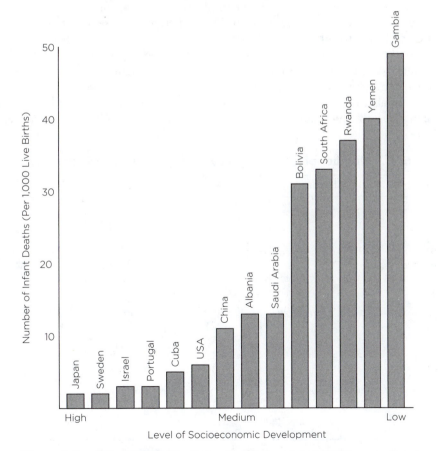

Figure 6.2. Infant Mortality Rates for 14 Countries, 2013
Source: World Bank Online Data, http://data.worldbank.org/indicator/SP.DYN.IMRT.IN.

The NCHS and similar agencies in Europe and Canada also report two additional measures related to infant and neonatal mortality. These are (1) maternal mortality rates and (2) fetal death rates (see U.S. Department of Commerce: Tables 123 and 124). The former rates account for the deaths that occur among women who are carrying, delivering, or who have just given birth ("puerperal" causes). The annual rate is calculated by dividing the total number of deaths among this group by the number of live births during the year, and it is expressed per 100,000. In 2007, the maternal mortality rate was 12.9 deaths per 100,000 live births.

Fetal mortality, also called "involuntary abortion" or "miscarriage," is death that occurs to a viable fetus whose period of gestation is understood to be twenty weeks or more. The annual rate is based upon the number of deaths of this type, per year, for every 1,000 live births. The U.S. fetal death rate declined steadily from 7.0 to 6.2 between 1995 and 2006. By way of comparison, rates of *voluntary* abortion also declined steadily between 1990 and 2005, as shown in Table 6.10.

Cause-Specific Rates

The decomposition of death rates by cause has important, and perhaps obvious, medical applications. Of course, we are always interested in knowing the rate at which members of a population are dying, and the ages at which death is more and less likely to occur. But, if we are also able to identify the major factors that put people at fatal risk, preventative measures can be attempted. For this reason, the study of **cause-specific mortality** is closely related to research on morbidity. In fact, the way in which both prevalence and incidence data are collected is, in part, based on the assumption that certain conditions are likely to become significant causes of death.

As with other specific death rates, cause-specific rates are calculated by dividing the number of deaths in a category by a population base. In most cases, cause-specific rates are stated annually and given per 100,000 members of the reference

Table 6.10. Number of Voluntary Abortions per 1,000 Pregnancies

Year	All Groups	European American	Others
1990	27.4	19.7	50.30
1991	26.2	18.1	50.85
1992	25.7	16.7	51.90
1993	25.0	16.1	48.75
1994	23.7	14.8	48.25
1995	22.5	14.2	44.45
1996	22.4	13.6	45.25
1997	21.9	13.2	44.10
1998	21.5	12.5	44.05
1999	21.4	11.9	44.30
2000	21.3	11.7	44.00
2001	20.9	11.3	42.65
2002	20.5	10.9	41.75
2003	20.2	10.8	40.90
2004	19.7	10.5	39.95
2005	19.4	10.5	39.10

Source: Stephanie J. Ventura, Joyce C. Abma, William D. Mosher, Division of Vital Statistics; and Stanley K. Henshaw, The Guttmacher Institute. "Estimated Pregnancy Rates for the United States, 1990–2005: An Update." *National Vital Statistics Reports* 58, no. 4 (October 14, 2009).

population.[7] For example, according to the NCHS, in 2010, 12,859 persons in the United States died from accidents (of all types, not just auto accidents). We will symbolize this as $D_{accidents}$. With a midyear population size, P, of 309 million, we can calculate $DR_{accidents,}$ the annual accident-specific death rate.

$$DR_{accidents} = (D_{accidents}/P) \times 100,000 =$$
$$(120,859/309,000,000) \times 100,000 = 39.1$$

All known causes of death vary significantly with age, gender, and socioeconomic characteristics. Thus, reports on the subject produced by the CDC and other organizations typically include information on such variables along with lists of diseases, other causes, and death rates. So, for example, the rate for the leading cause of death in the United States, heart disease, was 193.6 deaths per 100,000 persons. This is about five times the death-by-accident rate. Box 6.1 and Table 6.11 contain further information about the leading causes of death in the United States by gender and age.

SOCIAL AND ENVIRONMENTAL FACTORS

In Chapters 8 and 12, we discuss the current widespread fear of population explosion, and how it has been fueled by dramatic declines in mortality rates globally. The

---

Box 6.1   The 15 Leading Causes of Death in the United States

	(ABBREVIATION)
1 Diseases of heart*	(heart)
2 Malignant neoplasms*	(neoplasm)
3 Chronic lower respiratory diseases*	(pulmonary)
4 Cerebrovascular diseases*	(cerebrovascular)
5 Accidents (unintentional injuries)*	(accidents)
6 Alzheimer's disease*	(Alzheimer's)
7 Diabetes mellitus (diabetes)	(diabetes)
8 Nephritis, nephrotic syndrome, and nephrosis	(kidney)
9 Influenza and pneumonia	(flu and pneumonia)
10 Intentional self-harm	(suicide)
11 Septicemia	(septicemia)
12 Chronic liver disease and cirrhosis	(liver)
13 Essential hypertension and hypertensive renal disease	(hypertension)
14 Parkinson's disease	(Parkinson's)
15 Pneumonitis due to solids and liquids	(pneumonitis)

*See Table 6.11 for further data on causes of death 1–6.

Table 6.11. Death Rates per 100,000 Population in Specified Group (2010)

Group/Age	Heart	Neo-plasm	Pulmonary	Cerebro-Vascular	Accidents	Alzheimer's
All groups	193.6	186.2	44.7	41.9	39.1	27.0
Male	202.5	198.3	43.1	34.5	50.0	16.7
1–4	1.1	2.4	0.3	0.3	10.5	-
20–25	7.5	0.5	0.7	0.8	53.8	
30–35	14.1	-	1.0	1.8	50.8	-
50–55	147.7	154.1	13.4	18.5	59.5	-
60–65	320.7	431.5	57.7	42.3	51.7	-
70–75	685.8	957.5	216.4	121.7	68.4	31.6
Female	184.9	174.4	46.3	49.1	28.6	37.0
1–4	0.9	0.3	0.3	0.3	6.6	-
20–25	2.0	3.5	0.3	0.5	18.2	-
30–35	6.5	11.9	0.6	1.7	18.9	-
50–55	56.9	138.9	14.3	14.0	28.3	-
60–65	136.5	317.5	49.1	30.5	21.8	3.6
70–75	368.6	665.6	177.0	100.1	35.7	34.1

Source: Centers for Disease Control and Prevention, National Vital Statistics System, Mortality Table LCWK1, 2010.

likelihood of living a long life has increased considerably as the result of changes in our social and economic environments and our ever-increasing capacity to control the factors that cause death. In the process, longevity, the ability to prevent death from year to the next, has increased dramatically. This fact has deep social implications. Consider your own family. As more members survive to ages eighty and beyond, the likelihood increases that you will have living grandparents and great-grandparents (assuming that marriage patterns remain as they are). In the United States in 1900, about 80 percent of all persons lost their last grandparent by the time they had reached age 30. However, by the end of the twentieth century, 97 percent of all children were born with a living grandparent, and 76 percent of them will still have a grandparent alive by the time they reach age 30 (Uhlenberg 1996; Bengtson 2001).

Among the many social structural factors that influence the probability of death, we will focus here on three major categories, social class, ethnicity, and gender. Low SES is associated with low life expectancy, high IMRs, high rates of child mortality from injury, and high overall mortality rates (Adler et al. 1994; Pappas et al. 1993; Roberts 1997; Macassa, Hallqvist, and Lynch 2011). A now-classic study of mortality and class in Western Europe (Antonovsky 1967) tracked socioeconomic differences over several centuries. In the earliest period, up to 1650, no substantial differences in life expectancy were found across various social strata.

However, between 1650 and 1850, corresponding to the second stage of Europe's demographic transition (see Chapter 8), mortality differentials between classes increased sharply and significantly (Antonovsky 1967; Clarke et al. 2010). During this period, the average life expectancies of the middle and the upper classes increased at a much faster pace than in the lower classes. During the last period between 1850 and 1960, the third stage of demographic transition, these class-based differentials diminished once more.

Of course, Antonovsky's findings concerning long-range historical trends do not mean that there are no longer any differences between the mortality experiences of the rich and the poor. To the contrary, at the individual level, in comparisons between nations, and at most levels of aggregation in between, a clear inverse relationship exists between death rates and wealth, education, and occupational status (see Smith, Blane, and Bartley 1994). A recent prospective study of middle-aged British men found that the subjects with the greatest material assets also had the lowest mortality rates from all causes (Wannamethee and Shaper 1997; Ramsay et al. 2011).

The effects of SES on mortality are mediated by several factors. The main immediate determinants, or causal factors, are lifestyle and extent of access to health care. Cigarette smoking is perhaps the single-most-avoidable cause of death, and it is a habit that is inversely related to SES. George Orwell, author of *1984*, observed many years ago that cigarettes are the poor person's luxury. Unfortunately, that remains true today. Approximately 400,000 lives are lost each year in the United States because of smoking, of whom a disproportionate number are members of lower classes and poorer minority groups.

A second factor that affects the risk of dying is ethnicity. As discussed at some length in Chapter 3, data in this realm are often aggregated in terms of racial categories. But, because race is a subjective concept whose definition varies with time and between populations, measurement tends to be imprecise. This makes it difficult to assess the independent influences of "race" on mortality, if any exist. Nevertheless, even in advanced economies such the United States, members of certain minority groups are at significantly greater risk than are members of the majority (see Table 6.3). About nine out of 1,000 European American females die between ages 15 and 60; and for European American males and for African American females the rate is somewhat higher, at 16 percent. Recent evidence suggests that between-group differences in mortality from diseases such as stroke are more likely to be related to ethnicity than to social class. George Howard and associates (1995) found that SES explained less than one-quarter of the excess mortality from stroke among African Americans compared to European Americans. For women, the role of SES in accounting for the between-group differences in mortality was even less significant.

Gender differences in mortality are well documented. In general, females live longer than males. In the United States in 2008, the average life expectancy at birth for males was 73 years and for females it was 80.5 years. This pattern is also typical of Canada, the European countries, Japan, and several other nations. However, in societies in which women have low status, males tend to outlive females. In Western Asia and the Middle East (e.g., Afghanistan and Oman), the gap is very wide; but even in South Asia, the differences in life expectancies between males and females are either much smaller than those in the industrialized countries or they are reversed. For example, in 2010 life expectancy at birth for males in India was 66.4 years and for females it was 68.7 years.

MORTALITY IN THE UNITED STATES

We have already seen that one of the most important indicators of health in any population is infant mortality. Early in the twentieth century, around 1915, one in every 10 babies born in the United States died during the first year of life. Twenty-five years later, the IMR had declined by nearly one-half. The pace of infant mortality decline held over the succeeding 30 years, bringing down the rate to 20 per 1,000 infants born in 1970. Thus, the rate was again reduced by one-half between

1940 and 1970. By 1990, the rate had fallen well below 10 per 1,000 infants born. In sum, the chances of surviving increased at least tenfold between 1915 and 1990. With the rate at about 6.6 per 1,000 by the first decade of century, most of the traditional causes of infant death (parasites, malnutrition, etc.) had been eliminated. As we noted earlier, the current major factors include more recalcitrant conditions such as congenital defects and sudden infant death syndrom (SIDS) (*Morbidity and Mortality Weekly Report* 1997).

The Effects of Inequality

These low overall rates mask some important differences that have persisted throughout the course of infant mortality decline in the United States. In 1950, the African American IMR was at least 63 percent higher than that of European Americans. Although the rates for both African Americans and European Americans declined between 1950 and 2008, those in the latter group fell much faster. During this period, the European American IMR fell nearly 80 percent, whereas the African American IMR fell only 70 percent. These differences are indicative of the discrepancies between the general health conditions of the two groups. Higher rates of poverty, of drug use, and of teenage pregnancy among African Americans are among the leading factors (Pampel and Pillai 1987; Bhutta et al. 2012).

Another major indicator of a population's general health conditions is average life expectancy at birth. Principally because of high rates of infant mortality, life expectancy in the United States was in the range of 50 years or below until well into the twentieth century. With improvements in medical science, childcare, and nutrition and sanitation, this figure increased steadily until, as of 2010, the average for the general population was 78.7 years. As is typical of the industrialized nations, the average for women has for many decades exceeded that for men. By 2010, this difference among European Americans was more than six years, 76.1 for males and 81.3 for females.

Cause-Specific Death in the United States

We noted earlier that heart disease, lung cancer, and strokes are three of the leading causes of death in the United States.[8] The dominance of heart disease as the major killer is evident from the differences in the rates for this condition and for cancer, the second-leading cause. For example, in 1995, the rate of death from diseases of the heart was 280.7 per 100,000, whereas the rate for cancer victims was 204.9 per 100,000, a 37 percent difference (Anderson, Kochanek, and Murphy 1997; Towfighi and Saver 2011). Together, these two diseases account for more than one-half of all deaths in the United States, although the incidence rates for both are declining slowly. Between 2000 and 2010, the death rate from heart disease fell from 257.6 to 179.1 and the death rate from cancer fell from 506.0 to 518.8. These declines contributed to a slight improvement in average life expectancy. As the findings of the CDC and the *National Vital Statistics Report* indicate, men of working age (18 to 65) are about 3.5 times more at the risk of heart disease than women of the same age.

The prevalence rate suggests that one of every three persons in the United States will develop the disease during their lifetime. Men are at the highest risk of death from prostate cancer, whereas breast cancer is the most common killer among women. Prostate cancer is far more common among older men than among the young. Another common malignancy, which strikes both men and women, is cancer of the colon and rectum. Among all the sites at which malignancies occur, lung cancer has the highest overall mortality rate. It is now the second-most common cause of death among both men and women, although a disproportionately higher number of men are affected. According to the Fred Hutchison Research Center in Seattle:

> African Americans had the highest death rate and shortest survival time for most cancers of any racial and ethnic group in the nation as of 2005, the newest data available, according to the U.S. Department of Health and Human Services. Although the overall difference in cancer death rates among racial groups is decreasing, the death rate for all cancers combined in 2005 continued to be 33 percent higher in African American men and 16 percent higher in African American women than in Caucasian men and women, respectively. African American men also had the highest rates of cancer development of any race from 2001 to 2005.[9]

Stroke, the third most-common cause of death, has been concentrated regionally within the United States. During the early 1990s, the risk of stroke was significantly higher among populations living in the coastal plain regions of North Carolina, South Carolina, and Georgia, and in five other southern states. For persons between the ages of 35 and 54, stroke mortality in these states was twice the national average for the age group. In fact, public health experts referred to the region as "the **stroke belt**." However, the nation's population distribution, migration patterns, and other factors changed so substantially that, by the end of the decade, people living in northern and western states had become the most vulnerable (Howard et al. 1997; Galea et al. 2011).

Since the 1980s, HIV/AIDS has become one of the nation's (and the world's) leading killers, especially among young to middle-aged adults (ages 30–39). At the end of the twentieth century, it was the 15th-leading cause of death in the country. Between 1981 and 1996, more than 560,000 cases were reported, with the peak occurring in 1993 with 102,000 new incidents. The probability of death among those with the active HIV virus is very high. From 2008 through 2010, the annual estimated number and the estimated rate of diagnoses of HIV infection in the United States remained stable (see Box 6.2 and Table 6.12.)

Age Group

Between 2008 and 2010—the period covered in all of the statistical categories reported here, the mortality rates for persons aged 15–19, 20–24, and 25–29 decreased. The rates for persons aged 30–34, 35–39, 40–44, 45–49, 50–54, 55–59, and 60–64 decreased. The rates remained stable for children (aged less than 13 years) and persons aged 13–14, 15–19, 50–54, 60–64, and 65 and older. In 2011, the highest rate was for persons aged 20–24 years (36.4), followed by persons aged 25–29 years (35.2).

Suicide

We earlier noted that suicide is the eighth-leading cause of death in the general U.S. population (see Table 6.13). But this too varies by group and geographically.

- Suicide was the 10th-leading cause of death for all ages in 2010.
- There were 38,364 suicides in 2010 in the United States—an average of 105 each day.

- Based on data about suicides in 16 National Violent Death Reporting System states in 2009, 33.3 percent of suicide decedents tested positive for alcohol, 23 percent for antidepressants, and 20.8 percent for opiates, including heroin and prescription painkillers.
- Suicide results in an estimated $34.6 billion in combined medical and work loss costs.

Gender Disparities

- Suicide among males is four times higher than among females and represents 79 percent of all U.S. suicides.
- Females are more likely than males to have had suicidal thoughts.
- Firearms are the most commonly used method of suicide among males (56 percent).
- Poisoning is the most common method of suicide for females (37.4 percent).

Nonfatal Suicidal Thoughts and Behavior

Among adults aged ≥18 years in the United States during 2008–2009:

- An estimated 8.3 million adults (3.7 percent of the adult U.S. population) reported having suicidal thoughts in the past year.
- An estimated 2.2 million adults (1.0 percent of the adult U.S. population) reported having made suicide plans in the past year.
- An estimated 1 million adults (0.5 percent of the U.S. adult population) reported making a suicide attempt in the past year.
- There is one suicide for every 25 attempted suicides.
- Among young adults ages 15 to 24 years old, there are approximately 100–200 attempts for every completed suicide.
- In a 2011 nationally representative sample of youth in grades 9–12: 15.8 percent of students reported that they had seriously considered attempting suicide during the 12 months preceding the survey.

Native American and Hispanic Populations

- Among American Indians/Alaska Natives aged 15 to 34 years, suicide is the second-leading cause of death.
- The suicide rate among American Indian/Alaska Native adolescents and young adults ages 15 to 34 (31 per 100,000) is 2.5 times higher than the national average for that age group (12.2 per 100,000).
- Of students in grades 9–12, significantly more Hispanic female students (13.5 percent) reported attempting suicide in the last year than black, non-Hispanic female students (8.8 percent) and white, non-Hispanic female students (7.9 percent).

Mortality Decline: An Overview

The twentieth century saw a considerable reduction in the mortality levels of the U.S. population. This aspect of our demographic transition has been well documented, although no simple answers exist to the questions of why and how this change came

Box 6.2   HIV/AIDS: U.S. Profile

Source: Centers for Disease Control and Prevention. *HIV Surveillance Report, 2011*; vol. 23, Published February 2013.

Table 6.12.   AIDS/HIV-Related Deaths, United States, 2008-2010

Age Group	2008	2009	2010
13–14	0.0	3.0	2.0
15–19	48.0	31.0	34.0
20–24	182.0	184.0	169.0
25–29	518.0	484.0	364.0
30–34	858.0	801.0	672.0
35–39	1659.0	1407.0	1058.0
40–44	2845.0	2400.0	1861.0
45–49	3423.0	3222.0	2762.0
50–54	3233.0	3093.0	2749.0
55–59	2379.0	2414.0	2214.0
60–64	1369.0	1421.0	1428.0
65.0+	1435.0	1602.0	1439.0
Ethnicity			
European American	5307.0	5039.0	4556.0
African American	9241.0	8384.0	7195.0
Hispanic	2719.0	2602.0	2254.0
Others	684.0	1020.0	748.0

Source: Centers for Disease Control and Prevention. HIV Surveillance Report, 2011, vol. 23, Table 11a, http://www
.cdc.gov/hiv/library/reports/surveillance. Published February 2013. Retrieved March 5, 2015.

The following discussion presents a profile of the incidence of HIV/AIDS and AIDS-related deaths in the United States. The relevant data from the CDC highlight the differences between racial and ethnic groups, ages of those affected, transmission category, and sex. Although rates are well below the levels of the 1960s and 1970s, they remain high and/or increasing for several groups. The period covered in all of the statistical categories reported here is 2008 to 2010.

Age Group

The following table shows changes in the incidence rate (per 100,000 population):

Changes in HIV Rates by Age Group

Age	Change in HIV Rate	Age	Change in HIV Rate
< 13	Stable	40–44	Decrease
13–14	Stable	45–49	Decrease
15–19	Stable	50–54	Stable
20–24	Decrease*	55–59	Decrease
25–29	Decrease**	60–64	Decrease
30–34	Decrease	65 and above	Stable
35–39	Decrease		

*Highest rate: 36.4
** Second highest rate: 35.2

Race/Ethnicity

Between 2009 and 2010, the rate for Asian Americans increased, as did the rates for blacks/African Americans, Hispanics/Latinos, Native Hawaiians/other Pacific Islanders, and persons of multiple origins. Rates for Alaska Natives and whites remained stable.

HIV Incidence Rates by Racial and Ethnic Groups, 2011

Group	Incidence rate (per 100,000 Population)
Black/African American	60.4
Hispanic/Latino	19.5
Native Hawaiian/Other Pacific Islanders	15.3
Multiple Races	14.2
American Indians/Alaska Natives	9.3
Whites	7.0
Asian Americans	6.5

(Data for Native Hawaiians/other Pacific Islanders should be interpreted with caution because numbers are small.)

Sex

The rate for females decreased and the rate for males remained stable. In 2011, males accounted for 79 percent of all diagnoses of HIV infection among adults and adolescents. The rate for adult and adolescent males was 30.8, and the rate for females was 7.7.

Transmission Category

Among adult and adolescent males, the annual number of diagnosed HIV infections attributed to male-to-male sexual contact increased. The numbers of infections attributed to injection drug use, to male-to-male sexual contact and injection drug use, and to heterosexual contact decreased. Among adult and adolescent females, the numbers of infections attributed to injection drug use and to heterosexual contact decreased. In 2011, diagnosed infections attributed to male-to-male sexual contact (65 percent, including male-to-male sexual contact and injection drug use) and those attributed to heterosexual contact (27 percent) accounted for approximately 92 percent of diagnosed HIV infections in the United States.

Region

The rates of diagnoses of HIV infection in the Northeast and the South decreased. The rates in the Midwest and the West remained stable. In 2011, rates were 20.9 in the South, 18.1 in the Northeast, 12.0 in the West, and 9.3 in the Midwest.

Stage 3 (AIDS)

The annual estimated number and the estimated rate of infections classified as stage 3 (AIDS) in the United States remained stable. In 2011, the estimated rate of infections classified as stage 3 (AIDS) was 10.3.

Age Group

The following table shows the changes in AIDS rates between 2008 and 2010, by age group.

Changes in AIDS Rates 2008-2010, by Age Group

Age	Change in AIDS Rate	Age	Change in AIDS Rate
< 13	Stable	40–44	Decrease*
13–14	Stable	45–49	Stable**
15–19	Increase	50–54	Stable
20–24	Increase	55–59	Stable
25–29	Increase	60–64	Decrease
30–34	Stable	65 and above	Increase
35–39	Decrease		

*Highest rate: 22.7
** Second highest rate: 22.5

Race/Ethnicity

Between 2008 and 2010, rates for Asians, Hispanics/Latinos, whites, and persons of multiple races decreased. The rates for American Indians/Alaska Natives, blacks/African Americans, and Native Hawaiians/other Pacific Islanders remained stable. AIDS rates for 2011 by race/ethnic group are shown below.

Group	AIDS Rate (per 100,000 Population)
Black/African American	41.6
Multiple Races	12.9
Hispanic/Latino	12.2
Native Hawaiian/Other Pacific Islanders	9.3
American Indians/Alaska Natives	6.4
Whites	4.2
Asian Americans	3.3

Sex

The rate for adult and adolescent females decreased and the rate for males remained stable. In 2011, adult and adolescent males accounted for 75 percent of all infections classified as stage 3 (AIDS) among adults and adolescents. The 2011 rate for males was 19.1; the 2011 rate for females was 6.0.

Transmission Category

The annual number of infections classified as stage 3 (AIDS) among adult and adolescent males with HIV infection attributed to male-to-male sexual contact increased. The numbers of stage 3 (AIDS) classifications among males with infection attributed to injection drug use, to male-to-male sexual contact and injection drug use, and to heterosexual contact decreased. The number of infections classified as stage 3 (AIDS) among adult and adolescent females with HIV infection attributed to injection drug use decreased; the number with infection attributed to heterosexual contact remained stable.

Region

The rates of infections classified as stage 3 (AIDS) in the Northeast and the West decreased. The rates in the Midwest and the South remained stable. The following table shows the 2011 rates of stage 3 (AIDS) by region.

Region	Rate
South	13.7
Northeast	12.3
West	7.5
Midwest	5.8

Deaths of Persons with Diagnosed HIV Infection

In the United States, the annual estimated number and rate of deaths of persons with diagnosed HIV infection remained stable. In 2010, the estimated rate of deaths of persons with diagnosed HIV infection was 6.3. Deaths of persons with diagnosed HIV infection may be due to any cause (i.e., may or may not be related to HIV infection).

Age Group

The following table indicates the changes (2008–2010) in death rates from AIDS, by age category.

Changes in Death Rates from AIDS, 2008-2010, by Age Group

Age	Change in Death Rate	Age	Change in Death Rate
< 13	Stable	40–44	Decrease
13–14	Stable	45–49	Stable
15–19	Stable	50–54	Decrease
20–24	Stable	55–59	Stable
25–29	Decrease	60–64	Increase
30–34	Decrease	65 and above	Increase
35–39	Decrease		

Race/Ethnicity

The rates of deaths for persons of multiple races increased. The rates of deaths for American Indians/Alaska Natives, Asians, blacks/African Americans, Hispanics/Latinos, and Native Hawaiians/other Pacific Islanders decreased. The rate of deaths for whites remained stable. In 2010, the highest rate of deaths was for black/African Americans: 25.0.

Sex and Transmission Category

The rates of deaths for adult and adolescent males and females decreased. The numbers of deaths among males with diagnosed HIV infection attributed to injection drug use and to heterosexual contact decreased. The numbers of deaths of males with infection attributed to male-to-male sexual contact, to male-to-male sexual contact and injection drug use, and to perinatal transmission remained stable. The numbers of deaths of adult and adolescent females with infection attributed to injection drug use and to perinatal transmission decreased. The number of deaths of females with infection attributed to heterosexual contact remained stable. (Trend data for persons with infection attributed to perinatal transmission should be interpreted with caution because numbers are small.)

Region

Between 2008 and 2010, the rates of death in the Midwest and the West decreased. The rates in the Northeast and the South remained stable.

Rates of Death from AIDS by Region, 2010

Region	Rate
Northeast	10.0
South	8.1
West	3.6
Midwest	2.7

Table 6.13. Suicide Rates by Age, United States, 2000–2010

Age Group	2000	2005	2010
Under 1 year	4.3	4.0	2.7
1-4	-	-	-
5-14	0.1	0.1	0.1
15-24	0.2	0.2	0.2
25-34	0.6	0.7	0.6
35-44	1.6	1.7	1.8
45-54	4.4	4.8	4.9
55-64	12.8	13.5	13.9
67-74	38.0	38.8	39.3
75-84	100.8	110.2	115.7
85+	277.8	313.1	333.8

Source: Sherry L. Murphy, Jiaquan Xu, and Kenneth D. Kochanek, Division of Vital Statistics. "Deaths: Final Data for 2010," *National Vital Statistics Reports* 61, no. 4 (May 8, 2013): Table 9, p. 34.

about. Rather, public-health specialists, historians, and demographers have identified several interrelated causes. In a summary of some of this research, Robert Hoekelman and Barry Pless (1988) have proposed four major trends that have contributed the most to bringing about mortality decline. These are:

1. At the turn of the twentieth century, a decline occurred in the death rates of persons under 25 years of age. This was largely the result of programs that that lowered death rates from infectious diseases. These measures included purification of water and proper sewage disposal.
2. A decline in infant and general death rates began in the 1940s, and it continues, at a slower pace, to the present (see Table 6.14). These changes were the result of advances and new applications of medical technology. Especially significant were the development of vaccines (polio, measles, mumps, etc.) and the introduction of whole blood and blood products, which significantly reduced deaths from blood loss and electrolyte imbalances.
3. Despite persisting socioeconomic inequalities, an overall reduction of poverty and improvement in SES has occurred since the early 1900s. This has led to improved nutrition, safer environments, and greater access to health services, all of which have resulted in the lowering of death rates.
4. Finally, between 1970 and the present, the lifestyles of many Americans have changed for the better, from a medical point of view. More people exercise regularly, fewer people smoke cigarettes, and more eat healthy, reduced-fat and low-cholesterol diets. These factors have contributed to lower incidence rates of the major cause of death, heart disease, and have noticeably prolonged life expectancies.

As one considers the history of mortality in our country, it becomes clear that a definite shift has occurred, not only in the steady declines observed in crude, age-specific, and group-specific death rates, but also in the major causes of death. Just a few generations ago, most Americans died of pneumonia, enteritis, early childhood diseases, and the like. Today, infant mortality claims only a small fraction of the population every year, and pneumonia and similar diseases are viewed as almost

Table 6.14. Infant Mortality Rates by Ethnic Group, United States, 1915-2008

Year	Total	European American	African American
1915	99.9		
1940	47.0		
1950	29.2	26.8	43.9
1960	26.0	22.9	44.3
1970	20.0	17.8	32.6
1980	12.6	11.0	21.4
1990	9.2	7.6	18.0
1996	7.3	6.1	14.7
1997	7.2	6.0	13.7
2000	6.9	5.7	13.6
2005	6.9	5.8	13.6
2008	6.6	5.5	12.7

Source: T. J. Mathews and Marian F. MacDorman, Division of Vital Statistics, "Infant Mortality Statistics From the 2008 Period Linked Birth/Infant Death Data Set," *National Vital Statistics Reports* 60, no. 5 (May 10, 2012).

entirely curable. In the place of these causes of death, we now face the stress and lifestyle related illness: heart disease, cancer, and strokes.

Moreover, in the past, any one of several causes was equally likely to prove fatal; whereas today, well over one-half of the deaths in the United States are related either to cardiovascular disease or to cancer. These two conditions accounted for 58 percent of all deaths in 1990; but in 1900, the *eight* leading causes combined were responsible for this same percentage. These changes provide a meaningful measure of how the nation has been transformed over the years and decades, from a rural society largely at the mercy of a host of communicable infections to an urbanized people vulnerable to the pressures of industrialization and its pathogenic byproducts.

GLOBAL MORTALITY PATTERNS: PAST AND PRESENT

This section focuses on the broad historical patterns of mortality change at the international level. Over the course of several generations, beginning as early as the eighteenth century in Europe, public-health measures and socioeconomic development succeeded in bringing about changes in the causes of mortality. Several of the known killers, especially infectious diseases, were brought under control by improvements, first in sanitation and later in medical technologies. This period and the elimination of the traditional causes of high mortality associated with it are referred to as the **epidemiological transition**. This is closely related to the concept of *demographic* transition.

Epidemiological Transition in Europe and America

The epidemiological transition, like its demographic counterpart, occurred in three stages. The first, and longest, stage encompasses most of human history. It was characterized by universally high general mortality rates and IMRs, most of which can be traced to infectious diseases. Throughout the world, human populations struggled to maintain positive growth in the face of ever-present death and disease. Moreover, this "normal" situation was frequently punctuated by periods of epidemics and **pandemics** (such as the Black Death of fourteenth-century Europe), during which entire families, villages, and towns were wiped out. The second stage, called "receding pandemic," saw a decrease in the prevalence of the diseases associated with the first stage. In Europe and North America, this shift occurred in the period between the middle of the nineteenth and the middle of the twentieth centuries. The third stage, in which the industrialized nations now find themselves, is characterized by a high rate of degenerative and human-induced diseases such as cancer.

Explanations of the epidemiological transition take account of technological as well as social structural changes. During the preagricultural era, some 10,000 years ago, the principal mode of sustenance was hunting and gathering. Small bands of humans roamed through the countryside and forests, exposed to physical hazards as well as to uncertainties in their sources and supplies of food. Life expectancy was short and infant mortality very high. Although the social organization of the band facilitated strong interaction and mutual support, a high proportion of the deaths were the result of physical threats.

With the advent of agriculture, human populations became less nomadic. More complex, hierarchical forms of social organization were created to control the production and distribution of agricultural produce. New systems of control over land and labor resources took shape, and the old social units based on primary and egalitarian relationships were subordinated to the state and other large-scale institutions. The density of these populations increased dramatically, which led to greater contact with strangers and heightened competition for space and resources, especially with groups outside the social and physical space of the community. High density also created closer residential living arrangements, urban growth and migration, and the sharing of communal resources.

The emergence of towns meant increased dependency on common sources of water supplies. Knowledge of public hygiene was poor to nonexistent, and efficient and adequate systems for the disposal public waste and garbage were unknown. These conditions increased the likelihood of the emergence and the spread of infectious diseases. At the societal level, urban growth and large-scale poverty, brought about by inequalities in the distribution of power and wealth, increased the susceptibility of most members of the population to the diseases and famines inadvertently engineered by people. This situation characterized the human condition for centuries.

In the late seventeenth century, a series of related developments occurred in Europe that radically altered the probabilities of mortality and morbidity. This second stage of the epidemiological transition came about because of improvements in standards of living and working conditions. One key element was the establishment of overseas colonies and empires by Portugal, Spain, Holland, France, and, especially, England. New channels were provided to facilitate the inflow of wealth to these nations. Combined with technological changes, these resources helped fuel a second agricultural revolution that raised the nutritional and living standard of people throughout the continent. The colonial system and the improvements in agriculture, in turn, combined to trigger the great Industrial Revolution of the 1750 era. With each innovation, the proportions of the poor decreased, as employment opportunities expanded and wealth flowed relatively freely—for the first time in recorded history (Rosenberg and Birzdell 1986; Babones 2011). Mortality decline during the 1750 era was, in part, the result of increasing prosperity and improvements in nutrition (McKeown and Brown 1955). The Industrial Revolution was paralleled by many social revolutions, including the American Revolution, the emergence of democratic states, the French Revolution, and the foundation of social welfare (see Sen 1981). The expansion of welfare programs insulated the very poor from mass starvation and hunger. As rates of poverty fell, the prevalence of diseases decreased and the health of the populations improved considerably. In England, the production and distribution of more and higher qualities of food helped to reduce death rates, accompanied by further gains resulting from the control of waterborne diseases. In many parts of Europe and in North America during the later part of the nineteenth century, great strides were made in the public provision of potable water and sanitary systems. These public-health measures succeeded in further reducing mortality levels (Szreter 1988; Harper, Lynch, and Smith 2011).

Improvements in the standard of living continued into the third stage of the transition, beginning in about 1850. Technological refinements in public-health methods for fighting specific diseases were discovered and implemented. This was followed by discoveries of vaccines and antibiotics, and by vastly more effective methods of water treatment. Thus, through the late nineteenth and early twentieth centuries, and to the present, IMRs fell throughout Europe and in the United States. Scientific developments and the diffusion of mortality-control knowledge and technology characterize this later stage of the epidemiological transition. As a residue, so to speak, the major causes of death in these countries are diseases of advanced age and sedentary life styles: the "benefits" of living in a highly industrialized society.

With improvement in life expectancies and the process of modernization, we have thus entered the "age of degenerative and manmade diseases." Several structural factors, such as social-welfare activism, development of community sanitation, public-health education, and improvements in housing conditions continue to play a key role in prolonging the lives of the younger and the middle-aged segments of our populations. Now that average life expectancies are well over 70 years, chronic diseases claim a high proportion of lives.

Recently, demographers have suggested that we are seeing the advent of a second European demographic transition. Associated with this are declines in birthrates below replacement levels, small families, and growing numbers of unmarried persons. This trend, in combination with the aging of the population in the developed (and in the less-developed) world, has led to speculation about a fourth stage of the epidemiological transition. This stage is termed "the age of delayed degenerative diseases." It is, or would be, characterized by a large and growing proportion of persons over the age of 80, whose increased longevity puts them at an ever-increasing risk of degenerative diseases.

Transition in the Less-Industrialized Countries

Today's less-industrialized nations began their transition to the second stage approximately 200 years after Europe began its transition. These nations, located in Asia, Africa, and Latin America, did not benefit as Europe did from the colonial system and the subsequent agricultural and industrial revolutions. In fact, resources extracted *from* these areas helped to fuel the profound changes in Europe that eventuated in mortality decline. As a result, until well into the twentieth century, infectious diseases, epidemics, malnutrition, and infestation with parasites continued to claim the lives of infants and children at rates well over 100 per 1,000 live births.

When public-health technologies and modern medical practices did come to developing countries, slowly in the World War I period and with great rapidity after World War II, their impact was phenomenal. Reductions in general and infant death rates that occurred over the course of a century or more in Europe took just a few decades in the less-developed countries. For not only did the older methods of mortality control, such as swamp drainage and pest control, diffuse from the industrialized world, so too did penicillin, the polio vaccine, and a range of technologies that were developed very late in Europe's second stage. As a result of receiving this "complete package" of weapons to fight death and illness, mortality levels began to decline quickly and sharply, and the trend continues to this day.

In addition to the timing, there are several other differences between the manner in which today's more- and less-developed countries experienced the transition. One difference is that the causes and levels of mortality are far more varied in developing countries than they were in Europe. Many countries in Africa and Asia that are at the same level of socioeconomic development have quite different death rates. According to the PRB (1997), Mali and Nigeria both have very low per-capita GNPs, $250 and $260, respectively. However, Mali's IMR is more than twice that of Nigeria, 138 for the former and 68 for the latter.

Equally noteworthy is the variation between developing countries in the rate of transition. In the former British Colony of Hong Kong, for example, the death rate fell from 10.7 per thousand in 1940 to 5.0 in 1990, nearly a 50 percent reduction in 51 years. However, the colony's mortality rates from heart and degenerative diseases dramatically increased during this period: a sure sign of modernization.

The emergence in Asia, Africa, and Latin America of diseases such as HIV is an unprecedented event that has no counterpart during the epidemiological transition in Europe. Although AIDS/HIV now occurs throughout the world, its prevalence is by far the highest in the least-developed countries, especially in Africa. The cumulative number of cases in the world reported at the beginning of 1994 was about 17.2 million (Bongaarts 1996). Three million of these resulted in AIDS-related deaths before 1995. More than one-half of those infected who were alive at the end of 1994, 9.7 million cases, were in sub-Saharan Africa.

SUMMARY

The list of "Fifty Facts" about mortality that appeared in the United Nations' *World Health Report* provides a complex summary of what is, after all, a complex reality. It would certainly be impossible to say, in a word, if the picture of mortality that emerges from this chapter or from documents such as the "Fifty Facts" is one of optimism or of pessimism. Without question, mortality levels for the world and for virtually all regions and countries have never been lower. At the same time, the modern lifestyle has claimed millions of lives in the industrialized countries, and it is beginning to take its toll in developing countries. Suicide, HIV/AIDS, and lung cancer are frightening, fatal diseases of industrial society that are preventable but not yet prevented. Yet, more infants survive to adulthood today than could have been imagined by people just a few generations ago. A complex reality it is.

In an ironic way, part of the difficulty we have in easily comprehending the variations and impacts of mortality stems from our improved ability to track and measure the phenomenon. As we saw in the earlier sections of this chapter, there are several ways in which we can indicate the frequency and nature of the occurrence of death. And each way tells a slightly different story. Crude rates are just that, crude. Often they hide more than they reveal. Age and cause-specific rates allow us to focus on the details of the force of mortality, but such attention to detail can obscure the larger picture. IMRs and average life expectancy are quite different, in that the former measures death among only one age category and the latter takes account of deaths at every age. Yet, they are highly correlated with one another and both are highly accurate indicators of the levels of a population's wealth, health, and education.

With this introduction to the methods and facts of mortality analysis, we have now examined both of the vital events, or components, that make up natural increase. The symbol and formula for natural increase, $NI = B - D$, indicate the number of births minus the number of deaths that occur in a population during a year or another period. Under ordinary circumstances, natural increase plays the greatest role in determining how a population grows. The knowledge that you now have acquired about the forces of natality and mortality should help you to appreciate all of concepts, principles, and mechanisms that lie behind this simple-looking equation. Thus, we return to the topic of mortality when we observe how exactly birth and death do interact to create natural increase. First, however, we will take a closer look at the other two components that determine population growth, in-migration and out-migration. Although also counted as vital events, the two types of migration present some special challenges to demographers, both methodologically and in relation to their actual operation in society.

KEY TERMS

age-specific death rate (ASDR)
age-specific mortality
cause-specific mortality
central crude death rate
child mortality rate (CMR)
epidemiological transition
fetal mortality
incidence

infant mortality rate (IMR)
morbidity
natural increase
neonatal mortality rate (NMR)
pandemic
prevalence
"stroke belt"

NOTES

1. The website for Morbidity and Mortality Weekly Reports is http://www.cdc.gov/mmwr/index2015.html.

2. As in the case of births, in the United States deaths are registered at the local and state levels and then the data are transmitted to the NCHS in accord with the Federal-State Cooperative data-sharing program.

3. The latest revision ICD-10-CM was effective from October 1, 2015.

4. See http://www.cdc.gov/nchs/icd/icd10cm.htm#icd2014.

5. Another measure used is the incidence *ratio*, R. This indicates the number of persons who have contracted the disease during the year (etc.) compared to those who remain at risk. Here the denominator is not the total population size but the total population size minus

all members already affected. Thus, the denominator accounts for prevalence by subtracting the number already affected from the population size. This relationship makes it possible to express the incidence rate, I, in terms of the prevalence proportion, P, and the incidence ratio, R, as:

$$I = R \times (1-P)$$

6. A life table is a statistical model that describes the mortality experiences of a population, cohort by cohort. It presents the "life history" of a hypothetical birth cohort as it experiences depletion by death. We postpone further technical discussion until Chapter 9.

7. Data in this section are from NCHS *Vital Statistics Annual Report* reproduced in *Statistical Abstract of the United States, 1997*: Tables 125, 131, and 139.

8. Updated information on causes of death can be obtained directly from the Department of Health and Human Services (HHS) web site at http://www.hhs.gov (accessed November 20, 1998).

9. Fred Hutchison Research Center, "Cancer in our Communities," http://www.fhcrc .org/en/events/cancer-in-our-communities/african-americans-and-cancer.html.

CHAPTER
SEVEN

MIGRATION
Geographic and Social Psychological Components

Y ou probably do not need to be reminded that ours is a highly mobile society. Most employed people commute daily. Business and pleasure trips keep our airlines busy and our highways jammed. With easy access to cars, trains, and airplanes, it is now possible to travel often and widely, and to interact with people located very far from home.[1] With very few exceptions, Americans leave the home of their parents and establish a separate household when they graduate from college or get married. In fact, it is likely that a person of college age living in the United States today has already moved residences, across town or across the country, at least twice since birth. And the proportion of students who commute to campus from their family's home or their own house or apartment has been increasing steadily for decades.

Among all of these various movements, demographers are especially interested in certain types referred to as **in-migration** and **out-migration.** These involve the relocation of a person's residence from an area occupied by one population or subpopulation (called the "sender" population or "population of origin") to the area of another (the "receiver" population or "population of destination"; see McFalls 1998:16–17). Migration in this sense is viewed as an especially important type of movement, in two respects. From the purely demographic point of view, migration (in- and out- combined) is a component of change that, together with natural increase, determines the magnitude and rate of population growth. From a more sociological perspective, migration is significant because residential relocation brings about new activities and terminates old ones, with subsequent social and economic impacts at both the destination and the origin.

Several different forms of migration have been identified. At times, isolated individuals undertake such moves. Far more often, however, migration itself is a group activity, one that includes family members, neighbors, friends, and members of particular religious and ethnic groups. Migration may be temporary, long term, or permanent. At times, the move from a population of origin to a destination is temporary, because it is understood (by the migrants themselves) to be merely one link in a chain of migratory events. In such cases, the first destination becomes "home" only for a brief period, after which a new, second destination is reached, and so forth—thus the term "chain migration."

Demographers and other social scientists have identified myriad reasons for these moves, individual and group, permanent and temporary, single-step and chain-like. One of the most important ways of grouping these reasons is into the categories *voluntary* and **involuntary migration** (although most actual cases probably represent a mixture of the two extremes). Voluntary migration is undertaken willfully and with forethought. Migration is strictly involuntary, or "forced," if the decision to migrate is made by others, contrary to the will of the migrants; or if it is the result of external forces such as natural disasters.

This chapter presents the basic concepts and methods employed in understanding and measuring these various kinds of migration. The discussion includes consideration of:

1. Internal migration. These are movements between subpopulations within a larger population, such as between states within the United States.
2. Immigration. This refers to movements from one general population to another, such as from one country to another.
3. **Forced migration**, as discussed above.

These are the types of migratory activity that have been subject to the greatest share of rigorous demographic analysis and scrutiny.

There is another kind of population movement that has generally been neglected in population studies: tourism. To extend the reasoning behind the definition given above, if significant economic and social impacts of a population movement demand special attention, then tourism should also be considered a form of migration, or "near migration." The tourism industry is enormous, and it is expanding rapidly. Directly and indirectly, this "movement of people through space" generates employment for millions of workers throughout the world. Despite that fact that it is usually not associated with a permanent change of residence, tourism cannot be entirely ignored. Based on this reasoning, the topic of tourism is discussed in detail in Chapter 14.

With this noted, the following pages provide a discussion of each of the other three major types of migration, first in definitional terms and then in relation to its occurrence today and in the past. In each case, the descriptive sections are followed by a review of pertinent theories. These theories have been developed by social scientists to provide answers to key questions that take account of the analytical foundations (definitions) and knowledge of the facts (occurrence) of migration: Why do forced migrations occur? What factors influence internal migration? Why do people immigrate?

MEASURING MIGRATION

Although we can readily conceive of migration as a more-or-less permanent movement from one population (or subpopulation) to another, no universally accepted, technically adequate definition of the term exists. The United Nations has come closest to setting such a standard in defining a migrant as someone who has moved her or his residence from one geographic region to another for a period of at least one year. Nevertheless, among the four components of population growth, in- and out-migration are the least precisely observed and recorded.

In order to be understood effectively, the several aspects of migration that are of interest to researchers and policy makers must be clearly defined. Once this is achieved, relatively accurate measurement is possible. Scientists refer to this process of formulating definitions for the purposes of measurement as **operationalization**. Operationalization is essential in every branch of science; and, because of the special problems just noted, it is crucial in the study of migration.

Some Operational Definitions

Demographers generally distinguish between three levels of population movement, depending on the distance, or more properly the social distance, traversed.[2] The lowest level is a *move*, and it refers to a change of residence within a specific, regionally defined subpopulation. Examples of moves include changes of residence within the same block, neighborhood, suburb, and city or—in the United States—within the same county. In contrast, a move from one area associated with a particular regional subpopulation to another, but within a general population's territory, is referred to as *internal migration*. Examples include changes in residence from state to state, province to province, or city to city within a particular country. Finally, movement that involves crossing an official international frontier (from one recognized nation to another) is *international migration*. In this last case, we refer to two types of migrants, depending on the population at which the event is observed: **emigrants,** who move out a country of origin, and **immigrants**, who move into a country of destination.[3]

Other concepts used in the study of migration and their definitions are given below. As indicated, these definitions are intended to aid in the measurement of various aspects of population movements.

In-Migration

This is the movement of people into the territory occupied by a specific population or subpopulation for the purpose of residential relocation. The size of in-migration flows, symbolized as "I," is measured by counting the individuals who newly enter a geographic region for the purpose of changing residence, during a given interval of time (e.g., one year).

Out-Migration

This is the movement of people out of the territory occupied by a specific population or subpopulation for the purpose of residential relocation. In a manner similar to the case of in-migration, the size of out-migration flows, or "O," is measured by counting the number of individuals who depart from a region during a year or other interval.

Net Migration

Net Migration is the difference between the number of in-migrants and the number of out-migrants experienced by a population during a given interval of time (e.g., one year).

Gross Migration

This is the sum total of all in-migrations and out-migrations experienced by a population during a given interval of time. This total number of migrants is also referred to as the *volume* of migration in the geographic region of interest.

The risk of a migratory event is the probability that a member of a specific population will migrate during a year (or other interval of time). As in the case of mortality and birth, these are measured by rates, as follows.

1. In-migration rate = $(I/P) \times 1{,}000$
2. Out-migration rate = $(O/P) \times 1{,}000$
3. Net migration rate = $[(I - O)/P] \times 1{,}000$
4. Gross Migration rate = $[(I + O)/P] \times 1{,}000$

where "P" stands for the population size at midyear.

These migration rates are presented in crude form; that is, they refer to all members of a population regardless of structural characteristics. However, like fertility and mortality rates, they can be obtained for specific groups: males or females, members of given cohorts, members of various ethnic groups, social classes, and so forth. In this case, the events observed in the numerator refer to the group of interest; and the reference aggregate, the denominator, is the midyear size of that group. For example, gender-specific and age-specific in-migration rates are represented by formulas such as these:

Rate of in-migration for males = $(I_m/P_m) \times 1{,}000$
Rate of in-migration for females = $(I_f/P_f) \times 1{,}000$
Rate of in-migration for persons aged 20 to 29 years = $(I_{20-29}/P_{20-29}) \times 1{,}000$

Here, "m" represents males, "f" represents females, and "20–29" stands for that age category.

Measurement Problems and Estimation Methods

The data needed to identify migrants are not as readily available as is information about births and deaths. Many countries, including the United States, have no legal requirements to report either short- or longer-distance permanent moves from one's current place of residence. In these cases, there is no direct method to account for internal migration. All measurements thus provide indirect estimates, using data obtained from census reports.

Most national censuses ask two questions pertinent to the estimation of internal migration flows: (a) where were you born and (b) where did you live five years ago? If someone's place of residence five years ago differs from the place at which enumeration occurs, the person is identified as a migrant. A person born at a place different from that at which he or she is enumerated is considered to be a lifetime migrant. It is obvious that this method underestimates the volume of migration, as people can make several moves during the five years prior to the date of enumeration.

The simplest and most commonly employed way of estimating a population's net international migration rate between two census counts is the balancing equation method. According to the fundamental equation of demography, introduced in Chapter 1, growth (G) is defined as the number of individuals added to—or subtracted from—a population between an initial date (year 0) and a terminal date (year t). This is represented by the equation:

$$G = P_t - P_0 = (B - D) + (I - O)$$

Recall that (B – D) is the amount of natural increase that occurs between the two dates, or NI; and net migration between the dates is the difference between I and O.

Several years ago, U.S. Census demographers Henry Shryock and Jacob Siegel (1976) provided a classic illustration of the balancing equation method, using the case of Sri Lanka between 1963 and 1971. The problem was to determine the extent to which immigration and emigration were contributing to the overall (very rapid) growth of this small country's population. Here is a slightly revised version of that illustration.

1. Year 0 = 1963 and year t = 1971 (that is, the time interval of interest is 8 years).
2. The size of Sri Lanka's population in 1963, P_0 = 10,578,314.
3. The population size in 1971, P_t = 12,570,143.
4. Growth in the 8-year interval, G = (12,570,143 – 10,578,314) = 1,991,829.
5. The registered number of births in the 8-year interval, B = 3,069,360.
6. The registered number of deaths in the interval, D = 778,062.
7. Natural increase, NI = (B – D) = (3,069,360 – 778,062) = 2,291,298.
8. Therefore, net migration (I – O) = (G – NI) = (1,991,829 – 2,291,298) = –299,469.

The minus sign for net migration indicates that out-migration exceeded in-migration for this interval.

However, because this figure for net migration is just an estimate, we do not know how many persons actually immigrated and how many emigrated; that is, we have no information about the actual volume of migration. All we do know with this and related methods is that out-migrants exceeded in-migrants by 300,000. We cannot determine whether this was the result of 300,000 departures and no arrivals, 900,000 departures and 600,000 arrivals, 1 million departures and 700,000 arrivals, or some other combination.

INTERNAL POPULATION SHIFTS IN THE UNITED STATES

Internal migration involves the movement of people between specific territorially based subpopulations of a larger, general population. This is usually operationalized as a permanent change of residence from one administrative unit (a state, city, or county) to another within a nation-state. For example, within the developing countries, internal migration is mostly rural to urban, and its intensity has been highest in recent decades. As a result, urban growth rates there are the highest in the world (as discussed in Chapter 4). A majority of these rural to urban migrants are male, but there is wide variation in their age composition. For example, toward the end of the twentieth century 70 percent of the migrants in South Africa and Kenya were aged 15 to 24. However, in Tanzania and Senegal, a high percentage of the migrants have been children below 15 years of age. Poor rural infrastructure, low productivity of the farming sector, depletion of arable lands, and an education with an urban bias have contributed to these migration streams.

If the origin and destination of such a movement is within city boundaries—for instance, between neighborhoods, it is referred to as *intracity* move; whereas it is called *intercity* migration if the origin is one city and the destination another. These are the most common types of migration within the United States, whereby people can be expected to change residence approximately every seven years, or about 11 times during their lifetime. Thus, between 1996 and 1997, 13 percent of the population experienced either intra- or intercity migration (Long 1988; Gober 1993; McFalls 1998; Wolf and Longino 2005; Iceland and Scopilliti 2008; Frey 1998a, b). Although such movements can have important consequences at both origin and destination,[4] a third type of internal migration, namely interregional migration, may be even more significant.

The Great Migration

For historians of the U.S. population, the phrase "The Great Migration" is used to refer to one such highly consequential episode of interregional migration. This shift entailed the mass movement of African Americans, many of them children or grandchildren of slaves, from the southern and eastern to the northern and western states. It began at about the middle of the second decade of the twentieth century (the year 1916 is widely accepted as the formal start). Table 7.1 presents 1920 Census data on the distribution of the African American population (then referred to as "Negroes") by place of birth and region of residence at the time of enumeration.

At that time, nearly 343,000 eastern-born individuals in this group were living west of the Mississippi River. However, indicative of the major momentum of the movement, the number of southern-born, African-background persons residing in the North was more than twice as high, approximately 737,000. These figures illustrate that migratory movements are seldom unidirectional. The origins and destinations (of which there are ordinarily several) are somewhat like the poles of a magnet. They tend to repel each other and, as a result, migratory streams develop. The counter streams, as represented by the western-born individuals living east of Mississippi and those born in the North but living in the South at the time of enumeration, are quite small. Amidst all of the mobility, clearly, the strongest flow was from south to north.

Between 1910 and 1920, 13 states had a decrease in the number of African Americans, with Mississippi experiencing the largest absolute loss of about 75,000 persons. Georgia, which prior to the great migration had the largest African American population in the nation, experienced a decrease of 11 percent during the 1920s (Johnson and Campbell 1981). Nearly one-half of the migrants from the South came from three states: Alabama, Virginia, and Georgia. Five southern cities with large

Table 7.1. Summary of Results of Migration of the African American Population, East and West, and North and South, 1920

Region of birth	Number at enumeration	Net Gain/Loss region of enumeration
East	West	342,931 + 246,821
West	East	96,110 − 246,821
North	South	44,536 − 692,887
South	North	737,423 + 692,887

Note: The cumulative effects of interdivisional migration may be determined from data on state of birth as well.

Source: U.S. Bureau of the Census, *Population*, vol. 1: *General Report, Statistics by Subject, 1930* (adapted from Johnson and Campbell 1981:75).

African American communities (that is, 10,000 or more persons at the 1930 Census) experienced decreases: Louisville, Kentucky; Nashville, Tennessee; and Jackson, Vicksburg, and Meridian, Mississippi.

The most common destination in the North was Pennsylvania, where the African American population increased by more than 90,000 between 1910 and 1920. The next most-common northern destination states were Ohio, Illinois, Michigan, and New York. Between 1910 and 1920, the three cities that ranked highest in terms of relative increase in the size of their African American populations were Gary, Indiana; Akron, Ohio; and Detroit, Michigan.

A Reversal of Trends in the Late Twentieth Century

The Great Migration took place nearly 60 years after the U.S. Civil War of 1861–1865. Sixty years after the Great Migration, during the late 1970s and the 1980s, another interesting pattern of migration unfolded. Demographers consider it to be important not only because of its magnitude (several million people were involved) but also because its pattern represented a reversal of the direction of population flows that occurred prior to and during the Great Migration and throughout the subsequent several decades.

This recent movement was characterized by two separate but related trends. One, a large-scale migration from states in the northeastern and north central regions (the major receivers during the 1910–1920 era) to the southern and far-western states, continued—at a decelerating pace—into the 1990s. The other, consisting of moderate-sized flows from major metropolitan areas to "exurban" (that is, beyond the suburbs) and rural areas, more or less slowed to a halt in about 1990. The former trend, because much of it involved relocation of households from colder to warmer regions (especially California and Florida) came to be referred to as the "Snowbelt to Sunbelt" migration. The latter, which reflected the first declines in the U.S. urban population since the first census of 1790, has been called the "**rural renaissance**."

Table 7.2 shows the amount of net migration experienced by the four major regions of the United States during 1990–2004. The losses by the northeastern and mid-western states resulted in gains by the West and South. Approximately 86 percent of those who moved from the mid-western and northeastern states between 2000 and 2004 moved to the South. In the 1980s, states with the highest rates of growth in the nation were all in the Sunbelt: Arizona, Florida, Hawaii, Nevada, New Mexico, Texas, and California (which, although virtually saturated from large volumes of in-migration during earlier decades, continued to be a net receiver). In 2012, the top 10 states with large number of in-migrants were California, Missouri, Wyoming, South Dakota, Oklahoma, Texas, Oregon, Colorado, Arizona, and Nevada.[5] However, Cooke (2013) suggests that internal migration rates have declined considerably in the United States during the last decade. In 2006, 6.4 percent of the population moved between counties. But by 2006—annual intercounty migration rates had already declined to 4.7 percent, and by 2010 to 3.5 percent. Three factors have contributed to this decline: decreasing real income stemming from the financial crisis of the last decade, increase in dual-worker couples, and the growth of information and communication technologies.

In the 1990s, the booming metropolitan areas of Dallas-Fort Worth, Texas; Atlanta, Georgia; and Miami, Florida, began to attract African American migrants, especially between 1990 and 1996. With a high proportion of this group originating in the Northeast and Midwest, we see in these shifts signs of a reversal of The Great

Table 7.2. Net Migration (+ or -) for U.S. Regions, in Thousands, 1990-2000 and 2000-2004

Period	Northeast	Midwest	South	West
1990–2000	−314,457	−73,009	380,109	7,356
2000–2004	−246,816	−161,198	352,793	55,221

Source: U.S. Census Bureau, Population Estimates Program, 2004; compiled from Table 1 from Marc J. Perry, "Domestic Net Migration in the United States: 2000 to 2004," U.S. Census Bureau Current Population Reports, April 2006.

Migration (Frey 1998a, b; Haubert and Fussell 2006). Just as industrialization in the North served as a pull factor for African American migrants during the earlier part of the twentieth century, industrial growth during the last few decades of the century in Atlanta, Dallas-Fort Worth, and other southern metropolitan centers had a similar effect. In addition, like other Americans, members of this group expressed their preference for a warmer climate—if employment, housing, and other opportunities were comparable. Census estimates in 2013 indicate that the metropolitan areas experienced population growth, totaling about 2.3 million during 2012–2013. Regions benefiting from an energy boom or influx of retirees continue to record the steepest population gains. But other metropolitan areas without these advantages also gained in population principally because of immigration.[6]

Table 7.3 provides information on the numbers and percentages of persons in the older cohorts in two regions: the Northeast, a major sender region, and the South, a major receiver. Whereas the percentages of persons in the elderly cohorts are close to being equal across regions, the *number* of elderly persons in each cohort is greater in the South. Here we see clear evidence of how vital processes, in this case aging and migration, impact upon one another to affect the quality of the general population. The Snowbelt segment is smaller in absolute terms, declining in size, and old but getting younger. In contrast, the large and growing Sunbelt segment is young but becoming older.

The other aspect of the current migration flow, the rural renaissance, illustrates an even more dramatic case of demographic reversal (see Table 7.4). For a very long time, in the United States and in populations throughout the world, the general direction of migration flows has been from rural to urban areas. As we discussed in Chapter 4, this trend is closely associated with what Kingsley Davis first labeled "the urbanization of the human population." However, because of apparent demographic

Table 7.3 Numbers and Percentages in Elderly Cohorts for Two Regions, 2010

Age	Northeast		South	
	Number of Persons	Percentage of Total Population	Number of Persons	Percentage of Total Population
65–84	6,605,131	11.9	13,072,003	11.4
85+	1,199,702	2.2	1,821,982	1.6
65+	7,804,833	14.1	14,893,985	13.0

Source: U.S. Census Bureau, 2010 Census Summary File 1; compiled from Table 2 from Carrie A. Werner, "The Older Population: 2010," 2010 Census Briefs, November 2011.

Table 7.4. Migration between Nonmetropolitan Territory and Metropolitan Areas 1975-1990, 1985-1990, and 1995-2000

Flow	1975-1990	1985-1990	1995-2000
Metropolitan to Nonmetropolitan	6,618,849	6,020,438	6,166,532
Nonmetropolitan to Metropolitan	5,622077	5,969,024	5,656,044
Net Migration to Nonmetropolitan Territory	996,072	51,414	510,488

Source: U.S. Census Bureau, Decennial Censuses 1980, 1990, 2000.

saturation of the urban areas (there was simply no further room for expansion "near" the large cities)—and the associated decline in the advantages of centrality resulting from innovations in transportation and communication technology—this trend has been reversed. This was first substantiated for the United States during the 1970s, but it appears to be occurring in other highly urbanized populations as well.

THEORIES OF INTERNAL MIGRATION

In this section, we look more closely at the reasons why people migrate. We can already discern from the preceding discussion and examples that migration is largely a collective process. People move because employment or retirement opportunities for those in particular age categories are better in a new locale than they are at the place where they presently reside. Or they migrate because their ethnic group is discriminated against at home whereas the prospects for more equitable treatment are better elsewhere. Often, the decision to migrate is simply a matter of joining a relative who has already left home for "greener pastures." In this respect, it is appropriate and common to treat migration as a sociodemographic phenomenon, as we have done so far: a macroscopic shift in the geographic distribution of populations and subpopulations.

As useful as this approach may be, it is nevertheless a very partial and incomplete perspective. As indicated in the title of this chapter, migration is in fact both a demographic and a social-*psychological* phenomenon. This means that people do not simply follow economic and political trends, or follow one another for that matter, in an essentially mindless fashion as they relocate themselves and their families. Instead, the decision to migrate is ordinarily exactly that, a decision; one that is arrived at through deliberation, discussion, and no small amount of agony. Some of this deliberation is based on careful rational calculation of costs and benefits and, as is true of other kinds of human decision making, some of it involves emotions, wishes, fears, and fantasies.

Ravenstein's "Laws"

Perhaps the earliest scientific theory of migration was that proposed by the English geography professor E. Ravenstein (1889) and later updated by Edward M. Lee—see below. This is the theory that was first to suggest that migration is a **"push-pull" process.** It has been tested in various research sites throughout the world, with the result that its basic postulates still stand. Several of the more recent theories of migration are in fact respecifications of Ravenstein's, altered through the modification of some assumptions and the addition of new variables. Ravestein's laws can be summarized in five statements:

1. The major reason people migrate is economics: they seek better job and financial opportunities at a place different from their current residence.
2. The volume of migration, that is the number of persons who migrate, decreases as distance increases. Ravenstein predicted (correctly) that the distance over which people migrate and the volume of migration would increase with improvements in transportation technology.
3. Migration from origin to destination is rarely accomplished in one move. Rather, it typically occurs in several stages. For example, people might move from a rural area to a small town, from a small town to a larger town, and finally to a city. This has come to be known as "chain" migration, as noted earlier.
4. The risk of migration is not the same for all persons. It varies by demographic and social characteristics such as age, sex, literacy, and rural or urban place of residence.
5. Population movements are not unilateral. For every major stream of migration there is a minor counter stream in the opposite direction. Thus, large-scale movements, such as we saw in the case of the Great Migration in the United States, are bilateral or multilateral.

The Economic Opportunity Model

Several years ago, L. A. Sjaastad (1962) proposed a now widely used model based on the assumption that migration takes place in response to economic opportunities. This model is founded on neoclassical economic theory (later adapted by James Coleman and other sociologists as the "rational choice" theory), which assumes that individuals act rationally with the objective of utility maximization. Sjaastad believed that migration is especially strongly motivated by such economic incentives.

According to this model, the act of migrating has positive benefits if the difference between profits gained from migration (pm) and the cost of moving (cm) is positive: that is, if $pm-cm > 0$. Such a situation makes migration a likely prospect. Conversely, a move is unlikely to occur if $pm-cm < 0$. As in most models, benefits may be psychic as well as purely monetary. In addition, benefits may be realized either in the short term—for instance, with a new job upon arrival—or in the long term, such as improved educational opportunities for the migrants' children. Costs, too, may have a subjective component not readily measured in dollars and cents. An example of such a psychic cost is the feeling of loss related to breaking old social ties and entering an unfamiliar environment.

Lee's Theory of Push-and-Pull Factors

As noted, the sociologist Edward M. Lee (1966) extended Ravenstein's theory explicitly to include conditions that influence migration at the origin as well as at the destination. In addition, he specified a number of intervening constraints and barriers that restrict the migration process. Whereas Ravenstein focused on economic considerations as the primary motivation of population movements, Lee incorporated noneconomic as well as economic factors into the theory.

Some of these are push factors; that is, undesirable conditions in the sender population that make remaining at one's current place of residence unattractive. They might include lack of jobs, housing, schooling, or other social amenities, and ethnic prejudice, difficult political conditions, or natural disasters. Pull factors, conditions that make a potential receiver population attractive, include perceived economic, social, and political opportunities in a geographic area different from—but ordinarily close or adjacent to—one's current place of residence. The combination of better conditions (or the perception of such conditions) and close proximity to place of origin can exert a powerful attraction. This clearly was, and continues to be the case, in the millions of moves between rural areas and nearby towns and cities that have gone to create our urban world.

With this classification of the conditions that prompt or discourage migration as push-and-pull factors, every area of residence can be seen to have both desirable and undesirable features that bear on the decision to remain or to move. If undesirable conditions outweigh the desirable, people are pushed from the origin to the potential destination that exerts the greatest pull (distance considered). In principle, one's place of origin and potential destinations also have "zero" factors—neither pushes nor pulls, to which people are indifferent.

Lee also suggested that the volume of migration from an origin to a destination is influenced by a set of intervening obstacles. That is, the risk of migration is not the same for all individuals because of variations in personal, societal, political, and geographic circumstances. Thus, two households may live in very close proximity, even next door to one another, but they may be differently affected by pushes at the origin and the pulls from various potential destinations because they differ in employment status, ethnicity, or other features. Even perceptions of the advantages and disadvantages of moving, and the assumed desirability of one potential destination over another, may vary by socioeconomic status and other characteristics.

With such intervening obstacles taken into consideration, Lee's model—like Sjaastad's—views the decision to migrate as the outcome of an assessment of costs and benefits. Sometimes these are arrived at individually and sometimes as the result of a collective decision-making process. However, Lee recognized that it is impossible to specify *all* the benefits and costs associated with such a complicated undertaking and that, as a result, the decision to migrate is also influenced by imperfect information. That is, it often has an irrational component that can lead to regrets, attempts to return home, or the desire to move on to other destinations that have a more attractive constellation of pulls.

Social Network Theory

Social network theory suggests that international migration is a well-organized activity that is managed by new immigrants and closely associated potential migrants related by family or kinship ties. Emerging markets in industrialized countries attract these new immigrants. Douglas Massey (1988) (Massey, Goldring, and Durand 1994; Levitt and Jaworsky 2007; De Haas 2010) argues that this is a byproduct of development. As new markets are created, labor turnover increases. The emergence of new markets also brings about new consumerism and opportunities for those who are locally unemployed to achieve improvements in the standard of living. If one is not employed locally, one approach toward minimizing the risk of long-term loss of income is via international migration.

Once the process of migration is set in motion, it is perpetuated by two sets of factors, one personal and the other social. At the personal level, immigrants grow accustomed to opportunities for growth, high standards of living, and new consumer habits. Those who return are then more likely to immigrate. At the level of the family, the knowledge and experience of immigration of one member of the family reduces the risks associated with emigration for others who intend to leave home. The close relatives who choose to migrate will be initially helped and accommodated. This reduces the costs and minimizes the risk of immigration. Gradually, there emerges a network of immigrants and their close associates who intend to migrate. As the size of the network increases, the migration process itself becomes perpetuated and the flow takes on a momentum of its own.

Todaro's Migration Model

The geographer Michael Todaro (1976) has contributed to the development of migration theory with some general observations on the movement from rural to urban areas. In the tradition of neoclassical microeconomic theory, he views the response to urban-rural pushes and pulls in terms of expected rather than actual earnings. That is, his theory assumes that a potential migrant considers an array of opportunities in the labor market before choosing the one that maximizes expected gains (i.e., has the greatest pull). In the course of this process of deliberation, the decision to migrate or not is influenced by three factors:

1. The difference between expected income at the destination and income currently earned at the origin.
2. The costs of migration. These can be either monetary, or psychological, or both. Also, current improvements in transportation technology decrease the cost of migration.
3. The migrant's long-run assessment of the probability of securing employment at the destination.

Conditions 2 and 3, the cost of migration and the probability of finding a job, are influenced by social and demographic factors at the destination. However, the presence of a network of social and kinship ties into which the migrant may be absorbed upon arrival at the destination (a condition that is more common than many theories assume) decreases the psychological and monetary cost of migration. Furthermore, social networks play an active role in providing information about employment opportunities and aiding the migrant in actively pursuing job opportunities. These circumstances clearly influence the migrants' assessment of securing a job at their new place of residence. For example, in the United States, immigrants from Asian countries such as Philippines are more likely to move to cities with large Filipino communities.

THE VALUE EXPECTANCY MODEL

Each of the theories outlined here assumes that the intention to move is determined by a desire to achieve personally valued goals, along with an expectation that these goals can be realized through migration to one or more destinations. In extending these ideas, Gordon De Jong and associates (De Jong and Fawcett 1981; De Jong et al. 1983; Creighton 2013; Stecklov et al. 2005) have stressed that such goals and values may be as diverse as attainment of wealth, status, comfort, autonomy, and group affiliations. An individual's value system, life stage, aspirations, and available information about opportunities at various destinations influence desired goals. Thus, in the process of deliberation, potential migrants combine objective assessments with subjective values in determining the likelihood ("expectancy") of achieving specific goals at the origin and the destination(s).

It should be added in connection with this model that, although the intention to move is a strong indicator of migration behavior, it is possible that migrants may discover that valued goals can be achieved by making a few changes to their present social and economic arrangements. Thus, the model is not meant to predict migration outcomes but rather to determine various likelihoods or "propensities" to migrate. These may then be taken into account as the various pushes and pulls are reckoned.

INTERNATIONAL MIGRATION

International migration involves the movement of individuals and groups of individuals from one country to another. These movements may either be temporary or permanent. Unfortunately, the definitions of the terms *temporary* and *permanent* vary across countries. For example, based on the discussion at the beginning of the chapter, one could consider international tourists as temporary migrants. Also, in many parts of the world, citizens cross international borders on a regular basis for work or to visit friends and relatives. These kinds of temporary crossings are ordinarily not treated as a component of international migration. Those involved in such movements are often given passes that allow them to "migrate" without being counted as a migrant—provided that such travel is legal and the countries that share the border have friendly political relations.

Many permanent migrants hold work permits in the country of destination. In a pattern that has become increasingly common, these immigrants are soon followed by their immediate relatives, some of whom may also be granted work permits. International immigrants arrive at ports of entry in the country of destination, either by land, sea, or air. At these ports, the immigrants are expected to present visas and travel documents that permit them to enter the country of destination. In addition, international passengers provide demographic information and information on the origin and destination of their travels. National immigration departments process this information for the purpose of compiling statistics, and it is the major source of data employed by demographers and others who study population movements.

A Nation of Immigrants[7]

Among the earliest immigrants to North America were Africans, mostly from areas south of the Sahara, the first of whom arrived in the late sixteenth century. Beginning in the 1600s, these people began to be transported in large numbers by slave traders to work in large plantations in the South.[8] Because these slaves were violently forced by their captors in Africa and traders in America to enter the continent and, after 1776, the United States, theirs was clearly not a case of voluntary migration.

In contrast, a large-scale, essentially voluntary wave of European immigration to the United States began early in the nineteenth century, around 1820, and accelerated sharply at the end of the Civil War in 1865. Between 1820 and 1920, nearly 55 million Europeans immigrated to New World destinations, the most common of which was the United States. The pattern of the European influx into the United States between 1820 and the present has been described in terms of three major waves of immigration (Pedraza 1996). The first wave took place between 1820 and 1880. The second began some time after 1880 and ended in about 1930. The third, which is currently underway, began in the early 1950s.

Approximately 15 million persons immigrated in the first wave. During the first half of the nineteenth century, the largest proportion came from the British Isles, including many Irish immigrants fleeing the Great Potato Famine of the 1840s. Somewhat later, a large group arrived from Germany. A stream from the Scandinavian and Northwest European countries subsequently followed these, especially during the late 1800s. Supplementing this influx of Europeans, beginning in 1870 or so, a substantial number of Chinese laborers—about 133,000—arrived in the United States to work on the railroads and associated industries. This first large influx from Asia was abruptly halted by the Exclusion Act of 1882, which barred immigration of Chinese workers.

The second wave, which accounted for about 31 million persons, began in the mid- to late-1880s with the arrival of immigrants from southern and eastern Europe. These people, and the large groups that followed from Poland, Russia, Spain, and Portugal, were responding to the nearly irresistible pull of the U.S. Industrial Revolution and the subsequent enormous demand for workers it generated. During this period, which saw the greatest volume of international in-migration ever experienced by this (or any other) country, an average of more than 5,000 persons arrived—nearly all by boat—at U.S. ports of entry every *month*, year after year. Even this average is misleading, because most of the movement occurred between 1900 and 1920—the era that included World War I. During those two decades, the monthly average exceeded *60,000*!

The 1930s saw a considerable decline in the number of immigrants. This was partly the result of economic depression in the United States—and in most of the sender nations. But it also reflects the impact of the 1924 **Immigration and Nationality Act**, which favored immigrants from western and northern Europe while restricting immigration from southern and eastern European countries. The 1924 Act, passed by Congress in an attempt to protect the jobs of already-established U.S. workers, replaced the 1921 Quota Act. The 1921 Act had already set limits on the number of immigrants to be admitted from each country at 3 percent of the size of each ethnic group, as recorded in the 1890 Census.

The decline of the 1930s marked the beginning of a period of several decades during which international immigration virtually came to a halt. However, the demographic and sociological effects of the first two waves, especially the second, had already been established. As of 1955, the process whereby the United States was to become a nation of immigrants had been successfully completed—or so it appeared. However, a third wave began in the late 1950s and accelerated during the 1970s and 1980s. It came as something of a surprise to observers and policy specialists who believed that the growth of the nation's population from international migration had ceased. This wave saw the emergence of several new international migration streams that were sharply discontinuous with the past.

Table 7.5.   Origin of Migration Flows into the United States, 2005, 2008, and 2011

Year	Number of Migrants (in Thousands)	Total	European Origin		Asian Origin		Latin America
			N/W	S/E	E	W/C	
2005	11,222.57	6.88	2.76	4.12	9.60	2.35	26.08
2008	11,071.23	4.28	2.13	2.15	10.25	2.33	29.31
2011	10,620.34	3.60	1.75	1.85	10.11	3.32	25.00

Source: "Yearbook of Immigration Statistics: 2012," Office of Immigration Statistics, U.S. Department of Homeland Security, July 2013.

The influx of European migrants which, in conjunction with the importation of African slaves, had characterized the first two waves was no longer a significant factor. Instead, these groups were replaced by Latin American, Caribbean, and Asian peoples as the largest in-coming immigrant component in the country. In particular, Mexico emerged as the greatest source of both legal and illegal immigration (net illegal immigration during this period, most of it originating in or passing through Mexico, is estimated to be about 275,000 persons per year; McFalls 1998:20). A second major group of immigrants came from the Philippines. In all, nearly two-thirds of all immigrants to the United States since 1970 have come from Mexico, Cuba, El Salvador, Guatemala, Nicaragua, the Dominican Republic, and Haiti in the Caribbean Basin; and the Philippines, Vietnam, South Korea, China, Taiwan, and India in South and East Asia (Rumbaut 1996; Iceland 2009).[9]

Between 2000 and 2011, the foreign-born population grew from 31.1 million to 42.0 million, a 35 percent increase (see Table 7.5). Among the 29 million documented immigrants in 2010, 11.7 million came from Mexico, 29 percent of the foreign born. The second-largest group—amounting to about 7 million, 17 percent of all the foreign born—came from Asia. Thus Asian immigrants have displaced the Latin Americans as the second-largest share of the authorized immigrant population in the United States.[10]

Of the foreign born in 2010, nearly 11.1 million were undocumented. Of the 11.1 million undocumented immigrants, 6.5 million came from Mexico, 0.7 million from El Salvador, 0.5 million from Guatemala, 0.3 million from Honduras, and 0.2 million from China and the Philippines (Hoefer, Rytina, and Baker 2011).[11]

As shown in Table 7.6, nearly two-thirds of all immigrants resided in 12 counties in the states of California, New York, Texas, and Florida. Nearly 60 percent of the immigrants in 2012 lived in five states; California (10.3 million), New York (4.4 million), Texas (4.3 million), Florida (3.7 million), and New Jersey (1.9 million). Most Mexican immigrants reside in the West and Southwest, and more than 55 percent live in California or Texas. In 2012, the top five states with the largest proportion of Mexican immigrants were California (37 percent of the total Mexican immigrant population), Texas (22 percent), Illinois (6 percent), Arizona (4 percent), and Florida (2 percent).

Refugees: The Issue of Forced International Migration

Refugees are forced immigrants. Like the slaves who were brought from Africa to North America, their movements are not subject to the usual "pushes and pulls" or "rational choices," that influence other kinds of migrants. Instead, a refugee is

Any person who, owing to a well-founded fear of being persecuted for reasons of race, religion, nationality, membership of a particular social group or political opinion, is outside the country of his[/her] nationality and is unable, owing to such fear, willing to avail him[/her]self to the protection of that country; or who not having a nationality or being outside the country of his[/her] former habitual residence as a result if such events, is unable or, owing to such fear, is unwilling to return to it. (UNHCR 1992)

This definition was initially adopted at the 1951 United Nations Convention Relating to the Status of Refugees. The international oversight organization responsible for ensuring the right of refugees, the United Nations High Commission for Refugees (UNHCR), requires international border crossing as a precondition to assign a person to this category. For this reason, the many migrants who flee from their homes but do not cross an international border are referred to as "displaced persons."

The U.S. Department of Immigration and Naturalization Services (INS) considers for admission as refugees persons of special humanitarian concern who can establish persecution or a well-founded fear of persecution on account of race, religion, nationality, membership in a particular social group, or political opinion. The legal basis of the refugee admissions program is the Refugee Act of 1980, which embodies the American tradition of granting refuge to diverse groups suffering from

Table 7.6. U.S. Metropolitan Areas with the Greatest Net Influxes of Asian and Latino Migrants, 1985-1990

Rank	City	Asians	City	Latinos
Internal Migrants				
1	Los Angeles	31,804	Miami	48,270
2	Sacramento	11,203	Orlando	23,701
3	San Francisco	10,345	San Diego	19,711
4	San Diego	6,355	Las Vegas	6,216
5	Boston	5,364	Tampa-St Pete	13,763
6	Atlanta	4,760	Dallas	12,271
7	Seattle	3,990	Phoenix	11,127
8	Wash., DC	3,850	Sacramento	11,053
9	Orlando	3,840	Modesto,	10,072
10	Las Vegas	3,326	Wash., DC	9,912
International Migrants				
1	Los Angeles	219,652	Los Angeles	520,653
2	New York	190,512	New York	269,141
3	San Francisco	137,006	Miami	144,692
4	Chicago	44,823	San Francisco	86,222
5	Wash., DC	43,481	Chicago	72,719
6	San Diego	31,274	San Diego	54,704
7	Boston	27,219	Wash., DC	51,721
8	Seattle	26,817	Houston	50,433
9	Philadelphia	22,347	Boston	34,831
10	Houston	21,258	Dallas	34,662

Based on Frey 1995:743.

Source: Special Tabulation of full Migration Sample, 1990, US Census. Compiled at the Population Studies Center, University of Michigan.

or fearing persecution. The 1980 Act in essence adopted the definition of "refugee" contained in the 1951 U.N. Convention quoted above and its 1967 Protocol. The definition, which may be found in Section 101(a)(42) of the U.S. Immigration and Nationality Act (INA), as amended, is as follows:

> Any person who is outside any country of such person's nationality or, in the case of a person having no nationality, is outside any country in which such person last habitually resided, and who is unable or unwilling to return to, and is unable or unwilling to avail himself or herself of the protection of, that country because of persecution or a well-founded fear of persecution on account of race, religion, nationality, membership in a particular social group, or political opinion.[12]

As is clear from these definitions and protocols, the most important characteristic that distinguishes a refugee from an ordinary migrant is that the former has very little control over migration decision making. W. R. Smyser (1992:119) describes the difference in this way: "Migrants seek opportunity. Refugees seek haven. A migrant does not wish to return home; a refugee does not dare." Under such involuntary circumstances, the crossing of an international border for safety and/or life precipitates a long chain of events in which government(s) play an active role (W. R. Smyser 1992:119; Bloemraad 2006). Upon crossing, refugees may decide to seek asylum in the country of entry, or they may prefer to continue their trek, seeking entry elsewhere. In either case, the government at the point of arrival is obliged to make a number of decisions with respect to the survival and health of the refugees. It must decide where to house them, how long to keep them, and if long-term or permanent asylum is to be granted to those who seek it. National laws as well as relationships among the nations involved affect these matters, which at times even includes the hostile sender nation.

Explaining Forced Migration

When one considers the intensely political nature and demographic magnitude of the refugee situation today, it is natural to seek out explanations. Why are there so many refugees? Is the flow likely increase? What can be done about it? Unfortunately, our theories of migration are not adequate in this area, for several reasons. For example, as we have seen, all of the models and theories assume that, to some degree, migration is a voluntary undertaking; and that the most important factors are employment and the wage differential that exists between origin and destination countries. In addition most of our theories treat migration at the micro level. In this sense, migrants are understood to be individuals or family groupings who calculate costs and benefits, not large aggregates or categories of people subjected to a common stimulus. The reasons for migrating in the ordinary way may vary from individual to individual. But seeking refuge is a collective experience, especially when—as is usually the case—it is refuge from religious, ethnic, or political persecution.

Recent attempts have been made to formulate theories of forced migration that do take such factors into account (Mazur 1988; Schmeidl 1997; Bloemraad 2006; Eastmond 2007). These have mainly focused on the role of the state in refugee production. Along these lines, Charles Keely (1996) has identified political conflict as a major force behind increased refugee flows. According to Keely, one of the preconditions for this kind of conflict can be found in the recent political histories of several developing countries. In many parts of Africa and Asia, colonization led to the resettlement of ethnic groups. These resettlement projects brought about new contacts, and often disharmony, among groups with no shared past experiences. Then, with independence from colonial domination, new political boundaries were drawn and old ones reestablished. Some of these created socially arbitrary international frontiers that separated ethnic groups that had previously established amicable relations. Others brought together groups hostile to one another within one new, but essentially synthetic, nation. This process created new ethnic conflicts and rekindled old ones, ultimately resulting in refugee crises.

Human rights violations have been shown to be one of the most significant causes of refugee production (Pitterman 1986; also see ACLU 1997), and they are also the most immediate cause of refugee migration (Schmeidl 1997; Zottarelli 1998; Eastmond 2007). Such violations occur, and precipitate the flow of refugees, when governments sponsor violence against groups competing for political ascendancy, or when civil and international wars break out.[13] Wars and human rights violations are, in turn, influenced by several background factors, also referred to as "root factors" or "root causes." These include economic marginalization, ethnic competition, environmental degradation, hunger and overpopulation, and resource scarcities (Kane 1995:5; Jenkins and Schmeidl 1995; Kivisto and Faist 2009; Loescher and Milner 2005).

The idea of root causes with regard to refugee production suggests that underlying conditions and structures are in place and that they contribute to the creation of refugee movements long before people actually flee. The United Nations began to address the issue in the 1980s, in hope of formulating preventative measures (Clark 1989; Schmeidl 1997; Eastmond 2007; Salehyan and Gleditsch 2006), and it has continued to consider it an important factor.

SUMMARY

Migration is the most complex of all of the vital processes studied by demographers. Its impact upon population size and composition is often quite significant, especially in this mobile world that we now inhabit. Beginning with the simple idea that people move from place to place and thus regularly alter their activity and group-participation patterns, we considered numerous variations on the theme of geographic mobility, until we arrived at the politically charged issues surrounding the international refugee crisis. It may now be clearer why those who study population are quick to point out the paradox that one of the most important variables in their field is, at the same time, one of the most difficult to measure and explain.

KEY TERMS

emigrant	net migration
forced migration	operationalization
immigrant	out-migration
Immigration and Nationality Act (1924)	"push-pull" process
in-migration	"rural renaissance"
involuntary migration	

NOTES

1. In fact, with recent innovations in telecommunications technologies, people increasingly participate in groups throughout the world without ever leaving their chairs. This "virtual" travel and participation was first referred to as *tertiary relationships* by sociologist and demographer Janet Abu-Lughod. See Weinstein (2010:107, 110, 113, 132–33, 215, 218).

2. We say "social distance" because actual distance, as measured in kilometers or miles, does not adequately depict the character of migration as a demographic (not merely a geographic) change. For example, in large border cities such as Detroit, a family might move just a few blocks—into nearby Windsor, Canada—and they would be registered as having experienced international migration. In contrast, a second Detroit-area family might relocate a distance of 40 or 50 miles within Wayne County, say from a far southern suburb to a far northern suburb, and be considered only as movers—that is, no migratory event would be registered.

3. The inadequacy of these operational definitions is highlighted by the many possible exceptions. For example, in the past—and in some developing countries even today, when a family living in the village of one group of tribal people relocates a short distance to the village of another tribe, it is clearly experiencing a major change in group participation, activities, and in other ways. Yet, by the terms stipulated here, such a movement might not even qualify as migration—let alone international migration, which is what it most nearly resembles. On the other hand, when, in times of civil war, national boundary lines are drawn in the middle of metropolitan areas, as they were in Sarajevo in the early 1990s, what was once a simple visit to one's neighbor might become an international movement.

4. One of the most consequential instances of this type of migration is the massive population shift from the countryside, to the cities, to the suburbs experienced in the United States and other industrialized countries during the past few generations. Among the many significant impacts of this shift is a large-scale redistribution of the population that gave the suburbs the highest proportion of residents of the three settlement types.

5. See http://www.census.gov/hhes/migration/data/acs/state-to-state.html.

6. See http://www.governing.com/news/headlines/international-migration-immigration-driving-population-growth-for-metro-areas.html.

7. Information in this section is derived from Leon F. Bouvier and Robert Gardner (1986: Table 1) and U.S. Immigration and Naturalization Service (1992: Table 1.2).

8. Attempts were made to enslave the native Indians, but these were unsuccessful. It proved too difficult to subordinate a group of people whose homes—and, thus, relatives and places of refuge—were so nearby. The program to enslave Africans worked out much better (from the slave owner's point of view) because these people had been uprooted from their homes and relocated thousands of miles from kin and refuge.

9. This is in substantial contrast to the migration waves of the late nineteenth and early twentieth centuries. With very few exceptions these immigrants were from Europe.

10. http://www.pewsocialtrends.org/2012/06/19/the-rise-of-asian-americans/.

11. Estimates of the unauthorized immigrant population residing in the United States are from U.S. Department of Homeland Security (2010:4).

12. The Act continues:

or (B) in such circumstances as the President after appropriate consultation (as defined in section 207 (e) of this Act) may specify, any person who is within the country of such person's nationality or, in the case of a person having no nationality, within the country in which such person is habitually residing, and who is persecuted or who has a well-founded fear of persecution on account of race, religion, nationality, membership in a particular social group, or political opinion. The term "refugee" does not include any person who ordered, incited, assisted, or otherwise participated in the persecution of any person on account of race, religion, nationality, membership in a particular social group, or political opinion. For purposes of determinations under this Act, a person who has been forced to abort a pregnancy or to undergo involuntary sterilization, or who has been persecuted for failure or refusal to undergo such a procedure or for other resistance to a coercive population control program, shall be deemed to have been persecuted on account of political opinion, and a person who has a well-founded fear that he or she will be forced to undergo such a procedure or be subject to persecution for such failure, refusal or resistance shall be deemed to have a well-founded fear of persecution on account of political opinion.

13. The mass exodus from persecution and starvation may displace populations within national boundaries. However, the crossing of international boundaries is constrained by a number of geographic as well political factors that intervene between human rights violations and the entry into refugee status. These intervening factors are conditions that either inhibit or facilitate flight across a border (Schmeidl 1997; Clark 1989). For example, the presence of a porous international border increases the likelihood of refugee production.

CHAPTER EIGHT

POPULATION DYNAMICS IN HISTORICAL AND COMPARATIVE PERSPECTIVE

We have noted several times that the world's population size reached the 6 billion mark just prior to the end of the twentieth century. Considering that there were only 5 million people on earth in 8000 BCE, the era of the founding of the first cities, humanity has come a long way in a relatively short time (by geological standards in any case). It has also been suggested that this growth has not occurred in an even manner, either in terms of time or place. Rather, most of the increase in the size of the human population has happened very recently. As late as 1750, there were still fewer than 1 billion people on Earth, and some estimates put the figure closer to 600 million. Moreover, during some periods, certain regions of the world, such as Europe and especially North America, were experiencing rapid growth while in other places—for example, Africa—little or no population growth was occurring. At other times (such as today), the pattern has been reversed, with several countries in Europe experiencing negative growth while Africa's population is exploding.

This chapter presents an analysis of the phenomenon of population growth. It is designed to help us understand how the species *Homo sapiens* has increased to its current record-breaking size, what factors underlie the uneven character of this growth, and why some contemporary populations are in absolute decline whereas others are increasing at the fastest rates ever recorded anywhere.

The chapter begins with a discussion of the logic and mathematics of growth, in which we present several measurement techniques and models. Next we pursue a detailed historical examination of **demographic transitions**, the occurrence of prolonged and relatively permanent changes in population growth rates. This look into the past and the immediate present leads us to consider some of the issues surrounding future population growth. Here we present various projections of the population of the world and its regions through the middle of the twenty-second century. The following section takes up one of the main consequences of population growth and decline, changes in the age of a population. This discussion expands on some of the concepts and measurements introduced in Chapter 3. We conclude with an overview of population growth in the United States. There we find that, although the United States is experiencing a period of slow increase by historical standards, its population is still expanding at a rate many times higher than that in most other highly industrialized countries. The facts and tools presented in this chapter will provide a good foundation for the following part of the text, in which we discuss population models and their use in anticipating future growth.

MEASURES AND MODELS OF GROWTH

The fundamental equation of demography (see Chapter 2) indicates that a population grows or decreases in size as the result of the combined influence of births, deaths, in-migration, and out-migration. This way of looking at growth is referred to as the **components method**, because birth and the other vital events are the components of—the "parts that constitute"—change. With that in view, we will set aside the equation temporarily and approach the measurement of population growth at a simpler and cruder level, using what we call the **difference method** for reasons that will be obvious in a moment.

Measuring Growth by Difference

Following demographic conventions, we will refer to all change in the size of a population or other aggregate as "growth," even when an absolute loss or no change occurs. In such cases, we speak of negative or zero population growth (ZPG). If the size of a population, subpopulation, and so forth is known for two dates—date 0 for the earlier and date t for the later, then we can represent the population sizes as P_0 and P_t. The difference method defines G, *growth in the interval* between 0 and t, as:

$$G = P_t - P_0$$

To illustrate, let us consider the population of the world in 1950 and 2010, and for comparative purposes we will also look at the U.S. population for those two dates.[1] In 1950, the world's population size stood at about 2.5 billion and for 2010 we will use the figure of 6.9 billion. Thus, in the 50-year interval the growth was:

$$G = P_t - P_0 = 6.9 - 2.5 = 4.4 \text{ billion}$$

Three and one-half billion persons were added in the 50 years. The U.S. population size in 1950 was 152.3 million, and in 2010 it was approximately 309 million. The growth in the interval was:

$$G = P_t - P_0 = 309.0 - 153.2 = 155.5 \text{ million}$$

Although such information is interesting, comparisons between different eras or different populations are difficult to make when growth is measured in this way. For this reason, we ordinarily convert growth in the interval to *proportionate* or, more commonly, *percentage growth*. These are defined as G/P_0, for proportionate and $(G/P_0) \times 100$, for percentage. So, for the interval, the world's population grew by:

$$G/P_0 = 4.4/2.5 = 1.8 \text{ or } 1.8 \times 100 = 180 \text{ percent (it nearly doubled)}$$

For the United States, the comparable proportion and percentage are:

$$G/P_0 = 155.5/153.2 = 1.015 \text{ or } 1.015 \times 100 = 101.5 \text{ percent}$$

Now we can say that in the interval the U.S. population grew more slowly than that of the world; in fact, the world's population grew almost twice as rapidly.

Once percentage growth has been calculated, it is possible to derive the familiar annual growth rates. At this point, it is important to distinguish between actual annual rates and average annual rates. To derive the former, it is required that the two dates, 0 and t, are exactly one year apart. If this condition is met, then the annual rate is identical to proportionate or percentage growth. If this condition is met, then the annual rate is identical to proportionate or percentage growth. For example, Census Bureau estimates indicate that the U.S. population size in 2013 was 319.33 million and in 2014 it was 322.4233 million. Thus, growth in the interval was 3.09 million, and proportionate and percentage growth were 3.09/319.33 = .0096 and .0096 × 100 = 0.96 percent. Because the interval is one year, we can also say that the annual growth rate was 96 per 1,000 or 0.96 percent.

If the difference between the two dates is greater than one year, then it is necessary to make some assumptions, summarized in one of several *growth models* (also discussed in Chapter 10). In our illustration of the growth of the world's population, we found that there was a 180 percent increase during the 60 years between 1950 and 2005. But, in the absence of other information, we have no way of knowing how, in detail, the increase occurred. For example, the same number or the same proportion of persons could have been added in each of the 50 years. On the other hand, it is logically possible that little or no growth occurred during the first 25 years but then there was a real explosion beginning in 1975. Under those circumstances, all or most of the additional 3.5 billion persons since 1950 were actually added during the second half of the interval. Or perhaps a great population explosion occurred between 1950 and 1970, during which 5 billion people were added, but then there was a decline that left a residue of the additional 3.5 million. Well, you get the point; the possibilities are limitless. How, then do we know what the average annual rate, was? The answer is that we don't, but we can make an estimate.

As we will see in Chapter 10, several methods are available for estimating growth in an interval from data that cover only two periods. Here we introduce the two most common approaches, the **linear growth model** and the **exponential growth model**. The linear model, based on what Malthus referred to as "arithmetic growth," assumes that an equal percentage of persons is added to (or subtracted from) a population each and every year in the interval. This is identical to simple interest on money loaned or saved. The formula for this type of growth should be very familiar. If n stands for the number of years between the two dates, 0 and t, the (linear) average annual growth rate

$$r = (\text{proportionate growth})/n, \text{ or as a percent, } (\text{percentage growth})/n$$

Thus, for the world and United States between 1950 and 2010, the average annual rates were:

World: 1.80/60 = .030 or 3.0 percent
United States: 1.015/60 = .017 or 1.7 percent

We can say that by the linear model, the world's population was increasing by 3.0 percent per year while the United States population was increasing by only 1.7 percent. To derive P_t when P_0, r, and n are known, we simply multiply $P_t = P_0 \times (rn)$. So, for the United States,

$$P_{2010} = 153.2 + (153.2 \times .017 \times 60) = 309.46 \text{ million}$$

The other model to be considered is exponential growth. This is a more contemporary extension of Malthus's notion of "geometric increase" (which is also discussed in Chapter 10), and it is equivalent to interest compounded continuously. Under this assumption, the rate of population growth is not constant throughout an interval. Instead, increases occur slowly at first and then accelerate as the population base grows. Thus, the rate of increase is assumed to be greatest at the end of the interval. The annual average rate derived from this model takes account of the fact that the actual rate during a particular year differs somewhat from that of any other year. The formula for this rate is:

$$r = [\ln (P_t/P_0)]/n$$

where ln is the natural (base e) logarithm. The procedure for finding r is to (1) divide P_t by P_0, (2) find the natural log of the quotient with a calculator or a log table (3) divide the result by n. For the world population between 1950 and 2010,

$$r = [\ln (6.9/2.5)]/60 = [\ln (2.8)]/60 = 1.029/60 = .0171, \text{ or } 1.71 \text{ percent}$$

The comparable rate for the United States is:

$$r = [\ln (308.7/153.2)]/50 = [\ln (2.015)]60 = 0.700/60 = .0116, \text{ or } 1.16 \text{ percent.}$$

With this model, to find P_t when P_0, r, and n are known, the following formula is used:

$$P_t = P_0 \times e^{rn}, \text{ where e is the exponential constant} = 2$$
$$.71828 \ldots \text{ For the United States}$$

$$P_t = 153.2 \times \exp (.0116 \times 60)] = 153.2 \times (2.718 \times .696) =$$
$$1.532 \times 2.005 = 307.27 \text{ million}$$

You can also see that the exponential rates are lower than the arithmetic rates, which is ordinarily the case. Because this model better approximates the way population growth normally occurs, it is by far the most commonly employed. For this reason, all growth rates used in this book are exponential (unless indicated otherwise).

The final measure based on the difference model to be introduced here may be familiar to you. This is **doubling time**, an indicator of growth that is expressed in years rather than in rates or percentages. As the name suggests, it expresses the number of years it would take for a population to double in size at a given (exponential) rate. Technically, it is derived by solving for n (number of years) in the equation for exponential growth, assuming that Pt is twice as large as P_0. That is, with $P_t = P_0 \times e^{rn}$, let $P_t = 2P_0$. Then, $2P_0 = P_0 \times e^{rn}$. Dividing by P_0, we see that $\ln (2) = rt$. Dividing by r, we get t = ln (2)/r; and since ln (2) = .693, the amount of time it takes a population to double in size if it grows at the continuous rate of r (DT for doubling time) is DT = .693/r.

For the world's population, with a growth rate of .0171, the doubling time is .693/.0171 = 40.5 years. For the United States, at the rate of .0116, DT = .693/.0116 = 59.7 years. Obviously, because the U.S. growth rate is slower, it will take longer for the population size to double.

You can see that .693 is very close to .70, and we know that growth rates can be expressed as percentages (so that .0171 becomes 1.71 percent, and so on). For these reasons, one can always find a very close approximation of DT by what is called "the rule of 70." This says that doubling time can be estimated by dividing 70 by the (exponential) annual percentage growth rate. Thus a population growing at 1.0 percent per year will double in about 70 years, one growing at 2.0 percent will double in 35 years, 3.0 percent yields 23.3 years, and so on. Using the Census year 2010 as our base date, the world's population stood at 6.9 billion. Growing at about 1.8 percent per year, with no changes in the growth rate, there will be 13.8 billion people on this planet in the year 2048.

Growth by Components

We now return briefly to the Fundamental Equation:

$$G = (B - D) + (I - O)$$

The "G" used here is the same as that in the last section. It is the number of persons (not the percent or the rate) added or subtracted between two dates. You will recall from Chapter 7 that this formula indicates that population growth between the two dates comes from two sources, and that each of these sources consists of two components. The (B – D), births minus deaths, term is referred to as *natural increase*; and that the (I – O) term, in- and out-migration, makes up *net migration*. If we add together all the births that occur between the dates and the total number of in-migrants, we will have the incremental (increase-producing) part of growth. If we add together the deaths and the number of out-migrants, we will have the decremental (decrease-producing) portion. If the increments are greater than the decrements, positive growth occurs. If the two are equal, then ZPG has been achieved. If the decrements outweigh the increments, then growth is negative. Currently, one can find national populations in each of these three states of growth. For example, the United States is growing positively (see Table 8.1), Sweden is at ZPG, and Russia is experiencing negative growth.

We have already examined each of the components in detail, and we have applied the method in our discussion of measures of migration. Moreover, we will have an opportunity to employ component data in deriving population estimates and projections in Chapter 10. Thus, in the context of our present discussion of population dynamics, we have only limited concerns in reintroducing the subject. In fact, one of the main points of interest has already been made. That is, the components method is an alternative, and generally a more precise alternative, to other approaches such as the linear and exponential models just introduced. On the other hand, it is also a more demanding method because it requires access to vital statistics, which are not as readily available as information on population size, and to migration statistics, which are often even more difficult to find.

Table 8.1. Population Growth by Components, United States, 1980-2008

Year (time t)	Population Size (time t)	Births	Deaths	Natural Increase %	Net Migration	Growth	Population Size (t + 1)
1980	226.55	2.743	1.463	.71	0.724	1.900	228.45
1985	236.94	3.761	2.086	.70	0.649	2.171	239.11
1990	248.14	4.148	2.155	.81	0.566	2.549	250.66
1995	261.69	3.900	2.312	.87	0.888	2.475	264.16
2000*	281.42	0.989	0.651	.85	0.319	0.747	282.17
2001	285.08	4.007	2.430	.85	1.078	2.722	287.81
2005	293.05	4.121	2.433	.83	1.008	2.418	298.59
2008	301.58	4.263	2.486	.79	0.855	2,632	307.007

*April 1 to July1

Source: U.S. Census Bureau, Table 4 from *Statistical Abstract of the United States: 2012* and *Statistical Abstract of the United States: 1997.*

DEMOGRAPHIC TRANSITION AND SOCIAL CHANGE

Although data on the components of growth are not readily available for many countries, we do now have highly accurate estimates of the size of each nation's population and that of the world, thanks to the implementation of high-quality census operations globally. This was not always the case. Our knowledge of world population size even a few centuries ago is often unreliable because of a lack of records and the use of questionable methods of counting people. Nevertheless, and despite these obstacles, a fairly clear, albeit general, picture has been formed about our demographic past, at least for historical times (beginning in about 8000 BCE). This information is the result of some demanding research that combined the skills of demography, historiography, statistics, archaeology, and a fair measure of detective work on the part of several scholars. Among these, E. S. Deevey (1960), Nathan Keyfitz (1966), John Durand (1974), Ralph Thomlinson (1975), and Jean-Noel Biraben (1980) deserve special mention. Table 8.2 contains historical estimates of the world's population size based on the work of these people and others.

Early World Population Growth

According to Thomlinson, there may have been as many as 10 million people in the world as of 12,000 years ago, although it is likely that there were fewer, perhaps only 1 million. Deevey, who has provided the earliest estimates, suggests that there were a mere 25,000 members of *Homo erectus* in 1 million BCE. Using Thomlinson's higher figure, the estimated rate of population growth from that time up to the end of the Ice Age turns out to be a minuscule 0.0006 percent per year, that is, six ten-thousandths of 1 percent. The world's population in 4000 BCE is estimated to have been 7 million. With Thomlinson's lower figure for 10,000 BCE of 1 million, the average annual growth rate for the 6,000-year interval is still only 0.03 percent; and the higher estimate indicates a net loss of −.006 per year.

By 1000 BCE, the era of King David's reign in Judea and the spread of the Iron Age into Europe, the size of the human population had risen to 50 million. Growth in the preceding millennium occurred at an estimated annual rate of 0.06

Table 8.2. World Population Growth for Selected Dates

Date	Size	Growth Rate	Date	Size	Growth Rate
10000 BCE	5.5	0.0	1850	1,265.0	0.646
5000	12.5	0.006	1900	1,656.0	0.636
1000	50.0	0.060	1930	2,070.0	1.070
1 AD	285.0	0.122	1950	2,557.6	1.458
500	198.0	0.022	1960	3,042.8	1.346
1000	499.5	0.117	1980	4,450.9	1.865
1500	482.5	0.194	1990	5,287.8	1.569
1650	507.5	−0.148	2000	6,090.3	1.260
1750	795	0.094	2005	6,474.2	1.203
			2012	7,020.7	1.107

Notes: Sizes (in millions) are the averages of the highest and lowest estimates in cases in which more than one figure is provided. Growth rates are average annual rates in percentages calculated from the closest preceding date for which data are available.

Sources: "Historical Estimates of World Population," and "Total Midyear Population for the World: 1950–2050," U.S. Bureau of the Census.

percent. In the subsequent 1,000 years, to 1 AD and the height of Rome's Imperial power, improved sanitation and agricultural techniques obviously had their impact on population growth, even against a backdrop of constant warfare. By 1 AD, the population of the world had reached a size of something between 170 and 400 million. Taking an average of the two estimates of 285 million, the average annual rate of growth from 1000 BCE onward was just under 0.18 percent, which is extremely rapid by earlier standards.

For the next 1,000 years, which saw the defeat of Rome, the beginning of Europe's medieval era, and the center of world power move to Turkey and, after 500 AD, to the Arabic regions, world population growth was slow and irregular. The highest estimates indicate successive declines from 1 through 600 AD, and only a small recovery through 900. The lowest estimate for 1000 AD is 254 million and the highest is 345 million (following a dip to 206 million as of 600 AD). Thus, the growth rate during the first millennium of Christianity was approximately .005 percent: a significant decline. Overall, between 1000 and 1650 AD, the world's population increased very unevenly, from approximately 300 million to approximately 550 million, at an average annual rate of 0.09 percent. In the period between 1650 and 1750 (the date customarily designated as the start of the Industrial Revolution), one part of the world, the European colonizers, began to experience accelerated population grow. The other branch, the colonized populations outside of Europe, began a period of no growth and absolute declines.

The Four-Stage Process[2]

Prior to the Colonial Era, growth rates did not vary significantly between different regions of the world. Instead, on all continents, growth was equally slow and erratic. The exceptional cases, in which death rates were relatively low and consequently growth was rapid, were associated with urban settlements and their hinterlands (where the vast majority of people under the control of urban centers lived). From these accounts, it is clear that history of population growth until 1750 AD was characterized by a shift from a very long period of slow growth to one of high population-growth rates. This population explosion was followed by yet another period of slow growth in several parts of the world, especially Europe and North America. The term "demographic transition" has been coined to characterize these changes.

A demographic transition is a dramatic and relatively sudden transformation in a population's growth rates resulting from a combination of increases and decreases in one or more of the vital components.[3] When one change in growth rates is soon followed by another, the transition can be divided into stages: one prior to the first change, another between the first and second changes, another following the second change, and so on. The two basic types of transitions are (1) upward, a shift from low to high rates of growth and (2) downward, a shift from high to low rates. An upward shift can occur because of increasing fertility levels, declining mortality, and/ or increases in net migration, assuming all else remains the same. Downward transition is the effect of declining fertility, increasing mortality, or net migration loss (see Figure 8.1). When we indicate that the period from the beginning of history to about 1650 constitutes Stage I of Europe's demographic transition, we are pointing specifically to the fact that, after eons of slow growth, upward transition began to occur in England, France, and other countries. By referring to it as the *European* transition, we are underscoring the point that slow growth continued after 1650 in other parts of the world.[4]

From Stage 1 to Stage 2

During the first stage, population growth rates were low because of high morality, despite equally high levels of fertility. Death reigned and affected every aspect of human existence. The overriding concern was to ensure survival of the family by having a large number of children. Birth and death remained largely beyond human control, subject to the hazards of the environment—including the human environment. The second stage began in the mid-seventeenth century, when England and other parts of Europe were still overwhelmingly rural and dependent on a waning system of feudal agriculture. Two important advances were made at the beginning of this stage. They were (1) the founding of modern science by Sir Isaac

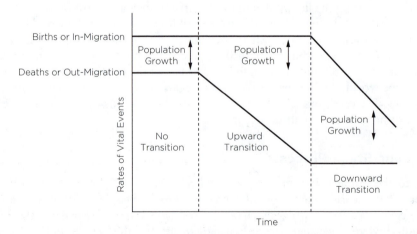

Figure 8.1. Demographic Transitions: Changes in Population Growth Rates Resulting from Changes in Vital Events

Newton and (2) the widespread introduction of the earliest modern technologies of **mortality control**.

Mortality control consists of practices that reduce death rates, in particular, infant deaths. These include improved standards of nutrition and sanitation, medical practices, and accident prevention. The changes in these practices that occurred during the century leading up to the Industrial Revolution were accompanied by the emergence of attitudinal and value changes (especially in the realm of theology) that supported human intervention in matters of life and death. The decline of fatalism and dependence on divine will provided an atmosphere supporting the spread and adoption of simple innovations such as boiling water, draining swamps, and safe disposal of garbage and human wastes. The demographic impact was dramatic. Between 1650 and 1750, Europe's population grew at nearly 0.4 percent per year, 10 times faster than the average for the preceding 1,500 years.

The Scientific and Industrial Revolutions mark the beginning of a new era in human history. From a demographic perspective, they accelerated significantly the rate of improvement and adoption of death-control ideals and techniques. As a result, death rates, which had been in a slow but selective decline for some decades, began to drop sharply. Between 1750 and 1800, Europe's population grew at an average annual rate of 0.6 percent—even though many parts of the continent were yet to emerge from feudalism. In the 200 years between 1600 and 1800, the population of Europe had thus doubled. More than 1,500 years were required for the doubling that began at the start of the Common Era, whereas the doubling that occurred during the early modern period took one-eighth as long.

The world's population reached 1 billion during the first decade of the nineteenth century. Of this total, Asia accounted for about 650 million, and another 150 million people lived in Africa. As new death-control technologies were discovered or invented, including antisepsis and anesthesia, England, the rest of Europe, and now the United States reaped the benefits in the form of authentic population explosions. In the colonized areas, however, death rates were still high and population growth remained in the Malthusian mode. By the 1800–1850 period, Europe clearly had the world's and history's fastest-growing population, at 0.84 percent per year. It reached the 274 million mark by the latter date. Although the rate at which growth rates were *accelerating* had begun to decrease at some point between 1850 and 1900, the growth rate itself reached an annual average of 1.2 percent during the interval. As events turned out, this was to be the most rapid growth ever achieved for Europe as a whole, to this day. As of 1900, Europe's population size stood at just over 423 million. Thus, another doubling had occurred, this time in 100 years—one-half as long as the previous doubling.

From Stage 2 to Stage 3

Europe's peak growth of approximately 1.2 percent annually was achieved within a few years before or after 1875. From that point until the present, growth rates have been in a generally steady decline—with the exception of the baby boom era of the 1950s. Between 1850 and 1920, most of the European continent, from northwest to southeast, from England and France to Germany, Italy, and beyond experienced declines in growth from 1.0 percent and above to 0.7 and below. The events that initiated this shift to the third, downward, stage of demographic transition are even more remarkable than those that had caused the earlier population explosion. For during the mid- to late-nineteenth century, for the first time in history, a prolonged and *intentional* decrease in fertility levels occurred. Just as people had taken control of the force of mortality more than a century earlier, they now were prepared technologically and ideologically to take control of the force of natality: that is, *birth (or fertility) control*. Although the ideals of family planning had been formulated in England prior to 1825 by Francis Place (and, some might argue, by Malthus), as of the 1860s and 1870s, people were prepared to put these ideals into practice.

The breakthrough in family planning resulted from a value shift among the urban middle classes of England and other countries, including the United States. This was a shift toward the acceptance of small family-size norms, or "stopping rules" (see Billari and Dalla-Zuanna 2013; Pampel 1993; Easterlin and Crimmins 1985; Banks 1954, 1968; also Keyfitz 1968; and Chapter 11, below). After centuries and millennia of **pronatalism**—the view that having many children is the most virtuous practice, it became apparent that this was an outmoded value, one better suited to a time when infant mortality levels were high and large families were a survival tactic.

With the spread of the conditions that make family planning accessible and the values that make it acceptable (after all, every major world religion and most local ones officially remain staunchly pronatalist), population growth rates have declined throughout the industrialized world. The decline has occurred in all of Europe, in North America, Oceania, Japan, and in a few other countries in Latin America and Asia. Between 1900 and 1920, Europe's average annual growth rate fell to 0.75 percent. This rate was sustained, with several fluctuations, through the late 1950s. By 1970, the continent's population size had reached 700 million, and the growth rate was about 0.66 percent per year. New technologies such as effective intrauterine devices, the pill, steroids, and cheap and effective sterilization procedures, contributed to the more recent declines, as they have made contraception close to 100 percent effective. In 1997, with a population size of 720 million, Europe as a whole reported its first negative rate of natural increase (RNI) since 1750 of −0.1 percent. Recently, 10 nations have reported an RNI below zero, including Estonia (−0.5), Latvia (−0.7), Hungary (−0.4), and Germany (−0.1). Six countries were at ZPG in 1997, including Sweden, Italy, and Portugal (Italy has since fallen well below ZPG). England's RNI was 0.2.

From Stage 3 to Stage 4

In more than just a symbolic sense, Europe has now completed its demographic transition full-circle (see Figure 8.2). As in the period prior to 1650, its growth is now slow, uneven, and rates often fall to zero or below. The difference, as we can see, is that during Stage I, this was the result of high birth rates, high death rates, and the ever-present threat that death rates would increase to cause a demographic collapse. Today, one finds low birth rates and low death rates, with the real possibility in dozens of countries that birth rates will fall below death rates (or they have already done so). Of course it is sheer fantasy, but if present growth patterns prevail, Europe will find itself unpopulated in a few centuries.

Demographic Transition in the Less-Industrialized Countries[5]

Asia's population doubled once between the beginning of the Common Era and the Age of Exploration, having reached about 370 million by 1600 AD. As of 1750, its average annual rate of growth was still only in the 0.06 percent range. Africa's population grew somewhat faster during this period, at about the same rate as Europe's. It

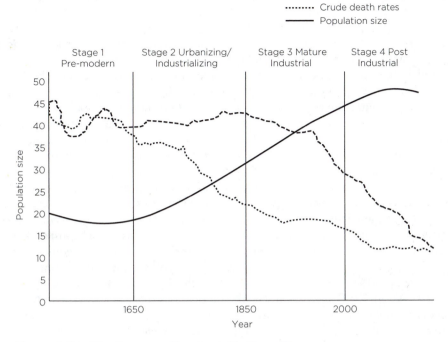

Figure 8.2. The European Demographic Transition
Sources: Based on Davis (1945, 1963); Thomlinson (1975).

had doubled twice since 1 AD, to reach the 100 million mark by 1750. Latin America experienced the most dramatic population fluctuations. With an estimated 3 million inhabitants in 1 AD and 7 million in 600 AD, the population size had reached 40 million by 1500 AD—the largest ever. Yet it was not quite large enough to resist the Conquistadors. With the coming of the Europeans, the size of Latin America's population fell to barely 7 million by 1650—the same size as in 600 AD. That is, 1,000 years of natural increase was eliminated in less than 50 years of colonization, from the usual causes: war, pestilence, and famine.

Industrial revolution, technological innovations, urban growth, and the other underlying causes of death control were generally not experienced outside of Europe. So, as England and its neighbors progressed through Stage II, the rest of the world remained in Stage I. Europe's growth rates rose to the 1 percent level between 1750 and 1850, whereas in the less-industrialized areas, they had risen to only 0.3 percent.

Beginning at about the turn of the twentieth century, the effects of improved sanitation and nutrition began to take hold in the colonized regions. At this point, Europe had had 200 years to perfect its technologies of mortality control. Thus, when they were at last exported to India, Southern Africa, and Latin America, they arrived in highly advanced forms. New antibiotics, vaccines, sewage systems, and related innovations made the prevention of infant and child death far more effective than had been the case when Europe began Stage II of its demographic transition. The consequences were profound. Between 1900 and 1950, the average annual growth rates in Asia, Africa, and Latin America reached the 1.0 percent level, with most of the increase occurring during the latter part of the period at substantially higher rates. These rates are comparable to the long-term average of Europe between 1650 and 1950. During the early 1900s, annual death rates in Europe and North America ranged between 14 and 24 per 1,000. Just prior to that time, death rates in the less-industrialized areas were still at the 40 to 50 per 1,000 level they had been for centuries. But then the gap began to close, and to close rapidly. So, at the end of World War I, virtually all of the world's populations were experiencing mortality declines.

Today's industrialized countries reached their maximum average annual growth rates of just above 0.5 percent per year approximately 200 years after the beginning of mortality declines. But the less-developed countries reached the same 1 percent levels in only 50 years, because of the high-growth potentials associated with their young populations and especially because of the rapid and wholesale innovations in mortality control. As Figure 8.3 indicates, growth rates in the two sets of countries have been equal twice—thus far. The first time was during the long period prior to 1650 when the entire world was growing at rates well below 0.1 percent per year. The second time was in 1950, when the two trajectories (the industrialized countries on the decline and the less industrialized on the incline) met at around 0.5 percent. Unlike England and the rest of today's industrialized countries, however, when the populations of the less industrialized reached this peak, they did not enter Stage III and the beginning of fertility declines. Instead, they continued to grow, with fertility levels about as high as they had always been (CBRs at the 40 per 1,000 level and above).

After World War II, medical and health innovations that were far more advanced than even those that had come to the less-industrialized countries earlier in the century were introduced, and they spread rapidly. Meanwhile, through the early 1900s, birth rates were essentially unchanged. In 1900, annual CBRs in India, Sri Lanka (then Ceylon), and Mexico were approximately 48, 39, and 45 per 1,000, respectively. These remained about the same through the 1950s until 1960, when they were

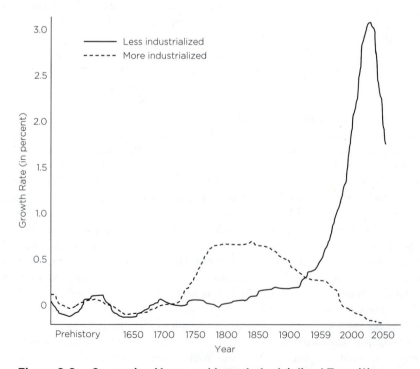

Figure 8.3. Comparing More- and Less-Industrialized Transitions

43, 37, and 46. As of 1972, annual CBRs in Africa averaged 46 per 1,000, ranging from 37 per 1,000 in Egypt (then the United Arab Republic) to 52 per 1,000 in Southwest African nations such as Niger. In West Asia, Saudi Arabia, and Pakistan for example, rates were also at or above 50 per 1,000. Latin America averaged 38 per 1,000, with rates as high as 49 per 1,000 in some Central American and Caribbean countries (PRB 1973).

The combination of rapidly declining death rates and continued high levels of fertility produced a population explosion that far surpassed Europe's experience a century or so earlier. Between 1950 and 1960, average annual growth rates in the less-industrialized areas climbed to the 2.0 percent level, and by 1970 they had reached 3.0 percent. At that point, the populations of countries in South and Central Asia, sub-Saharan Africa, and Central America were doubling every 22 years, and this included some of the world's most massive populations such as India, China, and Indonesia.

At the turn of the twenty-first century, almost every less-industrialized country had seen declines in population growth rates from their highest levels in the 1970s. In 1960, the size of the world's population was 3.03 billion. In the 33 years between 1927 and 1960, it had increased by 1 billion. However, it took only 14 years for another 1 billion to be added, with the world's population estimated at 4 billion in year 1974. But because of the downturns in growth rates in the less-industrialized countries during the 1970s, world population growth began to slow, stabilizing around 1980 at an annual average of 1.7 percent. This rate remained about the same through the 1980s; and by 1990 there were approximately 5.3 billion people in the world. By the late 1990s, the growth rate for the world had fallen to about 1.5 percent per year, with the less-developed countries at 1.8 percent and the industrialized countries at a mere 0.1 percent. The former group includes China, which in 1998 reported an RNI of 1.0 as the result of a CBR of 17 per 1,000 and a CDR of 7 per 1,000. This CDR is about the same as that of the United States.

Figure 8.4 summarizes recent world-population growth rates and the proportional shares of the industrialized and the less-industrialized nations. Table 8.3 shows the crude CBRs and CDRs and rates of natural increase for a set of less-industrialized nations. As indicated, all of these countries have experienced declines in growth rates since 1970, although in some—like China—the decline has been quite rapid whereas in others, such as Niger, it has been very slow.

THE PROSPECTS OF FUTURE POPULATION GROWTH

Recent projections indicate that by 2050 the world's population will have nearly doubled in size since 1990, from 5.3 billion to 10.02 billion. According to the medium UN projection, by 2150 the world will reach ZPG, at a size slightly under 11 billion. Accompanying these increases will be an almost certain geographic redistribution. For, as we have seen, rates of natural increase vary greatly between regions. For example, sub-Saharan Africa is growing at a rate of 2.9 percent per annum. Its population will double by 2025 at current rates. On the other hand, Europe's population is declining at a rate of approximately –0.2 percent per annum. As a result, the less-industrialized nations' share of the world's total, which was 72 percent in 1996, is projected to increase to 89 percent by 2025.

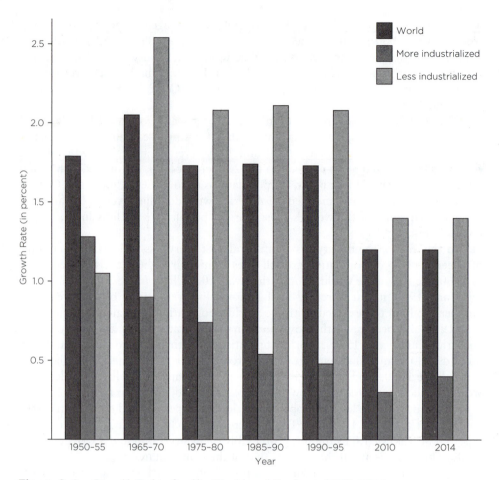

Figure 8.4. Growth Rates for the World and Regions, 1950-2014

Note: Average annual growth rates in percentages shown below.

Sources: El-Badry (1992); "World Population Growth," World Bank; *World Population Data Sheets*, 2010 and 2014, Population Reference Bureau.

The Redistribution of the World's Population

In Asia, Africa, and Latin America, mortality rates continue to decline much faster than birth rates, and this pattern is expected to continue for many years. Thus, the populations of most of the countries in these regions are very young. As of 2014, 42.1 percent of Kenya's population was below 15 years of age. On the other hand, the United States had only 19.4 percent in these cohorts. Another important difference is in average life expectancy at birth. In Chapter 9, we will show how this indicator summarizes the probabilities of dying at all ages and why it is, therefore, especially sensitive to infant mortality. Between 1980 and 2010, the world's average life expectancy increased from 61 to 67.2 years. In the more-developed countries, the average in 2013 was 75 years for males and 82 years for females (PRB 2013). In the less-developed nations, life expectancy is considerably lower: 67 years for males and 71 for females. In the poorest countries, such as Mozambique, Guinea, Gambia, and

Table 8.3. Less-Industrialized Countries in Transition, 2013

Country	Population Size	CBR	CDR	RNI	Rate of Decline
Brazil	202.8	15	6	0.9	M
Cameroon	22.8	39	12	2.7	S
China	1,364.1	12	7	0.5	R
El Salvador	6.4	20	7	1.3	M/S
Ghana	27.0	34	9	2.5	S
Haiti	10.8	28	9	1.9	M/S
Iran	77.4	19	5	1.4	R/M
Kenya	43.2	34	9	2.5	M
Malaysia	30.1	26	6	2.0	R/M
Nepal	27.1	22	7	1.5	M
Niger	18.2	50	11	3.9	S
Peru	30.8	20	5	1.5	M
Thailand	66.4	12	8	0.4	R
Uganda	38.8	43	5	3.8	S
Vietnam	90.7	17	7	1.0	M

Notes: Population size in millions, crude birth and death rates per 1,000, rate of natural increase in percentages. For rate of decline of growth rates, S = Slow, M = Moderate, and R = Rapid.

Source: Population Reference Bureau, *World Population Data Sheet* 2014.

Rwanda, averages for both men and women are below 67 years, with Mozambique reporting only 49 and 50 years for males and females, respectively (PRB 2013).

As of the year 2013, the world's population was growing at a rate of 1.2 percent per year. This represents a considerable decline from the levels that reached 2.0 percent and above during the 1960s. Nevertheless, continued high growth rates are anticipated in even the most conservative projections produced by the UN and other sources. Among the factors that lie behind this outlook, three characteristics of the populations in Africa and South Asia, especially, are cited most frequently. First, although the average family size in the less-industrialized countries has declined in recent decades, from six to three children per household, this number is still above the replacement level (of just over 2.0). Thus, without further fertility declines, each generation would be larger than the previous one. Second, mortality levels—especially levels of infant mortality—are expected to continue to drop, resulting in increases in average life expectancies. Third, populations generally grow for several years even if fertility were to fall well below the replacement level. Demographers refer to this phenomenon as *population momentum*, and it is an effect of a population's age-sex structure.

As we noted in Chapter 3, broad-based age-sex pyramids characterize high-fertility societies. These societies have very high proportions of their populations in the youngest cohorts. If birth rates remain high, the isosceles triangle-shaped structure will be reproduced generation after generation. If, at the same time, death rates fall, the broad base will become even more pronounced because more infants and children will survive. But a large population would be sustained even if the women in such a society were, instantaneously, to accept small-family norms, to practice effective birth control, and to have no more than two children in their lifetimes. For the large backlog of fertile and prepubescent women already alive would still produce more than enough children to maintain population growth for several a years to follow.

During the late 1990s, some demographers began to suggest that projected world population figures should be reassessed in the light of rapid fertility declines in many of the less-developed countries (Yea 2004; Eberstadt 1997). They hold that population growth will peak in the very near future and then register an indefinite decline in the subsequent generations. The United Nations' *World Population Prospects* (1995) provides three projections, the high, medium, and low variants. The low variant indicates that world ZPG will be achieved by 2040, and that depopulation will take place thereafter. This variant is based on a set of assumptions about the three population components, death, birth, and migration. First, it is assumed that in the more-developed countries, life expectancy at birth will rise from 75 to 81 years by the middle of the twenty-first century, and the less-developed regions are expected to make even greater gains. For these countries, average life expectancy is projected to increase from 64 to 76 years. Sub-Saharan Africa, which lags behind all other regions in terms of economic development, is expected to experience the greatest increase by 2050, from 52 to 72 years.

The projections of migration patterns focus on specific regions. Of course, migration has no direct impact on the world's population, as losses in one region will result in gains in another. The major assumption in this regard is that North America, Western Europe, Eastern Europe, and the European portion of the former Soviet Union will receive about 1.6 million migrants from the less-developed regions by 2025. The most important assumptions are related to future fertility patterns. The low variant assumes that the TFR in Europe, North America, and Japan will decline to 1.4 children per woman by the first decade of the twenty-first century (it was 1.6 as of 1997–1998). In the less-developed regions, the TFR is expected to decline steadily, reaching the replacement level by 2020 and declining further to 1.6 by 2050. Sub-Saharan Africa is expected to attain replacement by 2035.

Based on these assumptions, the U.N. projection indicates that the world's population will peak at 7.7 billion people around the year 2040. Population declines are predicted to occur after this date. Under this scenario, nearly all of the industrialized countries would experience negative growth rates before 2005, and the less-developed regions would begin to lose population about four decades later, by 2045. Sub-Saharan Africa is likely to have positive population growth beyond the year 2050, primarily as the result of population momentum. Because the rate of fertility decline is not uniform across all regions, relative population sizes are likely to differ from those of the predecline era. Table 8.4 lists the 10 most populous nations in 2013 and the 10 most populous nations in 2050 according to the low-variant projections. Several developing nations, Iran, Mexico, Zaire, Ethiopia, Bangladesh, and Nigeria, make their first appearance on the list for 2030. You can also see that by 2030 only one industrialized country (the United States) will be among the top 10.

United Nations' 2012 revised population forecast puts the world population at 9.6 billion by 2050 according to the medium scenario. The revised forecasts presents three types of population forecasts, medium, high, and low, under three separate sets of assumptions. The medium scenario assumes that the total fertility of each country will reach below replacement levels and will remain at the below level for about 100 years before attaining replacement levels. In the high scenario, total fertility after 2050 is assumed to be a quarter of a child higher than in the medium scenario. The fertility levels are assumed to remain at the attained level when the medium scenario stabilizes at replacement level. In the low scenario, total

Table 8.4. The World's Most-Populous Countries, 2013 and 2030 (Projected)

	2013		2030	
Rank	Country	Population	Country	Population
1	China	1,357	India	1,652
2	India	1,277	China	1,314
3	U.S.A.	316	Nigeria	440
4	Indonesia	249	U.S.A.	400
5	Brazil	196	Indonesia	366
6	Pakistan	191	Pakistan	363
7	Nigeria	174	Brazil	227
8	Bangladesh	157	Bangladesh	202
9	Russia	143	Congo, D. R.	182
10	Japan	127	Ethiopia	178

Note: Population sizes in millions.

Source: Population Reference Bureau, *World Population Data Sheet, 2013.*

fertility is assumed to be 0.25 of a child lower than in the medium scenario and to remain constant at 1.85 children per woman when the medium scenario remains at replacement level.

The revised medium forecast is an increase of 300 million people worldwide over the prior UN population growth forecasts. Of the 9.6 billion people in 2050, 8.2 billion will be in developing nations. The developed nations with a population of 1.3 billion are likely to stay more or less stable throughout the forecast period. The two population giants, India and China, will each have about 1.45 billion people by 2028. Beyond the late 2020s, the population of India is projected to grow much more slowly. The Nigerian population is expected to explode to 1.1 billion. Currently populous nations such as Indonesia, Tanzania, Pakistan, the Democratic Republic of Congo, Ethiopia, and Niger will each have more than 200 million by year 2100.

The most recent forecasts from a group of well-known demographers (Raftery Lalic, and Gerland 2014) suggests that the world population is likely to reach 11 billion by 2100, about 2 billion higher than prior UN world-population-growth projections. Unlike prior UN population-growth projections, this study quantifies the level of confidence in the projection. There is an 80 percent probability that the African population in 2100 will be between 9.6 billion and 12.3 billion.

The Third Stage in the Less-Industrialized Regions?

The slowing of world population growth and the impending aging of the population have been described in the social science literature within the framework of demographic transition. It is assumed that Stage III is the destiny of those nations that are currently in Stage II. However, this observation has not gone entirely unchallenged. For one thing, even though demographic transitions are among the most widely studied and best-documented events in population history, no scientific theory of the phenomenon that would allow for accurate law-based predictions has yet been formulated (see Cervellati and Sunde 2011; Coale 1973; Concepcion and Murphy 1973; Weinstein 1980). Kingsley Davis (1963) pioneered in developing the "theory of change and response" (also see Chapter 12, below), but neither he nor any of his successors has shown that entry into Stage III is a certain—or even a highly likely—outcome of mortality decline.

In addition, empirical research has uncovered several cases that are incompatible with the general course of events encompassed by transitions. Many African nations, including Gambia, Oman, and Rwanda, appear to have completed the second stage without any apparent movement toward the third. If a population does not make the transition to the third stage, even though it has achieved significant declines in general and infant mortality, one wonders how long it can endure the experience of explosive growth (Brown and Jacobson 1986). Finally, we might ask, what are the consequences of population pressures brought about by growth rates at or above 3 percent per annum? These are relevant questions because they have important policy implications. We need to assess our knowledge of demographic transition theory in terms of its value in making generalizations about population change. Instances of success and failure in this respect can provide guidance in selection among policy options in the realms of population education, foreign assistance, the promotion of family planning, and public-health initiatives.

Europe's transition from high to low rates of growth was accompanied by the transformation of a predominantly agrarian community into an industrial society (from **Gemeinschaft** *to* **Gessellschaft**, as sociologists put it). In particular, the combination of industrialization, urban growth, and secularization propelled England and the other countries of Europe toward history's first episode of intentional fertility decline. Recognition of these facts has led to an emphasis among policy specialists on *developmental* approaches to population control. According to this perspective, the single most important lesson to be learned from the European transition is that socioeconomic development is the most effective form of contraception. With development, couples want—indeed, they need—smaller families. The presence of easily accessible family-planning programs is an essential component in meeting the new demand for **birth control** methods. But, from the developmentalist point of view, the contributions of family planning to fertility decline are of secondary importance. A more crucial role is assigned to development in bringing about the economic, cultural, and psychological preconditions under which effective means of birth control are sought.

In some respects, there are some striking differences between current demographic events in some parts of the less-industrialized areas and the changes that occurred after 1850 in Europe. One that we have already noted is that population growth rates in parts of Asia, Africa, and Latin America are much higher than the maximum of 1.2 percent per year reached in Europe—in some instances, three times higher. Another substantial difference is in the importance and prevalence of marriage. By the mid-nineteenth century, Western Europe's hallmark pattern of relatively late marriage and a high proportion of single persons was well established. By contrast, in today's less-industrialized countries, marriage comes early and is nearly universal. The proportion of single adults is close to 0. In addition, the transition to low morality rates has occurred at a much faster pace in the less-industrialized regions than it did in Europe—about four times as rapidly. For example, in the 1970–1975 period, Egypt's CDR was 16 per 1,000. This fell to 9 per 1,000 between 1990 and 1995. Cameroon, whose CDR was 20 per 1,000 in the early 1970s, reported a decline to 13 per 1,000 by the early 1990s.

Although these differences are authentic, other evidence—often taken from other types of societies—suggests important similarities between the situation in today's less-industrialized countries' and Europe's experiences two centuries ago. Some population historians have questioned the argument that socioeconomic development is strongly linked to fertility decline. Whereas it seems clear that industrialization and the shift to small-family norms more or less coincided in England, the transition in France began earlier, during the late eighteenth century and before any significant industrial growth had occurred. Hungary and Bulgaria also appear to have undergone fertility declines with predominantly rural populations. Moreover, most of the inhabitants of Europe, England included, were illiterate at the commencement of the transition to Stage III.

We find similar conditions in Asia today. Birth rates have dropped significantly in several of India's states. These declines might have been expected in the economically advanced regions in the country. But, contrary to expectations, during the 1970s, fertility rates fell most impressively, to replacement levels, in the economically backward state of Kerala.[6] Countries such as Indonesia and Thailand also registered drops in birth rates despite the low per-capita incomes that prevailed. The wealthier nations of Southeast Asia, such as the former British Colony of Hong Kong, Taiwan, and Singapore have achieved rates of natural increase that are entirely comparable with those the industrialized world.

Another alleged difference that is in some dispute relates to the length of time required between the beginning and the end of Stage II. Apparently, the transition to low fertility in many parts of Europe occurred within the relatively short period between 1880 and 1910. In France, the transition probably came early, and in Ireland, it was late in coming, but in both cases only a few decades intervened between the drop in death rates and the drop in birth rates. In these and some other countries, the dates at which a decline in marital fertility of at least 10 percent occurred are: France: 1800, Belgium: 1882, Germany: 1890: Sweden: 1892, Ireland: 1929.[7]

Fertility transition in the less-industrialized countries began during the early 1960s: 1962 in Costa Rica, 1964 in Chile, and 1965 in China (Hardee et al. 2014; Donaldson 1991:13). Knowledge of family-planning methods is now nearly universal. During the European transition, birth-control techniques and ideologies diffused steadfastly through regions with low levels of cultural resistance: cities, less-traditional rural areas, and places undergoing secularization. This is true of the transition in Asia as well. For example, in Malaysia, birth rate declines began earlier among the ethnic Chinese and Indian groups than among the Malays.

As was true in Europe, a drop in voluntary fertility characterizes transition in the less-industrialized areas today. The lower demand for children is accompanied by a positive attitude toward control of one's own destiny and toward the use of technological means to achieve personal and familial goals. This shift from an external to an internal locus of control was and remains today a necessary condition for fertility decline. Organized family-planning programs and propaganda designed to make birth control desirable and legitimate have clearly begun to play a crucial role in bringing about and maintaining demographic transition in contemporary high-fertility populations.

Europe's Second Transition

Until fairly recently, observers believed that Stage III of Europe's demographic transition would be an indefinitely long and stable period of low fertility and mortality. It was assumed that fertility levels would fall to the replacement level and stay there.

Thus, population sizes and structures would remain more or less constant into the foreseeable future (see Chapter 9 for more on stable and stationary populations). During the Great Depression of the 1930s, this scenario was called into question, as fertility levels throughout Europe fell below replacement. These events raised concerns about the prospect of a shrinking European population. At that point, demographers began to refer to Stage III as the period of "incipient (forthcoming) decline." However, the baby boom of the post–World War II era appeared to refute such forecasts of population collapse, with the suggestion that the drop in birth rates of earlier decades was a response to unusually harsh economic conditions and widespread social dislocation. The baby boom was explained, in part, as the expression of delayed fertility that could now be actualized in a more prosperous environment.

But the baby boom subsided in the early 1960s, as birth rates began to decline once more. And they have continued to decline into the twenty-first century. Rather than being an aberration, the experience of below-replacement fertility levels of the 1930s appears to have been a harbinger of what is now referred to as the second European demographic transition (Van de Kaa 1987): an indefinite period of zero-to-negative population growth. Moreover, the absolute losses in population size are no long "incipient." As shown in Table 8.5, they are manifest throughout the continent: from Scandinavia to Italy, and from The Netherlands to Russia.

The continued declines in birth rates have been accompanied by changes in the rates of marriage, divorce, and cohabitation. By 1970, Sweden's total first-marriage rate had fallen to 584 first marriages per 1,000 single men below age 50, and 624 first marriages per 1,000 for women. In 1975, the total first-marriage rates for men in Denmark and Switzerland were 621 and 624, respectively, and for females the rates in these countries were 661 and 650. In Southern Europe, the greatest declines in total first marital rates occurred during the latter half of the 1970s. In Eastern Europe, there was a slight increase in these rates between 1965 and 1975, but they fell

Table 8.5.   Rates of Natural Increase in Europe, 1992-1993 and 2014

Country	1992–1993	2014	Country	1992–1993	2014
Albania	1.6	0.5	Malta	0.4	0.2
Austria	−.05	0.0	Netherlands	0.4	0.2
Belgium	−0.1	0.2	Norway	0.2	0.4
Bulgaria	.02	−0.5	Poland	0.5	−0.1
Czech Republic	.03	0.0	Portugal	0.3	−0.2
Denmark	0.0	0.1	Romania	0.4	−0.3
Finland	0.2	0.1	Russia	−0.5	0.0
France	0.3	0.3	Slovenia	-	0.1
Germany	−0.1	−0.2	Spain	0.4	0.1
Greece	0.2	−0.4	Sweden	0.1	0.1
Hungary	−0.1	−0.4	Switzerland	0.2	0.2
Iceland	0.8	0.9	UK	0.2	0.3
Ireland	1.0	0.9	Ukraine	-	−0.4
Italy	−.02	−0.1	Yugoslavia	0.5	0.1
Luxembourg	0.1	0.4			

Sources: *World Resources, 1992–1993*: Tables 16.2 and 16.3; Population Reference Bureau "Rate of Natural Increase," 2014.

during the late 1970s, particularly in Hungary and the former German Democratic Republic (GDR). These declines in marital rates were accompanied by increases in divorce among first-married couples. In the 1980s, as marriage rates continued to drop, divorce rates climbed to more than 11 per 1,000 married couples in Austria, GDR, Hungary, and Sweden (Van de Kaa 1987).

Changes in laws permitting divorce by mutual consent contributed to the increase in divorces in Northern and Western Europe. At the same time, rates of cohabitation as a form of marital union increased throughout Europe. Whereas cohabitation was rare prior to the 1960s, by the 1980s, it had become nearly as common as traditional marriage in Sweden and Denmark. Nearly every European country now reports rising divorce rates and a growing proportion of children living in single-parent families and stepfamilies (this is the case in the United States as well). The declining importance of marriage, increases in divorce, and growth in the number of nonmarital unions have resulted from and have contributed to further fertility decline, ensuring the continuation of the **second demographic transition** for many years to come.

The social-structural conditions that underlie these changes have not yet been clearly established, although some studies indicate that the emergence of individualistic values has contributed to the decline in fertility (Spaiser et al. 2014; Inglehart 1997). Current emphasis on using one's talents, realizing personal potentials, having quality children, and acquiring a good education have all helped to lower the demand for children. In addition, the increasing participation of women in the labor force and the consequent rise in the number of two-career families has increased the opportunity costs of having children. These and similar factors are significant, not only because they have the effect of further slowing population growth rates that are already at zero and below, but also because they are not likely to disappear. Unlike occasional wars and depressions, value shifts toward self-centeredness and structural improvements in the status of women are relatively permanent kinds of transformations that are reinforced by small-family norms. Under such circumstances, if there is to be a second, upward, stage of the second demographic transition, it will have to come in the wake of an authentic—and unlikely—social revolution.

THE AGING OF THE WORLD'S POPULATION

One of the major demographic consequences of fertility decline is that it causes a population to become older (Cleland 2013; Brandel and Gwatlun 1982). This is the outcome of steady decreases in the proportion of young persons, as the age-sex pyramid begins to lose its isosceles triangle shape. More than one-half of the 1 billion people in the world aged 55 and above now live in less-industrialized areas, where birth rates are high and are just beginning to fall. As fertility levels continue to drop, we can expect this percentage to increase significantly (Zhang, Guo, and Zheng 2012; Kinsella and Suzman 1992).

As discussed in Chapter 3, demographers use several indicators to measure the age of a population: median age, proportions in older and younger cohorts, dependency ratios, and so on. We also noted that average life expectancy *at birth* is not a measure of a population's age—but of its mortality levels. However, it is true that average life expectancy *at older ages* is closely correlated with other measures of age. In particular, if the average number of years remaining to older persons in a population increases from one date to another, then the population is getting older (see Bicknell and Parks 1989; United Nations 1990). In this case, the cause is not fertility decline but prolongation of life through the use of more effective death-control technologies

With this in mind, it is of interest to consider some recent estimates published by the United States Bureau of the Census (1997). Between 1975 and 2000, the average life expectancy at age 65 for the world rose from 13.5 to 14.3 years, an increase of 5.9 percent in the interval. But for the less-industrialized regions, it rose from 11.7 to 13.2, or a 12.8 percent increase. Thus, by this measure, the less-developed countries are aging twice as rapidly as the world as a whole. Africa registered the greatest increase of all the continents, from 11.1 to 12.7 years, which is a rate of 14.4 percent in the interval. Latin America's increase was the slowest, although it was still well above the world average: from 13.5 to 15.1, or 11.9 percent.

People aged 60 worldwide in 2010–2015 can expect to live 20 years or more. However, the number years they can expect to live varies across levels of development. In the more-developed countries, those who survive to age 60 will on average live 23 years more while in less-developed and least-developed countries they may expect to live an additional 19 years and 17 years, respectively.[8]

There is no universal consensus on the definition of "elderly." In most traditional societies, the timing of social role transitions, such as becoming a grandparent or losing the ability to reproduce, are used as a mark of old age. In many, the concept of "retirement age" does not exist (Szinovacz, Martin, and Davey 2014; Tout 1989, 1990, 1992), as people continue to work until they are physically unable. Only as cross-national data have become more available, have researchers begun to use a fixed chronological age (e.g., 60 or 65 years) to provide an operational definition of "old." During the 1980s, the number of elderly throughout the world was growing faster than the general population. This trend continued to hold into the 1990s for every region except Africa, reflecting both current worldwide declines in fertility and the large size of the cohorts now reaching old age. As of 2013, 30 percent of the world's elderly lived in East Asia, 24 percent in South Asia, and 7.7 percent in Latin America. The United Nations projects that by the year 2025, 29.9 percent of the world's population aged 60 and over will be living in East Asia, 27.4 percent in South Asia, and 8.3 percent in Latin America (*United Nations Chronicle* 1985). In most Latin American countries, by 2025 the population over 60 will be nearly four times the size of that group in 1980. In 1989, China had about 90.5 million people aged 60 and above. It is expected that this number will triple by 2025 (United Nations 1990).

In India, the elderly cohorts have been growing faster than any other segment for several years; and the country ranks fourth in the number of persons 60 and above among all countries with large elderly populations. By 2021, it is expected to be second in this category. In 1961, India's elderly population accounted for 5.6 percent of the total population and there were 24.7 million people in the age group. The number increased to 42.5 million by 1981. By 2011, of 1.2 billion people, 5 percent were aged 65 and above.

Although Sub-Saharan Africa's elderly population is not as large in size as in other regions, it still has considerable growth potential. The largest increase in the number of elderly in the world between 1980 and 2000 occurred in Asia and Africa. The number of Africans age 60 and older is expected to grow to 101.9 million in 2025. This represents two doublings in less than 50 years. In contrast, projections indicate that the elderly population in the industrialized countries will double just once during the same period (Habte-Gabr, Blum, and Smith 1987). In 1989, 2.8 percent of sub Saharan Africa's population was age 65 and older. This proportion is expected to increase to 3.4 percent by 2025. Thus, during the last two decades of the twentieth century, sub-Saharan Africa's elderly population increased by about 82 percent, and between 2000 and 2020, it is expected to increase by 93 percent (Nair 2014; Adamchak 1989).

Using the figure of 60 years and above, we can track the unprecedented growth in the number and proportion of elderly persons in the less-industrialized populations. In 1950, there were about 200 million people in this age group in the world, of whom about 100 million lived in the less-developed countries. Projections indicate that, as of the year 2000, there were 612 million elderly in the world and about 60 percent of them were living in Asia, Africa, and Latin America. Between 2000 and 2025, the number of elderly in the world is expected to double, with about 71 percent, or 860 million persons in the less-industrialized regions (UNESCO 1989).

In 2013, there were 841 million persons older than 60 years, and this population is projected to triple by 2050. About 66 percent, 554 million, of the older persons reside in less-developed regions, where the elderly population is expected to triple by 2050. The elderly population in developed countries was 287 million in 2013, and is expected to reach 417 million, about 32 percent of the population by 2050. In Japan, 24 percent of the population is already ages 65 and older. In the less-developed regions, the proportion of older persons was 9 percent in 2013 and is expected to reach 19 percent by 2050. In the least-developed countries, though the proportion elderly in 2013 was small at about 5 percent, it is expected to almost double to 10 percent by 2050.

THE U.S. POPULATION: GROWTH AND CHANGE

In our earlier section on the components method we observed that the annual RNI in the United States stood at about 0.6 percent as of the year 2000. Although this is the lowest RNI in U.S. history, it is still far higher than that of nearly all of the countries in Europe.[9] When we add in the approximately 800,000 immigrants who enter the country each year, we get a growth rate that approaches 1.0 percent. In addition, the United States is the only non-less-industrialized country projected to be among the world's 12 most populous nations by midcentury—and the only one that is expected to remain from the top 12 in 1950. For these and related reasons, the United States is clearly the exception to the rule that wealthy, highly urbanized industrial nations are experiencing a second demographic transition. The fact that it is a net receiver of immigrants—most of whom come from high-fertility, less-developed countries—partly explains this situation. But its birth rate of 15 per 1,000 also remains much higher than the average in Europe (which is 10 per 1,000), so migration cannot be the only factor operating. Rather, much of the answer to the question of why the United States is so lies in its population history.

The United States is one of the few countries in the world today that has a census-taking history that extends back more than 200 years. At the first Census in 1790, the new nation was home to about 4 million people (see Table 8.6). At that date, only six cities had more than 8,000 inhabitants: Philadelphia, New York, Boston, Charleston (South Carolina), Baltimore, and Salem (Massachusetts). According to Census Bureau estimates, colonial America experienced an enormous population explosion, with growth rates approaching 3.0 percent per year between 1700 and

Table 8.6. Enumerated Population Sizes of the United States, 1700-2010 (in Millions)

Year	Pop. Size	Year	Pop. Size	Year	Pop. Size	Year	Pop. Size
1700	0.280	1840	17.120	1900	76.094	1960	180.671
1790	3.929	1850	23.261	1910	92.407	1970	203.302
1800	5.297	1860	31.513	1920	106.461	1980	226.542
1810	7.224	1870	39.905	1930	123.188	1990	248.718
1820	9.618	1880	50.262	1940	132.122	2000	281.424
1830	12.901	1890	63.056	1950	151.684	2010	308.745

Source: U.S. Census Bureau, Statistical Abstract of the United States: 2012.

1790. Although there was some migration during the early part of the period, most of this growth was the result of natural increase. In 1790, Virginia had the largest population of the states, with nearly three-quarters of a million people.

At the turn of the nineteenth century, the population expanded rapidly toward the West. Between 1800 and 1840, western New York State, western Pennsylvania, Ohio, Michigan, Indiana, Kentucky, and Illinois were settled. These states and states-to-be absorbed much of the nearly 12 million people added to the nation's population. The annual growth rate remained near the 3.0 percent level, while the number of Americans doubled every 24 years. During the second half of the century, the largest component of growth was immigration. But with birth rates still high, the population continued to increase at or above 3.0 percent per year until the 1860–1870 period. The potato famine of the 1840s in Ireland brought more than 1 million Irish immigrants to the United States. Other early groups came from Germany and the northwest European and Scandinavian countries. In 1880, yet another wave arrived from southern and eastern Europe. At that Census, the 10th in U.S. history, the total population size had reached the 63 million mark and the growth rate was a still rapid 2.3 percent per year.

The stream of immigration lasted for about five decades. The process of westward expansion of the population that had begun in the early 1800s was hastened by the arrival of these new immigrants. In 1790, the median population center of the United States was 23 miles east of Baltimore, Maryland (see Chapter 3). By 1860, with California now in the Union, the center had moved a full 400 miles to the west, to south central Ohio; and by 1920, it was in Indiana. Migration from the East Coast and the expansion of the population from natural increase and immigration on West Coast helped to fuel urban growth across the continent. Between 1840 and 1860, the urbanization rated nearly doubled, from 10 to 20 percent, at a growth rate of more than 6 percent per year. Cities such as Chicago, Cleveland, Detroit, St. Louis, San Francisco, Los Angeles, and Seattle grew rapidly from villages to world-class metropolises during the late 1800s.

Immigration began to slow after 1880, although during the first decade of the twentieth century nearly 9 million people were admitted (this is close to the current number of admissions per decade). As these additional immigrants moved to the cities, and with even greater flows of domestic migration from the rural areas, the urban sector continued to expand. Largely because of reduced immigration, between 1890 and 1900 the general population growth rate fell below 2.0 percent per year for the first time in history. But by 1920 more than one-half of the population was living in cities. In this respect, the United States had caught up with Europe; and,

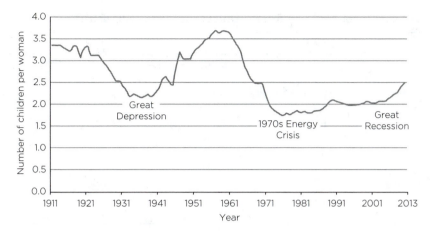

Figure 8.5.   Changes in Fertility Levels, United States, 1911-2011
*2013 rate was 2.5.
Estimated by Population Reference Bureau, data from National Center for Health Statistics.

with a "slow" annual growth rate of 1.9 percent between 1910 and 1920, its population was still expanding twice as rapidly.

Both mortality and fertility levels had been falling in the United States since early in the nineteenth century, as shown in Tables 8.7 and 8.8. But birth rates were so high during the early period that it was only after the Civil War of 1861–1865 that the impact of these declines was translated into slower population growth. According to the estimates of Ansley Coale and Melvin Zelnick, between 1800 and 1860 the TFR declined from 7.0 children per ever-married woman to 5.2 (see Figure 8.5 and Table 8.8). This is an average decrease of −0.5 percent per year. But, in the 1860–1870 period, the TFR fell to 4.6. This represents an annual rate of −1.2 percent, or more than twice as fast as in the years prior to the Civil War. By 1920, the TFR had been cut in half to 3.2 children per woman, at about a 1 percent annual decline. Between 1920 and 1930, the population growth rate fell once more, this time to a level below 1.5 percent per year, as the TFR also decreased to 2.5. As was the case in Europe, the era of the Great Depression had a definite demographic impact in the United States. During the 1930–1940 period, the population growth rate dropped below 1.0, to 0.7 percent per year. This is the slowest decadal growth the country has ever

Table 8.7.   U.S. Death Rates, 1900-2010

Year	Crude Death Rate	Year	Crude Death Rate
1900	17.2	1960	9.5
1910	14.7	1970	9.5
1920	13.0	1980	8.8
1930	11.3	1990	8.6
1940	10.8	2000	8.5
1950	9.6	2010	8.0

Sources: Department of Health and Human Services, National Center for Health Statistics, Centers for Disease Control and Prevention; *National Vital Statistics Report*, vols. 47–63. Retrieved on February 23, 2015 from *www.dhhs.gov and www.cdc.gov*.

Table 8.8. Total Fertility Rates, United States, 1800-2010

	TFR		TFR
1800	7.0	1910	3.4
1810	6.9	1920	3.2
1820	6.7	1930	2.5
1830	6.6	1940	2.2
1840	6.1	1950	3.0
1850	5.4	1960	3.5
1860	5.2	1970	2.5
1870	4.6	1980	1.8
1880	4.2	1990	2.08
1890	3.0	2000	2.06
1900	3.6	2010	1.93

Sources: Prior to 1917: Coale and Zelnik (1989). Between 1917 and 1980: National Center for Health Statistics, *Vital and Health Statistics, Series 21*, No. 28. Through 2010: "Births Final Data for 2012," *National Vital Statistics Reports* 62, no. 9 (December 2013).

experienced, to the present. Accompanying this decline was a decrease in the TFR to 2.2 children. Fertility levels were not to be this low again for 40 years.

The 1950 enumeration was the first to reflect the baby boom. With a total population size of more than 150 million, the U.S. growth rate had risen to nearly 1.4 percent (twice that of the previous decade). The TFR increased as well, to 3.0, which was about the same level as in the early 1920s. As the boom continued through the 1950s, so did the increases in population growth and fertility. As of 1960, with 70 percent of the population now living in urban areas, the general growth rate reached 1.75 percent per year and the TFR rose to 3.5—about equal to the rate in 1900. By the early 1960s the U.S. population size had climbed to 200 million, making it the fourth-largest population in the world, and still growing rapidly.

From that point until the end of the twentieth century, growth began to decelerate, until by 1990, the average annual rate had once more declined to below 1.0 (to 0.9). In addition, the TFR fell below replacement, to 1.8. At the turn of the twenty-first century, the United States was approaching the European pattern once labeled **incipient decline**. That is, population size was still increasing but, at current rates, it would not continue to do so for long.

This situation clearly suggests a point late in the third stage of demographic transition. However, continuing high rates of immigration have offset the prospects of a population decline. Legal immigration adds about 0.3 percent per year to the RNI of 0.6, which makes for a total increase of 2.3 million people annually. And this rate of growth is certainly an underestimate because of the large number of undocumented immigrants who enter the country. According to United States Census Bureau estimates, there were between 3.5 and 4.0 million such persons residing in the United States in 1994, of whom some 1.5 million were in California. The INS put the number at 5.0 million in 1996, estimating that 2.7 million came from Mexico (*Bureau of Statistics* 1997: Table 10). Based on the very rough assumption that about 100,000 "undocumenteds" enter the country every year, the general growth rate would be closer to 1.1 percent than to 0.9. During the 1990 and 2007 interval, the number of undocumented immigrants increased from 3.5 million to 12.2 million. In 2008 and 2009, the numbers fell to 11.3 million.[10] In any case, it seems that there will never be a time when fewer people seek entry into the United States than can be officially accommodated. So, even if population loss sets in, and if such a situation is deemed to be undesirable, the INS can always open wider what Emma Lazarus termed "the golden door."

SUMMARY

In this chapter we have attempted to indicate how and why human populations grow. Of course, at a very basic level the answers to these questions are obvious. A population grows if and when its size at a later date exceeds its size at an earlier date. Otherwise, it is experiencing ZPG, or decline—"negative growth." Moreover, such growth occurs when birth rates and in-migration rates exceed death rates and out-migration rates. Issues of measurement may need to be faced, but these are not very difficult. However, we were not entirely satisfied that the problems had been resolved at that point. Instead, with these *logical* premises in mind, we took the matter further to ask explore *sociological* and *historical* matters, such as why some populations grow at a particular time and others decline; why some periods in history are marked by very slow or negative growth and others by population explosions. As we observed, these kinds of concerns are not quite so straightforward.

Based on a review of the theories and principles of population change, we turned to empirical information about the growth of the world's population from the beginning of history (to the best of our knowledge) to the middle of the next century (as projections would indicate). During the course of this presentation, we took broad sweeps, moved in for a close focus, pursued tangents, and engaged in some outright speculation. The story that was revealed by these efforts is one that has captured the imagination, and often the doubts and fears, of demographers, policy specialists, humanitarians, and ordinary people alike. It is a story about how a few wandering bands of hominids have taken over the Earth, numerically at least. It is about explosive growth in areas of the world that can least afford additional mouths to feed, and absolute losses of citizens in some of the richest nations in the world. It is about the 6 billion of us who are around today and the 6 billion who will almost surely be added in your lifetime. But, perhaps most important of all, it is a story about life: about being born, forming families, moving to new states and cities, emigrating to foreign lands in search of opportunities, getting old, and dying. In this respect, the study of population growth is the very foundation of social science.

In contrast to the preceding discussion, in the following two chapters on the life table and population projection, we begin at the empirical level and move *back* to logical and mathematical concerns. The point of this exercise is to create realistic but relatively simple models of populations so that we may get a better idea of how the real thing operates. That is, we go from the concrete to the abstract to improve our understanding of the concrete. In combination with the part just concluded (Chapters 5 through 8), our knowledge of population models will prepare us for the very last set of discussion on policy and the like. At that point, we will have quite a bit more to say about what people are doing to *control* population growth.

KEY TERMS

birth control
components method
demographic transitions
difference method
doubling time
exponential growth model
Gemeinschaft

Gessellschaft
incipient decline
linear growth model
mortality control
pronatalism
second demographic transition

NOTES

1. Data in the section come from the U.S. Census Bureau's International DataBase and the Bureau's table, "Historical Estimates of World Population" at http://www.census.gov/ipc/www/worldhis.html.

2. In addition to the sources cited, data in this section are also derived from Weinstein (2010: chap. 3), Hernandez (1974), and Weinstein (1978).

3. Warren S. Thompson (1929), Kingsley Davis (1945), Frank Notestein (1945), C. P. Blacker (1947), and W. F. Wilcox (1953) conducted the pioneering research on the demographic transition. A substantial body of literature exists on the subject, extending from the late 1920s to the present. Major works from the 1960s, the 1970s, and more recent dates, include Beaver (1975), Coale, (1973), Concepcion and Murphy (1973), Stolnitz (1964), Taeuber (1960), van de Walle (1998), Donaldson (1991), Jones (1997), and Kalache (1997).

4. Strictly speaking, it was not exclusively European, for it also occurred in former colonial areas that became overseas-European enclaves, such as the United States, Canada, and Oceania. The last section of the chapter discusses the American version of the transition. After some delay, Japan also had a European-style, three-stage transition, as Irene Taeuber (1960) was among the first to note.

5. Data in this section come from several of the sources cited, especially Matras (1973), Durand (1974), and PRB (1973).

6. William Alexander (1998) makes a strong and convincing case that Kerala's fertility decline is the result of the high status afforded to women. Of special note, in his view, is the leading role played in Kerala by the matrilineal, matrilocal Nayar community. Where birth rates remain high in India, the alternative Rajput model of strong male domination continues to hold sway.

7. The source for these data is "Lessons from the Past: Policy Implications of Historical Fertility Studies," *Population and Development Review* 5, 2 (June), 1979: 221–22.

8. See http://www.un.org/en/development/desa/population/publications/pdf/ageing/World PopulationAgeing2013.pdf.

9. Japan, which in some ways is now demographically and sociologically similar to the United States, nevertheless has a European growth profile. With birth rates just under 10 per 1,000 and death rates about 7, its RNI is 0.2 (PRB 1998). With very little in-migration, its total population growth rate is approximately one-fifth that of the United States.

10. Source: Pew *Research on Hispanics.*

POPULATION MODELS

The following two chapters introduce a set of technical subjects with which all demographers are familiar. In fact, in some ways, these subjects define the field to the professionals who make the greatest use of its methods and data. Chapter 9 discusses one of demography's most powerful tools, the life table: its parts, its construction, its various forms, and its main applications. We have briefly mentioned this tool at several points in earlier chapters, and we discussed it at some length in Chapter 6 in connection with mortality. You will recall from the latter context that the life table is used to present information about death and that average life expectancies are derived from it. Here we present it in detail as a population model: an artificial depiction of how populations would behave under fairly strict and simplified circumstances.

Although every life table is based upon information taken from (or presumed to be taken from) an actual population, in itself it is only an array of various types of probabilities. Its value lies in precisely this quality. It is so simplified that actual population processes can be understood more clearly from it than is possible through observing real, but far more complex, populations.

A similar approach is used in deriving population estimates and, especially, population projections, as discussed in Chapter 10. Models are used in these contexts as well. Here, however, it is because we seek to understand features of populations for which data are not available. Thus we substitute an artificial, mathematical construction for a real phenomenon that we cannot observe. As we will see, estimation refers to a set of procedures whereby a reasonable, fact-based guess is made about the size or other characteristics of a population for a date (past or present) on which no enumeration has taken place. Projection consists of methods for anticipating the characteristics of a population at a date in the future. These two procedures have much in common, and each is pursued with one or more of several alternative techniques, types of data, and sets of assumptions. The chapter and this part on models conclude with a brief discussion of forecasting, a kind of future-gazing that is related to projection but that is also distinct from it in several important ways.

THE LIFE TABLE
An Introduction

If you are not familiar with the life table, you are about to be introduced to one of demography's most powerful and most interesting tools. This apparently simple aid to presenting mortality information has been known and used for generations, both within and outside of academic circles. We say *apparently* simple because, although it is not difficult to understand or even to construct a table (once you know the procedure), the more you contemplate and use it, the more it reveals about the dynamics of populations and the principles of population science. As we noted in Chapter 1, the origins of the life table extend back to the very foundations of demography in the seventeenth century, and to the work of Francis Place, John Graunt, and Edmund Halley, in particular. From that era to ours, most of the leading demographers have contributed to its refinement and application (see Namboodiri 1987).

This chapter is intended to provide an overview of the life table and its applications; principally so that you can understand its basic structure and functions, but also to point the way toward more advanced work on the subject. Anyone familiar with the life table is well aware of its practical value, in the fields of public health, actuarial science (Underwood 1950; Bell and Wade 1998), and in other areas as well. Toward the end of the chapter we provide some illustrations taken from realms that are somewhat remote from medicine and actuary, and that may at first seem unusual contexts in which this tool may be applied. In this same applied spirit, Chapter 10, which follows, demonstrates the use of life-table concepts and functions in developing projections of populations to future dates.

Before turning to these practical matters, however, we begin with some definitions and illustrations of the principles of the life table. Next, we define and derive the main functions: the surviving population, the **stationary population**, and so on. These explorations of the foundations of life table analysis are then used as the basis for considering several refinements: **abridged** and **unabridged tables**, survival rates, period versus cohort accounts, and the **Lexis diagram**. With these matters touched upon, we then move to the chapter's conclusion and to the topic of life table applications.

MEASURING MORTALITY

In our discussion of measures of mortality in Chapter 6, we began with the crude death rate (CDR), but soon observed that its value is limited. You will recall that this rate is derived by first establishing the number of deaths, which we will here label "D," that occur in a particular population during a time period: one year, five years, 10 years, and so on. This total is then divided by the size of the population at midinterval (for example, midyear), symbolized by "P." The resulting ratio is labeled "M" (for the force of mortality), and it is multiplied by 1,000 to produce the CDR: $D/P = M$; $M \times 1,000 = CDR$. For example, in the United States during 2010, there were approximately 2.47 million deaths throughout the country. The midyear population size, as established by the decennial enumeration, was 308.75 million. Solving for M and CDR, we find:

$$M = D/P = 2.47/308.75 = .008; CDR = M \times 1,000 = 0.008 \times 1,000 = 8$$

The symbol M expresses the probability that an individual alive at midyear (or other interval to which the data apply) will die at some point during the interval. Another way to think about what M measures is that it characterizes the average risk of death to which members of the population are exposed during the year. It is certainly an important and widely used variable, and one for which data are readily available.

However, M and CDR in these expressions are by no means the most accurate measures of the force of mortality. As noted in Chapter 6, they "average out" relevant characteristics of groups whose exposure rates are known to differ, principally age cohorts and the two sexes. Thus, if population A has a higher CDR than population B, it might be because A is a higher-risk aggregate, more prone to disease or other kinds of factors that cause death. Or it might be because A has more members in high-risk categories such as very young or very old age groups, even though overall it is less prone to risk factors than B. Moreover, because M and CDR do not account for age, they are insensitive to the differences and interactions between age in years, on one hand, and calendar date, on the other. For risk is related not only to whether or not a person is, say, 30 years old, it also depends on *when* the person is 30, in 1905, in 1955, or in 2015.

This chapter continues along these lines, analyzing and dissecting M and CDR into increasingly refined components. As we discuss the life table, its construction, and its derivations, it will help to keep this introductory discussion in view. If every individual in a given population had the same chances of dying as every other, regardless of age, or gender, or social characteristics, there would be no need for life table analysis. But, of course, risk factors vary significantly from person to person and group to group. Granting the many purposes to which the life table may be put, it is essentially designed to account for such variations, and to correct for the deficiencies of crude measures of mortality.

Definitions and Illustrations

A life table is a rectangular array of demographic information, consisting of rows and columns. In mathematics, such an array is called a **matrix** and each row and column is referred to as a **row vector** and a **column vector**, respectively. In addition to the single rows and columns, there are other ways to subdivide a life table into parts that contain several rows, several columns, or both. The process of subdividing is called *partitioning*. Another important distinction made in life table analysis is that between a period and a cohort (or generation) table. As in the case of fertility measures (Chapter 7), the former contains information for one date, or period, and refers to all cohorts at that date; the latter contains information about one cohort as it ages through several dates. In this section, only period tables are considered.

Observed Data

The numbers that make up a (period) life table refer to age structure, mortality, and usually sex structure. These are of two types: (1) data based on observations of an actual population at a given date, such as the U.S. population in the year 2015; and (2) sums, proportions, and probabilities derived from the actual population data. The first category includes the following items (see Figure 9.1)

- the ages that at least one person is observed to have attained by midyear of the relevant date, recorded as 1-year, 5-year, 10-year, and so on, cohorts and symbolized by "x";
- the number of persons alive at midyear for each age, symbolized as "$_nK_x$"; and
- the number of deaths that occurred among persons at each age during the course of the relevant year, symbolized by "$_nD_x$."

In general, these four data vectors occupy the first four columns of the array. Otherwise, the second and third are listed separately and do not even appear in the life table as such. In this chapter, we will keep them in the first three columns so that their relationship to the remaining vectors can readily be seen. The little "n" notation that precedes the K_xs and D_xs is included in some of the other **life table functions** and variables as well. It indicates the size of the cohort, such that $_5K_x$ means that we have a five-year cohort and $_5K_{10}$ includes all individuals between 5 and 10 years of age. Similarly, $_5K_{45}$ refers to everyone who has reached their 45th birthday but not their 50th at midyear, and so on. When cohorts are one year in length, the "n" is ordinarily omitted, and we simply use K_x, D_x, and the like. Thus, we know that D_0 refers to the number of deaths to individuals below age one (infant deaths), without having to write "$_1D_0$." Thus in most tables, a number is included under the symbol "n" to indicate the sizes of the cohorts: 1, 5, 10, and so on.

If we sum all of the entries in the second column to produce $\Sigma\,_nK_x$, we have the total population size—or the total size of the aggregate of concern, such as all females. Solving for $\Sigma\,_nD_x$ gives us the total number of deaths. So, the quotient, referred to as the "central death rate."

$$(\Sigma\,_nD_x/\Sigma\,_nK_x) = \,_nM_x; \text{ and } \Sigma\,_nD_x/\Sigma\,_nK_x \times 1{,}000 \text{ is the CDR}$$

The fact that we need to build *up* to find the CDR should already suggest how the life table dissects gross statements of risk to create smaller and more realistic indicators.

The column following the n_x vector does not contain directly observed data. Rather, each entry, $_nq_x$, is a probability that is based on the direct observations of each $_nD_x$, $_nK_x$, and therefore the $_nM_x$ vector. This variable plays a pivotal role. We have just noted that often the second and third columns are not displayed with the rest of the life table. This is because they do contain empirical information whereas the other columns do not, and it is held that the two types of entries should not

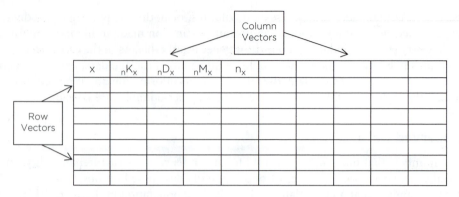

Figure 9.1.   Basic Outline of Life Table

be confused with one another. However, $_nq_x$ is almost always included in the table, despite the fact that it is more closely related to the observed data than the other functions. The reason for this special treatment will become obvious in a moment.

The $_nM_x$s give the probability of dying at age x, and they are derived in the following two steps: (1) We divide an element in the third column, an $_nD_x$, by its corresponding entry in the second column, $_nK_x$. This gives us $_nM_x$, the observed age-specific death rate—not multiplied by 1,000. (2) We solve for $_nq_x$ by assuming that the deaths to persons age x occur on the average at age x½ years.

That is, we spread the deaths evenly between those who have just reached the given age and those who are about to reach the next age. Spreading the deaths evenly is done for the sake of convenience, despite the fact that the younger the infant—or an individual in any age category—the greater the probability of dying. A more precise application would use a "separation factor," a set of numbers that add to 1.0. These would include .7 and .3, or .6 and .4, rather than the .5 and .5 indicated here; see Table 9.1. The formula for this is:

$$_nq_x = (2 \times {}_nM_x)/(2 + {}_nM_x)$$

Table 9.1.   Separation Factors for Ages 0 and 1-4, Selected European Countries

		Separation Factor for Age 0			Separation Factor for Age 1-4		
	Zones	Men	Women	Both Sexes	Men	Women	Both Sexes
Infant Mortality Rate > 0.100	I	0.33	0.35	.3500	1.558	1.570	1.5700
	II	0.29	0.31	.3100	1.313	1.324	1.3240
	III	0.33	0.35	.3500	1.240	1.239	1.2390
Infant Mortality Rate <0.100	I	.043	0.05	.0500	1.859	1.733	1.7330
	II	.0025	0.01	.0100	1.614	1.487	1.4870
	III	.0425	0.05	.0500	1.541	1.402	1.4020

(I) Iceland, Norway, and Switzerland; (II) Austria, Czechoslovakia, North-Central Italy, Poland, and Hungary; (III) South Italy, Portugal, and Spain

Sources: (1) PAHO. Technical Information System: Regional Mortality Database, AIS, Washington, D.C., 2003. (2) United Nations Population Division, World Population Prospects: The 2002 Revision, New York, 2003.

For example, the U.S. Census estimated that a total of 3,570,923 persons (male and female) ages 20–21 were living in the United States at midyear 1996; and vital statistics indicate that a total of 3,716 deaths occurred in that cohort during the year. This produces a death rate of:

$$(1)\ M_{20} = D_{20}/K_{20} = 3{,}716/3{,}570{,}923 = 0.001040$$

Next, we find the probability of dying at that age,

$$(2)\ q_{20} = (2 \times M_{20})/(2 + M_{20}) = (2 \times 0.001040)/(2 + 0.001040) =$$
$$0.00208/2.001040 = .001039$$

To review, life table analysis begins with observed data arranged into columns, as follows:

Column	1	2	3	4	5	6
Variable	Age	Number of persons	Number of deaths	Size of cohort	Central death rate	Probability of dying
Symbol	x	$_nK_x$	$_nD_x$	n	$_nM_x$	$_nq_x$
Data entries for each variable						

Occasionally, the $_nM_x$ vector is shown in the table, following the $_nD_x$s or at another point. This is ordinarily not done with unabridged tables, because q_x and M_x are typically very close in value. However, with abridged tables, in which mortality over several successive years is treated as a single entry, the $_nM_x$ and $_nq_x$ vectors can differ considerably and the former is included more often.

The Life Table-Proper

Beginning with the fifth column, we find a set of symbols known as the *life table functions*, which are derived from the $_nq_x$s. These functions create a model population that behaves as an actual population would if certain conditions were to prevail.[1] We emphasize that it is a model to distinguish it from the aggregate from which the $_nK_x$s, the $_nD_x$s, and thus the $_nq_x$s were taken, although it is closely tied to the actual population. Therefore, the fourth column divides the life table into two parts, the observed data and the life table-proper.

When we move from column 4 to column 5 and beyond, we say that we are "entering the life table," even though, loosely speaking, the first four columns are also part of the array. The major life table functions are: $_xl_x$, the surviving population;[2] $_nd_x$, the number of deaths in the surviving population; $_nL_x$, the number of person years lived, or the life table population; $_nT_x$, the number of life-years remaining, and, **average life expectancy**. Following are the life table functions as such:

Column	7	8	9	10	11
Variable	Number of survivors to age x	Number of deaths at age x	Number of years lived between l_{x-n} and l_x	Total years lived between 0 and x	Average number of additional years expected at x and beyond
Symbol	$_nl_x$	$_nd_x$	$_nL_x$	$_nT_x$	$_n\hat{e}_x$
Data entries for each variable					

As noted, life tables that use one-year age intervals, with n = 1, are referred to as unabridged or, sometimes, as *complete*; and those that use larger intervals, with n > 1, are called *abridged*[3] (and the functions in unabridged tables are usually not preceded by a subscript "n"). The main techniques for constructing and interpreting life tables apply equally to unabridged and abridged versions, but the latter present practical and technical challenges that have occupied researchers throughout the years. For this reason, we begin with unabridged data, usually focusing on only a portion of the complete table to avoid the unwieldiness of 85 or more rows. Then we move on to discuss entire tables with abridged data. For the sake of comparison, Table 9.2 shows a portion of an unabridged table; Table 9.3 shows a complete abridged table from a different source. In the next section, we discuss the life table functions in detail and demonstrate how they are derived.

DATA SOURCES AND FUNCTIONS

The data upon which a life table is based can come from any of several sources, depending on the purpose to which the table is to be put (Stolnitz 1956). In later sections, we focus on health and actuarial applications, and adaptations to educational administration. Some of these applications deal with special populations, for which information may best be drawn from surveys, official records, and/or local-area data sources. For most general purposes, however, the definitive source is national government census/vital statistics offices.

As discussed in Chapter 2, in the United States, the Census Bureau collects and publishes information on cohort sizes, $_nK_x$, and the CDC publishes mortality information, $_nD_x$, along with complete tables (see http://wonder.cdc.gov/). States and other local areas keep such records for their jurisdictions, and they also have access to the records of Federal agencies. Mortality data are collected continuously and are published in annual editions of *Vital Statistics of the United States*. These are usually presented in abridged format, so that the research often must go directly to NCHS or the Census Bureau to obtain one-year breakdowns. Census data are, of course, officially collected every 10 years. Thus, unless one happens to be creating a life table for 1990, 2000, or 2010, population estimates are required. These, too, are available

Table 9.2. Portion of an Unabridged Life Table, United States, 2010

Age	Probability of Dying between Ages x to x+1: q_x	Number Surviving to Age x: l_x	Number Dying between Ages x to x+1: d_x	Person Years Lived between Ages x to x+1: L_x	Total Number of Person Years Lived above Age x: T_x	Average Life Expectancy at Age x: $\hat{e}_x$
0–1	0.006123	100,000	612	99,465	7,866,027	78.7
1–2	0.000428	99,388	43	99,366	7,766,561	78.1
2–3	0.000275	99,345	27	99,331	7,667,195	77.2
3–4	0.000211	99,318	21	99,307	7,567,864	76.2
4–5	0.000158	99,297	16	99,289	7,468,556	75.2
5–6	0.000145	99,281	14	99,274	7,369,267	74.2
6–7	0.000128	99,267	13	99,260	7,269,993	73.2
7–8	0.000114	99,254	11	99,249	7,170,733	72.2
8–9	0.000100	99,243	10	99,238	7,071,484	71.3
9–10	0.000087	99,233	9	99,229	6,972,246	70.3
10–11	0.000079	99,224	8	99,220	6,873,017	69.3
11–12	0.000086	99,216	9	99,212	6,773,797	68.3
12–13	0.000116	99,208	12	99,202	6,674,585	67.3
13–14	0.000175	99,196	17	99,188	6,575,383	66.3
14–15	0.000252	99,179	25	99,167	6,476,195	65.3
15–16	0.000333	99,154	33	99,138	6,377,028	64.3
16–17	0.000412	99,121	41	99,101	6,277,891	63.3
17–18	0.000492	99,080	49	99,056	6,178,790	62.4
18–19	0.000573	99,032	57	99,003	6,079,734	61.4
87–88	0.105525	34,351	3,625	32,539	195,275	5.7
88–89	0.117007	30,726	3,595	28,929	162,736	5.3
89–90	0.129450	27,131	3,512	25,375	133,807	4.9
90–91	0.142873	23,619	3,375	21,932	108,432	4.6
91–92	0.157280	20,245	3,184	18,653	86,500	4.3
92–93	0.172661	17,061	2,946	15,588	67,847	4.0
93–94	0.188988	14,115	2,668	12,781	52,259	3.7
94–95	0.206214	11,447	2,361	10,267	39,478	3.4
95–96	0.224274	9,087	2,038	8,068	29,211	3.2
96–97	0.243080	7,049	1,713	6,192	21,144	3.0
97–98	0.262527	5,335	1,401	4,635	14,951	2.8
98–99	0.282492	3,935	1,112	3,379	10,316	2.6
99–100	0.302838	2,823	855	2,396	6,937	2.5
100+	1.000000	1,968	1,968	4,542	4,542	2.3

Source: *National Vital Statistics Report* 63, no. 7 (November 6, 2014).

at *census.gov*. Alternatively, researchers can create their own estimates, following the techniques to be presented in Chapter 10.

Regardless of the source of information, an annual period life table is *dated*, for example, "for the year 2000," and is built upon data on the size of each cohort at midyear (July 1). These begin with age 0–1 and extend to the oldest cohort in which at least one person was alive at midyear. The oldest cohort is usually symbolized with a "ω," the lower case omega (Ω), the last letter in the Greek alphabet. In practice, $_nK_\omega$, $_nD_\omega$, and so on, usually refer to an open interval that includes all individuals ages 65+ or 85+. Also required, from NCHS or another agency, is an accurate count of the number of deaths that occurred from the beginning to the end of the year of interest (from January 1 to December 31).

Table 9.3. A Complete Abridged Life Table, Brazil, 2002

x	n	D_x	P_x	$_nM_x$	$_nq_x$	$_nl_x$	$_nd_x$	$_nL_x$	$_nT_x$	$_n\hat{e}_x$
0–1	0	65,532	3,205,108	0.02045	0.02006	100,000	2,006	98,095	7,196,592	71.97
1–4	1	11,271	13,084,650	0.00086	0.00344	97,994	337	391,143	7,098,498	72.44
5–9	4	5,366	16,533,114	0.00032	0.00162	97,657	158	487,891	6,707,355	68.68
10–14	5	6,294	17,406,984	0.00036	0.00181	97,499	176	487,055	6,219,463	63.79
15–19	5	19,255	17,847,032	0.00108	0.00538	97,323	524	485,306	5,732,408	58.90
20–24	5	26,620	16,500,057	0.00161	0.00803	96,799	778	482,053	5,247,103	54.21
25–29	5	25,404	14,534,868	0.00175	0.00870	96,022	835	478,020	4,765,050	49.62
30–34	5	28,162	13,533,472	0.00208	0.01035	95,186	985	473,468	4,287,030	45.04
35–39	5	33,578	12,953,294	0.00259	0.01288	94,201	1,213	467,972	3,813,563	40.48
40–44	5	39,855	10,942,252	0.00364	0.01805	92,988	1,678	460,744	3,345,591	35.98
45–49	5	45,880	9,106,099	0.00504	0.02488	91,310	2,272	450,869	2,884,847	31.59
50–54	5	52,276	7,139,958	0.00732	0.03595	89,038	3,201	437,188	2,433,978	27.34
55–59	5	58,078	5,425,966	0.01070	0.05212	85,837	4,474	418,000	1,996,790	23.26
60–64	5	72,044	4,553,017	0.01582	0.07611	81,363	6,192	391,334	1,578,790	19.40
65–69	5	81,641	3,365,780	0.02426	0.11435	75,171	8,596	354,365	1,187,456	15.80
70–74	5	93,339	2,588,020	0.03607	0.16541	66,575	11,012	305,345	833,091	12.51
75–79	5	90,927	1,602,984	0.05672	0.24839	55,563	13,801	243,310	527,746	9.50
80–84	5	80,847	857,170	0.09432	0.38161	41,761	15,937	168,965	284,436	6.91
85+	+	103,085	460,928	0.22365	1.00000	25,825	25,825	115,471	115,471	4.47

Source: World Health Organization, *Epidemiological Bulletin* 24, no. 4)December 2003).

The use of midyear cohort sizes incorporates the assumption that on July 1 the number of persons alive was the average between the number alive on January 1 and the number alive on December 31. Thus, we assume that one-half of the deaths in each cohort occurred before July 1 and one-half occurred after that date. This is a fairly reasonable assumption for most cohorts, but when translated into life table functions, it is likely to be inaccurate for those ages 0 to 1 at the beginning of the year. The reason, discussed in Chapter 6, is that IMRs are much higher during the early months, especially during the first four weeks of life, for which special neonatal rates are derived. Thus, depending on how we treat the distribution of the ages of infants (month-by-month), as of July 1, the 50/50 assumption may need to be adjusted.

Age: x

In the life table and in demographic applications based on it, age is always symbolized by a lower case "x." This symbol refers to the exact age at midyear, for example, 20 years old on July 1, even for those who celebrate their 20th birthday on June 30 or their 21st on July 2. In unabridged tables, x stands for a single year: 1, 26, 38, and so forth; in abridged tables it stands for a range: 1–5, 5–10, and so on. As seen in Tables 9.1–9.3, the ages create the rows of the table, with each row containing a complete set of information for one cohort, from its size to its average life expectancy. This row-wise structure is divided into three segments that are treated somewhat differently: the top segment containing the youngest cohort or cohorts; the middle, which makes up the bulk of the table; and the bottom, consisting of the oldest cohort (for which x = ω). We discuss the reasons for this partition below.

The Observed Cohort Sizes, Deaths, and Probabilities of Dying: $_nK_x$, $_nD_x$, and $_nq_x$

As noted, the $_nK_x$ column lists the midyear sizes of each cohort in the observed population: $_nK_{20}$ is the number of 20-year-olds, $_nK_{50}$, the number of 50-year-olds, and $_nK_0$ is the number of infants. In each case, we refer to those who survived to July 1 but did not yet reach their next (21st, 51st, 1st) birthday by that date. The $_nD_x$ column contains the number of deaths at each age, and $_nq_x$ is the set of age-specific probabilities of dying derived from $_nM_x$ ($_nD_x/_nK_x$) as discussed above. Even without going further, it is evident that this technique produces results that are more highly refined and more informative about the manner in which the force of mortality operates than do M_x or the CDR.

Using the observed data on which Table 9.2 is based (not shown), the portion of an unabridged table for the U.S. population that covers ages 0 through 14, we did some calculations and found that $\Sigma {}_nK_x = 57,708,194$ and that $\Sigma {}_nD_x = 45,373$. Dividing $\Sigma {}_nD_x/\Sigma {}_nK_x$, we see that the force of mortality, $M = .00079$ and that the CDR (for this segment of the whole population) = 0.79 deaths per 1,000 persons. However, the $_nq_x$ column indicates that *none* of the 15 cohorts shown was actually exposed to that risk. The 1–2 group came close, with $q_1 = .000428$, but this and nearly every other probability listed is lower than the general M. Two cohorts, the 10- and 11-year-olds, are much lower—with less than one-fifth the risk of dying than the average of the 15 cohorts. The exception, and it is a significant one, is q_0, infant mortality. Here, the IMR in the observed population = 8.01 per 1,000, which is more than 10 times higher than the CDR. Thus we see that the general measures of mortality for a set of cohorts often conceal more than they reveal. In this case, what is concealed is the well-established fact that the probability of dying before age 15 is very low once individuals reach their first birthday.

The Surviving Population: $_nl_x$

With the set of $_nl_x$s, we enter the life table proper and the column containing the surviving (stationary) population. It is defined as the hypothetical number of individuals who survive to the beginning of the age x interval during the year. The first of these, l_0, is of special interest because it is an arbitrary figure upon which the rest of the table is based. Its function is the same as that of the "100" in percentages and the "1,000"—used in most demographic rates, in that it adjusts fractions of a whole to control for absolute size, "per 100," "per 1,000," and so on. Referred to as a *radix*, it could be any number; but for convenience we use 1,000, 10,000, or 100,000, depending on the size of the reference population. Unlike any other **radix** we have used to this point, however, the $_nl_x$ vector is dynamic: it changes size, always decreasing, as x increases.

We understand that any $_nl_x$ with x > 0 is the number of individuals who reach age x per whatever $_nl_0$ equals, for example, per 100,000, as in Figures 9.1 through 9.3. When put this way, we see that lo is a model birth cohort, because reaching age 0 is the same as being born. That is why $_nl_x$ is ordinarily expressed as "the number of survivors to age x for every 100,000 (etc.) born." This last form indicates how l_0 functions as the basis of the entire table, for it is the life table's imaginary population at "birth."

Assuming an unabridged table, once l_0 is selected, l_1 is derived as follows: (1) Multiply l_0 by q_0. That is, apply the observed probability of death for persons ages

0–1 to the imaginary starting number of, say, 100,000. This gives the number of deaths that occur in the surviving life table population to persons aged 0–1, which is also a kind of infant death rate. The number can be recorded in the d_x column, or d_x can be calculated directly from the l_xs, as discussed in the next section. (2) Next, subtract this number from l_0. Here we reduce the number "born" by the number of deaths, which yields the number of survivors to age 1–2, or l_1. In Table 9.2, we begin with $l_0 = 100,000$, and multiply it by $q_0 = 0.006123$. The result is 612, which can be seen as the first entry in the d_0 column. This is then subtracted from 100,000 to yield $l_1 = 99,388$.

To find the number of survivors to age 2, repeat the operation, this time multiplying l_1 by q_1 to find the number of deaths to members of the surviving life table population ages 1–2. This product is subtracted from l_1 to produce l_2. In Table 9.2, we multiply $l_1 = 99,388$ by $q_1 = 0.0428$ and get 43. This, subtracted from 99,388, is $l_2 = 99,345$. This process continues until l_ω is reached, at which point, $l_\omega = l_{\omega-1} - (q_\omega \times l_\omega - 1)$, and there are no survivors to a higher age: $l_{\omega+1} = 0$. Thus, the l_x column is completed, and all 100,000 of the original cohort have died. In general,

$$\text{for any } x > 0, l_x = l_{x-1} - (q_x \text{ times } l_{x-1})$$

For example, $l_{13} = l_{12} - (q_{12} \times l_{12})$; and, from Table 9.2, $l_{13} = 98,208 - (0.00016 \times 99,208) = 99,208 - 11.6 = 99,196$

Table 9.4. Creating an Abridged Table from Abridged Data: Age-Specific Death Rates for Adams County, Colorado, 2011

x	$_nK_x$	$_nD_x$	$_nM_x$	n	$_nq_x$	l_x	d_x	$_nL_x$	T_x	$\hat{e}_x$
0–1	7,172*	43	.0060	1	.00570	10,000	57	9.972	793,729	79.37
1–4	30,088	3	.0001	4	.00039	9,943	4	39,764	783,757	78.83
5–9	37,588	4	.0001	5	.00050	9,939	5	49,670	743,993	74.86
10–14	34,533	4	.0001	5	.00050	9,934	5	49,658	694,323	69.89
15–19	31,114	11	.0004	5	.00192	9,929	19	49,598	644,665	64.92
20–24	29,130	23	.0009	5	.00449	9,910	44	49,440	595,067	60.05
25–29	35,300	37	.0010	5	.00499	9,866	49	49,208	545,627	55,30
30–34	36,679	45	.0012	5	.00598	9,817	51	48,958	496,419	50.57
35–39	34,681	44	.0013	5	.00647	9,766	63	47,923	447,461	45.81
40–44	32,539	60	.0018	5	.00950	9,403	89	46,793	399,538	42.49
45–49	30,194	109	.0036	5	.01589	9,314	148	46,200	352,745	37.87
50–54	28,996	143	.0049	5	.02421	9.166	222	45,150	306,545	33.44
55–59	24,315	174	.0072	5	.03344	8,894	297	43,728	261,395	29.39
60–64	20,147	215	.0107	5	.04897	8,597	421	41,932	207,566	24.14
65–69	12,296	200	.0150	5	.07247	8,176	593	39,410	164,634	20.13
70–74	9,353	255	.0273	5	.12722	7,588	965	35,528	125,224	16.50
75–79	7,138	326	.0457	5	.20510	6,623	1,358	45,063	89,696	13.54
80–84	4,999	312	.0624	5	.26953	5,265	1,417	42,709	44,633	8.48
85+	4,165	608	0.146	*	1.000	3,848	3,848	19,240	19,240	5.00
All ages	451,576	2,616	.0058							

Note: Reed-Merrell method used for calculating $_nq_x$.

Source: Colorado Health Statistics, county data, http://www.chd.dphe.state.co.us/Resources/vs/2011/Adams.pdf.

* infant mortality based on live births, other rates based on midyear population estimates. Assumes no survivors beyond age 95.

This transition from empirical data ($_nK_x$, $_nD_x$, $_nM_x$, and $_nq_x$) to a model population ($_nl_x$) is the key operation in creating a life table. This is illustrated in Table 9.2. In effect, this procedure causes a model population to age and survive through time as if it were experiencing what is, in fact, a momentary force of mortality in the actual, reference population. In the reference population, q_x is the probability that persons age x will die during a specific year and q_{x+1} is the probability that persons age x+1 will die during that same year. However, in the case of the life table, beginning with the l_xs, we assume that l_0, a birth cohort of 100,000 individuals, experiences the passage of one year on the calendar, and those who survive make up l_1. Then, with the passage of another year, the survivors from l_1 become l_2, and so forth. Thus, in the life table, q_x is the probability that whoever has survived from the original 100,000 to l_x will not survive to l_{x+1}; and q_{x+1} is the probability that those who do survive to age x+1 will not reach x+2.

This property has led demographers to refer to l_x as the *stationary population*.[4] Of course, "stationary," means "unchanging," and the analogy here is that if a real population behaved as l_x does, it would be unchanging in certain important ways. Assume, as we do in a life table, that year after year a constant number of individuals—100,000—is born, and that age-specific mortality rates remain constant as well. Then, since $\Sigma _nd_x$ = 100,000, under these conditions, the population size would always remain the same. The total size would equal $\Sigma _nl_x$, and the size of each cohort would also be fixed at $_nl_0$ = 100,000, $_nl_1$, $_nl_2$, and so on.

The transition from actual to model populations is a somewhat subtle but powerful assumption that is critical to life table construction. It is quite evident when one moves from period to **cohort tables**; and it is the foundation of the components and matrix methods of projection, noted in the next chapter. In addition, the assumption effectively illustrates the paired concepts, *synchronous* and *diachronic*: "at the same time" and "through time"; and thus shows why the process is called "projection." In the actual population, $_nK_x$, $_nD_x$, and $_nq_x$ are synchronous. These data all pertain to one time period, thus the term **period table**. But, in the life table, $_nq_x$, $_nl_x$, and the other functions are understood to be diachronic; they pertain to a (hypothetical) process of aging from year to year. Figure 9.2 illustrates this difference.

The rectangle on the left represents the observed data and the one on the right the life table population. Notice that the q_x vector is included in both rectangles, but that it performs a different role in each. On the left side, it summarizes the relationship between observed cohort sizes and observed deaths, but on the right it is used to reduce the size of the surviving population as it ages "year by year." The arrow linking the two rectangles indicates that we take a vertical object and exert force, via multiplication, to create a horizontal object, as if it were a projectile being thrust ahead toward the future.

Deaths in the Life Table: $_nd_x$

The next column vector contains the number of deaths at each age that would occur if the observed probability of dying $2M_x/(M_x + 2)$ were experienced by the surviving population. It is derived by multiplying $_nq_x$ by $_nl_x$. For example, in Table 9.2, d_1, the number of deaths that would occur between ages 1 and 2 is equal to:

$$q_1 \times l_1 = .00048 \times 99{,}388 = 48$$

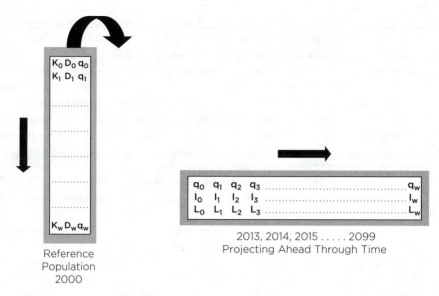

Figure 9.2.   Synchronous and Diachronic Applications of Mortality Data

We can conceive of this as 48 deaths at age 1 for every 100,000 persons born or, alternatively, 48 deaths at age 1 for every 99,388 persons surviving to age 1. Because of the way the $_n l_x$ vector is calculated (see above), we can also find the $_n d_x$s by subtracting. That is, for an unabridged table, $d_x = (l_{x+1} - l_x)$; and in general, $_n d_x = (_n l_{x+n} - _n l_x)$. This indicates that the number of deaths at a given age in the life table is equal to the size of the surviving cohort at the next higher age minus the size of the cohort at that age. So, in the abridged Table 9.4, we see that the number of deaths between ages 10 and 35 is:

$$l_{10} - l_{35} = 9,934 - 9,766 = 168$$

In fact, this is what is meant by the term "surviving population": the aggregate remaining from a younger age to an older age after the number of deaths has been subtracted.

The quantity $\Sigma _n d_x$, for all xs between two stated ages, for example, between 10–14 and 35–39, is the sum of the deaths to such individuals in the life table, in this case $4 + 11 + 23 + 37 + 45 + 44 = 154$. This can be compared to the second column of the tenth row in Table 9.2. If we divide that total by the sum of the surviving populations at those ages, we produce a probability of dying in the larger interval, a procedure that is used in constructing abridged tables. When the interval extends from 0 to w, the sum is equal to $_n l_0$, for example, 100,000; which is to say that the life table assumes that all members of the original birth cohort die by the time the oldest age is surpassed.

The Person Years Lived by the Life Table Population: $_n L_x$

Because $_n l_x$ is measured from the beginning of one age category to the beginning of the next, it does not take account of the deaths that occur in that cohort as of midyear. In particular, it overestimates the size of the cohort by not subjecting it to the force of mortality during the period of interest. For this reason, it cannot be used to derive the true size of the life table population or for related purposes, such as establishing certain rates. These types of applications require a truer measure of the numbers alive in the model population and, thus, the third life-table function. This is $_nL_x$, which adjusts the first function (the surviving population) by the second (the number of deaths) to produce a more accurate indicator of size and structure.

In general, the value of $_nL_x$ is based on the assumption that the deaths that occur at a given age, x, are equally distributed among those whose ages lie in the interval between exactly x and x + 6 months and those whose ages are in the interval between x + 6 months and x + 11 months and 29 (or 30) days. For example, in Table 9.2, we assume that the deaths to 13-year-olds are equally divided between the group aged 13 to 13½ and that whose ages are between 13½ and 14. The adjustment mentioned is reflected, for instance, in the difference between l_{13} and L_{13}, which is 99,196 versus 99,188. The reason that L_{13} is smaller, by 8 individuals, is that it reflects the true cohort size at midyear, at which point some (one-half) of those who do not reach the next age cohort had died.

Based on these assumptions, the general formula (for an unabridged table) is:

$$L_x = (l_x + l_{x+1})/\, 2; \text{ which, as we have just seen, is equal to: } l_x - (0.5\ d_x)$$

This formula can also be expressed as:

$$(0.5\ l_x) + (0.5\ l_{x+1})$$

This indicates that the life table population at a given age, x, is equal to the average of those who reach that age and those who reach the next higher age, x+1. Because it is an adjusted total, it represents the true number of persons alive at age x. This is why L_x is referred to as the number of "person years lived" at that age. So, for instance, we note that 98,848 person years are lived at age 9 for every 100,000 persons born; 98,802 person years are lived at age 12; and so on.

The "0.5"s in the formula are called **separation factors**, and are symbolized as f' and f", respectively. These apportion the deaths as follows:

$$f' = d_t /\ (d_t + d_{t+1}), \text{ and } f'' = 1 - f'$$

where d_t is the number of deaths that occur to those individuals born between July 1 and December 31 of the first year, and d_{t+1} is the number of deaths that occur to those born between January 1 and June 30 of the second year. If f" = f', we are assuming that the two groups experience the same number of deaths. Thus we can say, more generally, that $L_x = f''l_x + f'l_{x+1}$, and that f" = f' = 0.5. There are important exceptions, however, for which we know that the separation factors are not equal; and it is at this point that the three-part division of the life table mentioned earlier becomes effective.

The assumption of equal separation factors is valid for the middle portion of the table. But, for the upper portion, containing the youngest cohorts, we recognize that the number of deaths that occur during the first six months at a given age exceeds the number occurring in the last six months. This difference is especially

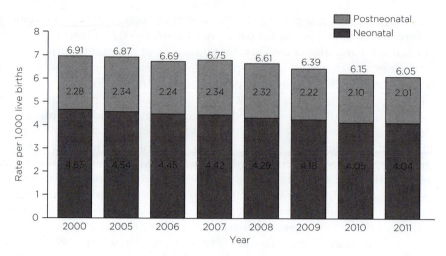

Figure 9.3. Infant, Neonatal, and Postneonatal Mortality Rates, United States, 2000 and 2005–2011

Sources: CDC/NCHS, National Vital Statistics System, mortality data set; U.S. Department of Health and Human Services, Health Resources and Services Administration, Maternal and Child Health Bureau. *Child Health USA 2011.*

pronounced in the 0–1, infant, cohort. For the lower portion of the table, containing the oldest cohorts, the opposite condition prevails: more deaths occur during the second six months at a given age than during the first. Although generally a trivial matter, the situation regarding older cohorts requires special consideration because, even in abridged tables, these tend to be stated in more-than-one year, or open, intervals.

Several methods have been devised for determining the appropriate f' and f" for the youngest and oldest age groups. In both cases, the most reliable approach is to observe $_nK_x$ and $_nd_x$ for n < 1 year, for example, monthly totals. In fact, neonatal mortality rates, such as those shown in Figure 9.3, are collected by the CDC and are often used for these purposes. However, for ages 1–2, 2–3, and so on, such data are generally not available. In these cases, various approximation methods have been employed, including those based on standard estimates and on overall infant mortality.[5] In Table 9.2, we assumed that infant mortality (ages 0 to 1) is distributed 70/30, for ages 1–2 it is 60/40, and for ages 2–3, 45/65 (with the remainder equal).

In the case of the oldest cohorts, there are two distinct approaches. In the more common situation, in which the oldest cohort is open, then the separation factors are accounted for as part of the abridging procedure, which we discuss in the next section. On the other hand, in the rare instances in which data are available for all older cohorts, including the one containing the oldest person (s) alive, then the deaths in that and possibly the next-younger group are apportioned as with the very youngest cohorts. For example, here are the last two rows of a completely unabridged table (Shryock and Siegel 1976:262, Table 15.2):

x	q_x	l_x	d_x	L_x	T_x	$\hat{e}_x$
108–109	.52810	1	0	1	2	1.35
109–110	.54519	1	1	1	1	1.29

You will note that although the probability of dying in the last interval is just under 0.55, the single individual to survive to age 109 from $l_0 = 100,000$ is assumed not to survive to his or her 110th birthday in that year. That is, one person year is lived at 109, but none beyond.

Total Person Years Remaining: $_nT_x$

The next life table function is the $_nT_x$ vector, which is interpreted as the total number of person years remaining at age x and beyond. In most applications, it is written without the preceding "n" subscript, although we retain it in this chapter. As the name indicates, it is a sum of $_nL_x$s that cumulates according to the value of x: $_nL_x + _nL_{x+n} + \ldots$ In Table 9.3, we see that $T_{30-34} = 4,278,030$. This means that just over 4.4 million person years in the life table can be counted between ages 30 and 35, 35 and 40, 45 and 50, and so on, up to and including 85+. The general formula is:

$$_nT_a = \sum_{x=a}^{w} {_nL_x}, \text{ where a is any given age and w is the highest age in the table}$$

As we move down the column, we can see how this function steadily decreases as the number of survivors declines, with its rate of decrease indicating how sharply mortality levels rise with age.

Average Life Expectancy: $\hat{e}_x$

The final life table function is perhaps the best known. This is $\hat{e}_x$, the average number of person years remaining to those who survive to age x. A small "∘" or "∧" is usually placed above the symbol to distinguish it from the exponential constant ("plain") e that we encountered in Chapter 8. Commonly referred to as "average life expectancy," this function is the basis of actuarial calculations of life insurance, and it has many other uses as well. The general formula is:

$$\hat{e}_x = {_nT_x}/{_nl_x} \text{ or, simply, } T_x/l_x$$

Table 9.4 illustrates the entire process from x to $\hat{e}_x$. We see that the function takes the total number of person years remaining at age x and averages them out (equally) among all of the survivors to that age. Thus, if an individual survives to a given age, say 30, then that individual is most likely to survive an additional $\hat{e}3_0$ years. According to Table 9.5, for example, for African American males $\hat{e}3_0 = 43,1$. If we add the age already attained, 30 years in this example, we get the total life expectancy for those who survive to that age; for example, 30 + 41.1 = 6733.1. Those who live to age 30 will, on the average, survive to age 75 and about 2 months. Demographers stress that this is an average because we know that some individuals who reach age x will not survive the full $\hat{e}_x$ number of years and, in contrast, some will live beyond the age indicated.

Average life expectancy at birth, that is $\hat{e}_0 = T_0/l_0$, is of special interest for both technical and practical reasons. Because l_0 is in the denominator, this measure makes explicit use of the table's radix of 1,000, 100,000, and so on. In this light, it can be interpreted as indicating that, on the average, a certain number of years of life remain at birth—for example, 79.6 for males and 53.56 for females in Table 9.6—to

Table 9.5. Comparative Probabilities of Dying (q_x) and Average Life Expectancies ($\hat{e}_x$) for Selected Ages for the United States, 2008

	White	Males	White	Females	Black	Males	Black	Females
x	q_x	$\hat{e}_x$	q_x	$\hat{e}_x$	q_x	$\hat{e}_x$	q_x	$\hat{e}_x$
5	.000167	71.6	.000125	76.4	.000270	66.7	.000190	73.2
10	.000068	67.6	.000082	72.4	.000095	61.8	.000129	68.2
20	.001145	56.9	.000398	61.6	.001767	52.2	.000537	58.4
30	.001311	47.6	.000577	51.8	.006370	43.1	.000981	42.8
40	.002096	39.2	.001248	42.2	.003444	34.2	.00225	39.4
50	.005155	38.3	.003034	32.9	.008585	25.7	.005549	30.6
60	,010870	29.3	.006623	24.1	.018943	18.5	.010701	22.6
70	024538	21,2	.016423	16.2	.036296	12.6	.022247	15.4
80	.063309	8.0	.055871	9.4	077689	7.6	.05123	9.4

Source: *National Vital Statistics Reports* 61, no. 3 (September 24, 2012): Tables 1, 5, 7, 8, and 9.

the 1,000, 100,000, and so on, individuals born into the table's model population. Because T_0 is in the numerator, this measure takes account of the entire set of mortality rates in the table. That is, $\hat{e}_0$ is a cumulative measure of survival at each and every age attained.

It may be apparent that an individual person born into a reference population during the reference year, for example a male born in India in 1980 would probably not have the actual average life expectancy at birth calculated, for example, about 53 years. This would probably differ, unless the deaths rate at age one in 1984 were the same as the death rates at age one in 1983, the rate at age 2 in 1985 were the same as the rate at age 2 in 1983, the rate at age 3 in 1986 were the same as in 1983, and so on. If these actually decreased, which is quite likely, then the true average life span for persons born in 1983 would be greater than the calculated 53 years. The tools of the Lexis diagram and cohort life tables help to clarify and resolve this synchronous/diachronic issue, as will see in later sections (also, see Shavelle 1996).

As a practical matter, $\hat{e}_0$ not only provides an especially accurate measure of mortality conditions, it is also one of the most effective indicators of overall socio-economic development. In our sample of 66 nations introduced in Chapter 3, the average life expectancy at birth ranged between 33 and 84 years, with means of 62.79 for males, 67.53 for females, and 65.14 for both sexes combined. The relationships between female life expectancy and seven crucial development variables are all very strong. In particular, where average life expectancy is high, per-capita gross national product, contraceptive use, and urbanization rates are also high, whereas death, birth, infant mortality, and TFRs are low.

Abridged and Unabridged Tables

Most life tables one is likely to encounter are abridged. Although, in principle, unabridged tables are more accurate and, of course, more complete, in human populations, the listing of information for each age, year-by-year, can be difficult to comprehend without careful study. Moreover, for most applications, the level of detail presented in unabridged tables is unnecessary; the number of deaths, probabilities of dying, and the other data contained in tables that use five- or even 10-year cohorts

Table 9.6. Separated Male and Female Life Tables for New Zealand, 2013 Base

Exact Age	Number Alive at Exact Age	Average Number Alive in the Age Interval	Number Dying in the Age Interval	Dies in the Age Interval	Central Annual Death Rate for the Age Interval	Proportion of Age Group x to x+5 Surviving another Five Years	Expected Number of Years of Life Remaining at Age
x	l_x	L_x	d_x	q_x	M_x	s_x	e_x
0	100,000	99,561	517	0.00517	0.00519	0.99899	79.6
1	99,483	397,753	90	0.00091	0.00023	...	79.0
5	99,393	496,813	61	0.00062	0.00012	0.99937	75.1
10	99,332	496,502	63	0.00063	0.00013	0.99808	70.1
15	99,269	495,550	318	0.00320	0.00064	0.99644	65.2
20	98,951	493,785	388	0.00392	0.00079	0.99612	60.4
25	98,563	491,868	378	0.00384	0.00077	0.99618	55.6
30	98,184	489,988	374	0.00381	0.00076	0.99533	50.8
35	97,811	487,698	542	0.00554	0.00111	0.99343	46.0
40	97,268	484,492	740	0.00761	0.00153	0.99031	41.2
45	96,528	479,797	1,138	0.01179	0.00237	0.98523	36.5
50	95,390	472,712	1,696	0.01778	0.00359	0.97814	32.0
55	93,694	462,379	2,437	0.02601	0.00527	0.96742	27.5
60	91,257	447,317	3,588	0.03931	0.00802	0.94862	23.2
65	87,670	424,335	5,605	0.06393	0.01321	0.91595	19.0
70	82,064	388,671	8,661	0.10553	0.02228	0.86290	15.1
75	73,404	335,384	12,654	0.17239	0.03773	0.77219	11.6
80	60,750	258,982	17,907	0.29477	0.06914	0.62778	8.5
85	42,843	162,584	20,652	0.48204	0.12702	0.37000	6.0
90	22,191	95,486	22,191	1.00000	0.23240	...	4.3
0	100,000	99,633	432	0.99568	0.00433	0.99914	83.3
1	99,568	398,100	87	0.99913	0.00022	...	82.6
5	99,482	497,307	41	0.99959	0.00008	0.99953	78.7
10	99,441	497,073	53	0.99947	0.00011	0.99899	73.7
15	99,388	496,573	147	0.99852	0.00030	0.99852	68.8
20	99,241	495,838	146	0.99852	0.00030	0.99855	63.9
25	99,094	495,120	141	0.99858	0.00028	0.99813	59.0
30	98,954	494,192	230	0.99767	0.00047	0.99736	54.0
35	98,723	492,889	291	0.99705	0.00059	0.99594	49.2
40	98,432	490,885	511	0.99481	0.00104	0.99334	44.3
45	97,922	487,616	797	0.99186	0.00163	0.98952	39.5
50	97,125	482,504	1,248	0.98715	0.00259	0.98478	34.8
55	95,877	475,162	1,689	0.98238	0.00356	0.97732	30.2
60	94,188	464,386	2,621	0.97217	0.00564	0.96522	25.7
65	91,567	448,236	3,839	0.95808	0.00856	0.94443	21.4
70	87,728	423,327	6,125	0.93018	0.01447	0.90388	17.2
75	81,603	382,635	10,151	0.87560	0.02653	0.83181	13.3
80	71,451	318,280	15,590	0.78180	0.04898	0.70664	9.9
85	55,861	224,909	21,758	0.61049	0.09674	0.41799	6.9
90	34,103	161,523	34,103	0.00000	0.21113	...	4.7

Source: Statistics New Zealand, New Zealand Abridged Period Life Table: 2012–2014 (provisional). Accessed May 12, 2015.

are usually adequate. The exception is the 0–1 cohort, which is ordinarily treated separately in even the most abbreviated tables, because infant mortality levels are always much higher than those at many other ages.

Reading and understanding an abridged table is not especially difficult; in fact we have already done so several times in the preceding section. We know that what makes a table abridged is the use of age categories greater than one year. Some tables, such as in Table 9.6 shown above, indicate the size of each interval with single numbers: 20, 25, 30, 35 . . . By the "closed-open" rule introduced in an earlier section, we know that this means: ages 20 to but not including 25, ages 25 to but not including 30, ages 30 to but not including 35. At times, as in Table 9.7, the intervals are stated: 20–25, 25–30, 30–35, with the same interpretation as the single-number style. Just as often, or more so, tables will state both limits as closed, as in Tables 9.3 and 9.4: 20–24, 25–29 . . . which is similarly interpreted: ages 20 through 24 but not including 25, ages 25 through 29 but not including 30. Tables with five-year intervals such as Table 9.6 are the most common, but 10-year intervals—as in Table 9.7—are also used.

One of the first features you notice about an abridged table is the three-part division between the youngest cohorts, the middle group, and the oldest cohort. The practice of treating each section separately is especially important when abridged data are used. The easiest of the three sections is the middle, because each interval is uniformly the same size (five or 10 years). Thus, all are interpreted and constructed in the same manner. The youngest cohorts require special treatment, on two grounds. These are: (1) separation factors f' and f" should not be equal at 0.5 each, because deaths among this age group occur more frequently in the earlier months at a given age; (2) the cohort intervals are not the same size as those in the middle section. In fact, the intervals of the two youngest cohorts are usually different from one another. Note that with five- and even 10-year abridgments, the youngest cohort—the infant category—has a one-year (0–1) interval but the next youngest is *four* years (1–4).

The third section, containing the oldest cohorts, is unique because it uses an open interval with no limit (65+, 80+, 85+, etc.). Thus, we cannot determine the highest age to which one or more persons survive. This makes it necessary either to estimate or approximate a limit, for example, 110, or simply to leave it indefinite with the omega (ω) or infinity (∞) symbol.

With this division in mind, the most important point to recall is that information about an age group between the upper and lower limits of an interval is inaccessible. For example, in Table 9.4, above, the observed mortality rates and average life expectancies for the 30–34 and 60–64 cohorts are .0012, 50.57 years and .0107, 24.14 years, respectively. However, we know nothing about the observed mortality rate or average life expectancy for people ages 32 or 63.[6] If such information is needed, one must either estimate or obtain unabridged data (which is often quite difficult; Stolnitz 1956). In the absence of these solutions, it is necessary to be careful how we state information drawn from an abridged table. Here are the abridged interpretations of the life table functions and some examples from Table 9.4 (male section):

1. $_nM_x$ is the total number of deaths to persons ages x to x+n during the year divided by the total number of persons alive at midyear who have attained the ages of x to x+n: $_5M_{15} = {_5D_{15}}/{_5K_{15}} = 0.00204$: just over two persons per 1,000 died between ages 15 and 20.

Table 9.7. Abridged Table with 1-, 4-, and 5-Year Intervals, India, 2006-2010

Age-Interval x to x+n	Total				Male				Female			
	$_nq_x$	l_x	$_nL_x$	$\hat{e}_x$	$_nq_x$	l_x	$_nL_x$	$\hat{e}_x$	$_nq_x$	l_x	$_nL_x$	$\hat{e}_x$
0–1	0.05227	100000	95781	66.1	0.05156	100000	95828	64.6	0.05308	100000	95802	67.7
1–5	0.01596	94773	375305	68.7	0.01317	94844	376252	67.1	0.01901	94692	374155	70.5
5–10	0.00598	93261	464909	65.8	0.00588	93595	466600	63.9	0.00608	92892	463047	67.8
10–15	0.00444	92703	462485	61.2	0.00429	93045	464226	59.3	0.00454	92327	460587	63.2
15–20	0.00683	92291	459981	56.4	0.00653	92645	461817	54.6	0.00718	91908	457991	58.5
20–25	0.00961	91661	456180	51.8	0.00970	92041	458075	49.9	0.00956	91248	454104	53.9
25–30	0.01050	90781	451572	47.3	0.01173	91147	453156	45.4	0.00921	90376	449809	49.4
30–35	0.01262	89828	446406	42.7	0.01504	90078	447156	40.9	0.01015	89544	445495	44.8
35–40	0.01647	88694	439910	38.3	0.02079	88723	439143	36.5	0.01193	88636	440574	40.3
40–45	0.01755	87233	432554	33.8	0.02246	86879	429782	32.2	0.01243	87578	435318	35.7
45–50	0.03318	85702	421873	29.4	0.04158	84927	416378	27.8	0.02334	86490	427755	31.1
50–55	0.04108	82859	406166	25.3	0.05216	81396	396799	23.9	0.02992	84471	416393	26.8
55–60	0.06097	79455	385987	21.3	0.07417	77151	372282	20.1	0.04835	81943	400615	22.5
60–65	0.10213	74611	355234	17.5	0.11853	71429	337175	16.5	0.08520	77981	374527	18.6
65–70	0.15611	66991	310042	14.2	0.17807	62962	287853	13.4	0.13455	71337	334087	15.0
70–75	0.23412	56534	250443	11.3	0.25625	51750	226178	10.7	0.21325	61739	276939	12.0
75–80	0.32714	43298	180901	9.0	0.35406	38490	157893	8.5	0.29999	48573	206602	9.5
80–85	0.42533	29133	113743	7.2	0.44900	24862	95287	6.9	0.40351	34001	134974	7.5
85+	...	16742	95820	5.7	...	13699	75297	5.5	...	20281	119839	5.9

Note: Average life expectancies in bold.

Source: SRS Based Abridged Life Tables 2003–2007 to 2006–2010, Office of the Registrar General and Census Commissioner, India.

2. $_nq_x$ is the probability that an individual who survives to age x will not survive to age x + n: $_5q_{55}$ = .072: Approximately 7 persons 1,000 who survive to age 55 will not survive to age 60.

3. $_nl_x$ (or l_x) is the number of individual in the life table per 100,000 (or another radix) born who survive to age x: $_5l_{40}$ = 9,403 persons per 10,000 born will reach age 40. Note that the interval size is not relevant for this function, since it denotes survival from the beginning of one to the beginning of the next interval, regardless of its size. For this reason, the l_x notation is usually written without the little "n," even in abridged tables.

4. $_nd_x$ is the number of deaths that occur (in the life table) to individuals who have reached age x up to but not including those who have reached age x + n: $_5d_{70}$ = 965 deaths occurred to persons between ages 70 and 75 (for every 10,000 born).

5. $_nL_x$ is the number of person years lived (in the life table) at each age between x and x + n: $_5L_{20}$ = 49,440: nearly 50,000 person years were lived at ages 20, 21, 22, 23, and 24. Note that this represents a *total* derived by adding the l_x for each year:

$$\sum_{a=x}^{x+n} l_a = l_x + l_{x+1} + l_{x+2} + l_{x+3} + l_{x+4}$$

When an abridged table is constructed from unabridged data (see Tables 9.2 and 9.3), this is how the $_nL_x$ vector is derived. When abridged data are used, this total must be estimated. In either case, $_nL_x$ is always approximately equal to, but somewhat less than, n times l_x.

6. $_nT_x$ (or T_x) is the total number of person years remaining to individuals who have attained age x.: $_5T_{60}$ = 207,566: More than 200,000 person years remain to persons age 60. Note that, as with l_x, we measure this function from the beginning of the interval. Thus, in our example, part of those 207,566 person years (207,566 – 264,076 = 42,932) are lived between ages 60 and 65.

7. $\hat{e}_x$ is calculated with the formula $\hat{e}_x = T_x/l_x$ It is the average number of years of life remaining to individuals who have reached age x: $\hat{e}_0$ = 52.75: life expectancy at birth is just under 53 years. $\hat{e}_{50}$ = 19.63; males who reach age 50 can expect an additional 19.6 years of life (including the five years between 50 and 55), and thus to reach age 69.6. This final function is also measured from the beginning of the interval, because it is based on l_x and T_x.

Survival Rates

One commonly used life-table function remains to be discussed: that is, **survival rates**. These rates ordinarily do not appear in the life table proper, but they are derived from it, and from either the l_x or the L_x vector, in particular. They are symbolized as follows: $_nS^{an}_x$, where "n" is the size of an interval, "x" is a given age, as usual, and "a" is an integer (1, 2, 3, . . .) to be multiplied by n to specify the number of intervals. In an unabridged table, the survival rate is written: S^a_x.

Interpretations

As the name implies, this function indicates the probability that a member of the life table population will survive from one age to another, from x to x + an; and in this respect it is a complement of nqx, the probability of dying. For example, in the unabridged case, if x = 7 and a = 6, then the whole expression S_x^a refers to the probability that an individual age 7 will survive six additional years, or to age 13; whereas the sum, $q_7 + q_8 + q_9 + \ldots q_{13}$, is the probability that an individual age 7 will *not* survive to age 13. In the abridged case, if x = 20, n=5, and a = 2, then the whole expression $_nS_x^{an}$ refers to the probability that an individual age 20 will survive an additional 2 times 5 = 10 years, or to age 30.

These rates can be calculated in one of two ways, depending on the interval of interest. If one wants to determine the probability of surviving from one *birthday* to the next, for instance, from the 7th to the 13th birthday or from the 20th to the 30th, then the rate is based on the l_xs. This is because the function measures the proportion of life table population that survives to the beginning of an age interval. The unabridged and abridged formulas, respectively, are:

$$(1) \; S_x^a = l_{x+a}/l_x, \text{ and } (2) \; _nS_x^{an} = l_{x+an}/_nl_x$$

From Table 9.2, with x = 7 and a = 6, l7 = 99,249 and l7+6 = l13 = 99,188; thus: the probability of surviving from age 7 to 13,

$$S_x^a = 99,188/99,249 = 0.9994$$

And, from Table 9.4, with x = 20, n = 5, and a = 2, l20 = 9,910 and l20+10 = l30 = 9,817; thus: the probability of surviving from age 20 to 30,

$$_nS_x^{an} = 9,817/9,910 = 0.9906$$

Because $l_{x+1} = l_x (1 - q_x)$, in the case of one-year survival, the formula $S_x^a = l_{x+1}/l_x$ can also be expressed as $S_x^a = l_x (1-q_x)/l_x = 1-q_x$. Again from Table 9.2, with l7 = 99,249 and l8 = 99,238, S_x^a (with a = 1) = 0.9999 = 1 – q_7 = 1 – 0.0001. That is, the probability of surviving from one birth date to the next is the same as 1.0 minus the probability of not surviving.

The alternative interpretation focuses on survival from the middle of one age interval to the middle of the next, and it uses the $_nL_x$s rather than l_xs. This approach, which is more commonly employed than "birth date" survival rates, exposes the life table population to an average risk of dying at both the initial and the terminal ages. The unabridged and abridged formulas, respectively, are:

$$(1) \; S_x^a = L_{x+a}/L_x, \text{ and } (2) \; _nS_x^{an} = _nL_{x+an}/_nL_x$$

From Table 9.2, with x = 7 and a = 6, L7 = 99,249 and L7+6 = L13 = 98,188; thus: the probability of surviving from 7½ to 13½,

$$S_x^a = 98,818/99,249 = 0.9957$$

And, from Table 9.4, with x = 20, n = 5, and a = 2, $_5L_{20}$ = 49,440 and $_5L_{20}$+10 = $_5L_{30}$ = 48,958; thus: the probability of surviving from approximately age 22½ to 32½,

$$_nS_x^{an} = 48,958/49,440 = 0.9760$$

Reverse Survival

All of these rates, whether abridged or unabridged and whether they use $_nL_x$ or l_x, refer to what is called "forward" survival. This terminology is based on the fact that the rates begin at a given age, x, and indicate the probability of surviving ahead a specified number of years: from 6 to 13, 20 to 30, and so on. It is also possible, however, to proceed in the opposite direction via the concept of *reverse* survival. In this case, the size of an observed cohort is known, as is the forward survival rate from a younger age. Reverse survival is then used to establish the size of the younger cohort and the number of person years lived at a younger age.

For example, following Table 9.2, with 99,345 survivors to age 2 (for every 100,000 born), we wish to establish the number of survivors to age 1. The procedure is to restore to l_2 those who did not survive between the two ages. From the life table, we find $l_2 = 99,345$ and S_1^a (with a = 1) = 0.999004. To determine the size of the surviving life-table population, we use the formula for forward survival, but in this case solving for lx. That is, if $S_x^a = l_{x+a}/l_x$, then $l_x = l_{x+a}/S_x^a$. Thus:

$$l_1 = l_2/S_1^a = 99,345/.0999004 = 99,444$$

With both l_1 and l_2 known, L_1 can be determined in the usual way: $L_1 = f'l_1 + f''l_2$, where f' = 0.4 and f'' = 0.6. So,

$$L_1 = (0.4 \times 99,366) + (.6 \times 99,345) = 99,353$$

Applications

Aside from average life expectancy, survival rates are the most extensively applied of the life table functions. Like the former, these rates summarize a considerable amount of information in a single measure, indicating at a glance the overall age-specific mortality conditions in a reference population. Because they are standardized to the arbitrary radix, $l_0 = 100,000$, and so on, they provide valid comparisons between the risk factors in two or more populations or in a single population between two dates.

To illustrate, from Table 9.6, we find that the birth-date, male survival rate from ages 0 to 1, S_0^a (with a = 1), in 2013 for New Zealand, was $l_1/l_0 = 99,483 /100,000 =$ .9948. From Table 9.7, we find that for India at a comparable date (2010) this rate was 99,849/100,000 = .9484. For New Zealand, the 35–45 midinterval rate, $_5S_{35}^{an}$ (with an = 10) = 479,797 / 483,087 = .9838; and for India this was 416,378/439,143 = .9482. From these rates, it is clear that the risk of mortality in India is substantially higher than that in New Zealand. This is especially clear in the infant cohort, whose members have a 5 percent greater chance of surviving in Sweden than India; but it holds for the older age groups as well.

Perhaps the most common use of survival rates is in deriving population estimates and projections. In this context, which we examine closely in the following chapter, forward survival rates are applied to cohort sizes for a base year in producing likely cohort sizes for a future year. Thus, as in the case of Adams County (Table 9.4), we see that in 2011 there were 29,130 persons ages 20 to 25; and we calculated, above, the 10-year survival rate to ages 30–35 as 0.9930. Assuming no migration and no changes in age-specific death rates, this would yield 0.9930 × 29,130 = 28,847 persons ages 30 to 35 in the year 2021. Because the 20–25 cohort in 2021 would have been ages 10 to 15 in 2011, we can project that group forward by multiplying its size in 2011 (34,533) by its 10-year survival rate = 49,440 / 49,650 = .9956 × 34,533 = 34,381. In some projection methods, this procedure is repeated until all cohorts are accounted for, and then those age groups not yet born in the base year (2011) are factored in through the use of estimated fertility rates.

In these and other ways, the idea of survival and the use of survival rates have proved to be especially useful in population studies. Reverse survival is often applied in the re-creation of historical populations, forward survival is routinely incorporated in matrix approaches to projection, and survival rates are extensively relied upon in public-health research and applications. In fact, the idea of demographic survival is so common that we often lose sight of its origins in the life table, that is, in a population *model*.

Cohort Tables and the Lexis Diagram

Here and at several other points, we have noted that the stationary life table population is not an observed population but rather a model *based on* observations. This is stressed because the (period) table assumes that observed death rates remain unchanged over the years, although we know that this is generally not true. In constructing a table, we begin with the set of $_nq_x$s, the probability that those who reach age x will not reach age x+n. Although these are not observed, they are calculated directly from observed age-specific death rates in the reference population, the $_nM_x$s. These death rates are given for a specific date (period), for example, 1996 in the Adams County example, and are then converted to $_nq_x$ by the formulas given above (depending on whether or not the data are unabridged). However, when the $_nq_x$s are applied to the l_x vector, the procedure assumes that as the life table population survives from one age to the next, it also is surviving from calendar year to calendar year.

At age zero/year zero, the life table population experiences the death rates of those age 0 in the reference population during the reference year (e.g., 2011). At age 1/year 1, it experiences the death rates of those age one during the reference year of 2011—not one year later, for example, 2012. At age 10/year 10, it experiences the death rates of those age 10 during the reference year, for example, not 2021, but 2011; and so on. Thus, when we derive average life expectancies at a given age, x, we do so with a certain understanding. Namely, that the actual number of years of life expected at that age in the reference population would equal $\hat{e}_x$ only if the age-specific death rates during the reference year were unchanged for every calendar year during which at least one person remains alive (85+ calendar years). Of course, this is a highly unlikely situation.

In some ways, this is simply a technicality that does not seriously detract from the utility and effectiveness of life tables. When we compare average life expectancies of one population with those of other populations, such as the set of $\hat{e}_0$s for selected nations shown earlier, we know that stationary models are being used, but that they are being used consistently. More important, perhaps, tables based on current data provide the best information available, because we cannot know how death rates may change in the future. Nevertheless, the built-in assumption of constant death rates limits the value of the period table as a model for understanding the complexities of actual population dynamics. As a supplement to the period table, two related models have been developed; and they are ordinarily considered in the context of discussing the assumptions on which period tables are based. These are: (1) cohort tables, also called "generation" tables, and (2) the Lexis diagram. The following sections present brief introductions to these two demographic tools.

The Cohort or Generation Table

In principle, it is possible to follow a cohort from the year of its birth to the point at which the last member dies, recording the number of deaths to its members each year. By establishing the origin of such a group as all persons in a selected population who had reached age 0 but not age 1 by midyear of a reference year, we can create a special kind of life table based on the survivorship of the cohort. This is in contrast to basing the table on the observed death rates of all cohorts during the reference year—as is done with period tables. The kind of table created in this manner is referred to as a *cohort* life table or, more loosely but more commonly, a *generation* life table.[7] The construction of such a table poses practical difficulties, because it requires access to a long series of data extending back to dates for which collection and storage methods may be less than adequate—or for which information is not available. But it also has distinct advantages over period tables in that the cohort method can incorporate actual changes in death rates that occur as individuals age. In this case, average life expectancies and survival rates reflect actual, dynamic, conditions, not a stationary model.

Table 9.8 shows a model cohort of size 30,015 that was age 0–1 at midyear 1900. During that year the death rate ($_1M_0$) for that age group was 0.1226. This produced a total of 3,680 deaths during the interval, with the remaining 26,355 surviving to their first birthday in 1901. Between 1901 and 1904, an additional 2,206 members of the cohort died, with 24,129 surviving to age 5 in 1905. The table follows the survivors of this cohort in this fashion through the years, until the last remaining individuals died between 1995 and 2000. Note that, contrary to what we see in a period table, each cohort in Table 9.8 is made up of the *same* individuals as they age through time, not different individuals having attained the various ages at the same time.

This type of table thus provides a diachronic view of the force of mortality, depicting the more realistic situation that, as individuals age, they are exposed to present risks, not to the risks that prevailed only during the year of their birth. So, although the cohort in Table 9.8 was subject to the (high) infant death rates of 1900, it also was subject to the (low) death rates characteristic of older groups in the 1990s. Because, as in this case, a population's death rates tend to decline over time, period tables in comparison to cohort tables ordinarily overestimate the probabilities of dying and underestimate survival rates and average life expectancies.

Cohort tables have several other distinctive features that follow from the fact that they track a true segment of a population through the years. Most significant, perhaps, is that the $\hat{e}_x$ vector no longer stands for average life *expectancy* at age x. Instead, it indicates the number of years of life actually *remaining* to those who have survived to x. It is a real, not a hypothetical, measure. For instance, from Table 9.8, individuals who reached age 50 in 1950 will, on the average, live an additional 23.6 years. This is quite different from saying, as we do with period tables, that individuals can expect to live a certain number of years if death rates remain unchanged.

Table 9.8. Life Table of a Model Cohort Born in 1900 and Surviving until 2000

Year	x	$_nK_x$	$_nD_x$	$_nq_x$	$_nl_x$	$_nd_x$	$_nL_x$	$_nT_x$	$\hat{e}_x$*
1900	0–1	30,015	3,680	0.1130	1,000	113	918.2	55,700	55.7
1901	1–4	26,335	2,206	0640	887	57	2,448.0	54,782	61.8
1905	5–9	24,129	355	0146	830	12	4,122.9	53,344	64.3
1910	10–14	23,774	175	0073	818	6	4,243.8	48,211	58.9
1915	15–19	23,600	223	0094	812	8	4,036.9	43,967	54.1
1920	20–24	23,377	264	0111	804	9	3,994.2	39,930	49.7
1925	25–29	23,113	250	0107	796	9	3,950.8	35,934	45.1
1930	30–34	22,863	322	0138	787	11	3,902.9	31,980	40.6
1935	35–39	22,541	409	0181	776	14	3,838.5	28,077	36.2
1940	40–44	22,132	586	0262	762	20	3,751.5	24,239	31.8
1945	45–49	21,545	795	0363	742	27	3,630.2	20,487	27.6
1950	50–54	20,750	1,167	0548	715	39	3,460.6	16,857	23.6
1955	55–59	19,583	1,630	0800	676	54	3,221.5	13,396	19.8
1960	60–64	17,953	2,280	0.1191	622	74	2,894.0	10,175	16.4
1965	65–69	15,673	3,017	0.1749	548	95	2,463.8	7,281	13.3
1970	70–74	9,043	3,711	0.2478	453	112	1,941.5	4,817	10.6
1975	75–79	5,331	3,004	0.3351	341	114	1,376.0	2,876	8.4
1980	80–84	2326	1,799	0.4354	226	98	849.0	1,500	6.6
1985	85–89	527	284	0.5495	128	71	434.1	651	5.1
1990	90–94	243	159	0.6540	58	38	173.5	214	3.7
1995	95–99	84	84	1.0000	20	20	38.1	38	1.9

l0 = 1,000.

Note: (*) in a cohort table, $\hat{e}_x$ refers to the (actual) average number of years remaining, not the (hypothetical) average life expectancy.

Sources: Rates to 1980 based on Shryock and Siegel (1996:258. Table 15-6). Later rates based on Table 9.5 and unpublished estimates.

The Lexis Diagram

A cohort table allows us to see how the force of mortality, which, itself, varies through time affects a group of age-mates. This can be illustrated with a diagonal motion, in which the cohort diminishes in size year-by-year as deaths occur. In contrast, the period table indicates the mortality conditions to which each of several cohorts is subject during a specific year:

As we know, in an actual population, the situations depicted in *both* of the above illustrations occur, and they occur simultaneously. Each year, a new cohort is born. As it ages, it joins other cohorts that have come before it; and, in turn, younger cohorts that follow join it. In the process, each experiences its own distinctive set of survival risks, depending on age, and on calendar time as well. This rhythm of births and deaths is what creates the complex dynamic of growth in a closed population (and, as we noted in Chapter 7, migration makes the process even more complex).

To illustrate this interaction between age and calendar time, demographers employ a diagram created by, and named after, the renowned German mathematician, Wilhelm Lexis (1837–1914; see Stigler 1986:222–24). The Lexis diagram, as shown in Figure 9.4, is a schematic representation that combines the properties of cohort and period tables, such as those illustrated above. If we were to add to a diagonal table that shows information for one cohort an additional diagonal for a second cohort, another for a third, and so on, indefinitely, we would be able to compare synchronous differences and diachronic changes in a single model.

The diagram uses lines to represent individuals or cohorts in such a way that distinctions such as those between exact age and beginning of an age interval, mid-year and throughout a year, can be made. It shows that during a specific year, some

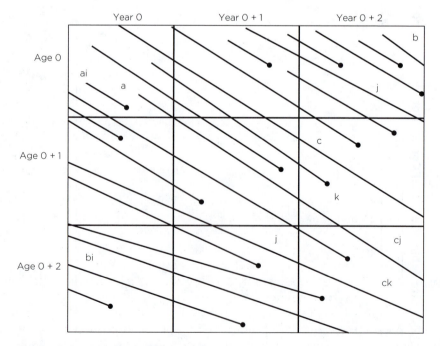

Figure 9.4. The Lexis Diagram
Lifelines show the relationship between age, calendar years, and mortality. Letters and combinations of letters indicate different types of outcomes.

people will begin life, as indicated with an "a," others will continue life from the previous year to the next, "b," and a third group will live part of the year but die before reaching the next year, "c." Similarly, each year, some individuals will experience a birthday and live through the year, marked with an "i," others will experience a birthday but not survive to the next year, "j," and others will live part of a year but die before their birthday, "k." Category "aj" represents infant deaths, whereas "bi" is the most common situation; and categories "cj" and "ck," together, refer to death at an age above 0–1, which is nearly everyone's ultimate fate.

LIFE TABLE APPLICATIONS

The value of life tables to medical researchers and insurance actuaries should be obvious. In the former instance, mortality information is often analyzed into cause-specific tables, closely related to the cause-specific mortality rates discussed in Chapter 5 (MIB 1998). Information derived from these kinds of tables helps to guide public-health policy, epidemiology, and other medical applications.

LIFE INSURANCE AND RELATED USES

In the case of insurance, life tables are a necessary part of the business, in determining prices and conditions for term and whole-life policies and for medical and disability insurance as well. Many of the procedures and considerations discussed in this chapter are reiterated on a day-to-day basis in these contexts.

In the insurance industry, however, additional sets of steps are performed once the appropriate tables are developed (Bell and Wade 1988; Underwood 1950). These involve associating monetary values with the probabilities and rates obtained from the tables. Thus, having calculated the survival rate from age x to x + n, the actuary must then take into consideration costs, the volume of business to be expected, and other economic factors in deciding what to charge customers for a policy that will cover them during the specific age interval. It will certainly matter if the customers are men or women, whether or not they smoke cigarettes, and if they are exposed to any of several other risk factors. In this way, insurance applications extend far beyond simply turning life tables into payment schedules. Nevertheless, the table is the foundation of all of the other elaborations that have made the business one of the most financially successful enterprises in capitalist societies (and actuaries among the highest-paid professionals).

In addition to these more obvious uses, life tables and life table functions have been applied in many other areas. These include population projection, which is discussed in the next chapter; social service administration, especially by those interested in how a population ages; and by labor and industrial relations specialists concerned with labor force size, composition, and turnover (Gamboa 1998; Hoon and Phelps 1996; Wilson 1997; Price and Mueller 1982). Urban and regional planners, especially those involved in housing and community development, are also making increasingly use of life table analysis. In fact, a substantial—and rapidly expanding—body of literature exists on how the life table may be employed for purposes beyond those traditionally associated with population studies.

One of the most fruitful of these nondemographic applications is associated with the technique known as **event history analysis** (Lauro 1977; Teachman 1983).

This relatively new approach uses the logic of cohort tables to explain changes in vital characteristics, cultural production, crime rates, and virtually any other phenomenon for which time-series data are available (Raftery 1993; Pandey 1987). At a web site that includes two- and three-dimensional Lexis diagrams, Brendan Halpin of Essex University (U.K.) provides this definition: "An event history is a sequence of events or states, the association between them, and their changes over time. Event histories of a similar type may be recorded for a number of individuals in a sample population" (Halpin 1996). If the "events" to which Mr. Halpin refers are deaths, and the "individuals in the population" constitute a cohort, then the event history is identical to cohort table analysis (Hoem 1993).[8]

We conclude this chapter with an example of a somewhat unconventional use, which is also an event history. Our purpose is to illustrate—with a realistic model population—further the basic principles of life table construction and interpretation. However, we also hope to show how the purposes to which these tools can be put extend far beyond traditional demographic theory and measurement.

THE CLASS OF '61

In a newsletter distributed a few years ago by the alumni club of a large Midwestern high school, it was announced that the last unmarried graduate of the class of 1961 had just been wed. Other information was provided about the year the other graduates had married, how many had married other members of the class, where they now lived, the fact that nearly all had eventually married, and other matters. In the course of a subsequent exchange among the alumni, additional questions were raised. How long after graduation could a typical member of the class expect to remain single (or to be married for the first time, in the case of those who were later divorced)? What was the peak period of weddings following graduation?

With the data that were available, it turned out that these and related questions could be addressed as problems in event history analysis, with the techniques of cohort life table construction. According to school records, a total of 699 persons graduated in midyear 1961. Between then and 1999, 18 graduates who had never been married died, and an additional three had entered religious careers that prohibited marriage. Subtracting these 21 from the total left 678 individuals whose marriage probabilities were tracked. The Table 9.9 summarizes this information with the

Table 9.9. Event History of Marriages for the Class of '61

Date	Years after Graduation	Single Persons	Number Married
1961	0–1	678	74
1962	1–5	604	198
1966	5–10	406	242
1971	10–15	164	97
1976	15–20	67	31
1981	20–25	36	18
1986	25–30	18	12
1991	30–35	6	4
1996	35+	2	2

date, number of years after graduation, number of single alumni remaining, and the number of marriages each one-, four-, or five-year interval:

With none of the class members married on graduation day, 74 did marry within one year of graduation. At the other extreme, at a point after 1996 the last two unmarried class members still alive had weddings, the very last of which was reported in the alumni news.

These data were then translated into a cohort life table by first calculating the year-after-graduation specific marriage rates ($_{nr}w_x$, as shown in Table 9.10). Next, the probabilities of marriage ($_nq_x$) were calculated. These are shown in the third column of the table. Because the reference population is small, an l_0 of 1,000 was chosen, which was multiplied by q_0 to begin creating the vector of unmarried alumni out of 1,000. With this completed, we determined the first three $_nL_x$s, the last set of T_xs and, via addition, subtraction, and division, the remaining $_nL_x$s, T_xs, and all of the $ê_x$s. This last function is the average number of years before marriage remaining to alumni who have stayed single x years after graduation.

The second column, containing the marriage rates, indicates that more than one peak period of marriages occurred. The rate during the first year after graduation, when 74 alumni were married, is nearly 11 percent, and in the succeeding four years, during which additional 198 class members were wed, the rate was almost 10 percent per year. However, in the 1966–1971 period, the rate was more than 18 percent, with 242 marriages—leaving well under one-half of the class still single. From that point to the more recent dates, the marriage rates declined until, during the last few periods, they rose again—in large part because so few single members remained.

These trends reveal distinct lifecycle changes. The first peak, just after graduation, reflects entry into adult careers and/or the results of postponement of even earlier marriages by this segment of the class. The 10 percent who married between one and five years after graduation appear to be in their early career- and family-formation stage, with a small proportion having just completed college. The next peak, between six and 10 years after graduation, represents college graduates and those who had established their professions and occupations. Nearly the entire remaining group married in the period between 10 and 20 years after graduation.

This pattern can also be seen in the years-remaining column. For the class as a whole at graduation, an average ($ê_0$) of nearly eight years remained before marriage.

Table 9.10. The Class of '61: Cohort Table Based on Marriage Statistics for the Class of 1961

Years After Grad (x)	$_{nr}w_x$	$_nq_x$	l_x	$_nw_x$	$_nL_x$	T_x	$ê_x$
0–1	0.109	0.093	1,000	93	966.0	7,811.4	7.81
1–5	0.099	0.264	907	239	2,966.3	6,845.0	7.55
5–10	0.181	0.608	668	406	2,251.0	3,879.1	5.81
10–15	0.179	0.604	262	158	959.4	1,628.1	6.20
15–20	0.124	0.470	104	49	358.8	666.5	6.38
20–25	0.139	0.510	55	28	191.0	305.0	5.55
25–30	0.220	0.683	27	18	82.9	114.2	4.23
30–35	0.220	0.683	9	6	25.6	31.3	3.47
35+	0.277	1.000	3	0	5.6	5.6	1.87

Note: $_rw_x$ stands for the marriage rate in the observed population for years x to x+n; $_nw_x$ stands for the number of marriages in the life table population during the interval.

Because the average age at graduation was between 17 and 18 years, this indicates that class members could expect to remain single until about age 25. For those who did not marry during the first year, the average ($\hat{e}_1$) was 7.55 years, or an age at marriage of more than 26 years. But for those who remained single through the fifth year after graduation, the average ($\hat{e}_5$) dropped to 5.81 years. This is another way to indicate that by the end of this second peak interval, a very large proportion of the class had been married. For subsequent periods, the average or age at marriage, or both, increase steadily.

Survival rates tell much the same story. The birth-date rate between 0 to 1 and 1 to 5 years, $_1S_0^{an}$ (an = 1) = 0.907, the rate between 1 to 5 and 5 to 10, $_4S_1^{an}$ (an = 4) = 0.736, reflecting the early peak period. However, the rate between 5 to 10 and 10 to 15, $_5S_5^{an}$ (an = 5), is a very low 0.392, and the 10-year rate between 0 to 1 and 10 to 15, $_5S_0^{an}$ (an = 10), is the lowest of all, at 0.262. This means that 10 years after graduation, in 1976, only 26.2 percent of the alumni remained single. The probability that a graduate would remain single until 1996—30 years after graduation, is the same as the survival rate $_5S_0^{an}$ (an = 30), = 3/1,000 = 0.003, or three-tenths of 1 percent. The feat of overcoming such odds certainly deserves a feature article in the alumni news!

SUMMARY

This chapter has introduced the basic concepts, principles, and terminology associated with life table analysis. We began with some definitions of the life table and its functions, along with a discussion of the role of this tool in the study of mortality. We have seen that the techniques of life table analysis use data on (1) the size of cohorts and (2) the number of deaths by age, in an observed population. With these data, age-specific death rates are created, and these, in turn, can be expressed as mortality rates—or the probability of dying before reaching the next year of age. From this point, a set of life table functions is created that indicates a range of rates and probabilities: the surviving or stationary population, person years lived, total years remaining, average life expectancy, and survival rates. From the discussion and illustrations of the life table and its functions presented here, it should not be difficult for you to read a table and understand what it is saying about the reference population on which it is based. You should also be able to compare two or more life tables in order to form judgments about relative risks of death, and even to create your own tables with the help of a calculator or a simple computer program.

It should be clear at this point that there are many different kinds of tables: male, female, and combined; unabridged and abridged; period and cohort (generation); general and cause-specific; and various tables for different dates and different kinds of reference populations: nations, states, counties, and special populations. In the last section of the chapter, we even noted ways in which nondemographic problems can be addressed with life tables. Nevertheless, as is true of most introductions to a subject, the seemingly wide range of topics treated here represents a small fraction of the material that has been developed during the centuries since the life table was invented.

Thus, we have said little or nothing about such matters as the mathematical relationships among life table functions. Nor have we discussed how these functions can be treated continuously with differential and integral calculus—better approximating the manner in which vital events actually occur. And we have only touched on neonatal and disease-specific tables, and the use of life tables in actuarial science and population projections. Unfortunately, all but the last of these topics lie beyond the scope of this book. But it is our hope that this discussion has sufficiently peaked your interest that you are motivated to pursue advanced studies, with the books listed in the reference section and by taking additional courses on the subject (many advanced courses in demography focus extensively on life table analysis). As for the last topic, life tables and projection, this is taken up in Chapter 10, to which we now turn.

KEY TERMS

abridged tables	period table
average life expectancy	radix
cohort table	row vector
column vector	separation factors
event history analysis	stationary population
Lexis diagram	survival rates
life table functions	unabridged tables
matrix	

NOTES

1. As discussed later in the text, one of the chief assumptions upon which most life tables are based is that the population of interest is closed; that is, no in- or out-migration occurs. Although a common premise, it is not necessary, as researchers in the United States and elsewhere have developed tables that do account for migration and its impact on host-population mortality conditions (Ledent 1980; Shavelle 1996).

2. Ordinarily, the "n" is omitted from l_x even in abridged tables, for reasons to be discussed in the text. However, in this chapter we retain it as a reminder that we are working with abridged data, even though this fact has no bearing on the value of l_x.

3. We rarely see life tables for human populations that use intervals of less than one year, although it is possible to construct them provided that the data on K_x and D_x are available at daily, weekly, or monthly rates. In nonhuman populations, especially those of very short-lived species, smaller intervals may be essential. Less-than-annual data are also required for the study of neonatal mortality but, as we note in the text, this information is ordinarily incorporated into tables with one-year or larger intervals via separation factors.

4. See Keyfitz (1968:5): "The set of l_x is spoken of as the *stationary population*, almost as though it had a real contemporary existence and $(l_x + l_{x+1})/2$ persons could be counted at age x last birthday." Similarly, Shryock, and Siegel (1976:251–52) note that "A stationary population is defined as a population whose total number and distribution does not change with time." One could argue that the L_x vector (not l_x) is the appropriate entity to refer to as the stationary population, since that is the true number of persons alive at the exact age at midyear. This may be true in the case of unabridged tables. However, because of the rules for forming abridged tables, the sum of the L_xs is many times

larger than the actual size of the stationary populations, so that l_x is generally the correct choice. A stationary population is a type of *stable* population, the latter being closed to migration and with unchanging fertility and mortality rates. When such a stable population also is at ZPG, with births equal to deaths, as in the case of a life table, then it is designated as stationary. Also, see Coale (1973), Impagliazzo (1985), and Stolnitz (1956).

5. The use of IMRs assumes that f' and f" are more nearly equal when IMRs are high and that f' is increasingly greater than f" as IMRs decline. See Shryock and Siegel (1976:236–39).

6. This situation is similar to that encountered with the use of grouped data in a frequency distribution. Without access to ungrouped information, the statistician makes certain assumptions about the values between the lower and upper limits of an interval. For example, consider this part of a frequency distribution of grades on an exam:

Grade	f
90–100	7
80–89	11
70–79	15
. . . . . .	

Since we don't know the exact score between 90 and 100 of the seven individuals in that category, nor do we know the exact scores between 80 and 89 of the 11 who were in that category, and so forth, an exact mean, standard deviation, and median cannot be derived. Instead, for the first two statistics, it is assumed that all 7, 11, and so on, individuals scored at the midpoint of their respective intervals. For the median, it is assumed that all 7, 11, and so on were distributed evenly throughout the interval. At a more general level, the techniques used both for abridged life tables and grouped frequency distributions are forms of mathematical interpolation.

7. We say "loosely" because *cohort* is the technically correct term. A generation, which has sociological as well as demographic properties, may or may not coincide with a cohort. A generation in the sense of a set of people who are distinguished from their parents and their offspring usually encompasses 20 or more years, and is thus much larger than a demographic cohort. In the sense of a group of people who experience the same dramatic event (such as a world war) at approximately the same stage of life, the size is even more indefinite. See Berger (1960).

8. For a guide to PC applications of event history analysis using the SAS software package, see Allison (1995).

CHAPTER TEN

POPULATION ESTIMATES, PROJECTIONS, AND FORECASTS

Early in Chapter 1, we observed that demography is not only a logically well-organized and highly quantified scientific discipline in its own right, but that it also is one of the most widely applied of all the academic social sciences: in government, business, and other areas. By this point in our discussion, it should be easier to see why this is so. For the methods and theories that help us understand the characteristics of current and past populations, from fertility analysis, to migration studies, to the interpretation and creation of life tables, have turned out to be very useful in many modern occupations and professions. To extend the theme further, in this chapter our attention is turned to a set of techniques that has been developed specifically with such practical applications in view; that is, approaches to anticipating the nature of future populations—or of present populations with past data. These have assumed a unique and indispensable niche in contemporary decision making, especially in the fields of urban and regional planning, public administration, and education, health, and social service management.

Demographers employ several techniques in attempting to understand how populations at a future date (or at a date later than that for which data are available) will resemble or differ from their current state. These are generally classed into three categories, each of which is based on a specific set of assumptions and mathematical formulations: (1) estimation, (2) **projection**, and (3) forecasting. Following a brief introduction, the following sections provide explanations of each type, in the order mentioned, along with extended mathematical derivations and illustrations using census data, current information from other sources, and formal models.[1]

Before we begin, however, it might help to clear away a source of possible misunderstanding. As interesting and useful as projection and the other techniques may be, they do not produce certain answers about tomorrow's populations; demographers do not possess crystal balls or tarot cards that let them "in" on what will happen in the future. Rather, all of these techniques use factual information about the present and the past to help provide educated guesses about what would occur if certain assumptions were to hold. In this way, they do reveal much authentic information about the nature of the present and past data on which they are based, but they do not and cannot produce "facts" about the future. Nathan Keyfitz (1968:27), one of the world's leading experts on population projection, put the matter succinctly. "The object [of projection] is to understand the past rather than to predict the future; apparently the way to think effectively about a set of observed birth and death rates is to ask what it would lead to if continued."

APPROACHES TO ANTICIPATING POPULATION CHARACTERISTICS

In ordinary conversation, we tend to employ certain words that refer to anticipating the future more or less interchangeably. Among the most frequently used are predict, estimate, project, and **forecast**. In scientific applications, however—including population science, each of these has a slightly different meaning which, if not respected, can lead to serious confusion.

Perhaps the most difficult of these four is the first, *predict* and the noun form, **prediction**. In ordinary usage, a prediction is a statement about what we think will happen in the future, based on fact or intuition; for example, "I predict that my car will hold up long enough to get me to work this morning." As we shall see, this is best called a "forecast" in scientific contexts. According to technical usage, a prediction is virtually identical to an explanation (see Rudner 1966). It is the outcome of a strict deductive process that need not even apply to the future at all. In contrast, a population *estimate* is an assessment of a population's size or other characteristics at a present or near-future date, for which we have no immediately current information. Estimates are actually updates of old data, based on the most recent data available. When census data are used, the procedure takes place either at an intercensal date (e.g., 1985, 1995, or 2005) or immediately following the most recent census count.

Estimates are necessary because it is practically impossible to collect data continuously, especially the amount and type gathered by government census operations. Even the kinds of surveys that are regularly conducted by the United States and other national census bureaus, which are very useful in validating estimates, are out of date the moment they are concluded: people are born, and migrate, and die whether or not interviewers are in the field. Yet, a continual demand exists for fresh information about population size, structure, and vital events from national, state, and local governments to allocate financial resources and for other purposes.

The point in time (usually the most recent point) for which authoritative data on demographic characteristics exists, such as Census years 1980, 1990, 2000, is referred to as the "**central date**." The size of a population at midyear of that central date, for example, July 1990, is used as the denominator of crude birth rates, death rates, and many other measures, as we saw in earlier chapters. But if we would like to know something about vital rates at a date between 1990 and 2000—for instance, birth rates in 1996—estimation is necessary so that the appropriate denominator can be determined (recall that information about the vital events in the numerator is continuously registered). To illustrate, the midyear 2010 U.S. population was enumerated at approximately 308,745,538. Based on this and other information, the following set of midyear estimates through 2013 (in thousands) was calculated by the Census Bureau:[2]

2010: 309,326
2011: 311,582
2012: 313,873
2013: 316,128

A *projection* depicts likely population characteristics at a future date based on a set of explicitly stated assumptions about what is expected to occur between the time the projection is made and the date to which it applies. The accuracy of a projection depends upon how closely the assumptions agree with the events that actually occur. Because it is usually difficult to assess future trends, several different scenarios are employed to account for a range of reasonable outcomes. This results not in one single projection but, instead, in a series of projections, of which one might assume slow growth, another moderate growth, and a third rapid growth. The U.S. Census Bureau has used this technique routinely for many years in its household projections, and the results are now regularly updated and posted at the *www.census.gov* web site.

More recently, projections of all the world's national aggregate populations for which information is available have been undertaken by the U.S. Census Bureau, national governments, the United Nations, and private organizations. Table 10.1 contains a set of moderate-growth projections for the total size of the world's population and selected nations to midyear 2025 and 2050, drawn from various sources by the Population Reference Bureau, Inc. The table shows that the world as a whole and most countries will continue to grow fairly rapidly well into the twenty-first century. However, a few countries are likely to experience little or no growth, and some—including Italy and Russia—are expected to experience significant population declines, as they were below ZPG at the time the projections were derived.

With the world's population size approaching 6.9 billion in 2010, the year on which the calculations were based, the total for the year 2025 was projected to be just over 8 billion. Using the 2010 world growth rate of 1.2 percent per year and the model of exponential growth (see Chapter 8), if no changes occurred in birth and death rates, the 2025 total would be slightly over 8 billion.

In the case of the United States' projection to 2025, with a rate of natural increase of 0.6 percent in 2010, the total projected population size in 2025 would be 351 million. In contrast, India's population growth is expected to decelerate over the projection period, from its then-current rate of 1.6 percent per year to 1.5 percent between 2010 and 2025. Nevertheless, with just about 1 billion people at the beginning of the projection period, this figure will probably reach 1.75 billion by the end of the period.

A *forecast* is neither fact nor sheer fiction (see Worrall 2014; Goodman 1983). Rather, it is an assessment of a future state of affairs, including the future state of population characteristics, based on any or all of several sources: projection, scientific theory, intuition, and even sheer guesses. It is the most idiosyncratic and least systematic of the three techniques, and often depends upon the personal viewpoint of the forecaster. Although a forecast is not as reliable as an estimate or a projection, and cannot replace these in attempting to anticipate tomorrow's demographic events, it does have its place in the larger scheme of things because it is so eclectic. We are well aware that the size, growth rate, rate of vital events, age structure, and other aspects of today's populations were affected not only by yesterday's size, growth rate, and so on, but also by a range of other, nondemographic factors. These include population policies and policy shifts, as discussed in Chapter 11, economic conditions, environmental changes, and even natural disasters. The same can be said of the range of possible causes today that will affect tomorrow's populations.

Table 10.1.   Projected Population Sizes (in Millions) of the World and Selected Countries to 2025 and 2050

Country	2010 Population Size	2025 Projection	2050 Projection
World	6892	8108.0	9485.0
United States	309.6	351.4	422.6
Canada	34.1	39.7	48.4
Mexico	110.6	123.4	129.0
Haiti	9.8	12.2	15.7
Jamaica	2.7	2.9	2.7
Puerto Rico	4.0	4.1	3.7
Argentina	40.5	46.2	52.4
Brazil	193.3	212.4	215.3
Peru	29.5	34.5	39.8
Australia	22.4	26.9	34.0
New Zealand	4.4	5.0	5.6
Papua New Guinea	6.8	9.1	13.4
Algeria	36.0	43.6	50.4
Egypt	80.4	103.6	137.7
Sudan	43.2	56.7	75.9
Ethiopia	85.0	19.8	173.8
Ghana	24.0	31.8	44.6
Nigeria	158.3	217.4	326.4
Kenya	40.0	51.3	65.2
Tanzania	45.0	67.4	109.5
South Africa	49.9	54.4	57.4
Israel	7.6	9.4	11.4
Saudi	29.2	35.7	49.8
Turkey	73.6	85.0	94.7
China	1338.1	1476.0	1437.0
India	1188.8	1444.5	1748.0
Japan	127.4	119.3	95.2
United Kingdom	62.2	68.6	77.0
France	63.0	66.1	70.0
Germany	81.6	79.7	71.5
Albania	3.2	3.3	2.9
Italy	60.5	61.9	61.7
Spain	47.1	48.4	49.1
Poland	38.2	37.4	31.8
Russia	141.9	140.8	126.7
Ukraine	45.9	41.9	35.3

Source: Haub, Gribble, and Jacobsen (2011).

When looking to the future, a forecaster can take these nondemographic factors into account and, under the right circumstances, provide a useful depiction of the shape of things to come. We have just noted that recent projections assume that India's growth rate will decline over the next few years, largely because of declining fertility rates. But it is within the realm of possibility that the political winds shift in India, and a new government is elected which, like that of Iraq, is strongly pronatalist and does not view the present growth rate as too high. Such a government might take steps to withdraw support from or even close down the country's extensive system of family planning clinics. Now, suppose further that some forecasters with keen political insight sense these changes just beginning to unfold and they include such information in their characterization of the country's future population size. If this were to happen, the old projections would prove to be less accurate than the forecast.[3]

POPULATION ESTIMATION

Several methods of estimation are used by government census offices and academic and private researchers. An estimate is an attempt at arriving at the size of the current population based on data that reflect current or recent conditions. Most of these rely on mathematical methods, including those based on simple growth models and on the fundamental equation of demography: Growth = Natural Increase + Net Migration. We have already employed the simple growth models in other contexts, but they are analyzed here for the first time.

Simple Growth Models

The simple growth model approach seeks to determine the unknown size of a population. This can be (1) at a specific point that lies between two dates for which information is available (e.g., an intercensal period), or (2) that occurs soon after a central date at which size is known (e.g., immediately following a census count). It uses one or more of several mathematical formulas to depict the nature of change and the estimated population sizes during a period for which we lack data via the procedure known as curve fitting. This technique is easily adapted for deriving projections, as will be shown in the following section.

Four models, the linear, geometric, exponential, and logistic, are commonly used, of which the first and third were introduced in Chapter 8 (also see Shryock and Siegel 1976: Chap. 13). Although there are infinitely many possible growth formulas, these four have been found most effective. One reason is that the curves associated with them are smooth. In the case of the first three, they assume that population growth occurs in a fairly even and regular manner rather than exhibiting dramatic peaks, valleys, reversals, and the like. In addition, records of population growth and growth rates taken from the Census Bureau and other sources verify that these give the most realistic picture of how populations actually change.

Arithmetic Growth

As we have seen, the linear model—also referred to as arithmetic growth—assumes that the rate of change between two dates will be constant throughout the interval. If the rate of growth at the beginning of a 10-year interval was 0.90 percent, then this model estimates growth as if the rate were 0.90 percent each and every year.

Arithmetic (linear) Growth: $P_t = P_0 + (P_0 \times GR \times t)$.

- P_t is the population size at a later date
- P_0 is the size at the earlier date
- GR is the growth rate
- t is the amount of time (number of years) between 0 and t

This is the same method that is used to determine simple interest on a savings account. A fixed rate is applied to the initial principal, say 10 percent per annum on $1,000, and that amount—$100, is added to the account each year. As shown in Figure 10.1, this equation traces a line to indicate the constant rate of change.

The population size of the United States was approximately 281,421,906 in midyear 2000, and the growth rate year was in fact 0.90 percent. Thus, if we wanted to estimate the population size in 2001, 2003, and 2005, when no Census counts were taken, we could use the linear model—provided that we were willing to make the constant-growth assumption. With t = 1, 3, and 5 for 2001, 2003, and 2005, respectively, the formulas would be:

$P_{2001} = 281,421,906 + (281,421,906 \times 1 \times 0.009) = 283,954,703$
$P_{2003} = 281,421,906 + (281,421,906 \times 3 \times 0.009) = 289,020,297$
$P_{2005} = 281,421,906 + (281,421,906 \times 5 \times 0.009) = 294,085,891$

To illustrate the use of the linear model between two dates for which we have data, we first need to rearrange the growth formula to solve for GR. This will then allow us to apply that rate (using the linear assumption) to any intervening year.

- First, we subtract P_0 from both sides, leaving: $P_t - P_0 = P_0 \times GR \times t$.
- Then, we divide both sides by P_0 and t, and switch sides of the equal sign.
- This gives us: $GR = (P_t - P_0)/(P_0 \times t)$.

Now, the enumerated U.S. population size in 2010 was just under 308,745,600, and we saw that the 2000 figure was 281,421,900. Thus the difference, or $(P_t - P_0)$, is 27,323,700. With t = 10 years $(P_0 \times t)$ = and GR, or $(P_t - P_0)/(P_0 \times t)$ = 27,323,700/2,814,219,000 = .0097 or 0.97 percent. Because this is slightly above the growth rate at the beginning of the interval, let us make some comparisons. We found that the 2005 estimate using the growth rate at one date (2000) was 294,085,891. But, if we apply the growth rate determined with two dates, then the 2005 estimate would be:

$$281,421,900 + (281,421,900 \times .0097 \times 5) = 295,070,862$$

Furthermore, since we know the 2010 enumeration total, we can compare that to the one-date estimate (with the rate of 0.90 percent) when t = 10 years. That is, $P_{2010} = P_{2000} + (P_{2000} \times .009 \times 10) = 281,421,900 + (281,421,900 \times .009 \times 10) = 306,749,871$. Thus, we find a difference of about 1,995,700 persons between the estimate and the enumeration, with the estimate about 2 million too low because it did not account for a slight rise in the growth rate during the intercensal period.

Although the linear model did not prove to be perfect when applied to recent dates from the United States, it does appear to be fairly accurate. However, the assumption of a constant growth rate is generally inappropriate when we deal with more volatile

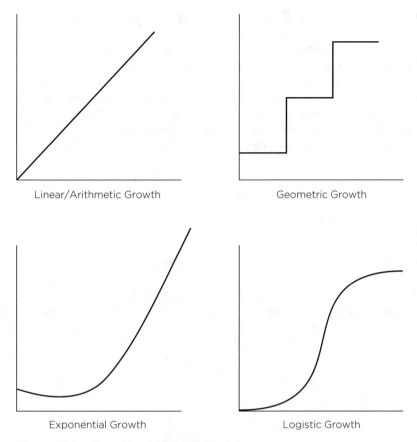

Linear/Arithmetic Growth

Geometric Growth

Exponential Growth

Logistic Growth

Figure 10.1. Four Simple Growth Models

populations and longer time periods. For example, in 1985 the population growth rate of Afghanistan was –2.8 percent per year, and its population size was 11,528,977. In 2010, the total population size was estimated at 28,397,812. During those intervening 25 years, the country, one of the poorest in the world, experienced:

- a civil war,
- a population explosion,
- a period of antinatalist policy, and
- an era of pronatalist Islamic fundamentalist family law, similar to Iran's under the Ayatollah Khomeini
- and a war with U.S. and Allied forces

Does the linear model explain its population growth? By the formula, the 2010 population size would be P_{2010} = 11,528,977+ (11,528,977 × –0.028 × 25) = 3,458,693, more than 25 million short. Obviously, Afghanistan's population did not grow arithmetically.

Geometric Growth

In Chapter 1, we noted that Thomas Malthus, who lived in an era during which his native England and other parts of Europe and America were experiencing civil war, revolution, and population explosions, argued that populations did not grow at the moderately slow pace depicted by the linear model. Rather, he believed that populations inevitably exhibited what he called "geometric" growth. That is, instead of expanding in an arithmetic series (with a constant rate of change) such as this: 1, 2, 3, 4, 5, and so on, he held that populations expanded in a geometric series (in which the rate of change itself increases), such as: 1, 2, 4, 8, 16, and so on. Although we now know that no single model or "law" applies to each and every population during any time period one chooses, it is true that **geometric growth** is often a more realistic assumption than the linear one. (It traces the step curve shown in Figure 10.1).

$$\text{Geometric Growth: } P_t = P_0 \times (1 + GR)^t$$

- P_t is the population size at a later date
- P_0 is the size at the earlier date
- GR is the growth rate
- t is the amount of time (number of years) between 0 and t

This model is applied to determine interest on savings compounded annually. A set interest rate, e.g., 10 percent, is applied to the initial principal, say $1,000, which at the end of the first year yields $100. For the second year, the rate is applied to the principal plus the interest, $1100, to yield $110 in interest, and so forth.

Let us illustrate, once again with recent U.S. Census data. Using the 2000 total of 281,421,900 and growth rate of 0.90 percent, we estimate the population sizes for 2001, 2003, 2005, and, for the sake of comparison, 2010.

$$P_{2001} = 281,421,900 \times (1 + .009)^1 = 283,954,703$$
$$P_{2003} = 281,421,900 \times (1 + .009)^3 = 289,088,888$$
$$P_{2005} = 281,421,900 \times (1 + .009)^5 = 294,315,904$$
$$P_{2010} = 281,421,900 \times (1 + .009)^{10} = 307,800,671$$

We can see that the geometric model yields estimates that are larger than those produced by the linear model (or larger in absolute value when growth is negative). The 2010 estimate of just over 307 million exceeds the linear estimate by about 1.05 million, and it is closer to the enumerated figure by about 0.9 million. This better, but still not perfect, estimate allows us to conclude that growth between 2000 and 2010 followed a course between linear and geometric, and closer to geometric.

Because geometric growth is more rapid than linear, it might be more helpful in explaining the situation in Afghanistan. Recall that the country's 1985 population size was about 11,528,977. Applying the geometric formula to estimate the 2010 total, we find that:

$$P_{2010} = 11,528,977 \times (1 - .028)^{25} = 5,668,233$$

which is still far below the estimate of more than 28 million. This leaves several possibilities, including that another model incorporating even a faster rate of increase would be more appropriate. Thus we are led to consider the third type of estimation curve, one that is believed to best fit populations undergoing explosive growth, the exponential model.

Exponential Growth

The assumption made by the geometric model, that increments ("interest payments") are added to the population base (the "principal") at the end of each year, is not realistic. In demographic applications, our attention is focused on vital events, births, deaths, and the comings and goings of migrants. These events occur continuously, hour by hour, day by day, and week by week. People don't wait until December 31st to bear children, or to pass away, or to change residence; yet, this is what geometric growth stipulates. When Malthus spoke of this kind of growth as being especially applicable to human populations, he almost certainly did not mean it literally. For the family of equations and curves based on the exponential model treats incremental (and decremental) factors as they actually occur. It is comparable to interest compounded daily, or even hourly, as close to momentarily as is practical. Most banks have adopted this method, and it is the kind of bank in which you want to keep your money.

Exponential growth traces the smooth, upward sloping curve in Figure 10.1. And its formula is

$$\text{Exponential Growth: } P_t = P_0 \times e^{GR \times t}$$

- P_t is the population size at a later date
- P_0 is the size at the earlier date
- GR is the growth rate
- t is the amount of time (number of years) between 0 and t
- e is the exponential constant = 2.71828

Just as we can determine the linear growth rate from its associated equation when both intercensal dates P_t and P_0 are known, exponential growth rates are determined by solving the preceding formula for GR. Using the algebraic concept of logarithms mentioned in Chapter 8.

$$GR = [\ln (P_t/P_0)]/t, \text{ where ln is the natural log (with the base e).}$$

Once again, we turn to the example of the U.S. population between 2000 and 2010. We have already seen that the geometric model assumes a rate faster than that actually achieved. Thus, we should expect that the estimates that anticipate exponential increase would be even higher and less accurate. With the 2000 population size and growth rate given, we solve for 2001, 2003, 2005, and 2010.

$$P_{2001} = 281,421,900 \times 2.71828^{(0.009 \times 1)} = 283,966,128$$
$$P_{2003} = 281,421,900 \times 2.71828^{(0.009 \times 3)} = 289,123,799$$
$$P_{2005} = 281,421,900 \times 2.71828^{(0.009 \times 5)} = 294,375,147$$
$$P_{2010} = 281,421,900 \times 2.71828^{(0.009 \times 10)} = 307,924,605$$

We see that these estimates are indeed the highest of the three sets, with the 2010 total close to the enumerated count.

Because all three sets of estimates based on the 2000 growth rate of 0.90 percent were inaccurate, it is most likely that actual growth in the 2000–2010 interval did not occur at that rate. When we assume exponential growth (a realistic model, as noted) we find that the associated growth rate is slightly below the 1980 figure. That is:

$$GR = [\ln (308,745,600/281,421,900)]/10 = 0.92 \text{ percent}$$

Recall that this is an annual average over 10 years.

When we fit Afghanistan's growth between 1985 and 2010 to the exponential model, we derive an estimate somewhat closer to the actual situation. For that country,

$$P_{2010} = P_{1985} \times 2.78128^{(-.028 \times 25)} = 5,764,488$$

Clearly, even the exponential estimate is low. In this case, it is reasonable to conclude that the growth rate at the beginning of the period of –2.80 percent did not continue at that level through to the end. In fact, we know that it fluctuated considerably with events. In 1985, it had gone to zero or even negative, at about –2.8 percent; by 1990, it had soared to 4.5 percent; in 1995 it was 6.5 percent; and in 2000 it was 3.00. Taking the exponential average for the period, we find that it is:

$$GR = [\ln (11,528,977/28,397,812)]/25 = 3.61 \text{ percent}$$

It is this rate which, when applied over the long range, that explains Afghanistan's uneven, but rapid, population explosion.

Logistic Growth

The logistic model assumes that neither absolute growth nor growth rates remain constant over the period under observation. Instead, it depicts a situation in which growth is rapid during the early part of the interval, then it slows until, during the last portion, it approaches or equals zero (or even goes negative). Its wide application in many fields in addition to demography has given the curve several names. One is the "S" curve, because of its shape. Another is the "saturation" curve because it is a model of how a permeable material, such as a sponge, fills up, taking on large amounts of liquid when it is dry but less as it fills and then none when it is saturated. A third is the "ogive," familiar to statisticians as the curve representing cumulative frequency. A fourth is "Pareto's curve" because it applies to a principle of economic saturation, Pareto's Law, developed by the early-twentieth-century Italian social scientist. It is also the mathematical model that best fits demographic transition, as Keyfitz (1968:76, 215) first suggested (also see Weinstein 1980:73).[4]

Table 10.2. Historical Population Data for the United States

Year	U.S. Population	Year	U.S. Population
1900	76,212,168	1960	179,323,798
1910	92,228,496	1970	203,302,031
1920	106,021,537	1980	226,542,199
1930	123,202,624	1990	248,709,873
1940	132,164,569	2000	281,421,906
1950	151,325,798	2010	308,745,538

Source: U.S. Census Bureau Fast Facts.

Box 10.1 Computations for Fitting Historical U.S. Population Sizes, 1900-2010, to the Logistic Curve

Notes: Computational Procedures

There are several computational procedures to choose from. The one used here is known as the method of selected points. Table 10.2 presents historical population data for 12 decades commencing from 1900. We selected three data points, 1900 (P_0), 1950 (P_5), and 2000 (P_{10}). The computation procedure involves estimating several coefficients which are used in the final projection formula.

1. Obtain the reciprocals for the selected years and multiply by 1 million.
   $(1/P_0) \times 1,000,000 = 0.131213$
   $(1/p_5) \times 1,000,000 = 0.006608$
   $(1/p_{10}) \times 1,000,000 = 0.003553$

2. Calculate the difference between the first two reciprocals, and between the second and the third.
   $D_1 = (1/P_0) - (1/P_5) = 0.006513$
   $D_2 = (1/P_5) - (1/P_{10}) = 0.003055$

3. Obtain coefficient "a" $= (1/r) \times [\ln(D_1) - \ln(D_2)]$, where "r" is 5 because the three points we chose are five units apart. a $= (1/5) [-5.033909 - 5.790975] = 0.1514133$.

4. Obtain the second coefficient, k, by first obtaining its reciprocal. $1/k = (1/P_0) - (D_1^2/(D_1 - D_2)) = 0.000861$. Therefore, k $= 1161.575091$.

5. Obtain the third coefficient, b. b $= [(k/P_0) - 1] = 14.241333$.

6. We will project the U.S. population to year 2015 first.
   $P_{(2015)} = (k/[(1+b) \times (e^{-aT})])$ where T is $(2015 - 1900)/5$
   $P_{(2015)} = 1161.57509/3.314488 = 350,453,803$ July 2015

The U.S. Population Clock estimates the population midday March 26, 2015 as 320,577,213.
P (2020) = 388,579,308.

The curve representing **logistic growth** is shown in the lower right panel of Figure 10.1, and its formula is:

$$\text{Logistic Growth: } P_t = k/[(1 + b) \times (e^{-aT})]$$

- P_1 is the population size at a selected date (for which data are unavailable)
- k is an estimate of the largest population size attainable over the observation period, based on but usually larger than P_0
- b is another estimated constant that represents the length of time between P_0 and the point at which growth begins to slow
- e is the exponential constant (indicating that this curve is related to the one for exponential growth

- a is an estimated average rate of growth for the entire period
- T is the number of five-year segments (our population data points are five years apart) in the duration to the projected date

Table 10.2 shows the results of applying this formula to the U.S. population, with the details of the calculations provided in the notes.

In Chapter 8, we saw how this type of change actually occurred in most of the populations in Europe between about 1700 and 1900. Just prior to the Industrial Revolution, following millennia of slow, uneven, "Malthusian" growth, general mortality rates and IMRs began to decline in England, France, and eventually other countries. As the effects of industrialization spread, this process accelerated, resulting in the highest rates of natural increase ever experienced in any human populations to that time. Then, around 1850, with the increase in the size and influence of the urban middle classes and the growing popularity of the family-planning movement, birth rates began to decline. They have continued to do so throughout Europe, the United States, and other parts of the world. With these declines came progressively slower population growth until, today, many countries are at or below ZPG.

One country that now appears to be in the midst of its transition is Brazil. With a total population size of 169 million in 1998[5] and a rate of natural increase of 1.5 percent, it is growing more rapidly than the United States and the European countries that have essentially completed their transitions. But it is growing more slowly than some of its neighbors such as Bolivia, Colombia, Paraguay, Ecuador, and Peru—and much more slowly than many Asian and African nations. Of even greater significance, Brazil's population growth rates have declined substantially over the past few decades when, as recently as 1960, the rate was nearly 3 percent.

Components Methods

Methods based on the fundamental equation of demography apply the fact that the size of a population at a date for which data are unavailable can be estimated. This requires information about (1) known population size at an earlier or a later date— or both—and (2) the volume of births, deaths, in-migrations, and out-migrations that occur between dates. The simplest of these, the **cohort survival method**, assumes a closed population in which net migration is set at zero. Under these conditions,

$$P_t = P_0 + B - D \text{ or } P_0 = P_t - B + D$$

where B is the number of births that occur between 0 and t, and D is the number of deaths in the interval. Note that we can either work forward from an earlier date, adding births and subtracting deaths, or from a later to earlier date by subtracting births and adding deaths. The assumption of a closed population does apply to the world, which experiences neither in- nor out-migration (thus far). It also characterizes populations in which there is negligible or no movement in or out, and it fairly closely approximates those in which in-migration exactly equals out-migration.[6] In general, when applied to today's dynamic national aggregate, state, provincial, and urban populations, this method is prone to inaccuracy, for which adjustments must be made.

Cohort Survival

This issue aside, the cohort survival method is more precise than the simple growth models because in the place of crude rates it employs age-specific measures, in a

Table 10.3. Components Method for Estimating Population Size

Age	Initial Population (P_0) Males	Females	Survival Rates Males	Females	ASFR	Estimated Population (P_t) Males	Females
0–9	20709.0	19841.0	0.995	0.996		23045.00	22141.00
10–19	21884.0	20834.0	0.975	0.980	0.04	20605.45	19761.63
20–29	21650.0	21038.0	0.965	0.970	1.60	21336.89	20417.32
30–39	20039.0	20104.0	0.950	0.960	0.51	20892.25	20406.86
40–49	21603.0	21997.0	0.930	0.950	0.02	19037.05	19299.84
50–59	20457.0	21506.0	0.920	0.940		20090.79	20897.14
60–69	18175.0	20357.0	0.900	0.930		18820.44	20215.64
70+	7267.0	11288.0	0.890	0.910		22824.00	29204.0

Note: Survival refers to forward survival. Thus, a woman's probability of surviving from ages 20–29 to 30–39 is .0.97, etc. This hypothetical model assumes higher survival rates for females at all ages and no fertility before age 15 or after age 49.

Source: P_0 based on data from Howden and Meyer (2010: Table 2).

manner similar to life table analysis. The three basic variables are: (1) the age-sex structure of the population: the size of each cohort of males and females taken separately, (2) the age and sex-specific survival rates, derived from the life table, and (3) age-specific fertility rates (ASFRs). The data can be unabridged, using one-year cohorts, 0–1, 1–2, and so forth; or, more commonly, abridged, using five- or 10-year cohorts (except for the 0–1 group). In the latter case, the highest age category is open and includes all individuals ages 65 and above, 70 and above, or 85 and above. Survival is measured by the forward rates (S_x), which indicate the probability of surviving from one age to another, for example, from 35 to 40.

The estimation procedure is illustrated in Table 10.3, which shows an initial population, P_0—that of the United States as enumerated in 2010, divided into cohorts for males and females separately. The total size is 308,749,000 with 151,784,000 males and 156,965,000 females. **Cohort survival** is employed to estimate the size of each cohort and of the population 10 years later, P_t (because we are using 10-year cohorts). Once this is accomplished, the exponential growth model is used to estimate the population size in various intervening years. The survival and ASFRs are realistic but hypothetical.

The procedure occurs in three steps. First, we obtain the estimated number of children in the 0–9 cohort in P_t. This is done by multiplying the age-specific birth rates by the female population of each cohort with a fertility rate above 0 (column 4) x (column 7), and summing the products. This sum is then multiplied by 0.51 to obtain the male births and by 0.49 to obtain the number of female births. (This assumes that there are 510 males in every 1,000 births.)

The second step is to derive the size of each of the remaining cohorts in P_t, from ages 10–19 to 60–69 (the size of the last cohort with an open age interval is calculated separately). This is accomplished by applying the survival rates to the respective cohorts, multiplying column 2 by column 4 to obtain the estimated age-specific male population, and column 3 by column 5 for the female population. For example, to estimate the number of 20–29-year-old males in P_t, the 10–19 cohort in P_0 is diminished by applying its 10-year survival rate. That is, 21,884,000 × .975 = 21,336,890.

The third step is to obtain the estimated size of the last age cohort. In P_t, this group will contain the base population in the age group 60–69 surviving to the next age category plus those in the 70+ category surviving the 10 years between time 0 and time t. For example, the projected female population age 70+ is obtained as follows: $(20,357,000 \times 0.930) + (11,288,000 \times 0.910) = 29,204,000$.

This procedure yielded a total size for P_t of 338,994,000, of whom 166,651,000 are male and 172,343,000 are female. Now, with two population sizes at two different dates, one actual and the other estimated, we can derive estimates for intervening dates. The exponential growth model indicates that the average annual growth rate for the interval, based on our assumptions, is:

$$GR = [\ln (338,994,000/308,345,000)]/10 = .00947 \text{ or } 0.947 \text{ percent}$$

Applying this rate in the formula:

$$P_t = P_0 \times e^{GR \times t}$$

where t = 2011, 2012, 2013, and 2014, we derive these estimates:

$P_{2011} = 342,219,000$
$P_{2012} = 345,475,000$
$P_{2013} = 348,762,000$
$P_{2014} = 352,081,000$

Because this method uses age- and sex-specific data, estimates can be derived not only for total population sizes but also for the sizes of cohorts, male, female, and combined, at dates between the base and terminal years. Two cohorts of special interest in planning and administrative contexts, one a school-age group (10–19) and the other seniors (70+), were selected and their sizes estimated for the same four dates, also assuming exponential growth. These are:

10–19 cohort: $P_{2010} = 42,717,000$ 70 + cohort: $P_{2010} = 18,555,000$
$P_{2011} = 43,123,000$ $P_{2011} = 18,731,000$
$P_{2012} = 43,533,000$ $P_{2012} = 18,909,000$
$P_{2013} = 43,942,000$ $P_{2013} = 19,089,000$
$P_{2014} = 44,366,000$ $P_{2014} = 19,271,000$

When we observe the estimates for the entire aggregate and the cohort sizes together, we see clearly how a population simultaneously grows and gets older, as is the case in the United States and other industrialized nations.

Components Methods that Include Migration

The more complex components methods take migration into consideration. In preparing its estimates, the U.S. Census Bureau uses this approach, choosing among several models that differ from each other with respect to the techniques used to estimate the net migration component.[7] These include (1) the components II method, (2) the administrative records method, and (3) the ratio correlation method. This section summarizes the first two of these approaches.

1. The components II method is widely used (Ferlay et al. 2013; CPR 1976; Raymondo 1992) and can be applied to national aggregates, regions, states, and other local areas. Like the cohort survival method, it begins by establishing the size and age-sex distribution of the central-year population from the most recent census data available. In this case, however, only the civilian population under age 65 is considered; that is, special groups such as members of the military, long-term hospital residents, and college dormitory residents are subtracted from the base total. Natural increase is derived by subtracting the total number of deaths from the total number of births during the period, using data obtained from vital-statistics registers.

2. The administrative records method is used by the Census Bureau to estimate the sizes of state, county, and subcounty (e.g., urban) populations. Like the components II method, it employs the demographic accounting formula. Thus it requires information about (1) population size for the estimate area (state, county, and so on) at a base date, and (2) the number of births, deaths, in-migrations, and out-migrations in the interval between the base date and the date for which an estimate is to be determined. These vital statistics are taken from the records of non-Census administrative organizations, and it is this practice that gives the method its name.

Data on deaths and births are obtained from the NCHS and the State health departments via the Census Bureau's Federal-State Cooperative Program for Population Estimates (FSCPE). The number of internal migrants is determined using Federal income tax returns provided by the Internal Revenue Service. Tax returns include the social security number and the address of the person filing, which can be compared at the base and estimate years. Those who file from two different addresses during the estimation period are classed as movers or as migrants, depending on whether the change of address is within a county (mover) or between counties (migrant), or

Table 10.4. Estimates Based on Components Method, 2013-2014 for the United States, Regions, and Selected States

	2013 Population Size	Total Population Change	Births	Deaths	Internat'l Migration	Domestic Migration	2014 Population Size
United States	316,497,531	2,359,525	3,957,577	2,593,996	995,944	(X)	318,857,056
Northeast	56,028,220	124,113	637,853	478,007	262,204	-286,696	56,152,333
Midwest	67,567,871	177,237	829,620	586,099	127,607	-182,057	67,745,108
South	118,522,802	1,249,132	1,511,280	1,007,640	358,956	365,289	119,771,934
West	74,378,638	809,043	978,824	522,250	247,177	103,464	75,187,681
Arizona	6,634,997	96,487	86,868	51,748	14,234	41,975	6,731,484
California	38,431,393	371,107	505,903	255,787	161,318	-32,090	38,802,500
Florida	19,600,311	292,986	214,567	187,102	112,306	138,546	19,893,297
Nevada	2,791,494	47,605	35,153	21,702	8,456	23,623	2,839,099
North Carolina	9,848,917	95,047	120,099	83,750	21,188	36,257	9,943,964
North Dakota	723,857	15,625	10,780	5,879	1,290	8,974	739,122
Pennsylvania	12,781,296	5,913	142,032	128,600	29,060	-31,448	12,787,209
West Virginia	1,853,595	-3,269	20,466	21,735	1,164	-2,749	1,850,326

Notes: NIM is net international migration, NDM is net domestic migration.

Source: U.S. Bureau of the Census: State Totals Vintage 2013 Estimates of the Components of Resident Population Change for the United States, Regions, States, and Puerto Rico: April 1, 2010 to July 1, 2013.

between states (interstate migrant). Taxpayers whose addresses do not change during the estimation period are classed as nonmovers.

International migration data come from the INS. The INS collects information on the state of intended residence. The number of immigrants during the estimation period, NIM (Net International Migration), is apportioned accordingly in areas with population sizes of 100,000 or more. For immigrant-residence destination areas with smaller populations, apportionment is done on the basis of the concentration of immigrants in the population as reported for the base year census.

Table 10.4 contains administrative records estimates for the United States, the regions, and selected states for the period between 2013 and 2014, using the 1990 enumeration as the base year. As the methodological note accompanying these data indicates, the state and regional (and national) totals are derived by cumulating county-level population reports and vital statistics from the sources identified. The estimated population size (at time t) is equal to the total population size at the base date (time 0), minus the special groups (sp), plus the number of domestic migrants, plus the number of international migrants, plus the number of births, minus the number of deaths.

METHODS OF PROJECTION

Most of the techniques used to derive population estimates can easily be adapted to produce projections. Whereas estimates are intended to apply either to an intercensal year or to a date immediately following an enumeration, projections are used to characterize the size, age structure, geographical distribution, or other characteristics of a population 10, 20, or more years into the future. In this case, the base population may be taken from the most recent census or from an estimate that updates census findings.

It is understood that the demographic characteristics obtained from projections are those that would be observed if specified conditions of fertility, mortality, and migration were to prevail between the date the projection is created and the date to which is meant to apply. The lack of certainty about future trends makes it necessary for demographers to take informed guesses about what is to be expected. The degree to which a projected population faithfully depicts the outcome depends upon several factors, including the accuracy of the base population figures and the initial vital rates employed. As noted in our chapter introduction, it is for these reasons that researchers ordinarily produce not a single result but rather a set of three, one low, one medium, and the third high. These are based on different possible rates at which growth components might (or might not) change over the course of the projection period. Each of the three components was used by the U.S. Census Bureau's projection of the population of United States for a period of 92 years, from the base year 1988.

Extrapolation from Simple Growth Models

Each of the four simple growth models discussed in the preceding section can readily be applied to projection, with the standard caution that a series of at least three "guesstimates" is preferred. This approach is sometimes referred to as *extrapolation.* In the most limited circumstance of having only one growth rate upon which to base our projections, we begin with the obvious assumption that the rate will continue into the future. We then and use it with each of the formulas: exponential growth

Table 10.5. Projections (in '000) for Selected Countries and the World by Four Methods, 2025 and 2050

Area			PRB Projections	
	P_{2025}	P_{2050}	P_{2025}	P_{2050}
Canada			39.7	48.4
Linear	36.146	39.556		
Geometric	36.204	40.003		
Exponential	36.208	40.016		
Logistic	29.994	32.46		
Kenya			51.3	65.2
Linear	41.620	44.320		
Geometric	41.650	44.555		
Exponential	41.653	44.561		
Logistic	41.252	44.551		
Germany			79.7	71.5
Linear	79.152	75.071		
Geometric	79.185	75.320		
Exponential	79.188	75.326		
Logistic	n.a.	n.a		
World			8108.0	9485.0
Linear	7016.056	7222.816		
Geometric	7017.103	7230.676		
Exponential	7017.179	7230.884		
Logistic	6707.145	7045.654		

Source: Kincaid (2010).

Kincaid, D. Population Reference Bureau (PRB). (2010). *World Population Data Sheet 20.*

will yield the largest projected population, the logistic formula will yield the smallest, and the arithmetic and geometric models will produce intermediate results (assuming positive growth).

However, if we were to use only one formula (for example, the exponential) and one growth rate, then the decisions as to whether we calculated a high, medium, or low future population size and how to derive the other two totals must be made in such a way that the method comes close to forecasting. That is, with such limited data, information from external sources—such as likely changes in family-planning policy, public-health procedures, or migration law—must be employed. On the other hand, if growth rates for several dates are available, then projection can incorporate these in anticipating future trends even with only one growth model.

In Table 10.1, we listed projections from the base year 2010 for the population sizes of the world and 36 countries. Along with this information, the Population Reference Bureau has provided RNIs for each country. These can be used as a substitute for growth rates in creating our own projections (that is, we assume 0 net migration or a closed population). Below we have selected a set of three countries, Canada, Kenya, and Germany, along with the world, to illustrate the **extrapolation** approach. For example, at the beginning of the period, Canada's population size was 34.1 million, and its RNI was 0.4 percent. We use the same projection intervals as the table, that is 12 and 27 years, or to 2025 and 2050; see Table 10.5.

Canada:
Linear: $P_{2025} = 34.1 \times (34.1 \times 0.0040 \times 15) = 36.146$ million
$P_{2050} = 34.1 \times (34.1 \times 0.0040 \times 40) = 39.556$ million.
Geometric: $P_{2025} = 34.1 \times (1+0.0040)^{15} = 36.204$ million.
$P_{2050} = 34.1 \times (1+0.0040)^{40} = 340.003$ million.
Exponential: $P_{2025} = 34.1 \times e^{0.0040 \times 15} = 36.208$ million.
$P_{2050} = 34.1 \times e^{0.0040 \times 40} = 40.016$ million.

The set of projections produced for Kenya is also shown in Table 10.5, whose population size in 2010 was 40.00 million with an RNI of 2.7 percent. Also included is Germany, with a population size of 81.6 million and an RNI of –0.2 percent. Finally, we show the projections for the world, with a population size of 6,892 million and a growth rate of 1.2 percent.

One of the first things you will notice is that all of the extrapolations for Canada for 2025 were low in relation to the PRB projections. There are several possible reasons for this discrepancy. But the most likely explanation is that each of the four growth models used here began with the assumption that the country's 2010 RNI provides an adequate estimate of its rate of growth during the projection period. However, Canada has one of the highest in-migration rates in the world, a factor that is ruled out when we assume a closed population. The PRB expects Canada to grow well into the twenty-first century, but principally because of migration, not natural increase (which actually declined during the late 1990s).

In the case of Kenya, the first three extrapolations are all considerably lower than the PRB projections. This is clearly because we assumed that the 2010 growth rate of 2.7 percent would continue for two or more decades. Germany's situation is interesting because its growth rate was negative in 2010. The linear, geometric and exponential and PRB projections are similar for 2025. However, the linear, geometric and exponential 2050 projections are higher than the PRB projection. The PRB projection assumes not constant (negative) growth, but further declines because of fewer births and possibly some net out-migration. Thus, by 2050 the two projections differ by about 4.0 million.

Finally, for the world, all five extrapolations except the logistic extrapolations concur that by 2025 about 1 billion people will have been added, raising the total to approximately 7 billion. Each of the first three sets of extrapolations is low in comparison to the PRB projection, because all employ a constant growth rate. Also there can be no discrepancies due to migration, such as those observed in the case of Canada.

Thus far, each example of the simple growth model-approach produced a set of projections based on one date, one growth rate, and three or four different equations. As noted, it is also possible to produce high, medium, and low projections even with only one model, provided that data for two or more dates are available. The United States Bureau of the Census International Data Base provides just such information for most nations in the world, extending back to 1950. Here we employ this source to illustrate the one-model/several-dates technique with three populations, Afghanistan, Brazil, and Russia. Although it is unlikely that a single growth formula will apply to all populations, especially those as different as the three selected (one rapidly expanding, the second in downward transition, and the third with negative growth), the exponential model usually yields the best first approximations.

We saw in the section on estimation that Afghanistan's population has grown very irregularly since World War II. Between 1950, when its size was 8.15 million, and 1960, its growth rate was 1.9 percent. Between 1960 and 1970, at the peak of its population explosion, that rate had increased to 2.4 percent. Between 1970 and 1980, it fell back to 1.9 percent. And, as noted earlier, in the civil war years between 1980 and 1990, growth went negative, to –0.1 percent. Early 1990, it had soared to 4.5 percent; and in 1995 it was 3.5 percent and in 2005 it was again at about 3.00 percent. The exponential average for the period was 3.61 percent. So, what can be expected in the future, in the years 2025 and 2050? The results of low, medium, and high exponential projections are shown below. The low-growth assumption is based on the average annual growth rate between 1950–2005, which was still negative at –0.58 percent. The medium-growth assumption extrapolates the 1990–1998 rate of 0.52 directly. And the high-growth assumption employs the exponential average rate between 1950 and 1998 of 1.019 percent. These are the results (in millions).

Afghanistan	Low	Medium	High
$P_{1998} = 24.79$	$P_{2010} = 23.13$	$P_{2010} = 26.40$	$P_{2010} = 31.15$
$P_{2025} = 21.20$	$P_{2025} = 28.54$	$P_{2025} = 41.42$	

The U.S. Census Bureau projects P_{2010} at 34.1 and P_{2025} at 37.9 million. These agree most closely with our high assumption, that for many years to come Afghanistan's population will continue to grow as rapidly as or more rapidly than it has done since 1950.

We have also had a chance to consider the growth of Brazil's population in our discussion of estimation. There we noted that researchers at the PRB now assume that the country is currently in a period of declining growth rates, based on figures such as these: Beginning in 1950, when the population size was 53.4 million, the growth rate was 2.9 percent, and this was sustained through 1970. Between 1970 and 1980, growth declined slightly to 2.5 percent, then to 2.1 percent 1980 and 1990. Finally, between 1990 and 1998, growth declined somewhat more sharply to just under 1.5 percent. For the following projections, the low assumption is based on a continuation of the decline observed between 1980 and 1998, such that the average rate in the 1998–2010 interval will be 0.9 percent and in the 1998–2025 interval it will be 0.6 percent. The medium assumption assumes a continuation of the average annual decline between 1950 and 1998 of .03 percent per year. The high assumption extrapolates the 1998 growth rate into the future (all totals in millions).

Brazil	Low	Medium	High
$P_{1998} = 169.81$	$P_{2010} = 192.93$	$P_{2010} = 198.70$	$P_{2010} = 203.14$
$P_{2025} = 217.13$	$P_{2025} = 266.95$	$P_{2025} = 254.16$	

The U.S. Census Bureau projections are $P_{2010} = 190.96$ and $P_{2025} = 209.33$. In this case, we find the closest agreement between the Bureau and our low series, indicating a continuation of declines in growth rates. In fact, because our low series exceeds the census totals (by about 2 and 8 million, respectively), it is evident that the latter anticipate that Brazil is about to experience the steepest growth-rate declines in recent history.

Our final example of growth-model projection uses the population of Russia, one of several in Europe that has fallen below ZPG. Between 1950 and 1990, when the country was part of the Soviet Union, growth was positive but in steady decline over the interval. Beginning in the 1950 to 1960 period (when its population size grew from 101.9 to 119.6 million), growth rates dropped from 1.6 percent, to 0.9 percent in 1960–1970, to 0.7 percent in 1970–1980, to 0.6 percent in 1980–1990, and finally to –0.1 percent in 1990–1998. Although a portion of this decline was the result of net out-migration, most of it was due to a decrease in birth rates below the level of mortality rates. The following low-projection series assumes that the most recent decline in growth rates, which average 0.07 percent per year will continue. The medium series assumes that the long-range average decline of 0.03 percent per year continues. And the high series extrapolates the current rate of –0.1 percent into the future (all totals in millions).

Russia	Low	Medium	High
$P_{1998} = 146.86$	$P_{2010} = 144.37$	$P_{2010} = 144.69$	$P_{2010} = 145.11$
$P_{2025} = 135.84$	$P_{2025} = 138.84$	$P_{2025} = 142.95$	

Obviously, given our assumptions, all projections anticipate absolute declines in the size of Russia's population. In fact, according to these and other projections, Russia's place as the world's sixth-most populous nation (after China, India, the United States, Indonesia, and Brazil) will be taken over by Pakistan, Bangladesh, and possibly Nigeria sometime in the early twenty-first century, thus relegating it to eighth or ninth place. The Census Bureau projects $P_{2010} = 143{,}918$ and $P_{2025} = 138{,}854$, both close to our medium and lowest series. The Bureau's assumption is that not only will the recent declines fail to abate but that they will accelerate somewhat to a steady –0.2 percent over the long range.

Projecting with the Components Method

Another of the mathematical methods discussed under estimation that can be used for projection is the components method. It is preferred to the simple growth-model approach because of its ability to determine not only likely future population size but also age and sex distributions. In applying the method earlier—to estimate the size and structure of the U.S. population between census dates, we assumed that net migration was zero. This is clearly an unrealistic premise considering the fact that the country does and will continue to receive significant numbers of immigrants from abroad. Nevertheless, by ruling out-migration as a growth component, it is easier to understand how one applies an already fairly complex technique. At this point, the assumption is relaxed, and our projection does take migration into account.

Table 10.6 contains information for a model population that represents a medium-sized city of approximately 85,250 persons as of enumeration year 1990. By the year 2000, the population had grown to just over 97,800, at an average annual rate of 1.3 percent. The increase of some 12,500 persons came from one or both of two possible sources, positive net migration or positive natural increase (a surplus of births over deaths). Our aim is to project the size and structure of the population to the year 2010 by components. Because we are basing the projection on two points of observation, not only are "stock" data available for the base year, 2000, but we also have information about the "flows" (the vital events) in the interval just prior to the base year, between 1990 and 2000.

Table 10.6. Components Method of Projection Using Population Model for Two Prior Dates

X(1)	2	3	4	5	6	7	8	9	10	11	12	13	14	15
0–4	3253	3161	.8860	.8951	3051	2928	.8982	.8996	2191	2107	1.390	1.390	2706	2656
5–9	3567	3440	.8875	.8903	3444	3123	.8987	.8991	2265	2158	1.520	1.451	2897	2683
10–14	3853	3715	.8967	.8976	3455	3261	.8962	.8984	2882	2829	1.198	1.153	3816	3660
15–19	3773	3653	.8949	.8976	4447	4079	.8933	.8977	3166	3063	1.405	1.332	4706	4063
20–24	3474	3341	.8892	.8962	4368	4134	.8928	.8977	3455	3335	1.264	1.240	3711	3377
25–29	3191	3111	.8856	.8955	4495	4274	.8930	.8973	3376	3279	1.331	1.303	.5579	4876
30–34	2631	2566	.8858	.8951	3788	3674	.8930	.8967	3089	2994	1.226	1.227	4930	4600
35–39	2449	2682	.8860	.8942	2968	2971	.8903	.8947	2825	2785	1.050	1.067	5344	4998
40–44	2741	2807	.8828	.8914	2540	2506	.8839	.8910	2330	2296	1.090	1.091	4148	4042
45–49	2712	2605	.8734	.8855	2407	2672	.8729	.8850	2169	2398	1.110	1.114	2776	2835
50–54	2393	2365	.8561	.8761	2675	2723	.8555	.8756	2419	2502	1.106	1.088	2447	2437
55–59	2148	2282	.8298	.8623	2423	2447	.8327	.8639	2368	2306	1.023	1.061	2331	2634
60–64	1928	2080	.7923	.8420	1919	2141	.7967	.8454	2048	2071	0.937	1.033	2530	2594
65–69	1447	1797	.7353	.8124	1621	1999	.7464	.8186	1782	1967	0.909	1.016	2064	2243
70–74	1058	1302	.6566	.7696	1210	1650	.6829	.7785	1527	1751	0.792	.942	1432	1871
75–79	756	1067	.5590	.7048	771	1229	.5943	.7065	1063	1459	0.725	.842	1100	1663
80–84	448	650	.4459	.6067	448	704	.4768	.5948	695	1002	0.644	.702	654	1210
85–99	307	505	.2450	.3497	340	643	.3575	.4648	696	1322	0.489	.487	529	1170
Total	42,124	43,129			46,370	51,432							53,700	53,612

Variables by columns: 1. Cohort; 2. Number of males, 1980; 3. Number of females, 1980; 4. Survival rates for males, 1990; 5. Survival rates for females, 1980; 6. Number of males, 1990; 7. Number of females, 1990; 8. Survival rates for males, 2000; 9. Survival rates for females, 2000; 10. Expected male population, 2000; 11. Expected female population, 2000; 12. 10-year migration rates for males; 13. 10-year migration rates for females; 14. Projected male population for year 2010; and 15. Projected female population for year 2010.

All of the data in the table are age- and sex-specific, so that columns 2 and 3 list the sizes of each five-year cohort[8] for males and females, respectively. Columns 4 and 5 contain age-specific survival rates based on a period life table; that is, the number of individuals alive at age x+5 in 1990 is divided by the number of individuals alive at age x in that year. Columns 6 and 7 show the observed sizes of each cohort, by sex, in 2000, as they were enumerated. Columns 8 and 9 contain the 10-year age- and sex-specific survival rates to 2000 based on cohort life-table calculations; that is, the number of persons age x in 2000 is divided by the number of persons age x–10 in 1990. Columns 10 and 11 show the expected age-sex-specific population for 2000, based on the application of the 1990 survival rates. Columns 12 and 13 show the age- and sex-specific 10-year migration rates. And columns 14 and 15 give the projected sizes of each cohort for 2010, accounting for the 1990–2000 survival rates and net migration. The projected total population size, derived by summing columns 14 and 15 and combining the two totals, is 107,312: that is, 53,700 males and 53,612 females. This indicates an annual growth rate of 0.9 percent between 2000 and 2010.

In detail, the projected population is derived in four main steps and several substeps:

1. The 1990 male age distribution is multiplied by the 1990–2000 (10-year) survival rates to obtain the expected 2000 age distribution: column 2 × column 10. Then, the 1990 female age distribution is multiplied by the 1990–2000 survival rates to obtain the expected 2000 age distribution: column 3 × column 5 to obtain column 11. The expected 2000 population in age cohort 0–9 is obtained by applying a general annual fertility rate of 52.5 births per 1,000 women in the 15–44 age range in 2000. The number of births is apportioned into male and female children by applying a sex ratio of 105 males born for every 100 females. The number of male infants in the 0–4 age cohort is survived by applying a survival rate of 0.9412 (the square root of .8860, from column 4). The assumed survival rate for female infants in the 0–4 age group is .9460 (the square root of .951, from column 5). The number in the oldest cohort, 85+ is the total of those survive from the 75–79 age group, plus those who survive from the 80–84 age group, plus those whose survive in the 85+ age group.

2. Net migration for each cohort, by sex, is found by taking the difference between the 2000 expected age distribution and the 2000 observed distribution, since the expected population is derived by adjusting the 1990 population for births and deaths. Column 6 minus column 10 gives the amount of net migration of males, and column 7 minus column 11 gives the amount of net migration for females. The net migration *rates* are obtained by dividing these amounts, for each cohort, by the numbers in the expected population. The net migration rates for males are in column 12 and for females in column 13.

3. The 2000 observed population is multiplied by the net migration rate first and then by the survival rates. That is, first multiply column 6 by column 12 for males, and column 7 by column 13 for females. Then, these products are multiplied by columns 8 and 9 (the 2000 survival rates) respectively. The results are found in columns 14 and 15, the projected population minus the youngest and oldest cohorts.

4. Finally, the size of the youngest age group is determined by applying the general fertility rate (52.5/1,000) and following the procedures presented in step (1). The number of males and females in the 85+ age group is also obtained by following essentially the same procedures as in step (1). That is, the number of survivors who were 85+ in 2000 is added to the number of survivors from cohorts whose members aged into the 85+ group over the projection period, using the rates in columns 8 and 9.

This application assumes that 10-year survival and general fertility remain constant over the projection period, but this is not required. Several techniques are available that allow the researcher to incorporate an increase or a decrease in either or both factors, such as assuming exponential growth (or decline) and then applying an annual average death or fertility rate. This would also affect net migration rates, because they are derived from information about observed and expected populations. By varying the rates of vital events, high, medium, and low series can be obtained. So, for example, one can build in a set of assumptions that (a) fertility rates remain the same over the interval, (b) the rates decline slightly, and (c) they decline sharply. With mortality and net migration assumed to be constant, this approach would of course yield three different growth rates and three different population sizes, as demonstrated with the simple growth models. In the case of the components method, however, we would also derive three different age-sex structures, information especially valuable in business and public-sector applications.

Once the idea of having rates vary over a projection period is considered, the possibilities are virtually unlimited, as we attempt to develop projection models that more faithfully capture the way in which real populations change. The components method does allow one to come closer to reality than most other approaches, but it still has limitations. Most serious perhaps, it requires several repetitive steps that are tedious and prone to mistakes, even when computer programs and programmable calculators aid us. In addition, although the components method can accommodate changes in vital rates and projections over successive periods, for instance, from 2000 to 2010 and then 2010 to 2020 and then 2020 to 2035, it does so in a mechanical rather than a logically and mathematically sophisticated manner. For solving these kinds of problems, demographers turn to another approach, the last to be discussed in this section. This is the matrix method, one of the most efficient and flexible tools in the demographer's repertoire. Its power derives from the fact that, in many ways, it is like the life table. But it is even more than that, because in effect it is a life table "in motion."

MATRIX-BASED APPROACHES TO POPULATION PROJECTION

Matrix-based methods were popularized by the leading U.S. demographer Nathan Keyfitz (1968, 1977). They can be used for any kind of projection, but they are computationally most efficient when projecting large populations over long periods with the use of computer programs. This approach employs the basic concepts and techniques of matrix mathematics, also called "matrix algebra" or "linear algebra." If you are familiar with this branch of mathematics, then you know that matrices are rectangular arrays of numbers (made up of rows and columns), and that they can be multiplied by one another to produce a product that (usually) is another matrix. This property is what makes the method so effective.

Suppose that we have a matrix, P_0, which contains the age structure of a given population—the number of persons at each age at an initial time. If we multiply it by another matrix, L (called the "Leslie matrix"), which contains information about birth and death rates between time 0 and time t, the product will be a matrix, P_t, which contains the projected age structure of the population at time t:

$$P_0 \times L = P_t$$

As stated, this technique assumes that the birth and death rates do not change and that no migration occurs between the two dates. However, these factors can be taken into account with more complex calculations. The main thing to be noted here is that we can further multiply L by P_t to produce a projected population twice as far into the future, and so on.

FORECASTS AND FORECASTING

Forecasts and projections, including matrix-based projections, both attempt to assess the size and/or composition of future populations, and they employ similar methods. The major difference between the two approaches is that projections suggest what *might* be the case five, 10, or more years from the projection date. These are always based on explicitly stated assumptions that can be altered to produce not one outcome but a set of possible scenarios, as we demonstrated earlier with the high, middle, and low series produced with simple growth models. A forecast, on the other hand, is based on what the forecaster believes to be the most likely condition that *will* prevail in the future. "When the author or the subsequent user of a projection is willing to describe it as indicating the most likely population at a given date, then he has made a forecast" (Shryock and Siegel 1976:439).

Considerable progress has occurred since the 1970s in deriving mathematical models for forecasting (see, for example, Hyndman and Athanasopoulos 2014; Furnam and Saxton 1989). However, as William Ascher (1978) has pointed out, the substantive knowledge required to make valid assumptions in demographic applications is not well developed. In most instances, the middle variant of a projection simply gets chosen as the most valid assumption. This certainly seems to be a reasonable way to proceed; that is, by eliminating the more extreme possibilities to determine what is most likely. However, we have seen that it can be the wrong decision in many instances, perhaps more often that it is the correct choice, because of the fluctuating character of fertility, mortality, and migration rates.

In this regard, some of the most advanced approaches to forecasting have been developed in the business fields of marketing and finance. Although not directly concerned with demographic processes and outcomes, the models used in these fields do rely heavily on information about the size of general and special populations, as well as their socioeconomic composition and growth rates. But, at the same time, this work incorporates information on economic trends, prospects in foreign markets, technological innovations, and many other factors. Jeffrey Jarrett (1991), for example, has provided several illustrations and suggestions concerning the value—and the limitations—of past population dynamics and other kinds of trends in business forecasting, which are directly relevant to the work of demographers.

As in the case of projections, population forecasts can apply to the short, middle, and long term. Forecasts for three or four time periods (usually years) are considered to be short term, whereas those that extend to twenty or more periods are long term. Anything in between is considered to be a middle-term forecast. Forecasting techniques are usually classed as either quantitative or qualitative, although as Jarrett and Spyros Makridakis—one of the world's leading experts in the field—stress, the best forecasts use both kinds of information (Berk and Bleich 2013; Makridakis, Wheelright, and Hyndman 1998). For several years, a group of researchers in the United States, led by Donella and Dennis Meadows, has been producing and disseminating forecasts of world-level trends, including but not only demographic ones

(Meadows et al. 1972; Meadows, Meadows, and Randers, 1992). These are known best by the title of one of the group's earliest books, *The Limits to Growth*. This work has received considerable attention, as well as some criticism, for academic and general audiences because of its earlier Malthusian forecasts of runaway population growth and global collapse. Through the years, the group's prognoses have been moderated by this criticism and by events, to the point at which its elaborate computer models increasingly resemble projection series, presented as alternative scenarios rather than certainties. In any case, this work represents the state of the art in multivariate forecasting, both quantitative and qualitative.

In addition to relying more on numeric data, quantitative approaches often assume that past trends in population characteristics will continue into the future. The most familiar quantitative method, time series analysis, is of this type. It is most useful in short-term forecasts because we know that past trends in fertility, and so on, are likely to continue into the immediate future. Thus, it is not necessary to consider all of the past characteristics of the relevant variable or variables in order to extrapolate a series into the future (Keyfitz 1982). This method was used to establish the middle variants of the projection of the world and national populations derived in our section on simple growth models.

Causal approaches employ some of the techniques of business forecasting developed by Makridakis and others. That is, they depend less on past data about population characteristics and more on available recent data that refer to other kinds of variables believed to be associated with population change in some casual fashion. In this respect, they are also closely related to the regression technique of population estimation discussed earlier, except that they seek to characterize the situation at middle- and longer-range future periods.

At times, numeric data on past trends may not be available and, as a result, quantitative forecasting approaches cannot be implemented. At this point, demographers sometimes turn to qualitative approaches developed in other fields, including technological forecasting (see Gonod 1990). Qualitative forecasting methods are not dependent on numeric time series data, although such information might be used in a supporting role. Instead, they are based on subjective assessments and experiences that suggest how current educational practices, research projects, business decisions, and the like will affect the course of social and cultural change.

Among the best know work in this area is that of John Naisbitt and associates (Naisbitt 1982; Naisbitt and Aburdene 1990), who use news reports to discern what they have labeled "megatrends." Another popular forecasting program, that of the World Watch Institute, uses much quantitative data but also information from various other sources to forecast the conditions that affect ecological and environmental conditions at the global level (see, for example, Brown, Renner, and Halweil 2014; Brown, Kane, and Roodman 1994). Although this method is interesting and often useful, one shortcoming is that population forecasts derived from it may vary widely among forecasters, who use different kinds of information they consider to be relevant.

With all of these variations in mind, it should be easier to understand why demographers consider projection and forecasting to be related but different procedures. Forecasting takes us beyond population science and into other fields such as business, economics, and technology studies. This is because the tools of demography in general, and projection techniques in particular, are designed to establish the facts of past and current population dynamics. When turned to the future, the best that these tools can do is provide a sense of what would occur if observed trends were to continue or were altered in specific ways. Determining the likelihood that a particular outcome *will* occur is not within our capabilities, although it is usually safe to assume that current patterns will prevail until tomorrow, next month, or perhaps next year. At the same time, forecasts that do not use demographic projections (if such projections or the data to derive them are not available) are ordinarily incomplete and inaccurate. In fact, the best forecasts begin with one or more series of projections and then add other data, qualitative information, experience, computer simulations, intuition, and more to suggest the most reasonable scenario for the future. And, of course, because no one can ever know everything that might affect the shape of our populations years ahead, even the most "complete" forecasts can turn out to be wrong.

SUMMARY

These comments on forecasting conclude our introduction to the principles and methods that demographers employ to look beyond their immediate data. We began by distinguishing between several concepts that apply to "future gazing," and then selected three for closer examination: *estimation, projection*, and the last-noted *forecasting*. We saw how each of these refers to an essentially inductive procedure, based on observed facts rather than some mysterious prophetic powers.

In the first two cases, we noted how the fundamental equation of demography plays a central role in a range of specific techniques, from the components method to matrix approaches. When faced with the problem of anticipating the size and/or structure of a population at a date for which information is unavailable, population scientists almost instinctively begin with the premise that change can only occur through the effects of fertility, mortality, and migration. Once this understanding is introduced, data are sought that will indicate trends in these components. This, in turn, leads to insight into the relationship between what is known about a population and what cannot (yet) be known. Because forecasting, at its best, relies heavily on projection, the fundamental equation is equally important in that realm, although indirectly and always in conjunction with other information.

The very first sentences of the chapter highlighted the fact these approaches to be considered have been developed with application in mind. They are intended to serve specific purposes in public administration, business management, and social planning in many realms. We now move directly to the subject of application, indicating how and at which points estimation, projection, and other demographic tools enter the real world. It may already be clear that the demography discussed in this chapter is an applied science. But in the next section, beginning with Chapter 11 on population policy, this phase of the field is featured "front and center."

KEY TERMS

"central date"	geometric growth model
cohort survival	logistic growth model
cohort survival method	prediction
extrapolation	projection
forecast	

NOTES

1. These techniques, especially estimation and forecasting, are not entirely unique to demography. Some engineering fields and, to a considerable extent, economics make use of approaches that are identical or very similar.

2. Source: See *Annual Estimates of the Resident Population: April 1, 2010 to July 1, 2013; 2013 Population Estimates* at https://www.census.gov/popest/data/cities/totals/2013/SUB-EST2013-3.html.

3. A symposium held at the University of Utrecht, Netherlands (Becker and Hermkens 1993) explored the impact of demographic and nondemographic factors on the characteristics of age groups. The contributors concurred that economic and social conditions are at least as important as birth and death rates in determining the size, structure, and geographic distribution of cohorts and generations.

5. Keyfitz (1968:76) and Shryock and Siegel (1976:215) credit the early-nineteenth-century Belgian statistician, P. F. Verhulst, with discovery of this curve, and Raymond Pearl and Lowell J. Reed (1920) with introducing it to demographers in the United States.

6. This is the estimate of the U.S. Census International Data Base, which is also the source of the historical information on Brazil's population used in this section. The Census estimates the 1997 population size at 167.7 million. The Population Reference Bureau (1998) has a somewhat lower estimate of 162 million for mid-1997.

7. As we saw in Chapter 7, net migration is the difference between in- and out-migration (I – O). It might equal zero because both I and O are zero, but it would also equal zero if they both equaled 1 million. With the cohort survival method and other demographic techniques that assume a closed population, *gross* migration, which is I + O, is the more important concept. The greater the gross migration between two dates, the more likely it is that the rate of natural increase changes (because migrants bring their birth and death rates with them); and the more that rates of natural increase change, the less accurate are estimates made with the cohort survival method.

8. A detailed discussion of estimation methodology is posted at the https://training.measureevaluation.org/non-certficate-courses/pap/lesson-8.The state-level method was used in producing the estimate included in Table 10.4 of this chapter.

The oldest cohort has a larger range (15 years) than the others do, but it is not open as in the earlier example. Instead, it is closed at 99 years on the assumption that no one above that age is alive. This is one common solution to the problems raised by using categories such as "65 and above."

DEMOGRAPHY IN APPLICATION

Each of the four chapters in this section considers a practical aspect of population science. Here the emphasis on methods, techniques, and data that characterizes the earlier parts of the book is replaced by a focus on how demography and population function in the world at large. In some respects, the tone of these discussions brings us back full circle to the level of discourse in Chapters 1 and 2, where our main concerns were demography and its subject matter, as such. Chapter 11, for example, explores population policy. It begins with a definition and some brief examples and then proceeds to analyze the policy process. The analysis includes a discussion of the aims of policy and a survey of how policies are created. This last topic is illustrated with the case of Zambia, a country in southern Africa whose leaders consciously, and successfully, undertook to create a policy with public and scientific input. Policy evaluation is also covered, with an illustration taken from a family-planning program in India. The chapter concludes with some comments on the role of values in the policy process.

Policy and values also play a prominent role in the interface between population and environment, the subject of Chapter 12. This chapter examines the many ways in which population affects and is affected by our ecosystems. The issues surrounding the depletion of resources are considered, with special emphasis on water, forests, and energy supplies. Much of the discussion is devoted to the measurement of environmental conditions and impacts on the associated growth of environmentalism as a social movement. The chapter concludes with the story of the Chipko movement in India and a comment on sustainable development.

Although such policy issues are implied in much of the material presented in Chapter 13, Accessing and Using Information about Population Science, its main concern is on intellectual resources. Here we discuss the information, the professional contacts, and the computer and Internet-related tools that are available to students and graduates interested in population studies. You have noted the several Internet sites referred to in earlier chapters. Some of these are repeated in this chapter, but we have also listed and described nearly 100 new, interesting, and useful Web pages of all sorts. Here we also provide a step-by-step guide to conducting demographic research and some concluding comments on how demography is applied in each of several professional fields. This Part, and the book itself, conclude with Chapter 14 and a further exploration of the practice of demography. Here, additional—especially historical—comments are offered on population policy and on the demography of tourism.

POPULATION POLICY
Controlling Demographic Processes

From the very earliest period in the history of demography, scholarly interest in fertility and the other vital events has been accompanied by a concern with how these affect social wellbeing, economic conditions, and political affairs. This interest in population's impacts has, in turn, typically been associated with efforts to control demographic changes for what is, or at least is considered to be, the better. The intricacies of population growth, changes in birth and death rates, the interplay between natural increase and the aging of a population, the pushes and pulls of migration, and the like certainly pose enough intellectual problems to challenge the curiosity of any scientist. But, in fact, practical issues motivate demographic research as much as if not more than sheer curiosity. As we observed in Chapter 2, when Malthus established the academic field in the early nineteenth century, it was under the label "political economy," reflecting its worldly—rather than pure-mathematical or logical—orientation.

This chapter focuses on the practical and political aspects of population with a close look at the policy realm. We begin with a definition and a summary of the basic theoretical underpinnings of population policy, and an illustration of the development of these policies in the countries with the world's largest populations, India and China. Next, we consider why we have such policies: in light of the potential conflict between individual and collective welfare, and through a discussion of the principal approaches to controlling population dynamics. The last two sections of the chapter examine (1) how population policies are created and (2) how they are evaluated. Related discussion can also be found in Chapter 14, where we review some of the major events in the history of population policy.

THE NATURE OF POPULATION POLICY: DEFINITION AND CASE STUDIES

Population policies are intended to achieve a specified goal or a set of objectives by manipulating one or more variables such as fertility, mortality, or migration. Ordinarily, policies are motivated by perceived social problems. If current population size, composition, or rate of growth is widely viewed as undesirable, the situation is conducive to the emergence of a social problem. Social problems, once recognized, then inspire "human responses" (Schneider et al. 1981; Jackson, Schuler, and Werner 2011), of which the most common is new or revised policy.

The fact that social problems need to be perceived, felt, and to inspire action before they are translated into policy raises two fundamental questions: policy *for* whom and *by* whom? As our definition suggests, the most important force involved in shaping policy is the government. In fact, it is perhaps the only agency at the national level that can realistically attempt to involve every citizen in implementing policy through its command over important resources such as the judiciary and media. For example, the population policies of the Republic of the Philippines are based on the understanding that "It shall be the responsibility of the State to achieve and maintain population levels most conducive to the national welfare" (Marcos 1982; David, Atun, and La Viña 2012).

The leading role played by national governments in the population-policy realm makes it very likely that either the focus or the objectives of policies will be influenced by the political ideology of the ruling powers. In this way, the type of constitution upon which a government is based, whether it is conservative, liberal, or radical, its geopolitical relations, and related conditions strongly influence policy formulation. Such factors enhance the likelihood that a particular country's population policy will be selective in terms of some demographic or social characteristics.

Perhaps no more dramatic example of the influence of ideology on policy can be found than in a comparison between two countries with enormous populations—in the range of 1 billion people: India and China. The first, a social-democratically oriented Republic, began its long-term process of policy development under British Colonial rule. It continues to struggle today to create an effective and acceptable approach to population control. The second, a Communist one-party autocracy, turned to policy-oriented control very late in its long history, arguing for many years that population control was an unnecessary and even a destructive course. Today, it has what may be the world's most-strict and—some believe—most-effective set of population policies, although they have been seriously questioned on human rights grounds.

India was the first country to have a population policy as early as 1952. The policy was formulated under the assumption that people would demand birth-control methods in the face of declining IMRs. The 1950s method was known as the "clinical approach." This approach saw the proliferation of family-planning clinics throughout the length and breadth of the country. The approach failed in the absence of the anticipated demand for birth control. Failure of the policy led to its modification and reannouncement in 1977, focusing on improving education and health as a two-pronged strategy to curb population growth. The latter component of the reformulated policy included the general as well as both maternal and child health. The tilt toward education[1] and health, health of mother and child in particular, coincided with a change of the phrase from "Family Planning" to "Family Welfare." The 1977 National Population Policy was pursued for nearly a quarter of century until the announcement of the National Population Policy 2000 (NPP 2000) alongside the formation of a new National Population Commission. The goals and objectives of NPP 2000 are given in Box 11.1.

As recently as the mid-1970s, China's ruling Communist Party officially rejected the Malthusian assumption that population growth is a threat to economic development. And its officials publicly opposed efforts to promote family planning in their country based on that assumption (especially efforts promoted by Western

Box 11.1   Selected Aspects of India's Population Policy

The overriding objective of economic and social development is to improve the quality of lives that people lead, to enhance their wellbeing, and to provide them with opportunities and choices to become productive assets in society.

On June 22, 2015, India's estimated total population was 1,294,764,959 (100 crore) people; this is 17.8 percent of the world's population (7,251,479,804), on 2.4 percent of the globe's land area. If current trends continue, India may overtake China by 2025 to become the most populous country in the world. Whereas global population has increased more than threefold since the beginning of the twentieth century, from 2 billion to 7.25 billion, the population of India has increased more than five times, from 238 million (23 crores) to 1.3 billion in the same period. India's current annual increase in population is large enough to neutralize efforts to conserve the resource endowment and environment.

Stabilizing population is an essential requirement for promoting sustainable development with more equitable distribution. However, it is as much a function of making reproductive health care accessible and affordable for all, as of increasing the provision and outreach of primary and secondary education, extending basic amenities including sanitation, safe drinking water and housing, empowering women and enhancing their employment opportunities, and providing transport and communications.

The National Population Policy, 2000 (NPP 2000) affirms the commitment of government toward voluntary and informed choice and consent of citizens while availing of reproductive health care services, and continuation of the target-free approach in administering family-planning services. The NPP 2000 provides a policy framework for advancing goals and prioritizing strategies during the subsequent decades, to meet the reproductive and child health needs of the people of India, and to achieve net replacement levels (TFR just above 2.0) by 2020 (in 2014, the TFR was 2.48 and declining). It is based upon the need to simultaneously address issues of child survival, maternal health, and contraception, while increasing outreach and coverage of a comprehensive package of reproductive and child health services by government, industry, and the voluntary nongovernment sector, working in partnership.

Objectives

The immediate objective of the NPP 2000 is to address the unmet needs for contraception, health care infrastructure, and health personnel, and to provide integrated service delivery for basic reproductive and child health care. The medium-term objective, which was not achieved, was to bring the TFR to replacement levels by 2010 through vigorous implementation of intersectoral operational strategies. The long-term objective is to achieve a stable population by 2045, at a level consistent with the requirements of sustainable economic growth, social development, and environmental protection.

In pursuance of these objectives, the following National Socio-Demographic Goals to be achieved in each case are formulated:

- Address the unmet needs for basic reproductive and child health services, supplies, and infrastructure.
- Make school education up to age 14 free and compulsory, and reduce dropouts at primary- and secondary-school levels to below 20 percent for both boys and girls.
- Reduce infant mortality rate to below 30 per 1,000 live births.
- Reduce maternal mortality ratio to below 100 per 100,000 live births.

Box 11.1   Continued

- Achieve universal immunization of children against all vaccine-preventable diseases.
- Promote delayed marriage for girls, not earlier than age 18 and preferably after 20 years of age.
- Achieve 80 percent institutional deliveries and 100 percent deliveries by trained persons.
- Achieve universal access to information/counseling, and services for fertility regulation and contraception with a wide basket of choices.
- Achieve 100 percent registration of births, deaths, marriages, and pregnancies.
- Contain the spread of Acquired Immunodeficiency Syndrome (AIDS), and promote greater integration between the management of reproductive tract infections (RTI) and sexually transmitted infections (STI) and the National AIDS Control Organization.
- Prevent and control communicable diseases.

Integrate Indian Systems of Medicine (ISM) in the provision of reproductive and child health services, and in reaching out to households.

Promote vigorously the small-family norm to achieve replacement levels of TFR.

Bring about convergence in implementation of related social sector programs so that family welfare becomes a people-centered program.

Source: From *National Population Policy, 2000*, National Commission on Population, Ministry of Health and Family Welfare, Government of India.

countries). As part of a group of eight developing countries, the Chinese endorsed the view that economic development rather than birth control should play a key role in population control (Winckler 2002).

However, "behind the scenes," these same officials were creating the most severe policy to limit family size the world has ever known (with the exception of cases of outright genocide). As mentioned in Box 11.2, this policy seeks to restrict the number of children a family may have to just one. Birth of a second and third child is strongly discouraged through a system of progressively harsh disincentives. One-child families are rewarded by state assurances of a number of long-term benefits, such as free medical care and free education. The policy was mainly restricted to the urban ethnic Han Chinese. Recognized ethnic minorities and people living in rural areas were exempt. The fact that negative sanctions are imposed on married couples for not complying gives the policy strict legal status, and it renders family-planning programs coercive. In contrast, India's population policy assumes that families are free to make decisions with regard to family size, in an attempt to bring about a voluntary reduction in the number of children born through education and improved access to family planning. The Chinese policy focuses not on decision making and access to fertility-reduction technologies (although these seem to be freely available) but rather on rewards for those who comply with and punishment for those who violate state dictates.

WHY ARE POPULATION POLICIES NECESSARY?

The need for population policies is inherent in modern-day living. Industrialization, technological innovation, expanded educational opportunities, and rapid urban

Box 11.2 Selected Aspects of China's Population Policy

In the early 1950s, an abortion was permitted only under certain conditions. At that time, official statements of the central Government indicated that abortion was allowed when continuation of the pregnancy was medically undesirable, when the spacing of children was too close, or when a mother with a child under four months of age had again become pregnant and experienced difficulties in breastfeeding. In such cases, a joint application of the couple and certification of a physician were required before the abortion could be performed. Under certain circumstances, special work or work (or study) that was too heavy could also be used as a legitimate reason for an abortion, but any request for the operation had to first be certified by the key personnel of the responsible organization and also approved by a medical organization. Abortions were to be performed as early as possible, preferably within the first month of pregnancy and at the latest not beyond the second month.

The results of data from the 1953 census contributed to the government decision to introduce and support the use of contraception and abortion to reduce the rate of population growth. On April 12, 1957, the Public Health Ministry announced that, from that date, all applications for abortion or sterilization would be free of restrictions concerning age, number of children, and approval procedures. However, an abortion could only be performed once a year and was permitted only within the first 10 weeks of the gestation period. The Government stressed the promotion of contraception as a preventive measure, with abortion to be used mainly as a backup measure in cases of contraceptive failure.

In the early 1970s, the Government of China began to incorporate population activities into the planning of its national economy. The planned-birth model was introduced, national goals were set, and an education model of communication was developed. The "Later-Longer-Fewer" (*Wan-Xi-Shao*) campaign was followed in 1979 by the one-child-per-couple policy. An article of the Chinese Constitution provided that individual couples were required to practice and the Government to support family planning. Since then, family-planning policy has been implemented primarily through a nationwide family-planning program that includes a strong information and education component, free contraceptive services, and a system of economic and social incentives and disincentives, which vary by province and between rural and urban areas.

Source: From *Abortion Policies: A Global Review*, United Nations Population Division, Department of Economic and Social Affairs.
© United Nations 2002
Also see the Population Policy Data Bank maintained by the United Nations Population Division

growth have vastly expanded our capacity to create, to consume, and to destroy. The effects of these forces have increased the level of societal complexity, making it possible for people to engage in a wide variety of social, political, and economic activities, at both private and public levels. However, these seemingly endless possibilities bring with them several contradictions. What is good and desirable at the individual level may not be in the common interests of the community.

Children, Families, and Communities

Around the time of the 1968 U.N. Human Rights Conference in Teheran and the appearance of Paul Ehrlich's *The Population Bomb* (1968), Garrett Hardin dramatically brought this contradiction to the attention of the public. Hardin, a radical neo-Malthusian, published an updated version of the classic parable known as "The Tragedy of the Commons (1973)" which underscores the tension between personal rights and collective welfare. The term **commons** refers to any resource, such as a sheep pasture, shared by a group of people. At some point, each of the owners thinks of adding one more animal to the flock, because the cost-benefit calculations indicate that this will result in increased profits. Not included in the individual calculations, however, are the costs of overgrazing. Thus, as the number of sheep increases, the carrying capacity of the pasture is reached and ultimately surpassed. Then, tragedy strikes. Without sufficient resources to sustain them, the sheep die; and the shepherds become impoverished because they followed what first appeared to be a financially wise course.

Similarly, Hardin argued, when people decide to have as many babies as they desire, they seldom share the resulting social costs of large families. As in the case of the shortsighted shepherds, this is bound to result in economic crisis. And, in order to prevent or minimize these costs, policies are needed. This argument is detailed in Box 11.3 by Paul Demeny, one of our most influential contemporary demographers. For Hardin and other neo-Malthusians, the most effective approach to this potential tragedy is to attempt to modify value structures that motivate high fertility. This is to be reinforced by the provision of means, such as family-planning programs and contraceptive technologies, whereby the new, small-family values can be put into practice (also see the discussion of W. P. Mauldin's work in the following section).

Malthus's belief that large population size is inimical to human welfare remains the basis of population control policies today. With very few exceptions, policy makers, social scientists, and educated people throughout the world agree that measures are needed either to cure a present population problem or to prevent one from occurring. Thus, an accurate assessment of current demographic conditions and associated cultural norms and values is a common and, in the opinion of most, a necessary part of contemporary public policy. For example, in Bombay, Nairobi, Rio de Janeiro, and Bangkok, the attempt to measure accurately areal population densities is taken very seriously. In these and most other primate cities of the developing world (see Chapter 4), the number of persons per unit of land is the highest ever experienced. These densities are increasing rapidly every month as the result of a combination of large inflows of migrants from rural areas and high rates of natural increase (which, in turn, are the result of dramatic declines in infant mortality).

Wherever such assessments have occurred, local and national governments have deemed urban densities to be too high relative to a desired ideal, lower level. Based on these comparisons, officials have considered a range of urban-density reducing policies. These include promotion of family-planning programs, as illustrated in the cases of India and China, above, and/or migration policies, as discussed briefly in a later section of this chapter and at greater length in Chapter 7.[2]

As we also observed earlier in the case of migration, strict standards with regard to "desirable" levels and trends in population characteristics often do not exist. Instead, such standards evolve, sometimes as the result of discussions held among concerned citizens and government officials or, more often, perhaps, bureaucratic officials impose them on the citizenry, especially the less-educated segments. The Malthusian ideology that continues to influence these standards implies the concept of an **optimum population size**. This concept underscores the importance of carrying capacity, the understanding that in any given nation/community the available base of renewable and nonrenewable resources can sustain a definite number of

Box 11.3   Contradictions Associated with Large-Family Preferences: Private Wants and the Common Good in Childbearing Decisions

by Paul Demeny

In 1977, in the midst of public debate on the effectiveness and ethical appropriateness of family-planning programs in the less-industrialized countries, Paul Demeny, founding editor of *Population and Development Review*, published a classic statement on the serious dilemmas that face population-control advocates. A section of this essay is reproduced here.

Since the birth of children reveals parental wants, the heart of the problem must lie in a contradiction between personal/private preferences, individual parents, and the desires of these same parents for the rate of childbearing in the society as a whole. That such a contradiction does exist is seldom well recognized. Parents are, of course, well able to express their private preferences with respect to fertility. But lacking the requisite knowledge and perception, the contradiction underlying the problem of population growth remains hidden to most actors in the drama: public preferences are not spelled out.

Besides ignorance, there are additional reasons that explain a lack of spontaneous interest in the matter. Perhaps the most obvious among these is the patent inability of individual couples to appreciably influence the level of childbearing in the nation as a whole. In my large community, the contribution of a single family to population growth is infinitesimally small, as is any possible impact it might exert on birth rates through influencing the fertility behavior of relatives, neighbors, or acquaintances. Given sufficient information concerning the economic and social implications a sustained high growth rate, the conflict between individual fertility desires and their aggregate manifestations could however be explicated.

If couples on the average raise four surviving children, population doubles in the short span of a single generation. The prospect of such doubling may be found an attractive one for any particular family, but it may be deemed dismal if applied to the nation as a whole. If each family had a choice, they might rather see their four children grow up into adulthood in a country that did not have to absorb twice as many people as claimed its resources a mere 25 years ago, and hence did not have to suffer the impact of such growth on employment, wage levels, urban amenities, and a host of other indicators of economic and social well-being. The inconsistency of private and public interests is rooted in the presence of negative externalities attached to individual fertility behavior. The birth of a child, perceived as a gain for the single family, imposes costs on all other members of the society in which it is born—costs that are not taken into account in the private decisions that determine fertility.

Similarly structured problems outside the population field are, of course, numerous. The man driving on a highway at high speed may be doing what he calculates as best for himself, but in the process he also imperils others on the road. While an obvious feedback mechanism—the driver's own sense of insecurity at high speeds—is likely to keep the problem within bounds far more effectively than in the case of fertility behavior, a government-enforced constraining of negative spillover effects—the introduction of speed limits—may be welcomed by all drivers as an improvement. The analogous solution with respect to excessive fertility is readily apparent: it consists of government-induced limitations of fertility calculated to balance public and private interests. But pronouncing a diagnosis and indicating the nature of the requisite solution is far from saying that an acceptable solution does in fact exist.

Source: From Demeny, Paul. 1975. "Population Policy: The Role of National Governments." *Population and Development Review* 1(1):147–61.

people, and no more. Renewable resources include such items as forests, which, when consumed at a rate faster than the rate of replenishment, are likely to collapse.

Population size and growth contribute to the rate of consumption, which then influences the stability of renewable resource systems. This complex chain of causes and effects raises many policy-relevant questions: What constitutes a nation's energy, soil, and water resources, in qualitative as well as quantitative senses? What is the most desirable level of consumption of these resources? What is a desirable standard of living? What is the correct population size for maintaining desirable standards of living and consumption? How should the social system be altered in order to ensure the long-term survival of the population? How should population size and distribution be altered, if at all, to achieve sustainable development? All these questions are now tied to the issue of a sustainable world in the wake of overwhelming data on global warming (Gunasekara et al. 2013).

These questions suggest, among other things, that optimum population size differs from a **sustainable population size**. The decision as to what constitutes an optimum population size is calculated through scientific manipulation of demographic data. In contrast, sustainable population size is influenced by community consensus on the average standard of living that can be sustained over a long period of time, not only by the current generation but also for future generations. For example, if a community decides that each household (on the average) should own two cars and five acres of residential land, the population size optimal for achieving these goals can be arrived at through relatively simple calculations using data on habitable land, available energy resources, and so forth. But, if the community decides to develop and use a new public-transportation system and low-cost housing in lieu of single-family estates, many more people than deemed optimal in the first instance can be accommodated.

The Legal Dimension: Policy Implementation and Fertility Determinants

Thus we find that a principal answer to the question of why population policies are created is that they are believed to help achieve desirable living standards and to prevent the erosion or collapse of economic and social systems. With this in mind, we now turn to some issues associated with the process of policy **implementation**. We have seen that population policies are typically formulated in general terms and that they aim to achieve goals that are stated very broadly: for instance, "reduce family size to improve the quality of life"; "slow growth rates to conserve natural resources." In contrast, specific aspects of policies, once created and ratified, are put into practice via sets of population laws. For example, in the case of broad policies of fertility limitation, associated laws pertain to matters such as age at marriage and the right of women to have medical abortions.

In principle, population laws can focus on any of the components of growth: birth, death, in-migration, out-migration, or on factors that indirectly contribute to these, such as marriage (and divorce). In fact, it is universally unethical and illegal to seek to sustain or increase morality rates in order to reduce population size or growth rates, although, tragically, this remains a preferred approach of those who perpetrate genocide. As Nobel Laureate Gunnar Myrdal (1970:152) urged several years ago: "complacency about or even tolerance of mortality because it slows down population growth is simply not permissible." Similarly, laws that entail compulsory controls on out-migration are widely considered to be at odds with basic human rights guarantees. Nevertheless, many countries do make it very difficult (if not impossible) for ordinary people to emigrate; and in parts of Africa, Asia, and Central Europe, large subpopulations have been expelled from their homelands for the sake of "ethnic cleansing"—despite international censure.

This leaves birth and migration as the vital events that may legally and ethically be manipulated to reduce population growth in a direct manner. Such laws are usually framed in terms of restrictive quotas for immigrants and support for fertility control—with sanctions ranging from permissive to coercive (as in China). We noted in Chapter 7 how immigration restrictions immediately raise issues with respect to which groups should and which groups should not be allowed to enter a country. Clearly, national political and economic interests, as well as labor policy and ethnic prejudices, play a major role in the decisions that affect how migration laws are written (and how they are enforced). During the era of rapid industrialization in the United States, these issues were at the forefront of national policy debates, especially during what we termed the first two "waves of immigration" of the nineteenth and early twentieth centuries. However, in today's developing countries, where population growth is most rapid and social problems most acute, the contribution of immigration to natural increase is relatively negligible. There, migration problems usually involve episodic influxes of refugees and displaced. For this reason, population law has come to be more or less equated with fertility-control measures.

In Chapter 5, it was suggested that the influence of all socioeconomic, cultural, and biological variables on fertility are mediated by a limited set of intervening variables and proximate factors. This well-known thesis was developed by two of America's most respected and influential demographers, Kingsley Davis and Judith Blake (1956). They observed that at three distinct points in the childbearing process, events—or proximate determinants—can occur that intervene between a woman's potential for procreation and the actualization of that potential in the form of offspring. If these determinants are effective, fertility levels will be reduced. The first point of intervention is prior to intercourse, and the proximate events include late marriage and abstinence. You will recall that these are the only forms of fertility control approved of by Malthus. The second point of intervention is between intercourse and conception. The proximate determinants here include traditional and modern forms of birth control: the pill, IUDs, male condoms, and antifertility steroids. The third point of intervention is between conception and birth; that is, voluntary abortion.

Among all possible events that can occur at each of the three points of intervention combined, Davis and Blake identified seven that account for most of the variation in contemporary aggregate fertility levels. These are: (1) the proportion of females married or in sexual unions, (2) contraceptive use and effectiveness, (3) the prevalence of induced abortion, (4) the duration of voluntary **postpartum abstinence** (avoidance of intercourse following delivery of a child),[3] (5) fecundability (the physical capacity to bear children), (6) spontaneous intrauterine mortality, and (7) the prevalence of permanent sterility (Bongaarts 1982).

Fertility-control laws now in effect seek to manipulate one or more of these determinants in order to slow population growth. However, among the seven, the later three—fecundability, spontaneous intrauterine mortality, and permanent sterility—are not readily manipulable (given universal ethical standards), nor do we clearly understand how they are influenced by socioeconomic and environmental factors. However, these play only a minor or negligible role in determining fertility differentials, apparently accounting for only 4.0 percent of the variation (Bongaarts

1982, 1993; Mcallister et al. 2012). Practically speaking, then, this leaves postpartum abstinence, access to abortion, contraceptive use and quality, and marriage norms, which together explain the remaining 96 percent of the variation, as the main targets of population legislation. The first and last of these determinants intervene at the initial point of the childbearing process—prior to intercourse, and thus constitute indirect means of fertility control. In contrast, contraception and abortion, which occur at the second and third points, respectively, are direct determinants. Let us briefly consider each of these, in order.

1. *Postpartum abstinence* is a traditional method of birth control throughout Africa and other parts of the developing world. In most countries, it is practiced to promote the survival of the newborn, on the grounds that pregnancy shortly after a birth is likely to diminish the mother's ability to nourish the child. The length of time the mother abstains from intercourse varies widely from country to country. In Zaire, the median in two rural and urban sites ranged from 4.5 to 8.8 months (Hassig et al. 1991; Nketiah-Amponsah, Arthur, and Abuosi 2012). Unfortunately, formal birth-control programs seldom explicitly promote postpartum abstinence. Nor do they credit those who practice it with being wise and, on that basis, discuss with the parents the possibility that a longer interval before the next conception (aided by contraceptives) might be even better for the health and well-being of the newborn.[4]

2. *Abortion.* Laws aimed at affecting access to abortion, the dissemination of birth-control information and technology, and the norms and practices associated with age at marriage are the principal direct means of implementing population control policies. Among these, government directives with regard to abortion are generally the most controversial. Nevertheless, induced abortion has a strong effect on fertility decline in today's rapidly growing populations, just as it did in Japan early in the twentieth century (Henshaw 1990; Sedgh et al. 2012). "(I)n settings where fertility is declining, abortion has an increasing influence over time; and . . . on average, the fertility-reducing influence of abortion is similar in magnitude to that of contraceptive use" (Johnston and Hill 1996:113; Shah and Åhman 2012).

Only a few countries strictly prohibit legal abortion as a fertility-reduction measure. Anika Rahman, Laura Karzive, and Stanley Henshaw (1998) report that a majority of the world's population, about 61 percent, lives in countries in which induced abortion is permitted, and about 25 percent live in nations that generally prohibit the procedure. Even where laws are very restrictive, induced abortion is usually allowed when the woman's life is endangered (Finer and Fine 2013). And in many cases, even where abortion is illegal, the operation is performed, but under unsafe conditions that increase the risk of maternal mortality. Rahman, Karzive, and Henshaw also point out that in nations with very liberal laws, access may still be limited by gestational-age restrictions, required third-party authorization, or limitations on the types of facilities that perform abortions.

3. *Contraception.* The most important component of fertility reduction today is artificial contraception: condoms, IUDs, the pill, and other mechanical and chemical methods of preventing pregnancy prior to or during intercourse. Just as fertility control has become the main focus of contemporary population law, modern types of contraception have become the methods of fertility control most favored in law and policy, especially in the less-developed countries. This focus on modern contraceptive use is also driven by the fact that a large number of pregnancies, nearly 40 percent of all pregnancies each year are unwanted (Singh, Sedgh, and Hussain 2010). These unintended pregnancies exert a huge toll on the reproductive well-being and health of women in developing countries. John Ross and Elizabeth Frankenberg (1993)

have shown that more than two-thirds of the world's population resides in eight densely populated countries, of which five have strong family-planning programs.

Most population-control policies are heavily slanted toward fertility control and hence the widespread popularity of family-planning programs (Ali et al. 2014). As family-planning programs rely on modern methods of birth control, innovations in the technologies of birth control developed in the United States initially facilitated it to play a key role in the propagation of family-planning programs in developing countries. Agencies such as the **United States Agency for International Development (USAID)** funneled billions of dollars into development of modern family-planning programs. Governments in developing countries were encouraged to develop population policies with U.S. technical assistance and support. If not for the external support and encouragement provided by the United States, initially it is doubtful that many governments in the developing world would have formulated their own modern population family-planning programs. Thus, the successful implementation of family-planning programs in the world, especially in developing countries, remains a good example of policies developed under external influence of power. The growth of support for family-planning programs is indicated by the increase in percentages of countries where it is supported directly by government policies, as presented in Table 11.1. In 1976, 63 percent of all countries in the world had government policies providing direct support for family planning. By 2011, this percentage grew to 80. During the same period, the percent of countries with no support for family-planning programs nearly halved, from 19 to 9.

In addition to distributing specific contraceptive devices, most family-planning programs also seek to provide service, information, persuasion, and legitimization, although the emphasis on each of these components varies from country to country. Both the public and private sectors are involved in these efforts; however, family-planning programs are nearly always financed and run by government agencies. The private sector plays a leading role in the manufacture of mechanical and chemical contraceptives, but, in most developing countries, it rarely undertakes direct distribution to the consumer. This, too, is understood to be the responsibility of government.

In the late 1980s, modern family planning was granted legal status in Iran and other countries in which such programs had previously been resisted on religious or political grounds. The Islamic Republic of Iran (IRI) was founded in 1979 following a prolonged revolution that overthrew the nation's pro-Western monarchy. This brought about abrupt changes in its population policies and laws, which until

Table 11.1. Percentages of Countries with Government Policies on Providing Support for Family Planning, 1976–2011

Year	Direct Support	Indirect Support	No Support	Not Permitted	Total
1976	63	11	19	7	100
1986	71	13	11	4	100
1996	76	10	14	1	100
2005	74	18	8	1	100
2011	80	11	9	1	100

Source: *World Population Policies 2011*, Department of Economic and Social Affairs, Population Division. United Nations: New York, 2013.

then had been modeled on the principles articulated by the United States at the Bucharest World Population Conference (see above). Shortly after the installation of the Ayatollah Khomeni, the revolutionary leader and a religious fundamentalist, as President of the Republic, the Family Planning Council of Iran ceased to exist (Aghajanian 1995; Gandevani, Ziaee, and Farahani 2014). The entire legislative framework affecting family relations, the status of women, and artificial contraception was altered to conform to what was interpreted to be traditional Islamic law. On the question of family planning in particular, the Ayatollah's position and that of the Roman Catholic Pope were essentially the same: that is, the practices of birth control and abortion are considered to be sinful.

In 1988, nearly nine years after the revolution, the IRI government reversed its position. At that time, it issued several declarations that clearly identified the large size and high growth rates of the country's population as detrimental to national development and a threat to health of mothers and children. In December 1988, Iran's High Judicial Council concluded that family planning does *not* violate Islamic law. This pronouncement cleared the way for legislative reforms that reinstated the country's family-planning program in 1989. A specially appointed undersecretary within the Ministry of Health now coordinates the program. According to the new policies and laws, women who do not want additional births are encouraged to obtain contraceptives from government health clinics and "health houses." The post-1989 program has three major components:

- Intervals of at least three to four years between births are encouraged.
- Special efforts are directed to lowering the fertility levels of adolescent and among women 35 years and older.
- Families are encouraged to limit reproduction to three children.

In addition, legal measures were considered to provide disincentives to couples who have more than three children (although it appears that these have not been enforced with the strictness or severity associated with China's program).

Several researchers have ranked nations according to the level of effort, extent of awareness, or the degree of support evidenced by national governments in relation to family-planning programs. These include the staff of the Population Reference Bureau (PRB 1997, 1998) and William Mauldin and John Ross (1991).

Mauldin and Ross have created a somewhat more-refined scale to determine program effort consisting of subscales measuring four separate dimensions: (1) policy- and stage-setting activities, (2) service and service-related activities, (3) record keeping and evaluation, and (4) availability and accessibility of fertility-control methods. The policy- and stage-setting activities include such components as: government's official policy or position concerning fertility/family planning and rates of population growth: favorable statements by leaders; level of family-planning program leadership; age-at-marriage policy; import laws and legal regulations regarding contraceptives; advertising of contraceptives in the mass media allowed; other ministries/government agencies involved; and in-country budget for program. The scale ranges between 0 and 120. Countries with scores greater than 45 are deemed to have moderate-to-strong programs. Those with scores below 45 are rated as having weak programs. In an attempt to show how the scale can discern trends, the researchers selected two dates, 1982 and 1989. They found that during this period, 18 countries had progressed from the weak to the stronger category. Upon analysis of these findings, they concluded that this progress had come about as a result of improvements in infrastructure, administration, training, and mass media support during the period of interest.

The study was replicated in 2004 and 2009 and the results reported by Ross and Smith (2011) show significant differences in mean scores on all four components between Asia and Africa as presented in Table 11.2 In 2009, Asia had the highest total score (61 percent of maximum), and Africa, the least. Latin American Average is also low, below 50 percent. On policy component score, both Asia and Middle East/Asia score high, above 50 percent.

4. *Age at marriage.* Laws that focus on age at marriage constitute the principal indirect means of implementing population-control policy. Such laws have been found to be effective for several reasons. First, women who delay marriage are more likely to continue their education, and the likelihood of being employed and pursuing a career outside the home increases as education increases. The combined effect of education and employment not only improves a woman's own wellbeing, but it also contributes to the health of her children and other family members. It also enables her to be more autonomous in making decisions with regard to contraceptive use and family size. As the leader of India's independence movement, Mahatma Mohandas K. Gandhi, once noted, "When you educate a man you educate a person, when you educate a woman you educate a family."

A second reason why age at marriage legislation is effective is perhaps the most obvious one: The older a woman is when she marries, the shorter is the time span during which she can bear (legitimate) children. It has been estimated that if the minimum age at marriage for females were universally fixed at 20 years, total fertility rates would be reduced by 12 to 20 percent, depending on level of development and other conditions (Dandekar and Rath 1970). As was pointed out in our discussion of fecundity (Chapter 5), a woman's capacity to bear children begins around age 12 and ends at about 45. If a woman marries in her late teens, a common practice in rural areas of the developing world, she is exposed to the risk of pregnancy for at least 30 years: more than adequate time to have 10 children, or more. Obviously, age at marriage is a good indicator of total fertility only if the time at which a young woman begins to be sexually active does not precede marriage.[5] This is less significant than it may at first seem, because in most countries with rapidly growing populations, premarital sex is strongly discouraged on moral and religious grounds. Unfortunately, in these same countries, early marriage continues to be the norm, perhaps to compensate for the serious restrictions on premarital relations.

Table 11.2. Total Score and Mean Score on Four Components of National Family-Planning Effort

Program	Asia	Mid-East/ N. Africa	Latin Am. Africa/ Anglophone	Africa/ Effort	Francophone
Total	60.7	56.7	45.8	43.0	45.4
Mean					
Policies	68.4	58.9	48.4	49.5	50.7
Services	59.9	53.7	40.4	40.0	43.2
Evaluation	62.7	63.8	49.3	46.1	50.1
Access	52.6	56.7	51.1	39.9	41.4

Source: Based on data from Ross and Smith (2011: Table 12).

What can be done to encourage young women and (of course) men to post-pone marriage and delay the beginning of their careers as parents? Enabling legisla-tion to create and support population-education programs offers one solution. Such programs can instruct young people about the benefits of delayed marriage and postponed child bearing. Another approach is to establish a minimum legal age at marriage. This course has been pursued in India and in several other countries, not necessarily for the sake of fertility control but, often, for health reasons. For there is considerable medical evidence suggesting that teenage childbearing is harmful to the physical condition of mothers as well as infants, resulting in high rates of spon-taneous abortion and maternal and neonatal mortality (Bankole and Singh 1998; Alexander and Guyer 1993).

Early marriage was a part of the culture of the country we now call India for most of its very long history. Reared in and deeply committed to this tradition, Mahatma Gandhi and his wife were mere children when they were wed, as was com-mon among their contemporaries. In response to such practices, and under British rule, the Child Marriage Restraint Act of 1929 was amended to make it an offense for a male 18 years or older to marry a female younger than 15. Following inde-pendence, the Hindu Marriage Act (of 1955) was passed, specifying a minimum age of 21 years for boys and 18 for girls. Gradually, and with variable impacts in rural and urban areas, these laws have succeeded in changing long-standing norms and behavior. As of 2008, the mean age at marriage, for males and females combined, was estimated to be 23 years, undoubtedly the highest ever recorded.

IMMIGRATION POLICY

When one mentions population policies, we almost automatically think of family-planning programs and similar approaches to fertility limitation. However, poli-cies and laws that affect the flow of immigrants into a country or region can also have substantial demographic and social impacts. The arrival of immigrants and the departure of emigrants immediately add to or reduce the size of a population. But such movements also affect other, more qualitative aspects of a population: its struc-ture, geographic distribution, growth rates, and more. International migrants are not random individuals who can be accounted for with mere numbers. Rather, they tend to be young, male, and occupationally skilled—although this pattern ordinarily does not apply to refugees. For example, whereas the number of immigrants in the United States in 2003 was less than 12 percent of the total population, they constituted nearly 16 percent scientists and engineers.

As in the realm of family planning, migration law and policy are strongly influ-enced by public perceptions and prevailing ideologies. In the case of migration, spe-cific economic and political concerns play an especially formative role. As we noted in Chapter 7, on several occasions in the history of receiver populations, including the United States, immigrants have been considered a threat to the jobs of estab-lished workers. Also, their "strange" cultural beliefs and practices, and their igno-rance of local ways, have made them unwelcome among their more conservative hosts. Consequently, public opinion about immigration remains deeply divided even today, and migration law continues to be a controversial issue. For example, in the United States, a 2014 Gallup poll revealed that almost twice as many Americans want a decrease in immigration as want an increase. In contrast, the American Civil

Liberties Union (ACLU) strongly advocates the view that the United States has a moral and political responsibility to provide asylum to all foreigners who seek relief from political oppression, economic hardship, or social unrest.[6]

The long-term impact of immigrants on the majority culture is a matter of concern that changes with social conditions. In the past, U.S. immigration law was clearly affected by feelings of white supremacy, racism, and xenophobia (fear of people who are different). At the turn of the twenty-first century, however, prevailing receptivity to cultural and ethnic diversity appears to be playing a key role in the shaping of immigration policies. Similarly, during periods of economic hardship, competition from immigrants for scarce jobs and opportunities is less likely to be tolerated than during times of economic prosperity.

These political, social, and economic concerns affect the role of migration law and policy as instruments for population control. Typically, immigration policies are designed to restrict the flow of immigrants into a country, in the United States and throughout the world. Current U.S. policy specifies a preference for three types of immigrants:

- those who come through family connections,
- those who come with employment assured, and
- refugees or asylum seekers.

Under the category of family connections, preference is given to persons 21 years or older, unmarried sons and daughters, married daughters and sons, and brothers and sisters of U.S. citizens. Each of the three types of family connections is subject to a specified allowable number every year, but there is no set limit on the number of spouses, parents, and children of citizens who may immigrate.

The second group of immigrants, employees, is subject to a numerical quota. Each year, no more than 140,000 employees are awarded permanent residency status. These permanent residents are classed into four categories: (1) priority workers with extraordinary abilities, researchers, and multinational executives and managers; (2) aliens who either have exceptional abilities or who hold advanced degrees; (3) skilled workers, professionals, and other workers; and (4) holders of diversity visas, awarded by a lottery system. The purpose of the lottery is to provide opportunities for those whose nationalities are consistently underrepresented in annual immigrant flows. About 50,000 visas are distributed annually through this system.

The third group, asylum seekers and refugees, is perhaps the most controversial, in part because it is often difficult to decide on the definition of a "legitimate" refugee (as opposed to someone who merely desires to improve his or her economic circumstances). A total of 73,293 people were admitted to the United States as refugees during 2010 and 21,113 individuals were granted asylum. The limits to the number of asylum seekers who may become permanent residents is set by the President in collaboration with Congress.

About three-fourths of the immigrants who enter the United States each year are drawn from the first two categories, family connections and employees. About 536,000—or almost half—of the Legal Permanent Residents (LPR) admitted in 2009 were immediate relatives of U.S. citizens. Next category composed of other relatives admitted under family-sponsored preferences accounted for 212,000 new LPRs (Ross and Smith 2011). Reflecting a distinctive history and unique social and economic conditions, current U.S. immigration policy is, nevertheless, very much like immigration policy throughout the world. It is restrictive and highly selective.

HOW POPULATION POLICIES ARE MADE

The creation of policy on any social issue is rarely a rational undertaking. And, despite the fact that demography is one of the most objective and thoroughly quantified of the social sciences, this is equally true of population policy.

A policy is the end result of decisions made by dozens of people who act as official policy makers. In democratic societies, elected or duly appointed officials who are accountable to their constituencies, and whose perceived interests they seek to represent, generally play this role. To this is added direct input from members of communities whose lives may be affected by the outcome of such deliberations. Because all human decisions are influenced to some extent by value judgments—opinions about what is right or wrong, good or bad, wise or foolish—personal preferences and group interests play a crucial role in the formation of policies. Thus, to understand how any particular policy is made, we need to consider the various values and interests that motivate the policy makers and concerned citizens who are involved. According to James Anderson (1984:163), "The policy making process in the United States is an adversarial process, characterized by the clash of competing and conflicting viewpoints and interests rather than an impartial, disinterested, or 'objective' search for the 'correct' solutions for policy problems."

Stages of the Policy Process

The process of policy formulation typically progresses through three stages: (1) agenda setting, (2) decision making, and (3) implementation. The first, **agenda setting**, stage is perhaps the most important in the life of a policy. At this point, issues related to the problem a policy is to address (recall that policies are born in response to perceived social problems) are brought to the surface. Through, often intense, negotiation, a subset of these issues is selected and considered for debate and further examination. Special-interest groups that seek to influence the content of the policy take action at this crucial stage, attempting to define the issues to be discussed and debated publicly.

Decisions concerning which items are to be included on the agenda also depend upon the severity of the social problem the policy addresses. In this regard, availability of and easy access to data that relate to the character and scope of the problem are important factors. Such data help policy makers and parties at-interest to convey the message to legislators that the problem is urgent, and that it is necessary to attempt to solve or mitigate it. In addition, problems that are considered in the agenda-setting stage are more likely to be translated into policy if they are in some way related to overall national goals. During the 1980s and 1990s in the United States, efforts to place broad "crime"-related issues on policy agendas were far more likely to succeed than other initiatives because of the Federal Government's stated commitment to stop the smuggling, dealing, and use of illegal drugs. In a similar manner, media play an important role in shaping public opinion. For example, TV and newspaper campaigns can succeed in forcing selected issues onto the policy agenda by eliciting the participation of celebrities and other public figures who support the cause.

The second, decision-making, stage has two key outcomes. These are: (a) formulating a clear definition of policy goals, and (b) creating strategies for achieving the goals; in other words, assertions concerning what is to be achieved and how to go about achieving it. Several pertinent decisions need to be made in this context, including the choice and specification of the policy objectives from among a number of alternative goals and strategies. This is far from being a rational and scientific process, for the values of decision makers and the views of celebrities, when they are involved, play a key role. Experienced policy makers are likely to draw comparisons between the current agenda and past policies in whose formulation they participated. In this way, current policies tend to be shaped by already-existing goals and strategies.

Once policy goals are determined, decisions must be made regarding budgetary allocations. Much of the deliberation that occurs during the decision-making stage relates to this issue, because budgets specify how money is to be allocated in support of the various programs and activities that constitute the strategies for achieving policy goals. The proportion allocated for each activity indicates its relative importance, as determined by the policy makers. Thus, at this point, ideological convictions, rhetorical skills, and political connections can be translated into financial resources—even for causes that may appear unworthy from a more objective perspective.

The last stage in the process is implementation, which includes all of the related activities that occur following official adoption of a policy. Soon afterward, there is a period devoted to the planning, organization, and staffing of agencies responsible for policy implementation. Next comes the development of rules, directives, and regulations intended to transform the policy statements into specific programs and initiatives. Then, activities are pursued that focus on providing direction and coordination of personnel and expenditures.

The implementation stage is perhaps the least stable of the three. Translation of policy into concrete action is always subject to legal challenge by opponents who now have an opportunity to question the way in which it actually affects people. In fact, it is unusual when a policy is *not* challenged upon implementation by groups or individuals who believe that their interests are threatened, and who attempt to delay or halt implementation in endless court battles. (Stockey and Zeckhauser 1978; Bardach 2011). In addition, poor communication, lack of resources, and the attitudes of bureaucratic officials often hamper policy implementation. Communication problems arise from the fact that policies are often translated into ambiguous rules and directives. As these vague orders pass through the layers of bureaucratic organizations, they serve to confuse officials, who subsequently make mistakes in interpreting the statements handed down "from above," or who simply ignore them. The adoption of new policies requires new staff members, some of whom may need training. But because personnel and resources for training are often difficult to find, months and even years may pass before the policies are actually put into practice. Finally, if the values and attitudes of the policy makers differ substantially from those of the people charged with putting the policy into practice, effective implementation can be delayed or permanently halted while the two factions attempt to work out their differences.

Creating a Population Policy: The Case of Zambia

In the southern African nation of Zambia, the central government is the key agency in the development of population policy, as it is in most countries. Government attention turned to population issues there in the early 1980s, when the nation's economy began a serious and rapid decline. The local currency, the kwacha, was devalued, and a severe shortage of food commodities occurred. In an attempt to restore economic stability, officials solicited the help of several international agencies, including the International Bank for Reconstruction and Development (IBRD), better known as the World Bank. The Bank assessed the long-term prospects of the Zambian economy and urged the Government to consider the impact of population growth on economic development. In response, permission was granted for the Bank to conduct a preliminary study on the status of the country's population, health, and nutrition.

In 1983, the World Bank submitted its preliminary report to the Zambian Government, which led to a two-part initiative intended (1) to prepare a response to the Bank, and (2) to study the extent to which the population variable should be accommodated in official social and economic development policies. The Government solicited the help of a wide range of national interest groups, including **nongovernmental organizations** (**NGO**s), to study the Bank's report. This meant that, for the first time ever, organizations not associated with the office of Zambia's President were involved in examining the population question. These included the United National Independence Party (UNIP), the National Commission for Development Planning (NCDP), the Planned Parenthood Association of Zambia (PPAZ), the University of Zambia (UNZA), various ministries, the Medical School in Zambia's Capital, Lusaka, and the Family Life Movement of Zambia (FLMZ). A steering committee consisting of selected members of these organizations was formed. This committee submitted its report in 1984 (National Commission for Development Planning 1984). Although the contents of the report were significant, it was even more important from a policy point of view that the investigation sensitized so many NGOs to issues surrounding rapid population growth.

A few months prior to the publication of the committee's report, the **United Nation's Fund for Population Activities** (**UNFPA**) submitted a document to the Zambian Government containing its assessment of population growth in Zambia and of UNFPA's role in providing monetary and personnel assistance for population control. The UNFPA report and the national committee's response to the World Bank provided considerable impetus for Zambia's participation in the 1984 World Population Conference in Mexico City. In preparation for the Conference, an African Regional Population Conference was held in Arusha, Republic of Tanzania, in January of 1984 (Economic Commission for Africa 1984). There, the Zambian Government gave its support to the "Kilimanjaro Program of Action on Population," which explicitly identified six principles that link population and development:

1. Population should be considered as a central issue in development strategies and plans.
2. Population and development are interrelated.
3. The right and responsibility of every country to solve its population problems should be recognized.
4. The formulation and implementation of population programs should exploit the African governments' commitment to self-reliant development and regional, interregional, and intercountry collaboration.
5. National population programs should aim at responding to nationally perceived problems as identified by empirical research findings.
6. International cooperation in the field of population should respect sociocultural values (UNFPA 1984:3, 4a).

The 1984 Conference in Mexico City was attended by very high-ranking Zambian officials, including Mrs. B. C. Kankasa, Chair of the Woman's Affairs Committee of the Republic and member of the Central Committee of Zambia. In a statement presented at the Conference, the President of Zambia, Dr. David Kaunda, declared that many of the consequences of the growth of the population are unobtrusive since they occur so gradually and pervade so much of life that they pass unnoticed. It is therefore our intention in Zambia that through the intensification and coordination of population programs, an observable impact on fertility and mortality rates shall be achieved. This implies incorporation of more demographic variables into the planning system to achieve growth rates of the economy that are consistent with the annual growth rate of the population . . . [I]t is therefore Zambia's policy to knit together isolated rural human settlements into socially acceptable and more economically viable communities through village re-grouping and rural re-construction centers.[7]

The Zambian delegation included the Minister of Health, a representative from the National Commission for Development and Planning, the UNFPA country representative, and as a participant, Father Cretins, who headed the Family Life Movement of Zambia. The head of the delegation, Mrs. Kankasa, stated that

the Government does have an implicit population policy which expresses itself in several categories of Government action ranging from regulative acts to executive statements and court decisions. Let me state that the Zambian Government views a population policy not in the narrow sense of being concerned only with efforts to affect the size, structure, and distribution; rather, because of the Government's recognition of the interrelationships between socioeconomic change and population, population policy is also conceived of in the much broader sense of also encompassing efforts to regulate economic and social conditions which are likely to have demographic consequences. Thus among the components of Zambia's implicit policies are: (a) free education for all, (b) free health service for all, (c) improved employment opportunities for women, (d) rural development including agricultural development, (e) family-planning information and services. . . . Mr. President, I should state that in order for Zambia to sustain a family planning program continued international assistance is necessary. However, we strongly believe that such assistance should not be made conditional on any particular family-planning policy; rather, it should conform with our cultural, social, and religious norms. For instance, while my delegation appreciates the importance of family life education, in our society we do not support the idea of providing contraceptive services to adolescents.[8]

As noted in the preceding section, social and political barriers often hinder the transition from an implicit to an explicit population policy. However, as we also observed, these barriers can be overcome if celebrities or respected political figures publicly support placing the issue on the agenda and moving it along the way toward becoming law. In Zambia, Mrs. Kankasa played this role in shaping public attitudes with respect to population education and birth control. The media also provided support in publicizing Mrs. Kankasa's statements and speeches on these subjects. Two of the country's leading newspapers, *Daily Mail* and *Times of Zambia,* ran stories on family planning, population control, and population policy. These stories featured strong statements in favor of an explicit population policy, including sex education in the schools, well-funded family-planning programs, child-spacing initiatives, and education to motivate couples to have smaller families.[9]

Soon after the 1984 Mexico City Conference, both internal and external pressures to formulate a population policy emerged. Internally, several prominent social activists and politicians publicly expressed their support. External proponents included donor agencies such as the World Bank and the International Monetary Fund, which introduced population planning as one component of its financial aid package to Zambia. Between December 8th and 11th, 1985, the NCDP held a population conference with the stated purpose of arriving at a draft policy after three days of deliberations. Several NGOs as well as private and religious organizations were invited to participate in the process. Despite the brief time period, a draft was produced, approved by those in attendance, and presented to the Zambian legislature for ratification.

The tone of the document was clearly and explicitly antinatalist in its unconditional support of "the policy option of slowing down the population growth rate as against other options of maintaining the status quo or increasing the population growth rate." In this spirit, several specific strategies were identified and framed as recommendations to the Government. These included: (1) "We recommend that the legal marriageable age be raised." (2) "We recommend family planning based on child spacing." (3) "We recommend that the present fertility rate of 7.2 children per woman be lowered to 4 children per woman within the next two decades."[10] A revised version of this draft was presented to the legislature, where it was passed in 1989. Shortly thereafter, it became an integral part of Zambia's fourth National Development Plan (Osei-Heidi and Osei-Heidi 1992; Robinson 2012).

International Organizations and Population Policy

Even as Zambia's population policy was being formulated, the Government was clear in its understanding that a large proportion of the initial investment for implementation would come from international organizations and foreign governments. Like most less-industrialized countries, Zambia now does receive substantial population-control program funds from wealthy nations such as the United States and Japan (nations that also happen to have slowly growing populations). In fact, the most important sources of funding for family-planning activities in Africa, Asia, and much of Latin America are private foundations and public agencies in the United States and other industrialized countries (Norman 1997; Meyer and Seims 2013). International population assistance organizations, such as the UNDP (United Nations Development Program) and the **International Planned Parenthood Federation (IPPF)**,[11] which have also traditionally been supported by the major donor countries, provide significant resources for birth-control programs in the developing world (Donaldson and Tsui 1990; Horn 2013). At the national level, government agencies, NGOs, and private hospitals and physicians finance family planning; and in some countries, state or provincial government agencies also contribute to the family-planning effort.

Since the end of World War II, the U.S. Government has been the leader in promoting family-planning programs abroad. Through the Office of Population of USAID, several *billion* dollars have been provided for population activities in developing countries. In fact, between 1969 and 1988, nearly one-half of the total contribution of all nations emanated from that agency (Donaldson and Tsui 1990.)

However, funding levels began to decline, slowly in the early 1980s and more rapidly in subsequent years, largely as the result of political opposition to the financing of birth-control programs in which voluntary abortions were performed. The United States was still at the top of the list of donors to the UNFPA in 1984, with a contribution of $38.0 million. However, five years later, it did not even make the top 10, with a contribution falling below 7 million. In 1991, 46 percent of all the international family-planning funds provided by OECD countries originated from USAID allocations, and the United States was the largest contraceptive supplier that year. Even as recently as 1995, the USAID budget for international family planning (to all recipients combined) was about $546 million. But by 1996, this was drastically reduced to a mere $76 million.

Between 1965 and 1990, both Democrats and Republicans in Congress supported U.S. Governmental assistance for international family planning. However, by the early 1990s, conservative factions had won the abortion debate, and support for such programs came to an abrupt end. The opponents of population aid appeared to be pleased that their moral values had been granted legal status. However, family-planning proponents pointed out that the significant reduction in the level of U.S. funding is likely to have negative effects on the reproductive health of millions of women in Zambia, India, and other countries with rapidly growing populations.

EVALUATING POPULATION POLICIES

As discussed in the preceding section, the Republic of Zambia adopted an explicit antinatalist population policy in 1989. The policy employs promotion of birth control as the principal strategy to achieve reductions in population growth rates. About 10 years later, in mid-1998, the Zambian Government sought to assess the program to determine whether or not it had been effective. Had the family-planning program succeeded in promoting the practice of birth control among couples of childbearing age? Were the funds and resources allocated to the program well spent? These questions, frequently asked by members of the Zambian public, are similar to those posed by people everywhere when they contemplate if and how costly public-policy initiatives actually work. In order to provide valid answers to such questions, contemporary social researchers pursue a scientific approach to generating relevant information known as *evaluation research*, or **program evaluation**.[12]

Evaluation research uses scientific techniques typically based on the experimental model to assess the implementation and outcomes of policy-driven programs. As a type of applied research, it is consciously undertaken with the goal of providing information upon which decision making will be based (for example, whether or not Zambia ought to continue supporting family-planning clinics; see Rutman 1984; Bauman and Nutbeam 2013). Because policy makers and affected citizens have an interest in a variety of impacts traceable to the resources committed to a program, several types of outcomes can be evaluated. In practice, however, evaluation researchers focus on only the three most important types of outcomes, which, although distinct, are also clearly interrelated: (1) process, (2) efficiency, and (3) impact.

As the name suggests, **process evaluation** is concerned with the activities and procedures associated with implementing a policy. Data are collected from personal interviews and relevant documents to determine if the strategies proposed by the policy have been followed, and if the groups and individuals who were meant to experience the impacts of new programs were, in fact, affected (Garcia-Nunez 1992; Rama-Rao and Mohanam 2003). These are obviously very important matters. Nevertheless, they still do not tell us if the program actually works. For it is quite possible to establish programs successfully and to follow procedures faithfully without ever delaying a marriage, or limiting the number of times a woman gives birth, or achieving some other clear policy goal. This is the main reason why the other types of evaluation research have been developed.

Efficiency evaluation is the most widely employed of the three types. The approach is used to investigate how well the allocated resources have been expended to achieve expected program outcomes. Financial data, as well as official reports and first-person accounts, are collected so that program expenditures can be compared to program results. The purpose of this work is to ensure that resources have been put to their most effective use (Stockey and Zeckhauser 1978).

Efficiency evaluation is very closely related to the well-known financial technique of cost-benefit analysis. To summarize in very simple terms, this technique focuses on investment decisions, such as the purchase of property, or bonds, or stock-market shares. The inputs (costs) of the investment are measured in dollar amounts and are compared to the outputs (benefits), also measured in dollars. If the benefits exceed the costs, all things considered (and here is where the technique can get quite complicated), the investment is considered sound; otherwise, it is viewed as a poor decision.

In the realm of policy evaluation, it is not always possible to perform a strict cost-benefit analysis, because dollar amounts cannot be assigned to every program output. For example, we know that some family-planning program activities have led to the practice of abstinence among young adolescents. When bookkeeping is adequate, the costs of such activities can be determined fairly accurately. However, the objective assignment of a monetary value to births averted is virtually impossible. How can we assess the amount saved by a couple who decide to forgo a pregnancy, or to balance that against the loss of potential social, economic, and political capital over the lifetime of an individual who was never born? Thus, with respect to program benefits, in the case of population policy and in general, problems arise that can only be approached subjectively.

Impact evaluation seeks to assess the changes that result from policies, quantitatively and in terms of direction. The approach assumes that the program activities specified in a policy will cause observable changes in the target population. Thus, it employs methods suitable for establishing a cause-and-effect relationship between program inputs and program outputs (Nachmias 1980). It is never a simple matter in any field of study to show that a causal relationship exists, and the problem is especially acute in program evaluation research. First, it must be shown that the cause actually did precede the effect in time. That is, a program activity, such as dispensing contraceptives, is initiated and later the effect occurs: birth rates decline.[13] Then, a significant correlation between cause and effect must be demonstrated: dispensing contraceptives and birth rate declines must occur in sequence, and if contraceptives are not dispensed, it must be shown that birth rates do not decline. Finally, and this is the most difficult condition of all for evaluators to satisfy, no other factor than that under consideration could have brought about the effect. In the case of contraceptive distribution and birth rate decline, this means that all other possible causes—acts that would make the distribution (or use) of contraceptives irrelevant—must be ruled out, including abstinence, sterilization, and abortion.

The preferred approach to establishing causality in the social sciences is the *experimental method*. As those who are familiar with the method know, it is best suited to a laboratory situation. Outside the lab in the real world, where most evaluation research is conducted, it is often necessary to make do with less-than-perfect conditions. In such instances, researchers attempt to come as close as possible with a range of strategies know as *quasi-* ("almost") experimental designs.

The experimental method is characterized by three conditions: (1) The experiment focuses on one presumed cause (the independent variable) and one presumed effect (the dependent variable). In population evaluation, the former would be something like the distribution of contraceptive devices, as in our example, which varies between "yes, distributed" and "no, not distributed." The latter would be the birth rates that are expected to decline. (2) The research has a clear "before" and "after" stage, to satisfy the first requirement for causality. The event that defines before and after is the introduction of the presumed cause. In our example, this would be the distribution of contraceptives. During the before stage, the dependent variable—birth rates—is observed and measured, and during the after stage it is measured again. (3) The researchers observe both an experimental and a control subject or group, which should be as much alike as possible. In true laboratory settings, this is achieved through random assignment, in which every subject has an equal chance of being assigned to either group. The cause is actually applied to the experimental group, but it is withheld from the control. In order to avoid the overt appearance of discrimination, which might bias the results, the control is often exposed to something that appears to be the cause (a "placebo").

Thus, a truly adequate evaluation of a birth-control-distribution program would require at least two clinics serving the same kinds of clients. One clinic would be randomly selected to distribute a real device, such as an antifertility pill, and another—identical in every way—would be randomly selected, to dispense nothing (or only a pill made of sugar). The birth rates of both sets of clients should be measured prior to distribution, and they should be equal. If, under these conditions, the clients of the clinic that dispenses real antifertility medication do, after an appropriate length of time, exhibit lower birth rates than when first measured, and the second set of clients does not, it can be concluded that the program is probably successful.

Probably successful? Not surely? Unfortunately, yes; for it is still possible that something else is responsible for the outcome. For example, the first set of clients might not have even bothered to take the pills. Perhaps this was because all of the men in that group underwent vasectomies at another clinic that gave color television sets to those who had the operation (this is only a slight exaggeration of something that actually occurred in India; see below). The lesson here is that even the most rigorous experiment cannot determine conclusively and absolutely that a presumed cause is responsible for an observed outcome. That is why scientific research—especially evaluation research—is always a never-ending, open-ended process in which one set of results must be confirmed by additional trials and follow-up studies.

Quasi-experimental designs are similar to the experimental method, except that the experimenter does not have complete control over all the factors that influence the outcome. Perhaps random assignment of subjects to control and experimental groups is not done. Or no control group is used. Or no information is available about the dependent variable at the before stage. Although we would like to perform classical experiments in population evaluation research, these are, in fact, the kinds of conditions that are ordinarily faced in the field. Fortunately, experts in research methodology have considered such shortcomings and have developed techniques that are highly effective under less-than-perfect conditions. Perhaps most influential among these experts are Donald Campbell and Julian Stanley, whose classic text on quasi-experimental design (Campbell and Stanley 1963) continues to guide the work of population-program evaluators and many other social scientists who seek to solve real-world problems.

THE ROLE OF VALUES IN POPULATION POLICY

We conclude this chapter on a somewhat subjective note. Having examined several dimensions of population policy, the various goals it is meant to achieve, how it is constructed, and how it is evaluated, we now step back from the realm of facts to consider some normative issues. In an earlier section, it was noted that the norms and values of policy makers and citizens play an important role in each of the three stages of the policy-implementation process. Here, these ideas are extended to scrutinize the value premises that underlie the family-planning movement in general.

Family-planning organizations, like other social service agencies, are bureaucracies. This has both positive and negative consequences. On the positive side, family-planning agencies can efficiently deliver birth-control information and improve their clients' access to contraceptive technologies. On the negative side, the combination of bureaucracy's rigid, impersonal mode of operation and the intimacy of the activities with which family planning deals has led to a range of political, social, and ethical controversies.

In the political realm, controversy over family-planning programs center on the issue of government control. Most governments of countries with rapidly growing populations are eager to limit reproduction, mainly on the grounds that a slower rate of growth, and fewer mouths to feed, will give their economic development programs a chance to succeed. Therefore, family planning is officially accepted as an effective tool to create the preconditions for improving standards of living. However, the outcome of this line of reasoning is a policy approach in which the government increasingly restricts the individual's choice to decide on the number of children to bear, especially among poor, rural, uneducated individuals. The belief that government officials know better, and that "the tragedy of the commons" is the inevitable outcome of leaving family-size decisions entirely to illiterate peasants, can lead to coercive state-controlled population programs. A nonpolitical and noncoercive policy would allow demand for birth control to be met by market mechanisms, with very little state interference. Yet, as noted in a more general context early in this chapter, population policies today are almost always formulated and implemented by central governments. Thus, restrictions on individual freedom in the name of development are not only likely today, they are a reality—and not only in China.

In societies in which official policy espouses, as essential conditions for the provision of family planning, voluntary fertility control and the freedom to choose the number of children one wants, the state nevertheless exercises considerable control over individual decisions to use contraceptive methods. For example, in the early 1970s, the Government of India, the world's largest democracy, established "vasectomy camps" designed to facilitate the sterilization of a large number of men in a short duration. Men were rewarded with transistor radios, other gifts, or small amounts of cash for undergoing the operation, in something like an assembly line. Family-planning workers were given monthly quotas, and those who failed to meet their quotas were penalized by salary reductions. In conjunction with this initiative, the authorities threatened to reduce the food rations allocated to households of Government employees who had more than two children and who refused to undergo sterilization. Prime Minister Indira Gandhi and her advisors (one of whom was her eldest son) defended the program on the grounds that the decision to have a vasectomy was strictly voluntary and left to the individual. However, the family-planning workers, conscious of their quotas, used coercive and insidious methods to gain recruits. Some simply "raided" neighborhoods and rounded up the men as if it were a police action.

Others gave people radios and other items as gifts in exchange for "taking a car ride." Then, without informing them how serious a vasectomy is, they channeled them to the camps. Thus, at the same time it was claiming to uphold its official policy of non-coercive fertility control, the Indian Government indirectly limited the capacity of its citizens to make voluntary and fully informed contraceptive decisions.

The family-planning movement in developing countries is also influenced by the mind-set of international donors who support local programs with personnel and money. As we observed earlier, for many years the United States was the strongest supporter of international family-planning programs. During the 1970s, the period during which the United States was the uncontested leader in providing population assistance abroad, the head of the USAID Office of Population was Dr. R.T. Raven-holt, a public-health physician. Dr. Ravenholt openly declared that his goal was to provide voluntary sterilization to at least 25 percent of the world's fertile women (Wagman 1977). The motivation behind this zeal has been referred to as the "medi-cal model" of fertility, although it would be equally correct to think of as a public-health model (Weinstein 1978). According to this view, high fertility is a "disease." And at some point in the 1960s, when it became apparent that population explo-sions were occurring throughout Asia, Africa, and Latin America, it was declared that this disease had reached "epidemic" proportions.

The medicalization of contraception brought with it a disregard for the social and economic factors associated with fertility. And it simply ignored a very basic demographic fact: The population explosion developing countries is not the result of some sort of pathological increase in fertility, but rather the effect of rapidly declin-ing *death* rates, especially IMRs, along with little change in traditional fertility levels. Nevertheless, if one follows out the public-health model to its logical conclusion, then the "epidemic" of high fertility must be countered with a program to provide at-risk women with a "vaccination" against getting pregnant. Based on this line of reasoning, that is exactly the course that U.S.-sponsored population policy abroad took during the Ravenholt regime. With the assistance of the Population Coun-cil, a hormone-bearing capsule with the brand name Norplant, which is inserted under a woman's skin, was developed and distributed in developing countries dur-ing the early 1980s. At about the same time, an ultimate public-health achievement occurred. USAID began to dispense an injectable antipregnancy hormone (a shot), known as Depo-Provera, in scores of countries (although it had been developed in the United States several years earlier but never distributed). Subsequently, it was discovered that, despite its significant advantages over other birth-control methods, Depo-Provera had serious side effects, although it has now been approved for use in the United States (Weeks 1992:104).

Programs that provide cash and in-kind incentives to promote contraceptive use have been defended on the grounds that incentives increase the desirability of contraception without coercion. However, this argument assumes that incentives are neutral, and that their value does not vary across socioeconomic levels. This assump-tion is not well founded. For a destitute peasant or slum dweller in any of dozens of countries in Asia, Africa, or Latin America, what would amount to a few cents in U.S. currency in the form of incentives could provide temporary relief from starva-tion. The very poor people who constitute the majority in developing countries have very limited choices. A small gift of a few rupees, kwachas, pesos, or bhats provided in exchange for undergoing sterilization forces the poor to forfeit future children to avoid despair (despite the fact that they may still accept the traditional belief that "children are the poor person's wealth").

Family-planning programs have been criticized for overemphasizing fertility reduction and paying too little attention to women's general health. The many health risks associated with going through the process of conception, gestation, and delivery tend to be ignored by clinicians who dispense birth-control information and devices and then consider their work done. However, we know very well that the distribution of birth-control methods does not guarantee that they will be used. Thus, the clinician's failure to consider reproductive health, or other aspects of their clients' physical and mental condition, is unfounded. In addition, the focus on preventing fertility with little if any emphasis on or concern for the rights of women to make reproductive decisions raises questions about the broad goals of family-planning programs and the movement for gender equality. As Angela Davis (1981:202) noted several years ago, "Birth control—individual choice, safe contraceptive methods, as well as abortion when necessary—is a fundamental prerequisite for the emancipation of women."

When the sole objective of population policy is fertility reduction, the physical, mental and social wellbeing of women during their reproductive years tend to be overlooked. It is for this reason that the 1995 Population Conference held in Beijing, China, called for a broader definition of family planning to include reproductive-health concerns (Pillai and Wang 1999). Along with the widely heralded breakthroughs and successes credited to the family-planning movement, the development of contraceptive technology has also taken place at the cost of ill health among many powerless and impoverished women. New drugs and methods for birth control, such as Norplant and Depo-Provera, are tested in countries in which poorly informed women participate in clinical trials that have resulted in illness. The story of Mrs. Li Aihai from China, reproduced in Box 11.4, dramatically underscores the potentially dangerous side of the family-planning movement today (Mosher 2002).

Box 11.4   The Story of Li Aihai

The Chinese Model

Li Aihai, happily married and the mother of a 2½-year-old girl, had a problem. She was four months pregnant with her second child. Sihui County family-planning officials had come to her home and told her what she already knew: she had gotten pregnant too soon. She hadn't waited until her daughter was four years old, as Chinese law required of rural couples. The officials assured her that, because her first child had been a girl, she would eventually be allowed a second child. But they were equally insistent that she would have to abort this one. It was January, 2010.

She pleaded that she had not intended to get pregnant. She was still wearing the IUD that they had implanted in her after the birth of her first child, as the law required. They were unsympathetic. Report to the family-planning clinic tomorrow morning, they told her as they were leaving. We'll be expecting you.

Aihai Fights to Save Her Baby

Aihai had other plans. Leaving her little daughter in the care of her husband, she quietly packed her things and went to stay with relatives in a neighboring county. She would hide until she brought her baby safely into the world. Childbirth-on-the-run, it was called.

When the county family-planning officials discovered that Aihai had disappeared, they began arresting her relatives. While her father-in-law managed to escape with her daughter, her mother-in-law and brother-in-law were arrested. Her own mother and father, brother and sister, and three other relatives were also imprisoned over the next few weeks. In all, nine members of her extended family were arrested, hostages to the abortion that was being demanded of her.

But Aihai, knowing that her family supported her pregnancy, stayed in hiding. And her relatives, each refusing to tell the officials where she had gone to hide, stayed in jail.

Three months later the family planning officials struck again. The date they chose, April 5, was an important one on the Chinese traditional calendar. It was the festival of Qingming, or "bright and clear," a day on which rural Chinese men, by ancient custom, "sweep the graves" of their ancestors. Starting with the grave of their own deceased parents, they visit in turn the graves of grandparents, great-grandparents, and ancestors even further removed. At each stop they first clean off the headstones and weed the plot, then set out a feast for the deceased, complete with bowls of rice, cups of rice liquor, and sticks of incense.

Why did the family-planning officials pick this day of all days? Was it a further insult to the family, several of whom were languishing in their jail? Or was the day chosen for a very practical reason: with most of the men and boys away in the hills feting their ancestors, the village would be half-deserted, and they could carry out their plan without opposition.

The family-planning officials came to the village in the company of a wrecking crew armed with crowbars and jackhammers. These fell upon Aihai's home like a horde of angry locusts. They shattered her living room and bedroom furniture into pieces. They ripped window frames out of walls and doors off of hinges. Then the jackhammers began to pound, shattering the brick walls, and knocking great holes in the cement roof and floors. By the time they completed their work of destruction, you could stand on the first floor of Aihai's home and look up through two stories and the roof to the blue sky above. The wrecking crew then moved on to her parents' house, and then to her in-laws'. At day's end, three homes lay in ruins. The family-planning officials confiscated the family's livestock and poultry, then disappeared.

Aihai remained in hiding, out of reach of the family-planning officials, for two more months. It wasn't until her child was actually born, she knew, that he would be safe. Abortions in China are performed up to the very point of parturition, and it is not uncommon for babies to be killed by lethal injection even as they descend in the birth canal. Only after she had given birth—to a beautiful baby boy—did she make plans to return home.

Aihai Returns Home

Aihai came back to find her family in prison, her home destroyed, and family-planning officials furious that she had thwarted their will. Underlying their anger was hard calculation: every "illegal" child born in their county was a black mark on their performance, depressing annual bonuses and threatening future promotions. But family-planning officials, like most Chinese officials, have access to other sources of income. If you want your relatives released, they now told Aihai, you must pay a fine of 17,000 Renminbi (about U.S. $2,000). Now this is a huge sum by Chinese standards, the equivalent of two or three years' income. It was many days before she was able to beg and borrow enough from family and friends to satisfy the officials' demands, and win her family's release.

No sooner had she paid one fine than she was told she owed another, if she wanted to regularize her son's status. He was currently a "black child," family-planning officials explained to her. Because he was conceived outside of the family-planning law, he did not exist in the eyes of the state. As a nonperson, he would be turned away from the government clinic if he fell ill, barred from attending a government school of any kind, and not considered for any kind of government employment later in life. He would not even be allowed to marry or start a family of his own. The government had decreed that "black children" would not be allowed to reproduce; one generation of illegals was enough. There was an out, however. If she was able to pay another fine of 17,000 RMB her son would be issued a national identity number, and would be treated like everyone else—almost. She would still be required to pay double fees for his school supplies.

She was not surprised when she was ordered to report for sterilization. The population-control regulations, she knew, were unyielding in this regard. Two children and your tubes are tied. This time she made no effort to resist the authorities. Having a second child had bankrupted her family. Having a third was out of the question. Her newborn son would have no younger siblings.

Source: From Mosher, Steven W. "The Population Controllers and Their War on People." *PRI Review: 2002* 12(5) September/October. Retrieved May 15, 2015 (http://pop.org/content/population -controllers-and-their-war-1422).

Along with the widely heralded breakthroughs and successes credited to the family-planning movement, the development of contraceptive technology has also taken place at the cost of ill health among many powerless and impoverished women. New drugs and methods for birth control, such as Norplant and Depo-Provera, are tested in countries in which poorly informed women participate in clinical trials that have resulted in illness.

SUMMARY

We introduced this chapter with the observation that, by the time you had finished reading it, you would be better sensitized to the fact that the study of human populations today is many times more complicated than the study of animal populations. The reasons for this higher degree of complexity should now be apparent. Like other animals, humans mate, reproduce, age, move from place to place, get sick, and eventually die. However, unlike other animals, people seek to control each of these processes, to "enhance" the natural flow of life, sometimes unconsciously, sometimes with definite purposes in mind; sometimes informally and on an individual basis, and sometimes formally and collectively. In the last case, formally and collectively, the main vehicles whereby we seek control are policies and the laws based upon them. Thus, as interesting and important as it may be to observe and measure a particular human population's fertility levels or migration patterns, it is equally necessary to understand that some members of that population are busy creating policies they hope will change the rates and patterns being observed.

KEY TERMS

agenda setting

commons

efficiency evaluation

impact evaluation

implementation

International Planned Parenthood
    Federation (IPPF)

nongovernmental organization (NGO)

optimum population size

postpartum abstinence

process evaluation

program evaluation

quasi-experimental designs

sustainable population size

United Nation's Fund for Population
    Activities (UNFPA)

United States Agency for International
    Development (USAID)

NOTES

1. Education is an important factor because the indirect pressure to have large families is nearly irresistible—even if a couple does not set out with a large family in mind.

2. The likely status of a population at a future date is often assessed through the use of projection techniques, as we noted in Chapter 10. If the projected size of the general population or an important subpopulation (such as urban dwellers) is deemed to exceed accepted norms, preventative policies may be initiated to avoid probable, undesirable changes.

3. This should be distinguished from postpartum *insusceptibility*, a highly variable physical condition of actual sterility following birth. Although it clearly has some effect on the spacing of children, some women appear not to experience it at all. In any case, it is insignificant in comparison to the purposeful avoidance of intercourse during the period of nursing.

4. This apparent lack of interest in promoting traditional methods of birth control is reminiscent of the elitist, pro-Western, prourban biases in family-planning programs identified several years ago in India by Mahamood Mamdani (1972).

5. In cultures and subcultures in which childbearing prior to marriage is considered acceptable, or is even encouraged, efforts to delay marriage do not, in principle, have an effect on total fertility. Nevertheless, single mothers do not consistently have large families—especially young mothers who continue to reside with their parents (London 1998; Lundberg and Pollak 2013).

6. ACLU, https://www.aclu.org/immigrants-rights.

7. Statement by Dr. David D. Kaunda to the World Population Conference, Mexico City, August 6–14, 1984. Document circulated at the National Seminar on Population and Development Policy, Lusaka, December 9–11, 1985.

8. Statement delivered by Honorable Mrs. B. C. Kankasa, M.C.C., Chairman of the Woman's Affairs Committee, patron of the Planned Parenthood Association of Zambia to the World Population Conference, Mexico City, August 9, 1984 (pp. 5–6). Document circulated at the National Seminar on Population and Development Policy, Lusaka, December 9–11, 1985.

9. "Kankasa Nods Sex Tips Call." *Times of Zambia*, March 30, 1984. "Family Planning Vital—PPAZ." *Times of Zambia*, April 1, 1984. "Women Told to Practise Child

Spacing." *Times of Zambia*, July 6, 1984. "Plan Your Family." *Daily Mail*, September 26, 1984. "Let's Have a Birth Policy." *Times of Zambia*, April 8, 1985.

10. Report of the Seminar on Population and Development Policy, Lusaka, December 9–11, 1985:23.

11. The IPPF is the oldest voluntary organization involved in promoting family-planning services globally.

12. Earl Babbie (1997, chap. 13) provides an excellent basic introduction that includes an outline of the approach, numerous examples and illustrations, and an extensive bibliography.

13. This is ordinarily fairly easy to show, but it is not automatic. Imagine, for instance, that a clever group of family-planning clinicians learns that birth rates are going down in a nearby village. They then rush to the village, set up a clinic, wait a reasonable amount of time, and take credit for the success of their program. Evaluation researchers must be alert to these and more subtle circumstances in which the sequence of events can be confused.

CHAPTER TWELVE

POPULATION AND ENVIRONMENT

This chapter is about people: about the 6 billion of us who now inhabit the planet, our production and consumption behavior, and the impact of this behavior on the environment. In the course of this discussion, we consider some of the major issues associated with the most essential of our resources. These include (1) water consumption, (2) **deforestation**, and (3) energy use. In light of these specific problem areas, we continue with a review of some of the leading current theories of the population/environment interface. Next, we take up the challenging problem of measuring environmental characteristics and impacts. The chapter concludes with an overview of contemporary environmental politics and policies, including a set of agenda items for **sustainable development**. Before turning to more technical matters, however, we begin with a personal anecdote about the complex relationship between production, consumption, and environmental impact to which you can all relate in one way or another.

THE TEA-SELLER'S DILEMMA

In 1994, one of the authors (VKP) was traveling in India from Mumbai to Pune in the State of Maharashtra. He had taken this scenic train route several times before, through the Western Ghats region well known to tourists for its steep hills and narrow river valleys. The train stops at several stations between Pune and Mumbai. At each station peddlers bring their goods to the doors and windows of the train to sell to the travelers: snacks, drinks, souvenirs, and the like. During all of his previous trips along this route, the author had joined many of his fellow passengers in purchasing tea from such vendors. And on each occasion, the tea was served in a small, unglazed kiln-fired cup. It had been common practice for the passengers to toss the cup on the ground of the station platform or on the tracks after they finished their tea. The cup shatters upon impact with the ground and, in a couple of days, it becomes dust—returning to the earth whence it came.

On the trip in 1994, the author was shocked to see his tea served in a Styrofoam cup. He noticed that, as usual, several passengers tossed their cups outside the train. But this time the cups did not shatter and begin to decompose. Instead, they either lay where they were thrown or local boys who hung around the station to scavenge collected them (and whatever else they could find). Of course, Styrofoam is not biodegradable like clay. It is mass-produced from scarce petroleum products and, by

Indian standards, it is relatively expensive. Clay cups are cheap and they are—that is, were—produced by local village women who earned their living making teacups and other small pottery items. Moreover, the clay cups are intended for a single use and are paid for by the consumer as part of the price of the tea. But the author could not be sure that his Styrofoam cup was never used before. If these cups were being recycled intact (which is likely, assuming that the scavengers have a market for their goods), then the switch to Styrofoam can easily contribute to an epidemic.

Clay cups are cheap and nonpolluting. Styrofoam cups are polluting, as they are not easily degradable. So, what is the attraction of Styrofoam? A large part of the answer to what is more or less the question of our era is that clay cups are old fashioned. They are an artifact of traditional, rural culture; they are crude (*kaacha*, in Hindustani), and they are not advertised in association with the "good life." A Styrofoam cup stands for that which is modern. It is manufactured, advertised, urban, and stylish. In comparison to the rough pottery formerly used, it is refined (*pukka*). The choice that the tea-sellers in the train stations of India have made symbolizes the kinds of choices being made by people everywhere and in a wide range of circumstances.

With modernity and affluence has come an apparent disregard for the environment in which we live and a lack of concern about conserving its resources. In the highly industrialized nations of the world, such as the United States, the capacity to exploit the environment has evolved to become a vast potential to destroy the air, the seas, and our other most valuable resources. Yet, for several decades it has been abundantly clear that the pressures of interpersonal relations and the powerful appeal of mass advertising have turned us into a society of **Waste Makers** (Packard 1971).[1] We consume frantically and then throw "away" the items we no longer want. But, as the pioneering environmentalist Barry Commoner once pointed out, there is no "away" to receive our waste; it all remains "here" (Commoner 1966). In the poorer developing countries like India, people appear to be in a big hurry to catch up with their wealthier cousins abroad. Now greatly assisted by cable TV and the Internet, models for the latest styles and fashions are instantaneously and widely available, including models of environmental destruction and wasteful consumption.

This chapter examines in some detail what might be termed the tea-seller's dilemma, which of course is everyone's dilemma. It is our hope that it will give you a clearer understanding of the complex dimensions of this relatively simple-to-describe set of issues; and that you will have a better idea of what you can do about it. Because this is a book on demography, our main interest is in how population growth and distribution enter into the environment/consumption dilemma. But, because of the complexity of the problems, it will also be necessary to place demographic factors in the background from time to time. We do this with the understanding that if there were fewer people in the world, if their habits and values were to change suddenly, and if the largest and poorest populations were not growing so rapidly, many of these problems would dissolve.

THE HOUSEHOLD OF NATURE:
THE PLIGHT OF NATURAL RESOURCES

The relationship between population growth and environment is complex. This complexity that is forcefully argued by the set of social scientific theories associated with the ecological paradigm. Early in the twentieth century, the evolutionary biologist Ernst Haeckel (1834–1919) coined the term **ecology** (Haeckel 1917).[2] It is taken from the Greek root word *oikos*, meaning "household," the same root as in *economics*. Ecology is the science of the household (and "economics" refers to its laws), in which the household symbolizes nature or a portion of nature, referred to as an **ecosystem** or, more broadly, an environment. The analogy here is that one's home is made up of parts, such as rooms (called *niches*), hallways, and so on, and that each part has specific functions and is reserved for certain occupants and their activities. In a well-functioning household, all of the parts and occupants exist in a harmonious balance, and things go smoothly. But, because each element depends on every other, when something goes wrong in one "room," the entire household is affected and can become imbalanced. These notions of (1) mutual influence among parts and the whole and (2) "a place for everything and everything in its place" constitute the core premises of contemporary ecological studies.

Today, ecology has developed into the science of the relationships among living things and their environments. The two parts, organisms and environments, are assumed to be inseparable. In addition, we understand that the environment of any given organism includes other organisms as well as geophysical features such as the land and water. As the organisms of an ecosystem reproduce, age, and die, the physical environment undergoes transformations (water is used, etc.), which in turn affect the activities and the well-being of the organisms. It is, in brief, a highly interactive (eco-) system.

Since the 1950s, or even earlier, the ecological perspective has influenced the study of the relationship between *human beings* and their environments. In the early 1950s, the sociologist and demographer, Otis Dudley Duncan (1954) introduced the concept of the *ecological complex* to emphasize the systemic, interdependent nature of the population/environment relationship. Figure 12.1 shows an updated version of Duncan's model and the associated POET acronym. Based on this model and the premises of mutual influence and a place for everything, three principles underlying the operation of ecosystems have been articulated:

1. Everything is related to everything else. The world is a web of relationships.
2. Nothing in nature grows indefinitely. This idea is contained in the concept of **carrying capacity** discussed earlier (see Carrying Capacity Network 1997). Checks and balances operate so that the number of prey-organisms in any given area is dependent upon the number of predators. If a very large increase occurs in the size of the predator population, the population size of prey will shrink rapidly and face extinction. As human populations grow, and more and more forestland is converted to agricultural uses, topsoil will be lost due to erosion.
3. Relationships between organisms and their environment are very complex. This means that interventions into such relationships between organisms and environment are likely to have more effects than are immediately apparent. Thus there are always unintended consequences (including negative consequences, or dysfunctions) of human actions aimed at altering the environment. Technological interventions are often based on simple models, which, according to ecologists, will yield unknown and often catastrophic results.

As we examine the relationship between population size and specific aspects of the physical environment, we will keep in mind these broad ecological principles. The last principle, in particular, tells us that many of the effects of population on

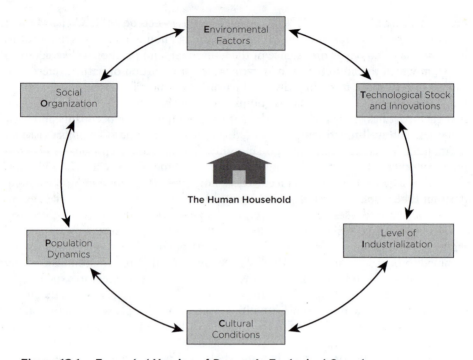

Figure 12.1.   Expanded Version of Duncan's Ecological Complex
Source: © United Nations Department of Economic and Social Affairs, 2014, https://sustainable
development.un.org/sdgsproposal (accessed May 15, 2015).

environment will remain unknown because of complexity. This should serve to warn us that those who claim to know how things will turn our in this realm (whether they are optimistic or pessimistic) must be speaking metaphorically or prophetically, but surely nor as empirical scientists. The following sections focus on a few of the more-publicized effects of population growth on components of our physical environment: water, forests, and energy. The first two obviously are necessary for sustaining life, per se; and the last, energy, is—for better or worse—a necessary part of modern-day life.

Fresh Water

In our discussion of urbanization in Chapter 4, we saw that throughout the world the earliest cities were established in river valleys. In fact, virtually all human settlements are located in areas where fresh water is available. When this is not possible, as in the cases of cities in Saudi Arabia and Israel's Negev region, technological solutions are implemented to overcome the scarcity. The main source of our freshwater supply is ultimately precipitation. Because of the well-known water cycle, the amount of water on the Earth remains a constant. Water evaporates from lakes and rivers, and from the seas as well. Trees transpire and put a large quantity of water into the air. The water in the atmosphere that accumulates through evaporation and transpiration precipitates and produces rain. The rain enters the lakes and rivers and is absorbed through the roots of trees. And so the cycle continues. In the past, the likelihood of pollutants entering into the water cycle was low. But today industries produce a considerable amount of chemical waste, which is likely to come in contact with the fresh water supply. Dangerous gases that are output into the atmosphere dissolve as precipitation occurs. These "acid rains" have significantly altered the chemical composition of lakes in Canada, the United States, the Scandinavian countries, and other places, making some inhospitable to any form of aquatic life.

The world's annual fresh water supply is about 110,000 cubic kilometers. Nearly two-thirds of this is lost to evaporation, leaving a net supply of about 40,000 cubic kilometers. Approximately two-thirds of this quantity, or 26,000 cubic kilometers, is not available for human consumption, either because it is held in swamps or wasted by floods. Of the 14,000 cubic kilometers of fresh water available for consumption, 5,000 cubic kilometers are lost in regions where human population is very thinly distributed. It is estimated that as of the year 2000 all of the available fresh water was in use (Ambroggi 1980; Gleick and Heberger 2011). Not only is water scarce, but the supplies that do exist are not equally distributed among regions and nations. Some nations, such as the United States, have adequate-to-plentiful water resources, but others suffer from acute water scarcity. The semiarid and arid regions with large populations and low levels of economic development, including Saharan Africa and India, do not receive adequate rainfall and chronically experience near-drought conditions. M. Fallenmark and associates (1989) have argued that by 2025 nearly 1.1 billion persons will be living in countries with widespread water scarcities. In addition, both developed and developing countries with plentiful fresh water are increasingly more likely to pollute supply systems.

As indicated earlier, water quality is very easily destroyed by pollutants, of which there are several types. Among the best known are industrial products, petroleum, sewage, inorganic chemicals, fertilizers, and radioactive substances. The three major sources of these pollutants are municipal wastes, industrial output, and agricultural byproducts. Municipal pollution originates from wastewater from homes and commercial establishments. The nature of industrial pollution varies from industry. Chemical industries generate a large amount of organic and inorganic effluence, which ultimately gets released into the river systems, whereas nuclear industries produce wastes with radioactive ingredients. Agricultural pollution consists of both organic and inorganic substances used as fertilizers and pesticides. Most fertilizers are composed of nitrates and phosphorous, both of which are highly destructive to fresh water systems. With increasing levels of development, corporate farming, and a rising demand for high-productivity yields, there has been a steady growth in the use of fertilizers globally. When rain falls over vast agricultural lands that are fertilized, run-offs are produced that contain high concentrations of chemicals.

The presence of inorganic elements and compounds, such as nitrates, in drinking water is harmful to health. Until a few decades ago, such problems were of little concern to the average person. But today, the threat of being poisoned by drinking from one's own kitchen tap is quite real. According to research recently conducted by students and faculty in an Iowa school district, in the Midwest a glass of drinking water during the first half of the twentieth century contained small traces of three or four different pesticides. A 1998 study of water quality in the Little Miami Basin found that a glass of sample water from the basin contained measurable amounts of different pesticides and metallic elements.[3] An Internet posting by Environment Canada, entitled "Clean Water—Life Depends on It," reports that over 360 chemical compounds have been identified in the Great Lakes.[4] Because of the increase in the number of chemical agents in tap water (and other factors as well, such as style), Americans now consume about 25 liters of bottled water per person annually.

Ultimately, water pollution is a side effect of the production, distribution, and consumption of goods and services. The amount of water pollution increases as population size increases, even when the production and consumption of goods does not vary or varies only slightly. The same result would be obtained if the consumption of goods and services increased while the population size remained stable. The magnitude of the global water-pollution problem can be gauged by considering the fact that it is the result of both increasing population size and increases in consumption brought about by modernization and development. Growing populations most directly impact municipal and agricultural pollution, whereas industrial pollution is the product of activities and practices stimulated by economic development and modernization.

Depletion of Forests

The term *deforestation* has been defined in several ways. One definition describes it as an essentially natural, peaceful process of gradual transformation from one land use to another. This emphasizes the fact of change from forest to agriculture, including shifting land from cultivation to use as pasture. Deforestation can also be a more dramatic type of change from forest to plantation, or to industry, or to urban land. And for some people, the term conjures a violent image of commercial lumbering firms employing mass-production methods to strip an area clean and then move on to the next stand of trees waiting to be exploited. Of the 6,750,000 square miles of forests that once covered the Earth, 60 percent has now been lost to deforestation—in all senses of the term. About 97 percent of the world's tropical forests are located in some 75 countries. Between 1976 and 1980, the average annual rate of tropical deforestation was about 0.6 percent. During the 1980s, this rate increased to just less than 1.0 percent annually. The deforestation rate is highest in Asia, followed by Latin America, and then Africa (FAO 1991:118). Several years ago, Norman Myers (1979) predicted that by year 2040, rainforests would have virtually disappeared if the present rate of deforestation continues. Thus far, there has been no reason to revise his forecast.

One of the most direct causes of deforestation is population pressure. As population density increases, the demand for shelter and inexpensive energy sources, such as firewood and charcoal, increases. This eventuates in the elimination of large tracts of trees and, eventually, the cutting down of entire forests. Increasing numbers of people raise the demand for food, which, in turn, creates the need to expand the acreage under cultivation. Forests are thus cleared to make room for agriculture. And the demand for land on which to grow food crops is not the only source of pressure. Most populations also depend on cattle and other stock animals as a source of food, so that the number and the size of domestic herds are likely to increase with population growth.

Such activity ordinarily results in overgrazing and the subsequent loss of soil. According to world resource experts Robert Livernash and Eric Rodenberg (1998:19), a leading study known as the Global Assessment of Soil Degradation (GLASOD) estimated that 17 percent of the Earth's vegetated land area was degraded; 10 percent was classified as moderately or severely degraded. Land is considered degraded if the chemical, physiological, or biological characteristics of the land have been altered and fertility compromised (Livermash and Rodenberg 1998; Sanderson 2013). GLASOD found the causes of land degradation almost equally divided among overgrazing of livestock, agricultural activities, and forest practices.

With diminishing quantities of nondegraded agricultural and pastureland, combined with an increasing demand for food, people turn back to the forests to clear additional plots. It is just this sort of viscous cycle that has brought about massive deforestation and loss of arable soil in the Andes of Peru, the Ethiopian Amhara Plateau, the Kenyan Rift Valley, and the Ugandan highlands.

Although population growth is a major cause of deforestation, it does not function in isolation from cultural, economic, and political conditions. If people are hungry because there are so many more mouths to feed, they *could* flee to a neighboring country as refugees, they *could* stop having so many children, they *could* become vegetarians, or they *could* move to the capital city and raid the supermarkets.[5] But they do not do these things because these are not viable options given the people's values, their economic conditions, and their political and social milieux. Thus, the reasonable—perhaps the only realistic—course of action is to clear more land.

In addressing the other parameters of the deforestation crisis, Robert Deacon (1994a, b) has argued that political insecurity and instability are associated with unstable ownership laws. When people feel insecure in protecting and safeguarding the properties and resources they own, their strategies of resource consumption are likely to be short term and oriented toward the immediate future (Deacon 1994a, b; Redo, Millington, and Hindery 2011). Both the type of political regime under which people live and the degree of political instability significantly influence the rates at which forest resources are consumed. In nondemocratic societies, property-ownership laws are weak and property is not secure. Deforestation rates are high in these societies. During political turmoil, resource consumption becomes intense and conservation for the future is less of a priority. Deforestation is more likely to occur during such periods of instability.

Socioeconomic development and urbanization are closely associated with deforestation. The demand for paper and wood increases in direct proportion to economic growth and to growth in the urban sector. In nearly every developing country, trees are cut without remorse to make way for parking lots and highways. Deforestation rates increase as modernization and industrialization introduce new technologies for cutting, felling, and transporting trees. Much of the deforestation currently underway in the Brazilian Amazon region is the result of an enthusiastic program of road-network expansion (Pfaff 1997).[6]

Although development specialists and local groups who realize immediate benefit from the removal of trees many not view their activities as detrimental, there are substantial costs involved. For example, deforestation threatens the sustainability of life by reducing the amount of rainfall annually. About one-quarter of the earth's land surface is forested. As we noted, these forests play a crucial role in the water cycle through the process of transpiration. The loss of forest will lead to a break in the water cycle. If this happens, the fresh water supply will be reduced dramatically. Another consequence of deforestation is the decrease in **biodiversity**. The removal of trees results in the destruction of habitats of rare species of animals, birds, and plants. Eventually, these species will vanish, as they are unable to adapt to their changed physical environment.

As suggested earlier, both population growth and development can lead to deforestation. The effects of these two well know causes are often indirect (Myers 1995; Humphreys 2014). The impact of population growth on denudation of forests depends partly on the diet of the people involved. Norman Myers (1995) has shown that there is a connection, which he calls "the hamburger connection," between the disappearance of forests in Costa Rica and the demand for beef in the United States. In 1960, Costa Rica possessed about 400,000 square kilometers of moist forests. Twenty years later, the country had lost nearly one-half of the forest area to cattle ranching, which emerged as the major export sector of the Costa Rican economy. The beef was exported to markets in the North America. Thus the connection: As the demand for hamburgers increased in the United States and Canada, the proportion of forest area in Costa Rica decreased. Here is further evidence that the relationship between population growth and deforestation is neither simple, nor direct, nor inevitable (see Pfaff 1977).

Energy

Energy, in its most basic sense, is the capacity to do work. It is required if we are to engage in the daily activities of life. The main source of energy for humans and other animals are the carbon compounds and trace minerals in food. Energy is also a necessary component in the production, distribution, and consumption of food. If all members of a population—including the world's population—consumed goods and services in the same proportion, then an increase in its size would translate into an increase in the use of energy. Increases in energy use also result when the members of a stable population increase the amount of goods and services they consume.

As in the cases of water and forests, the demand for energy is growing as a result of both of these causes. And, to make matters even more difficult, the proportional shares of energy consumption are grossly unequal: as the wealthiest one-third of the world's population consuming about three-fourths of the commercial energy (World Resources Institute 1992:144). World energy demand will increase to 820 quadrillion British thermal units in 2040 from 524 quadrillion in 2010, an increase of 56 percent. A large proportion of this increase will be due to energy demand from India and China. In 2010, these two countries accounted for 24 percent of world energy consumption. Table 12.1 provides a vivid sense of this imbalance with per-capita figures from 2010. Per-capita energy consumption in multiples of the per-capita consumption in low-income countries is presented in column. Middle-income countries consume about 3.5 times the energy consumed in low-income countries. The comparable figures for high income and the United States respectively are 14 and 20, approximately.

People have a wide variety of energy needs: household energy such as gas for cooking and heating; commercial energy for mass production of industrial goods; energy for daily transportation needs, and so on. In 2011, about 82 percent of the world energy resources was from fossil fuels, 11 percent from renewable other than large hydro, 5 percent from nuclear, and 2 percent from hydro.[7]

As Table 12.1 suggests, on average, individuals in high-income countries consume more than 13 times the commercial energy used by people from low-income regions. And such comparisons understate the differences because they assume that the sources of commercial energy are the same in the more and the less-developed countries, which is not true. It is well known that about 90 percent of the households in the rural villages of India and Africa use traditional fuels such as firewood, cow dung, and charcoal. Nearly all of the commercial energy sources are consumed by the industrial and urban sectors in such places. On the whole (not per capita), the dependence on oil as an energy source in developing countries is similar to that of

Table 12.1. Energy Consumption in Kilograms of Oil Equivalent Per Capita, 2010

Region	Per-Capita Energy Consumption	Multiples of Low-Income Per-Capita Energy Consumption
Low income	359.0	1.0
South Asia	555.0	1.54
Sub-Saharan Africa	681.0	1.90
Lower-middle income	686.0	1.91
Low and middle income	1179.0	3.28
Middle income	1280.0	3.57
Latin America and Caribbean	1292.0	3.60
Middle East and North Africa	1376.0	3.83
East Asia and Pacific	1671.0	4.65
World	1890.0	5.26
Upper-middle income	1893.0	5.27
Europe and Central Asia	2081.0	5.80
Euro area	3494.0	9.73
High income	4877.0	13.58
United States	7162.0	19.94

Source: U.N. Statistics Division and The World Bank, World Development Indicators.

developed countries. During the last decade, the developing world consumed roughly 66 percent of the oil as wealthier countries.

Consumption of energy resources such as oil and coal produces several undesirable chemical byproducts, including nitric oxide, particulate matter, and sulfur dioxide. These are extremely injurious to health, and excessive release of them into the atmosphere is a major cause of air pollution. Particulate matter may be the air pollutant that most commonly affects people's health. The amount of these pollutants released differs significantly between more- and less-industrialized countries, and they differ in *inverse* proportion to the relative rates of energy consumption. This indicates that in their sometimes desperate attempt to "catch up" with Western Europe, North America, and Japan, the governments and private sectors of the developing world are ignoring the serious costs of their ventures (as was the case during the early stages of industrialization in Europe, etc.). Table 12.2, which compares the rates of particulate matter in cities in the industrialized and industrializing countries, underscores this pattern.

The mean level of emissions in the industrializing countries is slightly less than twice that of the industrialized. Perhaps the most dramatic comparison is that between India, with an urban population size of 183 million and Sweden with about 2.6 million persons. The particulate-matter levels in the former are at least about seven times higher than those in the latter. Nearly all the cities in the industrializing countries have higher emission levels than their counterparts in Europe, North America, and Japan. With rapidly increasing levels of urbanization and consumption in the developing world, the pollution problem is bound to worsen in near the future. The difficult alternative is to follow the example of the developed countries, where pollution levels are kept under control with strict enforcement of emission laws—at a high cost and following decades of pollution at least as serious as that in Calcutta or Beijing today.

Table 12.2. Ambient Air Pollution in Industrialized and Industrializing Nations, 2004

Country	Urban Population (Millions)	(PM10) [μg/m^3][1]
Industrialized Countries		
Australia	13.51	18.0
Austria	3.01	33.0
Canada	24.09	22.0
Hungary	3.16	25.0
Japan	80.12	33.0
Sweden	2.64	13.0
Mean		24.0
Industrializing Countries		
Brazil	76.14	33.0
China	421.63	87.0
India	183.89	89.0
Iran	26.79	71.0
Korea, South	33.96	43.0
Venezuela	14.66	13.0
Mean		56.0

[1] Annual mean concentration of particulate matter of less than 10 microns of diamer.

Source: "Exposure Data by Country," Global Health Observatory Data Repository, World Health Organization.

THEORIES OF POPULATION AND ENVIRONMENT

The ecological principles and empirical observations we have been considering indicate that population size, socioeconomic development, and environmental quality are highly and complexly interrelated. To help us get a better understanding of this system, we now need to move to the theoretical level. We begin in a fairly abstract manner by focusing on only a few of the many possible variables that are involved. This approach enables us to isolate the key causal relationships, with the understanding that they do not exist in isolation from the other factors we are setting aside. As the discussion proceeds, we will then incorporate additional variables and connections that help to bring the theories closer to reality.

There are several theories that attempt to specify how population and development affect environmental quality. These may be grouped into two categories. The first category includes theories that focus on the *direct* relationship between population, development, and environment, which we will call "direct effect" theories. Those in the second category, which we will label "indirect effect" theories, consider several factors that intervene between the major components, operating "behind the scenes," so to speak.

Direct Effect Theories

The most popular explanation for environmental degradation today is the one inspired by the work of Thomas Robert Malthus some 200 years ago (see Chapters 2 and 11). Contemporary neo-Malthusians emphasize the negative effects of population growth on the environment and on a group's standard of living. A large and growing population is regarded as the principal determinant of poverty, water pollution, deforestation, degradation of air quality, and all other forms of environmental stress. As population size increases, it is argued, renewable resources are consumed at a pace faster than they can be replaced. Eventually, this race results in population crises. Malthus believed that these crises were manifested in war, pestilence, famine, vice and misery, which we refer to today as **ecological collapse** (UNFPA 2009; Pillai 1996). With an increase in death rates and a decline in reproductivity, the outcome of such a collapse is a decline in population growth and, ultimately, a decrease in population size—that is, until the next round of growth and crisis sets in.

The opposing school, represented by Julian Simon, argues in general that growth in population size is desirable. It suggests that societies have historically produced innovative solutions for social problems that confront them. From this perspective, as population size increases, so does the likelihood of solutions resulting from human ingenuity. Simon (1981) believed that the effect of population size on environment is poorly understood and that the negative effect of population size on environment depends upon a number of prevailing social and economic conditions. Although the neo-Malthusian position has captured the imaginations of many experts and laypersons alike, Simon's views are being taken with increasing seriousness. Livernash and Rodenberg (1998:24) report on a well-publicized confrontation between Simon and the leading neo-Malthusian and author of *The Population Bomb*, Paul Ehrlich, to make this point.

> In 1980, Paul Ehrlich made a public bet with Julian Simon about future trends in mineral resources. Ehrlich bet that increasing shortages would push up the prices of five metals—copper, chrome, nickel, tin, and tungsten—between 1980 and 1990. Simon bet that the prices would go down because of technological improvements in mining and resource use. Simon won the bet handily and gained considerable media attention. In the 1990s, known reserves of many natural resources are generally more abundant and prices generally higher than they were 20 years ago, despite rising consumption.

Between the extremes of the neo-Malthusian and the anti-Malthusian positions is a set of specialized theories that focus on one or more elements of the ecological complex (diagrammed in Figure 12.1). One such theory views environmental degradation as an inverse function of technological efficiency. That is, less-efficient production techniques use more scarce resources and produce larger quantities of pollutants that despoil water, air, and topsoil. This partly explains the differences in particulate matter output shown in Table 12.2, above. We see that the least-developed areas, which, one can presume, have the least-efficient industrial technologies, also have the highest rates of pollution. This perspective essentially leans in an optimistic direction because several technological solutions are currently available to reduce the amount of energy consumed and the pollutants produced. Moreover, environmental protection agencies in many developed countries, where most of the energy comes from fossil fuels (Gallopin 1992; Forsyth 2013) encourage industries to use efficient, energy-reducing technologies (Hughes 1991; Mosher and Corscadden 2012).

A related explanation proposes that the process of urban growth, resulting from industrialization in both developed and less-developed countries, produces environmental degradation. Proponents of this argument suggest that the effects of large-scale urbanization on the environment are more significant than the impact of sheer population size. Also, in comparison to those who live in rural areas, urban dwellers consume large amounts of energy, per capita, in order to sustain their life styles and higher standards of living. Thus, an increase in the proportion of a population living in urban areas increases the demand for energy and raises the levels of environmental pollution—and, in direct and indirect ways, it threatens forest resources (Teitelbaum 1974; Cassen 1976; Bongaarts and Sinding 2011).

Barry Commoner (1992) has proposed another theory that indicts modern life styles as the main source of environmental damage. He argues, flatly, that affluence causes pollution. This connection between population and pollution is expressed in the form of an identity:

$$\text{EI} = (\text{Population Size}) \times (\text{Level of Affluence}) \times (\text{Level of Technology})$$

EI stands for "Environmental Impact." In general, an increase in per-capita income is followed by an increase in consumption. And a change in consumption patterns tends to generate more pollution (Commoner 1992; Pearce, Barbier, and Markandya 2013). For example, it has been shown that economic growth rapidly increases the concentration level of carbon dioxide in the atmosphere (Legget 1990; Billett 2010). This perspective leans in the pessimistic direction, because it assumes that high levels of economic growth (per-capita income increases) are not sustainable environmentally. Supporters of the "affluence is polluting" argument suggest that the rapid economic development and standard of living to which the industrialized countries have become accustomed will cause ecological collapse in the long run. Furthermore, they warn, developing countries should not aspire to reach the level of affluence the developed countries have already reached (an argument that, as you can imagine, has not been well received in the developing world).

Indirect Effect Theories

The social demographer Ester Boserup (1981) has argued that Malthus did not foresee the technological revolution of the twentieth century. In her view, an increase in population growth rates and density does not inevitably lead to disaster. Instead, these changes trigger technological changes. The Green Revolution yielded multifold increases in agriculture production globally (see Karim 1986). It was made possible by innovations in the fields of agronomy, engineering, genetics, and in the use of fertilizers and pesticides. The Green Revolution saved millions of people from starvation and the disasters believed to be inherent in the exponential growth of population. Boserup reformulated the Malthusian argument by proposing technological change as an intervening variable according to the thesis: (1) population growth induces technological change, (2) the latter effects the environment to (3) increase productivity and, thus, (4) feed the growing population. Rather than forecasting certain crisis, this theory points to an economic response to population growth, as those affected attempt to increase the supply of food by improving technological efficiency.

The **multiphasic response model** (MRM) is essentially a modification of Boserup's theory, although its original formulation predates Boserup's work by several years. The model was originally outlined by Kingsley Davis (1963) in his foundation study of demographic transition. Davis observed that as the countries of Europe and North America achieved their maximum rates of population growth during the mid-nineteenth century, social and cultural changes took effect that eventuated in fertility declines and, soon thereafter, stabilization of population growth rates. The current version of the MRM proposes that increases in population size intensify competition for scarce resources and impose stress on the resource systems. The perception of pressure on resources induces a number of demographic changes, such marital fertility decline, out-migration, and delayed marriage (Bilsborrow 1979, Drummond and Loveland 2010). Richard Bilsborrow (1979), who is responsible for synthesizing the MRM model and Boserup's theory, suggests that economic response and demographic response are likely to occur together in the context of perceived stress on the environment (Boserup 1981; Jiang and Hardee 2011). The choice of specific strategies, according to Bilsborrow, will be influenced by factors such as cultural variables, level of technology, and level of infrastructural development (see Table 12.3).

Several combinations of responses are possible. For example, the demographic response may be weak when the economic response is strong. Consider Zambia, an agricultural society whose rural population density is low and whose agricultural technology is traditional. According to the MRM, the Zambian population is more likely to respond to resource pressure by agricultural intensification rather than by fertility reduction or rural out-migration. The possibility of agricultural intensification depends upon infrastructural variables such as credit availability and patterns of land ownership. Moreover, because it is known that agricultural intensification can lead to deforestation and soil degradation, the alternative responses may be more attractive in practice than in theory.

Another indirect-effect theory proposes that a country's degree of socioeconomic independence determines the impact of its population on the environment. Most of the poor countries of the South are dependent on the powerful economies of the North as export markets, for development assistance loans, and for tourism dollars. This relationship imposes constraints on the use of local resources because of low levels of infrastructural development and/or lack of proprietary control over local resources. Deforestation in Latin America and Southeast Asia, as well as the loss of valuable wildlife through poaching in Africa, is tied to powerful business interests in the industrialized countries. This is not to say that the other factors we have considered play no role. But, according to this perspective, environmental

Table 12.3. The Theory of Multiphasic Response and Alternate Responses to High Rates of Population Growth

Type of Response	Response	Determinants of Response
Demographic	Declining mortality Declining fertility Changes in timing and likelihood of marriage	Changes in the level of agricultural technology
Economic	Land-use change Intensification of agriculture Move toward cash crops Rent land	Changes in social cultural practices Infrastructural and development
Demographic/Economic	Out-migration	Institutional factors Natural resource endowments Policy and political factors

Source: Adapted from Bilsborrow (1979:5).

degradation and resource scarcities in the developing world would not be nearly as acute if these countries had more control over their own economic destinies. Under current circumstances, however, economic dependency plays a powerful role in shaping the demographic and the environmental conditions throughout Asia, Africa, and Latin America (Jolly 1991; Taylor 2011).

MEASURING ENVIRONMENTAL CONDITIONS AND IMPACTS

The test of the value of theories such as those just reviewed often depends on our ability to measure the variables they specify. Whereas we are fairly confident that the size, growth rates, and other characteristics of populations can be measured—especially after having nearly completed reading an entire book on the subject, the other side of the equation, environment and resources, presents special challenges. In general, measurement is possible provided that two conditions are met. First, what is being measured is specifically known and can be directly or indirectly observed. Second, the unit of observation is clearly stated. Because the extent to which these conditions are satisfied varies from theory to theory and study to study, we are about to embark on a slightly tangential discussion in which we review some current procedures for defining units, observing, and—when possible—quantifying these observations.

Although we cannot cover every aspect of this important subject, we can refer you to some of the several national and international organizations that routinely publish quantitative measurements of resources and of environmental conditions. Among these, the World Resource Institute in Washington, DC (http://www.world-watch.org) provides some of the most comprehensive information on many variables, including land use and deforestation. In the United States, the Environmental Protection Agency (http://www.epa.gov) gathers data on a regular basis and also publishes findings on a very large number of environmental indicators. And, as we mentioned earlier, Environment Canada publishes much useful material for people interested in ecological issues, regardless of where they live.

Environmental research typically focuses on either (1) a geographic area or territory or (2) the individuals who inhabit a particular territory. Here we begin with a discussion of issues in measuring the characteristics of territory, that is, the geophysical environment. This is followed by a look at problems associated with measuring the human environment, at the individual level. In the latter instance, there is great interest today in assessing the risks posed by hazards such as pollutants on human health. Thus, the human aspect of environmental measurement is illustrated with some comments on the procedures of health risk assessment.

The Geophysical Environment

A close relationship exists between economy and environment. Ideally, a healthy economy should lead to, and be supported by, high environmental quality. A "healthy" economy is not necessarily a vastly wealthy one. In ecological terms, the manner in which wealth is invested and saved is more important than the sheer amount. Five leading features characterize the kind of high-quality environment that reflects this sort of effective investment:

- A variety of species and communities (Dasmann 1971; Goudie 2013)
- Pollutant free
- Contains resources essential for setting life in harmony
- Productive
- Sustains the optimum population sizes of its species
- Supports and maintains diversity among species and communities

Where all of these conditions are satisfied, quality of life is high. Where they are all compromised, serious problems are imminent. Between these extremes we have a rough but useful gauge to measure the health of an ecosystem.

A more precise approach to measurement along these dimensions involves obtaining data on pollutants, on the quality of life-sustaining elements such as air and water, on the degree of biodiversity, and on the quality and quantity of renewable and non-renewable resources available. Analyzed in this manner, it is possible to measure a particular aspect of the environment across all geographic units that constitute an area of interest. As we noted in Chapter 4, the units can be either administrative (such as counties) or those created by Census definitions (tracts, CMSAs, regions, etc.). For example, in each state in the United States, one can measure the amount of forested land at the county level. Although this procedure is straightforward if the environmental variable is localized (as a forest is), variables characterized by movement are difficult to measure. Air pollution presents one of the greatest challenges. Particulates such as sulfur dioxide and hydrogen sulfide are carried by wind, so that the area affected changes from moment to moment. For this purpose, and for obtaining measures of water pollution as well, the process of *monitoring* is required. With this approach, the researcher samples the affected parts of the environment at regular intervals and then calculates an average over several observations. Based on such procedures, estimates are derived that convey as accurately as possible the momentary conditions.

Because a polluted environment is an unhealthy environment, and because healthy workers contribute to economic growth, any measure of an economy should take into account environmental quality. Unfortunately, this rarely if ever occurs. The most common indicators of economic performance are gross national product (GNP) and gross domestic product (GDP). Having discussed and used the GNP measure in earlier chapters, we need only add that GDP is equal to GNP minus the value of goods and services involved in imports and exports. Like GNP, the measurement of GDP ignores the losses incurred in producing wealth. Also, with both measures, the amount of natural resources used in creating wealth is treated as current income, and not as a permanent loss. Neither GNP nor GDP distinguishes between desirable and undesirable economic activity, such as pollution. Pollution and environmental degradation are simply ignored when they occur during the course of production. For these reasons, alternatives are currently being developed that are modifications of the traditional GNP and GDP measures. They do take into consideration the loss of environment that occurs during the course of creation of wealth. One organization that is active in this endeavor to include ecological concerns in deriving economic indicators is the Canadian University Services Organization-International (CUSO).

Individual-Level Measures

The procedures involved in measuring the effect of environment on an individual come from the discipline of risk assessment. With this approach, the environment is seen as a complex system of interrelated elements, including air, water, soil, solar radiation, and human artifacts (e.g., cars). According to a leading handbook published by the U.S. Council on Environmental Quality (Cohrssen and Covello 1989; Smith 2013), risk assessment consists of four steps: (1) hazard identification, (2) toxicity assessment, (3) study of exposure, and (4) risk characterization. A hazard is a condition that can potentially cause harm or injury to a person.

When applying this procedure to the measurement of water quality, the first step is to identify one or more toxic substances in the water system. If several toxins are present, a subset consisting of those known to be more harmful than the rest is selected on the basis of toxicity, concentration, or quantity. The toxins that pose the greatest threat are called "indicator chemicals." The second step involves measuring the levels of toxins that cause adverse effect in the organism that ingests it. The allowable levels of toxins in the environment are published by the Environmental protection Agency. In the third step the extent of exposure to a given toxin or set of toxins is assessed. The final step is to create an index that makes use of data on toxicity and exposure.[8]

ENVIRONMENTAL POLICIES AND POLITICS

You will recall from Chapter 11 that policies are the product of political decisions in response to perceived, pressing social problems. With this in view, two key factors need to be considered as we review current environmental policies. These are (1) the political processes that influence these policies and (2) the programs and strategies proposed to achieve desired environmental goals.

The Political Context

Environmental resources such as clear air and drinkable water are scarce commodities. The competition for a good environment in which to live and rear one's children is intense. With high rates of population growth, steadily rising levels of air and water pollution, and increases in per-capita consumption, the demand for uncontaminated spaces grows apace. One direct consequence of this is the increasing cost of real estate and commercial property that meet high environmental standards. Throughout the world, the point has been reached at which wealthy people can enjoy good air and water while the poor are being pushed into areas where conditions are less than desirable.

The emergence of a highly inequitable distribution of ecological resources in favor of the rich and powerful has clear political implications. In democratic societies such as the United States, new environmental coalitions representing the interests of the poor are emerging. From them, from the media, and from other quarters wherein public opinion is formed, has come a relatively new understanding. That is, in addition to the personal and economic problems that plague our most disadvantaged citizens, they must now also cope with breathing the dirtiest air, walking on the most contaminated ground, and drinking the most toxic water. As the twenty-first century begins, the marginalization of the poor to environmentally undesirable spaces has become a top political priority and a serious social problem.

Access to any type of scarce resource is subject to the changing distribution of power among groups. The distribution of formal power in the United States is regulated by the Constitution, which has safeguards to minimize the accumulation of control in a few hands.[9] The American political process is designed to provide access to many political and interest groups in the competition for power and to discourage the emergence of any one group or coalition of groups as a major power bloc. The process of competition is unregulated on the premise that all individuals have the right to promote their own self-interests. Governmental intervention to regulate competition is believed to be unnecessary, as individuals are assumed to be self-sufficient and rational beings. In addition, the federalist form of government makes it difficult to articulate all-encompassing policies. These factors—the presence of multiple interest groups, concern about the emergence of political elites, emphasis on bounded governmental intervention, and federalism—all act to limit the ability of government to formulate and to implement definitive national policies in all spheres, and environmental policies in particular.

The U.S. political system is designed to protect the freedom of the individual at the cost of the community if necessary, even when the latter's interests are more pressing. This value orientation has both advantages and disadvantages, depending on one's political ideology. Clearly, many environmentalists find it to be frustrating when they perceive the need to impose sanctions on a factory that is polluting the air and water, while the factory's management finds it profitable to pollute. Environmental politics everywhere are shaped by a focus on discrete, short-term issues within political institutions that are conservative and stability-oriented. But environmental realities are dynamic and highly interconnected. The web of relationships among the physical, geological, chemical, and biological systems that constitute the environment is fragile and complex. As a result, piecemeal and short-term approaches to solving environmental problems are unlikely to succeed.

Even when it can be clearly demonstrated that high population-growth rates and runaway consumerism lead to environmental degradation, it is extremely difficult to translate these findings into policies. Political factors have a significant, independent influence on the formulation of policies and programs that address environmental issues. Recognition of these obstacles has become the catalyst for a fundamental shift in values in the United States and elsewhere.[10] Just as individualism and liberalism have been traditional core American values for generations, environmental conservation and protection are now emerging as new principles (not necessarily to replace or to compete with traditional ways but in addition to them). This value change is fueling new governmental policies that can be uniformly implemented across the country and throughout the world.

Of course, new values do not emerge from a vacuum. New social institutions are being created that educate the public about the dangers of environmental degradation; about replacing old technologies with new, environmentally friendly ones; and about person-environment linkages that constitute the basis for environmental values. These value shifts and institutional changes originate from many sources. However, most observers agree that the most important part of the foundation was laid at two major international conferences held in the latter part of the twentieth century: one in Stockholm, Sweden, in 1972 and the other in Rio de Janeiro, Brazil, in 1992. Each of these conferences produced a major document on environmental policy, now widely known as the **Stockholm Declaration** and the **Rio Declaration**, respectively.

The Stockholm Declaration includes 26 environmental principles classed into three general categories: (1) general environmental rights, (2) the rights of the human family to a healthy and productive environment, and (3) responsibilities. Principles 1 and 2 proclaim that all human beings have are entitled to freedom, equality, and adequate conditions of life in an environment conducive to personal dignity and wellbeing. In this regard, the Stockholm Conference focused mainly on the containment and prevention of industrial pollution. The argument was put forward that although national governments have the freedom to exploit their own resources, they also have the responsibility to ensure that developmental activities do not lead to environmental damage in other nations. This recommendation became basis of current customary international environmental laws.

The Rio Declaration contains 27 principles for environmental protection. This document provides conceptual, ethical, and ideological boundaries within which to think and talk about international environmental policies. One concept employed at Rio that represents the key to the relationship between economic growth and environment is *sustainable development*. The concept refers to a future-oriented approach to the use of natural resources that can continue from generation to generation. This is in contrast to the common practice of grabbing all that one can for the moment with little or no regard for tomorrow. On the ethical side, the Declaration emphasizes the necessity to consider the environment as communal property. The community of nations has the responsibility for the overall maintenance of the world's ecosystem, whereas each individual member has an immediate commitment to take care of its own environment. Another characteristic of the Declaration is its ideological orientation. The declaration emphasizes the need to engage in participatory decision-making processes concerning environmental protection and management, processes that include women and men, migrant communities and indigenous peoples. Democratic forms of government are capable of achieving environmental goals more effectively than are autocracies, according to this perspective.

The Stockholm and Rio Declarations recognize that environmental policy is influenced by three main components. These are (1) the scarcity and quality of environmental resources such as clean air and water, (2) the nature of the bureaucratic systems within which political decisions are made, and (3) the emergence of new environmental values facilitated by international conferences such as those held in 1972 and 1992. Furthermore, international programs to manage our environment are likely to influence and to be influenced by the principles of sustainable development, international and interregional cooperation on the use and conservation of environmental resources, and the need to support democratic institutions universally.

Twenty years later, United Nations conference on sustainable development took place in Rio de Janeiro, Brazil in June 2012 attended by world leaders, participants from the private sector, NGOs, and other interest groups. This conference, now widely known as the Rio+20, recognized the need to muster the required political will necessary to promote sustainable development for achieving internationally agreed development goals, including the Millennium Development Goals. The stated goals are described in Box 12.1.

The broad concern of the conference was to reassess the progress made during the 20 years post-Rio on advancement of social equity and environmental protection and poverty reduction. These three issues steered the two main conference themes: how to build a green economy to achieve sustainable development and lift people out of poverty; and how to improve international coordination for sustainable development. The conference addressed a range of global issues including access to clean energy, food security, water, and sustainable transportation. More importantly, the final document called the "Future We Want" refocused and reemphasized rights-based strategies. The human-rights-based approach to sustainable development upholds five key values; participation; accountability; equality and nondiscrimination; empowerment; and rule of law toward ensuring basic individual rights to food, water, sanitation, health, housing, and education. The "Future We Want" contains

Box 12.1   Open Working Group Proposal for Sustainable Development Goals

Introduction

1. The Rio+20 outcome document, The future we want, inter alia, set out a mandate to establish an Open Working Group (OWG) to develop a set of sustainable development goals (SDGs) for consideration and appropriate action by the General Assembly at its 68th session. It also provided the basis for their conceptualization. The Rio outcome gave the mandate that the SDGs should be coherent with and integrated into the U.N. development agenda beyond 2015.

2. Poverty eradication is the greatest global challenge facing the world today and an indispensable requirement for sustainable development. The Rio+20 outcome reiterated the commitment to freeing humanity from poverty and hunger as a matter of urgency.

3. Poverty eradication, changing unsustainable and promoting sustainable patterns of consumption and production, and protecting and managing the natural resource base of economic and social development are the overarching objectives of and essential requirements for sustainable development.

4. People are at the center of sustainable development and, in this regard, Rio+20 promised to strive for a world that is just, equitable, and inclusive, and committed to work together to promote sustained and inclusive economic growth, social development, and environmental protection and thereby to benefit all, in particular the children of the world, youth, and future generations of the world without distinction of any kind such as age, sex, disability, culture, race, ethnicity, origin, migratory status, religion, economic, or other status.

5. Rio+20 also reaffirmed all the principles of the Rio Declaration on Environment and Development, including, inter alia, the principle of common but differentiated responsibilities, as set out in principle 7 thereof.

6. It also reaffirmed the commitment to fully implement the Rio Declaration, Agenda 21, the Programme for the Further Implementation of Agenda 21, the Plan of Implementation of the World Summit on Sustainable Development (Johannesburg Plan of Implementation) and the Johannesburg Declaration on Sustainable Development, the Programme of Action for the Sustainable Development of Small Island Developing States (Barbados Programme of Action) and the Mauritius Strategy for the Further Implementation of the Programme of Action for the Sustainable Development of Small Island Developing States. It also reaffirmed the commitment to the full implementation of the Programme of Action for the Least Developed Countries for the Decade 2011–2020 (Istanbul Programme of Action), the Almaty Programme of Action: Addressing the Special Needs of Landlocked Developing Countries within a New Global Framework for Transit Transport Cooperation for Landlocked and Transit Developing Countries, the political declaration on Africa's development needs, and the New Partnership for Africa's Development. It reaffirmed the commitments in the outcomes of all the major United Nations conferences and summits in the economic, social, and environmental fields, including the United Nations Millennium Declaration, the 2005 World Summit Outcome, the Monterrey Consensus of the International Conference on Financing for Development, the Doha Declaration on Financing for Development, the outcome document of the High-level Plenary Meeting of the General Assembly on the Millennium Development Goals (MDGs), the Programme of Action of the International Conference on Population and Development, the key actions for the further implementation of the Programme of Action of the International Conference on Population and Development, and the Beijing Declaration

and Platform for Action, and the outcome documents of their review conferences. The Outcome document of the September 2013 special event to follow-up efforts made toward achieving the Millennium Development Goals reaffirmed, inter alia, the determination to craft a strong post-2015 development agenda. The commitment to migration and development was reaffirmed in the Declaration of the High-Level Dialogue on International Migration and Development.

7. Rio+20 outcome reaffirmed the need to be guided by the purposes and principles of the Charter of the United Nations, with full respect for international law and its principles. It reaffirmed the importance of freedom, peace, and security; respect for all human rights, including the right to development and the right to an adequate standard of living, including the right to food and water; the rule of law; good governance; gender equality; women's empowerment; and the overall commitment to just and democratic societies for development. It also reaffirmed the importance of the Universal Declaration of Human Rights, as well as other international instruments relating to human rights and international law.

8. The OWG underscored that the global nature of climate change calls for the widest possible cooperation by all countries and their participation in an effective and appropriate international response, with a view to accelerating the reduction of global greenhouse gas emissions. It recalled that the United Nations Framework Convention on Climate Change provides that parties should protect the climate system for the benefit of present and future generations of humankind on the basis of equity and in accordance with their common but differentiated responsibilities and respective capabilities. It noted with grave concern the significant gap between the aggregate effect of mitigation pledges by parties in terms of global annual emissions of greenhouse gases by 2020 and aggregate emission pathways consistent with having a likely chance of holding the increase in global average temperature below 2° C, or 1.5° C above pre-industrial levels and it reaffirmed that the ultimate objective under the UNFCCC is to stabilize greenhouse gas concentrations in the atmosphere at a level that would prevent dangerous anthropogenic interference with the climate system.

9. Planet Earth and its ecosystems are our home and that "Mother Earth" is a common expression in a number of countries and regions, and Rio+20 noted that some countries recognize the rights of nature in the context of the promotion of sustainable development. Rio+20 affirmed the conviction that in order to achieve a just balance among the economic, social, and environmental needs of present and future generations, it is necessary to promote harmony with nature. It acknowledged the natural and cultural diversity of the world, and recognized that all cultures and civilizations can contribute to sustainable development.

10. Rio+20 recognized that each country faces specific challenges to achieve sustainable development. It underscored the special challenges facing the most vulnerable countries and, in particular, African countries, least developed countries, landlocked developing countries and small island developing States, as well as the specific challenges facing the middle-income countries. Countries in situations of conflict also need special attention.

11. Rio+20 reaffirmed the commitment to strengthen international cooperation to address the persistent challenges related to sustainable development for all, in particular in developing countries. In this regard, it reaffirmed the need to achieve economic stability, sustained economic growth, the promotion of social equity, and the protection of the environment, while enhancing gender equality, women's empowerment, and equal employment for all, and the protection, survival, and development of children to their full potential, including through education.

12. Each country has primary responsibility for its own economic and social development and the role of national policies, domestic resources, and development strategies cannot be

overemphasized. Developing countries need additional resources for sustainable development. There is a need for significant mobilization of resources from a variety of sources and the effective use of financing, in order to promote sustainable development. Rio+20 affirms the commitment to reinvigorating the global partnership for sustainable development and to mobilizing the necessary resources for its implementation. The report of the Intergovernmental Committee of Experts on Sustainable Development Financing will propose options for a sustainable development financing strategy. The substantive outcome of the third International Conference on Financing for Development in July 2015 will assess the progress made in the implementation of the Monterrey Consensus and the Doha Declaration. Good governance and the rule of law at the national and international levels are essential for sustained, inclusive, and equitable economic growth; sustainable development; and the eradication of poverty and hunger.

13. Rio+20 reaffirmed that there are different approaches, visions, models, and tools available to each country, in accordance with its national circumstances and priorities, to achieve sustainable development in its three dimensions, which is our overarching goal.

14. The implementation of SDGs will depend on a global partnership for sustainable development with the active engagement of governments, as well as civil society, the private sector, and the United Nations system. A robust mechanism of implementation review will be essential for the success of the SDGs. The General Assembly, the ECOSOC system, and the High-Level Political Forum will play a key role in this regard.

15. Rio+20 reiterated the commitment to take further effective measures and actions, in conformity with international law, to remove the obstacles to the full realization of the right of self-determination of peoples living under colonial and foreign occupation, which continue to adversely affect their economic and social development as well as their environment, are incompatible with the dignity and worth of the human person, and must be combated and eliminated.

16. Rio+20 reaffirmed that, in accordance with the Charter, this shall not be construed as authorizing or encouraging any action against the territorial integrity or political independence of any State. It resolved to take further effective measures and actions, in conformity with international law, to remove obstacles and constraints, strengthen support, and meet the special needs of people living in areas affected by complex humanitarian emergencies and in areas affected by terrorism.

17. In order to monitor the implementation of the SDGs, it will be important to improve the availability of and access to data and statistics disaggregated by income, gender, age, race, ethnicity, migratory status, disability, geographic location, and other characteristics relevant in national contexts to support the support the monitoring of the implementation of the SDGs. There is a need to take urgent steps to improve the quality, coverage and availability of disaggregated data to ensure that no one is left behind.

18. SDGs are accompanied by targets and will be further elaborated through indicators focused on measurable outcomes. They are action oriented, global in nature, and universally applicable. They take into account different national realities, capacities, and levels of development and respect national policies and priorities. They build on the foundation laid by the MDGs, seek to complete the unfinished business of the MDGs, and respond to new challenges. These goals constitute an integrated, indivisible set of global priorities for sustainable development. Targets are defined as aspirational global targets, with each government setting its own national targets guided by the global level of ambition but taking into account national circumstances. The goals and targets integrate economic, social, and environmental aspects and recognize their interlinkages in achieving sustainable development in all its dimensions.

Sustainable Development Goals

Goal 1: End poverty in all its forms everywhere

Goal 2: End hunger, achieve food security and improved nutrition, and promote sustainable agriculture

Goal 3: Ensure healthy lives and promote well-being for all at all ages

Goal 4: Ensure inclusive and equitable quality education and promote lifelong learning opportunities for all

Goal 5: Achieve gender equality and empower all women and girls

Goal 6: Ensure availability and sustainable management of water and sanitation for all

Goal 7: Ensure access to affordable, reliable, sustainable, and modern energy for all

Goal 8: Promote sustained, inclusive, and sustainable economic growth; full and productive employment; and decent work for all

Goal 9: Build resilient infrastructure, promote inclusive and sustainable industrialization, and foster innovation

Goal 10: Reduce inequality within and among countries

Goal 11: Make cities and human settlements inclusive, safe, resilient, and sustainable

Goal 12: Ensure sustainable consumption and production patterns

Goal 13: Take urgent action to combat climate change and its impacts

Goal 14: Conserve and sustainably use the oceans, seas, and marine resources for sustainable development

Goal 15: Protect, restore, and promote sustainable use of terrestrial ecosystems, sustainably manage forests, combat desertification, halt and reverse land degradation, and halt biodiversity loss

Goal 16: Promote peaceful and inclusive societies for sustainable development; provide access to justice for all; and build effective, accountable, and inclusive institutions at all levels

Goal 17: Strengthen the means of implementation and revitalize the global partnership for sustainable development

Source: © United Nations Department of Economic and Social Affairs, 2014, https://sustainable development.un.org/sdgsproposal *(accessed May 15, 2015).*

action plans for a number of strategies such as launching a systematic approach toward establishing sustainable development goals and recognizing the importance of voluntary commitments on sustainable development (see Box 12.1).

PROGRAMS AND STRATEGIES: THE RISE OF ENVIRONMENTALISM

All policies, including those directed at influencing the relationship between population and environment, reflect societal values. The emergence of new values, induced by specific social and economic conditions—contradictions, culture lags, and the like, thus ultimately leads to new policies. The experiences of poverty, rapid urbanization, high population turnover, growth of democratic institutions, and rapid technological changes are all relevant factors in this regard. For, as these kinds of conditions affect people's day-to-day lives and activities, they help to shape their attitudes toward their ecosystems. In addition, people everywhere are becoming increasingly aware of the ideals of environmental protection and conservation emanating from sources like the Rio Declaration. Widespread exposure to such experiences and ideals has given rise to a new, broad ideological program and its related strategies, a true social movement known throughout the world as **environmentalism**.

This movement seeks to transform existing cultural beliefs and values and to alter societal practices and institutions so that a new, ecologically informed person-environment relationship can be achieved. Environmentalism looks beyond preserving the distribution of power and welfare across social strata. A person is viewed as a member of a global society and thus entitled to all of the privileges and responsibilities of that membership. The movement is rooted in the belief that all people are equal and that each has an obligation to preserve and to enrich one's environment. This means that environmentalism is not only concerned with natural resources, but that it also has a definite agenda for sociopolitical change. In this respect, the movement is global in scope, uniting many very loosely connected groups of organizations and communities in an attempt to save and restore our environment.

Some proponents challenge social inequality, viewing it as an obstacle to the empowerment of disadvantaged individuals and groups that will allow them to preserve and create healthy environments. Poverty, it is argued, limits an individual's capacity to conserve and otherwise use resources with care. Many environmentalists connect large-scale deforestation and environmental pollution to the unequal distribution of wealth. They point out that, on one hand, members of the wealthy middle and upper classes engage in excessive consumption that contributes to pollution. On the other hand, the millions of poor people in southern Africa, Central America, and other regions cause deforestation in their bid to survive with cheap sources of energy. This ideological component of the movement differs in detail from nation to nation and from community to community. For example, some environmentalists are not directly concerned with social justice but believe, instead, that the best strategy is to practice vegetarianism or veganism. Others emphasize the preservation of the planet's biodiversity.

Although its roots extend far back in history, contemporary environmentalism arose during the late 1950s and early 1960s in Western Europe and North America.[11] The naturalist and author Rachel Carson is credited with playing a major role in the rebirth of the movement with her highly influential *Silent Spring* (1962). This study called attention to the dangers of the deadly pesticide DDT, which was later banned in the United States and many other countries. Professor Barry Commoner of Washington University in St. Louis, cited above, was also a leading figure in the early days of the movement. The post–World War II era brought sweeping technological and organizational changes, along with growing affluence, to the Western countries. These dramatically altered the places where people lived—as the rush for the suburbs gained momentum—and the ways in which they made their livings. The proportion of the population engaged in agriculture decreased precipitously, as the number of urban and suburban dwellers swelled. This was the coming of the postindustrial era (see Chapter 3). Old ways of preservation and careful use of resources (including wartime rationing) gave way to uncontrolled consumption.

The trend toward mass production and consumption removed people from the resource and manufacturing bases of the things they used. The middle classes became increasingly "alienated," as the buzzword of the 1950s and early 1960s termed the condition. Scientific reports brought to the masses new information about the negative effects of technology on health. It was in this context that Dr. Carson sold more than 1 million copies of her book. The environmental degradation brought about by atomic blasts (for this was also the heart of the Cold War era) and the threat of biological and chemical weapons provided an additional impetus to environmentalism. People learned that the impact of military conflict is global. Increasingly, it became a matter of common sense that the degradation of ecosystems cannot be localized.

Today we take very seriously the more recent lessons from the disasters of the 1980s in Bhopal, India (1984); Chernobyl, Ukraine (1986); and Valdez, Alaska (1989), and the reports in the 1990s of oil floods in Houston (1994), acid rains, holes in the Antarctic ozone layer, and global warming. Such events have made it abundantly clear to all that global action is needed for the sake of environmental protection. By now, nearly everyone has heard and can in some way relate to the phrase inspired by the environmental movement: "Think globally, act locally."

Organizations have sprung up all over the world to further the cause of environmentalism. These groups address local environmental issues, engage in education, and build active coalitions of resistance and protests groups to amend local legislation. One of the oldest environmental organizations is the U.S. National Audubon Society (NAS), which celebrated its 100th anniversary in 1999. Frank M. Chapman of the American Museum of Natural History, who was also first editor of its bimonthly magazine, *Bird Lore*, originally established it as a confederation of state-level bird-watching societies. In 1905, the group was rededicated for the "protection of wild birds and animals," and renamed in honor of the naturalist and wildlife painter John J. Audubon (1786–1851). During the following year, 1906, the Society joined forces with another then-new group, the Sierra Club, and its founder John Muir in urging Congress to incorporate California's Yosemite Valley into Yosemite National Park. Since that time, the NAS and the Sierra Club have helped to define the environmental movement in the United States and elsewhere, including taking the lead during the 1960s renaissance (see Graham 1998; Magness et al. 2011).

One of the most widely publicized of the newer groups is Greenpeace. This organization was founded in 1971 to protest against fallout from nuclear weapons testing. The organization espouses Gandhi's philosophy of nonviolence and engages in nonviolent protests against governments and private organizations that contribute to environmental degradation. The global reach of Greenpeace is apparent in the activities that it undertook during the 1980s and 1990s. Members protested against, and succeeded in stopping, the killing of whales in several places; they attempted to end French nuclear testing in the South Pacific; and they conducted successful protests against chemical companies that were dumping toxic wastes into rivers.

During the 1990s, the ideology of environmentalism spread from North America and Europe to the developing world. Among the factors that supported the emergence of the movement in the wealthier countries were industrial pollution, wasteful consumption patterns, and widespread knowledge of the harmful effects of technology. However, in the poorer nations, ecological deterioration—as symbolized by global warming and ozone depletion—and loss of sustenance have played a more important role (Shiva 1988, 2013). One does not find clear social concern about environmental protection in the developing world, where environmental problems are more often linked to general political and economic issues such as food scarcity. One well-known environmental movement in Asia that is pursuing just such a course is **Chipko**.

Embracing the Lessons of Chipko

The Chipko movement began in what was then the northern Indian State of Uttar Pradesh (see Weber 1989). The Uttarkhand region (now a state itself) lies in the foothills of the Himalayas and is home to two large ethnic groups, the Kumaon and Garhwal. In 1816, soon after the Anglo–Gurkha War, the region was incorporated into British India. The British administration soon initiated export of timber from the Uttarkhand forest. This marked the beginning of deforestation in the region. Timber from this and other forests was used to develop India's extensive railway system. When India became independent in 1947, the exploitation of natural resources for nation building became an accepted approach to development. As a result, the rate of timber extraction from Uttarkhand increased rapidly. More than a century of timber cutting under the British and large-scale growth of the postindependence lumbering industry denuded the forest region. As a result, the hill populations of Garwahls and Kumoans lost their traditional means of livelihood.

The introduction of a monetary economy in the region induced out-migration of young men in search of jobs, whereas women stayed behind and engaged in subsistence agriculture. The women were burdened with the dual responsibilities of plowing the land and childcare. But, meager returns from agriculture as well as remittances from the men who had emigrated enabled them to survive. As the forest steadily retreated, the women had to walk longer distances to collect water and wood for fuel. During the 1960s and 70s, under conditions of abject poverty, backbreaking work that resulted from deforestation, and the loss of traditional means of livelihood, the female suicide rate increased dramatically. Many people turned to alcohol. Meanwhile, continued deforestation led to soil erosion, massive landslides, and rampant flooding of the rivers and tributaries. The Uttarkhand ecosystem was experiencing a thorough collapse, one that swept in the human inhabitants (Guha 1990; Yeh, O'Brien, and Ye 2013).

It was during this critical period that two social workers from the Ghandi Foundation, Mira Behn and Sarala Behn, volunteered their time and energy to fight the spread of alcoholism. It soon was apparent to them that the problems of poverty in Uttarkhand had causes other than drunkenness. Rather, deforestation was identified as a major culprit. Under the leadership of Mira and Sarala, local women began to organize for the first time. Then, workers from Sarvodaya (a movement that encourages wealthy people to give up excess land voluntarily to the poor) joined the efforts of Uttarkhand women to engage in nonviolent protests against the forces of ecological destruction. In the early 1970s, two other activists, Sunderlal Bahuguna and

Chandi Prasad Bhatt, joined the movement. In 1974, under the leadership of an illiterate woman named Gaura Devi, local women entered the forest where felling operations were to begin and stood for days, clinging to the trees to prevent the workers from cutting them down.

The next time you read or hear the term "tree hugger," you will know how it originated. It is a term derived from this incident in Uttarkhand, India. And the incident is also the source of the name of the movement, because *Chipko* means, "embrace" (Weber 1989). Momentum gathered. In 1977, Bachni Devi, ironically, the wife of a lumbering contractor, led village women to save another forest in the Adwani region. And, in 1980, the movement forced the Government of Indira Gandhi to ban for a period of 15 years all felling operations in the Himalayan forests. Chipko had begun to make a difference in India.

The Chipko cause was carried out by a loose confederation of hundreds of locally organized and autonomous bodies, consisting of women who were engaged in saving their means of subsistence and their communities. This is an important point to remember. Chipko became an environmental movement as women clearly identified the source of their poverty and social problems as deforestation. Similarly, Hungary's first environmental group, the Danube Committee, emerged in the early 1980s to protest a state-sponsored proposal to build a dam on the Hungarian side of the Danube River. In 1978, the Hungarian and Czechoslovak governments signed a treaty to construct the Gabcikovo-Nagymaros Barrage system on the Danube, which is a thoroughly a chemically polluted river. The construction of the dam would have resulted in retaining large amounts of polluted water on the Hungarian side. Chemicals surely would have seeped through riverbeds and contaminated the groundwater system. As the Danube Committee began its protests, the movement spread, for people were concerned about their drinking water supply. Smaller groups, such as Friends of the Danube and The Blues, joined the movement. In the wake of mass demonstrations, the project was canceled in 1989 (Galambos 1993; Bernauer, Böhmelt, and Koubi 2012; Gallopin 1992; Forsyth, 2013).

Sustainable Development

The Norwegian Prime Minister Gro Harlem Brundtland first introduced the concept of sustainable development in a 1987 report to the United Nations entitled "Our Common Futures." Subsequently, it has come to be known as the Bruntland Report. In it, the author defined sustainable development as "that development which meets present needs without compromising future generations' capacity to meet their own." The term "development" is conventionally used to indicate an increase in the average consumption of goods and services (such as per-capita GNP, income, or GDP). In contrast, sustainable development de-emphasizes the need to register ever-increasing growth in material consumption. Moreover, poverty—which remains invisible as long as per-capita increases occur—is identified as a threat to sustainability. Sustainable development means improvement in real (not average) standards of living achieved through the elimination of poverty.

Although this aspect of the Brundtland Report was viewed as very innovative, perhaps the most important difference between old models of economic development and sustainable development is that the latter is explicitly environmentalist. This linkage marked the arrival of a new era. As noted earlier, the connection between economic growth and ecological concerns had already been articulated some years earlier at the Stockholm Conference. In the wake of Bruntland's report, the Rio Declaration served to ratify the model of sustainable development. Subsequently, environmental movements throughout the world have adopted the model, expanded upon it, and promoted it. So, we might ask, what can be done now to further the cause?

In the years that have passed since Rio, a set of priority items has been placed on the environmental agenda. Here are a few that appear to us to be among the most salient.

- The idea that goods such as air and water are "free" must be abandoned. The costs of despoiling the ecosystem do not equal zero. Rather, people who suffer the ecological and health risks absorb them. Those who pollute must, therefore, pay their fair share to repair the damage incurred. Unfortunately, some injuries are irreparable.
- We know that current economic indicators such as per-capita GDP ignore the role of environmental resources in production and consumption. New measures such "genuine savings" and "Green GNP" have been devised to correct this situation. The next step is to implement them in a policy-relevant manner.
- Sustainable development cannot be undertaken without environmental education. Programs of environmental education that provide opportunities to experience nature and develop skills to appreciate natural beauty are now being introduced in the schools. Such efforts should be supported and accelerated. The skills to conserve natural resources are essential for achieving sustainable development.
- New sustainability indicators must be developed. In addition to new measures of economic development to replace GNP, GDP, and the like, we need to find innovative ways to monitor growth toward sustainability. Indicators of market performances such as the consumer price index and interest rates are well known, and they receive the greatest attention when policies are made. But they convey little about the kind of progress that Brundtland or the signers of the Rio Declaration (including the U.S. Government) had in mind. The Netherlands is one of the very few states that have attempted to develop these indicators. Since 1991, The Government in The Hague has published data related to six environmental issues identified as important to the people of Netherlands. They are (1) climate change; (2) ozone layer depletion; (3) acidification of lakes and soils; (4) eutrophication of water bodies; (5) toxicity of soils, water bodies, and the ecosystem; and (6) accumulation of solid wastes. For each indicator, a scale is developed and the changes in the levels of the indicators over time are presented graphically. The level of each indicator is then compared with target levels. This informs the public about the gap between current performance and targets in terms of sustainable development.
- Finally, sustainable development is impossible without conservation. It is a practice that must be relearned. In the past, all peoples knew about conservation. But much of this knowledge was lost, as goods were mass-produced and consumption and production became clearly separated from activities within the household. Sustainable development means preserving the environment. Knowledge of traditional methods of conservation and recycling can greatly enhance the current store of know-how about strategies for environmental preservation.

SUMMARY

We would like to report that on our latest trip between Mumbai and Pune, India, the tea-sellers had reverted to using clay cups. Unfortunately, this rediscovery of the wisdom of traditional ways has not happened—yet. On the other hand, people in India and throughout the world now have a far better understanding of the costs involved in going the "Styrofoam route" than they did in 1994. As is true of population in general, the pace of events in the population-environment relationship is unprecedentedly rapid and it is accelerating. Similarly, our access to knowledge about these events is increasing exponentially. Without necessarily accepting either the optimistic or the pessimistic perspective, we can say that whatever we are presently doing to our ecosystems, we are no longer acting in ignorance. During the past several decades, people have abused natural resources, polluted the air, and poisoned the water. And people are doing it today as well. But no longer can anyone be excused for being innocent or naïve. Unless one has been living in a darkened cellar for the past 20 or 30 years, he or she can have no legitimate excuse for causing environmental damage, or for standing by while others do the dirty work. This should be heartening even to the most convinced neo-Malthusian (see Simon 1981; Cascio and Boudreau 2010).

KEY TERMS

biodiversity
carrying capacity
Chipko
deforestation
ecological collapse
ecology
ecosystem

environmentalism
multiphasic response model (MRM)
Rio Declaration
Silent Spring
Stockholm Declaration
sustainable development
Waste Makers

NOTES

1. For another early statement on the inherent tendency of our economies to promote waste, this from a Marxist perspective, see Baran (1967) and Gilpin (2011).

2. Haeckel was also a pioneer in the field of race science and believed that the differences between the ways various peoples thought and behaved could be explained biologically. This field later (long after Haeckel's death) played an important role in helping the Nazis justify their program of genocide (see Weinstein and Stehr 1999).

3. See the report entitled "Biological and Water Quality Study of the Little Miami River Basin, 1998" at http://www.epa.state.oh.us/portals/35/documents/LMR_Tsd.pdf.

4. The Environment Canada web site has much interesting information on pollution and resource conservation. Its home page is http://www.ec.gc.ca/?lang=En.

5. Citing demographer Richard Bilsborrow, Livernash and Rodenberg (1998:20) point out that "populations may respond to the shortage of agricultural land by reducing their fertility, changing technology, or migrating to another area."

6. It is not always the case that road construction leads to an increase in the rate of deforestation. A recent study in Belize, Brazil, Mexico, and Central Africa found that soil characteristics moderate the effect of road network expansion on deforestation rates (World Bank 1997). The International Center for Research in Agroforestry, Bogor, Indonesia, is participating in the research; and the Swedish and U.K. Trust Funds for the Social and Environmental Consequences of Growth-Oriented Policies are contributing funding for the project.

7. http://www.worldenergy.org/wp-content/uploads/2013/10/WEC_Resources_summary-final_180314_TT.pdf—World Energy Resources: by World Energy Council (2013).

8. For direct contact, go to http://www.epa.gov/risk_assessment/guidance.htm.

9. We emphasize *formal* power because things do not function in the same manner at the informal level. Ever since the publication of C. Wright Mills's classic *The Power Elite* (1956), sociologists have warned of the accumulation of power among corporate, military, government, and media leaders "behind the scenes." William Domhoff's influential studies have verified and updated our understanding of this tendency toward distortion of democratic process by the wealthy and the powerful (Domhoff 1970, 1983, 1990; Foster and Holleman 2010). More recently, political scientists have called attention to the excessive power wielded by special-interest and lobbying contingents, especially at that crucial juncture in the policy-formulation process and agenda setting. See Grady (1993).

10. The mechanism that lies behind this shift is *culture lag*. This concept, coined by the Chicago School sociologist William F. Ogburn (1922), refers to a situation in which the rate of change in one part of a sociocultural system—the policy-making process in our case—is seriously lagging behind the rate of another part—the technologies of environmental destruction. The contradiction between the two parts leads to a significant change in norms and values. A parallel situation occurred at the turn of the twentieth century, when cars began to take to the roads. Initially, there were no special traffic laws for motorized vehicles (because they weren't necessary). But after a "sufficient number" of people were maimed or killed, a change in our normative framework occurred. The current shift from values of production to values of conservation has been classed as a *postmodern* turn of events. We prefer to avoid the label because of the enormous "excess baggage" it carries (see Ritzer 1997: Chaps. 1 and 2).

11. The idea of environmentalism is very old, although it was not considered a movement until fairly recently. The ideal of a pristine land, with nature left intact and unspoiled by human contact, was a motivating factor during the early colonial era of the seventeenth and eighteenth centuries. It was clearly part of the "American Dream" from a very early date (see Marx 1970), given its best-known expression by Henry David Thoreau.

ACCESSING AND USING INFORMATION ABOUT POPULATION SCIENCE

It should be evident from the preceding chapters that the field of demography is information rich. Demographers have at their command dozens of data sources, both public and private. An ever-expanding range of procedures and programs for analyzing data and for communicating the results of research is now available. And there is a great and growing number of career opportunities that allow one to apply the knowledge and techniques of population science. This chapter explores these practical dimensions of the field. Our purpose here is to provide a perspective on the sources that demographers use in their research and how they are applied. With this goal in mind, the material is divided into several sections on accessible data, demographic organizations, publications—especially on the Internet, research design, and careers. In the Appendix are several web resources that relate to the subject matter of other chapters.

Before turning to these topics, however, a few disclaimers are necessary. We have provided the most up-to-date and most thorough overview possible of the resources under discussion. Nevertheless, our lists of journals, web sites, and the like are bound to be incomplete to some extent. This is simply inevitable given the incredible rate of change that characterizes information management today. For the same reason, some items on these lists will soon be outdated or invalid. Under the circumstances, it is wise to use this material with caution. Most of it will remain reliable for many years, but some must be understood as "suggestive," something to give you an idea about where to find a certain kind of software or which professions are hiring demographers.

Although we have attempted to be selective in keeping our references within the scope of the subjects covered in this book, some of the recommended sources are likely to take you far afield. Some demographic resources are easy to locate, but others are "disguised" under unclear labels. Similarly, some items that appear to be relevant, because they bear the title "demographics," for instance, may be only of marginal

Table 13.1. Growth in the Number of Web Sites, 2000-2014

Total Number of Web Sites as of December 2014: 1,142,735,777

Year	Web Sites
2000	17087182
2001	29254370
2002	38760373
2003	40912332
2004	51611646
2005	64780617
2006	85507314
2007	121892559
2008	172338726
2009	238027855
2010	206956723
2011	346004403
2012	697089489
2013	672985183
2014	1,142,735,777

Source: http://www.internetlivestats.com/total-number-of-websites/.

interest. With an estimated 1.1 billion Internet sites worldwide as of December 2014, one can never guarantee that one has hit the target with every try—especially when the target is moving at a rate approaching the speed of light (see Table 13.1).

DEMOGRAPHY-ORIENTED SOFTWARE

Software that is specifically designed for demographic applications, or which is widely used for these purposes, can be classed into four main categories. These are: **data sets and file transfer/file reading packages**, educational packagers, applications, and GIS tools.

Of these, the first and the last are the most abundant and the most readily available, although each category has many specific items, none of which is especially difficult to find. The following is a brief summary of the items in these categories.

Data Sets, Educational Packages, and Applications

We have already noted the value of the U.S. Bureau of the Census as a source of data for demographic research. The "American Fact Finder" links at the main U.S. Census site as well as two DVDs containing 2010 Census data include **Summary File 1**. These are publicly available. Summary File 1 contains the data compiled from the questions asked of all people and about every housing unit in the United States—thus the term, "complete enumeration." It is here that population researchers find data on the major demographic variables sex, age, race, Hispanic or Latino origin, household relationship, household type, household size, family type, family size, and group quarters.

Housing items, of interest to a wide range of population scientists, include occupancy status, vacancy status, and tenure (whether a housing unit is owner-occupied or renter-occupied). The DVDs also contain the 2010 Census Data Engine retrieval software for researchers to manipulate, display, and download data from the file. Geographical units associated with data were introduced in Chapter 4: these are the United States, regions, divisions, states, counties, county subdivisions (10,000 or more population), places (10,000 or more population), metropolitan statistical areas, ZIP Code Tabulation Areas, congressional districts (111th Congress), American Indian and Alaska Native Areas, and Hawaiian Home Lands.

Between 1878 and 2012, the unit within which the Census Bureau resides, the U.S. Department of Commerce, published an invaluable source of data, the annual *Statistical Abstract of the United States* (in hard copy and on CD-ROM). *The Abstract* included highlights of Census publications and information from the Department of Labor, Health and Human Services, and several other agencies. The U.S. Census Bureau terminated the collection of data for the Statistical Compendia program, which included the Statistical Abstract of the United States on October 1, 2011. However much of this information is now provided by other divisions of the Census Bureau and in the NCHS-CDC *Vital Statistics*. Researchers have found that the most efficient way to access Census data is at its home page. Here one finds a link to an index and a "search" panel. Using either, demographers may access and apply enumeration data from every U.S. Census count back to 1790. Advanced research often relies upon public use microdata sample (PUMS) results. Also included are state- and county-level data for several years, structural and geographic breakdowns, urban/rural data, estimates, projections, and a wide range of specialized data sets, and maps. Although the Department of Commerce and the Census Bureau are public, U.S. institutions, they maintain a wealth of international data covering virtually every country in the world. In addition to quantitative reports, census.gov provides informative material on Bureau definitions, procedures and protocol, as well as directives and press releases that contain news about the Bureau. There is also a catalog of software—mostly data sets and maps—available for a small charge.

Nearly all data from the Census Bureau web site that appear on the screen can be printed directly, and almost all can be downloaded. However, some of the data sets that are used in large-scale projects must be acquired in hard copy or by special electronic means. A related data source that has protocols similar to those of the Census, and which was discussed in earlier chapters, is the National Center for Health Statistics (NCHS)/U.S. Centers for Disease Control and Prevention (CDC). Data on U.S. births, deaths, and morbidity in this book and in other publications emanate from these organizations. The Internet and other developments in information technology have had a significant impact on the work of NCHS, to the advantage of those who require its software in population studies (e.g., life table construction and analysis) (Henman and Adler 2003). In fact, as one report noted, these technological changes view the NCHS and the state agencies that supply its data as "reinventing vital statistics." "The vital statistics system, one of the oldest sources of health data, is now on the threshold of a new era as a result of the information revolution" (Starr and Starr 1995:534). Among the new software products available is an updated version of the SETS (Statistical Export and Tabulation System) designer kit. This is a file-management package that comes with any of several data sets from the NCHS files. Also available are the Public Use Data Tapes containing survey data (some longitudinal) on several subjects (Smith 1995; Fleming 2003).

The mission of the CDC within the Department of Health and Human Services is to collect data and carry out many other missions within the United States. But it is also deeply involved through the Department of State in projects abroad, including an extensive research program in less-developed countries. Much research and application in population studies is comparative and as is true of the Census Bureau, essential international databases are available for printing and downloading from NCHS.

In addition, every state in the United States and hundreds of cities have web sites that provide useful, free data. Some of it is a duplication of material that can be accessed from the Census Bureau or the NCHS, but often the information is more up to date or organized in a better format. Detailed county-level data are usually easier to acquire from states than from Federal sources. In fact, information from state databases in Colorado, Arkansas, Texas, and Massachusetts has been used in this book.

There are several important sources of international demographic information, some of which have been mentioned earlier. The Princeton University Office of Population Research Data Archive is one of the leading academic centers for this purpose, and it has many U.S. data sets as well. Among nongovernmental organizations, the **World Bank**, a U.N. affiliate, collects and updates some of the most thorough "country profiles." These include birth and fertility rates, death rates, population sizes and composition, and multiple indicators such as the "development diamond" (see Chapter 3). Information for single nations or for several at a time can be acquired at no cost.

A United Nation's organizations that specialize in population information are the U.N. Statistics and the U.N. Population Information Network (POPIN), a branch of the U.N. Development Program. The latter has a large software catalog. Especially relevant items include (1) PC-Edit, which organizes and expedites data entry; (2) Xtable, which creates crosstabs; (3) PopMap, a population data utility program; and (4) MapScan, a GIS mapping aide. Training materials are available for the last two items. The University of Ulster (U.K.) is referenced by POPIN, and its business school also provides software over the Internet.

Another academically oriented center in Europe is the Interdisciplinary Demographic Institute (NIDI) in The Hague, the Netherlands. This institute was founded in 1973 with the mission of conducting research and developing software in conjunction with its research projects. Its home page, at http://www.nidi.nl/eu, has featured two software packages of interest, PopTrain, which teaches basic demography, and LIPRO (Lifestyle PROjections), a program to produce population projections that combines features of period and cohort tables. Several GeoSim modules are currently available, including MigPo. This module simulates the effects of population shifts on the U.S. House of Representatives. SnsPlace focuses on the characteristics of U.S. counties and states.

GIS Resources

As it has developed over the past few decades, GIS (Geographic Information Systems) has become a highly interdisciplinary field. From a demographic perspective, it affords the researcher an opportunity to work closely with geographers, city planners, and other professionals. A proper inventory of GIS resources would fill a chapter by itself. Although several sources were mentioned in Chapter 4, we will elaborate on two leading organizations. The first is also a U.S. Bureau of the Census project, **TIGER Map Serve**. You will recall from our earlier discussion that TIGER provides a range of software and services, including several data sets and programs that can be downloaded. Other than a selection of sample items, much of this material is stored in large data sets, and there is a charge for many of the packages.

The other organization is a private company in Redlands, California, Environmental Systems Research Institute (ESRI). ESRI describes itself as "the world's leader in GIS software," and this seems to be an accurate claim. The Institute provides Arc/Info packages, desktop ArcView software, online tutorials, digitizing programs, GIS references, and geographic databases. The programming software is sold via the web site and delivered via postal mail, but a considerable amount of data is available for free downloading.

As in other fields with high levels of "consumer" interest, including demography itself, GIS has spawned a set of master web sites whose main function is to provide links to other Internet resources related to the field. Massachusetts Institute of Technology Libraries provides a listing of number of help sources and tutorial. A large volume of material is available to anyone interested in learning basic GIS. Among the topics covered at the beginner's level are: finding data, using census data, geocoding addresses, and adding XY points. At a slightly advanced level they provide introduction to spatial statistics, map projections and making maps. In addition, they also provide an extensive listing of worldwide web links to spatial data.

On the commercial side is The Right Site also known by its logo name EASI. This company is a supplier to demographers and other users, including ESRI. Its site has links to other "demographic" web sites, which is here defined essentially as data sets organized for GIS applications. Included among the sets available directly from EASI is a package with data aggregated at the block group and county levels along with software for analyzing the data, and a database of 50 variables at the block group, tract, and ZIP code levels. Not all of their products are sold, for they advertise "1,000,000 pages of *free* easy-to-use Demographic Reports."

A small sample of other GIS-software providing sites of interest to demographic researchers includes the following:

1. Community 2020 Software. This is a low-cost package provided by the U.S. Department of Housing and Urban Development (HUD). The HUD general home page has numerous links, including some that can be downloaded.
2. The **United States Environmental Protection Agency** (**EPA**) GIS site. This is a useful site that will lead to all manner of mapping software.
3. GeoData at Berkeley. This is an interactive catalogue of database software and literature managed by the library of the University of California (Berkeley).
4. A rich collection of ecological applications of GIS is available from USGS Publications Warehouse. It includes a large number of articles on theory and how GIS is used.

DEMOGRAPHIC RESEARCH, APPLICATION, AND THE INTERNET

Professionals and students interested in learning more about populations and their characteristics and dynamics need only search the net for the subjects "population" or "demography." The results provide a wealth of information, resources, references, and organizational and personal contacts. In fact, demographic research designs, methods, and research findings are among the most extensively covered of the social sciences throughout the entire system, with hundreds of sites dedicated entirely or largely to demographic topics and issues. Following a general overview, this section lists and discusses some of the more useful among these resources.

Although this is a fairly long list, it does not include most of the college- and university-based pages now up and running, except for Centers and Institutes such as those at the University of North Carolina and Princeton University. One reason for excluding them is that there are so many. In fact, it would be safe to say that at just about any institution of higher learning is likely to have one or more demographers on the faculty. Many of these web pages are managed by teaching faculty, and include homework assignments and lectures posted by the professor.

Our focus is on topics covered in earlier chapters of this textbook. Thus, separate discussions are provided for many of the topics. However, several general sources are identified as well. This set of sites should serve as a starting point for exploring a vast, and somewhat uncharted, world of knowledge and resources in contemporary population studies.

The Internet: Roots and Branches

The Internet is the fastest, most user-friendly, and most abundant source of information now available. Unlike more traditional learning resources, the net is simply "there." Moreover, despite the fact that we capitalize the word with an "I," as Steele and associates have pointed out (Steele, Kepner, and Gotthoffer 1999:4), there is no company or institution that bears that proper name. Instead, "the word 'Internet' denotes a specific interconnected network of networks, and not a corporate entity." For these reasons, people sometimes have trouble conceiving of it as having a history, or of having a history that is recorded and well documented. Neither of these perceptions is accurate. Although it seems as if the Internet just "sprung up," it is the result of a series of events, sometimes connected, sometimes running on parallel tracks, that extends as far back as the historian's imagination wishes to go (cf. Segaller 1998; Clark 1999; and Wolinsky 1999). And these events are documented in several books and master web sites that have been created to help those interested "navigate" the literature on Internet history (Cotten 2001).

Demographic Research-Oriented Sites

The following overview of material with demographic content is organized from the general to the specific. We begin with items that *refer* to sites of interest rather than containing directly relevant information. These perform roughly the same function as does an index in a book. Next we move to sites of general interest that cover a wide range of topics. Finally we consider sites that specialize in areas discussed in earlier chapters.

Guides and Master Sites

As we have seen, many web sites and hard-copy items have been created to serve as clearinghouses and reference points for demographic researchers interested in particular subjects that are well covered on the net and in libraries. Demographers are among those with access to such resources. Although no single book is entirely and exclusively devoted to cataloging population-oriented web sites, specific sections of several references to these sites are included in the "Web Sites to Bookmark" section for each chapter in the Instructor's Manual.

The **Population Reference Bureau, Inc.** (**PRB**), whose data sets are used extensively in this book, maintains a site for directing population researchers to demographic resources, including many of its own. The Bureau is located in Washington, D.C. It has links to several sites and databases, including one for state-level information. The organization also publishes *Population Bulletin*.

A unique service is provided by Princeton University, which published the *Population Index* between 1936 and 2000. This journal, which first appeared in hard-copy format, was viewed as indispensable in the community of demographers. Since its founding, it has published references to relevant works in the field and abstracts of current articles on population that have appeared in other journals around the world, as well as some original commentary pieces. The *Population Index* web site now contains information online for the period 1986–2000, and the abstracts and articles can be downloaded at no cost.

General Interest Sites

The SocioSite is a member of the International Consortium for the Advancement of Academic Publications (ICAAP), which distributes listing of several web sites with demographic information at the national and international levels. The SocioSite is based at the faculty of Social Sciences, University of Amsterdam. Professional organizations, universities, and specialist groups maintain a set of general sites that often have links to additional resources. But their main focus is on providing quantitative data and other information directly to the user. Foremost among these is the **Population Association of America** (**PAA**). Located in the Washington, D.C. area (Silver Spring, MD), this group has over 3,000 members and is the main association of professional demographers in the United States. This group holds annual meetings that are attended by people from many countries, and it publishes *Demography*, the leading quarterly scholarly population journal in the United States (if not the world).

Equally influential in the discipline is the American Sociological Association (ASA) section on Population. There is considerable overlap between the PAA and this group, which also holds an annual conference as part of the ASA general meetings. The ASA home page includes information of general interest to sociologists as well as a link to the population section.

Several major universities maintain demographic sites. The following list includes some of the sites that were consulted in the preparation of this book. They are all excellent and, although each has certain areas of specialization, all are very comprehensive.

1. The Pennsylvania State University Population Research Institute (PRI)
2. The Princeton University Office of Population Research
3. The University of North Carolina
4. The University of California Library
5. The University of Minnesota Historical Integrated Public Use Microsample (IUPMS) Data
6. University of Virginia Library

Finally, there is a group of general interest sites maintained by various organizations, some governmental, some nonprofit, and others private. These have a somewhat narrower focus than the university centers, but they are still useful sources for information on population size, structure, geographic distribution, and vital events. The following list contains a representative sample of this type of site.

1. American Demographics published the popular magazine with the same name. Some interesting features and nicely presented tables, graphs, and charts can be found in this publication. Despite the title, the demographic content of the material is often limited, as the focus is on life styles and commercial implications of population trends.
2. Rural and Small Town Programme is a Canadian site that specializes in data on rural areas; that is, the neglected 20 percent of North America's population.
3. Urban Land Institute is the premiere nongovernmental urban planning "think tank" that specializes in data on the other 80 percent of the population.
4. HUD is not a primary data-collection agency. However, it provides very useful information about community revitalization, minority concerns, and many other population-related issues.

Additional Data Sources (Related to Chapters 1–4 of This Text)

1. The Population Research Bureau has an online glossary of demographic terms.
2. Two sites that provide general facts, including population information, are the U.S. Central Intelligence Agency and the World Health Organization (WHO). WHO is one of several organizations that have health information and vital statistics online at its home page. Related sources include the University of Michigan library, noted above, which maintains a health statistics site. This site provides FastStat A–Z and Statista. As noted, the *National Vital Statistics Reports* of NCHS can be obtained directly from the CDC site: http://www .cdc.gov/nchs/products/nvsr.htm. Three useful organizations among those that publish information on world population trends and related references are (a) the UNDP POPIN program, (b) PopNet, and (c) the private company, "Demographic.com."
   a. PopNet: The Directory for Global Population Information, the PRB, a nonprofit educational organization, aims "to increase the amount, accuracy, and usefulness" of population information available to the public.
   b. In addition to the Census Bureau and NCHS, several other U.S. Government agencies maintain web sites of interest to demographers. These include the Office of the U.S. President, the Department of Labor, and the Department of Housing and Urban Development (HUD).

The FAQ (Frequently Asked Questions) page of the U.S. Information Service (USIS— Department of State), USIA was terminated in 1999. But related information can be obtained from the U.S. Department of Justice's Bureau of Justice Statistics, the U.S. Department of Agriculture's Economic Research Service, and the U.S. Department of Labor's Bureau of Labor Statistics.

Migration and Refugee Information (Related to Our Chapter 7)

Resources for demographic research focused on migration and refugee issues are maintained by several governmental and nongovernmental organizations (NGOs).

These tend to have a substantive and, often, a political focus that distinguishes them for the U.S. Census Bureau, NCHS, and similar sites from which migration data are available. The leading organization of this type is the International Organization for Migration (IOM). This group provides access to quantitative information about migration worldwide as well as commentary on legal and human rights concerns.

The Canadian Government also maintains a multipurpose migration and refugee-oriented site with links to many national and international centers, institutes, and organizations in the field. The two leading NGOs that specialize in problems of international migrants and refugees, the **United Nations High Commission for Refugees (UNHCR)** and **Amnesty International**, maintain web sites. These contain data and commentary on the status of refugees, with particular emphasis on problem areas in Africa and Asia. The Amnesty International site is dedicated to concerns about the treatment of refugees. The U.S. Department of State also maintains a site with many resources and links, including data and several features on immigration problems and refugee status. A U.S.-based NGO, the U.S. Committee for Refugees (USCR), has a similar range of interests. It features a news-magazine format with articles on current issues throughout the world.

In addition to these internationally prominent agencies, several smaller organizations have postings on current crises and related human rights concerns. For example, *Forced Migration Review* (FMR) is the most widely read publication on forced migration. In a similar vein, audio recordings of—often-tragic—first-hand accounts of refugees from several countries are available at the RealAudio page of USCR.

Population Estimation and Forecasting (Chapter 10)

Several specialized sites discuss and demonstrate methods for population estimation, projection, or forecasting. Again, these tend to be professionally oriented specialized presentations that differ from the material offered by the U.S. Bureau of the Census or the U.N. Office of Population, from which specific projections and estimates can be obtained. As noted in earlier chapters, literature on population estimates and the projection methodology used by the Census Bureau are readily available.

The Census Bureau also provides graphic clocks that provide continuous U.S. and world population estimates. In addition, universities throughout the world are now posting lectures and assignments from their course offerings. Many of these are from population and demography classes, several of which discuss and illustrate projection techniques. For example, a site maintained by a demography course at San Jose State University gives a vivid description of the cohort survival projection method demonstrated in Chapter 10.

One additional source of world population forecasts is the site maintained as part of the UNDP POPIN program. Here, growth trends are analyzed and employed in creating long-range forecasts. This office is the source of the forecast that the size of the world's population will reach eleven billion before it achieves ZPG.

Population Policy (Chapters 11 and 14)

A substantial proportion of the population-oriented material on the Internet focuses on the discussion of policy issues. Topics range from abortion rights and prohibitions, to migration law, to the evaluation of family-planning programs. The United Nation's Department of Economic and Social Affairs maintains a comprehensive site with linkages to a vast number of population- and policy-related topics. Literature and information on the following subjects are available: aging, the environment, family planning, fertility, HIV/AIDS, international migration, marriage and unions, mortality, population policies, population trends, and urbanization. Although the majority of the policy-related sites cover one country or one area of the world (or one issue), several are dedicated to the formulation of world population policy. The World Bank is in some respects a definitive source in this regard, because of the extent of its operations and because of its internal policies that link population growth to socioeconomic development. The Population Council in New York City is one of the most influential NGOs in this area, for reasons that are similar to those that underlie the World Bank's prominence.

At several points in Chapter 11 we mentioned the U.N. World Population Conferences of 1974, 1984, and 1994. Among all of the organizations and conferences that have worked on the subject, these meetings come closest to serving as international policy tribunals: The National Association of Biology Teachers (United States) maintains another interesting discussion of world-level policy. Here you will find a position paper on world population growth prepared by a group of concerned educators.

Among the regions and countries covered most extensively by population policy sites are the nations of sub-Saharan Africa, where one finds the world's highest rates of population growth. The Organization for African Unity (OAU) has for many years been a proponent of pan-Africanism and of policies that would serve the interests of the continent as a whole. The POPIN program of UNDP has a link to the OAU position on population that can be accessed through its home page or directly. Also dedicated to policy in Africa is a comprehensive Internet resource with linkages to extensive research material. The population policies of specific African nations are also well covered by UNDP's POPIN via its Africa program.

Several sites are dedicated to especially controversial population policy-related issues. For example, China's widely discussed one-child policy was the subject of a radio talk show on station KZPG in California (February 16, 1996). The debate in the United States between proponents and opponents of abortion continues to rage at numerous sites and chat rooms on the web. The California Abortion and Reproductive Rights League established one site, which is highly informative and openly partisan on the prochoice side. On the other side, dozens of Christian Coalition sites provide the arguments against abortion.

Population and Environment (Chapter 12)

The final set of sites to be presented in this section contains material on environmental issues. This, too, is a vast area with several hundred governmental, NGOs, and privately sponsored sites. Not all of the information and commentary at these sites is of direct relevance to demography; although, from an ecological perspective, everything either impacts on or is impacted by population size, structure, distribution, and change. Each of the seven organizations selected here has extensive links to other resources in the field. Thus they can serve as a good starting point for professionals and students alike. Each also has some material explicitly focused on population dynamics.

Three sites maintained by the World Bank illustrate these connections. The first of these is the web site for NIPR (New Ideas in Pollution Regulation), which contains pollution data from the 2012 World Development Indicators. These indicators also include several demographic measures. The second World Bank site provides a general overview of the World Development Indicators, including not only those that measure environmental degradation. The third site maintained by the Bank is specifically focused on water quality and industrial water quality in India, in particular. You might recall from Chapter 4 that access to safe water is one of the four indicators that make up the "Development Diamond" (along with education, wealth, and infant mortality).

An online encyclopedia maintains a site that provides information on various aspects of environmental pollution, including news items on water quality. Water was also a major concern at the groundbreaking 1992 Rio Conference on Environment and Development (Rio de Janeiro, Brazil). Water pollution, air quality, deforestation, and several other issues were heatedly debated in the first real attempt to create a worldwide environmental policy. Among the U.N. organizations with environment-oriented data and commentary is the Food and Agricultural Organization (FAO). FAO has a strong emphasis on food production, but it has also been a major proponent of *sustainable development*. This subject and an essay on gender issues as the "key to sustainability and food security," are covered.

It would take many days to explore all of the resources discussed. As we have indicated, this is a mere sampling of what is available today.

MARKETING DEMOGRAPHIC SKILLS

Demography is a well-established academic discipline; but the field is not pursued *only* in colleges and universities. It is applied extensively in government, in the private sector, and in several professions in the United States and throughout the world. We have already had occasion to consider this side of population studies in earlier chapters; for example, in Chapter 9 in connection with the life table, Chapter 10 with reference to projection, and Chapter 11 in the context of policy formulation and evaluation. The concluding section of this chapter expands upon these earlier comments with a closer look at four fields that hire demographers and that apply demographic perspectives and techniques. These are (1) urban planning, (2) business, (3) **human services**, and (4) **actuarial science**.

Along with universities and academic research centers and the U.S. Bureau of the Census, the National Center for Health Statistics, and similar Government agencies (at Federal, state, and local levels), these are the major employers of demographers today. But even these do not exhaust all of the possible career opportunities in the field. For further information, you can contact any of three web sites that assist in job placements in this and related disciplines, two of which were given earlier in this chapter. These are the Population Association of America (www.populationassociation.org), the Population Research Bureau (http://www.prb.org), and the Association for Applied and Clinical Sociology (www.aacsnet.net).

Demography for Planners

Urban planning, which is also known as *city planning* and as *urban and regional planning*, is a highly interdisciplinary field that is practiced today in the United States and throughout the world. Its roots extend back to the family-planning movement in England and the United States (see Chapter 11), and to the early socialist writings and experimentation of Jean Meslier, Thomas Spence, William Ogilvie, and, especially, Robert Owen and William Godwin. Owen founded the first planned community at New Lanark, Scotland, in the early nineteenth century, and Godwin, as you will recall, was an early critic of Mathus's *laissez faire* philosophy. In the United States, planning developed as a profession in the mid- to late 1800s through the work of architects and engineers inspired by several related social movements: agrarianism, public health, Garden City, and City Beautiful (Krueckeberg 1983; APA 1990:83; Coop and Thomas 2007). In contrast to the situation in some other countries, planning's historical ties to civil engineering in the United States have given it a strong physical orientation. However, since the 1960s, it has become increasingly independent of architecture and engineering, and it has developed a distinct program of social improvement (APA 1990: Chap. 2).

Planning professionals generally work for state and local government, although hundreds of private consulting companies are owned or managed by planners and/ or hire them on a regular basis. Bachelors and doctoral degrees in planning are offered at several universities, but the most common entry-level degree in the field is the Masters in City Planning (MCP). The profession also has a certification procedure whereby a practicing planner can be awarded recognition by the American Institute of Certified Planners (AICP). The major professional organization in the United States is the **American Planning Association** (**APA**), which also administers the AICP. Information about the field, including employment opportunities, is available at http://www.planning.org. A separate association has been established for planners in academic careers (for which a PhD is usually required). This is the Association of Collegiate Schools of Planning (ACSP), whose web site also has job listings at http://www.acsp.org/jobs/jobs.html. The counterpart of the APA and ACSP is the Canadian Institute of Planning, with a site at http://www.cip-icu.ca.

Planning is a diverse field, with numerous branches and specializations. Nevertheless, virtually every planner and planning organization routinely uses demographic concepts, methods, and data. For example, transportation planners, zoning administrators, land-use planners, and neighborhood- and downtown-development specialists base most of their decisions and more comprehensive programming on information about the size, structure, and geographic distribution of the populations in their domains. Extensive use is made of Census data, especially at the tract and block levels, but planners also conduct their own surveys under local and state government jurisdiction. Such surveys are especially important in programs that attempt to measure and improve quality of life in local communities through citizen mobilization (Ronnby 1995; Nicodemus 2004).

Planning for commercial developments (such as shopping centers and malls), the construction of schools and human-service facilities, and residential single- and multifamily development programs depend crucially on population estimates and projections. Of special interest are projections of specifically targeted cohorts, such as senior citizens, young married couples, and school-age children. In step with related technological developments, planners are increasingly involved in work on spatial demography, especially techniques and data related to urban growth (see City of Los Angeles 1996; Summers, Cheshire, and Senn 1993; Brown et al. 2005) and—of course—GIS. In fact, the planning profession is one of the most active consumers of GIS hardware, software, and expertise. A person trained in demography, especially one with some knowledge of GIS programming and interpretation, is likely to be much appreciated and to find an interesting and challenging career as a city planner.

Demography and Business

From the smallest "Mom and Pop's" store to the most expansive multinational corporation, businesses depend on their markets. And knowledge of one's market—its size, structure, geographic distribution, and its dynamics—is a major key to business success. These facts underlie the extensive and growing use of demographic skills throughout the private sector. On a more specialized plane, medium- to large-sized capitalist enterprises must also be concerned with longer-range growth prospects, general economic trends, and changes in market shares among themselves and their competitors. Here, too, is a point at which business and population science intersect.

There are many ways in which for-profit organizations employ demographic techniques and population data. A casebook prepared by H. J. Kintner and associates (1994) provides more than 350 pages of case studies that demonstrate the extent of demographic involvement in business (some of the studies also refer to government agencies). Nevertheless, three areas are especially prominent: (1) marketing research, (2) business forecasting, and (3) employee relations. Of the three, marketing research clearly makes the greatest use of the concepts and techniques discussed in this book, and it does so in a number of ways.

Most directly, market researchers are interested in measuring the size of populations, the number of households and families in a particular area, and a wide range of structural characteristics: age, gender, occupation, ethnicity, and so on (Nichols 1990; Lipschultz, Hilt, and Reilly 2007). With such data in hand, a company can then target its advertising and sales strategies in the most efficient manner possible. As in the planning profession, marketing data are often taken from U.S. Census enumerations, estimates, and Current Population Surveys; but marketing researchers often conduct their own surveys (usually via random digit dialing—see Chapter 2) to tap into values, attitudes, and preferences. Another marketing-oriented use of demographic data is in the area of corporate decision making. As Louis Pol and Richard Thomas (1997) have noted, many important choices that routinely confront corporate executives are, or should be, guided by demographic insight. These include decisions concerning if, when, and where to relocate a business or to expand to new markets, and at what point a company should market new or alternative products and services.

The role of demography in business forecasting was briefly touched on in Chapter 10. There we noted that actual population dynamics, in contrast to simple projection models, reflect complex interactions among many variables, including economic conditions. With this in view, economists and other specialists in business administration have developed multidimensional models and formulas that are intended to anticipate long-range market trends, business cycles, and the like (some models are very long range; see (McRae 1995; Parameswaran 2001). Some refer only to the United States and local markets, but other research in this area covers different parts of the world (e.g., Tapinos and Bravo 1997; Granados 2005). The hallmark of many of these models is that they incorporate interaction between population and other factors, including demographic responses to economic change and economic responses to population dynamics. Knowledge of the principles and methods of demography is essential in the construction and the interpretation of such models (Haag, Mueller, and Troitzsch 1992). For this reason, the field promises good and growing employment prospects for those trained in population science.

Another aspect of business that is informed by demography is employee relations: hiring, disability, and retirement in particular. As the population ages, increasing proportions of the workforce are retiring. Managers and employees of any business large enough to have a pension plan, or that must replace workers who are disabled or have "aged-out," need to be aware of these numbers and the associated costs. Life tables, cohort analysis, and related tools can greatly assist in decision making in this area. Similarly, every fairly large company relies on knowledge of the size, composition, and geographic distribution of the labor force, especially when it is expanding, moving to a new area, or negotiating contracts. In this regard, every personnel officer is a part-time demographer—or has one on the staff. Finally, you will recall the illustration of the period life table that we used to represent the dynamics of turnover in a company (in Chapter 9). This type of adaptation of a traditional demographic technique to the business setting has virtually unlimited possibilities as a resource to aid management and workers.

Demography for the Human Service Professional

Among the many topics covered in this book, we have at various points discussed the family, aging, youth, birth, death, illness, minority groups, and occupational and income distributions. Because of our primary interest in demography, we have examined these insofar as they relate to population size, structure, and dynamics. Yet, from another point of view, these are also the major concerns of the several fields that make up the human-service professions: social work, public health, employment counseling, youth work, and related areas. People who work in these fields come into daily, face-to-face contact with individuals and groups who require assistance with issues of family, aging, and the rest. This considerable overlap between the research-oriented, macroscopic orientation of the demographer and the practical, micro-level focus of the human-service professional has given rise to a hybrid discipline, **demography for human service**. This area is filled with opportunities for people with a solid background in population science, especially those who are also interested in making a difference in the lives of others in need.

The connection between demography and public health is perhaps the most obvious. We have seen that knowledge of health statistics is essential for the study of fertility, morbidity, and mortality, in the construction of life tables, and in developing population projections and estimates. The NCHS and the CDC routinely employ demographers for work in the Washington, D.C. and Atlanta areas and for fieldwork as well, including fieldwork in developing countries. From the earliest period of Dr. R. T. Ravenholt's administration at the AID Office of Population (see Chapter 11) to the present, U.S. population policy has been guided by a combination of demographic and public-health perspectives. In addition, public-health professionals constitute a major component of the interdisciplinary corps of experts who pursue the important, and rapidly expanding, field of gerontology.

In fact, other than the largely quantitative databases generated by CDC/NCHS, most of the literature on demography for human service is about the aging process (see Joseph 1996; Cutler, Glaeser, and Vigdor 2008; Sadavoy, Meier, and Ong 2004; Bowling 2007). To this aspect of gerontology, the demographer brings expertise in measurement, in forecasting, and in working with historical and comparative data. Another leading issue in the study of the elderly, mentioned above in the context of business applications, is retirement (see Fogarty 1982; Bhattacharya, Mulligan, and Reed 2004). As is clear from our survey of age structure, mortality, and the life table, not only is the number of people who are nearing or at the age of retirement large and increasing, but people are living longer and longer after they retire. This has already had an impact on health-service delivery, Social Security and pension-fund management, recreation and leisure facilities, and family structure.

This last issue is especially challenging. For the presence of older parents, siblings, and more distant relatives (along with health care and the various needs associated with old age) has combined with other factors to alter the U.S. family in a significant and permanent way. These other factors, discussed in Chapter 3, include fewer children, single-parent households, and unmarried parents, all of which are also the concerns of social workers and their colleagues (see South and Tolnay 1992).

Challenges such as caring for the elderly and dealing with family problems are especially acute among minority groups, and no more so than among the Native American population. A recent study of American Indian demography commissioned by the Committee on Population of the U.S. National Research Council (NRC) (Sandefur, Rindfuss, and Cohen 1996; Simoni, Sehgal, and Walters 2004) provided the most detailed overview of the elderly, health care, family relations, and many other aspects of the group. The Sandefur report included discussions of the size and distribution of the population, fertility and mortality rates, and methodological notes on enumeration and sampling problems. Perhaps because Native Americans have such serious needs and because the U.S. Census Bureau has not been entirely effective in keeping track of this group and highlighting its special problems (see Chapter 3), the NRC study stands out as one of the most effective demography/human-service projects ever undertaken.

Just as management in the private sector makes use of demographic data and techniques, human-service managers also base their decisions in part on the facts of population (Healey, Pine, and Weiner 1989; Mary 2005). As the U.S. population becomes older, more ethnically diverse, less patriarchal, more mobile, and less inclined to form "traditional" families, those who administer service-providing organizations must be able to anticipate these changes, for these factors affect the nature of their client base, the number of professionals to be employed, the kinds of people they are, and the nature of their specialties. They also impact upon the locations, sizes, and types of facilities to which clients come. Thus, the linkages between the study of a population and the rendering of services to a population are especially strong at the management level. More information about this and other aspects of the interface between demography and human services, including a job link, can be found at the National Association of Social Workers (NASW) home page at http://www.naswdc.org.

Actuarial Science

Although we have mentioned the field of actuarial science earlier in this book, especially in Chapter 9, we end this section with a reminder about it. Those of you who are mathematically inclined and have found yourself particularly interested in the life table, a career as an actuary may prove to be both satisfying and rewarding (including in material ways). Actuaries work for a variety of businesses and governmental organizations, and many have established private practices. But the insurance industry is by far the largest employer of people in this profession. This is because actuaries are specialists in assessing risks based on inductive observations and theoretical principles. Their work intersects with that of demographers at a general level because they focus on probabilities; the likelihood that events will (or will not) occur, that an individual will belong to one or another group, that some quantities will increase, or remain the same, or decrease. More specifically, they share with demographers an interest in the analysis of fertility, mortality, and morbidity. And, in this vein, they are involved in constructing and interpreting life tables of various types.

Another noteworthy similarity between actuarial science and demography is that both fields trace their origins to the work of Sir William Petty, John Graunt, and Edmund Halley. If you recall our discussion of these people in Chapter 2, you will easily understand the reason. That is, the key breakthrough of the founders was that they were the first to express the probability of the occurrence of vital events in a logically organized and quantitative manner. This opened the way for the development of both risk assessment and population science, as we understand the two fields today.

Of course, there are many ways in which actuarial science differs from demography. For example, actuaries are more statistically inclined—more knowledgeable about significance testing and the like, and they are not especially concerned with policy issues and social problems. Most important, perhaps, actuarial science incorporates a considerable amount of applied economics, especially accounting. For at the point at which the demographer moves from the life table to projection and on to other life-table-based models, the actuary associates monetary values to average life expectancy and other functions (Hickman 2004).

If you would like to learn more about the evolution and the current practices of actuarial science, there is no better place to begin than with the comprehensive study edited by Steven Haberman and Trevor A. Sibbett (1995). This multivolume set includes Haberman's and Sibbert's *History of Actuarial Science*, plus volumes of life tables and an extended presentation of life insurance mathematics. This book is available at the University of Michigan library and at other major research universities. For a quicker but less-substantial introduction, the American Association of Actuaries maintains an "Actuary Network" web site. The site contains some historical material, an overview of the profession, a basic and an advanced tutorial, a substantial data base—including life tables—that can be downloaded, and a job link.

SUMMARY

This chapter has been about demographic resources. We began with some comments on computers and software and ended with a URL for a site dedicated to actuarial science. In a symbolic sense, these technical, quantitative, and information-oriented concerns also represent the beginning and the end—the alpha and the omega—of population science today. So, too, do the many Internet sites and the books, journals, manuals, and organizations that constituted the main focus of our discussion between the first and last sections. It seems to us that in emphasizing such matters we are providing you with a fair sense of what the contemporary tools of demography are like. In fact, the most difficult part of organizing these comments was in deciding what *not* to include. As mentioned at the very outset, demography is information rich. Under these circumstances, one wonders, "How many Internet sites do we include, knowing that there may be hundreds of relevant ones?" "How many software packages and databases should be mentioned, knowing that we are bound to leave out something that is very important?"

However, to speak of such tools and resources is also to say "merely tools," "only resources." Although one would find it virtually impossible to pursue demographic studies without computers, software, manuals, organizations, and web sites, the human element remains the most important part of the equation. Demography is a field by people, about people, and for people. This should be abundantly clear from our discussion of research and careers above and from the topics covered in earlier chapters.

KEY TERMS

actuarial science
American Planning Association (APA)
Amnesty International
data sets and file transfer/file reading
   packages
demography for human service
human services
Population Association of America
   (PAA)

Population Reference Bureau, Inc. (PRB)
Summary File 1
TIGER Map Serve
United Nations High Commission for
   Refugees (UNHCR)
United States Environmental Protection
   Agency (EPA)
World Bank

CHAPTER
FOURTEEN

DEMOGRAPHY AS AN APPLIED SCIENCE

D emographic knowledge and techniques have found widespread application in almost all spheres of purposive interventions to achieve desired goals and objectives. Demographers have a rich history of collaboration with social scientists dealing with various aspects of consumption and production under the direct or indirect influences of demographic characteristics. Though the number of disciplines and subdisciplines that benefit from demographic knowledge and techniques are plenty, a few selected disciplines such as urban planning, marketing, business, education, and epidemiology have well-established approaches and procedures for incorporating demographic methods and knowledge. In this section, we will describe a few selected areas where application of demographic knowledge and techniques are clearly recognized.

DEMOGRAPHY AND POPULATION POLICY

Demographers have made remarkable contributions to the area of family planning because of its relationship to fertility. Since the regulation of births involves controlling population changes, family-planning programs and policies are seen as a subset of population policies. Levels and rates of changes in selected demographic characteristics determine the programmatic content of population policies. In an expansion of some of the ideas and events introduced in this book's first chapter, this section examines the forces that shape population policies.

Population Policy in Historical Perspective

For most of human history, the aim of population policy in effect throughout the world was that summarized in the Old Testament injunction to "be fruitful and multiply." With death rates, especially infant mortality rates, so high that populations were perpetually on the brink of decline or outright collapse, pronatalism was the only realistic policy response to the perceived problem of imminent extinction. Thus, for many thousands of years, family planning simply meant to plan on having as many children as possible and to hope that at least a few of them would survive to adulthood.

As discussed in Chapter 8, this long-standing tradition experienced a dramatic and abrupt reversal in England, other parts of Europe, and the United States at the beginning of the **Industrial Revolution**. At that point, declines in infant mortality brought about by improvements in nutrition and sanitation led to steady increases in population size, heralding the first modern **population explosions**. This brought a new kind of population problem to the attention of philosophers and early social scientists, the problem of too many people. Since that time, policies aimed at controlling population growth have been formulated and put into practice in virtually every nation. Here we examine the history of these modern population policies with a look, first, at their origins and, second, at major landmarks in their development.

The Origins of Population Policy

Family-planning programs are generally thought of as a new approach to population policy and are common in today's developing countries such as India and China. However, the earliest attempts at population policy formulation took place in Europe and the United States during the late eighteenth and early nineteenth centuries, the era of the Industrial Revolution. During this period, various points of view were formulated with regard to the impact of population on social and economic life, especially in England.

Malthus wrote his *Essay on the Principle of Population* in 1798. In Chapter 1, we mentioned Malthus's older contemporary Sir James Steuart as the probable originator of the idea that food supplies cannot keep up with population growth. In addition, at about this time, several other well-known philosophers were also contemplating the significance of population for the wealth and health of nations. Among these were Adam Smith (1723–1790), William Godwin (1756–1836), and Marie Jean Condorcet (1743–1794). Smith, a classic liberal thinker who was born and lived in Scotland, is remembered as a founder of modern social science. Along with Malthus (who acknowledged Smith's contributions), he championed the intellectual movement that led to the separation between moral philosophy and the **political economy**. On the other hand, Godwin, an English writer, and Condorcet, a leading French intellectual, clearly identified with traditional philosophy and today are considered to be Utopians.

In 1793, Godwin published his most important work, a three-volume essay entitled *Enquiry Concerning Political Justice and Its Influence on Morals and Happiness* (1793 [1946]). In it, he claimed that the Industrial Revolution would bring about a wholly new type of society in which social and economic inequality would be greatly diminished. He believed that it would no longer be necessary for laborers to work long hours to provide for the life of the individual and community. He also forecast that in the future, there would be no wars or crimes. In his utopian society, the government would wither away and there would be an end to most of the physical and mental illnesses. In the realm of demographic policy, Godwin indicated in the *Enquiry* and later in his essay, *Of Population* (1820 [1964]), explicitly written in response to Malthus, that there would be enough resources to support a population of any size. Moreover, he believed that people would eventually be so healthy and would live so long that it would be unnecessary to have children in order to replenish their populations. He envisioned a time when people could simply take a pill to control their fertility (!).

Condorcet's essay, *Esquisse d'un tableau* ("Outline of a Viewpoint," 1795 [1796]), first appeared posthumously in 1795. As in Godwin's *Enquiry*, this work announced the coming of a new era of freedom and plenty. Condorcet believed that racial and national conflicts would subside, that there would be no inequality between the sexes, that everyone would be educated, and that the law and social institutions would identify with individual and collective interests. He foresaw the possibility of increased food production and a decrease in the incidence of disease.

Thomas Malthus, a minister of the Church of England, wrote his *Essay* during a period basically dominated by utopian thought such as that of Condorcet and Godwin. In contrast to this zeitgeist (spirit of the times), Malthus's viewpoint and predictions for the future were pessimistic. Looking at the history of population growth, he observed alternating periods of slow growth and decline, the latter usually precipitated by crisis or disaster. He held that this pattern would be repeated into the indefinite future, basing this view on two **postulates** ("postulata," logically necessary truths):

> First, that food is necessary for the existence of man. Second, that the passion between the sexes is necessary, and will remain in its present state. . . . Assuming then, my postulata as granted, I say that the power of population is indefinitely greater than the power in the earth to produce subsistence for man. (1798 [1960]:8–9)

This led Malthus to conclude that populations inevitably grow until they surpass what we now call their carrying capacity, that is, their ability to sustain life. At that point, external events emerge to slow or stop, to exert a "check" on, growth. In Malthus's words:

> Population, when unchecked, increases in a **geometrical** ratio. Subsistence increases in only an arithmetical ratio. A slight acquaintance with numbers will show the immensity of the first power in comparison with the second. By that law of our nature that makes food necessary to the life of man, the effects of these two unequal powers must be kept equal. This implies a strong and constantly operating check on population from the difficulty of subsistence. This difficulty must fall somewhere and must necessarily be felt by a large portion of mankind. (1798 [1960]:10)

The "difficulty" to which Malthus was referring entails a combination of direct causes: (1) war, pestilence (plagues of insects, rats, and the like), and famine and resulting social aberrations and (2) vice and misery. These, he believed, would surely and painfully diminish population size. Malthus's forecasts obviously differed from the optimistic views of Condorcet and Godwin.

Upon publication of Malthus's *Essay*, many readers, including Godwin, argued against this formulation on the ground that it was simply a rhetorical defense of policies to reduce welfare payments to the poor. That is, Malthus was understood to be saying that the poor will multiply steadily, efforts to cure poverty are expensive and likely to fail, and so, to prevent the above-named "difficulties," they should be allowed to die as nature dictates (this position was later called "social Darwinism"). In response to this and similar criticisms, Malthus revised the *Essay* several times over the years, each time moderating his views and granting a greater role for reason (and social welfare) in the larger scheme of things; although one would hardly call his later editions utopian.

By the end of his career, Malthus was endorsing what he termed "moral restraints" on population growth, late marriage, and abstinence. But, perhaps because of his religious background and training, he remained opposed to the precepts of family planning and to artificial means of fertility limitation. Thus, the title of "founder" of the family-planning movement must be given to Malthus's younger contemporary Francis Place (1771–1854). Place, who was one of England's first population scientists, wrote articles and books on a wide range of subjects, including one that came to be considered the family-planning manifesto, *Illustration and Proofs of the Principle of Population* (1822 [1930]). As might be assumed from the title, the *Illustration and Proofs* accepts most of Malthus's premises; however, Place disagreed strongly with the older scholar on the question of the inevitability of population crisis. Instead, he argued that people could be induced to plan in advance to limit the number of offspring and to achieve their goals through traditional practices such as the rhythm method and the use of mechanical means. The contemporary U.S. demographer William Petersen (1975:516) has credited Place with producing the family-planning movement's "first systematic theory and ethical rationale" (also see Miles 1988).

In 1832, about 10 years after the appearance of Place's study, Charles Knowlton, a physician from Massachusetts, published an influential book entitled *Fruits of Philosophy: The Private Companion of Married Couples* (1832 [1980]). This book is considered to be the most important work on contraception written during the nineteenth century. Dr. Knowlton practiced medicine in the small town of Ashfield where, in his work as a gynecologist, he observed that most people knew very little about contraception. In response, he prepared a manuscript on contraceptive methods that he loaned to several of his patients. When he realized how interested readers were in the subject, he published the manuscript in the form of a book. This was met with considerable opposition from the more conservative citizens of the area, who considered contraception to be morally wrong. As a result, he was arrested and fined $50.00 in the nearby town of Taunton. Nevertheless, the book sold well and went through nine editions during Knowlton's lifetime.

Dr. Knowlton is today considered to be the founder of contraceptive medicine in the United States. His *Fruits of Philosophy* was so popular that it made its way across the Atlantic to the United Kingdom. There, two English social reformers, Charles Bradlaugh, a well-known free-thinker of his time, and Annie Besant, remembered today for her participation in and leadership of the Indian independence movement, decided to reissue the book. This edition first appeared in 1877 and sold at the very affordable price of 6 pence. This increased access to contraceptive information for a large segment of society, including the middle class and the poor. However, on April 6, 1877, Bradlaugh and Besant were arrested for selling the book and, during the following June, were tried before Lord Justice Sir Alexander Cockbum. The trial lasted about five days, during which the defendants presented their case for population control and the necessity of bringing such knowledge to the poor public. The prosecution presented a less interesting argument, calling *The Fruits of Philosophy* a "dirty, filthy book." They contended that educated human beings would never possess such a tract. Ultimately, the case was decided in favor of Bradlaugh and Besant on technicalities, but the court officially questioned the publication of Knowlton's work on moral grounds. The trial was well covered by the press and well attended by the public. As often occurs in cases such as this, the associated controversy served to advertise Dr. Knowlton's book, and sales soared soon after the trial.

Perhaps coincidentally (or perhaps not), the following year, 1878, saw a dramatic decline in fertility in England. In any case, the trial contributed significantly to establishing the family-planning movement as a major component of English population policy. For example, the Malthusian League, which was originally founded as a voluntary organization in 1860, took on an activist orientation in the late 1880s. The League's new mission was to agitate for the abolition of penalties for public discussion of population questions and to spread among the people knowledge of Malthus's laws of population and their consequences. The Malthusian League played a key role in spreading what we now term neo-Malthusian ideas ("neo" because Malthus himself was opposed to family planning in the contemporary sense) across Europe and the erstwhile British colonies such as India.

Although *Fruits of Philosophy* was widely read in England, in the United States the popularity of the book was to an extent constrained by the Comstock Law. In 1872, Anthony Comstock, an American moralist and a reformer, led a movement to have Congress enact a bill that prohibited the mailing of "obscene" material. The term was broadly defined to include literature that provided information on the prevention of conception. Violation of the law resulted in five years' imprisonment and a fine of $5,000. Over the years, this law was ignored far more often than it was obeyed. But it did serve to keep communication about fertility control and sales of contraceptive devices such as condoms (which had to be advertised as "for the prevention of disease only") clandestine until 1970, when it was finally repealed (Weeks 1992:460). The major effect of the Comstock Law and the cultural milieu it represented was to make it difficult for the family-planning movement to be considered a morally and legally acceptable cause. Thus it took militant social reformers like Margaret Sanger to bring the issue to the attention of the public and, ultimately, to help give it legitimacy.

Sanger, one of the best-known social activists in the United States, had a profound impact on her country's family-planning movement. She was born in 1893 in Corning, New York, and trained as a nurse in a White Plains hospital. During her professional career, she observed that most of her patients desperately wanted information about birth control but did not have access to it for various reasons. Subsequently, she abandoned nursing and devoted her life to the dissemination of knowledge about family planning. In 1914, she was arrested under the Comstock Law for circulating the magazine *The Womens' Rebel*, which contained information on contraceptive techniques. When, in 1916, the case against her was dismissed, she immediately established America's first birth-control clinic, in Brooklyn. This was seen as a public nuisance and led to her arrest and thirty days imprisonment in the Queen's County Penitentiary. Undeterred, she continued her political campaign that included making it legal for physicians to provide birth-control information to women as well as founding the still-powerful Planned Parenthood Association of America.

The impact of Margaret Sanger's work was both widespread and long-lasting. For example, in England, Marie Stopes followed Sanger's example by opening a birth-control clinic specifically aimed at serving poor women and catering to their needs for birth-control information and technology. Based on Sanger's activities and arguments, during the early 1930s in the United States, the American Medical Association began officially to support family-planning services as an essential component of medical services. And further, substantial policy strides were achieved after World War II.

During the early 1900s, population policies were motivated by the perceived need to control the "quality" of population as well as population size. This led to the widespread adoption of the veterinary medicine principle of **eugenics** (literally, "breeding for the good") into the study and practice of fertility control (see

Weinstein and Stehr 1999). In England, fertility rates began to decline around 1850, slowly at first and then rapidly during the last two decades of the century. As discussed in Chapter 8, these declines occurred almost exclusively among the urban middle classes. This led to a concern about an increase in the size of the lower socioeconomic classes, which were often seen as lazy and apathetic. Thus, an increase in the number of poor people was perceived as a threat to national interests. Similar concerns also plagued the birth-control movements in the United States, especially during the first two decades of the twentieth century.

Ultimately, the concern for population "quality" came to be recognized as the product of class ethnocentrism and, in many countries, racism. The horrors of genocide during World War II considerably undermined qualitative approaches to population policy, and the focus on eugenics was essentially dropped from population control programs. Today, the objectives of family-planning policy are presented in terms of development, international peace, and improvements in standards of living. However, amidst all of this concern with development and the like, Sanger's founding doctrine that women bear children and therefore women's welfare is inextricably linked to the birth and health of children, has rarely come to the forefront. The relevance of women's issues, reproductive rights, and reproductive health as key components of population-control policies was at last addressed at the 1994 Conference on Population and Development held in Cairo, Egypt. The conference recommended that the focus of population policy should be shifted away from demographic targets and toward qualitative outcomes such as promotion of reproductive health. It was also suggested that population policy include socioeconomic measures that will bring about conditions in the lives of women conducive to having small families. These measures include providing women with better educational opportunities, equal access to employment, and improved health services.

Looking back on the developments that led to policy directives such as those formulated in Cairo, family-planning experts Peter Donaldson and Amy Tsui (1990) prepared a brief chronology of major landmarks in the history of the field. The revised and expanded version of that chronology presented here indicates just how far the field has come since the days of Godwin and Malthus. Originally a concern over quality of life shared by gentleman scholars at the dawn of the Industrial Revolution, it has become a high-priority item on the international agenda, on which hundreds of millions of dollars are spent annually.

The Early Advocates

Table 14.1 identifies the pioneers responsible for founding the family-planning movement, as discussed in earlier chapters and the previous section.

Post-World War II Developments

Following a period of relative quiet during the Great Depression and World War II, the family-planning movement gained momentum in the late 1940s (see Table 14.2). Among the several factors contributing to this revival were: (a) improvements in the status of women in the industrialized nations where women replaced men, and in some instances surpassed them in productivity, on the assembly line and in other occupations; (b) founding of the United Nations in 1945, which thereby created a world-level forum for considering population issues and policy; and (c) reaction to the eugenics movement that eventuated in mass slaughter in the name of "population control."

Table 14.1.   Earliest Contributors to Population Policy

Founder	Dates	Contribution
John Graunt	1620–1674	Pioneering Studies of Mortality
Edmund Halley	1656–1742	Inventor of Life Table
Sir James Steuart	1713–1780	Anticipated Malthusian "Laws"
Adam Smith	1723–1790	Founder of Political Economy
Marie Jean Condorcet	1743–1794	Incorporated Demography into Social Philosophy
William Godwin	1756–1836	"Utopian" Critic of Malthus
Thomas Robert Malthus	1766–1834	Developed the First "Laws of Population"
Francis Place	1771–1854	Founder of Family Planning
Charles Knowlton	1800–1850	U.S. Family-Planning Pioneer
Annie Besant	1844–1915	Family-Planning Advocate
Emilé Durkheim	1858–1917	Discovered Aggregate Effect
Margaret Sanger	1879–1966	Family-Planning Advocate
Marie Stopes	1880–1958	Family-Planning Advocate

Table 14.2.   Major Events in Population Policy Immediately Following World War II

Date	Event
1946	The United Nations Economic and Social Council establishes a population commission representing member governments and a population division within the Secretariat.
1951	India adopts family planning as part of its first Five-Year Plan.
1952	John D. Rockefeller III establishes the Population Council.
1953	Ratification of the constitution of the International Planned Parenthood Federation (IPPF), which was drafted one year earlier at an international conference in Cheltenham, England.

Rapid Program Expansion

Following the postwar renewal of interest in population issues, several innovations contributed to the worldwide institutionalization of the family-planning movement (see Table 14.3). Some of these were technological, some financial, and others political. Together, they helped to create the policy assumptions with which we are familiar today: acceptance of family planning on secular moral grounds (despite continuing prohibitions by some established religions), cheap and effective methods of fertility limitation, and international concern about the relationship between population growth and socioeconomic development.

DEMOGRAPHY AND TOURISM

Tourism has emerged as an important industry worldwide. Growth of the industry is profoundly related to demographic changes (Watson 2011). Declining fertility, population aging, improvements in life expectancy, urbanization, Women's liberation, increases in disposable income per capita, and availability of fast modes of transportation have contributed to the growth of the tourism industry.

Table 14.3 Major Events in Population Policy during the 1960s

Date	Event
1960	Oral contraceptives ("the pill") are introduced.
1961	Plastic intrauterine devices (IUDs) become available.
1967	The trust fund for the United Nations Fund for Population Activities (UNFPA) is established.
1968	The United Nations International Conference on Human Rights issues the Teheran proclamation, of which article 16 states: "Parents have a basic human right to determine freely and responsibly the number and spacing of their children."
1969	Pope Paul VI issues *Humana Vitae* banning the use of artificial contraception.
1969	Paul Ehrlich publishes his influential book *The Population Bomb*.

Given the importance of tourism to economies worldwide, building physical and economic structures such as hotels to cater to the diverse needs of tourists calls for planning. Demographers consider various characteristics such as age/sex composition, fertility rates, and value changes in various segments of the population with regard to tourism to forecast the demand for various services offered by the tourism industry. In the following section, we describe tourism as a form of migration and examine the various demographic characteristics that have implications for tourism planning.

Although touring, in itself, is obviously not associated with a change of residence, its social and economic impacts can be just as significant. Moreover, it can, and often does, lead to residential relocation, and in such instances may be viewed as a link in a special type of chain migration.

Tourism is a relatively modern phenomenon. Once only the privilege of the very wealthy (or the very adventurous), those whom Thorstein Veblen first labeled the **leisure class**, it has become a major aspect of life for millions of people throughout the world. According to M. Pretes (1995), it satisfies the need to experience "the hyper-real" and "the real." The hyper-real includes simulated theme parks and other contrived attractions, whereas the real constitutes the countryside and other natural attractions.

Several trends have contributed to the increase in tourism, thus creating a multibillion-dollar industry. These trends indicate that the activity and associated services will continue to expand. First and foremost is the increase in the amount of leisure time and disposable income available to those who are employed in the formal sectors of the economy. That is, to a considerable extent, tourism is an outgrowth of the rise of middle-class society whose members are willing and able to pay for hyper-real and real experiences. Second, tourism is one of the consequences of curiosity. The interest in exotic people and lands is likely to grow as more and more information about them becomes available via television, printed media, and the Internet. Third, the accessibility to new and potential tourist destinations has improved as the result of infrastructure development in the less-industrialized countries. Finally, diversification of the tourist industry will probably cater to different types of people who desire different modes of tourist experience.

The Dimensions of World Tourism

The World Tourism Organization (WTO) defines an international visitor as a person who travels for less than one year to a country other than that in which he or she usually resides. The purpose of such a visit is to engage in any activity or set of activities not remunerated in the country visited. The volume of tourism has risen dramatically since the 1970s and, according to WTO, the number of international arrivals will surpass the 1.6 billion mark by the year 2020. During the first two decades of the twenty-first century, the number of international arrivals is expected to grow at an annual rate of 4 percent.

The tourist industry is now an important component of the economies of many countries and of the global economy as a whole. Tourism industry's share in the world economy grew by 3.1 percent in 2013, accounting for about US$2.2 trillion. Between 2008 and 2011, the industry grew faster than the overall economic growth worldwide. One in 11 of all jobs in the world in 2011 was directly or indirectly related to the tourism industry.[1]

According to the U.S. Department of Commerce, international visitors to the United States spent an estimated $18.4 billion on travel and tourism-related activities during the month of July 2014; a 1 percent increase compared to the amount spent in July 2013. Travel and tourism-related exports increased more than $900 million per month between January and July 2014. Real spending on travel and tourism has increased at an annual rate of approximately 2.1 percent between 2012 and 2014. This spending supported 7.6 million jobs.[2] The United States is second only to France among the most-visited country in the world, with nearly 70 million tourists arriving in 2013. Spain occupied third position and Turkey sixth (see Table 14.4).

In 2013, the United States spent approximately $72 million on tourism marketing campaigns resulting in incremental international visitors spending of $3.4 billion. The return to investment was about 47 to 1.[3] Thus, the returns to investment on tourism promotion are very high, and for this reason alone the tourism industry is viewed as an important component of most national economies.

The Office of Research under the U.S. Travel and Tourism Administration (USTTA) is a chief source of international tourism statistics. To underscore the close ties between tourism and the more traditional types of migration, this agency obtains travel data from the INS, which collects completed INS forms from all overseas travelers entering the United States. These data are used to assess trends in international arrivals to the country on a yearly basis. The USTTA Research Office also conducts

Table 14.4. International Tourist Arrivals, 2012-2013

Destination Country	Ranking 2013	Number of Visitors in Millions, 2012	Number of Visitors in Millions, 2013	Percent Change 2012–2013
*France	1	83.0	83.0	1.8
United States	2	67.0	69.8	4.7
Spain	3	57.7	60.7	5.6
China	4	57.7	58.7	0.3
Italy	5	46.4	47.7	2.9
Turkey	6	35.7	37.8	5.9
Germany	7	30.4	31.5	3.7
United Kingdom	8	29.3	31.1	6.4
Russia	9	25.7	28.4	10.2
Malaysia	10	25.0	25.7	2.7

*2013 Data for France is unavailable; table shows 2012 data.

Source: Based on data from *Tourism Highlights 2014 Edition*, United Nations World Tourism Organization.

tourism surveys upon request from public and private organizations. In addition, the office conducts a monthly inflight survey that collects information on travel habits, demographic characteristics, and spending patterns of international air travelers (both U.S. residents and nonresidents) entering and departing from the United States.

The U.S. Department of Transportation also maintains a database on arrival and departure information from international travelers. This is the most important source of information currently available on the number of U.S. citizens traveling abroad. At the international level, the WTO, whose headquarters are located in Madrid, Spain, is a major clearinghouse for international tourism facts and figures. The WTO maintains country-specific databases on numerous aspects of international tourism.

The Impacts of Tourism

The presence of a large number of tourists acts, like more permanent forms of in-migration, to increase the population size at the destination, especially at places of historical, commercial, or recreational interest. As a result, there will be a more-or-less temporary increase of population pressure on local resources—more temporary where tourism is seasonal, less so where there is a steady flow of visitors year-round. The influx of tourists can result in crowded public-transportation systems and a lack of housing and other accommodations. In addition to these demographic effects, international tourism has several social impacts, some positive and others negative. The arrival of tourists at a destination results in social contacts among peoples of different cultures. The intensity of such contact varies depending upon the number of people who arrive and the duration of their stay. Interaction between the tourists and the resident population at the destination may bring about changes in quality of life, lifestyles, and value systems.

Tourism can contribute to the prosperity of economies at the destination, because money spent by tourists can increase employment. International tourism is also a foreign-exchange earner. Traditional arts and crafts industries in several developing countries owe their very existence to demand generated by international tourists. Countries such as Zambia advertise local culture festivals abroad in order to attract international tourists—and the money they bring. The well-known wildlife safaris in Tanzania, Zimbabwe, Zambia, and Kenya generate vitally needed income for the preservation of local ecosystems, animals, and flora. Indeed, without international tourism, the encroachment of human settlements into the forests of the world's tropical regions would have endangered the survival of very many rare animal species.

International tourists are informal cultural ambassadors. Mutual respect and regard between international visitors and people who reside at the destinations can pave the way for improving economic and political economic relations among nations. President Richard Nixon's landmark visit to the People's Republic of China in February 1972 was followed by several cultural and academic exchanges between U.S. and Chinese scholars for the first time in decades. These visits, in turn, led to normalization of political relations between the nations, and to President Bill Clinton's 1998 goodwill tour.

Negative impacts arise when social changes created by tourists and the tourism industry threaten, or are perceived to threaten, the wellbeing of the population at the destination. During the 1960s, there was a steady flow of tourists from the West to Asia in search of spiritual knowledge and the exotic aspects of Eastern cultures and religions. In this case and in similar instances in other developing countries, the lifestyles and behavior of the tourists, which were previously unknown to the population at the destination, came to be imitated in an unreflective manner, especially when the tourists originated from modern, industrialized societies. These new lifestyles and values often conflict with the traditional ways of life of the host peoples. Moreover, some tourists conduct themselves in a manner that is not tolerated in their own cultures, spreading new vices and exotic diseases. Unfortunately, in response to this pleasure-seeking behavior, several international destinations in Asia and Europe attract large numbers of tourists to their flourishing sex and drug trade.

The economies at major tourist destinations can become overly dependent on tourism, relying too heavily on this single source of revenue and failing to diversify into other industries and commercial undertakings. In the Placenitia region of the small Central American country of Belize, there has been a steady shift of the labor force away from fishing and agriculture to the tourism industry. As a result, revenues from fish exports have been considerably reduced, and the dependency of residents on international tourism for jobs has increased dramatically. Similarly, R. Sathiendrakumar and C. Tisdell (1989) have demonstrated that in the Republic of Maldives, development of a capital-intensive tourist industry has contributed very little to the solution of this island nation's poverty and has disguised unemployment problems.

Perhaps the best-known negative consequence of international tourism involves the threat to the ecological systems of the places of destination. In this regard, tourism has two highly identifiable characteristics. First are the products and attractions at the destination, such as relatively unspoiled natural environments—rain forests, sea shores, mountain ranges, and the like—that tourists are willing to spend considerable amounts of money and travel long distances to see, experience, and enjoy. Second are the people and organizations that provide the services for the visitors. So, for example, many international tourists travel to developing countries such as Costa Rica and Belize to see the plants, flowers, the land, and animals in their pristine, undisturbed settings. In response, a thriving tourist industry has developed to satisfy this demand. Ironically, however, as the number of tourists increases, these ecological systems that sustain tourism become used, then overused, and, ultimately, destroyed.

The concept of carrying capacity (discussed in earlier chapters) can help us understand the dilemma that arises from the delicate relationship between tourism and the preservation of natural attractions. Consider this example: The Luanga Valley in Zambia is the largest wild-game preserve in the country. Among its most popular attractions are the nighttime safaris. These involve visits to the forests in an off-road vehicle, under the supervision of a trained guide, to see nocturnal animals such as leopards. A particularly interesting aspect of these tours is to observe the leopard hunting. But the tourists cannot see the animals in action unless bright lights are used. However, these lights ordinarily blind the predator, scare the prey, and result in missed hunting opportunities. Some of these leopards starve to death because the nighttime safaris intrude into the pursuit of their prey. In this instance, the carrying capacity, as measured by the number of tourists that constitute "too many," may even be as low as zero, unless, that is, the practice of using bright lights is abandoned.

The effective management of tourist resources, whether economic, sociocultural, or environmental, ultimately involves people. Because people, as tourists and as hosts, bring with them their cultures and values, the preservation of culture is essential for the preservation of tourist attractions. This understanding has been incorporated in the relatively new movement known as ecotourism. According to proponents, visitors and people at destinations benefit through cooperation and mutual understanding of both the benefits and the costs of tourism and the tourist trade. In a recent editorial plea, Lisa Gosselin, editor of the *Audubon Magazine*, summarized the position of her influential organization:

> The mission of the National Audubon Society is to protect natural ecosystems for the benefit of humanity and the earth's biological diversity. Responsible eco-tourism not only helps us do this, it also offers a chance in some cases our last chance—to glimpse how the planet worked before humans altered it. (Gosselin 1998; also see Markels 1998)

Natural attractions can only be properly managed, and kept attractive, if those who engage in preservation are supported. Local economies are truly helped by tourism only when the revenues and other benefits thus generated are used wisely. And, as common sense would dictate, the people who reside at the destinations should be responsible for setting the boundaries for sharing their cultures. As indicated by the root word *ecos*, whose original meaning is "household," such respect for those who host others is an essential feature of ecotourism, or of responsible tourism whatever we may label it.

SUMMARY: APPLIED DEMOGRAPHY, A POSTSCRIPT

By now it is abundantly clear that demography possess all the characteristics of a scientific field. All scientific fields create knowledge which either directly or indirectly lead to improving human welfare and/or satisfying human curiosity. In the field of demography, a large number of demographers are engaged in building knowledge about population processes and outcomes. However, unlike many scientific disciplines, demographers have been historically involved in active translation of demographic knowledge into activities that solve problems at all levels of social aggregation such as groups, and communities. Demographers often team up with expert from several disciplines, aiding them make problem-solving decisions as they provide demography-based solutions to social problems for clients. This strong sense of involvement in solving problems has given rise to a specialized subfield within demography called applied demography.

The orientation toward engaging with clients has four implications for the field of applied demography. First, clients usually tend to be represent small groups, communities, and organizations. They seldom tend to be from large social aggregates such as a nation-state or regions and for this reason, applied demographers tend to be engaged with small-size populations. Second, its focus is on arriving at decisions of immediate interest to solving specific client-based problems. Third, applied demographers tend to focus on planning for a sustainable state of existence as desired by clients and communities. Finally, applied demographers are committed to manipulating demographic processes that preserve and promote human rights, human dignity, and social justice.

Applied demography is devoted to serving clients who bring problems that can benefit from demographic techniques and knowledge of population processes. In this regard, applied demographers bring to the problem at hand information and skills from two demographic knowledge domains, namely basic demography dealing with birth, death, and migration, and demographic indicators related to size, composition, and spatial distribution of populations. Applied demographers make use of innovative and purposive combining of knowledge from these two domains for attaining predetermined and selected goals on behalf of their clients. Most applied demographers are professional practitioners who are either employed by social/planning agencies or are practitioners who charge for their services. The rest volunteer their services to social organizations, groups, and communities.

Applied demographers very often use secondary data sets. They are used frequently to extract data at the level of selected aggregation (census tract) publicly available. Four well-known data sources in the field of applied demography are census, vital registration systems, population registers, and surveys. Among the four, population registers are least popular as there are only few countries which maintain these registers. In the United States, almost all survey data gathered with financial assistance from federal organizations are available to the public. Among these large-scale secondary data sets, a few such as the American Community survey, National Survey of family growth, current population survey, and National Health Interview survey are well known.

When secondary data sets are used, there is seldom any control over the quality of data. Quality of data is of great concern to applied demographers as a large measure of doing applied demography involves measurement and interpretation of data (Rives and Serrow 1984). Errors inherent in the data are likely to be compounded with additional errors that may occur during the course of data retrieval and preparation for analysis. In developing countries, availability of data may be restricted to only the census. Unfortunately, national census in most developing countries contains both coverage and content errors. This makes it difficult to obtain reliable estimates of parameters of interest to applied demographers.

Applied demographers are often under pressure from their clients to provide expert guidance in making decisions in a short period of time. They do not often have the luxury of collecting primary data, which is both costly and time consuming. For this reason, they often rely on available data sources as mentioned earlier such as census and surveys, which provide data for the specific area of interest to the client. Demographers may combine demographic data from different sources, such as census, Medicare, and new-housing data to arrive at reliable estimates. The growing demand for demographic statistics at the small-area level has now given rise to the development a number of related techniques variously called "**small-area estimation**" or **local demography**. The contributions of applied demographers have gained widespread recognition within the field of demography as is evident from the existence of the applied demography group in the Population Association of America. The group publishes a newsletter titled "Applied Demography" twice a year.

KEY TERMS

eugenics	political economy
geometrical	population explosion
Industrial Revolution	postulates
leisure class	"small-area estimation"
local demography	

NOTES

1. See http://mkt.unwto.org/.

2. See http://www.whitehouse.gov/blog/2012/09/19/administrations-efforts-promote-travel-and-tourism-are-working.

3. http://www.ibtimes.com/how-americas-first-ever-tourism-marketing-campaign-paying-1555431.

WEB RESOURCES DISCUSSED IN CHAPTER 13

United States Census Bureau: http://www.census.gov.

United States Centers for Disease Control and Prevention: http://www.cdc.gov.

U.S. National Center for Health Statistics: http://www.cdc.gov/nchs.

United States Census Bureau archive for state-level data: http://quickfacts.census .gov/qfd/index.html.

United Nations Statistics Division: http://www.un.org./popin.

United Nations Development Program population information software downloads: http://hdr.undp.org/en/data.

Interdisciplinary Demographic Institute (NIDI) in The Hague: http://www.nidi.nl/eu.

Population Training Software: http://www.nidi.nl/en/research/pd/140202 and http:// www.nidi.nl/en/research/al/270101 and http://geosim.cs.vt.edu.

M.I.T. library guides: http://libguides.mit.edu/content.php?pid=347508.

EASI GIS: http://www.easidemographics.com.

United States Department of Housing and Urban Development (HUD): http://www .hud.gov.

HUD software: http://portal.hud.gov/hudportal/HUD?src=/program_offices/public _indian_housing/reac/products/pass/pass_demo.

University of Wisconsin Directory for Global Population Information: https://scout.wisc .edu/archives/r16892/popnet_the_directory_for_global_population_information.

U.S. Census TIGER map division: https://www.census.gov/geo/maps-data/data/tiger .html.

U.S. Environmental Protection Agency GIS site: https://edg.epa.gov/metadata/catalog/ main/home.page.

The University of California (Berkeley) Library GIS Section: http://oskicat.berkeley.edu/search~S1/?searchtype=X&searcharg=GIS.

Population Index: http://popindex.princeton.edu.

POPNET: http://popnet.pacificsciencecenter.org/member-sign-in/.

SocioSite Population page: http://www.sociosite.net/topics/population.php.

CIC Refugee site: http://www.cic.gc.ca/EnGLish/refugees/index.asp.

American Sociological Association (ASA): http://www.asanet.org.

ASA population section: http://www.asanet.org/population/index.cfm.

Universities that maintain demographic data and analysis sites:

1. The Pennsylvania State University Population Research Institute (PRI): http://www.pop.psu.edu/.
2. The Princeton University Office of Population Research: http://opr.princeton.edu/.
3. The University of North Carolina Population Center: http://www.cpc.unc.edu/.
4. Stanford University Population Policy site: http://healthpolicy.stanford.edu/publications/the_us_global_health_initiative_informing_policy_with_evidence/.
5. The University of Minnesota Historical Integrated Public Use Microsample (IUPMS) Data: https://usa.ipums.org/usa/.
6. University of Virginia Library: https://www.library.virginia.edu/.
7. The University of Michigan: http://guides.lib.umich.edu/healthstats.
8. San Jose State University: http://www.sjsu.edu/faculty/watkins/cohort.htm.
9. Wichita State University: http://www.wichita.edu/thisis/wsunews/news/?nid=2358.

American Demographics: http://www.demographics.com.

Rural and Small Town Programme: http://www2.epa.gov/smart-growth/smart-growth-small-towns-and-rural-communities. This is a Canadian site that specializes in data on rural areas, that is, the neglected 20 percent of North America's population.

Urban Land Institute: http://www.urban.org. This is the premiere nongovernmental urban planning "think tank" that specializes in data on the other 80 percent of the population.

PopulationAssociation of America (PAA): http://www.populationassociation.org/.

Population Research Bureau (PRB): http://www.prb.org.

PRB glossary of terms: http://www.prb.org/Publications/Lesson-Plans/Glossary.aspx.

CentralIntelligenceAgencyWorldFactbook:https://www.cia.gov/library/publications/the-world-factbook/.

World Health Organization sites:

http://www.who.int/gho/publications/world_health_statistics/2014/en/.

http://www.who.int/en/.

Forced Migration Review: http://www.fmreview.org/.

U.S. Committee for Refugees and Immigrants: http://www.refugees.org/about-us/in-the-news/media-campaigns/refugee-voices.html.

Tourism sites:

> http://www.tourismcenter.msu.edu.
> http://www.nps.gov/index.htm.
> http://int.rendezvousenfrance.com/.
> http://www.paris-paris-paris.com/.
> http://www.atomictourism.net/.
> http://www.ecotourism.org.
> http://www.ecotour.com.

U.S. Census population projections:

http://www.census.gov/population/projections/files/methodology/methodstatement 12.pdf.

U.N. Development Program population projections:

http://www.un.org/en/development/desa/population/publications/manual/projection/index.shtml.

http://www.un.org/en/development/desa/population/theme/policy/.

http://www.un.org/popin/oau/poppolyc.htm.

World Bank population projections: https://openknowledge.worldbank.orghandle/10986/6788.

Population Council Research: http://www.popcouncil.org/research/population-policy-and-demographic-analysis.

U.N. International Population and Development site: http://icpdbeyond2014.org/.

U.N. Regional and National Population Information: http://www.un.org/popin/regional/africa/.

Prochoice/Prolife Debate:

http://www.naral.org/.

http://www.prochoiceamerica.org/what-is-choice/abortion/.

http://www.prolife.org/.

The World Bank datasets, databases, tables, etc.: http://data.worldbank.org/indicator#topic.

U.N. Food and Agricultural Organization Sustainable Development site: http://www.fao.org/nr/sustainability/sustainability-assessments-safa/en/.

Association for Applied and Clinical Sociology: http://www.aacsnet.net/.

Canadian Institute of Planners: https://www.cip-icu.ca/#.

GLOSSARY

abridged table A life table in which most of the age categories are grouped into intervals greater than one year (usually 4, 5, or 10 years)

actuarial science The field that focuses on the measurement of risk, especially mortality and other demographic events

administrative area A geographic area with official political status (a state, city, etc.) that also serves as a unit for the collection and reporting of census data

age-specific death rate (ASDR) A measure of mortality based on the ratio of the number of deaths that occur in a given cohort and the size of that cohort

age-specific fertility rate[s] (ASFR) A measure of fertility based on the ratio of the number of children born to women of a given age and the number of women at that age

age-specific mortality The occurrence of deaths in a population according to the age of the deceased

agenda setting The first and most important step in policy formulation, during which basic goals are established

aggregate A collection of items; in demography, examples of these items are individual human beings and households

Agricultural Revolution A dramatic increase in the production of food and other primary produce that contributes to the development and growth of cities

American Planning Association (APA) The leading organization of professional planners, which also administers the AICP (American Institute of Certified Planners)

Amnesty International A prominent organization that tracks migration, especially the legal and political issues associated with it

average life expectancy The life table function that indicates the (theoretical) average number of years of life remaining to individuals who reach a given age

baby boom The period of high fertility experienced in the United States and other countries following World War II

behavioral sink The pathological condition of population collapse as the result of crowding; from the work of behavioral psychologist, John Calhoun

biodiversity A wide range of species within a habitat; a high degree of biodiversity indicates a healthy system

biological (structure) The organization of a population based on sex or age categories

birth The events more precisely called a "live birth," of a child being delivered and surviving at least momentarily

birth (fertility) control The intentional lowering of fertility levels through family planning and related methods

Bureau of Labor Statistics (BLS) Branch of the U.S. Department of Commerce that collects and reports employment data

carrying capacity The theoretical maximum number of species and individuals that can be physically supported by a habitat

cause-specific mortality The occurrence of deaths in a population according to its causes

census A population count; from the word for "taxation"

central crude death rate An average of observed death rates for consecutive years

central date The date, often a Census year such as 1990 or 2000, on which population estimates are based; in this sense, the point of the procedure is to update central date information

central place theory The influential theory of Walter Christaller that focuses on the influence of a central place on the surrounding area

child mortality rate (CMR) A measure of the incidence of death among children during their first five years of life

child–woman ratio (CWR) A measure of fertility based on census or other survey data that compares the number of children at or below a certain age (e.g., five years) to the number of fertile women in the population

Chipko The women's movement against deforestation in India that gave rise to the term "tree hugger"

city-state (polis) A city that is politically autonomous and governs the population of its hinterlands

cohort An aggregate of persons in a population born at the same time

cohort measures Measures of fertility based on the observation of a group of women born or married at the same time as they proceed through their reproductive years

cohort survival A method of population estimation that uses age-specific measures over time

cohort survival method A technique of estimation and projection based on the life table in which observed birth and death rates are assumed to hold into the future

cohort table A life table based on information about a group of individuals born at the same time as they age with the passage of the years

column vector A column of a matrix; in a life table each column refers to a variable—such as the surviving population (lx) in the second column

commons Any property or commodity that is collectively owned

complete enumeration A census that presumes counting directly every member of a population

components method Approaches to estimation and projection that employ information about birth, deaths, and migration; the cohort survival method is of this

Consolidated Metropolitan Statistical Area (CMSA) An urbanized region of the United States consisting of a city with a population size of at least 1 million and its suburbs

crude birth rate (CBR) The number of infants born into a population per 1,000 persons (usually measured per year)

crude rates Rates that measure the occurrence of vital events in an entire population

cultural assimilation The blending of two (or more) populations in which one takes on the language and customs of another

data sets and file transfer/file-reading packages Large amounts of secondary demographic data available online

deforestation The large-scale cutting of forests to the point at which the land is denuded

demographic determinism The theoretical position that views population dynamics as the ultimate causes of sociocultural change

demographic transition A long-range change in population growth rates as the result of declining levels of fertility and/or mortality; especially Europe's three-stage transition that began in about 1650

demography for human service An interdisciplinary field that employs demographic data and techniques in human-service fields, such as Public Health

density The number of persons, households, and so forth per unit of area

dependency ratio A measure of the average number of people who must be supported by each member of a population's labor force

difference method The measurement of a population's growth by subtracting its size at an earlier date from that at a later date

doubling time The number of years it takes a population to double; it is approximately equal to 70 divided by the annual percentage growth rate

ecological collapse Environmental disaster resulting from misuse of resources and/or population pressure

ecological fallacy An erroneous conclusion that relationships observed at the aggregate level also hold true for the individuals making up the aggregate

ecology The interdisciplinary field that studies the relationships among occupants of *ecosystems*

ecosystem A natural habitat viewed as a system of interdependent parts

efficiency evaluation A type of evaluation research that focuses on how program funds are spent

emergence(ent) Characteristics of aggregates that exist independent of the characteristics of the individuals making up the aggregate ("the whole is greater than the sum of its parts")

emigrant An individual who moves from one nation to another, from the perspective of the sender nation

endogamy The practice of marrying only within one's own population or social group

environmentalism The social movement that focuses on the restoration, conservation, and appropriate uses of *ecosystems*

epidemiological transition The centuries long, three-stage shift in the most common causes of death

estimate A statement about the size and other characteristics of a population based on prior knowledge

eugenics A movement that encourages the selection of persons with desired genetic traits

event history analysis A research technique that is based, in part, on a cohort life table and which follows a phenomenon as its size diminishes (or increases) with the passage of time

exponential growth model The basis for estimates and projections that assume a continual increase in the rate of growth between two dates

extrapolation The process of estimating or projecting from a *central date* that assumes that growth will continue according to one of the growth models

fecundity The absolute physical capacity to bear children

fertility The actual process of childbearing during a woman's reproductive life

fetal mortality Death that occurs prior to birth through either spontaneous or voluntary abortion

forced migration Movement between populations motivated by violence or its threat

forecast A statement about what the characteristics of a population are likely to be at a future date

formal demography The approach to population studies that focuses on data collection, analysis, measurement, and projection; distinguished from *social demography*

Gemeinschaft and Gesellschaft Literally, "community and society;" a paired concept that emphasizes the difference between traditional rural life and modern urban society

general fertility rate (GFR) A measure that sums together all ASFRs in a population

geometrical A type of growth in which a population size continuously doubles over the course of time (e.g., each year)

geographic information systems (GIS) A computerized approach to mapping demographic and other types of information

geometric growth model The basis for estimates and projections that assume a periodic increase in the rate of growth between two dates

Gini Index (ratio) A measure of inequality in the distribution of wealth, and so on

gross migration The total number of in- and out-migrants entering/leaving a population during a year or other time period

gross reproduction rate (GRR) A measure of the capacity for a population to maintain its size over the course of generations; it does not account for child or maternal mortality

Guides and Master Sites Web sites that direct the user to a wide range of specialized sites

human services Assistance, such as food or housing, provided to persons in need

immigrant An individual who moves from one nation to another, from the perspective of the receiver nation

Immigration and Nationality Act (1924) An act of the U.S. Congress that established quotas favoring immigrants from western Europe

impact evaluation A type of evaluation research that focuses on the extent to which the goals of a program have been achieved

implementation The third and most difficult stage of the policy-formulation process, during which plans are put into effect

incidence A measure of the number of people recently diagnosed with a disease: for example, within a given year

incipient decline The term formerly used to describe the third stage of Europe's demographic transition, suggesting potential future population loss; this potential has now been realized throughout Europe

Industrial Revolution The transition to manufacturing as the basis of subsistence from agriculture during the first half of the nineteenth century

infant mortality rate(IMR) A measure of the incidence of death among infants during their first year of life

in-migration The entry of individuals into one part of a nation from another part of that same nation

intermediate variables The factors that limit fertility prior to intercourse, conception, or gestation

International Planned Parenthood Federation (IPPF) A well-established *NGO* that promotes family planning worldwide

involuntary migration Movement between populations contrary to the will of the migrant; forced migration is an extreme form of this

Lamarckian The belief that characteristics of parents acquired during their lifetimes can be passed on to their offspring; this is contrary to Darwin's law of natural selection

leisure class An elite group of people who accumulate and demonstrate their accumulated wealth in public spaces

Lexis diagram A graphic representation of the dynamics of cohort and period life tables

life chances The probability that the members of social groups will prosper, enjoy good health and longevity, and so on

life style The manner in which members of social groups conduct their daily round of life: how and where they work and live, how they spend their leisure time, and so forth

life table functions The variables contained in the columns of the life table-proper (l_x, e_x, etc.); based on observed data, these constitute a model of the observed population

linear growth model The basis for estimates and projections that assume a constant rate of growth between two dates

local demography A field within demography specifically dealing with demographic characteristics of small areas and populations

logistic growth model The basis for estimates and projections that assume that the rate of growth increases to a maximum and then decreases until it nears or reaches ZPG

Malthusian The theoretical position based on Malthus's principles of population change and crisis

matrix A rectangular array of numbers or other information made up of *row* and *column vectors*; a life table is a matrix

Metropolitan Statistical Area (MSA) an urban area consisting of a city or adjacent cities with a population of at least 50,000 and its (their) suburbs

morbidity The occurrence of disease in a population, especially a serious illness that can be fatal

mortality control The intentional lowering of death rates through the application of nutrition, sanitation, and public-health practices

multiphasic demographic response Behavior that mitigates the effects of relatively sudden increases in population growth

multiphasic response model (MRM) The ecological theory based on Kingsley Davis's model of demographic transition

natality The probability of the occurrence of births in a population

natural increase The component of population growth (or loss) resulting from the difference between the number of births and the number of deaths, symbolized as (B–D)

neo-Malthusian A Malthusian perspective that accepts family planning as a means to avert population crisis

neonatal mortality rate (NMR) A measure of the incidence of death among infants during their first month of life

net migration The difference between in-migration and out-migration

net reproduction rate The average number of female children born into a population and who survive to reproduce

nongovernmental organization (NGO) Such organizations now play a major role in population policy formulation

Office of Management and Budget (OMB) The branch of the U.S. government that regulates definitions of race, ethnicity, and other structural criteria

operationalization The act of defining a scientific term so that the term can be associated with clear observation

optimum population size The theoretically most appropriate number of persons that can be supported by a given base of resources

out-migration The exit of individuals from one part of a nation to another part of that same nation

pandemic An outbreak of a fatal disease that affects a very large proportion of a population

period measures Measures, such as crude death rates, that apply to members of a population at a given date (e.g., year)

period table A life table based on information about all members of a population at a given point in time (e.g., a specific year)

political economy A branch of economics focusing on the role of economic process in shaping public policy

population A kind of aggregate that shares a gene pool, bounded territory, and a sociocultural heritage

Population Association of America (PAA) The leading professional association of demographers in the United States

population explosion The unprecedented and exponential population growth rate resulting in large population size

population pyramid A bar graph representing a population's age and sex structures

Population Reference Bureau, Inc. (PRB) A private organization that provides demographic data (much free of charge)

Portable Document File (PDF) that contains data in a compact format

postpartum abstinence A variable period of time following delivery of a child during which a woman refrains from sexual intercourse

postulates Statements that are believed to be true across time and space

prediction A statement derived from observation and deduction that is equivalent to a scientific explanation; it indicates what would be the case if certain premises hold true

prevalence A measure of the number of people who are affected by a disease at specific point in time

process evaluation A type of evaluation research that focuses on the manner in which a program is implemented

program evaluation A type of research designed to determine if a program is effective

projection The depiction of the hypothetical size and structure of a population at one or more future dates based on explicit assumptions concerning the continuation of observed trends

pronatalism The belief that high fertility is desirable

"push-pull" process The principle of voluntary migration whereby prospective migrants compare the costs and benefits of a potential destination with those of their present residence

quasi-experimental design A type of research methodology that is applied when one or more components of the experimental method cannot be employed

radix A round number which, when multiplied by a proportion, allows comparisons between populations (or other collections) whose sizes are unequal: the "100" in percentages, the "1,000" in demographic rates, and so on

reductionist A type of theory that assumes that all aggregate characteristics can be reduced to the level of individuals—thus opposing the emergent position

relative deprivation The perceived lack of material items during a period following more prosperous times

reproduction The ability of a population to maintain or surpass its size in future cohorts

Rio Declaration Document produced by the 1992 environmental conference in Rio de Janeiro that promotes sustainable development

row vector A row of a matrix; in a period life table, each row refers to a cohort; in a cohort table, the rows refer to single ages or age categories

"rural renaissance" The movement during the late twentieth century that saw a reversal of the long-range trend in the United States of migration to cities from rural areas

sample survey Collection of demographic (and other) data from a part of a population (a sample) with the aim of generalizing the findings to the entire population

second demographic transition The shift observed in many industrialized populations toward below-replacement levels of fertility

separation factors A pair of decimal fractions that add to zero (0.5 and 0.5, 0.7 and 0.3, etc.) used to apportion deaths between adjacent cohorts in a life table

sex ratio The measure of a population's sex structure, defined as the number of males divided by the number of females times 100

sex structure The organization of a population consisting of two aggregates: all males and all females in that population

Silent Spring Title of an influential book by Rachel Carson that led to the banning of the pesticide, DDT

small-area estimation Methods of arriving at demographic estimates of small populations and areas

social aggregate A group of people who share common interests, values, and beliefs.

social demography The approach to population studies that focuses on facts, theories, problems, and policies; distinguished from *formal demography*

sociocultural (structure) The organization of a population based on nonbiological criteria: urban-rural dwellers, socioeconomic classes, occupational categories, for example

specific rates Rates that measure the occurrence of vital events in only part of a population: males and females (sex-specific), cohorts (age-specific), for example

stationary population The column vector of survivors to a given age (all l_xs) in which the number of births constantly equals the number of deaths

Stockholm Declaration Document produced by the pioneering environmental conference in Stockholm that established the concept of environmental rights

strata The hierarchically related aggregates of a stratification system

stratification Social inequality; a characteristic of sociocultural structure in which the aggregates (strata) are related to one another hierarchically

"stroke belt" The section of the southern United States traditionally known for high rates of stroke

structural effect The influence that the structure of a population has on its individual members

structure The organization of a population into two or more subpopulations according to sex, age, or any of several sociocultural characteristics

Summary File 1 The U.S. Census file that contains the data compiled from the questions asked of all people and about every housing unit complete enumeration

survival rates A measure derived from the life table indicating the probability that an individual will survive from one age to another (e.g., from 15 to 55)

sustainable development An approach to socioeconomic growth that emphasizes responsible management of the environment

sustainable population size The number of people that can be supported by a given resource base, over successive generations, in a manner that is acceptable in terms of community standards

Territorial Imperative The force which geographic factors exert on population characteristics and dynamics

TIGER Map Serve The U.S. Census service that compiles and distributes geographic data

total fertility rate The weighted sum of all age-specific fertility rates for a given period

unabridged tables Life tables that contain information for every single age in a population (0, 1, 2, 3, . . . etc.)

United Nations Fund for Population Activities (UNFPA) The UN agency responsible for family-planning programs

United Nations High Commission for Refugees (UNHCR) The world's leading organization in protecting the rights of and providing assistance to refugees

United States Agency for International Development (USAID) The branch of the Federal Government responsible, through its Office of Population, for family-planning programs abroad

United States Environmental Protection Agency (EPA) A data source from the U.S. Department of Environment (a GIS site)

vital events Natural occurrences that directly or indirectly contribute to population growth; these include births, deaths, illness, and—by extension—migration

vital registration The ongoing recording of births and other vital events by government and other authorities

voluntary migration Movement between populations that is purposely undertaken to benefit the migrants; the push-pull thesis and related theoretical models focus on this kind of migration

Waste Makers Title of a book by Vance Packard, which argues that wasteful behavior is deeply lodged in and encouraged by modern culture

World Bank The U.N.-affiliated agency that collects comprehensive demographic data sets

zero population growth (ZPG) The type of growth that occurs when births equal deaths, and thus the rate of natural increase = 0

REFERENCES

Abel, E. L. and M. L. Kruger. 2012. "Jewish Denominations and Longevity." *OMEGA—Journal of Death and Dying* 65:213–19.

ACLU. 1997. *The Rights of Immigrants*. New York: American Civil Liberties Union.

ACM. 1998. *Proceedings of the 6th International Symposium on Advances in Geographic Information Systems*. New York: Association for Computing Machinery.

Adamchak, D. J. 1989. "Population Aging in Sub-Saharan Africa: The Effects of Development on the Elderly." *Population and Environment* 10:162–76.

Adler, Nancy, Thomas Boyce, Margaret Chesney, Sheldon Cohen, Susan Folkman, Robert Kahn, and Leonard Syme. 1994. "Socioeconomic Status and Health: The Challenge of the Gradient." *American Psychologist* 49:15–24.

Aghajanian, Akbar. 1995. "A New Direction in Population Policy and Family Planning in the Islamic Republic of Iran." *Asia-Pacific Population Journal* 10:3–20.

Alexander, Cheryl S. and Bernard Guyer. 1993. "Adolescent Pregnancy: Occurrence and Consequences." *Pediatric Annals* 22:85–88.

Alexander, William M. 1998. "Female Sexuality Denied, Fatal Daughter Syndrome, and High Fertility Maintained." *Michigan Sociological Review* 12:117–31.

Ali, M., A. Seuc, A. Rahimi, M. Festin, and M. Temmerman. 2014. "A Global Research Agenda for Family Planning: Results of an Exercise for Setting Research Priorities." *Bulletin of the World Health Organization* 92: 93–98.

Allison, Paul D. 1995. *Survival Analysis Using the SAS System: A Practical Guide*. Cary, NC: SAS Institute, Inc.

Ambroggi, Robert. 1980. "Water." *Scientific American* 243:101–3.

Anderson, James. 1984. *Public Policy Making*. New York: Holt, Rinehart, and Winston.

Anderson, R. N., K. D. Kochanek, and S. L. Murphy. 1997. "Report of Final Mortality Statistics, 1995." *Monthly Vital Statistics Report* 45, 11:2.

Anderson, R. N., M. D. Kochanek, and S. L. Murphy. 1995. "Deaths and Death Rates for the 10 Leading Causes of Death in Specified Age Groups, by Race and Sex in the United States, 1995." *Report of Mortality Statistics, Monthly Vital Statistics Report* 45, 11: Supplement 2.1.

Andreasen, Robin. 1998. "A New Perspective on the Race Debate." *British Journal of the Philosophy of Science* 49:199–225.

Anker, R., M. Buvinic, and N. H. Youssef, eds. 2010. *Women's Roles and Population Trends in the Third World*. New York: Routledge.

Antonovsky, A. 1967. "Social Class, Life Expectancy and Overall Mortality." *Milbank Memorial Fund Quarterly* 45:31–73.

AP. 1999. "Supreme Court Bars Census Technique." *Associated Press*, January 25. Retrieved January 25, 1999 (http://www.mnbc.com/ news/ 235106.asp).

APA. 1990. *A Study Manual for the AICP Comprehensive Planning Examination*. Memphis, TN: Graduate Program in City and Regional Planning, Memphis State University.

Apt, N. A. 1989. "Grand Parenting Remains Important Role in Ghana." *Ageing International* 16:19–20.

Archives. 1998. "Sir James Steuart on the Causes of Human Multiplication." *Population and Development Review* 24:141–47.

Ardrey, Robert. 1966 [1997]. *The Territorial Imperative: A Personal Inquiry into the Animal Origins of Property and Nations*. New York: Kondansha Press.

Aridi, Naim. "The Druze in Israel: History & Overview." Jewish Virtual Library, online at http://www.jewishvirtuallibrary.org/jsource/Society_&_Culture/druze.html. Accessed August 31, 2015.

Ascher, William. 1978. *Forecasting: An Appraisal for Policymakers and Planners*. Baltimore: Johns Hopkins University Press.

Aveni, A. 2013. *Buried Beneath Us: Discovering the Ancient Cities of the Americas*. New York: Macmillan.

Babbie, Earl M. 2013. *The Practice of Social Research*. Belmont CA: Wadsworth.

Babones, S. 2011. "Middling Kingdom: The Hype and the Reality of China's Rise." *Foreign Affairs* 90:66–78.

Bachu, A. 1995. *Fertility of American Women. June, 1994* (U.S. Bureau of Census Current Population Report P20-482). Washington, DC: U.S. Government Printing Office.

Bailey, M. J. and S. M. Dynarski. 2011. *Gains and Gaps: Changing Inequality in U.S. College Entry and Completion*. National Bureau of Economic Research (No. w17633).

Bajos, N., M. Le Guen, A. Bohet, H. Panjo, H., and C. Moreau. 2014. "Effectiveness of Family Planning Policies: The Abortion Paradox." PloS on 9(3), e91539.

Bankole, Akinrinola and Susheela Singh. 1998. "Issues in Brief." *Support for Family Planning Improves Women's Lives*. New York: The Alan Guttmacher Institute.

Banks, J. A. 1954. *Prosperity and Parenthood: A Study of Family Planning among the Victorian Middle Classes*. London: Routledge and Kegan Paul.

———. 1968. "Population Change and the Victorian City." *Victorian Studies* 11:277–89.

Baran, Paul A. 1967. *The Political Economy of Growth*. New York: Monthly Review Press.

Bardach, E. 2011. *Practical Guide for Policy Analysis: The Eightfold Path to More Effective Problem Solving*. Thousand Oaks, CA: CQ Press.

Bates, Anna Louise. 1995. *Weeder in the Garden of the Lord: Anthony Comstock's Life and Career*. Lanham, MD: University Press of America.

Bauman, A. and D. Nutbeam. 2013. *Evaluation in a Nutshell: A Practical Guide to the Evaluation of Health Promotion Programs*. New York: McGraw Hill.

Bauman, Karl E., Claire I. Viadro, and Amy O. Tsui. 1994. "Use of True Experimental Designs for Family Planning Program Evaluation: Merits, Problems and Solutions." *International Family Planning Perspectives* 20:108–13.

Bautis, Michael. 1991. "Estimates Preparation: Methods and Procedures" in *Handbook of Population Estimates Methods*. Washington, DC: United States Census Bureau.

Beaver, Steven E. 1975. *Demographic Transition Theory Reinterpreted*. New York: Longmans.

Becker, G.S. 1981. A Treatise on the Family. Cambridge, MA: Harvard University Press.

Becker, Henk A. and Piet L. J. Hermkens, eds. 1993. *Solidarity of Generations: Demographic, Economic and Social Change and Its Consequences*. Amsterdam: Thesis Publishers.

Becker, S. O., F. Cinnirella, and L. Woessmann, L. 2013. "Does Women's Education Affect Fertility? Evidence from Pre-demographic Transition in Prussia." *European Review of Economic History* 17:24–44.

Belanger, Alain and Andrei Rogers. 1992. "The Internal Migration and Spatial Redistribution of the Foreign-Born Population in the United States: 1965–70 and 1975–80." *International Migration Review* 26:1342–69.

Bell, Daniel. 1976. *The Coming of the Post-Industrial Society: A Venture in Social Forecasting*. New York: Basic Books.

Bell, Felicitie C. (1998). *Actuarial Tables Based on the US Life Tables: 1989–1991 (No. 113)*. Washington, DC: Social Security Administration, Office of the Chief Actuary.

Bell, Felicitie C. and Alice Wade. 1998. *Actuarial Tables Based on the U.S. Life Tables: 1981–91*. Baltimore, MD: United States Social Security Administration, Office of the Chief Actuary.

Bengtson, V. L. 2001. "Beyond the Nuclear Family: The Increasing Importance of Multigenerational Bonds." *Journal of Marriage and Family* 63:1–16.

Berger, Bennett. 1960. "How Long is a Generation?" *British Journal of Sociology* 11:10–23.

Berk, R. A. and J. Bleich, J. 2013. "Statistical Procedures for Forecasting Criminal Behavior." *Criminology and Public Policy* 12:513–44.

Bernauer, T., T. Böhmelt, and V. Koubi. 2012. "Environmental Changes and Violent Conflict." *Environmental Research Letters* 7:15–60.

Berry, Brian J. L. 1965. *Central Place Studies: A Bibliography of Theory and Applications.* Philadelphia: Regional Science Research Institute.

Berry, Brian J. L. and Chauncey D. Harris. 1970. "Walter Christaller: An Appreciation." *Geographical Review* 60:116–19.

Bhattacharya, J., C. B. Mulligan, and R. R. Reed, 2004. "Labor Market Search and Optimal Retirement Policy." *Economic Inquiry* 42:560–71.

Bhutta, Z. A., S. Cabral, C. W. Chan, and W. J. Keenan. 2012. "Reducing Maternal, Newborn, and Infant Mortality Globally: An Integrated Action Agenda." *International Journal of Gynecology and Obstetrics* 119:S13–S17.

Bicknell, W. J. and C. L. Parks. 1989. "As Children Survive: Dilemmas of Aging in the Developing World." *Social Science and Medicine* 28:59–67.

Billari, F. C. and G. Dalla-Zuanna, G. 2013. "Cohort Replacement and Homeostasis in World Population, 1950–2100." *Population and Development Review* 39:563–85.

Billett, S. 2010. "Dividing Climate Change: Global Warming in the Indian Mass Media." *Climatic Change* 99:1–16.

Bilsborrow, Richard E. 1979. "Population Pressures and Agricultural Development in Developing Countries: A Conceptual Framework and Recent Evidence." Paper presented at the Population Association of America Annual Meeting, April 1.

Biraben, Jean-Noel. 1980. "An Essay Concerning Mankind's Evolution." *Population, Selected Papers*, December.

Blacker, C. P. 1947. "Stages in Population Growth." *Eugenics Review* 39:88–102.

Blau, Peter M. 1960. "Structural Effects." *American Sociological Review* 25:178–93.

BLM. 1993. *The Automated Digitizing System (ADS): User's Manual.* Denver: U.S. Bureau of Land Management.

Bloemraad, I. 2006. *Becoming a Citizen: Incorporating Immigrants and Refugees in the United States and Canada.* Berkeley: University of California Press.

Boden-Albala, B., E. T. Roberts, H. Moats, H. Arif, R. L. Sacco, and M. C. Paik. 2012. "Community Level Disadvantage and the Likelihood of First Ischemic Stroke." *Epidemiology Research International, 2012.* New York: Hindawi Publishing Corporation.

Bond, Lynne A., Stephen J. Cutler, and Armin Grams, eds. 1995. *Promoting Successful and Productive Aging* (No. 16). Thousand Oaks, CA: Sage Publications.

Bongaarts, John. 1982. "The Fertility-Inhibiting Effects of the Intermediate Fertility Variables." *Studies in Family Planning* 13:179–89.

———. 1993. "The Relative Contributions of Biological and Behavioral Factors in Determining Natural Fertility: A Demographer's Perspective" in R. Gray, H. Leridon, and A. Spira, eds., *Biomedical and Demographic Determinants of Reproduction.* New York: Clarendon Press.

———. 1996. "Global Trends in AIDS Mortality." *Population and Development Review* 22:21–45.

———. 2011. "Can Family Planning Programs Reduce High Desired Family Size in Sub-Saharan Africa?" *International Perspectives on Sexual and Reproductive Health* 37:209–16.

Bongaarts, J. and S. Sinding. 2011. "Population Policy in Transition in the Developing World." *Science* 333:574–76.

Bonilla-Silva, E. 2013. *Racism without Racists: Color-Blind Racism and the Persistence of Racial Inequality in America.* Boulder, CO: Rowman & Littlefield.

Boserup, E. 1981. *Population and Technological Change: A Study of Long-Term Trends.* Chicago: University of Chicago Press.

Bouvier, Leon and Robert Gardner. 1986. "Immigration to the US: The Unfinished Story." *Population Bulletin* 41.

Bowling, A. 2007. "Aspirations for Older Age in the 21st century: What is Successful Aging?" *The International Journal of Aging and Human Development* 64:263–97.

Bradburn, Norman M. 1998. "Fuss Over Census Sampling Simply Political Nonsense." *Houston Chronicle*, January 4, A33.

Brandel, S. K. and D. R. Gwatlun. 1982. "Life Expectancy and Population Growth in the Third World." *Scientific American* 246:57–66.

Brown, D. G., K. M. Johnson, T. R. Loveland, and D. M. Theobald. 2005. "Rural Land-Use Trends in the Conterminous United States, 1950–2000." *Ecological Applications* 15:1851–63.

Brown, Lester R. and Jodi Jacobson. 1986. "Our Demographically Divided World." *World Watch Paper* 74. Washington, DC: World Watch Institute.

Brown, Lester R., Hal Kane, and David Marlin Roodman. 1994. *Vital Signs*. Washington, DC: World Watch Institute.

Brown, L. R., M. Renner, and B. Halweil. 2014. *Vital Signs 2000–2001: The Environmental Trends That Are Shaping Our Future*. New York: Routledge.

Bureau of Statistics. 1997. *Statistical Abstract of the United States, 1997*. Washington, DC: U.S. Government Printing Office.

Burleigh, Michael and Wolfgang Wipperman. 1992. *The Racial State*. Cambridge: Cambridge University Press.

Burton, L. M., E. Bonilla-Silva, V. Ray, R. Buckele, and E. Hordge Freeman. 2010. "Critical Race Theories, Colorism, and the Decade's Research on Families of Color." *Journal of Marriage and Family* 72:440–59.

Butler, D. C., S. Petterson, R. J. Phillips, and A. W. Bazemore. 2013. "Measures of Social Deprivation that Predict Health Care Access and Need within a Rational Area of Primary Care Service Delivery." *Health Services Research* 48 (2) part 1:539–59.

Caldwell, J. C. 1982. *Theory of Fertility Decline*. London: Academic Press.

Calhoun, John B. 1962. "Population Density and Social Pathology." *Scientific American* 206:139–148.

Cambridge Group. 1974. *Original Parish Registers in Record Offices and Libraries*. Cambridge, UK: Cambridge Group for the History of Population and Social Structure.

Campbell, Donald and Julian Stanley. 1963. *Experimental and Quasi-Experimental Designs for Research*. Chicago: Rand McNally.

Cappuccino, Naomi and Peter W. Price, eds. 1995. *Population Dynamics: New Approaches and Syntheses*. San Diego: Academic Press.

Carey, James R. 1993. *Applied Demography for Biologists with Special Emphasis on Insects*. New York: Oxford University Press.

Carrying Capacity Network. 1997. *The Carrying Capacity Briefing Book*. Washington, DC: The Carrying Capacity Network.

Carson, Rachel. 1962. *Silent Spring*. Boston: Houghton Mifflin.

Cascio, W. and J. W. Boudreau. 2010. *Investing in People: Financial Impact of Human Resource Initiatives*. Upper Saddle River, NJ: Pearson Education.

Cassen, R. H. 1976. "Population and Development: A Survey." *World Development* 4:785–830.

Cazes, Marie Helene. 2006. "An Example of Demographic Anthropology, the Study of Matrimonial Exchanges—Endogamy, Choice of Spouse and Preferential Marriage." PuMed.gov (NCIH). *Collegium Antropologicum*. 30:475–78. September 30. Retrieved from http://www.ncbi.nlm.nih.gov/pubmed/17058510.

Census of India. 1991. New Delhi: Ministry of Home Affairs.

Cervellati, M. and U. Sunde. 2011. "Life Expectancy and Economic Growth: The Role of the Demographic Transition." *Journal of Economic Growth* 16:99–133.

Chandler, Tertius and Gerald Fox. 1974. *3000 Years of Urban Growth*. New York: Academic Press.

Chandrasekhar, S. 1966. "A Billion Indians by 2000 AD?" in S. Chandrasekhar and C. Hultman, eds., *Problems of Economic Development*. Boston: Heath.

Checkoway, B. and F. Morales-Martinez. 1990. "En La Tercera Edad: New Programs to Promote the Health of Older People in Costa Rica." *Ageing and Society* 10:397–411.

Cherlin, A. J. 2010. "Demographic Trends in the United States: A Review of Research in the 2000s." *Journal of Marriage and Family* 72:403–19.

Cho, Y. and B. Tien. 2014. "Sub-Saharan Africa's Recent Growth Spurt: An Analysis of the Sources of Growth." *World Bank Policy Research Working Paper* (6862).

Choi, J. K. and A. P. Jackson. 2011. "Fathers' Involvement and Child Behavior Problems in Poor African American Single-Mother Families." *Children and Youth Services Review* 33:698–704.

Choldin, Harvey M. 1978. "Urban Density and Pathology." *Annual Review of Sociology* 4:91–113

———. 1988. "Issues in Adjusting United States Census Counts." *Working Paper No. 6.* Urbana: Institute of Government and Public Affairs, University of Illinois.

———. 1995. *Looking for the Last Percent: The Controversy over Census Undercounts.* New Brunswick, NJ: Rutgers University Press.

Christaller, Walter. 1972. "How I Discovered the Theory of Central Places: A Report about the Origin of Central Places," in P. W. English and R. C. Mayfield, eds., *Man, Space, and Environment.* Oxford: Oxford University Press.

City of Los Angeles. 1996. *Annual Report on Growth and Infrastructure.* Los Angeles: Department of City Planning.

Clark, Jim. 1999. *Netscape Time: The Making of the Billion-Dollar Start-Up That Changed the World.* New York: St. Martin's Press.

Clark, Lance. 1989. *Early Warning of Refugee Flows.* Washington, DC: Refugee Policy Group.

Clarke, C. A., T. Miller, E. T. Chang, D. Yin, M. Cockburn, and S. L. Gomez. 2010. "Racial and Social Class Gradients in Life Expectancy in Contemporary California." *Social Science and Medicine* 709:1373–80.

Clarke, Lynda, Elizabeth C. Cooksey, and Georgia Verropoulo. 1998. "Fathers and Absent Fathers: Sociodemographic Similarities in Britain and the United States." *Demography* 35:217–28.

Cleary, Peter K. 1998. "Education Coalition Says Pro Sampling Coalition Misses Basic Flaws." *U.S. Newswire,* July 20.

Cleland, J. 2013. "World Population Growth; Past, Present and Future." *Environmental and Resource Economics* 55:543–54.

Cleland, John, N. Onuoha, and Ian Timaeus. 1993. "Fertility Change in Sub-Saharan Africa: A Review of the Evidence," in T. Locoh, ed., *The Course of Fertility Transition in Sub-Saharan Africa.* Liege, Belgium: International Union for the Scientific Study of Population.

Coale, A. J. 1973. "The Demographic Transition Reconsidered." Paper presented at the Conference of the International Union for the Scientific Study of Population. Liege, Belgium.

Coale, Ansley and E. M. Hoover. 1958. *Population Growth and Economic Development in Law Income Countries.* Princeton, NJ: Princeton University Press.

Coale, Ansley and Melvin Zelnik. 1989. *New Estimates of Fertility and Population in the United States.* Princeton, NJ: Princeton University Press.

Cockings, S., A. Harfoot, D. Martin, and D. Hornby. 2013. "Getting the Foundations Right: Spatial Building Blocks for Official Population Statistics." *Environment and Planning* 45:1403–20.

Coe, Michael D. 1985. *The Maya.* New York: Thames and Hudson.

Cohen, Joel E. 1997. *How Many People Can the Earth Support?* New York: Norton.

Cohrssen, J. J. and V. T. Covello. 1989. *Risk Analysis: A Guide to Principles and Methods for Analyzing Health and Environmental Risks.* Washington, DC: U.S. Council on Environmental Quality.

Coleman, James S. 1993. "Comment on Preston and Campbell's 'Differential Fertility and the Distribution of Traits.'" *American Journal of Sociology* 98: 1020–32.

Commoner, Barry W. 1966. *Science and Survival.* New York: Viking Press.

———. 1992. "Population, Development and Environment: Trends and Key Issues in Developed Countries." Paper presented at the United Nations Expert Group Meeting on Population, Environment, and Development, January 20–24. New York.

Concepcion, Mercedes B. and E. M. Murphy. 1973. "Wanted: A Theory of Demographic Transition." Paper presented at the Conference of the International Union for the Scientific Study of Population. Sydney, Australia.

Condorcet, Marie Jean, Maquis de. 1795 [1796]. *Outline of an Historical View of the Human Mind.* Early English translation of Equisse d'un Tableau historique des progress d'esprit humain. Philadelphia: Lang and Ustick (rebound).

Cook, Alan H. 1998. *Edmund Halley: Charting the Heavens and the Seas.* New York: Oxford University Press.

Cooke, T. J. 2013. "Internal Migration in Decline." *The Professional Geographer* 65:664–75.

Coop, S. and H. Thomas. 2007. "Planning Doctrine as an Element in Planning History: The Case of Cardiff." *Planning Perspectives* 22:167–93.

Correia, A. W., C. A. Pope III, D. W. Dockery, Y. Wang, M. Ezzati, and F. Dominici. 2013. "The Effect of Air Pollution Control on Life Expectancy in the United States: An Analysis of 545 U.S. Counties for the Period 2000 to 2007." *Epidemiology* 24:23.

Cotten, S. R. 2001. "Implications of Internet Technology for Medical Sociology in the New Millennium." *Sociological Spectrum* 2:319–40.

CPR. 1976. "Population Estimates and Projections." *Current Population Report.* Series P–25, Number 640 (November).

Creighton, M. J. 2013. "The Role of Aspirations in Domestic and International Migration." *The Social Science Journal* 50:79–88.

Crowell, Frank. 1995. *Measuring Inequality.* New York: Prentice Hall.

Cullen, M. R., C. Cummins, and V. R. Fuchs. 2012. "Geographic and Racial Variation in Premature Mortality in the US: Analyzing the Disparities." *PloS one,* 7:e32930.

Cutler, D. M., E. L. Glaeser, and J. L. Vigdor. 2008. "When Are Ghettos Bad? Lessons from Immigrant Segregation in the United States." *Journal of Urban Economics* 63:759–74.

Dandekar, V. M. and N. Rath. 1970. "Poverty in India" as quoted in David G. Mandelbaum, *Society in India* (p. 2). Los Angeles: University of California Press.

Dasmann, Raymond. 1971. "Population Growth and the Natural Environment," in N. Hinrichs, ed., *Population, Environment and People.* New York: McGraw Hill.

David, C. C., J. M. L. Atun, and A. G. La Viña. 2012. "Framing in Legislation: The Case of Population Policy in the Philippines." *Population Research and Policy Review* 31:297–319.

Davis, Angela. 1981. *Women, Race and Class.* New York: Random House.

———. 2003. "Racism, Birth Control and Reproductive Rights," in Reina Lewis and Sara Mills, eds., *Feminist Postcolonial Theory—A Reader,* 353–67. New York: Routledge.

Davis, Kingsley. 1945. The World Demographic Transition. *The Annals of the American Academy of Political and Social Science*: 1–11.

———. 1963. "The Theory of Change and Response in Modern Demographic History." *Population Index* 29: 345–66.

———. 1974. "The Migrations of the Human Population." *Scientific American* 231:95–105.

Davis, Kingsley and Judith Blake. 1956. "Social Structure and Fertility: An Analytic Framework." *Economic Development and Cultural Change* 4:112–35.

Deacon, Robert. 1994a. *Deforestation and the Rule of Law in a Cross Section of Countries.* Washington, DC: Resources for the Future.

———. 1994b. "Assessing the Relationship between Government Policy and Deforestation." *Journal of Environmental Economics and Management* 28:19–95.

Deevey, E. S., Jr. 1960. "The Human Crop." *Scientific American* 203:194–204.

De Haas, H. 2010. "Migration and Development: A Theoretical Perspective." *International Migration Review* 44:227–64.

De Jong, Gordon, R. G. Abad, F. Arnold, B. V. Carino, J. T. Fawcett, and R. W. Gardner. 1983. "International and Internal Migration Decision Making: A Value-Expectancy Based Analytical Framework of Intentions to Move from a Rural Philippine Province." *International Migration Review*: 470–84.

De Jong, Gordon, R. G. Abad, F. F. Arnold, B. V. Carino, J. T. Fawcett, and R. W. Gardiner. 1981. "International and Internal Migration Decision-Making: A Value Expectancy Based Analytical Framework of Intentions to Move from a Rural Philippine Province." *International Migration Review* 17:598–611.

De Jong, Gordon and T. T. Fawcett. 1981. "Motivation for Migration: An Assessment of a Value-Expectancy Model," in G. De Jong and R. Gardner, eds., *Migration Decision Making*. New York: Pergamon Press.

Domhoff, William G. 1970. *The Higher Circles: The Governing Class in America*. New York: Vintage Books.

———. 1983. *Who Rules America Now? A View for the 'Eighties*. Englewood Cliffs, NJ: Prentice Hall.

———. 1990. *The Power Elite and the State*. New York: Aldine de Gruyter.

Donaldson, Loraine. 1991. *Fertility Transition: The Social Dynamics of Population Change*. Cambridge, MA: Basil Blackwell.

Donaldson, Peter J. and Amy Ong Tsui. 1990. "The International Family Planning Movement." *Population Bulletin* 45:8.

Drake, Michael, ed. 1982. *Population Studies from Parish Registers: A Selection of Readings from Local Population Studies*. Matlock, Derbyshire, UK: Local Population Studies, Open University.

Drummond, M. A. and T. R. Loveland. 2010. "Land-Use Pressure and a Transition to Forest-Cover Loss in the Eastern United States." *Bioscience* 60: 286–98.

Duncan, Otis Dudley. 1954. "Human Ecology and Population Studies," in P. M. Hauser and O. D. Duncan, eds., *The Study of Population*. Chicago: University of Chicago Press.

Dunstan, John A. P. 1976. "Population Density, Crowding, and Human Pathology." *La Trobe Sociology Papers 36*. Bundoora, Australia: Department of Sociology, La Trobe University.

Durand, John D. 1974. "Historical Estimates of World Population: An Evaluation." *Analytical and Technical Reports 10*. Philadelphia: Population Center, University of Pennsylvania.

Durkheim, Emilé. 1895 [1962]. *The Rules of Sociological Method*. New York: The Free Press.

———. 1897 [1997]. *Suicide: A Study in Sociology*. New York: The Free Press.

Dyson, Tim and M. Moore. 1983. "On Kinship Structure, Female Autonomy and Demographic Behavior in India." *Population and Development Review* 9:35–60.

Easterlin, R. A. 1978a. "New Directions for the Economics of Fertility," in J. M. Yinger and S. J. Cutler, eds., *Major Social Issues: A Multidisciplinary View*. New York: The Free Press.

———. 1978b. "What Will 1984 Be Like? Socioeconomic Implications of Recent Twists in Age Structures." *Demography* 15:397–432.

Easterlin, R. A. and Eileen M. Crimmins. 1985. *The Fertility Revolution: A Supply and Demand Analysis*. Chicago: University of Chicago Press.

Eastmond, M. 2007. "Stories as Lived Experience: Narratives in Forced Migration Research." *Journal of Refugee Studies* 20: 248–64.

Eaton, Joseph W. and Albert J. Mayer. 1954. *Man's Capacity to Reproduce: The Demography of a Unique Population*. New York: Free Press.

Eberstadt, Nicholas. 1997. "World Population Implosion." *Public Interest* (Fall):3–22.

Economic Commission for Africa. 1984. *Survey of Economic and Social Conditions of Africa*. Addis Ababa: ECA.

Ehrlich, Paul. 1968. *The Population Bomb*. New York: Ballantine Books.

El Nasser, Haya, Kevin Johnson, Paul Wiseman, Mimi Hall, and Jessica Lee. 1998. "Sampling Supporter Tapped to Head Census Bureau." *USA TODAY*, June 23, p. 6A.

EPA. 1996. *Air Quality Criteria for Particulate Matter*. EPA/600/P–95/00lbf (April). Washington, DC: Office of Research and Development, U.S. Environmental Protection Agency.

ESRI. 1998. "Census Mapper." Optical CD (with data from Statistical Abstract of the United States, 1997). Redlands, CA: Environmental Systems Research, Inc.

Fage, J. 2013. *A History of Africa*. New York: Routledge.

Fallenmark, M., M. Lundquist, J. Widstrand, and C. Widstrand. 1989. "Macro Scale Water Scarcity Requires Micro Scale Approaches: Aspects of Vulnerability in Semi Arid Development." *Natural Resources Forum* 13:258–67.

FAO. 1991. Forest Resources Assessment 1990 Project, Food and Agricultural Organization of the United Nations, "Second Interim Report on the State of Tropical Forests." Paper presented at the 10th World Forestry Congress, Paris, September–October.

Fasel, N., Green, E. G., and Sarrasin, O. 2013. "Facing Cultural Diversity: Anti-immigrant Attitudes in Europe." *European Psychologist* 18:253–62

Feeney, G. and J. Yu. 1987. "Period Parity Progression Measures of Fertility in China." *Population Studies* 41:77–102.

Fergusson, D. M., G. F. McLeod, and L. J. Horwood. 2013. "Childhood Sexual Abuse and Adult Developmental Outcomes: Findings from a 30-Year Longitudinal Study in New Zealand." *Child Abuse and Neglect* 37:664–74.

Ferlay, J., E. Steliarova-Foucher, J. Lortet-Tieulent, S. Rosso, J. W. W. Coebergh, H. Comber, D. Forman, and F. Bray, F. 2013. "Cancer Incidence and Mortality Patterns in Europe: Estimates for 40 Countries in 2012." *European Journal of Cancer* 49: 1374–403.

Fernández, J. S. and R. D. Langhout. 2014. "A Community with Diversity of Culture, Wealth, Resources, and Living Experiences: Defining Neighborhood in an Unincorporated Community." *American Journal of Community Psychology* 53:122–33.

Finer, L. and J. B. Fine. 2013. "Abortion Law Around the World: Progress and Pushback." *American Journal of Public Health* 103:585–89.

Fleming, J. 2003. "Health Information on the Internet." *The Journal of the Royal Society for the Promotion of Health* 123:10–11.

Fogarty, Michael, ed. 1982. *Retirement Policy: The Next Fifty Years*. London: Heinemann.

Foley, E. E. and A. Hendrixson. 2011. "From Population Control to AIDS: Conceptualising and Critiquing the Global Crisis Model." *Global Public Health* 6, sup3:S310–S322.

Foote, Karen, Kenneth Hill, and Linda G. Martin, eds. 1993. "Demographic Change in Sub-Saharan Africa." *National Research Council, Panel on the Population Dynamics of Sub-Saharan Africa*. Washington, DC: National Academy Press.

Forsman, H. 2011. "Innovation Capacity and Innovation Development in Small Enterprises. A Comparison between the Manufacturing and Service Sectors." *Research Policy* 40:739–50.

Forsyth, T. 2013. *Critical Political Ecology: The Politics of Environmental Science*. New York: Routledge.

Foster, J. B. and H. Holleman. 2010. "The Financial Power Elite." *Monthly Review* 62:1–19.

Franklin, S. 2013. "Conception through a Looking Glass: The Paradox of IVF." *Reproductive Biomedicine Online* 27:747–55.

Frey, William. 1988. "Black Migration to the South Reaches Record Highs in the 1980s." *Population Today* 26:1–3.

———. 1995. *Immigration and Internal Migration "Flight" from U.S. Metropolitan Areas: Toward a New Demographic Balkanisation*. Ann Arbor: Population Studies Center, University of Michigan.

———. 1998(a). *Immigration and Internal Migration "Flight" from U.S. Metropolitan Areas: Toward a New Demographic Balkanization*. Ann Arbor: Population Studies Center, University of Michigan.

———. 1998(b). "New Demographic Divide in the U.S.: Immigrant and Domestic 'Migration Magnets.'" *The Public Perspective* 9:35–39.

Frey, W. H., K. L. Liaw, R. Wright, and M. J. White. 2005. "Migration within the United States: Role of Race-Ethnicity [with Comments]." *Brookings-Wharton Papers on Urban Affairs*, pp. 207–62.

Furnam, Nicholas R. and LaVerne Saxton. 1989. *Quantitative Forecasting Methods*. Boston: PWS-Kent Publishing Co.

Galambos, J. 1993. "An International Environmental Conflict on the Danube: The Gabcikovo-Nagymaros Dams," in A. Vari and P. Tamas, eds., *Environment and Democratic*

Transition: Policy and Politics in Central and Eastern Europe. Boston: Kluwer Academic Publishers.

Galea, S., M. D. J. Tracy, K. J. Hoggatt, K. C. DiMaggio, and A. Karpati. 2011. "Estimated Deaths Attributable to Social Factors in the United States." *American Journal of Public Health* 101:1456–65.

Gallopin, G. 1992. "Science, Technology and the Ecological Future of Latin America." *World Development* 20:130–40.

Gamboa, Anthony M. 1998. *The New Worklife Expectancy Tables: By Gender, Level of Attainment, and Level of Disability*. Louisville, KY: Vocational Econometrics.

Gandevani, S. B., S. Ziaee, and F. K. Farahani. 2014. "A Review of the Impact of Different Social Policy Incentives to Accelerate Population Growth Rate." *Women's Health* 1:e18967.

Garcia-Nunez, Jose. 1992. *Improving Family Planning Evaluation*. Hartford, CT: Kumarian Press.

Gardner, R. W. 1989. "Asian Americans: Growth, Change, and Diversity." *Population Bulletin* 40:n4.

Gerland, Patrick, Adrian E. Raftery, Hana Ševčíková, Nan Li, Danan Gu, Thomas Spooren-berg, Leontine Alkema, Bailey K. Fosdick, Jennifer Chunn, Nevena Lalic, Guiomar Bay, Thomas Buettner, Gerhard K. Heilig, and John Wilmoth. 2014. "World Population Stabilization Unlikely this Century." *Science*, September 18. DOI: 10.1126/science.1257469.

Gibb, S. J., D. M. Fergusson, L. J. Horwood, and J. M. Boden. 2014. "Early Motherhood and Long-Term Economic Outcomes: Findings from a 30-Year Longitudinal Study." *Journal of Research on Adolescence*. Wiley. Online Library. Article first published online March 20 (http://onlinelibrary.wiley.com/doi/10.1111/jora.12122/full).

Gillis, A. R. 1973. "Types of Human Population Density and Social Pathology." Discussion Paper, Population Research Laboratory 7. Edmonton, Alberta: Population Research Laboratory.

Gilpin, R. 2011. *Global Political Economy: Understanding the International Economic Order*. Princeton, NJ: Princeton University Press.

Gleick, P. H. and M. Heberger, M. 2011. "The Coming Mega Drought." *Scientific American* 306:14.

Gober, Patricia. 1993. "Americans on the Move." *Population Bulletin* 48:6–8.

Godwin, William. 1793 [1946]. *Enquiry Concerning Political Justice and its Influence on Morals and Happiness*. Toronto: University of Toronto Press.

———. 1820 [1964]. *Of Population: An Enquiry Concerning the Power of Increase in the Numbers of Mankind, Being an Answer to Mr. Malthus's Essay on that Subject*. New York: Kelly Books.

GOI (Government of India). 1952. Planning Commission, Government of India. "The First Five Year Plan–A Draft Outline (206–207)." New Delhi.

———. 1956. Planning Commission, Government of India, "Second Five Year Plan—A Draft Outline (156)." New Delhi.

———. 1962. Planning Commission, Government of India. "Third Five Year Plan—Summary (178–79)." New Delhi.

———. 1964. Information Service of India, Government of India. "The Family Planning Program in India," in S. Mudd, ed., *The Population Crisis and the Use of the World Resources*. New Delhi.

Gonod, Pierre F. 1990. *Technological Forecasting: Principles and Methods*. Vienna: United Nations Industrial Development Organization.

Goodman, Nelson. 1983. *Fact, Fiction, and Forecast*. Cambridge, MA: Harvard University Press.

Gosselin, Lisa. 1998. "Biophilia at Its Best (Editorial)." *Audubon Magazine* 100:8.

Goudie, A. S. 2013. *The Human Impact on the Natural Environment: Past, Present, and Future*. New York: Wiley.

Gove, P. B. 1981. *Webster's Third New International Dictionary of the English Language*, unabridged, vol. 1. Merriam-Webster.

Grady, Robert. 1993. *Restoring Real Representation*. Urbana: University of Illinois Press.

Graham, Frank, Jr. 1998. "The Dawn of Conservation." *Audubon Magazine* 100:33–34.

Granados, J. A. T. 2005. "Response: On Economic Growth, Business Fluctuations, and Health Progress." *International Journal of Epidemiology* 34:1226–33.

Guha, Ramachandra. 1990. *The Unquiet Woods: Ecological Change and Peasant Resistance in the Himalayas*. Berkeley: University of California Press.

Gunasekara, N. K., S. Kazama, D. Yamazaki, and T. Oki. 2013. "The Effects of Country-Level Population Policy for Enhancing Adaptation to Climate Change." *Hydrology and Earth System Sciences* 17:4429–40.

Haag, G., U. Mueller, and K. G. Troitzsch. 1992. *Economic Evolution and Demographic Change: Formal Models in the Social Sciences*. New York: Springer-Verlag.

Haberman, Steven and Trevor A. Sibbett, eds. 1995. *History of Actuarial Science*. London: Pickering and Chatto.

Habimana Kabano, I., A. Broekhuis, and P. Hooimeijer, P. 2013. "Fertility Decline in Rwanda: Is Gender Preference in the Way?" *International Journal of Population Research*, vol. 2013, Article ID 787149, 9 pages.

Habte-Gabr, E., N. S. Blum, and I. M. Smith. 1987. "The Elderly in Africa." *Journal of Applied Gerontology* 6:163–82.

Haeckel, Ernst. 1917. *Evolution in Modern Thought*. New York: Boni and Liverwright.

Halley, Edmund. 1693 [1942]. *Degrees of Mortality of Mankind*. Lowell J. Reed, ed. Baltimore: The Johns Hopkins Press.

Halpin, Reginald. 1996. "Event History." Essex University. Posted January 4, 1996. Retrieved November 13, 1998 (http://www.irc.essex.ac.ukl/brendan/ltr/strategy/html).

Handwerker, Penn. 1983. "The First Demographic Transition: An Analysis of Subsistence Choices and Reproductive Consequences." *American Anthropologist* 85:5–27.

Hanson, Susan, ed. 1997. *Ten Geographic Ideas that Changed the World*. New Brunswick, NJ: Rutgers University Press.

Hardee, K., J. Kumar, K. Newman, L. Bakamjian, S. Harris, M. Rodríguez, M., and W. Brown. 2014. "Voluntary, Human Rights-Based Family Planning: A Conceptual Framework." *Studies in Family Planning* 45:1–18.

Harder, Christian. 1998. *Serving Maps on the Internet: Geographic Information on the World Wide Web* (includes optical CD). Redlands, CA: Environmental Systems Research Institute, Inc.

Hardin, Garrett. 1973. "The Tragedy of the Commons," in Herman E. Daly, ed., *Toward a Steady-State Economy*. San Francisco: Freeman.

Harper, S., J. Lynch, and G. D. Smith. 2011. "Social Determinants and the Decline of Cardiovascular Diseases: Understanding the Links." *Annual Review of Public Health* 32:39–69.

Hassig, Susan, Jane Bertrand, Balowa Djunghu, Minuku Kinzoni, and Nlandu Mangani. 1991. "Duration and Correlates of Postpartum Abstinence in Four Sites in Zaire." *Social Science and Medicine* 32:343–47.

Hastings, A. 1997. *Population Biology: Concepts and Models*. New York: Springer.

Haub, C., J. Gribble, and L. Jacobsen. 2011. *World Population Data Sheet 2011*. Washington, DC: Population Reference Bureau.

Haubert, J. and E. Fussell. 2006. Explaining Pro-Immigrant Sentiment in the US: Social Class, Cosmopolitanism, and Perceptions of Immigrants." *International Migration Review* 40:489–507.

Hawthorn, Geoffrey. 1968. "Explaining Human Fertility." *British Journal of Sociology* 2:65–76.

———. 1970. *The Sociology of Fertility*. London: Collier-Macmillan.

Healy, Lynne M., Barbara A. Pine, and Myron E. Weiner, eds. 1989. "Social Work Leadership for Human Service Management in the 1990s: The Challenge of the New Demographic Reality." Proceedings of a symposium, October 8–9. West Hartford: University of Connecticut School of Social Work.

Heer, David. 1983. "Infant and Child Mortality and the Demand for Children," in R. A. Bulatao and R. D. Lee, eds., *Determinants of Fertility in Developing Countries*, 369–87. New York: Academic Press.

Heil, S. H., D. E. Gaalema, and E. S. Herrmann. 2012. "Incentives to Promote Family Planning." *Preventive Medicine* 55:S106–S112.

Henman, P. and M. Adler. 2003. "Information Technology and the Governance of Social Security." *Critical Social Policy* 23:139–64.

Hennekens, C. H., J. Drowos, and R. S. Levine. 2013. "Mortality from Homicide among
Young Black Men: A New American Tragedy." *The American Journal of Medicine*
126:282–83.

Hernandez, J. 1974. *People, Power, and Policy: A New View of Population*. Washington, DC:
National Press.

Henshaw, Stanley K. 1990. *Induced Abortion: A World Review, 1990 Supplement*. New York:
Alan Guttmacher Institute.

Herzfeld, M. 2014. *Cultural Intimacy: Social Poetics in the Nation-State*. New York: Routledge.

Hickman, J. (2004). "History of the Actuarial Profession," in Jef I. Teugals, ed., *Encyclopedia
of Actuarial Science*. New York: Wiley.

Hiller, Harry H. 1991. *Canadian Society: A Macro-Analysis*. Scarborough, Ontario:
Prentice-Hall.

Hoefer, M., N. Rytina, and B. C. Baker. 2011. *Estimates of the Unauthorized Immigrant Population Residing in the United States*. January 2009. Office of Immigration Statistics Policy
Directorate. U.S. Department of Homeland Security. January 2010.

Hoek, G., R. M. Krishnan, R. Beelen, A. Peters, B. Ostro, B. Brunekreef, and J. D. Kaufman.
2013. "Long-Term Air Pollution Exposure and Cardio-Respiratory Mortality: A Review."
Environmental Health 12:43.

Hoekelman, Robert and Barry Pless. 1988. "Decline in Mortality among Young Americans
during the 20th Century: Prospects for Reaching National Mortality Reduction Goals
for 1990." *Pediatrics* 82:582–95.

Hoem, Jan M. 1993. *Classical Demographic Methods of Analysis and Modern Event-History
Techniques*. Stockholm: Demography Unit, Stockholm University.

Hoon, Hian Teck and Edmund S. Phelps. 1996. "Low-Wage Employment Subsidies in a
Labor-Turnover Model of the 'Natural Rate.'" *Discussion Paper No. 9697–05*. New
York: Department of Economics, Columbia University.

Horn, D. M. 2013. "Locating Security in the Womb: U.S. Foreign Policy, Population Control,
and International Family Planning Programs." *International Feminist Journal of Politics*
15:195–212.

Horton, Hayward Derrick. 1998a. "Rethinking American Diversity: Conceptual and Theoretical Challenges for Racial and Ethnic Demography." Ms. Department of Sociology,
State University of New York at Albany.

———. 1998b. "Toward a Critical Demography of Race and Ethnicity: Introduction of the
'R' Word." Presented at the Annual Meetings of the American Sociological Association,
San Francisco, August 21–25.

Howard, George, R. Anderson, N. J. Johnson, P. Sorlie, G. Russell, and V. J. Howard. 1997.
"Evaluation of Social Status as a Contributing Factor to the Stroke Belt Region of the
United States." *Stroke* 28:936–40.

Howard, George, Gregory Russell, Roger Anderson, Gregory Evans, Timothy Morgan, Virginia Howard, and Gregory Burke. 1995. "The Role of Social Class in Excess African
American Stroke Mortality." *Stroke* 26:1760–63.

Howden, L. M. and J. A. Meyer. 2010. "Age and Sex Composition: 2010." *2010 Census Briefs,
U.S. Department of Commerce, Economics and Statistics Administration*. Washington
DC: U.S. Census Bureau

Hughes, G. 1991. "The Energy Sector and the Problems of Energy Policy in Eastern Europe."
Oxford Review of Economic Policy 7:77.

Hull, Charles Henry. 1896. *Graunt or Petty? The Authorship of the Observations upon the
Bills of Mortality*. Boston: Ginn and Co.

Humphreys, D. 2014. *Forest Politics: The Evolution of International Cooperation*. New York:
Routledge.

Hwang, S. S. and S. H. Murdock. 1998. "Racial Attraction or Racial Avoidance in American Suburbs?" *Social Forces* 77:541–65.

Hyndman, R. J. and G. Athanasopoulos. 2014. *Forecasting: Principles and Practice*. OTexts (https://www.otexts.org/)

Iceland, J. 2009. *Where We Live Now: Immigration and Race in the United States*. Berkeley: University of California Press.

Iceland, J. and M. Scopilliti. 2008. "Immigrant Residential Segregation in U.S. Metropolitan Areas, 1990–2000." *Demography* 45:79–94.

Impagliazzo, J. 1985. *Deterministic Aspects of Mathematical Demography*. Springer-Verlag Berlin Heidelberg.

Indian Ministry of Health and Family Welfare. 2000. *National Population Policy, 2000*. New Delhi.

Inglehart, Ronald. 1997. *Modernization and Post-Modernization: Cultural Political and Economic Change in 43 Societies*. Princeton, NJ: Princeton University Press.

Ioannides, Y. and S. Skouras. 2013. "US City Size Distribution: Robustly Pareto, but Only in the Tail." *Journal of Urban Economics* 73:18–29.

Irish Times. 1998. "Refugees Should Be Able to Work Survey." *Irish Times*, July 17, p. 1.

Jackson, S., R. Schuler, and S. Werner. 2011. *Managing Human Resources*. Independence, KY: Cengage Learning.

James, Patricia. 1979. *Population Malthus: His Life and Times*. London: Routledge & Kegan Paul.

Jarrett, Jeffrey. 1991. *Business Forecasting Methods*. Cambridge, MA: B. Blackwell.

Jeer, Sanjay. 1997. *Online Resources for Planners*. Washington, DC: American Planning Association.

Jefferson, Mark. 1909. "The Anthropography of Some Great Cities: A Study in the Distribution of Population." *Bulletin of the American Geographical Society* xii:537–66.

Jenkins, Craig and Susanne Schmeidl. 1995. "Flight from Violence: The Origins and Implications of the World Refugee Crisis." *Sociological Focus* 28:63–82.

Jiang, L. and K. Hardee. 2011. "How Do Recent Population Trends Matter to Climate Change?" *Population Research and Policy Review* 30:287–312.

Johnson, Daniel and Rex Campbell. 1981. *Black Migration in America*. Durham, NC: Duke University Press.

Johnston, Heidi Bart and Kenneth H. Hill. 1996. "Induced Abortion in the Developing World: Indirect Estimates." *International Family Planning Perspective* 22:108–14.

Johnson, M., W. P. Shively, and R. M. Stein. 2002. "Contextual Data and the Study of Elections and Voting Behavior: Connecting Individuals to Environments." *Electoral Studies* 21:219–33.

Jolly, C. 1991. "Four Theories of Population Change and the Environment." Paper presented at the Population Association of America Annual Meeting, Washington, DC, March 21–23.

Jones, Gavin W. ed. 1997. *The Continuing Demographic Transition*. New York: Oxford University Press.

Jones, Gavin W. and Pravin M. Visaria (Gujarat Institute of Development Research). 1997. *Urbanization in Large Developing Countries: China, Indonesia, Brazil, and India*. New York: Oxford University Press.

Joseph, Gillian M. 1996. *Difficult Issues in Aging in Difficult Times: An International Multi-Disciplinary Monograph*. Guelph, Ontario: Department of Family Studies, University of Guelph.

Jung, M. K. and Y. Kwon. 2013. "Theorizing the U.S. Racial State: Sociology Since Racial Formation." *Sociology Compass* 7:927–40.

Kalache, A. 1997. "Demographic Transition Poses a Challenge to Societies Worldwide." *Tropical Medicine and International Health* 2:925–26.

Kane, Hal. 1995. "What is Driving Migration?" *World Watch* 8:23–34.

Karim, M. Bazlul. 1986. *The Green Revolution: An International Bibliography*. Westport, CT: Greenwood Press.

Keely, Charles. 1996. "How Nation-States Create and Respond to Refugee Flows." *International Migration Review* 30:1046–66.

Kendall, P. L. and P. F. Lazarsfeld. 1955. "The Relation between Individual and Group Characteristics in The American Soldier," in P. Lazarsfeld, M. Rosenberg, eds., *The Language of Social Research*. Glencoe, IL: Free Press of Glencoe.

Keyfitz, Nathan. 1966. "How Many People Have Ever Lived on the Earth?" *Demography* 3:581–82.

———. 1968. *Introduction to the Mathematics of Population*. Reading, MA: Addison-Wesley.

———. 1977. *Applied Mathematical Demography*. New York: Wiley.

———. 1982. "Can Knowledge Improve Forecasts?" *Population and Development Review* 8:729–49.

Kincaid, D. 2010. *World Population Data Sheet 2010*. Population Reference Bureau.

Kinsella, K. and R. Suzman. 1992. "Demographic Dimensions of Population Aging in Developing Countries." *American Journal of Human Biology* 4:3–8.

Kintner, Hallie J. 1994. *Demographics: A Casebook for Business and Government*. Boulder, CO: Westview Press.

Kiser, Clyde Vernon, Wilson H. Grabill, and Arthur A. Campbell. 1968. *Trends and Variations in Fertility in the United States*. Cambridge, MA: Harvard University Press.

Kish, Leslie. 1995. *Survey Sampling* (Classic Edition). New York: Wiley.

Kivisto, P. and T. Faist. 2009. *Beyond a Border: The Causes and Consequences of Contemporary Immigration*. Thousand Oaks, CA: Sage Publications.

Knowlton, Charles. 1832 [1980]. *The Fruits of Philosophy: The Private Companion of Adult People*. Austin, TX: American Atheist Press.

Kodzi, I. A., D. R. Johnson, and J. B. Casterline. 2012. "To Have or Not to Have Another Child: Life Cycle, Health and Cost Considerations of Ghanaian Women." *Social Science and Medicine* 74:966–972.

Krahn, H., K. D. Hughes, and G. S. Lowe. 2010. *Work, Industry, and Canadian Society*. Independence, KY: Cengage Learning.

Krueckeberg, Donald. A. 1983. *Introduction to Planning History in the United States*. New Brunswick, NJ: The Center for Urban Policy Research, Rutgers University.

Kundu, A. 2013. "Processes of Urbanization in India: The Exclusionary Trends." *International Affairs Forum* 4:83–90.

Kunst, Anton, Feikje Groenhof, Johan Mackenbach, and the EU Working Group. 1998. "On Socioeconomic Inequalities in Health." *Social Science and Medicine* 46:1459–76.

Lakhan, V. C. 1996. *Introductory Geographical Information Systems*. Etobicoke, Ontario: Summit Press.

Lauro, Don. 1977. *Life History Matrix Analysis: Progress Report*. Honolulu: Population Institute, East-West Center.

Ledent, Jacques. 1980. *Constructing Multiregional Life Tables Using Place-of-Birth Specific Migration Data*. Laxenburg, Austria: International Institute for Applied Systems Analysis.

Lee, Everett S. 1966. "A Theory of Migration." *Demography* I:47–57

Lee, R. 2011. "The Outlook for Population Growth." *Science* 333:569–73.

Lee, Sharon M. 1998. "Asian Americans: Diverse and Growing." *Population Bulletin* 53:2–40.

Legget, G., ed. 1990. *Global Warming: The Greenhouse Report*. New York: Oxford University Press.

Leibenstein, Harvey. 1974. "An Interpretation of the Economic Theory of Fertility: Promising Path or Blind Alley?" *Journal of Economic Literature* 12:457–79.

Lesthaeghe, Ron. 2010. "The Unfolding Story of the Second Demographic Transition." *Population and Development Review* 36:211–51.

Levitt, P. and B. N. Jaworsky. 2007. "Transnational Migration Studies: Past Developments and Future Trends." *Annual Review of Sociology* 33:129–56.

Lipschultz, J. H., M. L. Hilt, and H. J. Reilly. 2007. "Organizing the Baby Boomer Construct: An Exploration of Marketing, Social Systems, and Culture." *Educational Gerontology* 33:759–73.

Livernash, Robert and Eric Rodenberg. 1998. "Population Change, Resources, and the Environment." *Population Bulletin* 53: 2–40.

Lobb, Michael and Garvin McCain. 1978. "Population Density and Nonaggressive Competition." *Animal Learning and Behavior* 6:98–105.

Loescher, G. and J. Milner. 2005. "The Long Road Home: Protracted Refugee Situations in Africa." *Survival* 47:153–74.

London, Rebecca A. 1998. "Trends in Single Mothers' Living Arrangements from 1970 to 1995: Correcting the Current Population Survey." *Demography* 35:125–31.

Long, Larry. 1988. *Migration and Residential Mobility in the U.S.* New York: Russell Sage Foundation.

Lorenz, M.O. 1905. "Methods for Measuring the Concentration of Wealth." *Quarterly Publications of the American Statistical Association* 9:209–19.

LSU. 1990. *Remote Sensing and Geographic Information Systems.* Baton Rouge, LA: Louisiana State University.

Lundberg, S. and R. A. Pollak. 2013. "Cohabitation and the Uneven Retreat from Marriage in the US, 1950–2010," in *Human Capital in History: The American Record.* Chicago: University of Chicago Press.

Lundgren, R., I. Sinai, P. Jha, M. Mukabatsinda, L. Sacieta, and F. R. León. 2012. "Assessing the Effect of Introducing a New Method into Family Planning Programs in India, Peru, and Rwanda." *Reproductive Health* 9 (17). doi:10.1186/1742-4755-9-17.

Lutz, W. ed. 2013. *The Future Population of the World: What Can We Assume Today.* New York: Routledge.

Macassa, G., J. Hallqvist, and J. W. Lynch. 2011. "Inequalities in Child Mortality in Sub-Saharan Africa: A Social Epidemiologic Framework." *African Journal of Health Sciences* 18:14–26.

Magadi, M. A. and A. O. Agwanda. 2010. "Investigating the Association between HIV/AIDS and Recent Fertility Patterns in Kenya." *Social Science and Medicine* 71:335–44.

Magness, D. R., J. M. Morton, F. Huettmann, F. S. Chapin III, and A. D. McGuire. 2011. "A Climate-Change Adaptation Framework to Reduce Continental-Scale Vulnerability across Conservation Reserves." *Ecosphere* 2: article 112.

Makridakis, Spyros, Steven C. Wheelright, and Rob J. Hyndman. 1998. *Forecasting Methods and Applications.* New York: Wiley.

Malthus, Thomas R. 1798 [1960]. *An Essay on the Principle of Population.* New York: Random House.

Mamdani, Mahamood. 1972. *The Myth of Population Control.* New York: Monthly Review Press.

Marcos, Ferdinand. 1982. "Philippines' Population Policy Statement." *Population Review* 26:55–39.

Markels, Alex. 1998. "The Great Eco-Trips: Guide to the Guides." *Audubon Magazine* 100:66–68.

Martin, David and Gary Higgs. 1997. *A Comparison of Recent Spatial Referencing Approaches in Planning.* Cardiff: Department of City and Regional Planning, University of Wales College of Cardiff.

Mary, N. L. 2005. "Transformational Leadership in Human Service Organizations." *Administration in Social Work* 29:105–18.

Marx, Leo. 1970. *The Machine in the Garden: Technology and the Pastoral Ideal in America.* New York: Oxford University Press.

Mason, J. Alden. 1968. *The Ancient Civilizations of Peru.* New York: Penguin Books.

Massey, Douglas S. 1988. "Economic Development and International Migration in Comparative Perspective." *Population and Development Review* 14:383–402.

Massey, Douglas S., Luin Goldring, and Jorge Durand. 1994. "Continuities in Transnational Migration: An Analysis of Nineteen Mexican Communities." *American Journal of Sociology* 99:1492–512.

Matras, Judah. 1973. *Populations and Societies.* Englewood Cliffs, NJ: Prentice Hall.

Mauldin, W. P. and Bernard Berelson. 1978. "Conditions of Fertility Decline in Developing Countries, 1965–75." *Studies in Family Planning* 9:89–148.

Mauldin, W. P. and J. A. Ross. 1991. "Family Planning Programs: Efforts and Results, 1982–89." *Studies in Family Planning* 22:350–67.

Mazur, Robert. 1988. "Linking Popular Initiatives and Aid Agencies: The Case of Refugees." Network Paper 2c, BRC/QEH *Working Papers on Refugees*. Oxford and London: British Refugee Council.

Mcallister, L., M. Gurven, H. Kaplan, and Stieglitz, J. 2012. "Why Do Women Have More Children Than They Want?" Understanding Differences in Women's Ideal and Actual Family Size in a Natural Fertility Population." *American Journal of Human Biology* 24:786–799.

McCave, Martha and V. A. Koeth. 1998. *Counting Heads and More: The Working of the U.S. Census Bureau*. Washington, DC: United States Bureau of the Census.

McFalls, Joseph A., Jr. 1998. "Population: A Lively Introduction." *Population Bulletin* 53, 3 (whole issue).

McKeown, T. and R. G. Brown. 1955. "Medical Evidence Related to English Population Changes in the Eighteenth Century." *Population Studies* 9:119–41.

McKinney, Michael L., ed. 1998. *Biodiversity Dynamics: Turnover of Populations, Taxa, and Communities*. New York: Columbia University Press.

McNicoll, Geoffrey. 1998. "Malthus for the Twenty-First Century." *Population and Development Review* 24:309–16.

McRae, Hamish. 1995. *The World in 2020: Power, Culture, and Prosperity*. Boston: Harvard Business School Press.

Meadows, Donella, Dennis L. Meadows, and Jorgen Randers. 1992. *Beyond the Limits: Confronting Global Collapse, Envisioning a Sustainable Future*. Post Mills, VT: Chelsea Green.

Meadows, Donella, Dennis L. Meadows, Jorgen Randers, and William H. Behrens. 1972. *The Limits to Growth*. New York: Universe Books.

Meyer, C. and S. Seims. 2013. "The Unique Role of U.S. Foundations in International Family Planning and Reproductive Health." *Journal of Women's Health* 19:1–8.

MIB. 1998. *Multiple Medical Impairment Study*. Westwood, MA: CMAS Books of Massachusetts Insurance Brokers, Inc.

Milanovic, B. 2011. *Worlds Apart: Measuring International and Global Inequality*. Princeton, NJ: Princeton University Press.

Miles, Dudley. 1988. *Francis Place, 1771–1854: The Life of a Remarkable Radical*. New York: St. Martin's Press.

Miller, Barbara. 1981. *The Endangered Sex: Neglect of Female Children in Rural North India*. Syracuse, NY: Syracuse University Press.

Moffitt, Robert A., Robert Reville, and Anne E. Winkler. 1998. "Beyond Single Mothers: Cohabitation and Marriage in the AFDC Program." *Demography* 35:259–78.

Montague, Ashley. 1970. *Man and Aggression*. New York: Oxford University Press.

Morbidity and Mortality Weekly Report. 1997. "Mortality Patterns: Preliminary Data, United States, 1996." *Morbidity and Mortality Weekly Report* 46:941–44.

Mosher, J. N. and K. W. Corscadden. 2012. "Agriculture's Contribution to the Renewable Energy Sector: Policy and Economics—Do They Add Up?" *Renewable and Sustainable Energy Reviews* 16:4157–64.

Mosher, Steven W. 2002. "The Population Controllers and Their War on People." *PRI Review: 2002* 12 (5) September/October. Retrieved May 15, 2015 (http://pop.org/content/population-controllers-and-their-war-1422).

Mu, Ch'ien. 1982. *Traditional Government in Imperial China*. New York: St. Martin's Press.

Murray, Christopher J. L. 1990. "Mortality among Black Men." *New England Journal of Medicine* 322:205–06.

Myers, Norman. 1979. *The Sinking Ark: A New Look at Disappearing Species*. New York: Pergamon Press.

———. 1995. "The Hamburger Connection. How Central America's Forests become North America's Hamburgers," in V. K. Pillai and L. Shannon, eds., *Developing Areas*. Providence, RI: Berg.

Myrdal, Gunnar. 1970. *The Challenge of World Poverty*. Harmondsworth, UK: Penguin.

Myrskylä, M., J. R. Goldstein, and Y. H. A. Cheng. 2013. "New Cohort Fertility Forecasts for the Developed World: Rises, Falls, and Reversals." *Population and Development Review*, 39:31–56.

Nachmias, David. 1980. *The Practice of Policy Evaluation*. New York: St. Martin's Press.

Nair, P. S. 2014. "Population Aging in Sub-Saharan Africa: Present and Prospects." *Gerontechnology* 13:266.

Naisbitt, John. 1982. *Megatrends*. New York: Warner Books.

Naisbitt, John and Patricia Aburdene. 1990. *Megatrends* 2000. New York: William Morrow.

Nalwadda, G., F. Mirembe, J. Byamugisha, and E. Faxelid. 2010. "Persistent High Fertility in Uganda: Young People Recount Obstacles and Enabling Factors to Use of Contraceptives." *B.M.C. Public Health* 10:530.

Namboodiri, N. Krishnan. 1987. *Life Table Techniques and Their Applications*. Orlando, FL: Academic Press.

National Commission for Development Planning. 1991. *Zambia's Population Policy*. Lusaka: Government of Zambia Press.

National Desk. 1998. "Blockbuster Census Sampling Lawsuit Hearing This Week." U.S. Newswire, August 3.

NCHS. 1993. "Advance Report of Final Statistics." *Monthly Vital Statistics Report*, 41, 7 (supplement). Hyattsville, MD and Washington, DC: National Center for Health Statistics, U.S. Department of Health and Human Services.

———. 1997. *U.S. Decennial Life Tables for 1989–91*. Hyattsville, MD and Washington, DC: National Center for Health Statistics, U.S. Department of Health and Human Services.

NHS. 2011. *National Household Survey*. Statistics Canada Catalogue. Number 99–012–X2011046. Ottawa.

Nichols, Judith E. 1990. *By the Numbers: Using Demographics and Psychographics for Business Growth in the '90s*. Chicago: Bonus Books.

Nicodemus, D. M. 2004. "Mobilizing Information: Local News and the Formation of a Viable Political Community." *Political Communication* 21:161–76.

Njogu, Wamucii and Teresa Castro Martin. 1991. "Fertility Decline in Kenya: The Role of Timing and Spacing of Births." Proceedings of the Demographic Health Surveys World Conference 3:1883–901. Columbia, MD: RD/Macro International.

Nketiah-Amponsah, E., E. Arthur, and A. Abuosi. 2012. "Correlates of Contraceptive Use among Ghanaian Women of Reproductive Age (15–49 years)." *African Journal of Reproductive Health* 16:155–70.

Norman, Dorothy. 1997. "Family Planning Program Resources: Focus on Funds," in Robert J. Lapham and George Simmons, eds., *Organizing Effective Family Planning Programs*. Washington, DC: National Academy Press.

Notestein, Frank. 1945. "Population: The Long View," in W. T. Schultz, ed., *Food for the World*. Chicago: University of Chicago Press.

NPP 2000. *National Population Policy of India*. New Delhi: National Commission on Population. Ministry of Health and Family Welfare, Government of India.

Office of Management and Budget (OMB). 1995. "Standards for the Classification of Federal Data on Race and Ethnicity." *Federal Register* 60, 166 (August 28): 44692.

Ogborn, M., A. Blunt, and P. Gruffudd. 2014. *Cultural Geography in Practice*. New York: Routledge.

Ogburn, William F. 1922. *Social Change*. New York: W. B. Heubsch.

Okun, Barbara S. 1997. "Innovation and Adaptation to Fertility Transition Jewish Immigrants to Israel from Muslim Africa and the Middle East." *Population Studies* 51:317–35.

Okun, B. S. and S. Kagya. 2012. "Fertility Change among Post-1989 Immigrants to Israel from the Former Soviet Union." *International Migration Review* 46:792–827.

Oppenshaw, S. 1984. "Ecological Fallacies and the Analysis of Areal Census Data." *Environment and Planning* 16:17–31.

Osei-Heidi, Kwaku and Bertha Osei-Heidi. 1992. "Reflections on Zambia's Demographic Profile and Population Policy." *Journal of Social Development in Africa* 7:87–97.

Packard, Vance O. 1971. *The Waste Makers*. Harmondsworth, UK: Pelican Books.

Pampel, Fred C. 1993. "Relative Cohort Size and Fertility: The Socio-Political Context of the Easterlin Effect." *American Sociological Review* 58:496–514.

Pampel, Fred C. and Vijayan K. Pillai. 1987. "Patterns and Determinants of Infant Mortality in Developed Nations, 1950–1975." *Demography* 23:525–42.

Pandey, Arvind. 1987. "Probability Models of Reproductive Events using Vital Statistics Data." *Carolina Population Center Papers*, No. 88–3. Chapel Hill: Carolina Population Center, University of North Carolina.

Pappas, Gregory, Susan Queen, Wilbur Hadden, and Gail Fisher. 1993. "The Increasing Disparity in Mortality between Socioeconomic Groups in the United States." *New England Journal of Medicine* 329:103–9.

Parameswaran, R. 2001. "Feminist Media Ethnography in India: Exploring Power, Gender, and Culture in the Field." *Qualitative Inquiry* 7:69–103.

Pearce, D., E. Barbier, and A. Markandya. 2013. *Sustainable Development: Economics and Environment in the Third World*. New York: Routledge.

Pearl, Raymond and Joseph F. Kish. 1940. "The Logistic Curve and the Census Count of 1940." *Science* 92:486–88.

Pearl, Raymond and Lowell J. Reed. 1920. "On the Rate of Growth of the Population of the United States since 1790 and its Mathematical Representation." *Proceedings of the National Academy of Science* 6:275–88.

Pedraza, Sylvia. 1996. "Origins and Destinies: Immigration, Race, and Ethnicity in American History," in S. Pedraza and R. Rumbaut, eds., *Origins and Destinies: Immigration, Race, and Ethnicity in America*. New York: Wadsworth Publishing Company.

Petersen, William. 1975. *Population*. New York: Macmillan.

———. 1997. *Ethnicity Counts*. New Brunswick, NJ: Transaction Books.

Pfaff, Alexander. 1997. "What Drives Deforestation in the Brazilian Amazon? Evidence from Satellite and Socioeconomic Data." *Working Paper Series* No. 1722. Washington, DC: Policy Research Department, The World Bank.

Pillai, Vijayan K. 1988. "Teen Fertility in Developing Countries." *Studies in Comparative International Development* 24:3–14.

———. 1996. "Air Pollution in Developing and Developed Nations." *International Planning Studies* 1:35–47.

Pillai, Vijayan K. and Guang-Zhen Wang. 1999. "Social Structural Model of Women's Reproductive Rights: A Cross-National Study of Developing Countries." *Canadian Journal of Sociology* 24:255–81.

Pillai, Vijayan K. and R. Gupta. 2006. "Cross-National Analysis of a Model of Reproductive Health in Developing Countries." *Social Science Research* 35:210–27.

Pillai, Vijayan K. and M. Salehin. 2012. "Spatial Divisions and Fertility in India." *International Journal of Population Research Volume* 2012 (2012), Article ID 235747, 6 pp. (http://dx.doi.org/10.1155/2012/235747).

Pitterman, Shelly C. 1986. *Determinants of Policy in a Functional International Agency: A Comparative Study of United Nations High Commission for Refugees (UNHCR) Assistance in Africa, 1963–1981*. Evanston, IL: Northwestern University. PhD dissertation. Photocopy, University Microfilms, Ann Arbor, MI.

Place, Francis. 1822 [1930]. *Illustration and Proofs of the Principle of Population*. Boston and New York: Houghton, Mifflin Company.

Pol, Louis G. and Richard K. Thomas. 1997. *Demography for Business Decision Making*. Westport, CT: Quorum.

Porter, John. 1971. *The Vertical Mosaic*. Toronto: University of Toronto Press.

PRB. 1973. *World Population Data Sheet*. Washington, DC: Population Reference Bureau, Inc.

————. 1978. "Declining World Fertility: Trends, Causes, and Implications." *Population Bulletin* 33.

————. 1997. *World Population Data Sheet.* Washington, DC: Population Reference Bureau, Inc.

————. 1998. *World Population Data Sheet.* Washington, DC: Population Reference Bureau, Inc.

————. 2013. *World Population Data Sheet.* Washington, DC: Population Reference Bureau, Inc.

Preston, R. E. 1985. "Christaller's Neglected Contributions to the Study of the Evolution of Central Places." *Progress in Human Geography* 9:177–93.

Preston, Samuel H., Irma T. Elo, Andrew Foster, and Hai-shan Fu. 1998. "Reconstructing the Size of the African American Population by Age and Sex, 1930–1990." *Demography* 35:1–21.

Pretes, M. 1995. "Postmodern Tourism: The Santa Claus Industry." *Annals of Tourism Research* 22:1–15.

Price, James L. and Charles W. Mueller. 1982. *Handbook of Organizational Measurement.* Cambridge, MA: Balinger.

Raftery, Adrian E. 1993. *Event History Modeling of World Fertility Survey Data.* Seattle: Seattle Population Research Center.

Raftery, A. E., N. Lalic, and P. Gerland. 2014. "Joint Probabilistic Projection of Female and Male Life Expectancy." *Demographic Research* 30:795.

Rahman, Anika, Lanra Katzive, and Stanley K. Henshaw. 1998. "A Global Review of Laws on Induced Abortion, 1985–1997." *International Family Planning Perspectives* 24:156.

Rama-Rao, S. and R. Mohanam 2003. "The Quality of Family Planning Programs: Concepts, Measurements, Interventions, and Effects." *Studies in Family Planning* 34:248.

Ramsay, S. E., R. W. Morris, P. H. Whincup, A. O. Papacosta, M. C. Thomas, and S. G. Wannamethee. 2011. "Prediction of Coronary Heart Disease Risk by Framingham and SCORE Risk Assessments Varies by Socioeconomic Position: Results from a Study in British Men." *European Journal of Cardiovascular Prevention and Rehabilitation* 18:186–93.

Ravenstein, E. 1889. "The Laws of Migration." *Journal of the Royal Statistical Society* 52:41–301.

Raymondo, James. 1992. *Population Estimation and Projection.* New York: Quorum Books.

Redo, D., A. C. Millington, and D. Hindery. 2011. "Deforestation Dynamics and Policy Changes in Bolivia's Post-Neoliberal Era." *Land Use Policy* 28:227–41.

Rees, Philip, Evert van Imhoff, Helen Durham, Marek Kupiszewski, and Darren Smith. 1998. "Working Paper 98/06: Internal Migration and Regional Population Dynamics in Europe: Netherlands Case Study." University of Leeds, White Rose University Consortium (http://eprints.whiterose.ac.uk/5035/1/98-6.pdf).

Rindfuss, Ronald R. and James A. Sweet. 1977. *Postwar Fertility Trends and Differentials in the United States.* New York: Academic Press.

Rives, N. W. and W. J. Serow. 1984. *Introduction to Applied Demography: Data Sources and Estimation Techniques (Vol. 39).* Beverly Hills, CA: Sage.

Ritzer, George. 1997. *Postmodern Social Theory.* New York: McGraw Hill.

Roberts, Ian. 1997. "Cause Specific Social Class Mortality Differentials for Child Injury and Poisoning in England and Wales." *Journal of Epidemiology and Community Health* 51:334–35.

Robinson, R. S. 2012. "Negotiating Development Prescriptions: The Case of Population Policy in Nigeria." *Population Research and Policy Review* 31: 267–96.

Roessler, M. 1989. "Applied Geography and Area Research in Nazi Society." *Environment and Planning D* 7:419–31.

Ronnby, Alf. 1995. *Mobilizing Local Communities.* Brookfield, VT: Avebury.

Rosenberg, Gerhard. 1982. "High Population Densities in Relation to Social Behavior." *Ekistics* 49:400–404.

Rosenberg, N. and L. E. Birdzell. 1986. *How the West Grew Rich.* New York: Basic Books.

Ross, John A. and Elizabeth Frankenberg. 1993. *Findings from Two Decades of Family Planning Research.* New York: Population Council.

Ross, John and Ellen Smith. 2011. "Trends in National Family Planning Programs, 1999, 2004 and 2009." *International Perspectives on Sexual and Reproductive Health* 37:125–33.

Rudner, Richard S. 1966. *Philosophy of Social Science*. Upper Saddle River, NJ: Prentice Hall.

Rumbaut, Ruben. 1966. *Origins and Destinies: Immigration, Race, and Ethnicity in America.* Belmont, CA: Wadsworth.

Rutman, Leonard. 1984. *Evaluation Research Methods: A Basic Guide.* Beverly Hills, CA: Sage.

Sadavoy, J., R. Meier, and A. Y. M. Ong. 2004. "Barriers to Access to Mental Health Services for Ethnic Seniors: The Toronto Study." *Canadian Journal of Psychiatry* 49:192–99.

Salehyan, I. and K. S. Gleditsch. 2006. "Refugees and the Spread of Civil War." *International Organization* 60:335–66.

Sample, Herbert A. 1998. "Census Sampling Goes to Court." *Sacramento Bee*, June 12, p. A10.

Sandefur, Gary D., Ronald R. Rindfuss, and Barney Cohen, eds. 1996. *Changing Numbers, Changing Needs: American Indian Demography and Public Health.* Washington, DC: National Academy Press.

Sanderson, Stephen K. 2013. *Social Evolutionism: A Critical History.* London: Blackwell.

Sanderson, W. C. 2013. *The End of World Population Growth in the 21st Century: New Challenges for Human Capital Formation and Sustainable Development.* New York: Routledge.

Sathiendrakumar, Rajasundaram and Clem Tisdell. 1989. "Tourism and Economic Development of the Maldives." *Annals of Tourism Research* 16:254–69.

Schmeidl, Susanne. 1997. "Exploring the Causes of Forced Migration: A Pooled Time Series Analysis, 1970–1990." *Social Science Quarterly* 78:284–308.

Schneider, Louis, Sheldon Ekland-Olson, Cookie Stephan, and Louis Zurcher, Jr. 1981. *Human Responses to Social Problems.* Homewood, IL: Dorsey Press.

Schoeni, Robert F. 1998. "Reassessing the Decline in Parent-Child Old-Age Coresidence During the Twentieth Century." *Demography* 35:307–13.

Schultz, T. P. 1981. *Economics of Population.* Reading, MA: Addison-Wesley.

Schwartz, J. and A. Marcus. 1990. "Mortality and Air Pollution in London: A Time Series Analysis." *American Journal of Epidemiology* 131:185–94.

Scott, Steve. 1998. "Race and Politics." *California Journal* 29:24.

Sedgh, G., S. Singh, I. H. Shah, E. Åhman, E., S. K. Henshaw, and A. Bankole. 2012. "Induced Abortion: Incidence and Trends Worldwide from 1995 to 2008." *The Lancet* 379:625–32.

Segaller, S. 1998. *Nerds 2.01: A Brief History of the Internet.* New York: TV Books, LLC.

Sen, Amertya. 1981. *Poverty and Famines: An Essay on Entitlement and Deprivation.* New York: Oxford University Press.

Shah, I. H. and E. Åhman. 2012. "Unsafe Abortion Differentials in 2008 by Age and Developing Country Region: High Burden among Young Women." *Reproductive Health Matters* 20:169–173.

Shavelle, Robert Michael. 1996. *The Semi-Longitudinal Multistate Life Table.* PhD Dissertation. Riverside, CA: Department of Statistics, University of California–Riverside.

Shinne, Margret. 1965. *Ancient African Kingdoms.* New York: St. Martin's Press.

Shiva, Vandana. 1988. *Staying Alive.* London: Zed Books.

———. 2013. *Making Peace with the Earth.* London: Pluto Press.

Shryock, Henry S., Jacob S. Siegel, and Associates. 1975. *The Methods and Materials of Demography* (2 vols., unabridged). Washington, DC: U.S. Bureau of the Census.

———. 1976. *The Methods and Materials of Demography, Condensed Edition* by Edward G. Stockwell. San Diego, CA: Academic Press.

Siegel-Hawley, G. 2013. "Educational Gerrymandering? Race and Attendance Boundaries in a Demographically Changing Suburb." *Harvard Educational Review* 83:580–612.

Sierra Club. 1998. "Population Ballot Question." Retrieved February 22, 1998 (http://www .susps.org/ref/ballotquest.html).

Simmel, Georg. 1969. "Metropolis and Mental Life," in R. Sennett, ed., *Classic Essays on the Culture of Cities.* New York: Appleton-Century-Crofts.

————. 1990. *The Philosophy of Money*. London: Routledge.

Simon, Julian. 1981. *The Ultimate Resource*, 2nd ed. Princeton, NJ: Princeton University Press.

Simoni, J. M., S. Sehgal, and K. L. Walters. 2004. "Triangle of Risk: Urban American Indian Women's Sexual Trauma, Injection Drug Use, and HIV Sexual Risk Behaviors." *AIDS and Behavior* 8:33–45.

Singh, S., G. Sedgh, and R. Hussain. 2010. Unintended Pregnancy: Worldwide Levels, Trends, and Outcomes. *Studies In Family Planning* 41, 4: 241–50.

Sjaastad, L. A. 1962. "The Costs and Returns of Human Migration." *Journal of Political Economy* 70:5680–93.

Smith, G. D., D. Blane, and M. Bartley. 1994. "Explanations for Socio-Economic Differentials in Mortality Evidence From Britain and Elsewhere." *The European Journal of Public Health* 4:131–44.

Smith, K. 2013. *Environmental Hazards: Assessing Risk and Reducing Disaster*. New York: Routledge.

Smith, Sandra S. 1995. "NCHS under Full Sail on the Information Highway." *Public Health Reports* 110:500–03.

Smith, T. E. 1960. "The Cocos-Keeling Islands: A Demographic Laboratory." *Population Studies* 14:94–130.

Smyser, W. R. 1992. "Refugees: A Never Ending Story." *Foreign Affairs* 64 (http://www.foreignaffairs.com/issues/1985/64/1).

South, Scott J. and Stewart Emory Tolnay, eds. 1992. *Changing American Family: Sociological and Demographic Perspectives*. Boulder, CO: Westview Press.

Spaiser, V., S. Ranganathan, R. P. Mann, and D. J. Sumpter. 2014. *The Dynamics of Democracy, Development and Cultural Values*. PloS one 9:e97856.

Stahl, David. 1995. "Mapmaker, Mapmaker." *America's Community Banker* 4:31–35.

Starr, Paul, and Sandra S. Starr. 1995. "Reinventing Vital Statistics: The Impact of Changes in Information Technology, Welfare Policy, and Health Care." *Public Health Reports* 110:534–44.

Stecklov, G., P. Winters, M. Stampini, and B. Davis. 2005. "Do Conditional Cash Transfers Influence Migration? A Study Using Experimental Data from the Mexican PROGRESA Program." *Demography* 42:769–90.

Steele, Stephen S., Teri Kepner, and Doug Gotthoffer. 1999. *A Quick Guide to the Internet for Sociology*. Boston: Allyn and Bacon.

Stigler, S. M. 1986. *The History of Statistics: The Measurement of Uncertainty before 1900*. Cambridge, MA and London: MIT Press.

Stockey, Edith and Richard Zeckhauser. 1978. *A Primer of Policy Analysis*. New York: Norton.

Stolnitz, George J. 1956. *Life Tables from Limited Data: A Demographic Approach*. Princeton, NJ: Office of Population Research, Princeton University.

————. 1964. "The Demographic Transition: From High to Low Birth Rates and Death Rates," in R. Freedman, ed., *Population: The Vital Revolution*. New York: Doubleday Anchor.

Strauss, Erich. 1954. *Sir William Petty: Portrait of a Genius*. London: Bodley Head.

Sullivan, Charles R. 1997. "The First Chair of Political Economy in France: Alexandre Vandermonde and the Principles of Sir James Steuart at the Ecole Normale of the Year III." *French Historical Studies* 20:635–50.

Summers, Anita A., Paul C. Cheshire, and Lanfranco Senn. 1993. *Urban Change in the United States and Western Europe: Comparative Analysis and Policy*. Lanham, MD: University Press of America.

Szinovacz, M. E., L. Martin, and A. Davey. 2014. "Recession and Expected Retirement Age: Another Look at the Evidence." *The Gerontologist* 54, 2: 245–57.

Szreter, S. 1988. "The Importance of Social Intervention in Britain's Mortality Decline c. 1850–1914: A Reinterpretation of the Role of Public Health." *The Society for the Social History of Medicine* 1:1–17.

Taeuber, Irene B. 1960. "Japan's Demographic Transition Reconsidered." *Population Studies* 14:25–38.

Tapinos, G., A. Mason, and J. Bravo. 1997. *Demographic Responses to Economic Adjustment in Latin America*. New York: Oxford University Press.

Taylor, P. W. 2011. *Respect for Nature: A Theory of Environmental Ethics*. Princeton, NJ: Princeton University Press.

Teachman, Jay. 1983. "Analyzing Social Processes: Life Tables and Proportional Hazard Models." *Social Science Research* 12:263–301.

Teitelbaum, M. 1974. "Population and Development: Is Consensus Possible?" *Foreign Affairs* 52:742–60.

Teune, Harry. 1990. "Comparing Countries: Lessons Learned," in E. Oyen, ed., *Comparative Methodology: Theory and Practice in International Research*. London: Sage Publications.

Thomlinson, Ralph. 1975. *Demographic Problems, Controversy over Population Control*. Encino, CA: Dickenson Publishing Co.

Thompson, Warren S. 1929. "Population." *American Journal of Sociology* 34:959–75.

Todaro, Michael P. 1976. *Internal Migration in Developing Countries: A Review of Theory, Evidence, Methodology, and Research Priorities*. Geneva: International Labor Organization.

Tout, Ken. 1989. *Ageing in Developing Countries*. Oxford and New York: Oxford University Press (U.K. and U.S. edition).

———. 1990. *Ageing in Developing Countries*. Oxford: Oxford University Press (U.K. edition).

———. 1992. "Does Third Age Plus Third World Equal Third Class?" *Community Development Journal* 27:122–28.

Towfighi, A. and J. L. Saver. 2011. "Stroke Declines from Third to Fourth Leading Cause of Death in the United States Historical Perspective and Challenges Ahead." *Stroke* 42:2351–55.

Turner, Michael Edward, ed. 1987. *Malthus and His Time*. Basingstoke, UK: Macmillan.

Turner, Stephen. P. 1986. "Beyond the Enlightenment: Comte and the New Problem of Social Science," in Steven Springer, ed. *The Search for a Methodology of Social Science: Durkheim, Weber, and the Nineteenth-Century Problem of Cause, Probability, and Action* (pp. 6–28). Berlin: Springer.

Uhlenberg, Peter. 1996. "Mortality Decline in the Twentieth Century and Supply of Kin over the Life Course." *The Gerontologist* 36:681–85.

Underwood, Reginald Edward. 1950. *The Elements of Actuarial Science*. London: Pitman.

UNESCO. 1989. *Second Review and Appraisal of the Implementation of the Intentional Plan of Action on Aging (E/1989113)*. New York: United Nations Economic and Social Cooperation Organization.

UNFPA. 1984. "Report on 'Second African Population Conference, Arusha, United Republic of Tanzania 9–13, January 1984.'" Document ST/ECA/POP/l UNFPA Proj. No. RAF/83/Po2. New York: United Nations Fund for Population Activities.

———. 2009. *The State of the World Population 2009*. New York: United Nations Population Fund.

UNHCR. 1992. *Handbook on the Procedures and Criteria for Determining Refugee Status under the 1951 Convention and 1967 Protocol Relating to the Status of Refugees*. Geneva: United Nations High Commission for Refugees.

United Nations. 1985. *The World Aging Situation: Strategies and Policies*. New York: The United Nations.

———. 1990. *1990 Demographic Yearbook*. New York: United Nations.

———. 1995. *World Population Prospects: The 1994 Revision*. New York: United Nations Publication. Sales No. E 95.XIII.16.

United Nations Chronicle. 1985. "Aging: An Update on the Elderly Worldwide." *U.N. Chronicle* 22:xxiiv.

United Nations Development Program. 1996. *Human Development Report*. New York: United Nations.

U.S. Bureau of the Census. 1983. "Geographic Mobility: March 1980 to March 1981." *Current Population Reports*, Series P–20, No. 377. Washington, DC: U.S. Government Printing Office.

———. 1992. *Heads of Families at the First Census of the United States Taken in the Year 1790*. Washington, DC: U.S. Bureau of the Census (Staff paperback).

———. 1997. *Current Population Reports*. Series P–2, No. 79.

———. 1998. "Money Income in the United States: 1997 (with Separate Data on Valuation of Noncash Benefits)." *Current Population Reports*, P60–200. Washington, DC: U.S. Government Printing Office.

———. 2004. *Statistical Abstract of the United States: 2004–2005*, 124th ed. Washington DC.

———. 2012. "Census Bureau Releases Estimates of Undercount and Overcount in the 2010 Census." *Newsroom Archives*, May 22.

U.S. Department of Commerce, Bureau of Statistics. 1975. *Historical Statistics of the United States: Colonial Times to 1970*. Washington, DC: U.S. Department of Commerce.

———. 1997. *Statistical Abstract of the United States, 1997* (I17 ed.). Washington, DC: U.S. Department of Commerce Press.

———. 2012. *Statistical Abstract of the United States, 2012* (I31 ed.). Washington, DC: U.S. Department of Commerce Press.

U.S. Department of Homeland Security. 2010. "Population Estimates." January. Office of Immigration Statistics.

U.S. Department of Immigration and Naturalization Service. 1992. *Statistical Yearbook 1992*.

U.S. House of Representatives. 1993. "White House Conference on Tourism, 1993; Joint Hearing before the Subcommittee on Aviation and the Subcommittee on Public Works and Transportation." U.S. House of Representatives, One Hundred-Third Congress, first session, on H. Con. Res. 110. Washington, DC: U.S. Government Printing Office.

U.S. Office of Management and Budget (OMB). 1995. "Standards for the Classification of Federal Data on Race and Ethnicity." *Federal Register*, August 28.

Van de Kaa, Dirk J. 1987. "Europe's Second Demographic Transition." *Population Bulletin* 42:1–59.

Van de Walle, Etienne. 1998. "Piercing the Fog of Time: Europe's Early Population History" (Review Essay). *Population and Development Review* 24:149–57.

Van de Walle, Etienne and John Knodel. 1967. "Demographic Transition and Fertility Decline: The European Case." IUSSP, *Contributed Papers: Sydney Conference, Australia, 21–25 August*. Canberra: Australian Government Printer.

Van Gennep, Arnold. 1977. The *Rights of Passage*. London: Routledge and Kegan Paul.

Volk, A. A. and J. A. Atkinson. 2013. "Infant and Child Death in the Human Environment of Evolutionary Adaptation." *Evolution and Human Behavior* 34:182–92.

Wagman, Paul. 1977. "U.S. Program to Sterilize Millions." *St. Louis Post-Dispatch*. April 22, pp. 1, 10.

Wallerstein, Immanuel. 1974. *The Modern World-System*. New York: Academic Press.

———. 2013. "Within the Capitalist World-Economy. Sociological Worlds." *Comparative and Historical Readings on Society* 142.

Wang, Wendy and Paul Taylor. 2012. *The Rise of Intermarriage: Rates, Characteristics Vary by Race and Gender*. Washington, DC: Pew Research Center.

Wang, Wendy, Kim Parker, and Paul Taylor. 2013. "Breadwinner Moms: Mothers Are the Sole or Primary Provider in Four-in-Ten Households with Children; Public Conflicted about the Growing Trend." Washington, DC: Pew Research Center.

Wannamethee, Goya and Gerald Shaper. 1997. "Socioeconomic Status within Social Class and Mortality: A Prospective Study in Middle-Aged British Men." *International Journal of Epidemiology* 28:532–39.

Watson, S. 2011. "Tourism and Demography," in *Tourism and Demography*, Ian Yeoman, Cathy Hsu, Karen Smith, and Sandra Watson, eds. Seattle: Goodfellow.

Weber, Max. 1900 [1958]. *The City*. New York: The Free Press.

Weber, Thomas. 1989. *Hugging the Trees: The Story of the Chipko Movement*. New Delhi and New York: Penguin.

Webster, Noah and Philip Babcock Gove, 1961. *Webster's Third New International Dictionary of the English Language: Unabridged*. London: G. Bell; Springfield, MA: G. and C. Merriam.

Weeks, John R. 1992. *Population: An Introduction to Concepts and Issues*. Belmont, CA: Wadsworth.

Weinstein, Jay. 1978. "Fertility and Social Service Access: Reconciling Behavioral and Medical Models." *Studies in Comparative International Development* 13:48–73.

———. 1980. "Do We Need a Theory of Demographic Transition?" *Humboldt Journal of Social Relations* 7:71–86.

———. 1991–1992. "Urban Growth in India: Demographic and Sociocultural Prospects." *Studies in Comparative International Development* 26:29–44.

———. 2010. *Social and Cultural Change*. Boulder, CO: Rowman & Littlefield.

Weinstein, Jay and Nico Stehr. 1999. "The Power of Knowledge: Race Science, Race Policy, and the Holocaust." *Social Epistemology* 13:3–36.

Westoff, L. and Charles Westoff. 1971. *From Now to Zero*. Boston: Little, Brown.

Wilcox, W. F. 1953. "Estimates of the Population of the World and Its Continents from 1650 to 1900." The Determinants and Consequences of Population Trends. *Population Studies* 17. New York: U.N. Population Division.

Williams, R. J. 2014. "Storming the Citadels of Poverty: Family Planning under the Emergency in India, 1975–1977." *The Journal of Asian Studies* 73: 471–92.

Wilson, Anthony A. 1997. *A Correlative Study of Employment Longevity with St. John's Regional Medical Center as Compared to Employment Longevity with Most Recent Employer*: MS Thesis. Pittsburgh, PA: Pittsburgh State University.

Winch, Donald. 1987. *Malthus*. Oxford and New York: Oxford University Press.

Winckler, E. A. 2002. "Chinese Reproductive Policy at the Turn of The Millennium: Dynamic Stability." *Population and Development Review* 28:379–418.

Wohlwill, J. F. and W. VanVliet, eds. 2013. *Habitats for Children: The Impacts of Density*. Hove, UK: Psychology Press.

Wolf, D. A. and C. F. Longino. 2005. "Our Increasingly Mobile Society? The Curious Persistence of a False Belief." *The Gerontologist* 45:5–11.

Wolinsky, Art. 1999. *The History of the Internet and the World Wide Web*. Springfield, NJ: Enslow Publishers.

World Bank. 1991. *The Challenge of Development: World Development Report 1991*. New York: Oxford University Press.

———. 1996. *World Resources*, 1996–1997. New York: Oxford University Press.

———. 1997. "Environmentally Sustainable Development: Causes and Consequences of Tropical Deforestation. Ref. no. 681–56." Washington, DC: The World Bank. (Responsibility: Policy Research Department, Environment, Infrastructure, and Agriculture Division: Kenneth M. Chomitz (kchomitz @worldbank.org), Klaus Deininger, David A. Gray, Charles Griffiths, Nlandu Mamingi, and Bart Minten, with Vivi Alatas, Princeton University; Upik Rosalina Wasrin, SEAMEO/Biotrop; and Xiaowen Huang).

———. 1998. *World Development Indicators 1998* (CD-ROM). Washington, DC: The World Bank.

———. "Data" online at http://data.worldbank.org/indicator/SP.POP.TOTL. Washington, DC. Accessed August 31, 2015.

World Energy Council. 2013. *World Energy Resources 2013 Survey Summary*. London: World Energy Council.

World Resources Institute. 1992. *World Resources: A Guide to Global Environment*. New York: World Resources Institute.

Worrall, J. 2014. "Prediction and Accommodation Revisited." *Studies in History and Philosophy of Science* Part A 45:54–61.

Wrigley, E. A. 1986. *Population and History: From the Traditional to the Modern World.* Cambridge: Cambridge University Press.

———. 1997. *The Population History of England*: 1541–1871. Cambridge: Cambridge University Press.

Yea, S. 2004. "Are We Prepared for World Population Implosion?" *Futures* 36:583–601.

Yeatman, S., C. Sennott, and S. Culpepper. 2013. "Young Women's Dynamic Family Size Preferences in the Context of Transitioning Fertility." *Demography* 50:1715–37.

Yeh, E. T., K. J. O'Brien, and J. Yee. 2013. "Rural Politics in Contemporary China." *Journal of Peasant Studies* 40:915–28.

Young, R. M. 2014. "Sixteen Evolutionary Biology and Ideology: Then and Now." *The Social Impact of Modern Biology* 12:199.

Youngs, F. A. 1991. *Guide to the Local Administrative Units of England. Volume II: Northern England.* London: Royal Historical Society.

Zhang, N. J., M. Guo, and X. Zheng. 2012. "China: Awakening Giant Developing Solutions to Population Aging." *Gerontologist*, 2:589–96.

Zottarelli, L. K. 1998. *Determinants of Refugee Production: An Exploratory Analysis.* PhD Dissertation, University of North Texas. August.

INDEX

abortion, *144*, 284
abridged tables: features of, 230; for India, *231*; information inaccessibility in, 230, 232; in life table, 213, 218, *220*, *222*, 228, 230, *231*, 232, 243n2; likelihood of, 228, 230; understanding, 230
academia, 6, 18–19
accuracy: of arithmetic growth model, 250–51; census, 23–24; of cohort survival method, 256–57; of specific rates, 40
actuarial science, 345, 349–50
administrative areas, 77
Afghanistan: age structure in, 44, *45*; gender in, 44, *45*; mean age for, 48; median age in, 48; population growth of, 251, 254, 263; population projections for, 263; population pyramid of, *45*, *46*; proportional age of, 48; SR of, 44
Africa, 122, 175, 196–97, 200, 204–5
African Americans: education of, 64; "Great Migration" and, *168*, 168–69; IMR for, 148; median family income for, 64; specific death rates for, 137, *137*; in U.S., *56*, *56*, *57*, *57*
age: average, 46, 50; components method and distributions of, 264, *265*, *266*; differences, 44; groups, 107, 149, *156*, *157*, 271n3; in life table, 220; at marriage, 287–88; mean, 48, *49*; median, 35, *36*, *37*, *38*, 46, 48, 48–50; proportional, 46, 48–50
agenda setting, 290
age-specific death rates (ASDRs): in Arkansas, 40; for California, 139, *139*, 140; for Canada, *138*; children's special rates in, 139–40, *141*, *142*; formula for, 39–40, 138; for HIV/AIDS, *151–55*; national, *138*; nature of, 138; NCHS on, 144; U.S., *138*, 140. *See also* infant mortality rate

age-specific fertility rates (ASFRs): age groups for, 107; fertility rates through, 107; formula for, 107; by nation, *110*; TFR from, 108–9; world fertility, *121*
age-specific mortality, 131
age structure: in biological structure, 43; cohorts in, 35, 48; gender and, 44, *45*; in Georgia, *38*; mean age for, 48, *49*; median age and, 35, *48*, 48–50; population pyramids and, 45–46; proportional age in, 46, 48–50; in Russia, 44, *45*; in Texas, *38*; U.S., 44, *45*
aggregates: applied demography and social, 364; definition of, 5; Durkheim on study of, 12; geographic, 79, 79–80; individuals and, 11–15; of living individuals, 5; population and other, 5–6; SR in sex structure, 34–35; subaggregates in, 43
aging population, 203–5. *See also* elderly
aging process, 248–49
Agricultural Revolution, 90–91, 94, 99nn6–7
agriculture, 90–91, 94, 95–96, 99nn6–7, 158
AIDS. *See* HIV/AIDS
Alaska natives, 76
American Indians: education of, 64; hierarchy of, 76; median family income of, 63–64; poverty of, 65; slavery of, 181n8; suicide among, 155; in U.S., *56*, *56–57*, *57*
American Planning Association (APA), 346
American Sociological Association (ASA), 341
Amnesty International, 343
ancient societies, 16–17
APA. *See* American Planning Association
Arabs, 62
Ardrey, Robert, 75, 77
arithmetic growth model, 249–51, *251*
Arkansas, 40
ASA. *See* American Sociological Association